Centre-State Relations in Indian Fiscal Context

Published by
ACADEMIC FOUNDATION
in association with

Centre for Economic and Social
Studies (CESS), Hyderabad

Centre-State Relations in Indian Fiscal Context

Editors

C.H. Hanumantha Rao

R. Radhakrishna

S. Galab

N. Sreedevi

ACADEMIC FOUNDATION

NEW DELHI

www.academicfoundation.org

First published in 2015
by

ACADEMIC FOUNDATION
4772-73 / 23 Bharat Ram Road, (23 Ansari Road),
Darya Ganj, New Delhi - 110 002 (India).
Phones : 23245001 / 02 / 03 / 04.
Fax : +91-11-23245005.
E-mail : books@academicfoundation.com
www.academicfoundation.org
www.academicfoundation.com

in association with
Centre for Economic and Social Studies (CESS), Hyderabad.

Disclaimer:
The findings/views/opinions expressed in this book are solely those of the authors and do not necessarily reflect the views of the publisher.

Cataloging in Publication Data--DK
Courtesy: D.K. Agencies (P) Ltd. <docinfo@dkagencies.com>

National Seminar on Centre - State Relations in Indian Fiscal Context (2012 : Centre for Economic and Social Studies, Hyderabad)
Centre-state relations in Indian fiscal context / editors, C.H. Hanumantha Rao, R. Radhakrishna, S. Galab, N. Sreedevi.
pages cm
ISBN 9789332701588

1. Intergovernmental fiscal relations--India--Congresses. 2. Fiscal policy--India--Congresses. I. Hanumantha Rao, C. H., editor. II. Centre for Economic and Social Studies, Hyderabad.host institution. III. Title.

DDC 336.54 23

Typeset by Italics India, New Delhi.
Printed and bound by The Book Mint, New Delhi.
www.thebookmint.in

B.P.R. VITHAL GARU

Contents

Section II: Federal Fiscal Sharing

Section III: State Finances: Specific Issues

Section IV : Sector Specific Issues

Section V: Local Finances

Section VI: Panel Discussion

Section VII: Personal Tributes to B.P.R. Vithal

List of Tables and Figures

Tables

Figures

About the Editors/Contributors

Editors:

C.H. Hanumantha Rao is presently, Chancellor, Hyderabad Central University; Chancellor, ICFAI Foundation for Higher Education (Deemed to be University), Hyderabad; Hon. Professor, Centre for Economic and Social Studies (CESS), Hyderabad and Institute of Economic Growth (IEG), University of Delhi. He did PhD (Economics) from the University of Delhi in 1962; was a Fellow, IEG, University of Delhi, 1961-1992, including as its Director (1997-1980) and Chairman (2002-2008). Founder-Member, CESS, Hyderabad, he was its Chairman during 1995-2007. He was President of the Indian Economic Association (2009); Member, National Advisory Council (2004-2008); Central Board of Directors, Reserve Bank of India (1994-2000); Planning Commission, Government of India (1982-1986); Economic Advisory Council to the Prime Minister (1983-1985); Seventh and Eighth Finance Commissions, Government of India (1977 and 1982). He was awarded Padma Bhushan by the President of India in 2004.

R. Radhakrishna held several important administrative positions—Chairman, National Statistical Commission, Government of India (2009-2012) in the rank of Minister of State; Director/Vice-Chancellor, Indira Gandhi Institute of Development Research, Mumbai (2001-2007); Vice-Chancellor of Andhra University (1998-2001); Member-Secretary, Indian Council of Social Science Research, MoHRD (1994-1997); Director, CESS, Hyderabad (1985-2004) and Professor of Economics, University of Hyderabad (1980-1985). He served as an expert consultant to several international organisations: International Institute for Applied Systems Analysis, Vienna (1978), Australian Centre for International Agricultural Research (1997); UNESCO's Management of Social Transformation (MOST) (2004);

UNDP Regional Bureau for Asia and Pacific (2005), World Bank, Asian Development Bank, UNDP, UNOP, FAO, etc. He was a Visiting Fellow at the University College of Wales, Aberystwyth (1976-77).

S. Galab is currently, Director, CESS, Hyderabad. His research encompasses the broad fields of rural development and agriculture. He has been the Project Director for Andhra Pradesh District Poverty Initiatives Project and Andhra Pradesh Rural Poverty Reduction Project. He is presently leading the Young Lives project, an International Longitudinal Project in Andhra Pradesh on childhood poverty. He has more than 30 research publications in national and international journals. He has also been teaching and supervising MPhil and PhD students. He was a member of the Welfare Commission on Farmers—a Commission appointed by the Government of Andhra Pradesh. He was also a member of the Working Group on Poverty Elimination and was associated with the Expert Group on Agricultural Indebtedness.

N. Sreedevi is presently an Associate Professor at CESS, Hyderabad. She has been working on state finances, central finances, local finances, and centre-state and state-local financial relations. Further, she has also analysed social sector expenditure in the framework of human development. She closely works with the state government on the contemporary issues like 'plan financing' component of Twelfth Plan Approach Paper; SC/ST Sub-Plan; revenue augmentation, public expenditure management; human development report and child budgeting. Besides public finance, her other areas of interest include interface of monetary policy and fiscal policy and macroeconomics.

Contributors:

K.S. Babu, Associate Professor, CESS, Hyderabad.

N.R. Bhanumurthy, Professor, National Institute of Public Finance and Policy, New Delhi.

V. Bhaskar, Former Principal Finance Secretary, Government of Andhra Pradesh, Hyderabad.

T.A. Bhavani, Professor, Institute of Economic Growth, University of Delhi, Delhi.

Santosh K. Dash, Project Associate, National Institute of Public Finance and Policy, New Delhi.

Haseeb A. Drabu, Columist, Mint, Wall Street Journal partner in India, the business daily.

Pradeep Kamble, Research Scholar, Department of Economics, University of Hyderabad, Hyderabad.

G. Pavan Kumar, Research Scholar, Department of Economics, Andhra University, Visakhapatnam.

Biswa Swarup Misra, Dean (Academics), Xavier Institute of Management, Bhubaneswar, Orissa.

Partha Mukhopadhyay, Senior Research Fellow, Centre for Policy Research, New Delhi.

Divya Parmar, Deputy Advisor, Planning Commission. New Delhi.

M. Govinda Rao, former Director, National Institute of Public Finance and Policy, New Delhi.

P. Padmanabha Rao, Associate Professor, CESS, Hyderabad.

A. Premchand, Economist, formerly associated with International Monetary Fund.

J.B. Rajan, Assistant Professor, Kerala Institute of Local Administration, Thrissur, Kerala.

C.S. Rao, IAS (Retired), former Chairman of the Insurance Regulatory Development Authority (IRDA).

N. Srinivasa Rao, Director, Department of Economic Affairs, Ministry of Finance, New Delhi.

R. Sudarsana Rao, Former Dean, Faculty of Arts and Chairman, BOS (PG), Department of Economics, Andhra University, Visakhapatnam

B. Shiva Reddy, Professor, Department of Economics, Osmania University, Hyderabad

G.R. Reddy, IES, former Financial Advisor in Central Revenue Ministry, Government of India.

K. Anji Reddy, Department of Economics, Mahatma Gandhi University, Nalgonda, Telangana.

M. Gopinath Reddy, Professor, CESS, Hyderabad.

Y.V. Reddy, former Governor, Reserve Bank of India.

Atul Sarma, Mahatma Gandhi National Fellow, ICSSR and Visiting Professor Institute for Human Development, New Delhi.

J.V.M. Sarma, Professor, Department of Economics, University of Hyderabad, Hyderabad.

Rekha Saxena, Associate Professor, Department of Political Science, University of Delhi, Delhi.

Tapas K. Sen, Professor, National Institute of Public Finance and Policy, New Delhi.

D.K. Srivastava, Chief Policy Advisor, Ernst and Young Pvt. Ltd. and Member, Twelfth Finance Commission.

M.L.K. Vaagdevi, Research Scholar, CESS, Hyderabad.

A. Vaidyanathan is Honorary Fellow at the Centre for Development Studies, Thiruvananthapuram. He has worked at the National Council of Applied Economic Research (1956-1962), Planning Commission (1962-1972), as Professor at the Centre for Development Studies (1976-1984) and Madras Institute of Development Studies (1984-2004), and as Economist, Food and Agricultural Organization and the World Bank.

Preface

This book is a collection of papers that were presented in a two-day National Seminar on "Centre-State Relations in Indian Fiscal Context", organised by the Centre for Economic and Social Studies (CESS) at its campus in Hyderabad on 5-6 November 2012, in honour of Sri B.P.R. Vithal, I.A.S (Retd), the founder of CESS, on the occasion of his 85th birth anniversary. The theme of the seminar is very appropriate because of his contribution in this area as a civil servant, member of various official committees, member of the 10th Finance Commission, and as a prolific writer. He inspired his colleagues in the finance and planning departments, several of whom consider him their guru.

Sri Vithal was, in his time, the longest serving Planning Secretary in the country. He initiated regional planning and formulated the famous proposition, "...Thus we have a situation where the rate of per capita income varies between an actual of 1 per cent and a target of about 3 per cent. This range is not fortuitous. This is the range within which alone the Hindu view of life will hold."

He was then the longest serving State Finance Secretary and a pioneer in wiping out the revenue deficit of Andhra Pradesh state. His views on this subject expressed in his book *Fiscal Federalism in India*, are relevant even today. In this book, he traces the evolution of the budgetary process from part I and part II schemes to Plan and Non-plan Outlays, and sets out his views on deficits in a scintillating statement:

> The Planning Commission was thus, from year to year, faced with...the disappearance of the BCR (Balance from Current Revenues) projected by the Finance Commission. ...Every Finance Commission has been confronted with deficits in the revenue budgets of the States which ought not to have been there according to the calculation of the previous Commission. The main difference between these two unanticipated gaps is that a Finance Commission, being a periodic body, has the consolation of being confronted with the sins of the State Governments committed during

> the interregnum only. On the other hand, the Planning Commission being a live and continuing body, is faced each year with the sins of commission of the State Governments and its own sins of omission. A Finance Commission's dispensation is like the Catholic Confessional; it condones past sins subject to certain penitence. The Planning Commission approving a Plan with a deficit is the Pontiff approving continued sinning. (pp.272-73).

His book, *The Gadgil Formula: For Allocation of Central Assistance to State Plans* is another important piece of work in public finance. With the expertise and experience in this subject, and association with every stage of the evolution of Gadgil Formula, Sri Vithal has provided an insight into the process through which the Gadgil Formula initially evolved and was subsequently modified. His recent book *A State in Periodic Crisis: Andhra Pradesh*, is an objective narrative of various economic and political developments in the state.

Sri Vithal's association with a number of official committees constituted by the Government of India and state governments is spread across issues relating to taxation policy, agricultural wealth and income, PSUs (public sector undertakings), expenditures, PRIs (panchayat raj institutions), ways and means advances to state governments, and its planning. As a member of the 10th Finance Commission, he was instrumental in recommending an alternative scheme of devolution which led to the amendment of the Constitution and facilitated sharing of all central tax revenues with states.

Regarding the seminar theme, the perennial debates—particularly in the domain of finances—across the federations on their bias in favour of the central government, the devolution of a part of the central government's revenue to the state governments, and *inter se* distribution among the latter with due regard to horizontal fiscal imbalances, are common in the Indian Union too.

The Indian Constitution laid out a few statutory provisions for the devolution of resources from the Union Government to the state governments, and a statutory body, the Finance Commission, to periodically review and recommend transfers to meet the budgetary needs of the states. But over a period of time, Centre's practice of resorting to levying of cesses and surcharges—the proceeds of which do not form part of the divisible pool of taxes—has somewhat constrained the Finance Commissions in dealing with the issue of vertical imbalances. However, encompassing local bodies by bringing in the 73rd and 74th amendments to the Indian constitution in 1993, and the consequent provision of grants for augmentation of their resources was a remarkable move. Pooling in all the central taxes for revenue sharing (as recommended by the Tenth Finance Commission and implemented through the Constitutional 80th Amendment) was another major step in the history of Indian fiscal federalism. Nevertheless, the wide variations in per capita income across states which reflect their differential fiscal capacities made the Finance Commissions' task of addressing horizontal fiscal imbalances (equity or efficiency) a challenging one. With regard the horizontal sharing, the approach adopted so far reflects plenty of ambiguity: whether and how the efficiency of the states should be rewarded, to what extent equity should be built, to what extent the state-specific factors and circumstances should be taken into account while assessing the fiscal management of the states, etc.

The impact of economic reforms on centre-state financial relations is quite evident. Of late, the Finance Commissions, notably the last four Commissions, have been entrusted with many tasks of macroeconomic and fiscal management. The basic objectives of fiscal restructuring would be not only balancing the receipts and expenditure on revenue account of all the states and the Centre, but also generating surpluses for capital investment and reducing fiscal deficit; raising the tax-GDP (gross domestic product) ratio for the Centre and tax-GSDP (gross state domestic product) ratios for the states; and in the context of debt reduction, suggesting corrective measures in regard to states' debt, consistent with macroeconomic stability and debt sustainability. The adjustment path suggested by the 11th and 12th Finance Commissions made a major impact on the fiscal performance of both levels of government although there were considerable slippages from the set targets. Hence, an important task of the Finance Commission should be to develop an integrated framework for restructuring public finances in order to address these interrelated objectives. Therefore, a need for fundamental institutional changes both in the form as well as the working of the Finance Commission.

So far 13 Finance Commissions have submitted their reports based on changes in the terms of reference and in the fiscal situation, both at the Centre and states. With the recent appointment of the 14th Finance Commission for the recommendation period 2015-2020, the stage has been set to review and discuss the challenges confronting the Finance Commission including: (a) vertical and horizontal distribution of resources (including specific purpose grants to important sectors such as education and health, to mention a few); (b) transfers to local bodies stipulated under 'other considerations'.

The Planning Commission—an additional channel of central transfers (grants and loans) to the States—assumed great importance since its inception and the transfers through this channel have increased enormously over the years with a gradual increase of central sector and centrally sponsored schemes, and marginalisation of formula-based transfers (modified Gadgil/Mukherjee formula). Relinquishment of central plan loans to state governments, as recommended by the 12th Finance Commission, changed the borrowing composition of the state governments and thereby, the composition of their plan financing. The Government of India and the Planning Commission, during the Twelfth Five Year Plan, intended to bring about greater flexibility in fiscal devolution for CSS. The transfer of these resources has an impact on revenue as well as state specific sector (health, education, etc.) expenditure patterns and trends of the state governments.

Emphasis on economic growth is the underlying rationale for all new economic policies, including financial sector policy reforms, mainly because of its contribution to social welfare—directly by raising the real incomes of people through employment generation, indirectly by making available the required resources to all levels of government, and also for federal-fiscal transfers towards undertaking the socio-economic activities. The recent economic slowdown raises issues that attempt to explain the effective inter-dependence of fiscal and monetary policies in economic stabilisation in recent years. However, there has been relatively less attention on the impact of global crisis on sub-central government finances and the fiscal relations between the central and sub-central government entities.

Though an attempt to statutorily bring the local bodies into the federal structure of the country through the 73rd and 74th amendments to the Indian constitution is a welcome feature, the pace of progress in this direction is nominal, i.e. the level of decentralisation particularly the fiscal decentralisation is far from satisfactory.

The papers included in this volume address all these important issues. We earnestly hope that this collection will be a remarkable addition to the ongoing debate on Centre-state relations in the Indian fiscal context.

The organising committee for the National Seminar consisted of Prof C.H. Hanumantha Rao (Chairman, Seminar Organising Committee); Prof R. Radhakrishna; V. Bhaskar, Principal Secretary, Finance Department, Andhra Pradesh; S.P. Tucker, Principal Secretary, Planning Department, Andhra Pradesh; Prof S. Galab, Director, CESS; Dr G.R. Reddy; Dr P. Padmanabha Rao; Dr N. Sreedevi and Prof Manoj Panda, the then Director, CESS (Convener, Seminar Organising Committee).

The holding of the national seminar and the completion of this volume became possible with effort and support from the academic community. The constant support of Dr Y.V. Reddy who considers B.P.R. Vithal his *guru* is acknowledged. The team is highly thankful to Dr Montek Singh Ahluwalia, the then Deputy Chairman, Planning Commission, for delivering the inaugural address and felicitating Sri Vithal. Special thanks are due to Dr Sanjay Baru for his initial help in holding this national seminar. The team acknowledges invaluable support from Prof K.L. Krishna (the then-chairman of the Centre) at every stage of the national seminar.

Various eminent people, by chairing the different sessions and panel discussion, and the paper contributors by their timely responses, despite their tight schedule, enriched the debates. Their participation and cooperation is gratefully acknowledged.

— The Editors

Introduction and Overview

I

Introduction

The debates on Centre-state relations and the experiences of federal systems show that the division of functions and powers between the Federal/Centre and the states, though defined constitutionally, has an inherent centripetal bias. It is more so in the domain of finances. Because of this vertical fiscal imbalance, the Central government devolves a part of its revenue to the state governments and distributes the same among the latter with due regard to horizontal fiscal imbalances—to offset the fiscal disadvantages of states and to ensure certain minimum levels of specific public services.

The Indian Union is not an exception to the above mentioned bias. Realising the built-in vertical imbalance, the framers of the Constitution made a few statutory provisions for the devolution of resources from the Union government to the state governments and also provided a statutory body, the Finance Commission (FC), to periodically review and recommend transfers to meet the budgetary needs of the states. The practice of the Centre resorting to the levy of cesses and surcharges, the proceeds of which do not form a part of the divisible pool of taxes, has somewhat constrained the FCs in dealing with the issue of vertical imbalances. The wide variations in per capita income across states which reflect their differential fiscal capacities made the FCs' task of addressing horizontal fiscal imbalances (equity or efficiency) a challenging one. So far 13 FCs have submitted their reports based on changes in the terms of reference (ToR) and changes in the fiscal situation both at the Centre and states. The remarkable move in the history of Indian fiscal federalism was encompassing local bodies by bringing in the 73rd and 74th amendments to the Indian Constitution in 1993 and consequent provision of grants for augmentation of their resources. With the recent appointment of the 14th Finance Commission (FFC) for the recommendation period 2015-2020, the platform has been set to review and discuss the challenges confronting the FC including: (i) vertical and horizontal distribution of resources (including specific purpose grants to important sectors such as education and health, to mention a few); (ii) transfers to local bodies stipulated under 'other considerations'.

The advent of Five Year Plans, with the introduction of development oriented multi-level planning, created the need for an additional channel of central transfers to the states—the Planning Commission. The state governments are required to prepare their plans within the framework of national priorities as formulated by the Planning Commission. However, each state proposes its plan keeping in view its own resources and the central assistance it receives. Plan assistance to states has assumed great importance since the First Five Year Plan. The resources transferred through the Planning Commission have increased enormously over the years. There has been a gradual increase of central sector and centrally sponsored schemes (CSS) and marginalisation of formula-based transfers (modified Gadgil/Mukherjee formula) to states with their implications over a period of time.

The 19 chapters in the volume (Section I to V), apart from the overview, examine Centre-state relations in the fiscal context, ranging from the global context to national, sub-national, and local finances. It also gives an overview of a panel discussion on "Issues Before Fourteenth Finance Commission" (Section VI). Section VII comprises "Personal Tributes to B.P.R. Vithal".

Background of the Theme

The impact of economic reforms on Centre-state financial relations is quite evident. At the Central government level, on the receipts front (particularly revenue account), the tax structure of both the direct (corporate tax and personal income tax) and indirect (customs and excise duties) were rationalised by reducing the rates as well as the number of slabs. The first phase of reforms on indirect taxation started with the introduction of Modified Value Added Tax (MODVAT) for selected commodities at the central level in 1986 and then its gradual extension to all commodities through Central Value Added Tax (CENVAT). The introduction of service tax further deepened this effort. With the success of state level Value Added Tax (VAT), executed in a phased manner since 2003, the Government of India (GoI) in 2007 evolved a roadmap for the introduction of destination-based Goods and Service Tax (GST) in the country. The review of the GST in the report of the 13th Finance Commission (ThFC) highlighted the significant benefits that it can provide to the Indian economy.

During 2003-2008, following the Fiscal Responsibility and Budget Management (FRBM) Act, state level VAT, the benefit of the Debt Consolidation and Relief Facility (DCRF) recommended by the 12th Finance Commission (TwFC), Debt Swap Scheme (DSS), etc., both the levels of government (central and state) have witnessed considerable improvement in the fiscal situation. However, it is clear that in spite of the improved performance in the first three years of the TwFC, the Centre could not achieve the FRBM Act targets. In addition, the impact of recent counter-recessionary measures on the fiscal stance not only led to the postponement of the implementation of FRBM Act targets but even to the amendment of FRBM Act in 2012.

Relinquishment of central plan loans to state governments, as per the recommendations of the TwFC, changed the borrowing composition of the state governments and thereby, the composition of their plan financing. In this context, it is relevant to discuss Centre-state financial relations and the issues related to plan transfers during the Twelfth Five Year Plan. Non-plan non-statutory transfers, though minor, also constitute a part of federal fiscal transfers.

Macroeconomic stabilisation and counter-recessionary actions are the primary responsibility of the Central government. The recent economic slowdown raises the issues that seek to explain the effective dependence on fiscal and monetary policies in economic stabilisation in recent years, in other words, interface between monetary and fiscal policies.

The key note address on "Centrally Sponsored Schemes across States", by Montek Singh Ahluwalia, the then-Deputy Chairman, Planning Commission, GoI, New Delhi, is summarised below.

II

Implementation of CSS: More Flexibility to State Governments

Over the years, states have been asking the Centre for greater freedom in the usage of funds given to them under various Centrally Sponsored Schemes (CSS) and also raising concerns at various forums about the lack of flexibility in CSS and related issues. The Planning Commission had constituted a sub-committee in March 2011 for suggesting restricting of CSS to enhance its flexibility and efficiency. The Committee observed that CSS covers the entire country and thus caters to extremely diversified demographic, geographical, economic and rural and urban needs. It is difficult to design schemes which will have parameters that will cater to the requirements of all the regions. The committee felt the need to have certain flexible components in the schemes for developing the specific schemes by the state governments. Hence, the Committee recommended that 20 per cent of budget allocation in all the CSS, (10% in flagship schemes) to be called 'Flexi Funds', should be earmarked in each scheme for this purpose.

In the Twelfth Five Year Plan, the Government of India and the Planning Commission are intending to bring about greater flexibility in fiscal devolution for CSS by allowing states their discretion to use 10 per cent of funds allocated to them. However, there will be guidelines on each scheme of the CSS. The issue of flexibility in the use of 10 per cent of CSS funds is to be taken to the Union Cabinet for its approval. After obtaining the cabinet approval, the Ministry concerned and the states assemble together and work on the utilisation of funds to reflect the realities of the states. But that does not mean states can divert funds of one scheme into another. Instead they would have the flexibility to use the funds innovatively within the framework of the scheme. With this amendment, states can soon have more flexibility in implementing the CSS and hence, lot of change in the execution of central schemes can be noticed. For each state, 10 per cent of the fund should be completely flexible. In the sense, the amount can be used for innovative steps in the sector for which they are intended.

Also, Dr Ahluwalia underscored the need for incorporating terms and conditions in allocations of funds for the central schemes so that the funds would be used for the purpose they were given for. Similarly the states should appreciate the need for greater freedom to the local bodies in the utilisation of state fund transfers.

The Share of CSS in Central Transfers

Referring to the general perception that Central government fund transfers to the states are small, he said most transfers from the Centre to the states are through CSS. Though CSS as a percentage of the total planned expenditure has increased only marginally between 2007-08 and 2012-13, it nevertheless comprises more than 60 per cent of the total expenditure. While in 2007-08, the share of CSS was about 60 per cent of the total expenditure of the centre, it has increased to 61 per cent by 2012-13. Its proportion in GDP (gross domestic product) has increased from 1.49 per cent in 2007-08 to 1.75 per cent in 2012-13.

More than 60 per cent of fund contribution is through various CSS like NREGA (National Rural Employment Guarantee Act), SSA (Sarva Shiksha Abhiyan), NRHM (National Rural Health Mission), ICDS (Integrated Child Development Service), PMGSY (Pradhan Mantri Gram Sadak Yojana), AIBP (Accelerated Irrigation Benefit Programme) etc. States such as Andhra Pradesh, Madhya Pradesh, Rajasthan, Maharashtra, Karnataka, and Chhattisgarh are getting more transfers per capita through CSS (all CSS) when compared with other states. Under the scheme NREGA, states such as Andhra Pradesh, Madhya Pradesh, Karnataka get a higher share per capita while Haryana, Punjab get a lower share. Andhra Pradesh gets more share in NRHM, ICDS as well. Dr Ahluwalia mentioned that the funds received by the Andhra Pradesh under the schemes such as SSA, NREGA, ICDS, PMGSY, AIBP, NHRM is more than that of Gadgil formula based transfers.

While states demand funds based on performance, the government and the Planning Commission want the rising growth to percolate to all the states. The Planning Commission has been increasingly pushed by the states to provide resources based on tax capacities. While states want central assistance based on tax capacities, the plan assistance normally is based on the Gadgil-Mukherjee (G-M) formula.

The real GDP growth rate during 2006-2011 was higher than in the period 2001-2006 in most of the states except Gujarat. While most of the states have shown sustained high rates of growth, several of the economically weaker states have demonstrated an improvement in their growth rates. Amongst them are Bihar, Rajasthan, Chhattisgarh, Madhya Pradesh, Jharkhand and Uttar Pradesh. While economically weaker states are catching up, there is a concern for the states which are doing well but their growth rates are low.

III

MACRO ISSUES

Global Financial Crisis and Sub-Central Government Finances (Y.V. Reddy)

According to Y.V. Reddy, in view of the significant impact of global financial crises, while there is considerable attention on the national economies concerned, there has been relatively less attention towards the impact of global crisis on sub-central government finances and the fiscal relations between the central and sub-central government entities. The finances of sub-central government entities are vital as the activities in their realm are meant for the well-being of the people in the absence of which a large number of people is directly affected, mainly the poorer sections. Though there is a huge diversity in the legal and institutional arrangements governing the sub-central government entities, broad generalisations may be made regarding recent trends, impact of crisis on their finances and their responses.

A glance at the recent trends reveals that relative to central government finances, there is stability and considerable improvement in state finances (partly reflecting the boom conditions during the pre-crisis period), significant recourse to public-private partnerships (PPP), land leases, to mention a few. Yet, the impact of the crisis on sub-central government finances is noticed in the reduction of own revenues and also the share in central taxes based on the sectoral and the industry linkages of the local economy with the developments in the global economy and the extent of deceleration in economic growth or recession in the national economy. Added to this was the increase in welfare payments/fiscal stabilisers wherever in place, along with inelastic expenditure commitments on their finances.

To withstand the global crisis, the Central governments supported the sub-central governments by: (i) increasing the share of taxes; (ii) extending special loans; (iii) implementing through sub-central government entities the stimulus packages of national priorities rather than local needs; (iv) greater access to debt markets by diluting the fiscal rules, improving the access to debt markets and providing guarantees. Alongside, one finds a cut in the quantity and quality of public services in the countries that were deeply affected by the crisis.

As a consequence of the global crisis, some broader issues with regard to the finances of sub-central governments, are emerging. The Central government's efforts, in some advanced economies, to manage the crisis-led fiscal stress, may result in lowering of its support to sub-central governments. Despite the shocks, the rising share of pension and other inelastic liabilities of sub-central governments (in advanced economies) is yet another crucial issue. In developing economies, the pace of economic growth may be impressive, even if slackening to lower than pre-crisis years, but it is likely to result in greater urbanisation with larger demands on local public services, and also in a higher proportion of economic activities at the level of sub-central governments.

Due to the global crisis, besides the national government, if the sub-central governments also go by the countercyclical policies related to the fiscal management at their level, then these policies become a shared responsibility of both. However, it is advantageous if the countercyclical fiscal policies are in the realm of the central government to get the benefit of pooled resources that meet the differentiated impacts on the sub-central governments which can be used as instruments of such countercyclical fiscal policies by central governments.

The currency markets could be much more volatile than in the pre-crisis period. Hence, those sub-central governments which have their debt denominated in foreign currencies may face significant foreign currency risk. There may be a need in some cases to explore the limits to foreign currency exposures of sub-central governments. It may also be useful to explore whether central governments should consider mechanisms for orderly debt restructuring of sub-central government debt. In the context of the possible new normal of the global economy, issues on fiscal transparency and managing implicit guarantees including contingent liabilities may have to be revisited.

Federal Finance: Operational Systems and Issues (A. Premchand)

The Constitution of India opted for a system with a strong government at the Centre with more elastic sources of revenues wherein the units would be given a large degree of autonomy, at the same time with financial reliance on the Central government, and so certain provisions were made for transfer of Central resources to the state governments. The states were also restricted to engage in public borrowing for so long as they owed money to the central government.

FC is the only statutory body that is to be appointed every five years to review the finances of state governments and to recommend statutory provisions for the devolution of resources from the Centre to the states. But, the introduction of the development-oriented multi-level planning not only paved the way for another channel of Central transfers to the states, i.e. the Planning Commission, but also made this channel a major vehicle to transfer the resources under the Constitution (Article 282) and the FCs had to accept their limited role. A. Premchand in this chapter suggests that, over a period of time, with the improved approaches in the FCs' response to the changing needs and administrative requirements of the state governments, the focus is on the changing operational approaches of the FC.

The work of the FCs, which begin with an assessment of the fiscal needs of the states for the next five year period for which the state governments submit their forecasts to the former for their scrutiny, has shown a major improvement in the methodology of estimates, assessing outlays, arranging devolution, grants-in-aid and central lending to states.

Yet, the focal issue of fiscal federalism—fiscal equalisation in the provision of public services—has not been formally aimed at in any form, including plan programmes, mainly because of the factors such as states' resource endowments, their fiscal policies, development plans, other outlays, central investments, foreign aid received, and the NRI remittances received and the patterns of their utilisation.

In India, as the Central government devises the fiscal policy, both the Commissions—Planning and Finance—consider the state units as accounting and administrative units, rather than as autonomous and cognate units. Otherwise, the Commissions' attention would have been towards the states' choices and patterns of resource allocation, related utilisation, and their implications for the financial status of the units during the next five years and also their capability of tracking down countercyclical policies.

The areas of major concern in the review of state finances are: (i) state-owned enterprises; (ii) the PPPs, entered into by states; (iii) the emergence of third party payments; and (iv) arrear component. The losses incurred by the first two are routinely guaranteed without legislative review and related accountability processes but included in the state governments' forecasts that are submitted to the FCs which goes without any review by the latter also. The services of the third party payments system have an enormous potential for fraud and consequent failure of expenditure controls. Another concern is that most state governments have massive arrears in payments of wages, and transfers to local bodies.

Role of Finance Commission in Macroeconomic and Fiscal Stability in India (Atul Sarma)

The tasks assigned to FC are specific in nature (vertical and horizontal distribution of resources); additional matters under sub-clause (d) have direct or indirect relevance to sound finance and have been referred to successive FCs right from the first one. One such matter is the issue of restoring fiscal balance and maintaining macroeconomic stability included in the ToR of the 11th and the following FCs.

It is in the backdrop of deep-rooted imbalances in government finances, that the 11th Finance Commission (EFC) was asked for the first time "to review the state of finances of the Union and the States and suggest ways and means by which the governments, collectively and severally, may bring about a restructuring of the public finances so as to restore budgetary balance and maintain macroeconomic stability."

Accordingly, EFC sketched an adjustment path for fiscal restructuring with a package of ways and means for implementation, the objectives of restoring macro stability and sustainable level of debt. Indeed, as Atul Sarma concludes in his paper, the adjustment path suggested by the EFC and 12th Finance Commission (TwFC) made a major impact on the fiscal performance of both the levels of governments *albeit* there were considerable slippages from the set targets. But the global slowdown, high inflation, rising current account deficit and falling growth in the first three years of the ThFC award period vitiated the macroeconomic and fiscal stability, and again drew attention to the strict adherence to the correction path recommended by the ThFC. Despite the unfavourable economic environment, the fiscal performance parameters at the aggregate States' level were closer to the targets set by the ThFC. Recognising the useful role played by the preceding three FCs in fiscal correction, a follow-up clause (clause 5) has been included in the ToR of the recently constituted FFC.

Indian Finance Commission: Need for Revamping and Restructuring (J.V.M. Sarma and V. Bhaskar)

Of late, the FCs, notably the last four Commissions, have been entrusted with many tasks of macroeconomic and fiscal management. The basic objectives of fiscal restructuring would be not only balancing the receipts and expenditure on revenue account of all the states and the Centre, but also generating surpluses for capital investment and reducing fiscal deficit; raising the tax-GDP ratio for the Centre and tax-GSDP ratios for the states; and in the context of debt reduction, corrective measures with regard to states' debt may be suggested, consistent with macroeconomic stability and debt sustainability. Therefore, J.V.M. Sarma and V. Bhaskar argue that an important task of the FC should be to develop an integrated framework for restructuring public finances to address these interrelated objectives. Hence, a need for fundamental institutional changes both in the form as well as the working of the FC.

In the absence of an independent institutional arrangement for the evaluation of the fiscal performance of the Centre and the states against targets/norms prescribed by the FCs and for monitoring the implementation of the recommendations, especially those relating to matters other than devolution and grants-in-aid, the TwFC recommended the setting up of a high-level monitoring mechanism in every state and that the committee should meet at least once in every quarter to review the progress and issue directions for mid-course corrections.

For strengthening the fiscal architecture, the ThFC has identified the following areas: indirect tax reform in the form of adopting the GST; strengthening and empowering the local bodies and finding ways of involving them in the devolution process; extending the sharing process to non-tax revenues such as profit petroleum, profit gas, revenues from spectrum; dynamic updating of the horizontal sharing parameters; improving governance to enhance the quality of public expenditure; strengthening the data base; introducing environmental dimension into inter-governmental fiscal arrangements; basic reforms of the fiscal accounting procedures, creation of council of Finance Ministers, a fiscal council, a local body ombudsman, national debt management agency; and reform of revenue—capital classifications. Sarma and Bhaskar thus suggest the need for a thorough overhaul of the institution of the FC.

Institutional Mechanisms of Fiscal Federalism: A Case Study of National Development Council (NDC) in India (Rekha Saxena)

As mentioned earlier, the introduction of development-oriented multi-level planning not only paved the way for another channel of Central transfers to the states, the Planning Commission, but also made this channel a major vehicle to transfer the resources under the Constitution (Article 282). In this regard, NDC was created with a specific politico-economic mandate to formally approve five-year plans and related issues of economic development in the country like objectives, priorities, financing pattern, inter-sectoral allocation, etc. It may be reiterated that instead of creating the NDC under Article 263 of the Constitution or under a Parliamentary Statute, it was set up by a Cabinet Resolution. Though lacking in constitutional or statutory status, it has been more functional than the Inter-State Council (ISC) belatedly set up in 1990 under Article 263.

May be because the NDC is devoid of any constitutional or statutory status, plans are invariably launched without the stamp of its formal approval; its meetings too are not held for considerable lengths of time. For instance, the Draft Ninth Five-Year Plan prepared by the Planning Commission, provisionally implemented in 1997, was belatedly approved by the NDC only in 1999, after a lapse of two years. It is precisely for this reason that the Sarkaria Commission recommended that the NDC should be reconstituted as National Economic Development Council (NEDC) by a Presidential Order under the provisions of Article 263 so as to have moorings in the Constitution.

It is necessary to study the importance and working of the NDC in the context of the gradual shift from the 'emphasis on public investment' in the initial stages of development planning to paving the way for 'private investment', strategic economic development, and also Union-State relations. In conclusion, Rekha Saxena suggests that the NDC as an important inter-governmental mechanism can play a creative political role in the planning as well as political processes. It can facilitate a process of multi-level planning—planning for the Central government, state governments, local levels—and laying out an indicative framework for the private sector.

Measuring Financial Access in India: A Macroeconomic Growth Approach (T.A. Bhavani and N.R. Bhanumurthy)

Emphasis on economic growth is an underlying reason for all the new economic policies, including financial sector policy reforms, mainly because economic growth contributes to social welfare directly by raising the real incomes of people through employment generation and indirectly by making available the required resources to all the levels of government and also for federal-fiscal transfers towards undertaking socio-economic activities.

Financial sector development and its accessibility contribute to economic growth by providing financial resources to all the sectors. A comprehensive empirical analysis undertaken by T.A. Bhavani and N.R.

Bhanumurthy for different sectors shows that in terms of availability and adequacy, accessibility of the formal financial system to the agriculture sector, and unorganised service and manufacturing enterprises is limited and unequal. Regardless of several policy measures, financial access continues to be limited in India and the oft-mentioned reasons include high risk and high transaction costs, particularly to the unorganised sector. However, as shown by the authors, existing policies are not adequately focusing on reducing risk and transaction costs.

FEDERAL FISCAL SHARING

Central Tax Reforms: Implications for States (C.S. Rao and G.R. Reddy)

In the initial years of tax reforms, there was a reduction in the states' share in Central taxes as a percentage of GDP because of lower growth of revenue from both income tax and excise duties, which were shareable with states. With the introduction of the service tax, deepening of tax reforms, economy shifting to a higher growth trajectory and the Constitutional amendment enabling the states to share the proceeds of all Union taxes, there was an improvement in the states' share in Central taxes from 2000-01. But, as pointed out by C.S. Rao and G.R. Reddy, this improvement was not commensurate with the increase in the tax revenues of the Centre because of greater recourse to the levy of cesses and surcharges and tax expenditures. The moderation in tax rates was not accompanied by a reduction in tax concessions and exemptions resulting in revenue loss. The authors thus conclude that the levy of cesses and lack of follow-up on reforms in removing tax exemptions has resulted in near stagnant share of states in the gross tax revenue of the Centre.

The FRBM Act: Impact on Central Finances and its Transfers (N. Sreedevi and M.L.K. Vaagdevi)

While introducing the FRBM (Fiscal Responsibility and Budget Management) Bill (2000) in Lok Sabha in December 2000, the Union government had really watered down the recommendations of the Committee on Fiscal Responsibility Legislation (January 2000) by not adding in the bill its key proposal of setting up a Fiscal Management Review Committee. The major targets of the Central government, as per the Bill, were to reduce the revenue and fiscal deficit to nil and not more than two per cent of GDP respectively within a period of five financial years i.e., March 2006. The delay of the FRBM Bill (2000) to take the shape of an Act in 2003 and the notification of the Act and Statutory Rules in July 2004 resulted in the postponement of the targeted year to 2007-08 and subsequently to 2008-09. In brief, the FRBM which started with amendments from the status of a Bill (2000) to an Act signed up for another amendment in 2012.

According to N. Sreedevi and M.L.K. Vaagdevi the fiscal targets which the Union government has achieved may not be totally attributed to FRBM. Diversion of huge loan recoveries under DSS (2002-2005) towards bulk repayments to National Social Security Fund (NSSF) reduced the interest burden and thus lowered revenue and fiscal deficits. Moreover, the yearly growth rate of gross transfers in 2005-06 was lower than the preceding two years. The fall in the deficit indicators during 2006-2008 may be attributed to robust economic growth-led revenue augmentation. Thus in any year of the post FRBM period, the effort of the Union government in improving its fiscal responsibility is not clearly seen.

The FRBM Act does not specifically discuss the issue of Federal Transfers to the State Governments. As per rule 6 of the FRBM Rules 2004, the Union government is mandated to submit the statements of receivables and guarantees and a statement of assets, at the time of presenting the Annual Financial Statement (AFS). Based on the reporting year 2010-11, the revenue through principal taxes raised but not realised (under dispute and not under dispute together) amounted to ₹ 249,443 crores of which 85 per cent fall under the recent 5 year period. Its further break-up shows that 53 per cent of the total uncollected revenues falls during the period 2006-2009 when the growth rates of both tax revenue and GDP were high (barring 2008-09).

The authors show that the total uncollected revenue constitutes nearly 7 per cent of the Centre's gross tax revenue, 9 per cent of the Centre's net tax revenue and nearly 26 per cent of states' share in central taxes. The break-up of the uncollected amount shows that the proportions under dispute were higher.

Federal Fiscal Sharing and Fiscal Accountability in India: An Integrated Approach (J.V.M. Sarma and Pradeep Kamble)

The basic function of the FC relates to the sharing of Central taxes under Article 270 and determination of grants for the states as provided for under Article 275. In due course, though the FC made substantial changes or improvements in the principles and methods considering the changing economic structure and policy environment, streamlining of the primary functions of the FC is required to make it more objective and scientific.

With regard to the objective of vertical sharing, the FCs adopted incremental approaches and increased the share of the states under each successive FC. However, the important development was the combining of all the Central taxes for revenue sharing based on the recommendation of the 10th Finance Commission subsequently put into practice through the Constitutional 80th Amendment. While the exclusion of the several central revenue sources which remained outside the divisible pool (cesses and service tax proceeds) becomes the focal point on the tax front, demand for the inclusion of non-tax revenues into the divisible pool started gathering momentum. Some states desire that a minimum guaranteed devolution of the central taxes from the Centre to the states should be fixed.

Regarding horizontal sharing, Sarma and Kamble make the point that the FCs are inclined to get convinced by the importance of progressivity instead of attempting to consider, as per the theory, how fiscal capacities can be equalised. Every FC tried to introduce a host of criteria in tax devolution and each FC tries to do better than its predecessor by appearing to be more 'progressive'. The selection of the indicators, the quantification methods, the weights assigned for each of the criteria etc., however, remain subjective. Successive FCs tends to use similar formula albeit with modifications that made the formula even more subjective and more inconsistent. Also, there is confusion regarding equity *versus* efficiency.

Fiscal accountability measures (reducing and restricting the deficit and debt indicators) recommended by the recent FCs and adopted by the Centre and the states are similar to the task of the FC transfers to a state to reduce its fiscal gap (defined as 'own revenue-total expenditure' and can be viewed as a variant of fiscal deficit). Given the commonality in the objectives, it is only proper that the criteria should be more or less the same.

STATE FINANCES: SPECIFIC ISSUES

Fiscal Transfers to Andhra Pradesh in the Post-Fiscal Reform Period of the State (R. Sudarsana Rao and G. Pavan Kumar)

While the aggregate states' share in central taxes and duties was increased by the successive FCs, the share of Andhra Pradesh in central tax revenue has been decreasing from the 11th Finance Commission (EFC) onwards. This happened in the case of some other states too, mainly due to the criteria adopted and the weights assigned to them for the horizontal distribution of resources.

As far as Article 275(1) grants-in-aid are concerned, the state was not eligible to get non-plan revenue deficit grants under the EFC, TwFC and ThFC and also grants-in-aid for education and health under the TwFC mainly due to the criteria adopted by the Commission. According to Sudarsana Rao and Pavan Kumar, had the Commission taken the physical indicators like literacy levels and health into account, Andhra Pradesh would have got grants-in aid for these two essential social services. However, the state could receive grants-in-aid for upgradation of essential social and administrative services, local governments, and special problems and to meet calamity relief expenditure. With regard to grants for relief expenditure, there has been a wide gap between the central grants and the actual expenditure incurred for calamity relief operations.

An analysis of growth rates of different components of fiscal transfers reveals that shared tax revenue recorded a growth rate of 12.3 per cent while total grants-in-aid a growth rate of 13.9 per cent during the period 1995-96 to 2011-2012 (RE). This is mainly due to the fast growth of grants-in-aid for CSS and non-plan grants. It is interesting to note that the growth rate of FC grants is greater than the Plan grants. A comparison of percentage of total transfers under the three FCs (EFC, TwFC, and ThFC) to southern states reveals that the mean percentage share of Andhra Pradesh is slightly higher than for the other southern states of Karnataka, Kerala and Tamil Nadu.

Plan Financing in Andhra Pradesh: Trends and Concerns (G.R. Reddy)

With the deterioration in state finances in the late eighties, a vicious circle had set in. The dependence on borrowings for plan financing had increased considerably with the balances from current revenuers turning negative. In the absence of commensurate direct returns to the state from plan investments, increasing pressure was felt on the non-plan revenue account to service the outstanding borrowings resulting in further deterioration in the balances from current revenues. According to G.R. Reddy, the situation would have further deteriorated but for the enactment of fiscal responsibility legislation and introduction of VAT (value added tax) in 2005-06, DCRF recommended by the TwFC, turnaround in economic growth and resultant higher growth in central as well as state revenues and higher transfers to states. Following these developments, the balances from current revenues turned positive reducing somewhat the dependence on borrowings for plan financing. However, the situation is far from comfortable. The author highlights a number of concerns with regard to financing of the Twelfth Five Year Plan which need to be addressed to meet the financial requirements and to realise the objective of achieving faster, inclusive and sustainable growth. These concerns relate to the declining share of state plans in total plan outlays, change in the composition of plan assistance, debt servicing burden during the period of the Twelfth Plan and more importantly to the deceleration in economic growth being witnessed in recent years. With the focus on social sectors and the bulk of the plan expenditure becoming committed, there is limited scope for taking up new schemes.

Fiscal Imbalances and Indebtedness (Tapas K. Sen and Santosh K.Dash) and Debt Sustainability (N. Srinivasa Rao and Divya Parmar) in Indian States

In India, under Article 293(3) of the Constitution, a state may not without the consent of the Government of India (GoI) raise any loan if any part of a loan is still outstanding which has been made to the state by the Government of India or by its predecessor government, or in respect of which a guarantee has been given by the GoI or by its predecessor government. Most transfers awarded by the Planning Commission to the larger states are block transfers, composed of loans (70%) and grants (30%). The Centre also on-lends bilateral and multilateral agency lending at the same terms as for regular plan assistance.

Besides working for the basic objectives of vertical and horizontal distribution of central resources, FCs started a tradition of writing-off of central loans to the states. The 6th, 7th and 8th Finance Commissions gave substantial debt relief to the most indebted states in the proportion of their indebtedness relative to the size of their economies. The 10th Finance Commission (TFC) recommended two new incentive schemes for debt relief, one tied to improvement in fiscal performance in the current account, and a matching debt relief scheme tied to the amount of state public enterprises divestment proceeds used to retire state debt. The long-term goal for the Centre and the states as suggested by the TwFC was to bring down and maintain the debt-GDP (gross domestic product) ratio at no more than 28 per cent each.

Until the mid-2000s, debt composition of the states (also borrowings) was mainly constituted by Central government component. The composition of public debt has changed in recent times particularly with: (i) the implementation of rule based fiscal consolidation, (ii) the availability of market loans at a lower rate of interest, (iii) DSS (2002-2005) and (iv) Centre's relinquishment of plan loans to states from 2005-06 onwards. (v) DCRF introduced during 2005-06, based on recommendations of the TFC.

The adjustment path, recommended by the EFC and TwFC—fiscal restructuring with a package of ways and means for implementation, the objectives of restoring macroeconomic stability and sustainable level of debt—impacted both the levels of governments *albeit* there were considerable slippages from the set fiscal deficit and debt targets particularly at central level. The state governments could achieve the FRBM targets in the last decade. As there are different ways of achieving fiscal adjustment, obviously the results vary with each one of them. Accordingly, its impact on the state economy varies.

The ratio of revenue deficit to GSDP (gross state domestic product) for general category states for two periods (averages 2000-2004 and averages 2007-2011) shows that almost all the states have reduced revenue deficit/ GSDP ratios in the second period. Among the general category states, the decline in revenue deficits/GSDP ratios is substantially larger in the low income states. For the special category states, though, no clear pattern is visible. The scenario with respect to fiscal deficits is very similar to that regarding revenue deficit in general category states. With respect to special category states, the picture relating to fiscal deficits is qualitatively different from that relating to revenue deficits.

In the process of adjustment, in general, states have not reduced the expenditure on capital outlay; instead it has increased. Therefore, the fall in fiscal deficit is lower than that in the revenue deficit in most states. However, there was a cut in net lending which may not necessarily be a bad development; in many cases such lendings were only to perpetuate dysfunctional public enterprises that also had become financial liabilities. The fiscal adjustments could have proved to be the necessary catalyst for public enterprise reforms. In the general category states, the pattern of fiscal adjustment with respect to fiscal liabilities, by and large, replicates the adjustment in fiscal deficits with some notable exceptions.

The authors conclude that it is indeed the low-income states that have undertaken a greater extent of fiscal adjustment than both high- and middle-income states in terms of all deficit indicators. At the sub-national level, fiscal indicators including indebtedness are at levels far less worrisome than before, obviating the need for stringent measures.

SECTOR SPECIFIC ISSUES

Grants from the Centre flow through the channels of planning and FCs. FCs, besides the grants under Article 275, also recommend sector-specific (education and health etc.) and state specific grants. Similarly Planning Commission channelises certain grants to the states under: (i) state plan schemes (ii) central plan schemes, and (iii) CSS. The transfer of these resources has an impact on the revenue as well as expenditure patterns and trends of the state governments.

Financing of Elementary Education in India: A Study of Sarva Shiksha Abhiyan (SSA) (B. Shiva Reddy and K. Anji Reddy)

Elementary education in India is being funded under various programmes including the on-going SSA. SSA, a flagship programme to universalise elementary education in India by: (i) enrolling all children in the age-group 6-14 in school, (ii) bridging gender and social gaps, (iii) retaining all children in school till they complete elementary education, and (iv) providing education of satisfactory quality.

The role of the Central government in financing of education in general and financing of elementary education in particular increased in the last few decades. As a per cent of GDP the Central government budget for education increased from 0.67 to 0.94 during 2001-2013. As a per cent of total budget also the education budget of Central government increased from 2.4 to more than 5.3 during the same period. The Central Government's budget for education increased more than the increase in state governments' budget for education. The Central government's share in the education budget increased from about one-sixth to one-fourth in the last decade.

About half of the education budget of the Central government is allocated to elementary education in recent years. The increase in Central government's role in financing of education is more in the form of CSS, particularly to SSA under elementary education. In spite of the significant increase in the funds for SSA in the last decade they are far from adequate and whatever the amount released or actually spent is much less than the approved outlay. The costs of SSA were shared in the ratio of 75:25 in the beginning and 65:35 currently by the Centre and states, the corresponding ratio for the north-eastern states is 90:10. Many states including Andhra Pradesh face problems such as: (i) delay in the release of SSA funds by the Centre to the state Governments, (ii) release of SSA funds in more than stipulated two instalments, (iii) unequal distribution of SSA funds—inter-state and intra-state, and (iv) regressive distribution of SSA funds—educationally and economically developed states receive relatively more than the backward states.

The authors observe that while there is some progress in quantitative terms, such as increase in number of schools, enrolment and retention, in qualitative terms the performance of SSA is far from satisfactory. The learning levels of students as measured by achievement scores in subjects like language, mathematics and environmental studies have not improved since the launching of SSA in 2001.

Why Government Should Prioritise Spending on Health (Biswa Swarup Misra)

There is a deficiency in health infrastructure and health personnel in India due to very low public expenditure on health which has resulted in poor health outcomes. The poor health status in turn constrains the economy to achieve its potential growth. The Twelfth Five Year Plan has projected the Indian economy to grow at a slower pace between 2012-13 and 2016-17. The low growth scenario is going to put pressure on government resources and in the process health care spending may suffer. The TwFC had provided for an equalisation grant to states in health care spending. The ThFC, however, has replaced it by an incentive grant for reduction in IMR (infant mostality rate). Though there have been positive interventions to improve health outcomes, it falls short of the requirement.

The empirical findings suggest that higher growth promises higher public spending on health which in turn contributes to improved health status in the country.

Role of Central Government Finances in Improving Health Services in India with Special Focus on Andhra Pradesh (K.S. Babu)

Higher health budgets in various countries have helped in achieving good health outcomes. In India, however, public health expenditure accounts for just about one-sixth of total health expenditure. It accounts for nearly one per cent of GDP and private health expenditure accounts for five per cent of GDP. India's health indicators are very discouraging compared to other countries. According to the United Nations Development Programme (UNDP's) *Human Development Report (HDR) 2010*, out of 193 countries, India ranked 143rd in IMR. Limited financial resources of the states are mainly used to meet their committed liabilities toward wages, salaries, interest payments and pensions, leaving little scope for spending on health sector. Many states do not have good health infrastructure. Hence, it is necessary for the Central government to introduce specific-purpose transfers to the states to ensure minimum standard of basic health services. Health infrastructure in Andhra Pradesh is neglected when compared to Karnataka,Tamil Nadu and Kerala. Andhra Pradesh has a sufficient number of sub-centres, but there is acute shortage of Primary Health Centre's (PHCs) and Community Health Centres (CHCs), and also health manpower. The situation however, is better in the other three states.

Financing of Flagship Programmes in Andhra Pradesh (P. Padmanabha Rao)

The share of social sector expenditure in total expenditure or in state income shows its importance in the priorities of the government. The aggregate picture regarding the components of social sector expenditure in Andhra Pradesh shows inconsistent trends in these ratios—decline in one period and increase in another period and again fall in the subsequent period—which may not help in achieving the objectives of social development by making the best use of scarce resources. The flagship programmes are centrally sponsored and launched by GoI with an objective to ensure that growth is widely spread so that its benefits, in terms of income and employment, are adequately shared by the poor and weaker sections of the society.

On Total Sanitation Campaign (TSC), more than 50 per cent of respondents in a survey felt that the state should pay for improving sanitation. Households were generally found to be dissatisfied with the existing poor level of sanitation and cleanliness but were unaware that these were also caused by widespread unhygienic practices.

The coverage of habitations with water supply and sanitation under National Rural Drinking Water Programme (NRDWP) changes with time. Despite improvement in rural water supply and increased outlay by the Government, particularly in the last decade, the level of general satisfaction is quite low at the community level. Despite huge investments, the objective of providing access to water and sanitation to the entire population has remained far from fulfilled. Changing technologies, availability of sustainable drinking water sources and sustainable service delivery are becoming increasingly challenging.

National Social Assistance Programme (NSAP) envisages the pension schemes, National Family Benefit Scheme (NFBS) and scholarship to up to two children of BPL (below poverty line) families studying in classes 9th to 12th. There has been an enormous increase in the number of old age pensions. The Government is also giving greater importance to widow and disabled pension schemes, indicating a shift in its priorities.

The number of houses constructed per lakh population under Indira Awas Yojana (IAY) in Andhra Pradesh has always been higher than the corresponding national figure for the reference period. The position of the state improved from 13 to 7 at the national level with respect to this indicator.

Under Pradhan Mantri Gram Sadak Yojana (PMGSY), Andhra Pradesh has shown considerable growth in the release of funds. Another flagship programme implemented in Andhra Pradesh is Mahatma Gandhi National Rural Employment Guarantee Act (MGNREGA). Assets created under this scheme are land development, restoration of minor irrigation tanks, rural connectivity (roads), de-silting of canals, field channels & feeder channels, percolation & mini percolation tanks, earthen bunding, farm ponds, horticulture, bund plantation, gram panchayat buildings and social audit.

The aim of the Jawaharlal Nehru National Urban Renewal Mission (JNNURM) is to encourage reforms and fast track planned development of identified cities. Focus is on efficiency in urban infrastructure and service delivery mechanisms, community participation, and accountability of urban local bodies/parastatal agencies towards citizens. Benefits of the programme seem to be impressive across the State of Andhra Pradesh.

Local Finances

This section presents an overview of local finances in India in general covering the experiences of two state governments—Kerala and Andhra Pradesh.

It was a red letter day in the Indian fiscal federalism when the 73rd and 74th Amendment was made to the Constitution giving due place to the local governments (both rural and urban) in 1993—a legal foundation for the third layer of government in the federal structure of the country. The Constitutional Amendment Act (CAA) mandates to devolve power to local self government institutions (LSGIs) so as to provide public services including drinking water, sanitation, street lights, roads, etc.

Article 243G of the Constitution authorises *panchayats* to function as institutions of self-government in the preparation of plans and implementation of schemes for economic development and social justice in their realm for various matters along with those listed in the 11th Schedule. Like the division of powers and functions enumerated in the Union List and State List, no clear demarcation exists between the state and *panchayats*. It is the state legislature that has to make laws with respect to the devolution of powers and functions to the *panchayats*. Almost all states and union territories claim that they have transferred responsibilities in varying degrees to the *panchayats*, by enacting laws in conformity with the CAA. However, the functional domain of *panchayats* still pertains only to traditional civic functions in several states.

According to finance-follows-function rule, fiscal decentralisation allows the LSGIs to deliver the public services that are devolved to them. Based on this rule there are four pillars of fiscal decentralisation—assignment of expenditure responsibilities, assignment of revenue sources, the allocation of intergovernmental fiscal transfers or grants, rules on sub-national budget deficits and the incurrence of sub-national debt. The shares of total expenditure of local governments in India either in terms of total expenditure or in terms of GDP is meager compared to the higher levels of governments (Centre and the states). The major portion of revenue of PRIs (panchayati raj institutions) in India is from grants and other revenues.

Considering the spirit of the 73rd and 74th CAA in general and Article 280(3) (bb and c) in particular, the federal fiscal system needs to be revamped. The constitutionally created third tier of government—LSGIs—need to be given due place. Like the states, LSGIs are constitutionally eligible to get financial support.

Devolution Index for Major States

IIPA's survey constructed an index for all the 23 States. As per this devolution index, Kerala is ranked first with value close to 75 per cent followed by Karnataka (69.5), Tamil Nadu (68.9) and West Bengal (66.5). The scores of Maharastra and Madhya Pradesh are lower around 60 per cent whereas Gujarat and Andhra Pradesh scores are above 50 per cent.

PRIs and CSS

Substantial tied funds are being transferred to the *panchayats* through the CSSs and additional central assistance (ACAs). Till recently, the CSS transfers were administered and utilised mainly by the line departments. In recent years, the *panchayats* are identified as implementing institutions for the plan schemes of line ministries. The most important scheme in this regard is the MGNREGA. However, as CSSs get mostly tied funds, PRIs have very little say on spending them.

Status of Local Finances: Andhra Pradesh Experience (M. Gopinath Reddy)

The general fund budget or untied resources for the three tiers of local government derive from two sources: transfers from the state and local revenues. In practice, internal revenue mobilisation at the *panchayat* level is weak. Higher dependence on upper levels of governments for resources, particularly tied funds, limited their role with regard to expenditure. Thus, according to Gopinath Reddy, Andhra Pradesh remains one of the 'decentralisation deficit' states in the country. In spite of the fact that on devolution index it scores 50 per cent, yet it is lagging behind the southern states. Most of the recommendations of the first and second State Finance Commissions (SFC) are not honored by the government. Although DPCs have been constituted, their functioning as institutions for the preparation of comprehensive district plans may be said to be poor.

Kerala Experience (J.B. Rajan)

As enumerated by J.B. Rajan, Kerala is the 'trend setter' with regard to the extent of decentralisation as assessed at national level based on 3Fs (i.e., devolution of functions, functionaries, and finance). The hallmark of decentralisation in Kerala is the transfer of well-defined developmental responsibilities to local governments. Regardless of the fact that Kerala is far ahead in decentralisation when compared with other Indian states, it remains a loser as far as the Union Finance Commission (UFC) grants are concerned. Paradoxically, there is a gap between the extent of devolution—represented by devolution index—by the states and the general basic grants provided to them by UFCs.

Section I: Macro Issues

1 Global Financial Crisis and Sub-Central Government Finances

Y.V. Reddy

Introduction

The global financial crisis had and is continuing to have a profound impact on fiscal conditions, especially in major advanced economies. There is considerable attention on these issues in view of the significant macroeconomic implications for the global economy and the national economies concerned. However, relatively less attention has been given to the impact of global crisis on finances of sub-central government entities, and the fiscal relations between sub-central government entities and central governments.

Sub-central government entities may fall into two broad categories: those in federations, and those in unitary forms of government. In the case of federations, the relationship between the Centre and the provinces which are sub-central government entities is determined by the Constitution, while the relationship of both the central government and the provincial governments, if any, with the local self-governments is determined normally by legislation, but in a few cases by constitutional provisions. In some countries, especially developing economies, large urban conglomerates often have special legal and institutional arrangements, but they still constitute sub-central government entities.

It is necessary to recognise the huge diversity in the legal and institutional arrangements governing the sub-central government entities. Moreover, the available data is limited, often out-of-date, and not easily comparable. The three major sources of data on this subject are the International Monetary Fund (IMF), the World Bank, and the Organisation for Economic Cooperation and Development (OECD). At a country level, the data in regard to federal fiscal relations is more easily available than the data pertaining to local self-government entities. The sub-central governments and their finances have an important place in the economic and social well-being of the people and hence, need to be considered despite these data limitations.

Importance

The finances of sub-central government entities are important because they undertake activities which are collectively critical for the well-being of the people. These usually include water supply, sanitation, street lighting, schooling, roads, public transport, etc.

Second, the number of people directly affected by their activities are large because most of them provide public goods, and are of special relevance to the poorer sections.

Third, public policies in the recent decades have resulted in the rebalancing of the public sector functions in favour of the market, and in the process, the share of sub-central governments in public expenditure has been increasing in most countries. For example, about 30 per cent of the expenditures in the government sector are incurred by sub-central governments.

Fourth, their share in public investment appears to be significant, and in most cases, it amounts to about 60 per cent of the total, although some of such public investments are undertaken on behalf of or at the behest of the central governments.

Fifth, the public debt incurred by them has been increasing at a faster pace than that of the central governments till the onset of the crisis. At the time of the crisis, the share of their public debt stood at around 30 per cent. This magnitude, no doubt, includes utilities such as power and road transport, which are often technically separate but owned by the sub-central governments.

Sixth, the sub-central government debt markets have been expanding rapidly in many countries.

Recent Trends

There are significant variations among countries in the performance of the sub-central government entities, but a few broad generalisations may be appropriate, considering the status in the years leading to the crisis.

First, relative to central government finances, they have been more stable. Second, fiscal improvement in their finances has been considerable, partly reflecting the boom conditions during the pre-crisis period. Third, in most cases, though not all, fiscal rules governing local self-governments have been tightened and effectively enforced by the central governments. Fourth, there has been significant recourse to public-private partnerships. Finally, land leases and other ways of innovative, though somewhat non-transparent funding the activities of local self-government, have been taken up.

Impact of Crisis on Sub-central Government Finances

It is difficult to make a quantitative assessment on a global scale of the impact of the crisis on the finances of sub-central government entities. However, on the basis of data and the anecdotal evidence, a few generalisations can be made.

First, a reduction in revenues has been noticed, depending on the sectoral and the industry linkages of the local economy with the developments in the global economy.

Second, there has been a reduction in the receipt of taxes shared with the central government, but the magnitude of reduction depended on the extent of deceleration in economic growth or recession in the national economy.

Third, welfare payments increased where fiscal stabilisers were in place and, in some cases, as a result of the crisis there was additional stress on their finances.

Fourth, many of the entities had relatively inelastic expenditure commitments. This had to be met somehow and was done with considerable difficulty in many cases.

Fifth, the value of investments made by them in financial markets, especially investment of their pension funds, has been adversely impacted where the financial intermediaries failed them or the financial markets faced erosion of values of assets that the entities were owning.

Sixth, in regard to some countries, there has been a downgrading of the credit rating of the national economies, and automatically some of the sub-central governments had to suffer a downgrade since the rating of sovereign entities generally operates as a ceiling. In addition, there has been considerable downgrading of sub-central governments by rating agencies in view of the pressure on their finances.

Finally, and in extreme cases such as in Spain, there has been a separatist sentiment among the inhabitants of sub-central governments fuelled by the pressure on their finances, consequent upon the financial or sovereign debt crisis.

Responses

The fiscal responses of the sub-central governments to the global crisis consisted of one or a combination of the following.

First, support from central governments was made available to them in terms of an *ad hoc* increase in the share of taxes or extending special loans.

Second, support of central governments was forthcoming not only in terms of loans from central governments but also greater access to debt markets done by diluting the fiscal rules, improving the access to debt markets, and providing guarantees. In some cases, evergreen funding was also encouraged.

Third, stimulus packages of central governments were implemented through sub-central government entities. However, in most cases, these stimulus packages were linked to national priorities rather than local needs.

Fourth, there have been cutbacks in the quantity and quality of services provided by them in the countries that were seriously affected countries.

Finally, debt defaults have been reported in a few cases.

Emerging Issues

As a result of the global crisis, some broader issues in regard to the finances of sub-central governments are emerging. These may be summarised as follows.

First, a large national public debt has been incurred in some advanced economies to manage the crisis, and that is likely to result in stress on the fiscal position of central governments. In such cases, the support of the central governments to sub-central governments may not be forthcoming at the same level as it was during the pre-crisis period. In other words, the new normal of the finances of central governments of advanced economies may be less benign than it was before the crisis. Increasing share of pension liabilities of sub-central governments in advanced economies, and inelasticity of their liabilities in the face of their shocks is yet another important issue in advanced economies. In developing economies, however, the pace of economic growth may be impressive even if subdued relative to pre-crisis years, but it is likely to result in greater urbanisation with larger demands on local public services. The increase in urbanisation is likely to result in a higher proportion of economic activities at the level of sub-central governments.

Second, as a result of the global crisis, there is an acceptance of the relevance of countercyclical fiscal policies. It is necessary to take a view as to whether the sub-central governments will also follow suit and adopt countercyclical policies in the fiscal management at their level. In such a case, countercyclical fiscal policies are treated as a shared responsibility between central and sub-central governments. However, there are advantages of restricting the countercyclical fiscal policies to the central government, such as having the benefit of pooled resources for meeting differentiated impacts on sub-central governments. In any case, the sub-central government entities can be used as instruments of such countercyclical fiscal policies by central governments.

Third, the currency markets could be considerably more volatile than in the pre-crisis period. Hence, those sub-central government entities which have their debt denominated in foreign currencies may face a significant foreign currency risk. Under those circumstances, in some countries, there may be a need to take a view on incorporating limits to foreign currency exposures of sub-central governments in the fiscal rules.

Fourth, there has been increasing recognition of the need for orderly debt restructuring mechanisms for sovereign debt, and the Stiglitz Commission has also made a similar recommendation. Such arrangements are expected to be of value in avoiding irresponsible lending. It may be useful to explore whether central governments should consider mechanisms for the orderly debt restructuring of sub-central government debt.

Fifth, the importance of guidelines for interface between sub-central governments and the financial markets could be incorporated in the fiscal rules. Furthermore, the frameworks for regulation of the sub-central government debt markets may have to be reconsidered in view of the growing importance of such debt.

Finally, as part of the general review of fiscal management in the context of the possible new normal of the global economy, issues relating to fiscal transparency, and managing implicit guarantees including contingent liabilities, may have to be revisited.

Conclusion

The global crisis is having a profound impact on macroeconomic thinking and on fiscal management for the future. The new normal with regard to the global economy and national fiscal policies may be different from the pre-crisis frameworks in some ways. It will be useful to explore them in the context of sub-central governments even if one were to conclude that the current frameworks may not change much, or need not change much in the near future.

2 Federal Finance

Operational Systems and Issues

A. Premchand

Introduction

Federations are broadly divided into two groups—aggregative and devolutionary. The Indian system is a part of the second group. Federalism envisages, in principle, the coexistence of a central government and several autonomous units (provinces or states) working together in a country. The autonomy of States in India has, over the years, been largely circumscribed, and there has emerged a vertical integration which is at work now. There are several constitutional and informal mechanisms that facilitate the regular functioning of the system. A schematic presentation of these mechanisms is given in Table 2.1.

From the early days when constitutional reform was envisaged in the transition of a colony to a dominion status and eventually to complete independence from the colonial government, there was never any unanimity of opinion about the issue whether India should be a federation or a union. It was feared that if India were to be a federation some of the units might seek a separation and aim at forming independent states. The alternative to this was a system in which the units would be given a large degree of autonomy while being financialy dependent on the central government. Moreover, any separation was to be approved by Central Legislation. In addition, the powers of the states were restricted in some spheres so that the supervision of the central government could be strengthened. Accordingly, the more elastic sources of revenues were assigned to the central government, and the states were not permitted to engage in public borrowing for so long as they owed money to the central government. It was further envisaged that the annual needs of the states would be met through a division of the central revenues through formulae designed for the purpose.

Some of these elements were a part of the provincial autonomy arrangements introduced in 1937. To meet the fiscal needs of the Provinces, an award specifying the percentage of resources that would accrue from a divisible pool (comprising central revenue sources assigned for the purpose) was issued. The award was later updated immediately after Independence and pending the formulation of a Constitution for the country.

The Constitution provided for only a Finance Commission to be appointed for every five years to review the finances of State governments and to recommend formulae for the devolution of resources, and the principles governing the grants-in-aid. In due course however, a Planning Commission was set up at the Centre to formulate development plans for the country as a whole. It became the major vehicle for economic development and under its aegis centrally sponsored and centrally assisted programmes came to be taken up. Most of the programmes so formulated were financed by transfers under Article 282 of the Constitution. The relative place and role of each Commission, Finance and Planning, became a controversial issue in that the 3rd Finance Commission spent a good deal of effort to retrieve the ground lost to the Planning Commission to no avail. The Finance Commissions appointed from the 4th Commission onwards accepted the *de facto* limited role and confined their activities to the determination of the non-plan revenue budget gap and to evolving devolution formulae aimed at providing a degree of autonomy, and financial stability for each five year period assigned to them.

Over the years the Finance Commissions made several improvements in their approaches in response to the changing needs and administrative requirements of the state governments. It is important to note that while the working of these commissions and that of the Planning Commission may not conform to the classic model of federalism, they have created a model that is well understood by the participants and the stakeholders alike; it is a model that has stood the test of the time. While no federal structure is sustained by financial arrangements alone, it is now accepted that the arrangements that evolved over the last six decades have proved to be, on balance, stabilising factors in the maintenance of Indian federalism.

In looking at the daunting tasks ahead, it is necessary to keep in view, the changes made in the operational approaches of the Finance Commission during the last half-a-century. The focus here is on the transformational changes (that impacted both the commissions, and the state governments) and not the transactional changes.

Changing Operational Systems

Assessment of Fiscal Needs

The work of the Finance Commissions starts with an assessment of the fiscal needs of the states for the next five year period (which after the 4th Finance Commission was changed to synchronise with the Plan Period). Towards this end, the state governments submit their forecasts to the Finance Commission for their detailed scrutiny. This scrutiny has varied over time and major improvements, listed below, have been made.

Methodology of Estimates

During the first one and a half decades, greater reliance was placed on the forecasts submitted by the state governments. Since the 4th Commission, however, improved statistical techniques, such as least squares, were adopted so as to be more consistent and less arbitrary. During these years, there was little reliance on macroeconomic variables, and it was implicitly assumed that the features of the base year would continue to prevail during the next five year period. Some adjustments were made from time to time to reflect major changes in the economy or in the policies of governments. Thus, committed expenditures were added on by the 2nd Finance Commission to reflect the additional expenditure needed to maintain the completed projects and programmes. Similarly, provisions were also made for national calamities.

In subsequent years, three far-reaching changes were made in regard to the assessment of fiscal needs. First, in lieu of the previous approaches that treated revenues and expenditures as somewhat autonomous, now greater emphasis is laid on macroeconomic factors. With the availability of data on state GDP, forecasts of needs and outlays are made keeping in view their relationships with other variables of the domestic product. This approach has admittedly added some additional measure of verisimilitude to the forecasts. It is true that every forecast has its own vulnerabilities but to some extent they have been minimised through the extensive use of macroeconomic data.

Second, the first few Finance Commissions did not have the benefit, except in a very superficial fashion, of the forecasts of the central government of its own revenues and likely outlays. This meant that the Finance Commissions had no means of knowing the likely impact of their recommendations on the financial condition of the central government. This area of darkness did not however, prevent, the first few Commissions from completing their assigned tasks. Rather, the central government had to bear the brunt of adjustment and did so without any input of its own into the formulation of the recommendations of the Commission. The claimants were given full opportunity but it was denied to the major player in the game. This area came to be illumined now with the submission of central government's own revenues and expenditures. It helps in harmonising the respective needs and in balancing the fiscal distribution.

A third major development also needs to be noted here. This relates to the introduction of fiscal responsibility and budget management legislation both at the centre and in most states. The intent was partly to signal the formulation of fiscal policy with particular attention to deficit containment over the medium term, and partly to persuade the foreign investors and international financial institutions that earnest efforts were being made to reduce the budget deficits. In theory, the medium term policy indications were to guide the making of the annual budget both at the centre and in the states. The impact of this legislation at both levels is an issue that is unlikely to receive a unanimous verdict. Some contend that it was more of a formality with little substance and as a self-regulating mechanism it did not have much force. Enforceability was left to the respective governments. The central government which was supposed to lead the way by setting an example did not give the needed weight to the legislation. In fact, during some years, the implementation of the deficit reduction goals was put on a `pause'. On the other hand, it can be argued, counterfactually, that were it not for this legislation, deficits would have been higher.

The future uses of this legislation would partly influence the direction of fiscal policy in the country. Meanwhile, a couple of the limitations of the operational systems also need to be noted. First, the forecasts of the Finance Commission are necessarily incomplete in that they are limited to the revenue budget of the state governments. Plan outlays and capital outlays are excluded from the purview of the Finance Commission. Second, the forecasts that were used as the basis for the determination of the devolution formulae, and related quantum of grants-in-aid are rarely made public. As far as the state governments, they prepare the budgets for the five year period as if the forecasts did not exist at all. In other words, the forecasts cease to be a limitation on the policies of the state governments. Second, the forecasts do not also include the servicing of the new borrowings to be undertaken during the next five year period although that burden falls on the revenue budget of the state.

Assessing Outlays

It has been noted earlier that the estimated rate of expenditure growth during the next five years period is a linear projection of the previously recorded rates of growth. To that extent, the implicit patterns of outlays are accepted as fully merited and therefore need to be continued for the foreseeable future. By the same token, it also means that there is little scope for rationalisation of expenditure so as to ensure accrual of benefits of efficiency. The important element is the quantum, rather than the quality of expenditures. This element, in turn, introduces an upward bias in expenditures. The pursuit of fiscal policy would then depend on the revenue side of the budget and not the expenditure side. This approach therefore sets aside all considerations of economy and efficiency of expenditures. Indeed, the state governments, being at the receiving end, have every incentive to spend every rupee at their disposal. In such a context, the pursuit of a fiscal goal of containing the budget deficit remains moot.

In partial recognition of the above phenomenon, the 13th Finance Commission was asked to develop expenditure norms for the consideration of the state governments. The action taken on the recommendations of the Commission is not clear, and at any rate, little impact is discernible in the field. No bold initiatives have been announced by any state government in any area concerning public expenditure. As a result the high administrative costs so clearly brought out by the 12th Finance Commission continue to operate as earlier.

In extenuation some factors affecting the state approaches need to be noted.

(a) Most development programmes are evolved by the central government, and are, for the most part, funded by them. More important, the financing is done, not from the current revenues of the central government but from the proceeds from borrowing both from domestic markets and from international financial institutions. Economies in this context can be procured only when there is a change in the design of the programmes. Frequently, however, the design evolved in the central government, is hardly susceptible of change, as the programmes are intended for uniform application throughout the country regardless of local variations. The programmes may not address the local needs at all but are accepted by the state governments partly under the impression that the funds released by the central government are fungible and thus can be used for other purposes as well. It is important to recognise that there is little incentive for the state governments to envisage changes in the design of the programmes and to that extent do not make any efforts to procure any gains through active management of the implementation process. Moreover, in many cases, the funds released may be intended to the lower level of governments where much of the implementation may be taking place.

(b) Any attempt at formulating norms should also recognise that conditions at the field level tend to vary from state to state. Sparcity of population, location of SC (scheduled caste) and ST (scheduled tribe) sections of the population, and administrative traditions (such as the establishment of nodal agencies) tend to add to local costs. Moreover, norms may be complied with through reliance on false reporting, as was the case with numerous development projects, most notably, the community development programme initiated and too quickly abandoned in the 1950s. This is not to say that norms should be done away with. Rather, the point is that norms are an instrument of day-to-day management and are best employed so as to serve as a handmaiden of local management.

(c) In this sphere, there is a major role for the central government to perform as an exemplar whose experience may be emulated at the sub-national government through an educational campaign. In this respect, the record of the central government leaves a lot to be desired. A bad model cannot be a good policy guide. Practice goes a long way than precepts or preaching from the high pulpit.

Arranging Devolution

In the 1950s, the most important source of revenue for the central government was the income tax closely followed by the proceeds from customs duties. During this period, the most important and stable source of revenue for the state governments was the land revenue. Income tax was a more elastic revenue than land revenue whose revision, apart from political opposition, was a long-drawn-out administrative process. It was evident then that sooner or later, the divisible pool which drew much of its strength from the income, would need expansion through the addition of other sources of central revenues. Accordingly, in due course, Union excises were added to the divisible pool. A decade later, the pool was expanded to include all the central revenues which came to be shared between the centre and the states on the basis of the formulae recommended by the Finance Commissions.

As one looks into the medium term, it is clear that the resources available would not be adequate to finance the growing needs at the national and sub-national level. Mobilisation of additional revenues at the sub-national level has become an anathema to the policymakers. Each level hopes that the other level would make efforts to be fiscally sustainable. In practice, this issue is being addressed in two ways. First, at the centre far too much reliance has been placed on surcharges than on the revision of basic rates and thus avoid the divisible pool criterion. Second, at the sub-national level it has become politically more convenient to demand the inclusion of surcharges in the divisible pool. Such a demand has obvious limitations, in that the central government which has the constitutional responsibility for the fiscal policy of the country is already under heavy pressure to reduce the size of its fiscal deficit. If surcharges become divisible, it is more than likely that the deficit would increase and so would be the level of borrowing. At the same time, both the centre and the states are forced to recognise the growing limitations of public borrowing. For one, such increased borrowing could crowd out corporate investment. Also, borrowing would become more expensive and a greater share of budget outlays would need to be devoted to debt servicing. More important, there would be greater pressure from the international and domestic creditors to change the content of fiscal policies. The full details of this scenario need to be worked out with utmost care. Meanwhile it needs to be recognised that borrowing can no longer be a soft option. For all these years, the appetite for borrowing has become an addiction, or in Plato's words, 'Pleonexia'—a hunger for more and more. But this fiscal profligacy has the potential of adversely affecting, indeed seriously eroding the strength of the state (at national and sub-national levels) in the citizens' minds. Should that happen, the very strength of the state, which is vital for its continuation, may be in danger.

This is not an idle mind's doomsday scenario. It is a recognition of a fiscal reality and what it portends for the future.

Grants-in-aid

At the time of the framing of the Constitution, the full contours of grants was not fully known. They could be specific and conditional, or they could be of the nature of a general subvention. The general understanding was that the broad category could be used to accommodate all kinds of transfers other than those relating to the devolution of resources from the specified revenue categories.

Accordingly, the first two Commissions made grants both for budgetary support and for developmental as well as non-developmental purposes. By the time of the 3rd Commission, however, the distinction between budget support grants and development grants became abundantly clear and the latter came to be administered by the Planning Commission through the invocation of Article 282 of the Constitution. This did not however, prevent the Finance Commissions from making specific and conditional grants for some purposes (such as the strengthening of the state treasury systems), although it must be noted, to the credit of the Finance Commissions, that this was not a well-treaded path. The transfers so made are relatively minor and do not have any importance of their own.

The important grant made by the Finance Commission is for budget support, and is specified for the whole five year period with no variation during the period. In principle, it means, that during periods when revenues are not buoyant, the grants-in-aid do not in any way compensate for the revenue short-falls. The fixed nature of the grants offers a degree of certainty to the policy-makers at the state level. As an extension, it has to be recognised that the lack of flexibility to vary with the changing economic conditions imposes some degree of hardship on the state governments. But, so far, no Finance Commission has envisaged a varying grant formula. It is presumably best to leave it unchanged.

Central Lending to States

A unique feature of Indian federalism is the fact that the Central government makes loans to the state governments both as a part of the annual Plan formulation and its related financing and *ad hoc* loans from time to time. Prior to the entry of the international financial institutions into the activity of direct lending to the state and local governments, development borrowing by the Centre was also transmitted in part to the state governments depending on the project or programme selected for financing by the international financial institution.

The process of Central lending to the states has its origins in two factors. First, a major part of the development plan was and is financed by borrowing by the Central government both from the domestic market and from abroad (including the international financial institutions). The funds so borrowed and utilised for development purposes are then relent (at enhanced rates, in some cases, to cover the risk factor) to the state governments to finance the plan programmes. These programmes have both a loan and a grant component. Second, it is recognised that the Centre has greater financial clout in the financial market and as such is better placed to borrow from the market.

The plan projects can both be self-liquidating and self-financing. In the case of the former, the state governments should have no difficulty in servicing the loan. In practice, however, there are long lags between the completion of projects and the flow of benefits, and between the flow of benefits and the actual utilisation of benefits, leading to enhanced fiscal capacities: owing to these lags, the state governments experience many problems in servicing the loans. It may also be noted, that many states also borrow from the Centre for general purposes, in the form of miscellaneous development plans (a catch all residual category). This is simply a way of avoiding borrowing from the markets. As a result of these approaches, the amount to be repaid is substantial. Viewed from the point of the states, the amounts are so huge that they can never be repaid in full and that in the meantime, the net transfer of resources from the Centre (after adjustments for repayments due) is not much.

In addition, many of them have been demanding a write-off of outstanding loans, and the need for making a new beginning. Although no thought has been given to the latter, the Central government has selectively written off outstanding loans (as was the case with Punjab). With this discretionary action, the issue has moved into the political arena.

Although the terms of reference may not require a mandatory investigation into this area, it is necessary, given the magnitude and the importance of the issue, to look into the process and analyse the patterns of future relationships, with particular reference to the following aspects:

What are the areas where the Centre should lend monies to the state governments?

(i) If the Centre is to be a lender of the last resort, what alternatives may be envisaged?

(ii) Should the terms of Central lending be uniform or should some weight be given to economic and financial factors?

Issues

Fiscal Equalisation

A common goal in the functioning of the federal systems is to achieve fiscal equalisation in the provision of the public services. So far this has not been formally aimed at in any form, including plan programmes, in India. A main reason for not doing so are the range of factors at work at the ground level. Such factors include—the resource endowment of the states, fiscal policies of the states, development plans of the states, central investments and other outlays in the states, foreign aid received, and the NRI remittances received and the patterns of their utilisation.

While the reluctance to address the issue is understandable, a beginning needs to be made in this direction to illustrate the efforts that need to be made in the future.

States and Financial Management

Accounting Unit versus Fiscal Entity

In an ideal set up every unit in a federation has its own territorial jurisdiction, and autonomy in the mobilisation of fiscal resources, and in the allocation and effective use of those resources. While the pursuit of fiscal policy may involve some degree of coordination with other units and with the Central governments the units themselves have the principal responsibility for the formulation and implementation of fiscal policies. This may involve conflicts with the Central government and fiscal perversity may be the assured outcome. Notwithstanding such divergences, the fact of complementarities between the national and sub-national levels needs to be recognised.

In India, the responsibility for the formulation of fiscal policy rests with the Central government. As a consequence, the sub-national levels have come to be treated both by the Planning and Finance Commissions as accounting and administrative units, rather than as autonomous and cognate units with a major responsibility to complement the role of the Central government while performing their own tasks and responsibilities. In the former capacity as accounting units, their budgets are for all intents and purposes supervised by the Central agencies, and the budget deficits are financed by transfers from the Centre, although the sub-national units have their own legislatures to which they are accountable. The accounting and auditing of the fiscal transactions of the sub-national governments are undertaken by the Indian Accounts and Audit Department, an agency of the central government. As an administrative unit, the sub-national units perform many agency functions for which reimbursements are made by the central government. As a result of these unique arrangements, the sub-national governments have never attained the fiscal autonomy that was implicit in the arrangements envisaged by the Constitution.

If, however, the sub-national governments are viewed as autonomous fiscal units, then it would be necessary to pay attention to the patterns of resource allocation, and related utilisation. Such an attention and related analysis would reveal the choices made, and their implications for the financial status of the units during the next five years. As a complementary feature, their capability for the pursuit of countercyclical policies would also come to the fore for consideration. None of these aspects have been given the attention due, in view of the traditional, lopsided emphasis on the accounting aspects and associated fiscal dentistry.

There is a need to depart from the previous practices and initiate a detailed analysis of the resource use and address the issues that emerge from such an analysis.

Public Sector Undertakings (PSUs) and Public Private Partnerships (PPP)

Three areas of major concern in the review of State finances relate to the financial working of the state-owned enterprises, the PPPs, entered into by states and the emergence of third party payments. The losses incurred by the PSUs, and any liabilities from the PPPs are routinely included by the state governments in their forecasts submitted to the Finance Commissions. This means that the losses incurred are routinely underwritten, without any review, by the Commissions. Similarly, the liabilities from the PPPs are also underwritten by the Commissions, and to that extent, both types of transactions tend to be financed from the national resources without legislative review and related accountability processes. As an extension of PPPs, there has emerged a third party payment system. In this system, the services are mandated by the government but are provided by private parties which are then paid by the government. This system has enormous potential for fraud and consequent failure of expenditure controls. These aspects merit further attention.

It is appropriate to raise the issue whether this practice should be continued or whether the Finance Commission should examine these areas in view of their potential impact on the state as well as national finances.

Arrears in Payment

Since the revenue and capital budgets are respectively underwritten by the Finance and Planning Commissions, it holds that there would be no liquidity problems at the sub-national governments. Nothing could be further from the truth. Most state governments have, on any given day, massive arrears in payments of wages, and transfers to local bodies. Some of these arrears are more than one year old suggesting that accumulation of arrears has become an accepted tool of liquidity management at the sub-national level. The damage that it does to the credibility of the governments is immense. In due course, this contributes to an increase in the borrowing costs. Equally, the actions underlying arrear accumulation are arbitrary and constitute an involuntary lending to governments. It is necessary that these aspects are brought out into daylight.

Table 2.1

Functioning of Federal System in India: A Schematic Presentation

Constitutional Aspects		*Resource Transfer Management*		*Other*
Constitutional Mechanism	*Statutory Mechanism*	*Regular Administrative Machinery*	*Consultative Machinery*	*Central Activities Impacting State Fiscal Status*
• Central, State and Concurrent Lists • Quinquinnial Finance Commission • Other periodic commissions to review the functioning of the system	• Finance Commission • Special dispensation by Central Governments	• Planning Commission • Central Assistance for Plan Projects • Centrally sponsored • Miscellaneous development assistance (ad-hoc) • Natural calamity assistance • Processing of foreign aided projects	• National Development Council • Planning Commission Reviews • Zonal Meetings • Monthly letter from PM to Chief Ministers • Ad-hoc Meetings • Ad-hoc Ministerial Committees	• Central policies toward pay revision • Central investment in public undertakings and its locational impact • Negotiation of foreign aid • Selective write-off of Central loans to State governments
State Governments				
• Finance Commission to review local finances and to recommend devolution formulae		• Parallel machinery on the lines of Central Government with selective modification • Local bodies receive direct assistance from Central Government • Local bodies can borrow from the market subject to clearances by State and Central Governments	• For the most part under the direct supervision of the Finance Departments (including Audit) and concerned administrative agencies	• Impact varies depending on the state policies towards pay and allowances structures

3 Role of Finance Commission in Macroeconomic and Fiscal Stability in India[1]

Atul Sarma

Introduction

A Finance Commission's terms of references are clearly specified in the Constitution itself under Article 280. To be more specific, Finance Commission (FC) is required to make recommendations every five years to the President of India as to: (a) the distribution between the Union and the states of the net proceeds of the divisible taxes (prior to the 80th Constitutional Amendment in 2000, only Personal Income tax compulsorily and Union Excise duties, if needed, were divisible) and the allocation of the respective states' shares in the divisible pool and (b) the principles that should govern the grants-in-aid of the revenues of the states out of the consolidated Fund of India. Later two sub-clauses were added under (bb) and (c) vide the 73rd and 74th Amendments of the Constitution in 1992. Under these, FC is required to recommend the measures needed to augment the Consolidated Fund of a state to supplement the resources of the *panchayats* and the municipalities in the state on the basis of the recommendation of the respective States' Finance Commission (SFC). The other sub-clause (c) replaced as sub-clause (d) by the Constitution (74th Amendment) Act 1992 relates to any other matter referred to the Commission in the interest of sound finance.

Even if the tasks assigned to FC are specific in nature as noted above, additional matters under sub-clause (d) that have direct or indirect relevance to sound finance have been referred to successive FC right from

1. Based on the presentation made at the Asia-Pacific and Latin American Interregional Forum for Results Decentralisation and the Changing Role of Central Finance Agencies, Manila, Philippines (November 28-29, 2012).

the first one. This paper addresses one such matter *viz.*, the issue of restoring fiscal balance and maintaining macroeconomic stability included in the Terms of Reference (ToR) of the Eleventh Finance Commission (EFC) and the following three FCs. It discusses the circumstance in which the matter was first referred to the 11th Finance Commission (EFC), indicates the broad scheme of restructuring public finances recommended and their impact on the finances of the Union and the States as observed and ways of improving them further as recommended by the subsequent two FCs.

The Context

Large fiscal deficits were fuelled increasingly by deficits in the revenue budgets of the Union Government for nearly two decades since 1979-80. Since then financing current expenditure by borrowing became a feature in Union budgets. Since 1987-88, first, the fiscally weaker states and then even the better-off among the states slipped into revenue deficit. Revenue deficits were only visible manifestations of multiple and deep-seated imbalances in government finances. What was a matter of serious concern were five key fiscal trends:[2] (i) decline in the tax-GDP ratio, (ii) large pre-emptive claims of interest payments relative to revenue receipts, (iii) high revenue deficit to GDP ratio, (iv) large and unsustainable fiscal deficit to GDP ratio, and (v) falling levels of capital expenditure.

For example, taking the combined finances of the Union and the states, tax-GDP ratio fell from a level of about 16 per cent during three year average of 1987-1990 to 14.4 per cent during 1999-2002 three year average. Interest payments relative to revenue receipts rose nearly by 13 per cent to reach the level of 34 per cent during the corresponding periods; revenue deficit increased to 6.5 per cent of GDP by a margin of 3.5 per cent during the same period; combined fiscal deficit which was 8.8 per cent in late eighties rose by 0.7 per cent during 1999-2002 and climbed above 10 per cent in 2002-03; capital expenditure slumped to 2.8 per cent from 3.3 per cent of GDP during the reference period.[3]

It is in this context that the EFC was asked for the first time "to review the state of finances of the Union and the States and suggest ways

2. Report of the 12th Finance Commission (2005-2010), p.22
3. Ibid.

and means by which the governments, collectively and severally, may bring about a restructuring of the public finances so as to restore budgetary balance and maintain macroeconomic stability."[4]

The EFC while addressing this task, (i) considered the relevant parameters of macroeconomic stability; (ii) based on the parameters chosen, outlined the contours of the restructured public finances of the country with suitable disaggregation between the Union and the states needed to ensure macro stability; (iii) specified the contents of restructuring; and (iv) spelt out the ways and means by which such restructuring can be brought about by the Union and State governments, collectively and severally.[5]

In the context of the task of formulating the ways and means for achieving budgetary balance, the EFC was subsequently asked "to draw a monitorable fiscal reforms programme aimed at reduction of revenue deficit and recommend the manner in which grants to cover the assessed deficit in their non-plan revenue account be linked to progress in implementing the programme."[6]

Keeping in view the objectives of restoring macro stability and sustainable level of debt, the EFC reviewed the state of the Union and state finances and attempted to identify the basic and proximate causes of the deterioration of their public finances. It also considered issues of macroeconomic stability with a focus on implications for intergovernmental transfers. It finally outlined an adjustment path for fiscal restructuring as also put forward a package of ways and means for implementation, keeping in view a medium term goal of fiscal consolidation both at the level of the Union and the state governments.

With a view to moving Indian public finances away from chronic deficits and unsustainable debt, the EFC designed a restructuring plan. It aimed at: (i) bringing the combined revenue deficit of the Union and the states to a level not more than 1 per cent of GDP by 2004-05 over a period of five years (2000-05); (ii) containing combined fiscal deficit to a level less than 6.5 per cent—Centre's target being 4.5 per cent and States' 2.5

4. Report of the EFC (2000-2005), p.18
5. Ibid.
6. Ibid.

per cent;[7] (iii) restoring the tax-GDP ratio to 17 of GDP; (iv) enhancing non-tax revenue by 0.75 per cent of GDP; (v) reprioritising expenditure towards basic needs like elementary education, primary health, water supply and sanitation and essential infrastructure; and (vi) increasing capital expenditure on the combined account to around 6.6 per cent of GDP. As for debt reduction, the combined debt-GDP ratio of the Union and states was to be brought down to 55 per cent in 2004-05 from the current (1999-2000) level of 65 per cent. The EFC also suggested setting a limit of borrowing from all sources by both levels of government under Articles 292 and 293 of the Constitution.

The EFC designed a detailed scheme of restructuring[8] of different aspects of public finances to make it possible to achieve the above targets together with an output growth rate of 7.0-7.5 per cent and inflation rate of 5.5-5.5 per cent. The very comprehensive restructuring design covered restructuring of revenue sources, both tax and non-tax, restructuring of government expenditure, reform in the method of financing plan expenditure, desirable role of government, enhancing the efficiency of government expenditure, restructuring of public sector enterprises, institutional reforms comprising federal fiscal relations, management and control of debt and constitutional and legal changes and restructuring of finances of special category states.

The strategy that the EFC has suggested was anchored on:

(i) "Widening the tax base and in particular, bringing services fully under the tax net in a properly designed scheme which requires, among listing among other things, listing of services, in the Concurrent List,

(ii) "Using profession tax as also taxation of farm incomes to augment revenues in the States,

(iii) "Gearing up administration for better exploitation of the tax bases, without unduly increasing tax rates,

---

7. Separate target for the Centre and the States can be seen from Table 3.2: Fiscal Adjustment: Centre and States in the Report of the EFC (2000-2005), p.25.

8. See Report of the EFC (2000-2005), pp.27-36.

(iv) "Relying on user charges for enhancing non-tax revenues by index linking them to changes in input costs;

(v) "Reviewing the policy towards fixation of royalty rates of minerals by index linking them to inflation for augmenting the revenues of the states;

(vi) "Bearing salaries and other allowances a relationship with the revenue expenditure of the Centre and the States. The ratio may be worked out by an Expert Committee;

(vii) "Building up infrastructure in every State, particularly in the special category States, for the generation of economic activities on a substantial scale which alone can provide them with a strong revenue base;

(viii) "Cutting subsidies and making them explicit and transparent;

(ix) "Transferring Centrally Sponsored Schemes to the States along with funds;

(x) "Revising the present system of determining and providing assistance to State plans;

(xi) "Resizing the governments at all levels by redeployment and downsizing;

(xii) "Improving budgetary procedures and procedures for evaluation and monitoring of public expenditure programmes;

(xiii) "Introducing comprehensive structural reforms for public sector enterprises;

(xiv) "Reviewing the assignment of tax powers between the Centre and the States for better exploitation and revenue yield;

(xv) "Suggesting limits on borrowing close to a fixed norm regarding the ratio of interest payment to revenue receipts, as also the size of debt relative to output (GDP/GSDP), and suggesting the need for bringing relevant legislation by the Centre and by each State for fixing the limits to borrowing and guarantees; and

(xvi) "Restructuring finances of the special category States by changing the method of providing plan assistance and direct

> Central participation in building up infrastructures in these States."[9]

The fiscal transfers that the EFC designed kept in view the objectives of restructuring as outlined, provided incentives to prudent fiscal behaviour and debt relief with improvements in fiscal performance. The EFC also designed a scheme through fiscal reform facility to evaluate fiscal performance in terms of reduction of revenue deficits of the states through monitorable measures.

Fiscal Responsibility and Management Budget Act (FRBM), 2003

In view of the unsustainable state of government finances, the Union Government enacted FRBM, 2003[10] in the broad framework of the recommendations of the EFC on fiscal consolidation. The Act came into effect from July 4, 2004. It sought to introduce the fundamentals of fiscal discipline at different levels of government. The FRBM Act aimed at eliminating revenue deficit, prohibiting government borrowings from the Reserve Bank of India (RBI), and reducing the fiscal deficit to 3 per cent of GDP within a time frame. The main purpose was to eliminate revenue deficit of the country (building revenue surplus thereafter) and bring down the fiscal deficit to a manageable level of 3 per cent of the GDP by March 2008. However, due to the 2007 international financial crisis, the deadlines for the implementation of the targets in the act was initially postponed and subsequently suspended in 2009. In 2011, given the process of on-going recovery, the Economic Advisory Council (EAC) publicly advised the Government of India to reconsider reinstating the provisions of the FRBM.

Since the act was primarily for the management of the governments' behaviour, it provided for certain documents with regards to the country's fiscal policy to be tabled in the Parliament annually along with the Annual Financial Statements and demands for grants. These included:

(i) A document titled *Medium-term Fiscal Policy Statement:* This report was to present a three-year rolling target for the *fiscal*

---

9. Government of India (2000).
10. Government of India (2003).

indicators with any assumptions, if applicable. This statement was to further include an assessment of sustainability with regards to *revenue deficit* and the use of capital receipts of the Government (including market borrowings) for generating productive assets.

(ii) A document titled *Fiscal Policy Strategy Statement:* This was a tactical report enumerating strategies and policies for the upcoming financial year including strategic fiscal priorities, taxation policies, key fiscal measures and an evaluation of how the proposed policies of the Central Government conform to the 'Fiscal Management Principles' of this act.

(iii) A document titled *Macroeconomic Framework Statement:* This report was to contain forecasts enumerating the growth prospects of the country. GDP growth, revenue balance, gross fiscal balance and external account balance of the balance of payments which were some of the key indicators to be included in this report.

The Act further required the government to develop measures to promote fiscal transparency and reduce secrecy in the preparation of the Government financial documents including the Union Budget.

Fiscal Management Principles

The Central Government, by rules made by it, was to specify the following:

(i) A plan to eliminate revenue deficit by 31 Mar 2008 by setting annual targets for reduction starting from day of commencement of the Act.

(ii) To reduce annual fiscal deficit of the country.

(iii) To set annual targets for assuming contingent liabilities in the form of guarantees and the total liabilities as a percentage of the GDP.

It is important to note that the FRBM provided the institutional framework that can support fiscal reforms. The Tenth Plan pleaded for adoption of FRBM at the State level. Accordingly, several States enacted fiscal responsibility legislations. The Twelfth Finance Commission (TFC) suggested that the rest of the States should also draw up medium term reform programmes with specific monitorable targets in the context of Medium Term Reform Facility (MTRF) instituted on the basis of the recommendations of EFC.

Twelfth Finance Commission (2005-2010)

Like the EFC, the TFC was also required to "review the state of finances of the Union and the States and suggest a plan by which the Governments, collectively and severally, may bring about a restructuring of the public finances restoring budgetary balance achieving macroeconomic stability and debt reduction along with equitable growth."[11] Unlike the EFC, the TFC was required to address the objectives of debt reduction and equitable growth in addition to achieving budgetary balance and macroeconomic stability. We would, however, largely deal with the issue of restoring budgetary balance consistent with macroeconomic stability and debt reduction, it being the main thrust of this paper.

Reviewing the restructuring plan recommended by its predecessor, the TFC observed improvement in fiscal balance even if there were considerable slippages in achieving the stipulated targets by both the levels of government. This failure was due to deficiency in revenue efforts, slackness in expenditure controls in addition to slowdown in growth in the first three years of the EFC period.

Fiscal correction that the TFC recommended required increasing by 2009-10, the combined tax-GDP ratio to 17.6 per cent, primary expenditure to a level of 22 per cent of GDP and capital expenditure to nearly 7 per cent of GDP. Revenue deficit should be eliminated by Centre and States by 2008-09 and the fiscal deficit should be fixed at 3 per cent GDP for each level of Government. Debt-GDP ratio should be brought down to at least 75 per cent against 81 per cent.[12]

Debt restructuring recommended had two components: a consolidation of all outstanding State debt to the Centre at the end of 2004-05 at an

---

11. Report of the TFC (2005-2010), p.50
12. The TFC set targets for the fiscal variables that should be achieved over a five-year period by 2009-10 from the base year of 2004-05 both in combined finances as well as separately in the Union and State Finances through its suggested restructuring. See Tables 4.12 and 4.13, Report of the TFC (2005-2010), pp.74-75.

interest rate of 7.5 per cent and a debt relief scheme linked to achievement in reducing deficits. The precondition for availing the benefit of the scheme was the requirement "to enact the fiscal responsibility legislation that provides for eliminating revenue deficit in their respective states no later than 2008-09, incorporates annual targets for reduction of fiscal and revenue deficits, and presents to the respective legislatures a consolidated growth and fiscal strategy statement along with their budgets."[13] The other component relates to the process of accumulation of debt to the Centre. To arrest this process the TFC recommended that the Centre should not act as an intermediary and allow the States to approach the market directly. That would impart fiscal prudence since the market would evaluate fiscal performance.

With the system of on-lending being stopped over time the long term goal for the Centre and States should be 28 per cent each.

The reforms that the TFC recommended presented an adjustment path which aimed at achieving over a five-year period (2004-05 -2009-10) a macroeconomic scenario as given in Table 3.1.

Table 3.1

Macroeconomic Scenario: Current and Forecast

Macro-Indicators	*Per cent to GDP*	
	2004-05 (estimate)	*2009-10 (projection)*
GDP growth (constant prices) per cent p.a	6.5	7.0
Inflation rate (per cent p.a)	6.0	5.0
Saving rate	24.0	26.0
Investment rate	24.5	27.5
Current Account Deficit	-0.5	1.5
Fiscal Deficit	8.9	6.0
Revenue Deficit	4.5	0.0
Government Capital Expenditure	5.6	6.6

Source: Report of the TFC, Table 4.11, p.73

The core strategy of fiscal adjustment recommended by the TFC was anchored on raising the trend growth rate by enhancing the savings ratio through reduction of government dis-savings which, in turn, required elimination of revenue deficit by the both levels of government.

13. Report of the TFC (2005-2010), p.84

The restructuring recommended by the TFC covered the following areas:[14]

(i) Taxation reforms aimed at paving the way for non-distortionary revenue elastic system with low tax rates, limited rate categories.

(ii) Non-tax revenues: In the case of user charges, reforms aimed at recovering current cost in the short term and full recovery of costs compatible with acceptable efficiency levels in the longer run; in the case of services where there is no clear case of subsidisation, ensuring rates of return on investment covering the average cost of borrowing.

(iii) Expenditure restructuring covering both its size and sectoral allocations aimed at eliminating inefficiencies by improving design, implementation and delivery of services.

(iv) Rationalising subsidies to a reduced magnitude by making them explicit and transparent and by improving targeting.

(v) Public sector restructuring towards reducing government's involvement leaving aside natural monopolies and strategic ones.

(vi) Fiscal transfer system with greater weight on equalising transfers and larger transfer to local bodies.

(vii) Suggesting a reformed role for the planning process.

(viii) Strengthening the role of local bodies to enable them to become effective institutions in local public goods delivery.

(ix) Phasing out the Union government's intermediation in borrowing by the states as also suggesting the need to set annual ceiling of borrowing for each state and implementing a hard-budget constraint; and

(x) Suggesting institutional frameworks that include ceiling on debt and deficits and mechanisms for their monitoring through a fiscal responsibility legislation at the state level.

While suggesting the scheme of restructuring, the TFC pre-supposed determined and coordinated effort by the Central and State governments.

14. See for details, Report of TFC, pp.76-85.

Thirteenth Finance Commission (2010-2015)

Recognising the improvement in fiscal performance at the levels of the Union and the states in the preceding years, the ToR of the Thirteenth Finance Commission (ThFC) was differently worded. The ThFC was required to "review the roadmap for fiscal adjustment and suggest a suitably revised roadmap with a view to maintaining the gains of fiscal consolidation through 2010-2015." The Commission was also required to "review the state of finances of the Union and the States, keeping in view, in particular, the operation of the States' Debt Consolidation and Relief Facility (DCRF) 2005-2010 introduced by the Central Government on the basis of the recommendations of the TFC and suggest measures for maintaining a stable and sustainable fiscal environment consistent with equitable growth."

While addressing this ToR, the ThFC observed that the Centre and the states recorded a commendable fiscal improvement. It observed that the two key indicators of macro-fiscal performance, *viz.*, the combined fiscal deficit and debt to GDP ratio of the Union and the states fell consistently from 7.3 and 91.7 per cent respectively in 2004-05 to 5.0 and 81.9 per cent in 2008-09 (B.E). Against this, TFC targets set for 2009-10 were 3 per cent for fiscal deficit and outstanding debt to GDP ratio of 75 per cent. The aggregate revenue deficit of the Centre and the states was also estimated at 0.4 for 2008-09 (B.E) against the TFC recommendation of zero revenue deficits to be achieved by 2009-10. The ThFC noted that the previous FCs' strategy of linking debt relief incentives to fiscal corrections delivered improved fiscal health in State finances. However, there was a global slowdown subsequent to the budget for 2008-09. The adverse macroeconomic circumstances that prevailed in 2008-09 continued even in 2009-10.

ThFC's roadmap for fiscal correction path had set the following fiscal rules:

(i) The revenue deficit of the Centre at 4.8 per cent in 2009-10 should be progressively brought down to zero by 2013-14, followed by emergence of a surplus of 0.5 per cent of GDP in 2014-15.

(ii) All states should maintain zero revenue deficit. Only three general category states, *viz.*, Kerala, Punjab and West Bengal recorded revenue deficit in 2007-08. The ThFC suggested an adjustment path for these states beginning from 2011-12 to eliminate revenue deficit by 2014-2015.[15]

(iii) As for special category states, it was observed that all of them had revenue surplus over the 2005-08 for a very peculiar situation. It was that these states were highly dependent on Central grants and Central grants were classified as revenue receipts while capital expenditure out of Central grants were not treated as revenue expenditure. This meant that revenue balance had little significance for the purpose of fiscal adjustment. Therefore, ThFC recommended fiscal deficit adjustment path for six out of the eleven special category states[16] with a base level higher than 3 per cent to reduce it to 3 per cent by 2014-15.

(iv) The combined fiscal deficit should be brought down to 5.4 per cent by 2013-14 and maintained at that level in 2014-15. To conform to this target, Centre's fiscal deficit should be brought down to 3 per cent by 2013-14 from 6.8 per cent in 2009-10 and maintained at that level in the subsequent year while that of the states' to 2.4 per cent from 2.8 per cent in 2009-10.

(v) The capital expenditure of the Centre should be raised from 2.1 per cent in 2009-10 to 4.5 per cent of GDP by 2014-15.

(vi) Keeping in view the projected medium-term macroeconomic situation, and feasible and desirable fiscal correction, ThFC set the combined target of 68 per cent of debt- GDP ratio by 2014-15 with the target of 45 per cent for the Centre against the level of 54.2 per cent in 2009-10 and 25 per cent for states by 2014-15 against the level of about 27 per cent in 2007-08. It indicated the year-wise target for the Centre and the individual States within this overall target.

---

15. See, Report of the ThFC (2010-2015), p.138.
16. These are: J&K, Manipur, Mizoram, Nagaland, Sikkim and Uttarakhand.

Strengthening Institutions

The states' enactment and amendment of their (Fiscal Reform Legislations) FRLs incorporating the targets set should be a conditionality for release of all state specific grants.

ThFC recommended that the Central Government should revise the existing medium term fiscal policy statement with a more detailed Medium Term Fiscal Plan (MTFP) which would provide a fiscal roadmap for three years into the future. This would ensure tighter integration of the MTFP and the annual budget exercise and it would then make the MTFP more a statement of commitment than merely one of intent.

Drawing a lesson from the implementation of the FRBM during 2005-2010, the THFC recognised the need for built-in-flexibility in the fiscal system to adapt to exogenous shocks. Accordingly, it recommended three changes in the design of the fiscal responsibility to address such challenge. First, the THFC recommended that the MTFP should make "the values of the parameters underlying expenditure and revenue projections and the band within which these parameters can vary while remaining consistent with FRBM targets."[17] Second, the FRBM should specify the nature of shocks that would call for relaxation of FRBM targets. Finally, it should be explicitly recognised that macroeconomic and counter-recessionary actions are the primary responsibility of the Union Government. The associated cost of such occurrences should entirely be borne by the Central Government. In the event of occurrence of such a situation, instead of relaxing the borrowing limits for the states, the Central Government should assume the responsibility of mobilising additional resources and pass on the resources so mobilised to the states in the form of increased devolution on the basis of the horizontal formula recommended by the Finance Commission.

The ThFC recommended that all states should include independent review/monitoring as some states already have done as a feature of the FRBM. It also recommended that the Central Government should set net borrowing limits for states based on the fiscal deficit path recommended for each state.

---

17. For further elaboration, see, Report of the ThFC, p.136.

In short, the roadmap for fiscal consolidation that the ThFC recommended was essentially based on the following premise. It is that the key to successful consolidation "lies in maintaining the growth dynamism of our economy. There is a two-way relationship between growth and fiscal consolidation; or what is called the 'strategy of expansionary fiscal consolidation' where fiscal consolidation leads to higher growth due to higher levels of public and private investments which in turn, further facilitates maintenance of fiscal stability."[18]

Concluding Remarks

Given the fact that the FC has come to enjoy high respectability as an independent institution, both the Union and the state governments do give serious consideration to its deliberations and recommendations. That is probably the reason why the issue of restructuring public finances in the context of deteriorating fiscal situations was included for the first time in the ToR of the EFC and later in the ToR of the subsequent FCs in one form or the other.

Indeed, the adjustment path recommended by the EFC and TFC made significant impact on the fiscal performance of both the Union and the state governments even if there were considerable slippages from the targets set by them.

But the exceptional circumstances of 2008-09 and 2009-10 disrupted the fiscal consolidation process. High inflation, rising current account deficit and falling growth in the following three years which were the first three years of the ThFC award period as can be seen in the table below vitiated macroeconomic and fiscal stability which in turn has threatened strict adherence to the correction path recommended by the ThFC.

18. Report of the ThFC, p.141.

Table 3.2

Macroeconomic Scenario in 2010-11 and 2011-12
(First Two Years of the ThFC Award Period)

	2010-11(RE)	2011-12(BE)
GDP Growth 2004-05 prices(per cent p.a)	9.3	6.2
Inflation (per cent)(WPI average)	9.6	8.9
Gross domestic saving (current market price as % of GDP)	32.3	30.8
Current Account Deficit as % of GDP	2.8	4.2
Fiscal deficit as % of GDP	7.81	6.75
Revenue Deficit as % of GDP	3.73	3.16
Tax revenue as % of GDP	16.46	16.64
Government capital expenditure as % of GDP	4.49	4.24

Source: (1) *Economic Survey* 2011-12 and 2012-13.
(2) *Indian Public Finance Statistics 2011-12.*

Even so, the fiscal performance parameters at the level of the states in aggregate were closer to the targets set by the ThFC. For example, against the target of zero revenue deficit, the Centre's revenue deficit stood at 3.52 per cent of GDP in 2010-11 (RE) and 3.52 per cent in 2011-12 (BE) while the states' were 0.22 per cent and revenue surplus 0.26 per cent respectively in the corresponding years. Similarly, against the target of fiscal deficit at 3 per cent of GDP, the Centre's fiscal deficit was 5.23 per cent of GDP in 2010-11 (RE) and 4.60 per cent in 2011-12 (BE) while the states' fiscal deficit was a little higher in 2010-2011 but lower than the target of 2.4 per cent in 2011-12, 2.62 per cent and 2.16 per cent of GDP in the corresponding years.

Recognising the useful role that the preceding three FCs played in fiscal correction, a kind of follow-up clause (clause 5) has been included in the ToR of the recently constituted 14th Finance Commission. It runs as: "The Commission shall review the state of the finances, deficit and debt levels of the Union and the States, keeping in view, in particular, the fiscal consolidation roadmap recommended by the Thirteenth Finance Commission and suggest measures for maintaining a stable and sustainable fiscal environment consistent with equitable growth including suggestions to amend the Fiscal Responsibility and Budget Management Acts currently in force..............."

References

Government of India (2000). *Report of the Eleventh Finance Commission (2000-2005)*. New Delhi: Ministry of Finance. pp.35-36.

———. (2003). *The Fiscal Responsibility and Budget Management Act, 2003*. No. 39 of 2003, The Gazette of India, Extraordinary Part II. New Delhi: Ministry of Law and Justice. August 26.

4 Indian Finance Commission

Need for Revamping and Restructuring

J.V.M. Sarma and V. Bhaskar

Introduction

Since 1951, it has been a routine quinquinnial exercise to appoint a Finance Commission (FC) to recommend resource sharing between the Central (Federal Government) and the State (Provincial) Governments. "The President of India is required under Article 280(1) of the Constitution to constitute within two years from the commencement of the Constitution and thereafter at the expiration of every fifth year, or at an earlier time as he may consider necessary, a Finance Commission consisting of a chairman and four members appointed by him" (First Finance Commission, 1952).

Over the last two decades, the Indian economy has been experiencing significant growth along with structural transformation, necessitating vital economic reforms not only for sustaining the economic growth but also to bring about necessary changes in the policy environment to cope with the structural changes in the economy. The federal fiscal system, being a crucial aspect of the Indian economy, also needs fundamental revamping. Gone are the times when the basic function of the Indian Finance Commission was to merely recommend vertical and horizontal sharing of revenues collected by the Centre with the constituent States.

Even with the present form there is a need to bring certain changes in the working of the FC. For example, with the implementation of the GST (goods and services tax) it may be expected that the revenue collections and consequently, the fiscal imbalances between the Centre and states will undergo major change and perhaps the existing vertical and horizontal sharing methods will have to be streamlined.

In addition, the FC is being increasingly entrusted with many other tasks including overall macroeconomic and fiscal management of the country. This calls for fundamental institutional changes both in the form as well as the working of the FC. It is therefore imperative that some thought should be given to this aspect and sufficiently debated. The purpose of this note is to underline the need for revamping and restructuring of the FC, especially to re-examine the issue whether the FC should be made a permanent organ of government administration and, if made permanent, how its role can be enhanced.

After exploring the need for streamlining the approach of the FCs in view of the impending changes in the revenue imbalances, this paper emphasises the need for enhancing the role of the FC. The issue of making the FC a permanent organ of the Government is discussed and thereafter the possible additional roles for the FC other than recommending revenue sharing between the Centre and states are discussed. In particular, the enhanced responsibilities could make the FC to be:

(i) The macroeconomic manager of the country that devises policies for growth and macroeconomic stability, suggests ways of controlling fiscal deficit and debt management, and also designs the fiscal framework for economic reforms;

(ii) An instrument to closely monitor the economy;

(iii) An economic think-tank for the Government; and

(iv) Manager of the fiscal data base.

In what follows, these points are elaborated.

Streamlining the Primary Functions of the Finance Commission

Like all other federations the Indian federation is also facing the problems of vertical and horizontal imbalances. The Constitution of India, in recognition of these two problems, facilitates the balancing of finances between the Centre and the states through various Articles (especially Articles 268, 269, 270, 275, 282 and 293) that specify ways and means of sharing the resources. In addition, the Constitution also provides an institutional framework in the form of the FC to facilitate the transfers.

Thus, the FC came into existence in 1951 under Article 280 of the Indian Constitution.

The main duty of the FC relates to the sharing of Central taxes under Article 270 and determination of grants for the states as provided for under Article 275. The Commission is constituted to make recommendations to the President about the distribution of the net proceeds of taxes between the Union and states and also the allocation of the same amongst the states themselves. The Commission's mandate and the terms of reference (ToR) are contained in the Presidential order for the FC. Over time, the principles and methods adopted have undergone substantial changes and rightly so in keeping with the changing economic structure and policy environment. However there is a need to bring more fundamental changes in the approach to make it more objective and scientific.

Vertical Sharing

A feature of federal systems in the world including India is that the constituent provinces (States) have relatively large constitutionally-assigned spending responsibilities but fewer own-revenue sources while the reverse is true at the federal (Central) government level. For example, in India, the Central government collects about 70 per cent of the total revenue raised at all levels of government in the country while its share in total government spending is only about 45 per cent. The difference between the relative revenue and spending responsibilities of the federal and provincial governments is reflective of the VFI (vertical fiscal imbalance).

The vertical sharing formula for example, albeit inadvertently, follows an incremental approach. FC after FC the objective appears to increase the share of the states. There is no evidence of any scientific derivation of the share. An important improvement has been the combining of all the Central taxes for revenue sharing as recommended by the 10th FC and implemented through the Constitutional 80th Amendment. Yet, several Central revenue sources such as the cesses, the service tax proceeds, are left out of the shareable pool. The 11th FC for example, notes that: "The share to be given to each State is only in respect of taxes and duties which are leviable in that State in the relevant year... The Union Ministry of Finance has informed us that at present all taxes except the expenditure tax and service tax are leviable in every State of the country. Expenditure tax and

Service tax are not leviable only in the State of Jammu & Kashmir. We have kept this position in view while determining the *inter-se* share of the States in the distribution of Central taxes" (11th Finance Commission, 2000). The 12th and 13th FCs followed suit.

Thus, there are significant sources of revenue that are at present kept out of the sharing. The exclusion of the revenues on account of cesses and also the service tax proceeds from the fiscal sharing has been drawing critical attention from the states. Of late, opinion is gathering momentum in favour of the inclusion of other revenues possibly including the non-tax revenues into the divisible pool, and adopting an integrated approach for vertical sharing. Long ago (Guhan, 1995) went even a step further and recommended the inclusion of plan grants and specific purpose grants as well into the divisible pool, "...except for natural calamities, grants for specific purposes such as upgradation, special problems and local bodies are not logically sound or practically necessary..."

Horizontal Sharing

As regards horizontal sharing, the approach adopted so far reflects some inherent confusion: whether and to what extent states' efficiency should be rewarded, to what extent equity should be built, to what extent the state-specific factors and circumstances should be taken into account while assessing the fiscal management of the States etc.

For example, as Sarma (1997) pointed out, "In several cases the transfers are subject to a great deal of experimentation and frequent modification. Often, the lack of agreement on the criteria has led to dominance of political considerations rather than economic rationale. ... the debate shows that an objective transfer mechanism has eluded the policy-makers so far. Although significant efforts have been made by the last two Finance Commissions (10th and 11th FCs) to integrate the system of tax devolution and enlarge the divisible pool to include all union taxes, with regard to the horizontal revenue sharing however, not much attention has been paid." Sarma (1997) then proceeded to develop a method of objectively identifying the criteria and deriving of weights for deciding the horizontal revenue shares within a fiscal behavioural framework.

Use of 1971 Population

The practice of using the 1971 population was started since the 4th Finance Commission and has become a permanent item of the ToR of the subsequent FCs. It was obviously intended to not reward the states which failed in population control. However, given that population has been used as an indicator of 'need/adequacy' of a state, denying resources to the state on this front would lead to a distortion in the allocation pattern. It is time that a better alternative is prescribed. In fact, there are instances where the FC considered the actual population instead of the 1971 population. An obvious instance is where the tax devolutions are based on 'distance' or 'inverse' formulae.

Taxation of Services

Although there is no explicit mention of services in the 7th Schedule of the Constitution, taking its cue from Entry 97, the Central government has been levying taxes on services under this entry. The selective taxation started with three services (telecommunications, non-life insurance and stockbrokers) in 1994 and was progressively extended to 26 services by 2000-01. In the 2001-02 budget, the tax was extended to 14 more services. Subsequently more and more services are added and presently about 100 services are taxable. Out of these, telecommunication, non-life insurance, brokerage, advertising and courier contribute over 90 per cent of the revenue from service tax.

There has been considerable discussion on sharing of the power to levy the tax on services between the Centre and states. Two alternative models are suggested for sharing of tax powers with the states. One model is to clearly distinguish between services having nation-wide ramifications and those with regional spread and assign the latter to the states. This can lead to several harmonisation complications. The alternate approach to sharing tax powers with the states is to give concurrent power to levy tax on all services to the centre as well as states. This would require the amendment of the Constitution to place taxation of services in the concurrent list. In the past, several states expressed their desire through their Memoranda to the 12th Finance Commission[1] that service tax should be in the state

1. Assam, Gujarat, Haryana, Kerala, Nagaland, Tamil Nadu, Tripura, Uttar Pradesh.

list but the service tax should be collected by Centre and transferred to the state. When GST will be introduced, the service tax is expected to be merged with it.

Inclusion of Surcharges and Cesses, Cost of Collection, Non-tax Revenues

Even with the current provisions of tax devolution under Article 270 some issues do remain. For example, it has been argued that the power to levy surcharges, instead of meeting any emergent requirements of a specific nature, is used as a normal source of revenue. Article 271 gives the power to levy surcharge on all Union taxes and not merely on income tax and the taxes specified in Article 269 as was the position before the 80th Amendment to the Constitution. Surcharge levied on any tax is not shareable, and therefore, to the extent that the power to levy surcharge is used as a revenue raising measure, it affects the states. The concept of net proceeds, instead of gross proceeds of Union taxes, does not provide any incentive to the Union to reduce the collection cost.

Also, over the years, the non-tax revenue of the Union has increased significantly. The non-tax revenue is non-shareable. Hence, the Union Government is now better equipped, financially, to meet its expenses and therefore there is a scope for higher devolution of union taxes to the states. Some states desire that at least 30 per cent/proportionate share of the shareable pool for distribution among Special Category States.

Some states desire that a minimum guaranteed devolution of the Central taxes from the Centre to the states should be fixed.

Other Issues

It has been a well-known practice to keep the working of the Finance Commission from the public. "Each finance body has to start its work practically *de novo.* No member of one Finance Commission sits on another, such is the convention. All the working papers are destroyed after the Commission has finalised its report. The reason is that the Commission's report in effect amounts to an award and no documents showing how it was arrived at need to be kept" (Sarkar, 1969). Therefore, there is a need for making the working of the FC—the methods employed to arrive at the recommendations—should be open and transparent and the room for subjectivity should be minimised. Further, there remains a need to coordinate the recommendations of the Finance Commission with those of the Planning Commission, which itself needs fundamental revamping. In addition, there are several thorny issues of fiscal reforms that the FC is called to examine—implementation of GST, reform of the service tax, off-budget expenditures, and so on.

The Changing Role of the FC and the Debate on the Permanency Issue: Need for Revamping the FC

Over time however, there has been steady widening of the Commission's mandate and in the terms of reference (ToR). Gone are the times when the basic function of the FC was to merely recommend vertical and horizontal sharing of revenues between the Centre and the constituent states. Of late the FC has also been entrusted with many tasks of macroeconomic and fiscal management. Besides macroeconomic management, there are issues like calamity relief to states, the need for ensuring reasonable returns on investments in power, transport and industrial enterprises (Eighth Finance Commission, 1988). More notably, the last four Commissions were required to go into the fiscal management aspects more deeply. They include tasks such as:

(i) Identifying structural and cyclical factors causing fiscal imbalances in states and Centre such as erosion of tax-GDP ratio, stagnation in non-tax revenue, upward shifts in pay and pensions, interest and subsidies and so on.

(ii) Assessing expenditure needs on account of the non-salary component of maintenance and upkeep of capital assets and the non-wage related maintenance expenditure on plan schemes and recommend norms on the basis of which specific amounts are recommended for the maintenance of the capital assets and the manner of monitoring such expenditure.

(iii) Assessing the need for ensuring the commercial viability of irrigation projects, power projects, departmental undertakings, public sector enterprises in the states through various means including adjustment of user charges and relinquishing of non-priority enterprises through privatisation or disinvestment.

(iv) Reviewing the Fiscal Reform Facility introduced by the Central Government on the basis of the recommendations of the 11th Finance Commission (2000), and suggest measures for effective achievement of its objectives.

(v) Recommending basic tax reforms and implementation of the taxes like GST (Thirteenth Finance Commission, 2009). There have been basic reforms targeted at the tax system by way of the goods and services tax, streamlining the income tax etc. Implementation of these reforms can bring substantial change in the revenue capacities of the Centre and the States.

(vi) Reviewing the arrangements as regards financing of Disaster Management with reference to the National Calamity Contingency Fund and the Calamity Relief Fund and making appropriate recommendations thereon.

Indeed, the 13th Finance Commission has explicitly recognised the need "to respond transformationally, rather than incrementally, to national and global imperatives that are causing fundamental changes to the national development agenda" (Thirteenth Finance Commission, 2009: 255). It emphasised the need for a "fiscal framework equipped to meet the challenges of the future and to enable India to make the most of its demographic dividend." All this calls for a thorough overhaul of the institution of the FC. In an attempt to indicate the areas of strengthening the fiscal architecture, the 13th Finance Commission has identified the following areas.

(i) Indirect tax reform in the form of adopting the GST.

(ii) Strengthening and empowering the local bodies and finding ways of involving them in the devolution process.

(iii) Extending the sharing process to non-tax revenues such as profit petroleum, profit gas, revenues from spectrum.

(iv) Dynamic updating of the horizontal sharing parameters.

(v) Improving the governance to enhance the quality of public expenditure.

(vi) Strengthening the data base.

(vii) Introducing environmental dimension into the inter-governmental fiscal arrangements.

(viii) Basic reforms of the fiscal accounting procedures.

(ix) Creation of council of Finance Ministers, a fiscal council, a local body ombudsman, national debt management agency.

(x) Reform of revenue—capital classifications.

Thus, there is indeed a need for a thorough overhaul of the institution of the FC.

The Debate on the Permanency Issue[2]

An aspect that has received persistent attention is whether the Finance Commission should be a permanent body like the Planning Commission, or continue to be in the present form. This issue has been debated over the years since the 2nd Finance Commission itself. However, the issue was somewhat misunderstood as a step towards the transfer of an increasing amount of funds from the Centre to the States.

Irresponsible Fiscal Strategies by States

The setting up of the Finance Commission at five-year intervals has been leading to a variety of immature acts on the part of the states. For example as observed by Sarkar (1969), "The Uttar Pradesh Government, for instance, hustled its Pay Commission to conclude its work, issued a Government order on the pay body's report and sent copies of the order and of the report by a chartered plan to New Delhi, only to meet the deadline for submission of Statements set by the Fourth Finance Commission. The West Bengal Government raised the dearness allowance of its staff by Rs 9 crores on March 27 1969, to show the amount as committed expenditure for the last financial year which was to expire in another three days."

Besides, "Many State Governments are also known to submit one set of financial statements to the Finance Commission and another for the Planning Commission. In the former, they normally try to show an inflated figure of deficits in non-plan revenue account, the obvious intention being to reinforce their demand for a larger share of divisible taxes and grants

2. This section draws from Sarkar (1969).

in aid. In statements for the planning body, they quite often draw a much more elastic estimate of their resources to justify their demand for a big State plan... Every effort is made at present to shake off even the faintest suggestion of continuity between successive Commissions" (Sarkar, 1969).

Argument against Permanent FC

Yet, a potent argument against a permanent Finance Commission is that it will induce states to show perennial deficits in their revenue accounts. Not only will they refrain from taking measures to make up the deficits but they will manipulate the figures in such a way that the deficits continue. But it has been pointed out that when there is a permanent body, keeping vigil on the states' performances round the year, the states in turn would have less scope for putting pressure on the Commission to secure higher allotments. And the Centre can always make them feel that they cannot live by deficits alone. Secondly, there could be perennial litigation between the Centre and states with regard to the sharing.

The important question is whether a permanent Commission will be able to inspire states to put in a little more effort to mobilise resources. A permanent Commission can take up these matters with the states, and make them implement reforms such as the tax reforms, and GST.

As a permanent body, the role and powers of the FC needs to be specified more carefully. The permanent FC can be expected to be the country's macroeconomic manager, as an apex instrument body to monitor the economy of the country as well as the states and local bodies, and as the think-tank for the design of the important economic policies.

Admittedly, a permanent body by itself will not solve all problems. But it will at least help generate in the states a sense of confidence that any 'injustice' done to them need not be endured for five long years. The pattern of devolution can be continued, if necessary, by a permanent Commission for periods longer than one year and then the situation will nearly be the same as the one existing at present. But it will have an advantage over the present system in that the mere existence of a standing body like this, to which appeals can be made at any time, will by itself calm down irate nerves. Financial administration in a federation is bound to generate a lot of steam, and it is better to let it off as and when it develops, rather than allow it to grow. In fact, Dr Rangarajan, Chairman of the 12th Finance Commission also felt that "If the Finance Commission is made a permanent body, the way grants are made will change. Annual projections can be used to allocate funds to the states instead of five-year projections."

Views of FC on Permanency

Actually, even the 1st Finance Commission suggested the setting up of a small organisation preferably in the Secretariat of the President for conducting continuous study of the finances of the state governments, working of state undertakings, etc. This was indeed accepted by the Government but all that was done was to set up a small cell in the Finance Ministry. The 2nd Finance Commission also suggested that a nucleus staff with experience of the work of the Finance Commission should be retained within the Finance Ministry and its services be made available to future Commissions. The 3rd Commission also stressed the importance and necessity of arranging the compilation of reliable statistics. The cell, maintained in the Finance Ministry, consists of only some ministerial staff. No data except the Central and state budgets are kept. So the Fourth Commission suggested that the cell should be strengthened by the addition of personnel with suitable research experience who would be able to continue to collect and analyse the relevant material. The 8th Finance Commission did not agree to the suggestion put forward by some states that the Finance Commission should be made a permanent body. It, however, suggested that there should be a permanent secretariat which should continue to function during the intervals between one Commission to the next. Such a secretariat may function as a division in the Ministry of Finance during the intervening period.

International Experience

Such permanent bodies are in fact in existence in some countries with federal Constitutions. The Australian Federal Grants Commission, which bears some similarity to our FCs in terms of its functions, is a permanent institution. In the US, there are two permanent agencies to look after inter-state and Federal-State financial issues. While the Council of State Governments (CSG) deals mostly with issues arising between States, the Advisory Committee of Inter-Governmental Relations performs somewhat extended functions. In fact, the World Bank has for long, voiced that making Finance Commission a permanent body (as it is in Australia for example) would improve coordination and data collection.

Possible Additional Roles for the Revamped Finance Commission

FC as Overall Macroeconomic Manager

The fiscal health of the nation as a whole, irrespective of whether it is the Centre, the state or local bodies should be of primary concern. The FC has to take cognizance of the prevailing fiscal and macroeconomic situation, particularly the need to sustain the growth momentum, while bringing about fiscal consolidation.

The issue of macro fiscal management has been explicitly figuring in the terms of reference of the FC since 1968. For example from the 5th Finance Commission onwards, the FC was required to link the grants-in-aid to better fiscal management "as also for economy consistent with efficiency which may be effected by the States in their administrative maintenance, developmental and other expenditure" (Fifth Finance Commission, 1970). Indeed the 5th Finance Commission went into conceptualising fiscal management. "Fiscal management is a multi-dimensional concept. ... Briefly stated, in assessing sound fiscal management one should have regard both to the manner in which the State has endeavoured to raise the resources needed for meeting its commitments and also the manner in which it has deployed the resources so raised so as to get the best possible results for the expenditure incurred. A review of fiscal management in this broad sense will call for a comprehensive and critical survey of the fiscal policies and administration of State Governments over a period of time" (Fifth Finance Commission, 1970: Chapter XIII).

Since the 11th Finance Commission it has become customary that the Finance Commission is asked to "suggest a plan by which the Governments, collectively and severally, may bring about a restructuring of the public finances restoring budgetary balance, achieving macroeconomic stability and debt reduction along with equitable growth" (Twelfth Finance Commission, 2005). The ToRs of the 11th Finance Commission onwards included reference to budgetary balance and macroeconomic stability. The plan for restructuring is required to also address the objectives of debt reduction and equitable growth.

"The requirement implies that revenue sharing between the centre and the states cannot be decided in isolation but must be anchored to a macro framework defined by parameters of fiscal adjustment in the desired directions along with incentives to induce prudent and efficient fiscal management. Also, restructuring calls for spelling out directions of reform over a wide front spanning fiscal policy, budgetary practices and design of intergovernmental transfers but also the monetary, legal and administrative systems within which budgets operate, in order to facilitate the implementation of the restructuring Plan" (Vithal and Sarma, 2002).

The basic objectives of fiscal restructuring would be not only balancing the receipts and expenditure on revenue account of all the states and the Centre, but also generating surpluses for capital investment and reducing fiscal deficit; raising the tax-GDP ratio for the Centre and tax-GSDP ratios for the states; and in the context of debt reduction, that corrective measures in regard to states' debt may be suggested, consistent with macroeconomic stability and debt sustainability. Therefore an important task of the FC should be to develop an integrated framework for restructuring public finances to address these interrelated objectives.

Fiscal restructuring aimed at macroeconomic stabilisation requires a broad analytical framework. The impact of the size and composition of government expenditure on growth, inflation, interest rate and the external account has to be considered in a framework that takes into account relevant inter relationships and feedbacks. The structure of public finances relates, apart from other features, to the size and composition of expenditure.

Macroeconomic management aims at keeping the economy to its long term growth with stabilisation while keeping the inflation rate within acceptable limits. It is desirable to design public finances to remove the structural constraints such as supply bottlenecks and bring potential output closer to full employment levels. In this context, the structure of government expenditure, particularly the share of capital expenditure and its allocation becomes important. In regard to the second issue, in achieving stabilisation, the management of aggregate government demand in response to the cyclical movements of potential output along its growth path becomes relevant.

Finance Commission as Monitoring Instrument

Yet another vitiating factor is the absence of an independent institutional arrangement for the evaluation of the fiscal performance of the Centre and the states against targets/norms prescribed by the FCs and for monitoring the implementation of the recommendations, especially those relating to matters other than devolution and grants-in-aid.

The FC should be entrusted with the responsibility of monitoring the economic adjustments recommended by it. The past practice of such Commissions has been to consider their duty done once they submitted their report. The 12th Finance Commission, broke with this passive tradition and urged the setting up of a high-level monitoring mechanism in every state headed by the Chief Secretary and comprising the Finance Secretary and Secretaries/Heads of Departments as Members to lay down at the beginning of each year financial and physical targets with definite time frames to achieve specific milestones for ensuring proper utilisation of the grants. The Commission also stipulated that the committee should meet at least once in every quarter to review the progress and issue directions for mid-course corrections.

It is not enough to keep a watch over the mode of utilisation of grants by states. The entire mind-set of the parties and alliances ruling the states needs to be attuned to the spirit of mutually cooperative and supportive fiscal federalism. States should check their tendency to squander away thousands of crores of rupees of precious resources on freebies and seek to plug the gap by unconscionably heavy borrowings in the hope of being bailed out by the Centre. The states must realise that they bear an equal, if not greater, responsibility to augment their revenues and avoid infructuous expenditure. The axe should mercilessly fall on unjustifiably high expenditures incurred by the state governments and their agencies on salaries and perks of employees without establishing correlation with norms of performance.

The 12th Finance Commission could only be said to have let off the Centre lightly, without insisting on any monitoring and review mechanism and without binding the Government to any parameters of revenue mobilisation or expenditure control. This is strange because, actually, it is the Centre that should be called upon to set an example in whatever it preaches to state governments. Far from living up to that obligation, it has been giving an impression of adopting a business-as-usual attitude.

Finance Commission as a Think-tank and Fiscal Data Manager

Unfortunately, the functioning of the FCs suffers from two major handicaps. The first is the absence of a permanent secretariat with cells for collection and maintenance of databases and for undertaking research studies on issues coming within the purview of the Commissions. Recommendation to this effect had been made in the reports of one or the other Commission in the past but with no perceptible follow-up other than a 50-page long note written in the Finance Ministry containing an academic discussion of the ramifications and implications.

Indeed, it can be argued that the nodal ministry/department for dealing with the FC matters should not be the Ministry of Finance, but the Cabinet secretariat or the Inter-State Council. The states are also strongly of the view that they should be effectively consulted in the drafting of the terms of reference of the FC. Whether this has been done for the current Commission is not known.

Over all, the right thing to do is aim at creating a think tank for economic management in the form of the FC. Its main functions could be revenue sharing, revenue reforms, expenditure management, monitoring the economy. The FC can have different divisions looking into these aspects. May be it is time for a total revamping of the federal fiscal sharing system.

The 11th Finance Commission had earmarked more than ₹ 10,000 crore for creation and computerisation of databases at the district, state and Central levels on the finances of local bodies and accounts of village and intermediate-level panchayats and the CAG was made responsible for prescribing the necessary formats for the compilation of data. Again, a shadow has fallen between intention and execution.

The 12th Finance Commission emphasised the need for statistical agencies to design and implement a plan to produce more timely data on Gross State Domestic Product (GSDP). The 12th Finance Commission clearly brought out the difficulties of working without reliable data. "We have been constrained to use the latest available estimates of GSDP which are for years less recent than we would have liked. This is an issue that requires most urgent attention in order to eliminate time lags in the availability of data and to bring to a close the cumbersome process of generating comparable GSDP data. There should, in our view, be no hesitation on the part of all agencies concerned, whether at the Central, State or district level, to put aside any perceived questions of mandate or primacy and collectively agree to a blueprint and methodology for delivering comparable GSDP data on a regular and timely basis. It is equally important that the Central Statistical Organisation (CSO) assume greater responsibility for producing GSDP at market prices, and for generating estimates of income accruing to States inclusive of net inward remittances. It is important to recognise that data is vital for the business process underpinning effective policy making, monitoring and devolution, and that the availability of quality data is a factor that will determine whether future policy making is able to rise to the challenges posed by a rapidly changing social and economic environment" (Twelfth Finance Commission, 2005).

Conclusions and Recommendations

(i) Entrust the FC with the duty of not only making recommendations for revenue sharing but also closely monitoring it.

(ii) Entrust it with overall macroeconomic management.

(iii) Revamp the taxing powers of the Centre and states.

(iv) Institute expenditure management techniques.

(v) Combine the economic advisory councils with the FC and make FC the think-tank for the Finance Ministry.

(vi) Streamline the off-budget expenditure schemes and find ways of incorporating them into the state level budgets.

(vii) The FC should be an apex body advising the Finance Ministry with sufficient fiscal management plan.

References

Eighth Finance Commission (1988). *Report of the Eigth Finance Commission.* New Delhi: Government of India.

Eleventh Finance Commission (2000). *Report of the Eleventh Finance Commission.* New Delhi: Government of India.

Fifth Finance Commission (1970). *Report of the Fifth Finance Commission.* New Delhi: Government of India.

First Finance Commission (1952). *Report of the First Finance Commission of India.* New Delhi: Government of India.

Guhan, S. (1995). "Report of the Tenth Finance Commission", *Economic and Political Weekly*: 877, April 22.

Sarkar, J. (1969). "A Permanent Finance Commission?", *Economic & Political Weekly*: 1311-5, August 9.

Sarma, J.V.M. (1997). "Federal Fiscal Relations in India: The Issue of Horizontal Transfers", *Economic & Political Weekly*: 1719-23.

Thirteenth Finance Commission (2009). *Report of the Thirteenth Finance Commission: Volume I.* New Delhi: Government of India.

Twelfth Finance Commission (2005). *Report of the Twelfth Finance Commission.* New Delhi: Government of India.

Vithal, B.P.R and J.V. M. Sarma (2002). "Twelfth Finance Commission: Framing its Terms of Reference", *Economic and Political Weekly,* August 24.

5 Institutional Mechanisms of Fiscal Federalism

*A Case Study of National Development Council in India**

Rekha Saxena

Introduction

This paper examines intergovernmental relations (IGRs) in the contemporary Indian federal governance. Being a variant of Westminster influenced parliamentary federation, IGRs are dominantly noticeable in the form of executive federalism. Since 1989, India is witnessing a shift from a one-party dominant system to a multi-party configuration at the national level and an extremely diversified set of party systems at the state level. This changed political scenario has engendered the phenomenon of 'divided government' such that the two houses of Parliament and state legislatures are controlled by different sets of coalition governments at the union as well as in many states. Further, economic liberalisation and globalisation have also resulted in new jurisdictional conflicts between the union and states. The upshot is that intergovernmental negotiations and policy harmonisation have acquired critical importance. The distinctive forums of these relations are the National Development Council (NDC), the Inter-State Council (ISC), and more frequent meetings of executive heads of governments in India, and ministerial and secretarial conferences from the union and the states.

Though the acceleration in the neo-liberal economic reforms in India since 1991 did necessitate some change in the nature of economic policies and planning processes, yet the important role of the NDC in Union-State

* Part of it earlier published in Rekha Saxena, *Situating Federalism: Mechanisms of Intergovernmental Relations in Canada and India*, 2006.

relations hardly diminished. If anything, with the increasing federalisation of the Indian polity and assertion of state autonomy, localism, and ethnic identities, its role in India's cooperative federalism is likely to become even more crucial.

This paper discusses the background of NDC, its functioning under various regimes till 1989 and thereafter till date.

Background

It was as early as in 1946 when the interim government set up the Advisory Planning Board (APB) under the chairmanship of K.C. Neogy that the desirability of a consultative body representing the provinces, the princely states and some other interests to advise the Planning Commission was pointed out. Consequently, the NDC came into being with the object of ensuring "uniformity of approach and unanimity in its working" (Sen, 1961).

The Planning Commission in the Draft Outline of the First Five Year Plan also made the following suggestion: "In a country of the size of India where the States have, under the Constitution, full autonomy within their own sphere of duties, it is necessary to have a forum such as National Development Council, at which from time to time, the Prime Minister of India and the Chief Ministers of states can review the working of the Plan and its various aspects" (Government of India, 1975). The NDC was thus set up in August 1952 "to strengthen and mobilise the effort and resources of the nation in support of the Five Year Plans, to promote common economic policies in all vital spheres and to ensure the balanced and rapid development of all parts of the country."[1] The Council was assigned the following functions:

(i) to review the working of the national plan from time to time;

(ii) to consider important questions of social and economic policy affecting national development; and

(iii) to recommend measures for the achievement of the aims and targets set out in the national plan, including measures to secure

1. National Development Council, Cabinet Secretariat, Department of Cabinet Affairs, Resolution No.65/15/CF-67, New Delhi, 7 October 1967.

> the active participation and cooperation of the people, improve the efficiency of the administrative services, ensure the fullest development of the less advanced regions and sections of the community and, through sacrifice borne equally by all citizens, build up resources for national development.[2]

The Study Team of the Administrative Reforms Commission (ARC) in its Interim Report observed that in the future set-up of planning in the country, the NDC would have to play a much more dynamic role. It pointed out that in the emerging political situation in the country, the NDC has to be developed as the most important instrument for ensuring all-India support for the National Plan. As the supreme political body giving guidance to the formulation of the Plan, the Council would have to operate ceaselessly (without interruption) and its working would have to be more systematised than in the past (Paranjape, 1970).

The ARC also supported this viewpoint and recommended that the NDC should be reconstituted to include the Prime Minister, the Deputy Prime Minister, 10 Ministers of the Central Cabinet in charge of major ministries, the Chief Ministers of all the States and Members of the Planning Commission. In a note of dissent, H.V. Kamath, one of the members of the ARC, expressed concern that a plethora of ministers would make the NDC too unwieldy. He was of the view that besides the Prime Minister and the Deputy Prime Minister, only ministers of finance, home affairs, agriculture, industry, and irrigation and power should be honoured as Members of the Council. He further suggested that in view of the rapidly changing political landscape, the Chief Ministers of the Union Territories and the Chief Executive Councillor of Delhi should invariably be invited to attend the meeting of the Council (Paranjape, 1970). The ARC also suggested that the functions of the NDC be redefined. The most important change suggested was that the NDC should be specifically required "to prescribe guidelines for the formulation of the National Plan" (Paranjape, 1970).

The government considered the recommendations of the Commission and decided to reconstitute the NDC and redefine its functions. To this

2. National Development Council, Cabinet Secretariat Resolution No. 62/CF/50, dated 6 August 1952.

effect, a Resolution was passed on 7 October 1967. The revised functions of the NDC were:

(i) to prescribe guidelines for the formulation of the national plan, including the assessment of resources for the plan;

(ii) to consider the national plan as formulated by the Planning Commission;

(iii) to consider important questions of social and economic policy affecting national development; and

(iv) to review the working of the plan from time to time and to recommend such measures as are necessary for achieving the aims and targets set out in the national plan, including measures to secure the active participation and cooperation of the people, improve the efficiency of the administrative services, ensure the fullest development of the less advanced regions and sections of the community and, through sacrifice borne equally by all citizens, build up resources for national development.[3]

The NDC would now comprise the Prime Minister, Chief Ministers of all states and Union Territories and Members of the Planning Commission. Delhi Administration was represented in the Council by the Lt. Governor and the Chief Executive Councillor, and the remaining Union Territories by their respective Administrators. It further provided that other Union Ministers could also be invited to participate in the deliberations of the Council. The Secretary of the Planning Commission would act as Secretary to the NDC and the Planning Commission would provide administrative and other assistance for the smooth functioning of the Council. It also required the Council to meet "as often as may be necessary and at least twice in each year" (Paranjape, 1970).

In the past, when it comprised the Prime Minister, the Chief Ministers of the states and Members of the Planning Commission, it was considered as too unwieldy for an effective discussion of problems (Paranjape, 1970). To facilitate a more effective deliberation, a Standing Committee was set up in 1954 with Members of the Planning Commission and Chief Ministers

3. National Development Council, Cabinet Secretariat Resolution No. 65/15/CF-67, dated 7 October 1967.

of nine states. It did serve a useful purpose at the time of the formulation of the Second Five Year Plan but met only twice subsequently—in 1957 and 1958—and thereafter in 1963, after a long gap of five years. The Standing Committee henceforth, became almost defunct. Moreover, over the years, in addition to regular members, a large number of Central and state Ministers were invited thus making the body too unwieldy. Against this background, the ARC Study Team recommended the continuance of the earlier composition of the NDC. Also, to make the NDC operationally more effective, it suggested that "sub-committees of the NDC may be appointed from time to time, and especially at the time of formulating a Five Year Plan" (Government of India [GoI], 1967). It further recommended the constitution of counterparts of these NDC committees at the official levels also "so that there is adequate consultation, communication, and therefore mutual understanding and cooperation between the States and the Union in all matters pertaining to Planning" (GoI, 1967).

In regard to the effective utilisation of the sub-committees as recommended by the Commission, the question of constituting a sub-committee of the NDC for examining the principles and patterns of Central Assistance was duly considered by the NDC in May 1968, but the exclusion of any Chief Minister from the sub-committee was found impracticable. Only the Central Cabinet Ministers were excluded from the sub-committee. A number of sub-committees, of a purely *ad hoc* nature, were appointed from time to time to investigate problems of national importance, a prominent example being the setting up of the Mehta Committee in 1957 to evaluate the performance of the Community Development Programme (CDP). Unfortunately, the recommendations of these committees were not faithfully followed by the Central Government, thus defeating the very purpose of their establishment. As a reaction to lack of action on these recommendations, Biju Patnaik, the Chief Minister of Orissa, who was also the Chairman of the Austerity Committee, tendered his resignation in 1992 (Das, 1997). The official level committees for regularly discussing and examining plan problems had also not developed, though in the past meetings were held to discuss particular problems between the Planning Commission and the state government officials such as Planning Secretaries. Two working groups were appointed under the auspices of the NDC in 1968 to examine and make recommendations on certain problems of inter-state disputes (Paranjape, 1970: 10).

The Study Team of the ARC also found that the measures of consultation and examination of issues by the Council were 'inadequate' because certain aspects of perspective-planning and possible alternatives were not placed before the Council in sufficient detail. It highlighted the shortcomings in its conferencing procedures, namely, short duration of meetings, delays in the circulation of agenda-papers, use of the Council as "a forum for the ventilation of individual grievances rather than for collective discussion of principles and polity" etc., and suggested a more systematic and an in-depth involvement of the Council in all basic questions of planning policy, particularly those pertaining to goals and objectives, alternative frameworks, strategy and crucial sectors, and helping in arriving at a national consensus. It was further suggested that the Council should be assisted by a Standing Advisory Committee (SAC) consisting of official advisors from each State, the Central Ministers concerned and the Planning Commission (Government of India, 1967).

The Sarkaria Commission on Union-State relations also highlighted some deficiencies in the Council: the NDC meets only at the initiative of the Planning Commission which determines its agenda; the Council has been approving the Approach Paper and the Draft Plan but not keeping track of the progress of the Plan (for instance, the consideration of other policy questions affecting national development which is one of its stated functions has been infrequent and insufficient); the frequency and duration of its meetings are very inadequate; the Planning Commission does not always put before the Council alternative sets of perspectives, strategies and targets along with the assumptions made to enable it to decide among the choices available; the conferencing procedure consists of set speeches made by Chief Ministers with very little of mutual discussion; the summing up of deliberations often does not reflect the diversity of views; the time given to States for crystallising their views is often insufficient; and the Standing Committees and the Special Committees are not formed or convened on a regular basis for in-depth analysis and consideration of issues.[4]

Due to the reasons mentioned above, the NDC was perceived as a forum deficient both in effective participation and systematic deliberation of alternatives. As a policy-making body it was not able to guide the

4. *Commission on Centre-State Relations, Report*, Part I, pp.380-81.

Planning Commission and also failed to carry out a critical appraisal of the implementation of the plans and policies. This sorry state of affairs led to some rethinking about the reorganisation of the NDC. It was suggested that a constitutional or a statutory status would improve the functioning of this body. These reappraisals suggested, among other things, the following: the NDC should exercise greater control over the Planning Commission and should have a say in determining the composition of the Planning Commission as well; some supported the idea of representation of experts on this body. However, a view had been expressed that the experts should be on the Planning Commission and the role of the NDC should be political decision-making and laying down national guidelines on planning; some were of the view that the NDC should express its opinion on all matters of national development and may be actively involved in evolving policies of industrial development, trade and commerce, prices, etc; and one State Government even suggested that the NDC should approve the guidelines for preparation of the plans, the Approach to the Five Year Plan and the quantum and allocation of Central Assistance for State Plans.[5]

The Sarkaria Commission finally made the following recommendations: the NDC should be made to function more effectively and emerge as the highest political level inter-governmental body for giving a direction and thrust to planned development of the country. Being the supreme inter-governmental body for all matters related to socio-economic development, it is necessary that the NDC should be renamed and reconstituted as National Economic Development Council (NEDC) by a Presidential Order under the provisions of Article 263 so as to have moorings in the Constitution; the NEDC should be involved in the formulation of the plans right from the beginning. Selection of studies and setting up of various working groups should be done under the guidance of the Standing Committee of the NEDC; the draft Approach Paper containing all relevant data and alternative strategies should be circulated to the States at least two months in advance of the meeting of the NEDC to consider the same; a preparatory meeting should be held by the Planning Commission, with all Deputy Chairmen and/or Secretaries of the State Development Boards two weeks prior to the NEDC to consider the Approach Paper/ Draft Five Year Plan for identifying the main issues and firming up the

5. Ibid.

agenda for the meeting of the NEDC; deliberations in the NEDC should be so structured as to facilitate meaningful discussions on each item of the agenda; the NEDC or its Standing Committee should meet regularly to consider important economic issues of national significance in addition to the usual developmental issues; the NEDC should formulate its own procedures to enable it to discharge its responsibilities; the Secretary of the Planning Commission shall act as Secretary to the NEDC and the Planning Commission shall provide such administrative or other assistance for the work of the Council as may be needed and a Standing Committee of the NEDC should be constituted consisting of the Prime Minister, Finance Minister, three other Union Ministers nominated by the Prime Minister, Deputy Chairman of the Planning Commission and Governor, Reserve Bank of India, and six Chief Ministers, one from each zone selected by rotation or consensus. This Standing Committee should be constituted under Article 263 along with the NEDC. It may, however, set up other committees or sub-committees to advise it or the Standing Committee on special issues.[6]

Working of the NDC under Various Regimes until 1989

The Nehru premiership was the first formative phase of governance during which the NDC was founded and its procedures and rules of business were devised. One textual factor to bear in mind for this phase is that there were at least two forums that more or less mirrored each other in terms of composition. One was the Congress Working Committee (CWC), a party forum that included the most influential Union Ministers and State Chief Ministers along with other party functionaries, and the other was the NDC that included the key Union Ministers and all Chief Ministers. Since the Congress during that period was the dominant political force in New Delhi and practically in all States of the Union, these two forums had by and large a similar party political configuration. The relevance of this fact of Union-State relations is that either of the two forums could be used for Union-State policy-making and harmonisation. Yet, the very fact that the NDC was set up underlined its essential intergovernmental character, authoritatively representing the two orders of government in the Indian Federation. Nonetheless, it would appear that a certain air of superfluity

6. Ibid.

would be inescapable for the NDC which would tend to get partially eclipsed not only by the apex party forum but also by the Parliament to an extent. This was because in the period of one-party dominance under a charismatic Prime Minister, the Parliament would naturally shine with a more authoritative glow of power, especially at a time when the travails of the nationalist movement were over and the centre of political gravity had shifted from the movement to the party in power, and from the latter to the government.

The brief tenures of Lal Bahadur Shastri and Indira Gandhi as Prime Minister between 1964 and 1971 were more or less a continuation of the trend of Union-State relations in the preceding Nehru era. However, the period did witness the growing importance of regional party leaders and State Chief Ministers in the early post-Nehru period. A series of omnibus non-Congress coalition governments came to be formed in all major north-Indian States, but since they included all sorts of parties ranging from the Right-Centre to the Left, they could not manage to work out a stable and an effective front of non-Congress State governments against the Congress-controlled Centre. Indeed, the Congress Party at the Centre misused its overriding constitutional powers to destabilise the fractious non-Congress coalition governments in the States (Brass, 1968). Nevertheless, these rumblings were heard when the Congress Party more or less still provided the main common political framework in the country either as the ruling or the opposition party. Hence, the political repercussions of the above changes were felt within the Congress Party itself that developed a more collective leadership rather than a politically differentiated federal framework in terms of different political parties ruling in New Delhi and the State capitals (Brecher, 1966; Singh, 1981). Two factors put additional pressure on the declining Congress party to close ranks and manage its internal differences within the house rather than outside. The first of these factors was the Chinese aggression in 1962. For example, in the 22nd meeting of the NDC held on 6 September 1965, the Chief Ministers wanted that at a time when the country was facing external aggression, the Council need not waste time discussing the various aspects of the Plan. Instead they decided to leave it to the Prime Minister's discretion to reorient, alter or amend the Plan (as and when necessary) to meet the emergent situation and safeguard the country's security and long-term interests. It may be noted that in 1964-65, the country was also facing a serious drought and food crisis.

The second factor was the growing internal division within the Congress Party which was somehow managed amicably by the Congress Working Committee (CWC) dominated by regional party bosses under Congress Party President, K. Kamraj, who successfully coordinated the Shastri succession from Nehru and the Indira Gandhi succession from Shastri. The expanded CWC including most Union and state Chief Ministers virtually turned into what Brecher called the "Grand Federal Council" of the Indian Republic (Brecher, 1966). By the end of 1969, however, despite the growing external challenge from opposition parties, unity in the Congress finally ruptured as Indira Gandhi decided to take on the dominant party bosses (using her entrenched position in the government and the Congress Parliamentary Party) and forced the Right-wing old-guard Syndicate leadership out of the party (Singh, 1981).

The Fourth General Elections in 1967 altered the parameters of politics in the country by unseating the Congress government in half of the States of the Union. Despite the fact that most of these non-Congress state governments—barring the Left-wing coalition in Kerala and the Right-wing coalition in Odisha—were unstable, a new federal ferment was conspicuously evident: the new political scenario required a re-negotiation of Union-state relations as well as a review of the planning machinery.

In this new context, the need for an adequate planning machinery was acutely felt by political analysts. The Report of the ARC (1957) also underlined this point. In fact, the then Deputy Chairman of the Planning Commission, D.R. Gadgil, also reportedly felt the same way. "He would like to fix the Central Assistance (which forms roughly 50 to 60 per cent of the States' plan outlays) according to Plan priorities and let the States decide the size of their plans on the basis of their resources" (Singh, 1981).

Nevertheless, a perusal of the speeches of the Chief Ministers during these years in the NDC suggests that the opinions expressed did not strictly follow major party lines, especially the Congress/non-Congress cleavage. If the non-Congress Chief Ministers were critical of the Draft Fourth Plan prepared by the Planning Commission, some Congress Chief Ministers too were not really sparing in their critical comments.

Union-State relations during Indira Gandhi's premiership from 1971 to 1977 developed in four contextual aspect. First, the internal politics in the Congress Party happened to be in turmoil as can be seen from the fact that the brief phase of collective leadership under Shastri and early years of Indira Gandhi was gradually replaced by the latter's dominance at the culmination of a round of factional politics that resulted in the great split of Congress towards the end of 1969. Second, State politics in major north Indian States witnessed a period of unstable non-Congress coalition governments that provided an opening for federal forces by giving the non-Congress opposition parties an opportunity to enjoy power at the State level. Third, pluralistic and federal tendencies released by the foregoing two contexts could not develop into a long-term trend as these possibilities were thwarted by assertion of leadership claims (on her behalf) by Indira Gandhi who not only managed to force her factional opponents in the Congress Party out in the 1969 split, but also managed to bring about a great political mobilisation in the country in the 1971 mid-term Lok Sabha elections which she fought on the slogan of *garibi hatao*. Facing challenge from her Right-wing Syndicate opponents in the party, she took a series of populist pro-poor measures such as nationalisation of 14 major commercial banks, abolition of Privy Purses for the *maharajas*, promises of bank credits and jobs to the unemployed and the poor, and speedy land reforms.

These policies yielded rich dividends and she was voted back to power with a thumping majority which enabled her to checkmate opposition both within the national Congress Party and in the north Indian States that were lost to the Congress since 1967. Fourth, though Indira Gandhi emerged as the dominant political leader in the Congress Party and the country in the electoral legislative arenas, she had to contend with a new development in the larger arena of mass politics. The Nav Nirman movement launched by the opposition Congress leader, Morarji Desai, in Gujarat, and the anti-corruption movement triggered off by the youth in Bihar—which drew Jayaprakash Narayan from virtual political retirement to offer his leadership to both these movements—confronted Indira Gandhi with a great mass movement against her. Thus even with massive legislative majorities, she found it difficult to govern and claim larger democratic legitimacy. This contradiction of parliamentary and mass politics eventually culminated in the proclamation of Internal Emergency in June 1975 with large-scale arrests of leaders of the mass movements and opposition parties.

The above stated conditioning factors naturally affected the working of the NDC as the major intergovernmental forum. For example, no meeting of the NDC took place between 27 March 1970 and 28 May 1972. Another major gap is noticeable during the pendency of the Internal Emergency—the period between the 30th meeting in December 1973 and the 31st meeting in September 1976. With the kind of political dominance Indira Gandhi was able to command in the country during this phase, it was natural for the Central Government to enjoy the upper hand both in the formulation of the plans and in the NDC meetings. However, a survey of the speeches delivered in the NDC indicates that critical voices were not entirely unheard. And, interestingly, these critical opinions on the Plan documents did not come only from the non-Congress Chief Ministers; even Congress Chief Ministers expressed reservations against the Plans presented for the approval of the NDC. It may thus be seen that issues of underdevelopment and regional disparities did not find expression strictly along party affiliations.

The post-Emergency 1977 Lok Sabha elections proved to be a turning point in Indian politics. This was so because it altered the parameters of politics in the country, especially in terms of Union-State relations. The Janata Party that was hurriedly formed on the eve of the elections with improper merger of major non-Congress and non-Communist opposition parties, won political power in major north-Indian states. It was essentially a confederal political formation that formed government in New Delhi as well as in Uttar Pradesh, Bihar, Madhya Pradesh, Haryana, Himachal Pradesh, Rajasthan, Gujarat, Odisha, etc. The areas of its electoral success were broadly the same as those that had suffered the excesses of the Emergency the most. The Congress-ruled states in the South re-elected the Congress Party except in Tamil Nadu where one of the Tamilian parties again won. This was thus a fairly variegated political scenario in the country with the Janata Party in power at the Centre and a broad spectrum of parties ruling in the states. After 1967, this was another major opening for the state-level political forces to experience a more federalised context than before. One crude index of this federalisation is that there was a greater regularity in the NDC meetings which were convened annually in contrast to the preceding periods in which its meetings were not held for years. Also, the fiscal federal policies and Centrally Sponsored Schemes (CSS) were seriously reviewed at these meetings.

Yet, since the Janata Party could not emerge victorious in the South, the full extent of federal possibilities could not materialise. This could be attributed largely to the existence of the overarching unity in the Janata Party, primarily a north-Indian party, thanks to the painful memory of suffering together under the emergency authoritarians, and the moderating presence of JP until his death.

The 32nd Meeting of the NDC held in March 1978 and chaired by Prime Minister Morarji Desai was in sharp contrast to the preceding meetings under Congress Prime Ministers. Commenting on the meeting, an analyst observed:

> The NDC is no longer a rubber-stamping body which would promptly accept any 'consensus' dictated by the Central Government from time to time. The present political landscape and the alignment of forces precludes that happening. If anybody in the Central Government or the Planning Commission entertained the idea of going through with the conventional pattern of obtaining the old type of consensus, he must have become much wiser after the event (Economic and Political Weekly, 1978).

With the return to power of the Congress under Indira Gandhi in 1980, a new phase of Congress dominance began. However, this was a dominance with difference. To start with, it was a mellowed Indira Gandhi who had learnt some lessons from the Emergency and its aftermath. Sanjay Gandhi's premature death in an air-crash also precluded some of her proclivities for personal and familial rule, though she did try to fill this void by inducing her reluctant elder son Rajiv Gandhi to join politics. Secondly, starting from the early 1980s, the Congress Party began to lose in popularity in a number of states which was amply reflected in the assembly elections. However, the Party continued to rule until around the end of the decade, first under Indira Gandhi and subsequently under Rajiv Gandhi. Thus, during this phase, Indira Gandhi experienced a number of electoral defeats at the state level; besides she also encountered growing regional ethnic mass movements led by the Akali Dal in Punjab and the Sons of the Soil movement in Assam. The dominant feature of this term of Indira Gandhi's rule therefore was an enhanced degree of regional assertion on the part of non-Congress parties and mass movements. This enlarged opening for federal forces in the political system is also reflected in the meetings of the NDC during this period. It met four times in five years with rather heavy agendas that included the Sixth Five Year Plan, Approach to the Seventh Five Year Plan, Indira Gandhi's new 20-point programme, law and order situation, river-water disputes, and finances of States and Plan implementation.

Rajiv Gandhi's succession to Indira Gandhi as Prime Minister took place in the wake of the latter's assassination. So severe was the distorting impact of this calamity on the political process that President Zail Singh proceeded to swear him in the Prime Minister's office with unseemly hurry—even before the Congress Party had formally elected Mr Gandhi as its leader. In the past also, President S. Radhakrishnan had opted for a provisional appointment of the seniormost cabinet colleague as the Prime Minister, pending the election of the Congress Parliamentary Party leader, striking examples being Shastri's succession to Nehru and Indira Gandhi's to Shastri. On both the occasions, Gulzari Lal Nanda served as provisional Prime Minister before the regular incumbent took over (Brecher, 1966; Singh, 1981).

Rajiv Gandhi's approach to federal politics was somewhat different in the sense that even though he did follow Indira Gandhi's centralising approach in the Congress-ruled states, yet he was more amenable to regional demands in non-Congress states where he signed a series of ethnic accords with dominant regional parties in Punjab, Assam and Mizoram.

The tempo of the NDC meetings seen in the immediately preceding phase remained more or less unchanged during this period as well. Three meetings took place during Rajiv Gandhi's premiership during the course of which the Draft Seventh Five Year Plan, New Education Policy and the Mid-Term Appraisal of the Seventh Plan were discussed. A review of the proceedings of the NDC meetings during this phase suggests that this was by far the most vigorous articulation of the critical views of state governments, presumably because almost half of the states (of the Union) were then ruled by non-Congress parties.

Rajiv Gandhi introduced a new style in the conduct of the meeting which was held after a gap of two years in March 1988. He insisted that the Chief Ministers should speak impromptu and the time allocated to each was only 10 minutes. The Chief Ministers agreed initially but soon got disillusioned as they were neither allowed to make lengthy speeches nor permitted discussions on the few points they had made.

NDC Meetings in the Post-1989 Phase

The 1989 Lok Sabha elections was a turning point in Indian politics, especially in Union-State relations and patterns of federal politics. The year witnessed the transformation of the one-party dominance system into a multi-party system. The Congress Party whose fortunes were gradually declining over the 1980s, was decisively routed. It yielded power to a multi-party federal coalitional formation comprising the Janata Dal, some major regional parties, and major Communist parties. The last named group of parties was part only of the legislative coalition, as it did not join the Cabinet. An unlikely parliamentary ally of the ruling coalition was the right-wing Hindu nationalist party, BJP, which decided to reluctantly support the coalition government with the motive of keeping the Congress out of power. The National Front Government headed by V.P. Singh was thus a minority coalition government dependent on the outside support of the right and left-wings of the party system. This new political dispensation in New Delhi and a variety of political parties in power at the state level in different states fundamentally altered the parameters of federal politics in India. This new political configuration occasioned a re-negotiation of Union-state relations in which the Union for the first time felt the compulsion for a new strategy of accommodating state governments and regional political forces. Some regional and national parties in power at the state level also brought a direct representation in the federal coalition Cabinet. This enormously increased the influence of regional political parties in the government at the Centre. As a result of all this, a big avenue was opened for the operation of federal forces and tendencies in the political system.

Another dimension of increased federalisation around this time was a more differentiated or variegated pattern of party representation in the election of the President of the Republic. Until then, the Presidency and the Union Cabinet overlapped in terms of party representation in such a manner that the head of the State, the head of the government and the cabinet generally came from the same party. In the 1990s, for the first time, this pattern changed. In the initial years of the decade, with the exception of the term of the Rao Congress Government, the Presidency continued to be occupied by Congress nominees whereas the Union Cabinet came to be formed by non-Congress Coalition Governments. In the later years of the decade, the Cabinets were formed by left of the centre or right of the centre non-Congress coalitions, but a former Congressman was elected to the Presidency in K.R. Narayanan with an all-party consensus. These new trends engendered a tendency towards activist Presidency or at least a more unrestrained and open expression of differences between the Prime Minister and the President. Although there was no radical departure from strictly constitutional construction of Presidential power, there were occasions when the President had a final say on some issues because the Union Cabinet chose not to press its point of view. Around the same time, there was also evidence of greater discretion in the exercise of a Governor's power and some other constitutional offices like the Election Commission of India. There was also a radical shift in judicial behaviour in as much as the Supreme Court for the first time in the S.R. Bommai case established judicial review of proclamation of President's Rule in States in 1994.

This naturally had an impact on intergovernmental relations and mechanisms. For one thing, the NDC became diverse in terms of party representation than before. This was so both because of the coalitional nature of the Cabinet at the Centre and because different sets of parties came to form governments in the states. For another, the V.P. Singh Government, in pursuance of the National Front election manifesto, proceeded to appoint for the first time ever the ISC under Article 263 of the Constitution in 1990. Thus, instead of a single intergovernmental mechanism in the NDC, there was now another, namely the ISC.

During the tenure of the National Front Government headed by V.P. Singh, two meetings of the NDC were convened (in June and October 1990) to discuss the Approach Paper to the Eighth Five Year Plan, distribution of Central budget support for states' plan expenditure, issues relating to right to work and impact of the Gulf crisis on India's balance of payments.

In the 42nd meeting of the NDC in October the same year, it was unanimously agreed to modify the Gadgil formula for resource allocation among the States. The amendment cut down the weightage given to population and stepped up that to per capita income. Under the Dandavate formula, devolution of resources for non-special category States was 55 per cent on the basis of population; 25 per cent on the basis of per capita income; 5 per cent on the basis of fiscal management and 15 per cent on the basis of special development problems.[7] The criteria set by the Gadgil formula for resource allocation was: population, 60 per cent; per capita income, 20 per cent; tax effort, 10 per cent; and special problems, 10 per cent. Tax effort was redefined as 'fiscal management', including both revenue and expenditure. Thus the NDC took a collective view that the performance of each state in this area should be evaluated in the light of a variety of related indices and not just taxation effort. The NDC also decided to appoint a committee to suggest lasting solutions for the financial problems of all special category states. It was also decided to give Assam and Jammu & Kashmir the same grant-loan ratio (90:10) as for other special category states.[8] The non-special category states got grants and loans in the ratio of 30:70.[9]

The P.V. Narasimha Rao Congress government, the only one to complete its full five year term, was partly in tune with the general tenor of politics during the 1990s and partly different. It started as a one-party minority government dependent on parliamentary support of some other parties and gradually transformed itself half-way through its term into a one-party majority government through accretion of support as a result of favourable election results in Punjab and manipulative realignment of political parties in the Parliament. The Rao government convened four meetings of the NDC—in December 1991, May 1992, April 1993, and September 1993. The agenda at these meetings included the Approach Paper and the final document of the Eighth Five Year Plan, review of centrally-sponsored developmental schemes, distribution of central assistance and open-market borrowings among the states during the Eighth Plan, population control policy, consideration of the NDC committee reports on austerity, population, employment and illiteracy, micro-level planning, etc.

---

7. *Economic Times*, 12 October 1990.
8. Ibid.
9. For a detailed account of the proceedings of the above meeting, see Government of India, Planning Commission, Summary Record of the 42nd meeting of the NDC held in October 1990, New Delhi.

The Rao regime was followed by two United Front Governments headed by H.D. Deve Gowda and I.K. Gujral respectively. Both these governments were rather short-lived. Deve Gowda called the 47th meeting of the NDC in January 1997. The Gujral Government did not convene any meeting, presumably because much of his attention was directed to foreign policy concerns as also because of its short duration.

The premature termination of the United Front regime was followed by two BJP-led Coalition Governments, both led by Atal Behari Vajpayee. The Vajpayee Government held the 48th Meeting of the NDC in February 1999 after a gap of over two years. The delay was apparently caused by the fall of two United Front Governments led respectively by Deve Gowda and I.K. Gujral in 1997 and 1998. This resulted in a delay in finalising the Ninth Plan. But the Draft Ninth Plan was provisionally kicked off pending its subsequent approval by the NDC which could be done only in the 1999 meeting.

The second meeting of the NDC under Vajpayee's premiership was held on 1 September 2001 in New Delhi during the course of which the Draft Approach Paper to the Tenth Five Year Plan (that envisaged an 8% annual growth in the next five years) was unanimously approved. It was also decided in the meeting that the Prime Minister and all the Chief Ministers would have a "Davos-type informal retreat to mull over the future of economic reforms."[10]

The third NDC meeting (which was overall the 50th meeting) held during the premiership of Vajpayee took place on 23 December 2002 in New Delhi. On the Golden Jubilee of the NDC meetings, Prime Minister Vajpayee in his opening address emphasised pushing ahead with the economic reforms programme and announced the setting up of four sub-groups of the NDC to work out the modalities to improve governance, implement policies and programmes, bring down barriers to internal trade, create an investor friendly climate and provide more resources to the panchayati raj institutions.[11]

During the Congress-led UPA governments since 2004, seven meetings of the NDC have taken place under the premiership of Prime Minister

10. *The Hindu*, 2 September 2001.

11. *http://www.hinduonnet.com/2002/12/22 Stores/2002 122204160100.htm.*

Manmohan Singh. The 51st meeting was the first meeting held during UPA-I on 27-28 June 2005 to discuss the mid-term appraisal of the Tenth Five year Plan. They also discussed the challenges facing policy making in the remaining years of the Tenth Plan and the run-up to the Eleventh Plan. It was also agreed to set up a NDC sub-committee on "Agriculture and Selected Issues" under Union Agriculture Minister Sharad Pawar to give suggestions regarding problems faced by the agriculture sector.[12] The 52nd meeting of the NDC took place on 9 December 2006 to approve the Approach Paper for the Eleventh Five Year Plan and Annual Plan for 2007-08.[13] Two meetings took place in 2007 in May and December. The 53rd meeting was held on 29 May 2007 which discussed the slowdown of agricultural sector due to "technology fatigue". The Prime Minister stated that small and marginal farming had become an unviable proposition and until farming was made viable at this scale, it would be virtually "impossible" to reduce rural poverty and distress.[14] There was consensus on improving the conditions of farmers and performance of agriculture. The goal of 4 per cent annual growth in agriculture and allied activities in the Eleventh Five Year Plan was considered feasible. However, there were differences in the requirements of highly irrigated states and relatively dry states with low rain fall. It was resolved to allow states to draw up their own plan with immediate objectives and medium-term goals for 4-5 years.[15]

The NDC in its 54th meeting held on 19 December 2007 considered the Eleventh Five Year Plan (2007-2012) with the aim to increase the economic growth to 9 per cent from 7.6 per cent in the Tenth Plan; to make economic growth inclusive; reduce poverty; generate employment, and reduce unemployment to less than 5 per cent. The next meeting of the NDC took place after almost two and a half years on 24 July 2010.[16] In this 55th meeting, the Mid-term Appraisal of Eleventh Plan was considered. It was emphasised that there was a need for fiscal consolidation, higher investment in infrastructure, faster growth in agriculture, strengthening panchayati raj and urban bodies, improve social sector programmes for

---

12. *www.planningcommission.nic.in/aboutus/speech/spemsa/msa.*
13. *planningcommission.nic.in/plans/planrel/52ndc/Bihar1.doc.*
14. *articles.timesofindia.indiatimes.com/2007-05-29/india/*
15. Ibid.
16. *planassam.in/reports/ndc_54thMeeting.htm* .

weaker sections and improving governance.[17] Tamil Nadu Deputy Chief Minister M.K. Stalin argued that concessions already formulated under the SEZ (Special Economic Zone) policy should be continued and amendments proposed in the revised DTC (Direct Tax Code) need to be modified. He also reminded the Centre that the state had been urging the Centre to initiate talks with state governments, particularly southern States, for inter-linking of rivers.[18]

The 56th meeting of the NDC took place last year on 22 October 2011. There was consensus that objectives laid down in the Approach Paper and challenges identified should be the basis for finalising the functioning of the Twelfth Five Year Plan. States had grievances that CSS were not flexible to accommodate specific issues facing each state. The Centre assured that it was been examined by B.K. Chaturvedi Commission and they will take their concerns into consideration. Other important issues related to fiscal burden faced by states due to range of national flagship programmes and inadequate consultation with the states regarding fiscal sustainability of these initiatives.[19]

The last (57th) meeting of the NDC was held on December 27 to consider the draft Twelfth Five Year Plan. Several CMs realised that lowering of growth target to 8 per cent is only a realistic refection of the external constraints on growth. Though some asserted that they will aim for a higher growth rate. Several Chief Ministers stressed the significance of sectors such as agriculture, power, other infrastructure, health, education and skill development. The Twelfth Five Year Plan document reflects these priorities. Many also focused on the need for special consideration for backward states, and also for backward areas within states. The Prime Minister in his concluding speech shared this concern. He argued that states with low-income levels already get more resources under the formula used by the Finance Commission, and also the Gadgil-Mukherjee formula, which is used by the Planning Commission to distribute normal central assistance.[20]

---

17. *hpplanning.nic.in/55th%20NDC%20meeting%20CM%20Speech.pdf.*
18. *www.thehindu.com/news/states/tamil-nadu/article532110.ece.*
19. *planningcommission.nic.in/plans/planrel/56NDC/PM_concl..*
20. "PMs Closing Remarks at 57th Meeting of NDC", Press Trust, Submitted by editor on December 27, 2012 - 22:30. *www.presstrust.com.*

He further added that under the Backward Regions Grant Fund (BRGF), a large number of districts received special assistance in the Eleventh Plan. There were also State Specific Packages for Bihar, KBK (Kalahandi; Balangir Koraput) districts of Odisha, Bundelkhand district of Madhya Pradesh and Uttar Pradesh, and most recently West Bengal. The Planning Commission is currently working on a restructured design of BRGF, which will come into effect from next year. Chief Minister Jayalalitha however walked out of the meeting as to register her "strong protest" against being asked to wind up her address when she was reading out the 10th page of the 28-page speech. Referring to it as "shabby treatment" by the Centre, she argued that a Chief Minister could not speak on the voluminous Twelfth Plan document in just 10 minutes. She alleged that there have been occasions when Chief Ministers "supporting" the UPA government have been allowed to speak even for 30 minutes or more.[21]

Analysis

The NDC serves—and with certain reforms it can serve even better—as a useful instrument of intergovernmental relations in matters relating to economic development and fiscal policy related issues in the Indian federal set-up for it provides a unique forum for bringing together the executive heads of the two orders of governments in the country. As already mentioned, it was created with a specific politico-economic mandate to formally approve five year plans and related issues of economic development in the country like objectives, priorities, financing pattern, inter-sectoral allocation etc. It may be reiterated that instead of creating the NDC under Article 263 of the Constitution or under a Parliamentary Statute, it was set up by a Cabinet Resolution. Despite lacking in constitutional or statutory status, it has been more functional than the ISC belatedly set up in 1990 under Article 263.

Since 1952, the NDC has met 56 times until the time of writing (October 2012). In the realm of development planning, one can venture to say that the NDC has been more functional with a concrete agenda than the Parliament. Admittedly, the Rajya Sabha as a federal chamber can claim to represent the interests of the states but its composition is not

21. "Jayalalithaa 'humiliated,' walks out of NDC", *The Hindu*, 27 December 2012.

intergovernmental as those of the ISC and the NDC that represent the executive heads of the two orders of government. A member of the Rajya Sabha clearly represents the people or legislators of a state rather than the government of the state, whereas the NDC/ISC represent the executive heads of the Union and the state governments respectively.

Table 5.1

NDC Meetings from 1952 to October 2012

Government	*No. of Years*	*No. of Meetings*	*Average per year*
One-Party Dominant Phase 1			
Jawaharlal Nehru (1952-64)	12	20	1.67
Lal Bahadur Shastri (1964-66)	1.5	2	1.33
Indira Gandhi (1966-77)	11	9	0.82
Janata Interregnum			
Morarji Desai (1977-79)	2.5	2	0.8
One-Party Dominant Phase II			
Indira Gandhi (1980-84)	4	4	1.0
Rajiv Gandhi (1984-89)	5	3	0.6
Multi-Party Coalition/Minority Governments Phase I			
V.P. Singh (1989-90)	1	2	2.0
One-Party Congress Minority Government			
Narasimha Rao (1991-96)	5	4	0.8
Multi-Party System Phase II			
Deve Gowda (1996-97)	1	1	1.0
Atal Behari Vajpayee (1998-2003)	5	3	0.6
Manmohan Singh (2004-2012)	7		

Source: Saxena, 2006.

During the 37 years of one-party government phase (Congress dominance and Janata Party government phase), the NDC had 40 meetings which works out to an average of 1.1 per year. In 22 of multi-party coalition/ minority governments since November-December 1989, it had seventeen meetings—an average of 0.77 per year (See Table 5.1). It may appear to be paradoxical that the frequency of meetings between the two phases has declined by 30 per cent in terms of averages for one would have expected a greater frequency during the latter phase given the greater commitment and representation of state-level political parties in the Union Government as indicated by a more differentiated set of parties ruling at the Union and in the states since 1989. However, this paradox can probably be explained by referring to two factors. First, coalition and minority governments have been very unstable and short-lived, resulting in delays in launching of the plans. Second, different sets of parties, including the regional ones, ruling in the states, have been partners in the federal coalition governments. This has allowed them direct access and opportunities for representation of their views in the Union Cabinet. In this political format thus the Chief Ministers came to enjoy considerable political clout and could influence decisions at the federal level informally rather than through formal channels like the NDC. The Union Government found itself to be dependent on their support but then different Chief Ministers had their own vested interests and viewpoints. Their influence on the federal government would therefore ultimately depend on the realpolitik.

In the context of the frequency of the meetings, it is relevant to recollect that the NDC's organisation and role were reconsidered by a government resolution in October 1967 which stated that it should meet "as often as may be necessary and at least twice in each year." This was the time when from Chandigarh to Calcutta, non-Congress governments were in power. However, the 1967 coalition experiments were very short-lived. In 1971, Indira Gandhi came back to power with a thumping majority; the actual impact of non-Congress governments therefore was not considerable.

There is of course a point of view that maintains that the NDC has been meeting whenever there is an issue that must specifically be discussed by it. In defence of this argument, for example, it may be stated that the 48th meeting of the NDC was called urgently by the Prime Minister (at a very short notice) at the request of some Chief Ministers to discuss, among other things, the approval of the Plan Document, increase in the administered price of food grains, etc. (Saxena, 2006). Apologists of this point of view also argue that the NDC does not lose anything by not having constitutional or statutory status. It is directly under the Prime Minister who is its Chairman. Thus by virtue of being under the highest political executive in the country, a special status is imparted to it in the government.[22]

22. Interview with Rajeev Malhotra, Deputy Advisor, Planning Commission, New Delhi, August 2001.

Because the NDC is devoid of any constitutional or statutory status, plans are invariably launched without the stamp of its formal approval; its meetings too are not held for considerable lengths of time. For instance, the Draft Ninth Five Year Plan proposals prepared by the Planning Commission, which was provisionally implemented in 1997, was belatedly approved by the NDC only in 1999, after a lapse of two years.[23] It is precisely for this reason that the Sarkaria Commission recommended that the NDC should be reconstituted as NEDC by a Presidential Order under the provisions of Article 263 so as to have moorings in the Constitution.

For a proper understanding and explanation of the role and relevance of the NDC, it is necessary to examine its working not only in the context of Union-state relations, but also in the context of the strategy of economic development in the country. Development planning in India started in the Nehru era. In order to be more effective, it is imperative that it adapts itself to changed contexts and policy shifts. These changes began to be reflected from the Fourth Five Year Plan onwards. On the one hand, there has been a new kind of politics which may be called 'populist' politics in which politicking has elbowed out rational economic planning. Vested interests of particular classes, especially those who are influential in political terms, have come to adversely affect the process of planning. On the other hand, the policy-shifts that go by the nature of economic liberalisation have also changed the context of planning in India. In the initial stages of development planning expansion, emphasis was on public investment; the bulk of investments then emanated from the State. But subsequently, public investment began to decline in size and started making way for private investment. So the planning process ought to be reoriented keeping in mind the needs of an economy in which the role of the private sector is constantly expanding.

There is a line of thinking according to which state planning has no place in a liberalised economy. Yet in the rethinking process of the Planning Commission, planning continues to hold relevance in a developing country like India, and the process of planning must be adjusted to a changed economic structure. In other words, the planning process needs to be geared to the restructuring of the economy. In view of the expanding private

---

23. 48th meeting of the NDC held on 19 February 1999.

sector some sort of indicative planning for this sector is needed which has to be different from the planning for the state sector. In the entire process, the NDC emerges as a key agency, especially in the new setting where the importance of the state governments and the private sector is on the increase. Earlier, the Planning Commission (a central agency) planned mainly for the Union that included the plans for the states as well, which easily fell in line. However, exception was made in the case of West Bengal which, because of its different (Leftist) ideological leanings, has a somewhat different perspective on planning. State Planning Boards/Commissions have been set up in all the states, with the exception of Sikkim. Some states have also established district planning units. In the states, besides the Planning Departments and Boards, other development departments and agencies (such as Directorates of Economics and Statistics, research institutions and universities, finance corporations and voluntary agencies)[24] also participate in the planning process.

Most states have expressed their dissatisfaction at not being given due opportunity to participate in national planning. In the present situation, the states are consulted only after the broad features of the five year plan have been formulated. Though the majority of State Planning Boards lack expertise, yet the states are now politically more assertive and desire a greater say in the planning process. The Sarkaria Commission recommended, on the basis of a suggestion made by a state government, that "State Planning Boards should perform functions for the State governments as the Planning Commission does at the national level. ...The Chief Minister should be the Chairman of the State Planning Board as his active involvement would be necessary for the success of the State level planning" (Government of India, 1987-88).

With the 73rd and 74th amendments relating to panchayati raj and nagar raj, the third tier of the government, that is, the grassroots level, has also become relevant for political and developmental processes. The question that now arises: is how to involve the Zila Parishads, Block level and the Gram Panchayats in the process of planning right from the stage of formulation of plan, setting up of priorities, raising of resources, devising implementation strategies, review or appraisal of plan implementation

24. Ibid.

and feedback of these exercises into the planning process. The Sarkaria Commission has also stressed the need for the strengthening of institutions like Zila Parishads and elected Municipal Corporations both financially and functionally. It also stated that regular elections and sessions of these institutions are a must, and means for ensuring the same in all the states uniformly should be evolved by the Union Government in consultation with the NEDC. The National Commission to Review the Working of the Constitution (NCRWC) also recommended to strengthen the institutions of intergovernmental relations in the true spirit of cooperative federalism.[25] Furthermore, Punchhi Commission, given the constitutional and semi-judicial tasks envisaged in the Constitution and the case law but so far denied to it, strongly emphasises that "with the full range of functional empowerment under Article 263, the Council should have functional independence with a professional Secretariat constituted with experts in relevant fields of knowledge supported by central and state officials on deputation for limited periods."[26] The Secretary of the ISC should be designated ex-officio Secretary of the Department of States reporting directly to the Union Home Minister who is to be ex-officio Deputy Chairman of the Council." With this amount of significance and power in intergovernmental relations, the functions of the NDC may also be finally transferred to the ISC.[27]

There is need to correlate macroeconomic indicators and the ground realities at the grassroots level. States differ from one another in many respects. Some states are relatively more developed, while others are backward. In economically developed states, there is a class of industrial bourgeoisie; in agriculturally developed states, there is a class of agrarian capitalists. Also, some states have larger tribal population or other backward classes. So state-level and grassroots level situations vary and the planning process must take into account these variations. Different classes have vested interests; they are politically influential and like to

25. *Commission on Centre-State Relations, Report*, Part I, *op.cit*, Chapter XI.

26. *Commission on Centre-State Relations, Report*, Vol.II, Constitutional Governance and the Management of Centre-State Relations, Chair Justice M.M. Punchhi, New Delhi: Government of India, March 2010..

27. *Report of the National Commission to Review the Working of the Constitution* (NCRWC) 2002.

influence political and economic processes. What is therefore important is that the processes of politics and economic planning must coordinate these differential needs and aspirations. The states must aggregate local level factors into a cohesive framework of policies. The national or federal political process must aggregate diversities and disparities among states. So there is a creative role for politics in the entire process. The NDC is the crucial intergovernmental mechanism in all these processes.

Starting from the Fourth Plan, the planning process began to demand a kind of planning that involved the states' sector, the private sector, civil society, a much greater assertive set of state governments, and constitutionally entrenched local-level political institutions. It is precisely for these reasons that the process of planning needs to be seriously reoriented and agencies like the NDC must be made more functional.

The planning process has now assumed another dimension: it has become much more bargaining in nature. States have come to believe that if the Finance Commission is not able to fulfil their aspirations, an effort could be made to get things done through the Planning Commission. This accent on the bargaining process has projected the NDC as the principal bargaining forum.

The planning discourse has taken a quantum leap but India continues to remain wedded to the obsolete development discourse concerned with issues such as GDP-based thinking, growth, investment, savings, capital-output ratio, that is, purely economistic planning. It is not much concerned with development disparities and their implications for the state, society, administration, quality of life, human development indicators, etc. The NDC and its role must be reconceptualised within these altered parameters of planning. K.N. Kabra in this context visualises two circles of planning: the inner and the outer. The NDC is located as a pivotal agency in the inner circle (of planning), but it must be sensitive to and concerned with the implications of planning for the outer circle, e.g., the impact of globalisation on agriculture, industry, backward regions, poorer sections, etc. and of central pay revisions on the finances of the state governments, etc. The NDC as an important intergovernmental mechanism can play a creative political role in the planning as well as political processes. It can facilitate a process of multi-level planning—planning for the central government, state governments, local levels and indicative laying out of the framework for the private sector.[28]

The NDC is pre-eminently a political body where divergent and conflicting politics of development and planning are reconciled. The work of the Planning Commission is a highly technocratic exercise which does not adequately reflect conflicting interests, aspirations, etc. NDC has thus developed into a forum where political conflicts are resolved in such a manner that the consensus that emerges is realistic and effective and has a close bearing on its implementation. This in fact is the most important role of the NDC.

The NDC with a permanent secretariat and a permanent Finance Commission must function constantly as the key intergovernmental mechanism, where diversity of perspectives is debated, conflicting interests are articulated, and different preferences into a coherent policy-framework of public policies are aggregated.

The above projection of the role envisaged for the NDC—a discerning reader would know—is more in the future than in the past. Lack of a constitutional status is a handicap which ought to be removed to enable it to actualise the potentialities projected. Indeed, as has been argued later, it would be more appropriate to merge the NDC with the ISC and provide proper infrastructural support.[29] In fact, the suggested merger could be brought about without any formal amendment either in the Constitution or the Presidential Order setting up the ISC under Article 263 (Saxena, 2002). For neither the Constitution nor the Presidential Order exclude the functions assigned to the NDC by the 1952 Cabinet Resolution allocating specific functions to it in the domain of economic development and planning.

---

28. *Commission on Centre-State Relations, Report*, Part I, *op.cit*, Chapter XI.

29. Interview with K.N. Kabra, Indian Institute of Public Administration, New Delhi, August 2001.

References

Brass, Paul (1968). "Coalition Politics in North India", *American Political Science Review* LXXII, December.

Brecher, Michael (1966). *Nehru's Mantle: The Politics of Succession in India*. New York: Praeger.

Das, Geetanjali (1997). "National Development Council and Regional Development: A Study of its Role and Functional Dimensions in Indian Federal Polity", Ph.D. thesis in Political Science. Orissa: Berhampur University. pp.75-78.

Economic and Political Weekly, 25 March 1978, p. 542.

Government of India (1967). Administrative Reforms Commission, *Report of the Study Team on Centre-State Relationship*. Vol. I. pp.11, 100-07.

Government of India (1987-88). *Commission on Centre-State Relations: The Report*. Part I and II. Volume I. Government of India Press, Nasik.

Paranjape, H.K. (1970). *The Reorganised Planning Commission: A Study in the Implementation of Administrative Reforms*. New Delhi: The Indian Institute of Public Administration. p.7.

Planning Commission (2002). "Prime Minister's Foreword"', *Ninth Five-Year-Plan, 1997-2002— Vol. I: Development Goals, Strategy and Policies*. New Delhi: Government of India.

————. (n.d.). *Draft Outline, First Five-Year Plan* New Delhi: Government of India. p.253.

Saxena, Rekha (2002). "Role of Intergovernmental Agencies", *The Hindu*, Jan. 29, 2002.

————. (2002). "Strengthening Federal Dialogue: Role of NDC & ISC", *Contemporary India* 1(3), July-Sept.

————. (2006). *Situating Federalism: Mechanisms of Intergovernmental Relations in Canada and India*. New Delhi: Manohar.

Sen, S.R. (1961). "Planning Machinery in India", *Indian Journal of Public Administration*, VII(3): 233, July-September.

Singh, M.P. (1981). *Split in a Predominant Party: The Indian National Congress in 1969*. New Delhi: Abhinav Publications.

6 Measuring Financial Access in India

*A Macroeconomic Growth Approach**

T.A. Bhavani and N.R. Bhanumurthy

Introduction

The basic proposition of this paper is that the financial sector reforms in India toward liberalisation of hitherto heavy-handed quantitative controls, would have led to the development of the sector which further would have improved financial access. The post-1991 financial sector reforms include, apart from liberalisation measures, market-oriented regulations such as prudential regulations over banks aiming at ensuring soundness of the financial system. These regulations combined with increasing market competition due to liberalisation are expected to force incumbent financial institutions to restructure themselves by way of reorganising their assets, exiting from some activities/areas and/or entering into new activities/areas or, limit their activities due to capital adequacy norms, which might have an adverse impact, initially, on financial access. However, it is anticipated that reforms over time increase competitiveness of the financial system and expand financial access through efficiency improvements and cost reductions. In this background, we examine the extent of financial access in post-reform India.

Macroeconomic Growth Approach

Financial access broadly refers to making financial services (such as savings, credit, insurance and payments) available to all potential users

* This paper is part of a larger study "Impact of Financial Sector Reforms in India" funded by the British High Commission, New Delhi and prepared at the Institute of Economic Growth, Delhi, which is published as a book titled *Financial Access in Post-reform India*.

without any barriers—price or non-price. It requires availability of financial services (i.e., physical access), eligibility and affordability of users (World Bank, 2008).

We approach the issue of financial access from the macroeconomic growth perspective. In the literature, financial access has mostly been approached in the name of financial inclusion, from the microeconomic angle focusing on individuals/households for welfare reasons. Microeconomic welfare approach is appropriate, in our view, for developed countries such as United Kingdom (UK), which have well-developed financial systems that include all production organisations and majority of individuals/households leaving only a tiny portion of people outside the formal financial system.[1] In developing countries, however, a significant percentage of not only individuals/households but also production organisations is not covered by the formal financial system.[2] For these countries, financial access or inclusion has important growth implications besides having welfare consequences.

We adopt a macroeconomic growth approach to analyse financial access given the importance of economic growth in the Indian context. India has been placing critical emphasis on sustainable and rapid growth (Planning Commission, 2006) and growth has been the underlying reason for all the new economic policies including financial sector policy reforms.[3] Emphasis on growth has been motivated by the fact that economic growth is considered as a pre-requisite for welfare. Economic growth contributes to welfare directly by raising the real incomes of people through employment generation and indirectly by providing the required resources to government for undertaking welfare enhancing measures including provision of basic services.

---

1. In the most developed countries, more than 90 per cent of households use bank accounts to save and make payments (CGAP, 2009: 11). Only 7 per cent of households in Britain lack any financial products at all (FSA, 2000: 1).
2. Less than 50 per cent of the population in many developing countries has bank accounts (Beck *et al.*, 2008a: 8). In developing countries, SMEs (small and medium enterprises) particularly micro and small enterprises have great difficulty in obtaining the necessary financial resources to effectively scale up their business (Zavatta, 2008: 1; OECD, 2006; Dinh *et al.*, 2010).
3. See *Budget Speech 1991* by Manmohan Singh, which has set the stage for systemic economic policy reforms in India.

Rapid growth, however, requires significant acceleration in investments especially of private investments, which further depends on the financial system and its ability to intermediate savings to potential investments including the level of financial access. For instance, the Eleventh Five Year Plan forecasts the average annual growth rate to be 9 per cent, which requires an estimated investment rate of 35.1 per cent. Half of this investment is expected to come from the private sector (Planning Commission, 2006: 12-13, 15-16), which depends on financial access. For example, private investment in agriculture depends significantly on numerous farmers' access to the formal financial system. So is the case with the micro and small enterprises (MSE) that account for about 40 per cent of industrial production.[4]

The macroeconomic growth approach links financial sector development and access to economic growth through productive investments such as investments in physical capital accumulation, human capital formation, technological progress and other investments required to sustain production of goods and services. While financial development determines the aggregate financial resources, financial access decides the actual flow (magnitude and distribution) of resources for productive investment purposes. We, therefore, analyse financial access in terms of the formal financial system providing financial resources for productive investment requirements of the growth process in India.

Financial access acquires critical significance as internal finances are not adequate for maintenance and expansion of production organisations and formal sources of finance are superior to informal sources. External financing is an essential complement to internal finance for production organisations to manage their production activities and/or to realise their growth potential irrespective of their size. Internal financing constraints are considered stringent for MSE and agricultural activities[5] although large corporate firms too have finance problems. Large corporate firms are in a better position both in terms of internal resource generation and

4. *Annual Report 2008-09*, pp.9, 12-13, available at *http://msme.gov.in*.

5. These constraints are well recorded in the case of Indian agriculture and small enterprises. For international evidence, one can refer to Carpenter and Petersen (2002), which provides a good review of the studies in the area—theoretical and empirical. Also see Dinh *et al.* (2010).

procurement of external resources and face constraints mainly in financing potential investments. Further, external financing from formal financial system is considered superior to informal sources of finance in terms of cost and available amount of finance. Although some international studies show that avoidance of regulatory obligations such as taxes is one of the reason for firms obtaining finance form informal sources (Mehnaz and Wimpey, 2007; Ayyagari *et al.*, 2008), it may not hold good for Indian firms given the high cost of informal (*vis-à-vis* formal) sources of finance.

Measurement of Financial Access

Following the definition mentioned in the beginning, literature tried to assess financial access along the dimensions of: (i) availability (supply side) and usage of financial services; (ii) cost and other barriers to avail the services; and (iii) availability and quality of the services at the individual/ enterprises level. The last two aspects require detailed information about the potential users, which can be obtained only through primary surveys. Hence, the majority of studies measured supply side availability and usage of financial services using geographic and demographic penetration ratios of bank branches, number of deposit and loan accounts, and other such aggregate parameters due to easy availability of data.

Since we are approaching the issue from the macroeconomic growth perspective, we assess financial access in terms of the use of one of the financial services i.e., provision of financial resources from the formal financial system for productive investment purpose. We confine ourselves to actual use of formal financial resources for productive investment as it is difficult to assess potential use given the lack of information about affordability and eligibility aspects of financial access. Actual use of formal financial resources in relation to need serves as the best possible indicator of financial access and improvements in the use of formal financial resources can be taken as improvements in the financial access. We consider 'need' in terms of actual investment undertaken, which can also be taken as an indicator of absorptive capacity of productive organisations. Further, the use of the formal financial system is examined at two levels: one, production organisations obtaining financial resources such as credit from the formal financial system for the purpose of productive investment; two, adequacy of financial resources from formal financial sources in taking care of the investment requirements of productive organisations.

Adequacy of resources obtained from the formal sources of finance is measured in terms of 'financial resource gap' (FRG) defined as: [1–(finances availed from formal financial sources/investment undertaken)].

Financial resources mainly come in the form of credit for agriculture and micro enterprises (both in industry and services sectors) but these resources include credit and others like equity funds for corporate firms. The ratio of financial resource gap ranges between zero to one (100 in percentage terms), which indicates full financial inclusion and exclusion respectively. Although *ex ante* potential investment would be more relevant for the analysis of financial access, we have confined to *ex post* investment undertaken for reasons of data availability. We take it that actual investment can be less but not more than the potential investment (i.e., investments required for the production organisation to realise growth potential) given the fact that the majority of enterprises (large and small in both industry and services sector) and farmers in a developing country like India are resource constrained. This means the use of formal financial resources for actual investment may overestimate but not underestimate the financial access.

The study attempts to measure financial access at different levels of aggregation i.e., economy, segment (organised and unorganised) and sector (agriculture, industry and services) level. Industry and services sectors are divided into organised (corporate) and unorganised segments given their differential access to the formal financial system. We take it that financial access is not a problem for the organised (corporate) sector and hence their FRG (financial resource gap) to be zero as this sector is well integrated with the formal financial system—domestic as well as international.[6] For the unorganised segment in the industry and services sectors, financial access is examined at two levels mentioned earlier, namely, availability and adequacy of credit for the productive investment needs of the enterprises. We have

6. This can be taken as a reasonable assumption. See, for instance, WEF (2009: xiii) states based on international comparison of 55 countries that "larger enterprises in developing countries appear to enjoy access to financial services (such as equity offerings and private credit) that rivals access seen in developed countries".

measured FRG for the sectors, segments and economy in several steps. First, we have calculated the share of the group of 'enterprises not having any external loan' and 'enterprises having loan only from informal sources' (say Group 1) in the total gross value added of the enterprises surveyed by the National Sample Survey Organisation (NSSO) (details of NSS data are given in the next section). Further, we take FRG for this group to be 100 as these enterprises do not have any loans from the formal financial system. Next, we have calculated the value added share for the group of 'enterprises having loan from formal financial institutions' (say Group 2) in the total valued added of the unorganised enterprises surveyed by NSS and its FRG. Second, we have computed FRG for the unorganised segment of the specified sector (industry/services) as weighted average of the FRG of the two groups (Group 1 and Group 2), weights being their value added shares in the segment. Three, taking FRG for the organised segment to be zero, we have arrived at FRG for the industry and services sectors as the weighted average of the FRG of the organised and unorganised segments of the concerned sector weights being their shares in the sectoral GDP (gross domestic product). For this purpose, GDP shares of the organised and unorganised segments in the specified sectors are taken from the National Commission for Enterprises in the Unorganised Sector [NCEUS] (2007). We have estimated FRG for the agriculture sector using macroeconomic data due to lack of disaggregated information. Four, we have computed FRG for the organised/unorganised segment as the weighted average of FRG of the respective segments of the three sectors, weights being sectoral shares in the unorganised and organised segments. This sectoral composition of the unorganised segment is given in the NCEUS (2007) and the sectoral composition of the organised segment is calculated by applying the share of organised segment in different sectors given in NCEUS (2007) to GDP data. Finally, we have measured FRG for the economy as the weighted average of the sectoral FRG, weights being sectoral shares in GDP. FRG for the economy and organised and unorganised segments is measured for the year 2004-05 as GDP shares of the unorganised and organised segments for the three sectors are available for this year.[7]

7. GDP shares of the unorganised and organised segments in the three sectors: agriculture, industry and services, have been estimated by the Sub-Committee on the Contribution of the Unorganised Sector to GDP (NCEUS, 2007: Table 2.8, p.8).

Data

For the agriculture sector, we have used aggregate economy level data for GCF (gross capital formation) and direct institutional credit for the agriculture sector.[8] GCF refers to the aggregate additions to fixed assets and changes in stock and hence taken as investment in the sector. We have taken private investment in agriculture from the *Indiastat.com* which has compiled this data from the Ministry of Agriculture, Government of India. Since we have got private investment in fixed assets, we have used direct institutional credit for long term investment purpose in agriculture and allied activities provided by the Reserve Bank of India (RBI). To make it compatible with investment—a flow variable, we have made use of loan issued rather than outstanding credit (RBI, 2009). FRG for the agriculture sector is estimated using private investment and direct institutional credit for the period of 1992-93 to 2004-05. The major limitation of this data set is that it does not include working capital that constitutes a significant part of investment due to lack of readily available data.

For the unorganised segments of industry and services sectors, we have made use of unit level data of relevant National Sample Surveys (NSS). NSS has been conducting quinquennial surveys of the unorganised manufacturing enterprises since long through various rounds. We have made use of unit level data of the 51st and 62nd Rounds of NSS as these cover the initial (1994-95) and latest available time points 2005-06 in the reform period.[9] NSSO conducted a comprehensive survey of unorganised

8. Initially, we have tried to use PLP (potential-linked credit plan) projections as potential investment and GLC (ground level credit) flows collected by National Bank for Agriculture and Rural Development (NABARD) annually at district level. It could have been ideal for our purpose as it not only provides potential investment but also available in details such as potential crops, required agricultural machinery and implements, irrigation, livestock and crop expenditure at district level. After putting in substantial efforts, we had to discard the idea of using this data due to lack of complete and uniform information for all the states in one place say, NABARD Headquarters, Mumbai, and inconsistencies between PLP and GLC data.
9. There is a difference in the coverage of the specified rounds. Most of the activities classified as manufacturing activities in the National Industrial Classification (NIC) 1987 and hence covered by 51st Round, have been classified under services sector in the NIC 1998 and 2004 and thus not covered by 56th and 62nd Rounds. This may explain the large difference in the number of enterprises surveyed in the two rounds. We take it that these differences will not have any impact on the quality of the analysis.

service enterprises for the first time as a part of the 57th Round with the reference year of 2001-02 and hence we have data for only one time point for the unorganised segment of the services sector.[10]

NSS unit level data include among other variables, fixed assets—owned and hired—working expenses and borrowings. Further, the data source provides borrowings credit agency-wise, which are classified into institutional and non-institutional sources. Institutional sources of credit include government, cooperative society/bank, commercial banks including regional rural banks, insurance, provident fund, financial corporations and institutions. Since all these institutional sources of credit form a part of the formal financial system, we refer to these as 'formal sources' of finance in the study. Non-institutional sources of loans include money lenders, landlord, traders, friends and relatives and others. Most of these sources are a kind of informal arrangements as their main job is not supplying finances. For money lenders, lending may be one of their occupations but we presume that these are not registered sources of finance. We refer to all these sources as 'informal sources' of finance. The main limitation of this data is that fixed investment and loan are provided as stock variables whereas working expenses is given as a flow variable.

For the organised segments of the industry and services sector, the entire external financing comes from the formal financial system implying that the financial resource gap is zero. Hence, we examine the pattern of financing in the organised segment just to have an idea whether there is any change in the pattern if so in which direction, as it has implications for the financial access of unorganised segment. If the large organised enterprises use more of non-bank sources of finance such as capital markets, we would expect more of bank funds to be available for non-corporate, unorganised enterprises. We have calculated the relative shares of different sources of funds in the total funds for the period of 1994-2008 based on company level balance sheet data provided by capitaline for the organised segment in both industry and services sector. In both the sectors, internal source of funding is the main source of funding. External financing is dominated by debt especially from the banks, although the size and importance of

10. Since we have not used multiplier provided, data refers to the sample surveyed but not to the population of enterprises.

stock markets have grown significantly in the recent years. Loan funds are higher for manufacturing companies in comparison with that of service companies.

In addition to the data limitations that have been mentioned, data are available with a considerable time lag. Notwithstanding this we have used it as primary surveys would limit the sample substantially on many dimensions including area coverage and hence may not provide overall picture. Given the limitations, estimates of this study may be taken as indicative values for the financial resource gap and hence the status of the financial access in the economy.

Empirical Analysis

Agriculture Sector

Private investment, direct institutional credit and financial resource gap in the agriculture sector for the post-reform years of 1992-93 to 2004-05, are given in Table 6.1. The table indicates that financial resource gap in agriculture has come down from 55 per cent in the initial year (1992-93) to 37 per cent by the year 1998-99 and goes up to 70 per cent in the year 2001-02 only to come down again to 40 per cent by the year 2004-05. This evidence does not show any trend—upward or, downward, in the financial resource gap of the Indian agriculture sector.

The evidence implies that financial resource gap persists in the reform period ranging between 40–70 per cent despite the priority sector lending and other policy measures. However, financial resource gap estimates of the agriculture sector, being based on macroeconomic aggregate data, might not reveal much about microeconomic details.

To have an idea about the microeconomic situation, we combine this evidence with that of the households in the occupational category of 'self-employed in agriculture'.[11] Mean FRG for the group of 'self-employed in agriculture' remains large although it declined over time (from 92% in

---

11. We have estimated financial resource gap for different households in our main report using 5th and 6th All India Debt and Investment Surveys (AIDIS) conducted by NSSO as a part of its 48th and 59th Rounds with 1992 and 2002 as reference years respectively.

the year 1992 to 72% in 2002). This explains the dependency of Indian agriculturalists on costly informal sources of finance such as moneylenders and the resulting indebtedness.

Table 6.1

Private Investment, Institutional Credit and FRG in Agriculture, India

Year	*Private investment*[1] *(₹ Crore)*	*Direct Institutional Credit*[2] *(₹ Crore)*	*Financial Resource Gap (FRG %)*[3]
1992-93	10804	4864	54.98
1993-94	10331	5261	49.08
1994-95	12381	6841	44.75
1995-96	14605	8419	42.36
1996-97	17119	9389	45.15
1997-98	19087	10007	47.58
1998-99	19131	12087	36.82
1999-2000	41481	15968	61.51
2000-01	38558	15346	60.20
2001-02	51285	15612	69.56
2002-03	52319	19887	61.99
2003-04	49249	23834	51.61
2004-05	55662	33555	39.72

Notes: 1. Private Investment refers to gross capital formation in the private sector in agriculture and allied sector in India (at current prices). Data are available separately for public and private sectors.

2. Direct Institutional Credit refers to long term loans issued directly to the beneficiary/borrower by the financial institutions.

3. FRG = 1- [Loan from formal financial institutions/productive investment].

Source: *Indiastat.com* (compiled data from Ministry of Agriculture) for Private Investment.

RBI (2009). *Handbook of Statistics on Indian Economy*, Table 56, p.112 for credit.

Service Sector

Table 6.2 reveals that the NSS survey covers little more than 0.36 million service enterprises, of which only 10 per cent of the enterprises had loan from external sources. Of the enterprises that availed loan, almost 60 per cent had taken loan from the formal financial system. Around 40 per cent of the enterprises that had external financing obtained their loan from informal sources of finance. Effectively, only 6 per cent of the service enterprises surveyed availed loan from formal financial institutions.

In the rural areas, around 88 per cent of the surveyed service enterprises have not availed any loan from external sources. Of the 12 per cent of enterprises that had loans in the rural areas, almost 60 per cent had borrowings from the formal financial system. The remaining 40 per cent of the enterprises had borrowed entirely from the informal sources of finance. Surprisingly, higher percentage (91%) of urban (*vis-à-vis* rural) enterprises did not avail any external financing though their average investment is much higher than that of rural enterprises. Sixty per cent of the urban enterprises that have reported borrowings had borrowed from the formal financial sources.

Table 6.2

Use of Formal Financial System by Unorganised Service Enterprises in Rural and Urban Areas: 2002

Enterprises	*All-India*	*Rural*	*Urban*
Enterprise Surveyed (no)	361776	138145	223631
(%)	100	100	100
Ent. No loan, + invest.[1] (%)	89.41	87.54	90.51
Ent. having loan[2] (%)	10.37	12.16	9.28
Ent. Having loan from:			
- formal + informal sources[3] (%)	4.03	3.73	4.28
- formal sources only[3] (%)	55.78	55.44	56.06
- informal sources only[3] (%)	40.19	40.84	39.66

Notes: 1. Percentage of enterprises had a positive investment but availed no loan in the total number of enterprises surveyed; 2. Percentage of enterprises having positive loan in the total number of enterprises surveyed; 3. Percentages are in the total number of households having loan.

All these rows may not exactly tally as good number of enterprises got eliminated in the process of data cleaning such as those enterprises that did not have investment or, specify the source of loan or missing values.

Percentages of enterprises having loan from formal financial institutions is the total % of enterprises having loan from formal as well as informal sources and % of enterprises having loan only from formal financial sources.

Source: NSS 57th Round Unit Level Data.

Table 6.3 highlights that FRG1 is much higher and only about one quarter of the investments is taken care of by the formal financial system. If one had to purchase the hitherto hired assets, FRG2 becomes much more. FRG in the urban enterprises (75%) is larger than that of rural enterprises (73%) contrary to expectations.

Table 6.3

Financial Resource Gap (%): Unorganised Service Segment in Rural and Urban Areas, 2002

	All-India	*Rural*	*Urban*
FRG1	74	73	75
FRG2	79	76	80

Notes: FRG1 includes owned fixed assets and working capital in investment;
FRG2 includes owned + hired fixed assets and working capital in investment
Loan includes loan amount taken from only formal financial sources.

Source: NSS 57th Round Unit Level Data.

Manufacturing Sector

Table 6.4 reveals that only 15 per cent of unorganised manufacturing enterprises surveyed in the year 2005-06 had taken external loan. Of these, 55 per cent of the enterprises had loan from formal sources of financing and the remaining 45 per cent had taken loan from informal financial institutions. In comparison with the earlier time point i.e., 1994-95, a little higher percentage of enterprises availed loan from the formal financial system in 2005-06. By the year 2005-06, only around 14 per cent of rural manufacturing enterprises had availed loan from an external source and half of these had taken loan from formal financial sources, which is smaller in percentage terms than that of the earlier years of the reform i.e., 1994-95. Of the urban enterprises surveyed in the year 2005-06, around 17 per cent had shown loans from external sources. Of the urban enterprises that had reported external loans, 60 per cent had taken loans from formal financial sources. At the all-India level, and also for rural and urban sectors, the percentage of enterprises that had external source of loan has increased over time. However, rural enterprises that availed loan from formal financial institutions had come down over time pulling down the all-India percentage too. Urban enterprises that had taken loan from the formal financial system increased over time in percentage terms (see Table 6.4).

The evidence shows that FRG has definitely come down for all the categories of manufacturing enterprises over time but the gap is still large. Only 30 per cent of the investments made by the unorganised manufacturing enterprises that availed loans from formal financial institutions is taken care by the financial system at the all-India level. The gap is smaller for rural enterprises in comparison with the urban enterprises (see Table 6.5).

Table 6.4

Use of Formal Financial System by Unorganised Manufacturing Enterprises: Rural and Urban Areas, 1994-95 and 2005-06

Enterprises	*All-India*		*Rural*		*Urban*	
	1994-95	*2005-06*	*1994-95*	*2005-06*	*1994-95*	*2005-06*
Enterprise Surveyed (no)	192029	82882	120609	42045	71420	40837
(%)	100	100	100	100	100	100
Ent. No loan, + investment[1] (%)	87.37	84.18	87.60	85.32	87.73	83.01
Ent. having loan[2] (%)	11.84	15.47	11.93	14.39	11.70	16.54
Ent. Having loan from:	100	100	100	100	100	100
- formal + informal sources[3] (%)	7.67	17.50	7.04	11.39	8.76	22.97
- formal sources only[3] (%)	50.20	37.01	53.40	38.01	44.72	36.12
- informal sources only[3] (%)	42.11	45.49	39.56	50.60	46.52	40.92

Notes: 1. Percentage of enterprises having positive investment but availed no loan in the total number of enterprises surveyed. 2. Percentage of enterprises having positive investment and positive loan in the total number of enterprises surveyed. 3. Percentages are in the total number of households having loan.

All these rows may not exactly tally as good number of enterprises got eliminated in the process of data cleaning such as those enterprises that did not show investment or, specify the source of loan or missing values.

Percentages of enterprises having loan from formal financial institutions is the total % of enterprises having loan from formal as well as informal sources, and % of enterprises having loan only from formal financial sources.

Source: NSS 51st and 62nd Round Unit Level Data.

Table 6.5

Financial Resource Gap (%) for Unorganised Manufacturing Enterprises: Rural and Urban Areas—1994-95 and 2005-06

Enterprises	*All-India*		*Rural*		*Urban*	
	1994-95	*2005-06*	*1994-95*	*2005-06*	*1994-95*	*2005-06*
FRG1[1]	78	70	78	67	75	72
FRG2[2]	81	74	81	71	80	77

Notes: 1. FRG1 includes owned fixed assets and working capital in investment; 2. FRG2 includes owned + hired fixed assets and working capital in investment.

Source: *NSS 51st and 62nd Round Unit Level Data.*

Unorganised Segment and Economy

Table 6.6 provides GDP shares and FRG for the three sectors. The table presents the financial resource gap for the organised and unorganised segments and for economy. Table 6.6 shows the largest FRG for the agriculture sector (49%)[12] followed by the services sector (41%) as larger part of these sectors is unorganised. The industry sector that has limited unorganised segment in terms of value added, indicates the smallest resource gap (22%).

Table 6.7 exhibits that at the economy level FRG is around 39 per cent meaning that 60 per cent of the investment needs are taken care of by the formal financial system. FRG is the largest for the unorganised segment of the economy (68%) and only 32 per cent of its investment requirements are financed by the formal financial institutions. The organised segment does not have any problem in obtaining resources from the formal financial system. In sum, the unorganised segment consisting of numerous small and widely dispersed firms/farms, has been having limited access to formal financial system that is acting as a big hurdle for these units to grow and thus contribute to economic growth.

Table 6.6

Sectoral Financial Resource Gap (%): 2004-05

	Unorganised	*Organised*	*Sector Total*
Agriculture			
GDP Share of Segments	0.95	0.05	1.00
Financial Resource Gap	51.61	0.00	49.00
Industry			
GDP Share of Segments	0.29	0.71	1.00
Financial Resource Gap	76.03	0.00	22.00
Services			
GDP Share of Segments	0.45	0.55	1.00
Financial Resource Gap	91.16	0.00	41.00

Notes: GDP shares of organised and unorganised segments of the three sectors are taken from NCEUS (2007); Financial resource gap is computed based on NSS unit level data for the unorganised segment of the industry and service sectors and RBI data for the agriculture.

Source: NSS 61st and 62nd Rounds unit level data.

12. We would expect it to be much larger had we included working capital requirements.

Table 6.7

Financial Resource Gap, 2004-05: Segments and Economy

	Agriculture	*Industry*	*Services*	*Total*
Unorganised				
Sectoral GDP Share	0.38	0.15	0.47	1.00
Financial Resource Gap	51.61	76.3	91.16	67.53
Organised				
Sectoral GDP Share	0.03	0.30	0.67	1.00
Financial Resource Gap	0.00	0.00	0.00	0.00
Economy				
Sectoral GDP Share	0.19	0.21	0.60	1.00
Financial Resource Gap	49.00	22.00	41.00	38.53

Notes: Sectoral GDP shares of the unorganised segment are taken from NCEUS (2007); We have computed sectoral GDP shares of the organised segment using NCEUS (2007) GDP shares of the organised segment in different sectors. Financial resource gap is computed based on NSS unit level data for the unorganised segment of the industry and service sectors and RBI data for the agriculture.

Summary Findings

We summarise below the significant findings of the study.

(i) FRG for the agriculture sector varied from 40 to 70 per cent during the period of 1992-93 to 2004-05.

(ii) Only 10 per cent of the unorganised service enterprises reported loans in the year 2001-02. Of these, about 60 per cent reported taking loans from formal financial institutions. FRG for the unorganised service enterprises that took loans from the formal financial system was around 75 per cent.

(iii) Around 15 per cent of unorganised manufacturing enterprises reported loans in the year 2005-06. Of these, 55 per cent availed loans from the formal financial system. FRG for the unorganised manufacturing enterprises that took loans from formal sources was around 70 per cent indicating that only 30 per cent of investments made by these enterprises were financed by the formal financial system.

(iv) For the year 2004-05, the agriculture sector revealed the larget financial resource gap (49%) followed by the service sector (41%) because a large segment of these two sectors is unorganised. The industry sector with a larger organised segment showed a resource gap of only 22 per cent.

(v) In sum, the agriculture sector, and unorganised service and manufacturing enterprises had limited access to the formal financial system in terms of availability and adequacy (given by the FRG) of loans. Empirical evidence indicates not only limited financial access but also unequal access across enterprises.

(vi) At an aggregate economy level, the financial resource gap was estimated to be 39 per cent in the year 2004-05. As expected, FRG was the largest for the unorganised segment of the economy (68%) and only 32 per cent of its investment requirements were financed by the formal financial system.

Policy Recommendations

Empirical analysis of the study clearly indicates that the unorganised segment covering agriculture, MSE (in industry as well as services sector), have limited financial access with wide FRG. The often-cited reasons for the limited financial access of the unorganised segment are—high risk and high transaction costs.

Lending to unorganised entities is associated with higher production as well as behavioural risks. Lack of expertise of small producers in the required areas such as technology and marketing is considered as one of the main reasons for production risk. Added to this is the risk of crop failure due to weather in the case of agriculture. Behavioural risk originates from the lack of reliable information. Collecting and processing information for a large number of small entities is quite costly. Documentation and processing of loan applications, distribution and monitoring of loans, etc. for a large number of small borrowers incur high transaction costs. Hence, the solution for the problem of limited access lies in reducing risk and transaction costs.

The majority of the existing policies are not focusing on reducing risk and transaction costs. The major policies that are in operation in respect of lending to agriculture, micro and small enterprises are: priority sector lending (PSL), credit guarantee schemes (CGS), refinance schemes, interest/capital subsidy programmes, and other schemes of state and central government such as Swarna Jayanti Grameen Swarojgar Yojana (SGSY). Although CGS reduces the lender's risk by government absorbing the risk, and thus encourages credit flow to the specified segment, it suffers from the problems of adverse selection and moral hazard. Long-term loans with subsidies for purchasing fixed assets (i.e., government bearing a part of the fixed cost) reduces the cost of capital but induces corruption and hence misallocation of capital. Government, however, cannot absorb risk and cost forever given ever-increasing demands on its limited resources. Availability of timely and adequate capital is a problem for small producers as much as cost of credit as the former is essential for the smooth operation of production activities.[13] Cost of capital provided by the formal financial system is as such lower than that provided through informal sources of finance. Policy measures that do not reduce risk and transaction costs are not sustainable. For instance, evidence shows that although banks at large attained the overall targets of priority sector lending but not the sub-targets of lending to sectors like agriculture. At end-March 2009, out of 27 public sector banks, three banks have not attained priority sector lending target of 40 per cent and 13 public sector banks have not attained the 18 per cent target for agriculture. In the case of domestic private sector banks, 5 out of 22 banks have not reached targeted amount for overall priority sector lending and 14 banks have not fulfilled the target for agriculture sector. Out of 27 foreign banks, three have defaulted on priority sector lending and 6 banks have not attained sub-targets for each of the two segments i.e., export credit and small enterprises.[14] Banks whenever enforced to lend to high risk borrowers like farmers and micro enterprises, try to reduce risk by having collateral (mainly land), which itself limits financial access.[15]

13. Author's own survey of small enterprises in and around Delhi a decade ago showed the same (IDPAD study done by IEG). Many committees on the issue have repeatedly brought out this fact including the recent Prime Minister Task Force on Micro, Small and Medium Enterprises (January 2010).

14. *Report on Trend and Progress of Banking in India 2008-09*, RBI, Mumbai, pp.288, 91 and 94.

15. Author's personal interaction with the farmers in some villages of Krishna district of Andhra Pradesh (AP), shows that both the scheduled commercial banks and cooperatives lend only to those farmers who provide collateral, which is mainly land. Even with collateral, banks do not provide adequate credit. For instance, with collateral of one acre, which is valued at three lakh rupees by the government of AP, banks provide a maximum loan of ten thousand rupees whereas cost of paddy cultivation in the *Kharif* season in these areas is approximately sixteen thousand rupees in the year 2009.

For these reasons, despite numerous policy measures, financial access remained limited in India. At the same time, policy measures like PSL not only restrict risk diversification by banks but also not encourage banks to specialise in lending to the specified sectors. Lending to agriculture, and MSE requires specialisation as it enables cost reductions—information, transaction and others. Policy measures such as PSL and subsidised schemes may not encourage new private sector banks to come up and specialise in lending to agriculture and small enterprises.

Policy measures should be devised to reduce transaction costs and risk in lending to small producers. This can be attained by:

(i) Encouraging the local area banks with local employees and decentralised decision-making procedures. If young, high school graduates from the local areas are employed and provided the required training they can be of great help as they are expected to have the necessary knowledge of local conditions. Given their limited education and skills, and wage bargaining power, wages and salaries of these employees are expected to be much less than that of national banks. The attrition ratio of these employees is also expected to be low given their limited education and opportunity costs. At present, employees of the national level banks although having higher education and skills, and higher wages and salaries, lack local knowledge and their standard information collection procedures may not give them the required information. Coupled with the centralised decision-making procedures, national banks may not be suitable for lending to scattered small producers.

(ii) Banks linking borrowings to savings through innovative deposit schemes and insurance products and thus reducing risk.

(iii) Removal of priority sector lending or, issuing PSL certificates, which are tradable in the market as these may allow some of the banks to specialise in the unorganised segment. Specialisation is essential for reducing the cost of lending so as to expand financial access to unorganised segments.

References

Ayyagari, Meghana, Asli Demirguc-Kunt and Vojislav Maksimovic (2008). "Formal versus Informal Finance: Evidence from China", *Policy Research Working Paper* 4465. The World Bank.

Beck, Thorsten (2008). "*The Econometrics of Finance and Growth*", *Policy Research Working Paper* No. WPS4608. Washington, D.C.: World Bank. April.

Beck, Thorsten, Asli Demirguc-Kunt and Patrick Honohan (2008). "*Access to Financial Services: Measurement, Impact and Policies*". May. *www.worldbank.org*

Bhavani, T.A. and N.R. Bhanumurthy (2012). *Financial Access in Post-reform India*. New Delhi: Oxford University Press.

Carpenter, Robert E. and Bruce C. Petersen (2002). "Is Growth of Small Firms Constrained by Internal Finance", *The Review of Economics and Statistics* 84(2): 298-309, May.

CGAP (2009). *Financial Access 2009: Measuring Access to Financial Services around the World.* Consultative Group to Assist the Poor. Washington, D.C.: World Bank.

Chidzero Anne-Marie, Karen Ellis and Anjali Kumar (2008). *Indicators of Access to Finance: Through Household Level Surveys (Comparison of Data from Six Countries).* World Bank, DFID and FinMark Trust.

Dinh, Hinh T., Dimitris A. Mavridis and Hoa B. Nguyen (2010). "*The Binding Constraint on Firms' Growth in Developing Countries*. Policy Research", *Working Paper* WPS5485. Washington, D.C.: World Bank.

FSA (2000). "*In or Out? Financial Exclusion: A Literature and Research Review*", *Consumer Research* No. 3. UK: Financial Services Authority.

Mehnaz Safavian and Joshuva Wimpey (2007). "*When Do Enterprises Prefer Informal Credit?*", *Policy Research Working Paper* No.4435. Washington, D.C.: World Bank.

NCEUS (2007). *Report on Financing of Enterprises in the Unorganised Sector.* New Delhi: National Commission for Enterprises in the Unorganised Sector, Government of India.

OECD (2006). *The SME Financing: Theory and Evidence. Volume 1*. OECD Browse it Editions.

Planning Commission (2006). *Towards Faster and More Inclusive Growth: An Approach to the 11th Five Year Plan.* New Delhi: Government of India.

Reserve Bank of India (RBI) (2009). *Handbook of Statistics on Indian Economy*. Mumbai.

World Economic Forum (WEF) (2009). *Financial Development Report 2009.* Geneva.

World Bank (2008). *Finance for All: Policies and Pitfalls in Expanding Access.* Washington D.C.

Zavatta Roberto (2008). *Financing Technology Entrepreneurs and SMEs in Developing Countries.* Washington, D.C.: InfoDev/World Bank. Available at *http://www.infodev.org*

Section II: Federal Fiscal Sharing

7 Central Tax Reforms

Implications for States

C.S. Rao and G.R. Reddy

Introduction

In the Indian Constitution, taxation powers are assigned to the Centre and the states based on the principle of separation. Most taxes with a nation-wide base are assigned to the Centre. These include taxes on income and wealth from non-agricultural sources, taxes on manufacturing excluding those on alcoholic liquor and customs duty. In addition, the Centre is vested with the power to levy taxes unspecified in the Constitution. The revenue potential of the taxes assigned to the Centre is much greater because of their broader base and higher buoyancy. Though a large number of taxes are assigned to states, their revenue potential is much lower with the exception of taxes on sale of goods and duties of excise on alcoholic liquor. The allocation of functions in the Constitution broadly follows the pattern in other major federations with functions relating to defence, foreign relations, macroeconomic management, atomic energy, space, communications and subjects involving inter-state ramifications assigned to the Centre and subjects like agriculture, public order, health, water supply and sanitation, irrigation, education, and industry assigned to the states. Some of the functions which do not figure either in the State List or the Union List are listed in the Concurrent List, over which both the Centre and the states have concurrent responsibility. By an amendment of the Constitution, education and forestry were shifted from the State List to the Concurrent List. As the subjects assigned to states involve huge expenditure commitments disproportionate to the revenue potential of taxes assigned to them, the Constitution provides for sharing of central tax revenue and grants from the Centre to states.

Though the assignment of tax powers between the Centre and the states in India is based on the principle of separation with both of them having exclusive jurisdiction over taxes assigned to them, tax reforms at the Centre will invariably impact the state finances because a part of the Central tax revenue is shared with the states as provided for in the Constitution. This paper attempts to analyse the impact of reforms in central taxation on the states' share in central taxes. After an overview of the reforms in central taxation, the impact of tax reforms on central tax revenues and on the transfers to states are analysed. Though the reforms undertaken by the Centre resulted in an improvement in tax buoyancy considerably thereby increasing the resource flows to the states, certain policies of the Centre such as the indiscriminate resort to the levy of cesses and surcharges and tax exemptions have resulted in lower revenue sharing with the states. These issues are analysed and finally the conclusions are presented.

An Overview of Central Tax Reforms

Tax reforms are an on-going process. However, it can be said that serious efforts for reforming the Indian tax system started from the mid-eighties. Major tax-wise reforms in the Indian tax system since the mid-eighties are presented below. This is not an exhaustive account of the reforms in central taxation but gives a synoptic view of the direction of major reforms.

Income Tax

By 1973-74, there were 11 different income slabs with tax rates ranging from 10 to 85 per cent. With a surcharge of 15 per cent, the effective top marginal rate was at a confiscatory level of 97.5 per cent. During the next 10 years, the peak income tax-rate was brought down to 62 per cent and the number of slabs was reduced to 8. Even after such reduction, the burden of income taxation combined with wealth tax was perceived to be very high and often exceeded 100 per cent of income in higher income and wealth tax brackets. In 1985-86, the peak marginal rate of income tax was reduced from 62 per cent to 50 per cent and the wealth tax from 5 per cent to 2 per cent. The number of income tax slabs was reduced from 8 to 4. The next wave of tax reforms started with the initiation of broad-based economic reforms in the country in 1991. Following the recommendations of the Tax Reforms Committee (TRC) (Chelliah Committee), the income tax slabs were reduced to 3 and the rates were brought down to 20, 30 and 40 per cent. The rates were further reduced to 10, 20 and 30 per cent.

In addition to reduction in the number of slabs and income tax rates, there was a significant improvement in tax administration resulting in better tax compliance. Reforms in tax administration include extension of scope of tax deducted at source, introduction of one by six criteria and TIN (Tax Information Network). In order to broaden the tax base, two by four criteria was introduced which was later converted into one by six criteria. Under this criterion, every individual covered under any one of the six conditions, *viz.*, owning a house, owning a car, having a membership in a club, owning a credit card, foreign travel and subscribing to a telephone connection is required to file income tax return. This has considerably increased the number of income tax payers in the country. Following the recommendations of the Task Force on Direct Taxes (Chairman, Dr Vijay L. Kelkar, December, 2002), TIN was put in place in collaboration with the National Securities Depository Limited (NSDL). Under the TIN, all returns of TDS (tax deducted at source) and other information is stored in a central database. TIN receives online information on collection of taxes from the banks through Online Tax Accounting System (OLTAS), which also flows into the central database.

To take the reform process further, the Government of India (GoI) had released a draft Discussion Paper on Direct Taxes in August 2009, indicating the broad contours of further reforms proposed for feedback from the public. Based on the feedback, a revised discussion paper was put out by the Government seeking comments from the public. The issues covered under the discussion paper related mainly to tax treatment of savings, taxation of income from property, capital gains, salary income and retirement benefits as far as the taxation of income is concerned.

Corporate Income Tax

The taxation of corporate income remained complex. There was a distinction between widely held companies and closely held companies, and the tax rate varied from 45 per cent to 65 per cent in 1973-74. Despite the higher nominal rates of taxation, the effective rates were substantially lower because of liberal allowances for depreciation and investment. There were also tax incentives for industrial units located in certain specified backward areas. This resulted in some companies not paying any tax on their profits. In 1985-86, the basic corporate tax rate was reduced to 50 per cent and the rates applicable to different types of closely held companies were unified at 55 per cent. Following the recommendations of the TRC, the distinction between the closely and widely held companies was done away with and a uniform rate of 40 per cent was adopted in 1993-94. This was followed by a further reduction in the tax rate to 35 per cent and shifting of 10 per cent dividend tax from individuals to companies in 1997-98. To address the problem of zero tax companies, the Government introduced the Minimum Alternate Tax (MAT) in 1996-97. Under this dispensation, while the companies can take advantage of tax preferences, they are required to pay 30 per cent tax on their book profits. In 2005-06, the corporate tax rate was reduced to 30 per cent and at present it remains at this level.

Wealth Tax

Wealth tax was introduced in India in 1957. The wealth tax rate was reduced from 5.0 per cent to 2.5 per cent in 1976-77. This was reversed in 1979-80 and the rate returned to a maximum of 5.0 per cent. Major reform in wealth taxation took place in 1992-93 when all the financial assets were taken out of computation of wealth tax and the rate was reduced to 1.0 per cent. The exemption limit was raised to ₹ 15 lakh in 1993-94 and further to ₹ 30 lakh in 2010-11. The yield from wealth tax continues to remain very insignificant. The revenue from wealth tax is budgeted at ₹ 1244 crore in 2012-13, which is just 0.01 per cent of the budgeted gross tax revenue of the Centre. In view of its low yield and high administrative costs, several committees have recommended its abolition. Both the TRC and the Task Force on Direct Taxes recommended its abolition.

Central Excise Duties

Central excise duties were initially levied on select goods which by 1975-76 were extended to all manufactured goods. The structure of excise taxation remained complex with as many as 24 rates varying from 2 to 100 per cent. While some commodities were subject to specific duties, others were subject to ad valorem duties. The process of converting specific duties into ad valorem was completed by 1993-94. Now there are very few commodities which are subject to specific duties. As the excise duties were levied based on the releases from the warehouses, both inputs as well as final goods were subject to taxation resulting in cascading of tax burden. To address the problem of cascading, the Government introduced Modified Value Added Tax (MODVAT) in 1986 to give credit to the taxes paid on the inputs. It was initially restricted to a few select items and only by 1996-97 it was gradually extended to cover most of the commodities listed in the excise tariff. There were further reforms in excise duties following the recommendations of the TRC which included unification of rates and reliance on company accounts rather on physical verification of goods. The rates of excise duties were reduced from 11 (ranging from 5% to 40%) to three rates (8, 16 and 24%), with a few luxury goods subject to an additional non-rebatable tax of either 6 or 16 per cent. Further unification took place in 2000-01 when the three rates were merged into a single rate of 16 per cent called Central Value Added Tax (CENVAT). Along with CENVAT, non-rebatable special excise duties at the rates of 8, 16 and 24 per cent were introduced on a few select luxury goods.

Customs Duties

The system of customs duties remained complex till 1990-91 with wide dispersal of rates ranging from 0 to 400 per cent, wide ranging exemptions and quantitative restrictions (QRs) on imports. It can be said that serious attempts at reforming customs duties started in 1991-92 with the reduction in the peak rate of customs duties on non-agricultural goods to 150 per cent. This rate was further reduced in stages to 15 per cent by 2005-06. Another reform was the reduction in the number of duty rates from 22 in 1990-91 to 4 in 2003-04. Some items are outside the ambit of these four rates and are subject to higher duty rates. Coupled with rate reduction, there was also a major easing of QRs resulting in liberalisation of foreign trade in the country.

Service Tax

In the Indian Constitution, service tax is neither assigned to the Centre nor to the states. Because of the growing importance of the service sector in the national economy, the Centre introduced service tax under the residuary powers in 1994-95 on three services, *viz.*, insurance other than life insurance, stock brokerage and telecommunications. The Constitution was amended in 2004 (88th amendment) to vest the power to levy the service tax with the Centre. In terms of this amendment, the proceeds from the service tax shall be shared between the Centre and the states in accordance with the principles to be determined by Parliament. The list of services liable to service taxation was increased in a phased manner to over 70 by 2004-05. The tax initially levied at 5 per cent was increased to 8 per cent in 2003-04 and further to 10 per cent in 2004-05. There was a major rationalisation of service taxation in the Budget for 2012-13 with the extension of the tax to all services except those in the negative list. The negative list comprises 17 heads and includes all services provided by the government or the local bodies, with the exception of a few specified services where they compete with the private sector, school education, recognised higher and vocational education, renting of residential buildings, agriculture, animal husbandry, etc. In addition to the negative list, there is a list of exemptions which include health care, services provided by charitable and religious institutions, journalists, advocates providing services to non-business entities, sports persons and performing artists in folk and classical arts. The rate of tax now stands raised to 12 per cent.

Impact of Tax Reforms on Central Tax Revenue

The reforms in central taxes have contributed to a significant improvement in Central tax revenue in the post 2000 period. There has also been a significant change in the composition of central tax revenue. These are briefly analysed in this section.

Contrary to expectations, there was a fall in central revenues as a percentage of GDP from 9.82 in 1990-91 to 7.97 in 2001-02. While the revenue from direct taxes improved from 1.88 per cent of GDP in 1990-91 to 2.95 per cent in 2001-02, revenue from indirect taxes witnessed a sharp decline from 7.94 per cent of GDP to 5.02 per cent in the same period. Within the direct taxes, revenue from both income tax and corporation tax as a percentage of GDP recorded an increase, with the latter performing better than the former. In the case of indirect taxes, revenue from both union excise duties and customs declined as a percentage of GDP between 1990-91 and 2001-02. Customs revenue declined sharply from 3.52 per cent of GDP in 1990-91 to 1.71 per cent in 2001-02. In the same period, revenue from excise duties declined from 4.18 per cent of GDP to 3.09 per cent. Trends in central tax revenue are presented in Table 7.1.

The improvement in direct tax revenue is attributed to better compliance following the reduction in the marginal tax rates. The decline in the proportion of excise revenue to GDP was on account of the rate structure adopted following the allowance for input tax credit not being revenue neutral. The decline in the ratio was also on account of continued exemptions for small scale sector and area based exemptions. Besides, poor information system resulted in excess claims for input credit. Furthermore, during this period, the service sector which remained outside the tax net contributed largely to the GDP growth, while the growth of manufacturing was sluggish. Revenue from customs as a proportion of GDP declined because of the lowering of tariffs and continued exemptions even after tariff reductions, despite a substantial increase in imports.

There was a reversal of the declining trend in the proportion of tax revenue to GDP during the period 2002-03 to 2011-12. This reversal in the overall tax revenue took place despite a fall in the proportion of indirect tax revenue to GDP. A significant improvement in direct tax revenue contributed to such an overall improvement. Within the direct taxes, while revenue from income tax recorded a modest improvement from 1.46 per cent of GDP in 2002-03 to 1.88 per cent in 2011-12, revenue from corporation tax as a proportion of GDP more than doubled from 1.82 per cent to 3.70 per cent in the same period. The indirect tax revenue to GDP ratio declined from 5.24 per cent in 2002-03 to 4.58 per cent in 2011-12. Within the indirect taxes, while revenue from customs witnessed a marginal decline from 1.77 per cent of GDP to 1.73 per cent, revenue from excise duties declined significantly from 3.25 per cent of GDP to 1.69 per cent in the same period. The decline in the ratio of excise revenue to GDP is more perceptible since 2008-09, a year which witnessed a significant fall in the growth of GDP (from 9.3% in 2007-08 to 6.7%), and more particularly in the growth of the manufacturing sector (from 10.3% in 2007-08 to 4.3%). It is noteworthy that an improvement in the revenue from service tax from 0.16 per cent of GDP to 1.07 per cent in the same period could not contain the declining trend of revenue from indirect taxes (Table 7.1).

Table 7.1

Trends in Gross Tax Revenue and its Composition

Years	*Direct Tax Revenue*			*Indirect Tax Revenue*				*Total Gross Tax Revenue*
	Income Tax	*Corporation Tax*	*Total Direct Taxes*	*Union Excise*	*Customs*	*Service Tax*	*Total Indirect Taxes*	
	Gross Tax Revenue of the Centre as Per cent of GDP							
1990-91	0.92	0.91	1.88	4.18	3.52	-	7.94	9.82
1991-92	1.00	1.17	2.28	4.17	3.30	-	7.72	10.00
1992-93	1.02	1.15	2.34	3.98	3.07	-	7.29	9.64
1993-94	1.02	1.13	2.28	3.56	2.49	-	6.22	8.50
1994-95	1.15	1.32	2.58	3.57	2.56	0.04	6.25	8.83
1995-96	1.27	1.34	2.74	3.28	2.91	0.07	6.33	9.07
1996-97	1.28	1.31	2.74	3.17	3.02	0.07	6.40	9.07
1997-98	1.09	1.27	3.07	3.05	2.56	0.10	5.78	8.85
1998-99	1.12	1.36	2.58	2.95	2.25	0.11	5.39	7.97
1999-2000	1.27	1.53	2.88	3.08	2.41	0.11	5.66	8.54
2000-01	1.46	1.65	3.15	3.16	2.19	0.12	5.55	8.70
2001-02	1.36	1.56	2.95	3.09	1.71	0.14	5.02	7.97
2002-03	1.46	1.82	3.29	3.25	1.77	0.16	5.24	8.55
2003-04	1.46	2.24	3.70	3.20	1.71	0.28	5.26	8.96
2004-05	1.52	2.55	4.08	3.06	1.78	0.44	5.33	9.41
2005-06	1.55	2.74	4.40	3.01	1.76	0.62	5.52	9.95
2006-07	1.75	3.36	5.24	2.74	2.01	0.88	5.79	11.03
2007-08	2.06	3.87	6.26	2.48	2.09	1.03	5.63	11.89

contd...

...contd...

Years	*Direct Tax Revenue*			*Indirect Tax Revenue*				*Total Gross Tax Revenue*
	Income Tax	*Corporation Tax*	*Total Direct Taxes*	*Union Excise*	*Customs*	*Service Tax*	*Total Indirect Taxes*	
	Gross Tax Revenue of the Centre as Per cent of GDP							
2008-09	1.88	3.79	5.68	1.93	1.77	1.08	5.07	10.75
2009-10	1.90	3.79	5.69	1.59	1.29	0.90	3.98	9.67
2010-11	1.81	3.89	5.71	1.79	1.77	0.93	4.62	10.33
2011-12	1.88	3.70	5.59	1.69	1.73	1.07	4.58	10.18
2012-13	1.88	3.70	5.60	1.92	1.85	1.23	5.09	10.69
	Percentage Composition of Gross Tax Revenue of the Centre							
1990-91	9.33	9.27	19.16	42.58	35.86	-	80.84	100.00
1995-96	14.02	14.82	30.18	36.13	32.15	0.78	69.82	100.00
2000-01	16.84	18.93	36.22	36.33	25.21	1.39	63.78	100.00
2005-06	15.60	27.56	44.18	30.27	17.71	4.66	55.46	100.00
2010-11	19.61	39.19	55.28	17.36	17.12	8.95	44.71	100.00
	Buoyancy of Central Tax Revenue							
1990-91 to 1999-2000	1.217	1.291	1.292	0.697	0.731	2.483	0.713	0.869
2000-01 to 2010-11	1.282	1.793	1.597	0.447	0.889	2.834	0.875	1.036

Source: (Basic Data) Government of India, *Receipts Budgets*, Various Years and Central Statistical Organisation.

As a result of continuous improvement in its performance, revenue from direct taxes overtook the revenue from indirect taxes in absolute terms for the first time in 2007-08. The share of revenue from direct taxes in total tax revenue witnessed a significant improvement from 19.16 per cent in 1990-91 to 54.95 per cent in 2011-12. The overall impact of reforms on revenue growth is positive though in the initial years of reforms there was a decline in the ratio of tax revenue to GDP. With the extension of taxation to all services with the exception of those in the negative list, it is likely that the declining proportion of indirect tax revenue to GDP will be halted.

Impact of Tax Reforms on Transfers to States

Initially, the Constitution provided for the sharing of only two central taxes with the states. Article 270 provided for mandatory sharing of the net proceeds of income tax levied and collected by the Union with the states. Such proceeds assigned to States did not form part of the Consolidated Fund of India (CFI). Under Article 272, sharing of union excise duties was permissible, if Parliament by law so provided. The shares of the states in union excise duties were to be paid from the CFI. This position continued till the 80th amendment of the Constitution in 2000 which provided for sharing of the proceeds of all union taxes and duties with the states, except the central sales tax, consignment taxes, surcharges on central taxes and earmarked cesses. This was done following the recommendation of the 10th Finance Commission to enable the states to derive the advantage of sharing the buoyancy of all Central taxes, to ensure greater certainty in the resource flows to the states and to facilitate increased flexibility in tax reforms. Following the Constitutional amendment, states started getting a share in the total tax revenue of the Centre from 2000-01 onwards. The analysis of states' share in central tax revenue is done separately for two periods, the first one from 1990-91 to 1999-2000 representing the period when proceeds of only income tax and excise duties were shareable with the states, and the second from 2000-01 onwards during which states started getting a share in the total tax revenue of the Centre.

States' Share in Central Taxes: 1990-2000

States' share in central tax revenue during the period 1990-91 to 1999-2000 was based on the recommendations of the 9th (1990-91 to 1994-95) and the 10th (1995-96 to 1999-2000) Finance Commissions. The 9th Financc Commission recommended the states' share in the divisible pool of income tax and excise duties at 85 per cent and 45 per cent, respectively. The states' shares recommended by the 10th Finance Commission were 77.5 per cent and 47.5 per cent in respect of the divisible pool of income tax and excise duties, respectively. States' share in central taxes as a proportion of GDP declined from an average of 2.50 per cent during the period 1990-1995 to 2.39 per cent in the period 1995-2000. While the average states' share in income tax improved from 0.79 per cent of GDP during 1990-1995 to 0.97 per cent during 1995-2000, share in union excise duties declined from 1.73 per cent of GDP to 1.43 per cent in the same periods, despite an increase in the states' share in excise duties from 45.0 to 47.5 per cent. Because of its low base relative to union excise duties and reduction in the states' share from 85.0 to 77.5 per cent, a higher income tax-GDP ratio could not contain the declining ratio of tax transfers to GDP. Thus, in the initial years of excise tax reforms, states were adversely affected. But it would be incorrect to place the blame on the reforms as other factors, such as declining share of manufacturing and continuation of exemptions even after rationalisation of tax rates contributed to revenue loss (Table 7.2).

States Share in Central Taxes: 2000-2012

The 11th Finance Commission (2000-2005) recommended that 29 per cent of the divisible pool of central taxes be assigned to States. This was raised to 30.5 per cent by the 12th Finance Commission (2005-2010) and further to 32 per cent by the 13th Finance Commission (2010-2015). The Central tax-GDP ratio witnessed a significant improvement from 8.70 per cent in 2000-01 to 11.89 per cent in 2007-08. Because of global developments and deceleration in GDP growth, tax-GDP ratio declined to 9.67 per cent in 2009-10 but recovered to 10.18 per cent in 2011-12. This improvement as well as the increase in the states' share in central taxes has resulted in the states' share-GDP ratio improving from 2.38 per cent in 2000-01 to 2.86 per cent in 2010-11 (Table 7.3). But this improvement

Table 7.2

Trends in States' Share in Central Taxes, 1990-2000

Years	*States' Share in Central Tax Revenue (₹ Crore)*			*States' Share in Central Taxes as Per cent of GDP*		
	Income Tax	*Union Excise Duties*	*Total*	*Income*	*Union Tax*	*Total Excise Duties*
1990-91	4121	110414	14535	0.70	1.78	2.48
1991-92	5104	12093	17197	0.76	1.79	2.55
1992-93	6057	14465	20522	0.78	1.87	2.65
1993-94	7768	14473	22241	0.87	1.62	2.50
1994-95	8357	16283	24840	0.82	1.56	2.38
1995-96	11274	18011	29285	0.92	1.47	2.39
1996-97	13516	21545	35061	0.95	1.52	2.47
1997-98	21102	22446	43548	1.34	1.43	2.77
1998-99	14480	24665	39145	0.80	1.37	2.17
1999-2000	16523	26958	43481	0.82	1.34	2.16
Average States' Share/GDP 1990-95				0.79	1.73	2.50
Average States' Share/GDP 1995-2000				0.97	1.43	2.39

Source: Government of India, Ministry of Finance, *Receipts Budget*, various issues.

Table 7.3

Trends in States' Share in Central Taxes, 2000-11

Years	*(₹ Crore)*	*As % of GDP*
2000-01	51688	2.38
2001-02	52842	2.25
2002-03	56122	2.22
2003-04	65766	2.32
2004-05	78595	2.42
2005-06	94385	2.56
2006-07	120330	2.80
2007-08	151800	3.04
2008-09	160179	2.85
2009-10	164832	2.55
2010-11	219303	2.86
Average States' share in Central Taxes/GDP 2000-05		2.32
Average States' share in Central Taxes/GDP 2005-10		2.76

Source: Government of India, Ministry of Finance, *Receipts Budget*, various issues.

has lagged much behind the improvement in the tax-GDP ratio of the Centre. That this should happen despite an increase in the states' share in Central taxes is a matter of concern to the states. The position becomes very glaring if we look at the states' share in central taxes in relation to the gross tax revenue of the Centre. States' share in the gross tax revenue of the Centre hovered between 26 and 27 per cent during the entire 20 year period from 1990 to 2010. It is only in the recent years that it has inched upwards by a percentage point.

It is quite clear that reforms coupled with higher growth of the economy have resulted in higher revenue growth in the post-2000 period. But this has not resulted in a commensurate increase in the transfers to states by way of their mandated share in central taxes. This is the result of increasing recourse to cesses and surcharges by the Centre, more particularly from the year 2002-03 onwards. The continuation of tax exemptions, despite the lowering of tax rates has also deprived the states of their due share in central taxes. These issues are discussed in the next section.

Cesses and Surcharges

Under the Constitution, proceeds from earmarked cesses and surcharges do not form part of the divisible pool of central tax revenue to be shared with states. While cesses are supposed to be levied for meeting the funding requirements of a very limited number of activities on a dedicated basis, surcharges are meant to be levied for meeting certain unexpected contingencies and are expected to be abolished once the contingency is met. Contrary to these established practices, the GoI started extending the levy of cesses to more and more commodities almost on a permanent basis. In the initial years, levy of cesses was resorted to a very limited extent, that too to meet the development or regulatory needs of certain commodities like tea, coffee, jute, mica, *bidis*, etc. The extension of the scope of cesses started in 1988 when the Government levied a road cess on petroleum products following a resolution passed in Parliament to fund the construction and maintenance of national highways. The Central Road Fund Act was enacted in 2000 to give statutory status to the road fund established following the resolution in Parliament. This was followed by the levy of primary education cess on all major taxes in 2004-05 to provide and finance universal quality basic education in the country. A separate cess was levied in 2006-07 to fund secondary and higher education. A National Calamity Contingency Duty (NCCD) was levied for the first time in 2000-01 on *pan masala* and certain tobacco products and later it was extended to cover motor cars, two wheelers, multi-utility vehicles, petroleum crude and mobile phones. NCCD was imposed to replenish the National Calamity Contingency Fund (NCCF). The yearly accretion to the NCCF enables build-up of its corpus. Though termed as a duty, NCCD is no different from a cess as the proceeds do not form part of the divisible pool of taxes. These four cesses along with the cesses on certain commodities account for a predominant share in the total proceeds from cesses. Surcharges are currently levied on corporation tax and in the form of special additional duty of customs and excise on motor spirit. In addition, there is also a surcharge on *pan masala* and tobacco products. The surcharge on income tax was abolished in the Budget for 2012-13. As compared with the revenue from cesses, revenue from surcharges is not very significant.

Revenue from cesses and surcharges increased from 3.45 per cent of gross tax revenue of the centre in 2001-02 to 10.85 per cent in 2010-11, the period selected for the analysis. Cesses are predominantly levied in the case of excise duties. Revenue from cesses and surcharges in respect of excise taxation increased from 7.92 per cent of total revenue from excise duties in 2001-02 to 32.99 per cent in 2010-11. Of these, road cess alone accounted for 2.17 per cent of excise revenue in 2001-02 which increased to 12.49 per cent in 2010-11. Following the road cess, cesses on commodities, education cess and NCCD accounted for 6.63 per cent, 3.56 per cent and 2.15 per cent of total excise revenue, respectively, in 2010-11 (Table 7.4).

Proceeds from road cess are credited to the CRF which is utilised predominantly for the maintenance of national highways. In addition, road fund is also used for the development of rural roads and improvement of state roads. The proceeds of primary education cess are credited to Prarambhik Siksha Kosh (PSK), a dedicated and non-lapsable fund for funding Sarva Siksha Abhiyan (SSA). Initially, the matching share of the states was fixed at 15 per cent which was progressively raised to 35 per cent. The secondary education cess is used for promoting secondary and higher education under the Rashtriya Madhyamik Abhiyan (RMA). The proceeds from NCCD are credited to the National Disaster Response Fund (NDRF), earlier known as NCCF. This fund is meant for assisting the states in the case of occurrence of major calamities which are beyond the coping capacity of states. The fact that the proceeds of road cess, education cess and NCCD are used to partly/fully assist the states does not fully justify the levy of these dedicated cesses. While these cesses confer the advantage of a dedicated source of revenue to the Centre, the states are saddled with a matching contribution or additional allocation in most cases. In the absence of the cesses, the states would have gained access to higher untied revenue by way of a higher divisible pool of central tax revenue, in which their share is 32 per cent (from 2010-2015 as per the recommendations of the 13th Finance Commission). The greater resort to the levy of cesses and surcharges has distorted the Constitutional scheme of tax sharing considerably. It has in a way neutralised the higher states' share in central taxes recommended by the successive Finance Commissions. While the states' share in central taxes recommended by the Finance Commissions increased from 29.5 per cent (2000-2005) to 30.5 per cent (2005-2010) and further to 32 per cent (2010-2015), their share in the gross tax revenue of the Centre stagnated at around 26 per cent in the period of 10 years from 2000-01 to 2009-10. In 2010-11 and 2011-12, the states' share was around 28 per cent of the gross tax revenue.

Tax Expenditures

The Indian tax system is charactrised by a number of tax concessions and exemptions to serve numerous objectives like balanced regional development, incentivising savings and investments, protection of small scale industry, promotion of exports, promotion of charitable institutions and various other social and economic objectives. As observed by Amaresh Bagchi (1974) from book publishing to family planning, not to mention fostering of growth, export promotion, agricultural development, refugee rehabilitation and scientific research, there is hardly any item on the national agenda that does not find some support somewhere in the tax structure. Tax expenditures are revenue losses attributable to tax provisions that provide for exemptions and concessions and the use of the tax system

Table 7.4

Non-Shareable Tax Revenue Accruing to the Centre from Cesses and Surcharges

(₹ crore)

Tax	*2001-02*	*2004-05*	*2005-06*	*2006-07*	*2007-08*	*2008-09*	*2009-10*	*2010-11*
Corporation Tax								
1. Surcharge	289	2630	3733	5337	6532	9269	9776	8218
2. Education Cess	-	1167	2010	2828	5694	6217	7060	11501
Total	289	3797	5743	8165	12226	15486	16836	19719
Income Tax								
1. Sucharge	267	706	924	797	1718	2405	1553	373
2. Education Cess	-	637	1204	1495	3113	3244	3674	6526
Total	267	1343	2128	2292	4831	5649	5227	6899
Customs Duties								
1. Surcharge	-	-	350	435	105	390	290	2588
2. Cess on Exports	154	189	187	260	1320	1779	454	133
3. Road Cess	-	14	175	370	570	670	490	2643
4. Education Cess	-	735	1248	1712	2088	1795	1340	4727
5. NCCD	-	365	500	545	625	790	900	1121
Total	154	1303	2460	3322	4708	5424	3474	11212

contd...

...contd...

(₹ *crore*)

Tax	*2001-02*	*2004-05*	*2005-06*	*2006-07*	*2007-08*	*2008-09*	*2009-10*	*2010-11*
Excise Duties								
1. Road Cess	1573	4806	8095	10901	14041	14577	16204	17201
2. SADE on Motor Spirit	21	3886	3761	4071	6987	8760	10099	10154
3. Clean Energy Cess	-	-	-	-	-	-	-	1066
4. Cess on Commodities	3464	6386	6089	8382	8118	8164	8335	9135
5. Education Cess	-	1451	2138	2416	3987	3778	3499	4908
6. Duty on *Pan Masala*	-	-	114	328	516	946	1068	1115
7. NCCD	686	1484	1275	1728	2268	2320	2620	2967
Total	5744	18013	21474	27826	35917	38545	41825	46546
Service Tax								
1. Education Cess	-	186	442	729	1337	1769	1625	1945
Other Taxes								
1. Education Cess	-	-	94	102	205	227	66	4
2. Water	-	149	56	-	191	229	207	236
3. Central Acts	-	3	104	170	3	4	5	6
4. R&D Cess	-	157	177	190	266	316	418	592
Total	-	309	431	462	665	776	696	838
Total-All Cesses and Surcharges	6454	24951	32676	42796	59684	67649	69683	87159
Cesses and Surcharges as % of Gross Tax Revenue	3.45	8.18	8.86	8.97	9.98	11.02	10.99	10.85

Note: SADE: Special Additional Duty of Excise Duty on Motor Spirit.

Source: Government of India, Controller General of Accounts, *Union Government-Finance Accounts*, various years.

to promote social and economic goals without incurring direct expenditures. The way tax expenditures are structured determines as to who will benefit from them and how much revenue loss they involve. Tax expenditures take the form of outright exemptions, special rates of tax, deductions from the taxable income, rebates, tax deferment or tax credits (Sarma, 2006).

Tax expenditures have a number of deficiencies which have been well documented. Tax expenditures make the tax system complicated imparting subjectivity to the interpretation of provisions. As these involve hidden subsidies, it is difficult to estimate the revenue loss and to assess whether these have really subserved the objectives for which they are meant. Apart from the revenue loss, there are two more serious issues. First, tax expenditures facilitate spurious claims being put forward to avoid and evade tax. Secondly, it imposes immense burden on the tax administration in terms of processing and verification of claims. Swift *et al.* (2003) have observed that tax expenditures are seldom subjected to scrutiny as that of public expenditure. Even in more developed countries which have developed sophisticated systems of reporting tax expenditures, the gap between the level of scrutiny and transparency of tax expenditures compared with direct public expenditure remains very wide. Therefore, it is widely felt that tax exemptions should be resorted to only in exceptional cases and that direct transfers would facilitate better targeting and therefore serve the objectives much better.

Despite its limitations, tax expenditures serve certain objectives. These mainly relate to incentivising private participation in economic activities, promoting private decision-making in desired directions and reducing the inefficiencies associated with government spending. Thus, there is merit in selective use of tax exemptions instead of the present system of spreading the tax expenditure net far and wide without adequately analysing the implications and their suitability in sub-serving the objectives.

For the first time, the Union Budget for 2006-07 presented a tax expenditure statement or statement of revenue foregone as an annex in the Receipts Budget. The tax expenditure statement in the Budget for 2006-07 related to 2004-05. Since then, the practice of presenting the tax expenditure statement in the Union Budget is continuing. In the case of the corporation tax, the tax expenditure for the year 2010-11 was based on the returns submitted by 4,59,270 companies electronically. Based on the estimated loss of revenue in 2010-11, projection was made for the year 2011-12. The estimates of income tax foregone are based on the various claims for tax preference in the 68,62,807 returns filed electronically in 2010-11. The estimates of revenue foregone in respect of excise is based on the Automation of Central Excise and Service Tax (ACES) database and its extrapolation. The estimate of revenue foregone under various exemptions in respect of customs duties is based on the data generated from the bills of entry filed in the Indian Customs Electronic Data Interchange System (ICES) at various Electronic Data Interchange (EDI) locations. Since the EDI does not cover all ports, suitable adjustments have been made.

Estimates of tax expenditures presented in the Union Budget represent the difference between the notional tax revenue applying the standard rates of taxation and the estimated tax revenue applying the effective rates of taxation after duly accounting for tax concessions and exemptions. There is a possibility of tax expenditures being overestimated as revenue from additional economic activities following tax exemptions is not taken into account. There are also a number of methodological issues in estimating tax expenditures. In India, the methodology used for estimating tax expenditure has undergone numerous changes making the estimates non-comparable over time. Despite the estimates suffering from various limitations, they broadly indicate the extent of loss of revenue.

Any analysis of the trends in tax expenditures is subject to the above limitations. The revenue foregone as percentage of gross tax revenue has gone up from 52.03 per cent in 2004-05 to as high as 77.25 per cent in 2009-10 and moderated to 58.72 per cent in 2011-12 (Table 7.5). It is still high by any yardstick. This clearly establishes the fact that tax exemptions are all pervasive and have eroded the tax base considerably thus adversely affecting the tax buoyancy. The explanatory note given with the tax expenditure statement in the Budget for 2010-11 pointed out that the amount of revenue foregone continued to increase year after year as a percentage of aggregate tax collection and called for a reversal of this trend by way of an increase in the tax base.

Table 7.5

Trends in Tax Expenditure

(₹ *crore*)

	2004-05	*2005-06*	*2006-07*	*2007-08*	*2008-09*	*2009-10*	*2010-11*	*2011-12*
1. Corporation Tax	57852	34618	45034	62199	66901	72881	57912	51292
2. Income Tax	13229	15182	32143	38057	37570	45142	36826	42320
3. Excise Duties	30449	66760	75475	87468	128293	169121	192227	212167
4. Customs	57131	90140	87060	97328	181335	195288	172740	223653
Total	158661	206700	239712	285052	414099	482432	459705	529432
Tax Expenditure as Percentage of Total Revenue Collections under the Tax								
1. Corporation Tax	69.97	34.18	31.20	32.24	31.35	29.78	19.39	15.65
2. Income Tax	26.85	26.49	42.80	37.08	35.43	36.86	26.48	25.39
3. Excise Duties	30.72	60.02	64.17	70.76	118.12	164.21	139.60	141.37
4. Customs	99.17	138.53	100.85	93.48	181.55	234.37	127.19	146.18
As Percentage of Gross Tax Revenue of the Centre								
Total Tax Expenditure	52.03	56.25	50.62	48.06	68.41	77.25	57.97	58.72

Source: Government of India, Ministry of Finance, *Receipts Budget*, various issues.

Of the four taxes for which estimates are made available, revenue foregone in respect of corporation tax had come down from 69.97 per cent of tax revenue in 2004-05 to 15.65 per cent in 2011-12. In the case of income tax, revenue foregone after increasing from the level of 26.85 per cent of the tax revenue in 2004-05 has come down marginally to 25.39 per cent in 2011-12. The major concern is with regard to excise duties and customs duties, which continue to record revenue losses exceeding 100 per cent of tax collections. In the case of excise, the situation had worsened so much that revenue foregone had gone up steeply from 30.72 per cent in 2004-05 to 141.37 per cent in 2011-12. In the same period, revenue foregone from customs increased from 99.17 per cent to 146.18 per cent of tax collections. Because of the methodological changes, year to year estimates of revenue foregone may not be strictly comparable. This paper has not examined the methodological issues and changes in them over the years. Despite this limitation, one cannot but come to the conclusion that the revenue foregone remains unexceptionally very high eroding the tax base and depriving the Centre as well as the states their due share in tax collections.

Conclusion

Tax reforms per se did not adversely affect the states' share in central taxes. With the positive impact of tax reforms taking effect in the post-2000 period, there was an improvement in tax buoyancy which improved the states' share in central taxes as a percentage of GDP. But there is a near stagnation in the states' share in gross tax revenue of the Centre and that this should continue despite major reforms and growth in central tax revenue is a major concern for states. The indiscriminate extension of the scope of cesses and surcharges which in 2010-11 accounted for over 10 per cent of the gross tax revenue of the Centre eroded the divisible pool of taxes, thus adversely impacting the transfers to states. Tax expenditures which account for nearly 59 per cent of the gross tax revenue had further eroded the tax base adversely impacting the states. With the moderation of tax rates, there should have been a rationalisation of concessions and exemptions and their pruning to a considerable extent. The continuation of exemptions and concessions had moderated the positive impact of tax reforms to a large extent. Thus, it is the lack of follow-up on reforms rather than reforms per se which had adversely impacted the states' share in central taxes. With the follow-up on reforms, states would have gained much more along with the Centre.

A number of committees have recommended reduction in the number and scope of the cesses and surcharges. The Sarkaria Commission on Centre-State Relations and its successor, the Puncchi Commission expressed strong reservations regarding the levy of surcharges and cesses and recommended that the Central government should review all the existing cesses and surcharges with a view to bringing down their share in the gross tax revenue. A similar view was expressed by most central Finance Commissions. The Constitutional Review Commission expressed hope that public policy would move decisively in the direction of doing away with the surcharges as part of the Union's fiscal armoury. Despite the consensus, there has been no move so far at least to review the existing cesses and surcharges. There is hope that with the introduction of Goods and Services Tax (GST), all cesses and surcharges will be merged with the basic rates. The exact contours of such merger are not yet known. Nevertheless, this should result in a major relief to the states. Despite strong evidence that many of the concessions and exemptions have outlived their utility and are proving counterproductive, the GoI has not moved in a decisive manner for their rationalisation. It is hoped that this would be done without further loss of time and considerable revenue.

References

Acharya, Shankar (2005). "Thirty Years of Tax Reforms in India", *Economic and Political Weekly*, May 14.

Bagchi, Amaresh (1974). "Efficacy of Tax Incentives", *Economic and Political Weekly*, June 15.

Government of India (1992). *Tax Reforms Committee: Final Report Part-I.* Chairman: Raja J. Chelliah. New Delhi: Ministry of Finance.

————. (1993).*Tax Reforms Committee: Final Report Part-II.* Chairman: Raja J. Chelliah. New Delhi: Ministry of Finance.

————. (2002a). *Report of the Task Force on Direct Taxes.* New Delhi: Ministry of Finance. December.

————. (2002b). *Report of the Task Force on Indirect Taxes.* New Delhi: Ministry of Finance. December.

————. (2002c). *Report of the National Commission to Review the Working of the Constitution*. New Delhi: Ministry of Law. March.

————. (2010). *Report of the Commission on Centre-State Relations.* New Delhi: Ministry of Home Affairs. March.

————. (various years). *Receipts Budget.* New Delhi: Ministry of Finance.

Rajaraman, Indira (2004). "Fiscal Restructuring in Context of Trade Reform", *Economic and Political Weekly*, June 26.

Rao, Govinda and Kavita Rao (2005). "Trends and Issues in Tax Policy and Reforms in India", *India Policy Forum 2005-06.*

Sarma, E.A.S. (2006). "How Useful Is New Tax Expenditure Statement?", *Economic and Political Weekly*, April 8.

Swift, Z.L., H.P. Brixi and C. Valenduc (2003). "Tax Expenditures: General Concept, Measurement and Overview of Country Practices", in H.P. Brixi, C. Valenduc and Z.L. Swift (eds.), *Tax Expenditures: Shedding Light on Government Spending Through the Tax System—Lessons from Developed and Transition Economies.* The World Bank.

8 The Fiscal Responsibility and Budget Management (FRBM) Act

Impact on Central Finances and its Transfers

N. Sreedevi and M.L.K. Vaagdevi

Introduction

India embarked upon major economic and fiscal policy reforms in the early 1990s in the wake of a serious BoP (balance of payments) crisis.[1] The first generation reforms[2] played out in over a decade, with liberalisation happening, across key areas of fiscal policy, trade and exchange rate regime, industrial and foreign investment policy and financial sector among others. On the receipts front, particularly revenue account, the tax structure of both the direct (corporate tax and personal income tax) and indirect (customs and excise duties) were rationalised by reducing the rates as well as number of slabs. Several irritants and unnecessary procedural obligations were also abandoned. On the expenditure front, the major step was the appointment of Expenditure Reforms Commission (ERC) that dealt with four specific issues—food subsidy, fertiliser subsidy, autonomous institutions and optimising staff strength and pensions.

---

1. Though the immediate trigger for the BoP problem was the oil price shock and the dwindling remittances from West Asia due to the Gulf war, the legacy of excessive economic controls, high cost import substitution policies and heavy dependence on external commercial borrowings during 1980s was to blame.
2. The impending crisis forced the government to initiate far-reaching policy reforms to attain macroeconomic stability and higher rates of growth. The decade-long reform process which can be divided into two phases of crisis management and stabilisation (1991-92 to 1993-94) and the post-stabilisation phase (1994-95 to till date) sought to transform India from an over-regulated and closed economy into a fairly open one with a greater role for the private sector and market forces in the allocation of resources.

In an attempt to bring about fiscal discipline upon itself, another major reform that was initiated by the Central government was the FRBM Bill in the year 2000 which took the shape of an Act in 2003. Has the expediting of the FRBM Act influenced central finances? Has it impacted central transfers to the states?

Regarding the first question, the very initiation of FRBM Act is to influence the central finances. Regarding the second question, FRBM Act of the Central government may not be directly related to federal transfers. But the steps taken by the Central government towards revenue augmentation/ expenditure management in order to achieve the targets in FRBM may have an impact to a certain extent on federal transfers. Withdrawal of central plan loans to the states, on the recommendation of the 12th Finance Commission, was one such measure with which the Centre's expenditure composition changed which in turns reflected in its deficit indicators. On the other hand the same measure has changed the states' borrowings/debt composition.

In the context of the appointment of the 14th Finance Commission (for the period 2015-2020) and the just started Twelfth Five Year Plan (2012-2017), it is intended to review the FRBM Act and its impact on central finances and subsequently on the share of central taxes to states. Central transfers—particularly grants and loans—are outside the purview of the study. To study the impact of FRBM Act on central finances, the present paper compares the broad fiscal indicators before and after the implementation of FRBM Act. The discussion is focused mainly on the ratios of fiscal and revenue deficits, broad aggregates of receipts and expenditure w.r.t. GDP (gross domestic product). For this purpose, the study covers the period from 1993-94 to 2011-12RE. As the fiscal year 2012-13 is the year of amendment of FRBM Act, it is not taken into account. To understand the deprivation of states' share in the central taxes (also Central government's share), the paper has focused on Rule 6 of the FRBM Rules 2004 under which the Union government discloses the revenue raised but not collected from principal tax sources. For this purpose, the data is based on the table given in the Receipts Budget, 2012-13 and the reporting year of the above data is 2010-11.

The main data sources are *Handbook of Statistics on Indian Economy*, *Handbook of Statistics on State Finances*, *Study of Budgets: State Finances* which are published by Reserve Bank of India (RBI), *Union Audit Reports* published by the Comptroller and Auditor General of India (CAG) and also *Union Budget* documents. Simple statistical tools such as percentages are used in the study.

The paper begins with a review of the expedition of FRBM right from its inception. Then it discusses the trends in Central government finances before and after the implementation of FRBM Act. It also discusses the disclosure of revenue raised but not realised by the Central government from the principal taxes sources and the composition of unrealised amount (under dispute and not under dispute), its share in central tax revenue and states' share in central taxes and estimated accruals of both the centre and the state governments.

Expedition of FRBM Act: A Review

One of the major causes for the BoP crisis of 1990-91 had been fiscal profligacy (Virmani, 2001). Though the reform measures helped tide over the immediate crisis, with deficit indicators showing signs of improvement (Figure 8.1), fiscal consolidation became a challenge by the end of the 90s. Hence, the Central government brought out FRBM Act as a measure to bring upon itself fiscal responsibility and to create a strong need for an institutional mechanism that would help effective fiscal planning and the management of the fiscal deficit[3] and thus bring about fiscal responsibility in the system.

FRBM Bill (2000)

A Committee[4] on Fiscal Responsibility Legislation (FRL) was constituted on 17 January, 2000 by the Central government to look into various aspects of the fiscal system and recommend draft legislation on fiscal responsibility. This was followed by an announcement in the Budget 2000-01 for a strong institutional mechanism embodied in a

3. Ministry of Finance, 2007: Chapter 21, p.18.
4. Budget speech for 2000-01 announced the set up of a Committee (Chairman: E.A.S. Sarma), Government of India, 2000.

"Fiscal Responsibility Act" and to bring the necessary legislative proposals to the House during the course of the year. Accordingly the FRBM Bill, 2000 was introduced in Lok Sabha in December, 2000. While doing so, the Union government had significantly watered down the Committee's recommendations on FRL by not including its key proposal of setting up a Fiscal Management Review Committee (FMRC) in the bill.[5]

As per the Bill, the Central government, along with the annual Budget in each financial year has to present the following statements—(i) Medium-term Fiscal Policy Statement; (ii) Fiscal Policy Strategy statement and; (iii) Macroeconomic Framework Statement. The major targets of the Central government, as per the Bill, were to reduce the revenue deficit by 0.5 per cent of estimated GDP per annum to nil within a period of five financial years from the initial financial year 01 April, 2001 and ending on 31 March 2006. Similarly, with regard to the fiscal deficit, a progressive reduction to not more than 2 per cent of GDP within a period of five financial years, following the promulgation of the law, was proposed in the Bill. Though these targets, in a way, were good to bring the fiscal situation on track, "it is moot if 2 per cent level of borrowing meets the development needs of the economy" (Karnik, 2002).

Further, the Central government was supposed to ensure within a period of 10 financial years, beginning from the initial financial year on the 01 April 2001, and ending on 31 March 2011, that the total liabilities (including external debt at current exchange rate), do not exceed 50 per cent of the estimated GDP for that year. Direct borrowings from the RBI were also prohibited after three years of the initiation of the Act except for WMA (ways and means advances). The Central government was to take suitable measures to ensure greater transparency in fiscal operations and to minimise, as far as practicable, secrecy in the preparation of the annual budget.

FRBM Act (2003) and its Amendments

The FRBM Bill (2000) had taken the shape of an Act in 2003. In other words, the idea of self-restraint on fiscal front took three years to come into

5. *http://expressindia.indianexpress.com/fe/daily/20001223/fec23066.html*

force, may be partly due to discussions which took place for about three years and related procedural delays. The law became operational with the notification of the Act and Statutory Rules in July 2004 (Annexure Box A-8.1) and hence postponement of the targeted year to 2007-08. However, the targeted year was further postponed by another year i.e., 2008-09 with an amendment to the Act[6] even before its implementation. Leaving aside the targeted years, the act was incomplete in two respects: first, not defining a debt-GDP ratio that would be required for keeping the economy on its potential growth path, and secondly, not defining the suitable limits of departure from the medium-term stance to cope with cyclical fluctuations (Rangarajan and Srivastava, 2005).

While presenting the Union Budget 2012-13 in the Parliament, the Union Finance Minister announced again the amendments to the FRBM Act, 2003 as part of the Finance Bill 2012. This includes two major components. One is introduction of the "effective revenue deficit" (that brings out the difference between revenue deficits and grants for creation of capital assets) and elimination of the same by March 2015; associated with it is the goal of meeting a revenue deficit of not more than two per cent of GDP by March, 2015.[7]

The second one is the introduction of the Medium Term Expenditure Framework Statement (that spells out a three year rolling target for prescribed expenditure indicators along with the underlying assumptions and risks associated. The statement should contain expenditure commitment of major policy changes—involving new services, schemes and programmes, explicit contingent liabilities, detailed break-up of grants for creation of capital assets). The authority to review the compliance to the Act and the authority to share these reviews with the Houses of the Parliament was entrusted to the CAG. Is this (amendment) different from Article 151 of the Constitution of India according to which the audit done

6. As amended through the Finance Act 2004. (*http://rbidocs.rbi.org.in/rdocs/Content/PDFs/DHOLA140809.pdf*) and the Finance Act 2004: *http://indiabudget.nic.in/ub2004-05(I)/fb/fbill.pdf*

7. Union Budget (2012-13): *MTFP Statement*. See also *Union Budget Speech 2012-13.*

so far by CAG[8] in scrutinising various kinds of transactions, according to the provisions of the audit code?[9]

As per the amendment, the fiscal deficit/GDP ratio was projected to decline to 4.5 per cent in 2013-14 and 3.9 per cent in 2014-15. The deficit levels that were projected are higher than the 13th Finance Commission's recommendations.[10] That means fiscal targets are further postponed. Now the 14th Finance Commission, as per the ToR (Terms of Reference), has to "......suggest measures for maintaining a stable and sustainable fiscal environment consistent with equitable growth including suggestions to amend the FRBM Acts currently in force...." (GoI, 2013).

In brief, the expediting of high spirited draft FRBM legislation started with a diluted Bill (2000) before becoming an Act in 2003. The Act was carried on with incompleteness without indicating the debt-GDP ratio required for keeping the economy on its potential growth path, and its stand to cope with cyclical fluctuations with another amendment in the Act in 2012.

Trends in Central Government Finances: Pre and Post FRBM Act

FRBM Act had been introduced with tremendous hope that it will help bring about fiscal responsibility with regard to both revenue augmentation and expenditure management within the government. It is customary to demarcate the study period before and after any significant occurrence. The

---

8. Under the provisions of the Constitution of India (article 149 to 151) and Comptroller and Auditor General's (Duties, Powers and Conditions of Service) Act, 1971, the CAG is the sole auditor of the accounts of the Central (Union) Government and the State Governments. The Article 151 which is about Audit Reports says that:

   (1) The reports of the CAG relating to the accounts of the Union shall be submitted to the President, who shall cause them to be laid before each House of Parliament.

   (2) The reports of the CAG relating to the accounts of a State shall be submitted to the Governor of the State, who shall cause them to be laid before the Legislature of the State.

   http://saiindia.gov.in/english/home/about_us/mandate/Constitutional/Constitutional.html
9. The audit done by CAG is broadly classified into Regularity (Compliance) Audit and Performance Audit. *http://www.cag.gov.in/html/unionaudit.html*
10. 13th Finance Commission put the cap of fiscal deficit/GDP ratio at 3.0 per cent in 2014-15.

present study has also done a similar breakup i.e., before and after FRBM Act. The proportion of revenue and fiscal deficits in GDP which were high before the implementation of FRBM Act showed a declining trend after its implementation (Table 8.1). Similarly, the Centre's gross and net tax revenue w.r.t. GDP and also their growth rates increased after FRBM implementation. However, total expenditure/GDP ratio, because of higher revenue expenditure, has not decreased in the later period. Expenditure growth rates were also higher in the later period.

Annexure Tables A-8.1 to A-8.4 and Figure 8.1 to Figure 8.4 give the year-wise details of the trends in deficit indicators, receipts and expenditures before and after the implementation of FRBM Act. Year-wise break-up also showed that before the implementation of FRBM Act, GFD (gross fiscal deficit)/GDP and RD (revenue deficit)/GDP ratios were higher ranging between 5-7 per cent and 3.0-4.3 per cent respectively (barring 1995-1997) while the corresponding ratios after the FRBM Act, particularly during the period i.e., 2003-04 to 2007-08, ranged between 2.5-4.0 per cent and 1.1-3.5 per cent respectively. It is to be verified whether the improvement/change in the fiscal situation may be attributed to the implementation of FRBM Act or to the acceleration in GDP growth or both.

Pre-FRBM Period

During the period 1994-95 to 1996-97 the Union government could reduce the revenue and fiscal deficits (Annexure Table A-8.1 and Figure 8.1), not because of a marginal increase (decrease) in gross (net) tax revenue receipts (revenue expenditure) (see Figures 8.2 and 8.3), but mainly by curtailing the capital expenditure (Annexure Table A-8.3 and Figure 8.4). But during 1997-1999 Union government experienced a reversal in the above indicators due to the net effect of decline in gross (net) tax revenue, particularly indirect taxes (Annexure Table A-8.2 and Figure 8.3), an increase in total expenditure—revenue as well as capital (Annexure Table A-8.3 and Figure 8.4). Under revenue account there was a sharp rise in salaries and pensions following the acceptance of the Fifth Pay Commission (See also Kumar and Soumya, 2010) recommendations in 1996-97 while under capital account, the component of loans and advances increased. The decline in revenue and fiscal deficits again in 1999-2000 was due to an improvement in gross revenue (both tax and non-tax) and

Table 8.1

Central Government Finances: Pre and Post FRBM Period

	As % of GDP		*Year on Year Growth Rate (%)*	
	1993-2003	*2003-2012*	*1993-2003*	*2003-2012*
Gross Tax Revenue	8.5	10.3	12.6	17.6
Corporation Tax	1.5	3.5	18.9	24.8
Personal Income Tax	1.3	1.8	17.5	18.7
Customs	2.3	1.7	9.1	16.5
Union Excise Duties	3.2	2.2	11.3	7.5
Less States Share	2.3	2.7	11.3	18.7
Net Tax Revenue	6.2	7.5	13.2	17.2
Non-Tax Revenue	2.6	2.0	14.3	10.8
Total Net Revenue	8.8	9.6	13.4	14.9
Loan Recoveries	0.7	0.4	24.2	7.5
Disinvestment Receipts	0.1	0.3	-1119.2	1278.2
Non-Debt Capital Receipts	0.8	0.7	30.7	95.5
Total Expenditure	15.2	15.1	12.7	14.0
Plan	4.0	4.5	11.2	16.4
Non-Plan	11.2	10.6	13.4	13.0
Revenue Expenditure	12.3	13.0	13.6	14.9
Defence	1.6	1.3	11.9	11.5
Interest Payments	4.4	3.4	13.9	10.0
Subsidies	6.0	4.7	16.4	21.4
Capital Expenditure	2.9	2.1	10.4	13.9
Loans and Advances	1.7	0.4	8.3	9.2
Capital Outlay	1.2	1.5	9.7	22.0
Defence (Capital)	0.6	0.8	9.6	20.1
Gross Fiscal Deficit	5.6	4.9	11.0	23.2
Revenue Deficit	3.5	3.4	15.5	43.1
GDP at current market prices	100.0	100.0	12.4	14.9

Note: For details see Annexure Tables A-8.1 to A-8.3.

also decline in total expenditure particularly loans and advances because of the modification in accounting procedures by shifting the loans to states against small savings collections from the Consolidated Fund of India (i.e., from the budget) to National Small Savings Fund (NSSF) (i.e., outside the budget). But in 2000-2002, there was again an increase in the fiscal and revenue deficits because of the higher (lower) growth rate of expenditure (revenue receipts). An increase in the capital expenditure during this period was mainly due to increased loans and advances.

Figure 8.1

Fiscal and Revenue Deficits of the Centre: Pre and Post FRBM Era

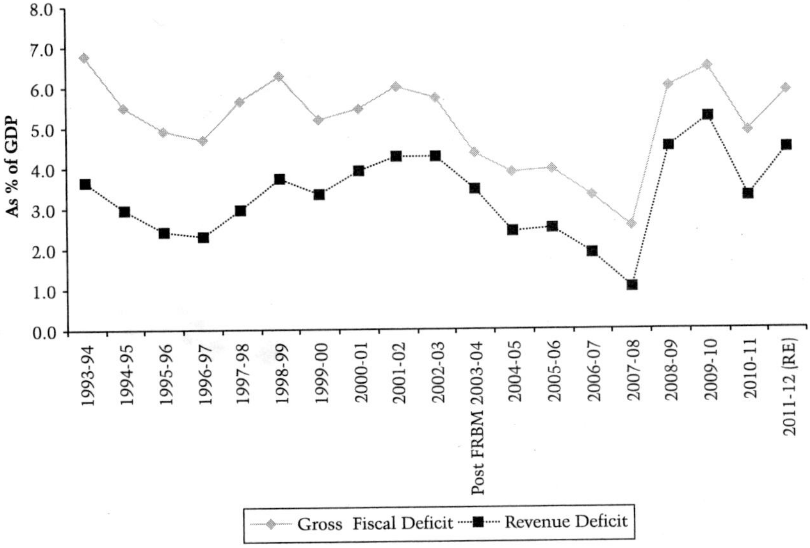

Source: As per Annexure Table A-8.1.

During 2002-2005, the Union government experienced an improvement in the fiscal situation through the higher growth rate in gross revenue on receipts front and loan recoveries (component of non-debt capital receipts) from the state governments during 2002-03 to 2004-05 due to the Debt Swap Scheme (DSS)[11] formulated by the Central government.[12] Total expenditure increased during the 2002-03 mainly on account of increased revenue expenditure (particularly subsidies) and capital expenditure (particularly repayment of NSSF loans and capital

11. As far as the states are concerned, this scheme is debt neutral and results in a change in the level and the composition of capital expenditure and receipts. See RBI (2004). *State Finances: A Study of Budgets of 2003-04*, Box 1.
12. The 12th Finance Commission also recommended that outstanding central loans to states be consolidated and rescheduled for a term of 20 years at 7/5 per cent rate of interest. This consolidation and rescheduling has been made subject to a state enacting a fiscal responsibility legislation, which should aim at completely eliminating the revenue deficit by 2008-09. The Commission further recommended a debt write-off scheme, which is linked to a reduction in the revenue deficit of states. These measures would imply a relief to states in terms of lower interest payments and repayments.

Figure 8.2

Trends in Central Receipts: Pre and Post FRBM

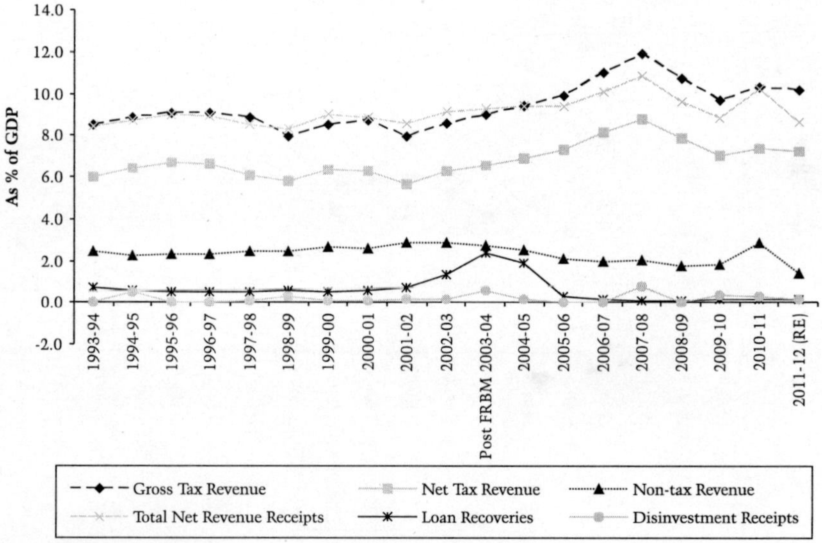

Source: Same as Figure 8.1.

Figure 8.3

Trends in Central Tax Revenue Receipts: Pre and Post FRBM

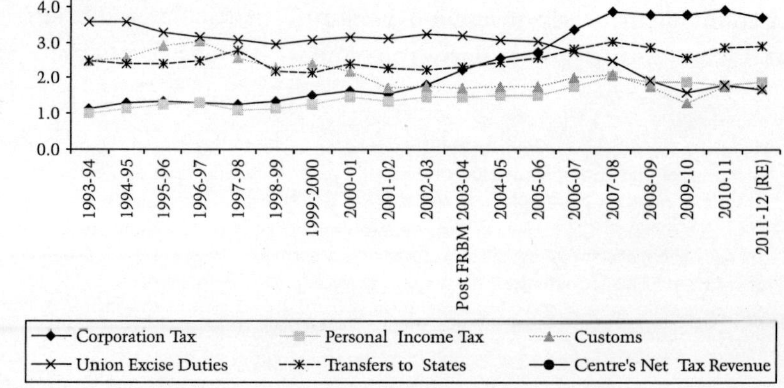

Source: Same as Figure 8.1.

Figure 8.4

Trends in Centre's Expenditure: Pre and Post FRBM

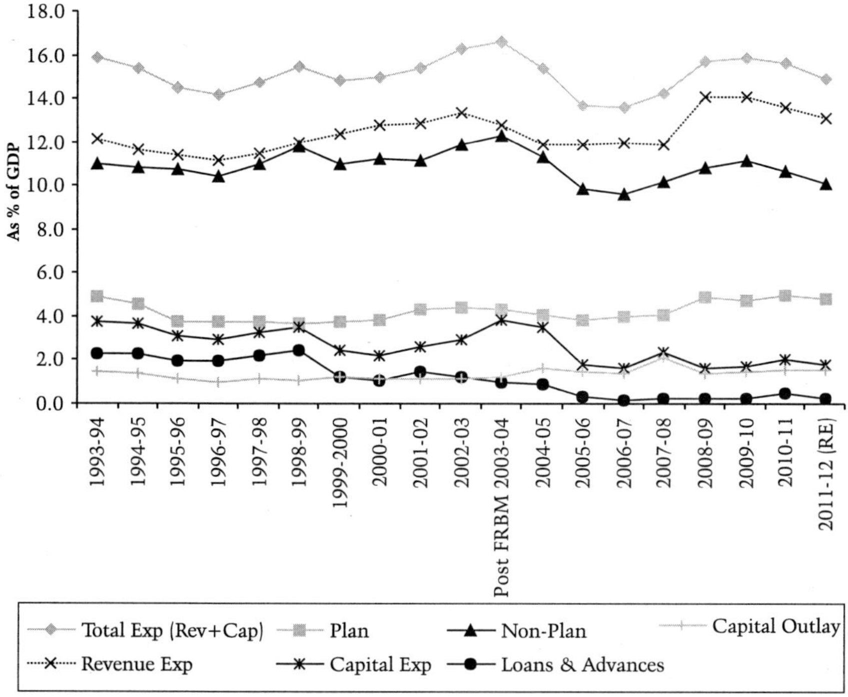

Source: Annexure Table A-8.3.

outlays). However, the growth rate of increased expenditure was relatively lower than that of receipts and hence the net result was the decline in the revenue and fiscal deficits.

In brief, though there were fluctuations in the revenue as well as fiscal deficits in the 1990s i.e., ever since the reforms started, the fiscal situation had shown signs of revival. The decline of deficit indicators had instilled a sense of confidence. However, by the end of the nineties the GFD and the RD began to rise almost until the initiation of the FRBM Act.

Post–FRBM Period

The FRBM Act has been effective since July, 2004. Looking at Annexure Table A-8.1 and Figure 8.1 it can be seen that in the very first year of implementation, 2004-05, the GFD and the RD as percentages of

GDP showed a decline. Analysis of the data (Annexure Tables A-8.1 to A-8.3) clearly points towards an encouraging beginning. The fall in GFD/GDP ratio by 0.4 percentage points and RD/GDP ratio by 1.1 percentage points had been possible through the curtailment of the total expenditure/GDP ratio by 1.2 percentage points of which revenue and capital expenditures constituted 0.9 per cent and 0.3 per cent respectively. The decline in revenue expenditure was mainly due to a decline in the interest payment burden because of bulk loan repayments to NSSF. These bulk repayments to NSSF were possible only through the loan recoveries under DSS. There was also a marginal increase in the revenue. It is important to note that though the year on year growth rate of revenue expenditure during the period had slowed down, the slowdown in the growth of capital expenditure was huge. The revenue augmentation was largely on account of the rising contribution of personal income tax and customs duty which has been possible because of the cyclical upswing.[13]

However the succeeding year (2005-06), once again saw a deviation from the FRBM targets as there were marginal increases in the deficit numbers. The proportion of non-tax revenues to GDP had declined by 0.4 percentage point to 2.1 per cent. The Centre's gross (net) tax revenue as a percentage of GDP had registered a marginal rise which was largely on account of improved receipts through the corporation tax, despite the poor performance of most of the other taxes during the period (Annexure Table A-8.2). Expenditures during the period were curtailed largely through reduction in capital expenditure[14] which registered, in fact, a negative growth to the extent of 41.7 per cent over the previous year (Annexure Table A-8.3) which was mainly on account of the declining capital outlays, lowered repayments to NSSF and also loans and advances. While decrease in the repayments to NSSF may be due to closure of DSS, decrease in loans and advances was mainly due to the implementation of one of the recommendations of the 12th Finance Commission—the stoppage of plan loans from the Centre to the states—which reduced financial burden on the Centre.[15] It's also interesting to note here, that during this period there was

13. Ministry of Finance, 2006: Chapters 21 and 22.
14. Capital expenditure includes capital outlay and loans and advances to the sub-national governments.
15. See *Report of the 12th Finance Commission*, Chapter 10, p.174.

also a reduction in the non-plan loans given out by the Central government (Annexure Table A-8.4). Thus, the total expenditure as a percentage of GDP did fall during the period, though the revenue expenditure during the period was maintained at 11.90 per cent of GDP as in the preceding year. Can the decline in the plan loans or non-plan loans be attributed to FRBM Act?

The Finance Minister, in his budget speech for the year 2005-06 (GoI, 2005), postponed the target year by pressing the pause button of FRBM Act saying: "Consequent to accepting the recommendations of the Twelfth Finance Commission and the drastically changed pattern of devolution and funding, there has been a considerable strain in making the Budget for 2005-06. I was left with no option but to press the 'pause' button *vis-á-vis* the FRBM Act." Hence one may call this 'an impact of central (Finance Commission) transfers to states' of FRBM Act.

The 12th Finance Commission has increased the states' share. However, it is important to highlight here, that one of the recommendations of the Commission which the Centre implemented—stoppage of plan loans from the Centre to the States—had reduced the financial burden of the Centre. In fact comparing states' share in central taxes *vis-á-vis* plan loans from the Centre, the former had increased from ₹ 78,550 crore to ₹ 94,024 crore, while the latter had fallen from ₹ 23,754 crore to ₹ 8,062 crore (Annexure Table A-8.4). In other words, a year on year growth of states' share in central taxes was 19.70 per cent *vis-á-vis* a fall of plan loans by 66.06 per cent. In fact it is also interesting to note that in this year, there was a substantial reduction of 98.59 per cent (from ₹ 2,403 crore to ₹ 34 crore) in the non-plan loans given out by the Central government. Thus, despite a fall in the plan and non-plan loans, the Centre was unable to reduce the fiscal and revenue deficits during the year probably due to increase in non-plan grants by ₹ 17,236 crore of which those recommended by the Finance Commission constituted 58.5 per cent while other non-plan grants and grants for relief on account of natural calamities constituted 35.1 per cent and 6.4 per cent respectively. The effect of increased states' share in Central taxes and grants has been nullified by the decreased plan and non-plan loans to states and the year on year growth rate of gross transfers was 10.7 per cent which was lower than the preceding two years.

In 2006-07 and 2007-08 the deficit indicators, as percentages of GDP, once again declined. In 2006-07 this was possible due to an increase in Centre's tax revenue (particularly corporation tax, personal income tax and customs duties) on the one hand and nominal reductions (increase) in capital (revenue) expenditure (Annexure Table A-8.3). In 2007-08, the Central government finances reflected a slight variation in the trend. The revenue expenditures as percentage of GDP exhibited the most awaited decline (on account of decline in defence expenditures and interest payments as percentages of GDP). However rising capital expenditure (rise on account of both loans and advances as well as capital outlay) pushed up the total expenditure as a percentage of GDP. On the other hand rise in total revenues on account of increased tax and non-tax revenue ensured a fall in the deficit. Therefore, during the two year period 2006 to 2008 the deficit indicators showed a fall largely on account of resource mobilisation/ revenue augmentation (Annexure Table A-8.3) which has largely been possible because of robust economic growth. Where does the FRBM Act figures in this?

The year 2008-09 was a huge setback in terms of achievement of the FRBM targets. The fiscal situation deteriorated with the GFD registering a year on year growth of 165.53 per cent, the revenue deficits 382.30 per cent and as a percentage of GDP they stood at 6.0 per cent and 4.5 per cent respectively (Annexure Table A-8.1). The huge deficits had been largely attributed to the deliberate fiscal measures undertaken to pull the economy out of the slowdown. The economy which was growing at the rate of 8 per cent had slowed down to 6.7 per cent due to rising global commodity prices and the global financial crises.[16] This was a period of poor revenue augmentation, particularly GTR with a year on year growth rate of mere 2 per cent and rapid rise of revenue expenditure (on account of both defence and subsidies). Apart from the deliberate measures of fiscal expansion through tax cuts and expenditure hikes, the implementation of the Sixth Pay Commission recommendations, supplementary demand for grants on account of farm loan waiver and funding on projects prioritised in the Eleventh Five Year Plan were cited as reasons for the huge deficit numbers.[17]

16. Ministry of Finance, 2009: Chapter 1.

17. Ibid.: Chapter 3.

Though the government asserted to abide by the FRBM norms in the years 2006-07 and 2007-08, in the subsequent year high social sector expenditure, implementation of the Sixth Central Pay Revision Commission's recommendations and the impact of global slowdown were shown as the major causes for not reaching the set targets of FRBM. However, one should remember the fact that while preparing the policy documents, particularly related to fiscal, the government has to take into account the commitments which are repetitive in nature. All public finance professionals, policy makers, executives of government know the quinquennial appointment of the Union Finance Commission and decadal appointment of the Central Pay Revision Commission whose recommendations are obviously implemented. Hence, they should not be shown as obstacles in achieving the self-imposed targets.

By 2009-10, the deficit figures reached new heights on account of rising expenditures on revenue and capital accounts as well as falling gross revenues (Annexure Table A-8.1). In fact the *Economic Survey* (2009-10: Chapter 3) states that the huge deficit figures are a result of "conscious policy-driven stimulus to counter the demand slowdown."[18]

The recovery of the economy in 2010-11, the subsequent rise in both the tax and non-tax revenue and with curtailment of the revenue expenditure (on account of defence and subsidies) the deficit figures finally showed the much awaited decline in 2010-11 (Annexure Table A-8.1), only to rise again in 2011-12. In accordance with the revised estimates for the year 2011-12 expenditures declined, (largely contributed by a decline in capital expenditure specifically on account of loans and advances, Annexure Tables A-8.7 and A-8.9) and the gross revenues as well showed a decline. On the backdrop of inflationary pressures, rising costs and weakening manufacturing activity, revenues through taxes had fallen (Annexure Table A-8.2) With no substantial gains on the non-tax revenue front, deficits once again shot up in the year (Annexure Table A-8.1). A failure to meet these numbers would only highlight our inability to factor in the 'externalities' and meeting the FRBM targets would remain a mere mirage.

The analysis of the trends in Central government finances in the post-FRBM period raises the thought that the notion of FRBM though

18. Ministry of Finance, 2010, Chapter 3.

appreciable, the implementation remains questionable. The results which the Union government has achieved may not be totally attributed to FRBM. The effect of DSS (2002-03 to 2004-05) because of which loan recoveries from the states have increased on the receipts front of the Centre, declining interest burden because of the bulk repayments to NSSF for which the source was again the loan recoveries from the states is quite different from the FRBM Act. The effect of increased states' share in central taxes and grants has been nullified by the decreased plan and non-plan loans to states and the year on year growth rate of gross transfers in 2005-06 was lower than the preceding two years. Attributing Finance Commission transfers to giving pause to FRBM Act targets is illogical. The reason for the fall in the deficit indicators during 2006-2008 may be attributed to robust economic growth led revenue augmentation. Thus in any year of the post-FRBM period, the effort of the Union government in improving its fiscal responsibility is not strikingly seen. The fiscal measures that were undertaken may go well even in the absence of FRBM Act. Whatever fluctuations were found in the fiscal indicators before FRBM Act also appeared even after the implementation of the Act (Table 8.1).

FRBM Rule 6: Revenue Accruals of Centre and States Governments

On account of the well accepted vertical and horizontal fiscal imbalances between the Centre and the states, the framers of the Indian Constitution made a few statutory provisions for the devolution of resources from the Union government to the state governments and also provided a statutory body, the Finance Commission, to periodically review and recommend transfers to meet the budgetary needs of the states. The other channels of central transfers to states are the Planning Commission and the Central ministries. The central financial transfers to the states may be categorised into share in central taxes, grants (statutory, plan and non-plan) and loans (plan and non-plan).

The FRBM Act does not specifically discuss the issue of federal transfers to the state governments. However adherence to the FRBM specifications has broader implications. For greater transparency in the budgetary process, FRBM rules mandate the Central government to disclose changes, if any, in accounting standards, policies and practices that have a bearing on the fiscal indicators. The Union government is also mandated to submit the statements of receivables and guarantees and a statement of assets, at the time of presenting the Annual Financial Statement (AFS). This would imply greater transparency in the system and access to data that would enable us to comprehend the areas with blockage of revenues. Resolving the identified issues would lead to a significant accentuation in the revenue (e.g., through clearance of revenue blockages) leading to higher divisible pool of resources and thereby higher transfers to the states. Based on Rule 6 of the FRBM Rules 2004, the Central government is giving the details (in the annexure of Receipts Budget Volume) regarding the tax revenue raised but not realised. This helps us to understand the extent of blockage of revenue receipts particularly tax revenue in which the states have a statutory share.

In the nineties, a series of measures were undertaken by the Central government in an attempt to rationalise the tax rates and structure. In the early 2000s changes such as the introduction of rule based fiscal management and administrative changes such as the implementation of the TIN (Tax Information Network) significantly transformed the fiscal scenario.[19] It is noteworthy to highlight that during the four year period 2003-04 to 2007-08, the gross tax GDP ratio went up by over three percentage points. This has been attributed to the high economic growth and better tax administration.[20] However data available in the budget documents (Annexure Tables A-8.5 to A-8.7) hint that significant amounts of tax that have been raised have not been realised during this period.

Based on the reporting year 2010-11, as given in the Receipts Budget 2012-13 of the Union government, the revenue through principal taxes raised but not realised (under both dispute and not under dispute together) amounted to ₹ 249,443 crore (Annexure Table A-8.5). About 15 per cent of the uncollected amount (about 13% falls during a 5-10 year period and nearly 2% was more than a decade old) was old arrears and the remaining 85 per cent fell under the recent five year period. A look at a cross-section

19. Significant rise in the tax compliance has been realised and for the first time in the history of Indian Public finance, tax collections from direct taxes exceeded that of the indirect taxes in the year 2007-08....as stated in the Report of the Thirteenth Finance Commission (2010-2015). Volume 1. p.45.
20. Report of the Thirteenth Finance Commission (2010-2015). Volume 1. p.45, paragraph 4.14.

of the total uncollected amount of ₹ 249,443 crore shows that about 75 per cent i.e., ₹ 1,88,010.2 crore was blocked under dispute in spite of the better tax administration as mentioned in the above paragraph. While the remaining 25 per cent i.e., ₹ 61,432.7 crore which was not under dispute was also not collected (Figure 8.5).

Figure 8.5

Central Tax Revenue Raised But Not Realised: Principal Taxes

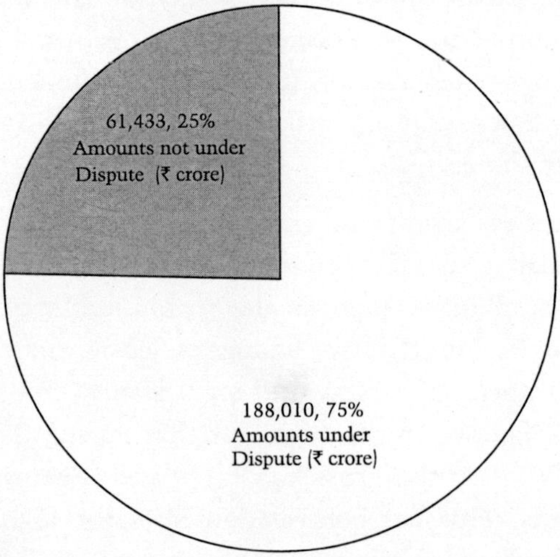

Source: Annexure Table A-8.5.

Segregation of the total uncollected amount into different time periods with a break-up of the amount under dispute and amount not under dispute shows that of the total amount nearly 32 per cent (20% under dispute and 12% not under dispute) falls within the recent two year period when the economy was facing a crisis. But 53 per cent of the total uncollected revenues (47% under disputes and 6% not under dispute) falls during the period 2006-07 to 2008-09 when the growth rates of both tax revenue and GDP were high (barring 2008-09). Annexure Table A-8.5 shows the composition of total uncollected revenue across the periodic break-up—under dispute and not under dispute—and also shows that the recent five years have higher proportions.

The proportion of total uncollected revenue (under dispute and not under dispute) constitutes nearly seven per cent of the Centre's gross tax revenue, 9 per cent of the Centre's net tax revenue and nearly 26 per cent of states' share in central taxes (Figure 8.6 and Annexure Table A-8.6). The proportion of amount under dispute constitutes about five per cent of the Centre's gross tax revenue, 7 per cent of the Centre's net tax revenue and nearly 20 per cent of states' share in central taxes. The proportion of the amount not under dispute, which is lower in the total uncollected tax revenue, obviously constitutes a lower share i.e., about 1.6 per cent of the Centre's gross tax revenue, 2.2 per cent of the Centre's net tax revenue and 6.3 per cent of states' share in Central taxes.

An attempt is made to estimate the proportions of revenue accruing to the Centre and the states (Annexure Table A-8.10) if there was no uncollected revenue under disputes (not under disputes too) or if the entire amount was collected. The estimated proportion of total uncollected amount to GDP accruing to the Centre and states for the entire period was 0.5 per cent and 0.18 per cent respectively. But the corresponding proportions for the recent two years constituted 0.9 per cent and 0.33 per cent respectively. During the recent five years (more than 2 years and less than 5 years), the corresponding proportions were 0.66 per cent and 0.23 per cent respectively. The break-up of the uncollected amount shows that the proportions under dispute were higher.

Probing further and looking into the reports of the CAG, during the above period 2006-07 to 2008-09, with regard to the direct taxes, the extent of appeals[21] not disposed of at the level of the CIT Commissioner of Income Tax (Appeals) is alarming. It ranges from 61.5 per cent to 70.4 per cent.[22] The efficiency of collection, measured in terms of total demand pending as a percentage of net tax collection, during the same period (2006-07 to 2008-09) ranges between 39.8 per cent and 65.0 per cent.[23] This shows that even during the period of economic boom significant amounts were blocked and this is a matter of concern. According to the

21. "An aggrieved tax payer has the right to dispute a tax demand with the Income Tax Department through the Commissioner of Income Tax (Appeals)". Also see *Report no. 26 of 2010-11 (Direct Taxes)*, Comptroller and Auditor General of India.

22. Computed from *Report on Direct Tax: the Union Audit Reports* 2010-11 and 2011-12.

23. Ibid.

Figure 8.6

Proportion of Total Uncollected Revenue (Under Dispute and Not Under Dispute)

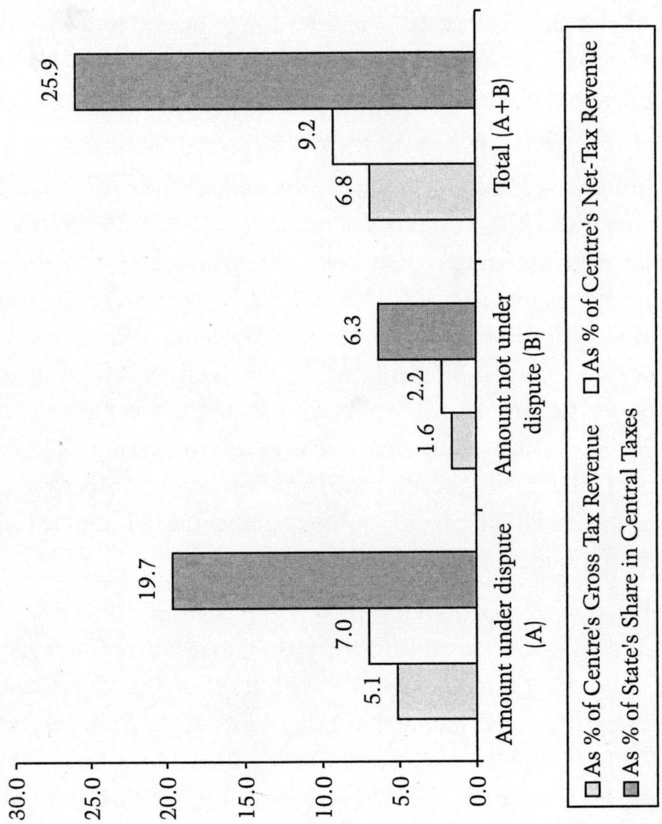

Source: Annexure Table A-8.6.

latest available Union Receipts Audit Report 2011-12, the position of appeals pending at the CIT (Appeals) has risen to 72.6 per cent and the efficiency of collection has significantly deteriorated to 65.25 per cent in 2010-11, thus showing no encouraging signs. Further, the tax effect of cases that are time barred during the last five years (2006-07 to 2010-11) amount to ₹ 5,334.46 crore.[24]

With regard to the audits made on the indirect tax front, considering a period of five years from 2006-07 to 2010-11, the percentages of recovery out of the accepted audit observations have been as low as 13.13 per cent in the case of excise duties, 23.75 per cent in the case of customs and 38.26 per cent of service tax, implying a blockage of funds to the extent of ₹ 2,014.74 crore (Annexure Table A-8.8). Such low percentages of recovery are clearly a matter of concern and necessitate an in-depth study into the causes and measures to speed up the process of recovery.

Though the gross tax revenue has grown significantly in the FRBM era (Annexure Table A-8.2) considering just the above cases of blockage of funds both on the direct and indirect tax front nearly 0.93 per cent of gross tax revenue of the year 2010-11[25] has remained blocked. This clearly implies that the rise in the tax revenues was largely due to the economic boom that existed during a larger part of this period and not due to improved fiscal responsibility on the part of governments. A minimisation/removal of these blockages would definitely lead to greater resource mobilisation at the Centre, a larger divisible pool of resources and thereby more transfers to the states.

Conclusion

With the implementation of the FRBM, the system has clearly become more transparent in respect of availability of data. However, much more needs to be done. The originally set FRBM targets had never been achieved, there have been periodic postponements of the target dates and amendments to the Act have been made to bring in greater focus and clarity towards ensuring a fiscal balance. In an attempt to improve the fiscal situation, several measures have been adopted to raise the revenues (such

24. *Report on Direct Tax: Union Audit Report 2011-12*, CAG.
25. *Union Audit Report* for receipts is 2010-11, 2013. *http://www.saiindia.gov.in*

as widening the tax base, consolidating the tax rates and simplifying the administrative procedures). Though steps have been taken towards effective management of expenditure, (e.g., setting up of the Expenditure Reforms Committee, stoppage of loans from the Centre to state) much work on this front is yet to be done (including factoring in and providing fiscal space for the periodic liabilities that arise such as from pay commission recommendations).

The initiation of the FRBM Act is appreciable but implementation of the FRBM Act itself has been very feeble. As a result, the extent of rise in the resources attributable to fiscal responsibility has been limited—as evident from the blockages of funds. Thus, though the impact of the FRBM act on federal transfers has been limited in the current period, the future seems promising, provided: (i) there is more clarity on the tax policies so that amounts locked up in disputes can be minimised, and (ii) there is more active participation of the authorities in clearing up tax appeals so that the tax revenues raised can be realised to its maximum potential, thus contributing to a larger pool of resources to the Centre and to the states.

Annexure Box A-8.1

The Fiscal Responsibility and Budget Management Rules, 2004

- Reduction of revenue deficit by an amount equivalent of 0.5 per cent or more of the GDP at the end of each financial year, beginning with 2004-05.
- Reduction of fiscal deficit by an amount equivalent of 0.3 per cent or more of the GDP at the end of each financial year, beginning with 2004-05.
- No assumption of additional liabilities (including external debt at current exchange rate) in excess of nine per cent GDP for the financial year 2004-05 and progressive reduction of this limit by at least one percentage point of GDP in each subsequent year.
- No guarantees in excess of 0.5 per cent of GDP in any financial year, beginning with 2004-05.
- Specifies three fiscal indicators to be projected in the medium term fiscal policy statement. These are, revenue deficit as a percentage of GDP, tax revenue as percentage of GDP and total outstanding liabilities as percentage of GDP.
- For greater transparency in the budgetary process, rules mandate the Central government to disclose changes, if any, in accounting standards, policies and practices that have a bearing on the fiscal indicator. The Government is also mandated to submit statements of receivables and guarantees and a statement of assets, at the time of presenting the Annual Financial Statement, latest by Budget 2006-07.
- The rules prescribe the form for the quarterly review of the trends of receipts and expenditures. The rules mandate the Central government to take appropriate corrective action in case of revenue and fiscal deficits exceeding 45 per cent of the budget estimates, or total non-debt receipts falling short of 40 per cent of the budget estimates at the end of first half of the financial year.

Source: *Economic Survey 2004-05*, chapter 27; *http://indiabudget.nic.in/es2004-05/chapt2005/chap27.pdf*

Annexure Table A-8.1

Trends in Aggregate Receipts, Expenditures and Deficits

(in %)

Year	GTR	Net Tax Revenue	NTR	TNR	TRE	Loan Recoveries	Dis-investment Receipts	TCE	TE	GFD	RD
						As Percentage of GDP at Current Market Prices					
1993-94	8.5	6.0	2.5	8.5	12.1	0.7	0.0	3.8	15.9	6.8	3.7
1994-95	8.8	6.5	2.3	8.7	11.7	0.6	0.5	3.7	15.4	5.5	3.0
1995-96	9.1	6.7	2.3	9.0	11.4	0.5	0.0	3.1	14.5	4.9	2.4
1996-97	9.1	6.6	2.3	8.9	11.2	0.5	0.0	3.0	14.2	4.7	2.3
1997-98	8.9	6.1	2.4	8.5	11.5	0.5	0.1	3.3	14.8	5.7	3.0
1998-99	8.0	5.8	2.5	8.3	12.0	0.6	0.3	3.5	15.5	6.3	3.7
1999-00	8.5	6.4	2.6	9.0	12.4	0.5	0.1	2.4	14.8	5.2	3.4
2000-01	8.7	6.3	2.6	8.9	12.8	0.6	0.1	2.2	15.0	5.5	3.9
2001-02	8.0	5.7	2.9	8.6	12.8	0.7	0.2	2.6	15.4	6.0	4.3
2002-03	8.5	6.3	2.9	9.1	13.4	1.4	0.1	2.9	16.3	5.7	4.3
1993-2003	8.5	6.2	2.6	8.8	12.3	0.7	0.1	2.9	15.2	5.6	3.5
						Post-FRBM					
2003-04	9.0	6.6	2.7	9.3	12.8	2.4	0.6	3.8	16.6	4.3	3.5
2004-05	9.4	6.9	2.5	9.4	11.9	1.9	0.1	3.5	15.4	3.9	2.4
2005-06	9.9	7.3	2.1	9.4	11.9	0.3	0.0	1.8	13.7	4.0	2.5
2006-07	11.0	8.2	1.9	10.1	12.0	0.1	0.0	1.6	13.6	3.3	1.9
2007-08	11.9	8.8	2.1	10.9	11.9	0.1	0.8	2.4	14.3	2.5	1.1
2008-09	10.8	7.9	1.7	9.6	14.1	0.1	0.0	1.6	15.7	6.0	4.5
2009-10	9.7	7.1	1.8	8.9	14.1	0.1	0.4	1.7	15.9	6.5	5.2
2010-11	10.3	7.4	2.8	10.3	13.6	0.2	0.3	2.0	15.6	4.9	3.3
2011-12 (RE)	10.2	7.3	1.4	8.7	13.1	0.2	0.2	1.8	14.9	5.9	4.5
2003-12	10.3	7.5	2.0	9.6	13.0	0.4	0.3	2.1	15.1	4.9	3.4

contd...

...contd...

Year	*GTR*	*Net Tax Revenue*	*NTR*	*TNR*	*TRE*	*Loan Recoveries*	*Dis-investment Receipts*	*TCE*	*TE*	*GFD*	*RD*
					Year on Year Growth Rate (%)						
1994-95	21.9	26.2	7.4	20.7	12.9	2.5	-10679.2	14.7	13.3	-4.2	-5.2
1995-96	20.5	21.5	19.3	20.9	14.5	2.5	-92.9	-0.6	10.9	4.4	-4.2
1996-97	15.8	14.4	15.6	14.7	13.6	15.9	5.0	9.5	12.8	10.8	9.8
1997-98	8.1	2.1	17.3	6.0	13.5	10.3	140.0	22.9	15.4	33.3	42.2
1998-99	3.3	9.4	17.3	11.7	20.0	27.8	544.1	21.6	20.4	27.4	44.2
1999-00	19.4	22.6	18.7	21.4	15.1	-4.7	-70.7	-22.1	6.7	-7.6	0.9
2000-01	9.8	6.5	5.1	6.1	11.5	18.9	23.3	-2.5	9.2	13.5	26.1
2001-02	-0.8	-2.3	21.1	4.5	8.5	36.2	71.6	27.4	11.3	18.6	17.5
2002-03	15.6	18.7	6.7	14.7	12.4	108.4	-13.6	22.5	14.1	2.9	7.7
1993-2003	12.6	13.2	14.3	13.4	13.6	24.2	-1119.2	10.4	12.7	11.0	15.5
2003-04	17.6	17.9	6.3	14.3	6.9	96.4	26.2	46.4	14.0	-15.0	-8.9
2004-05	19.9	20.2	5.7	16.0	6.1	-7.6	438.0	4.4	5.7	2.0	-20.3
2005-06	20.5	20.2	-5.4	13.4	14.3	-82.8	-73.9	-41.7	1.5	16.4	17.8
2006-07	28.9	29.9	8.3	25.2	17.1	-44.6	-64.3	3.6	15.4	-2.6	-13.1
2007-08	25.3	25.2	23.0	24.7	15.5	-13.5	-66.2	71.9	22.2	-11.0	-34.5
2008-09	2.0	0.9	-5.3	-0.3	33.5	20.4	7165.0	-23.7	24.0	165.5	382.3
2009-10	3.2	3.0	19.9	6.0	14.9	40.3	-98.5	25.0	15.9	24.2	33.7
2010-11	27.0	24.8	88.0	37.6	14.1	44.2	4242.9	39.0	16.9	-10.7	-25.6
2011-12 (RE)	13.7	12.7	-42.9	-2.7	11.6	14.8	-7.1	0.1	10.1	39.7	56.6
2003-12	17.6	17.2	10.8	14.9	14.9	7.5	-32.2	13.9	14.0	23.2	43.1

Note: GTR = Gross Tax Revenue, NTR = Non-Tax Revenue, TNR = Total net revenue, TRE = Total Revenue Expenditure, TCE = Total Capital Expenditure, TE = Total Expenditure, GFD = Gross Fiscal Deficit, RD = Revenue Deficit

Source: Calculated from *Handbook of Statistics on Indian Economy 2012*, RBI and various *Receipts Budgets*, GoI.

Annexure Table A-8.2

Tax Revenue Composition of the Central Government

(in %)

Year	Centre's Gross Tax Revenue	Of which: Corporation Tax	Personal Income Tax	Customs	Union Excise Duties	Less States' Share	Centre's Net Tax Revenue	GDP at Current Market Prices
		As Percentage of GDP at Current Market Prices						
1993-94	8.5	1.1	1.0	2.5	3.6	2.5	6.0	100.0
1994-95	8.8	1.3	1.2	2.6	3.6	2.4	6.5	100.0
1995-96	9.1	1.3	1.3	2.9	3.3	2.4	6.7	100.0
1996-97	9.1	1.3	1.3	3.0	3.2	2.5	6.6	100.0
1997-98	8.9	1.3	1.1	2.6	3.1	2.8	6.1	100.0
1998-99	8.0	1.4	1.1	2.3	3.0	2.2	5.8	100.0
1999-00	8.5	1.5	1.3	2.4	3.1	2.2	6.4	100.0
2000-01	8.7	1.6	1.5	2.2	3.2	2.4	6.3	100.0
2001-02	8.0	1.6	1.4	1.7	3.1	2.3	5.7	100.0
2002-03	8.5	1.8	1.5	1.8	3.3	2.2	6.3	100.0
1993-2003	8.5	1.5	1.3	2.3	3.2	2.3	5.5	100.0
				Post-FRBM				
2003-04	9.0	2.2	1.5	1.7	3.2	2.3	6.6	100.0
2004-05	9.4	2.6	1.5	1.8	3.1	2.4	6.9	100.0
2005-06	9.9	2.7	1.5	1.8	3.0	2.6	7.3	100.0
2006-07	11.0	3.4	1.7	2.0	2.7	2.8	8.2	100.0
2007-08	11.9	3.9	2.1	2.1	2.5	3.0	8.8	100.0
2008-09	10.8	3.8	1.9	1.8	1.9	2.8	7.9	100.0
2009-10	9.7	3.8	1.9	1.3	1.6	2.6	7.1	100.0
2010-11	10.3	3.9	1.8	1.8	1.8	2.9	7.4	100.0
2011-12 (RE)	10.2	3.7	1.9	1.7	1.7	2.9	7.3	100.0
2003-12	10.3	3.5	1.8	1.7	2.2	2.7	7.5	100.0

contd...

...contd...

	Centre's Gross Tax Revenue	*Of which*				*Less States' Share*	*Centre's Net Tax Revenue*	*GDP at Current Market Prices*
		Corporation Tax	*Personal Income Tax*	*Customs*	*Union Excise Duties*			
Year on Year Growth Rates								
1994-95	21.9	37.4	31.8	20.7	17.8	11.7	26.2	17.3
1995-96	20.5	19.3	29.7	33.5	7.6	17.9	21.5	17.3
1996-97	15.8	12.6	16.9	19.8	12.0	19.7	14.4	15.7
1997-98	8.1	7.8	-6.2	-6.2	6.6	24.2	2.1	10.8
1998-99	3.3	22.5	18.4	1.2	11.0	-10.1	9.4	14.7
1999-00	19.4	25.1	26.7	19.1	16.3	11.1	22.6	11.6
2000-01	9.8	16.3	23.8	-1.8	10.7	18.9	6.5	7.8
2001-02	-0.8	2.6	0.8	-15.3	5.9	2.2	-2.3	8.3
2002-03	15.6	26.1	15.2	11.4	13.4	6.2	18.7	7.8
1993-2003	12.6	18.9	17.5	9.1	11.3	11.3	13.2	12.4
Post-FRBM								
2003-04	17.6	37.7	12.3	8.4	10.3	17.2	17.9	12.1
2004-05	19.9	30.1	19.0	18.5	9.2	19.5	20.2	14.2
2005-06	20.1	22.5	13.6	12.9	12.2	20.1	20.2	13.9
2006-07	29.3	42.5	34.1	32.7	5.7	27.5	29.9	16.3
2007-08	25.3	33.7	36.7	20.6	5.1	26.2	25.2	16.1
2008-09	2.0	10.6	3.3	-4.1	-12.1	5.5	0.9	12.9
2009-10	3.2	14.7	15.5	-16.6	-5.2	2.9	3.0	14.7
2010-11	27.0	22.1	13.5	63.0	33.7	33.0	24.8	18.8
2011-12 (RE)	13.7	9.7	19.9	12.7	9.0	16.5	12.7	15.4
2003-12	17.6	24.8	18.7	16.5	7.5	18.7	17.2	14.9

Source: Calculated from various *Receipts Budgets*, GoI; GDP taken from *Handbook of Statistics, 2012*.

Annexure Table A-8.3

Major Heads of Expenditures of the Central Government

(in %)

	Total Exp (Rev+Cap)	of which		Rev Exp	of which			Cap Exp	of which		Defence (Capital Outlay)	GDP at Current
		Plan	Non-Plan		Defense	Interest Payments	Subsidies		Loans & Advances	Capital Outlay		
As Percentage of GDP at Current Market Prices												
1993-94	15.9	4.9	11.0	12.1	1.7	4.1	1.3	3.8	2.3	1.5	0.8	100.0
1994-95	15.4	4.5	10.8	11.7	1.6	4.2	1.1	3.7	2.3	1.4	0.7	100.0
1995-96	14.5	3.8	10.8	11.4	1.5	4.1	1.0	3.1	2.0	1.1	0.7	100.0
1996-97	14.2	3.8	10.4	11.2	1.5	4.2	1.1	3.0	2.0	1.0	0.6	100.0
1997-98	14.8	3.8	11.0	11.5	1.7	4.2	1.2	3.3	2.2	1.1	0.6	100.0
1998-99	15.5	3.7	11.8	12.0	1.7	4.3	1.3	3.5	2.4	1.0	0.6	100.0
1999-00	14.8	3.8	11.0	12.4	1.8	4.5	1.2	2.4	1.2	1.2	0.6	100.0
2000-01	15.0	3.8	11.2	12.8	1.7	4.6	1.2	2.2	1.1	1.1	0.6	100.0
2001-02	15.4	4.3	11.1	12.8	1.6	4.6	1.3	2.6	1.5	1.1	0.7	100.0
2002-03	16.3	4.4	11.9	13.4	1.6	4.7	1.7	2.9	1.3	1.1	0.6	100.0
1993-2003	15.2	4.0	11.2	12.3	1.6	4.4	6.0	2.9	1.7	1.2	0.6	100.0
Post-FRBM												
2003-04	16.6	4.3	12.3	12.8	1.5	4.4	1.6	3.8	1.0	1.2	0.6	100.0
2004-05	15.4	4.1	11.3	11.9	1.4	3.9	1.4	3.5	0.9	1.6	1.0	100.0
2005-06	13.7	3.8	9.9	11.9	1.3	3.6	1.3	1.8	0.3	1.5	0.9	100.0
2006-07	13.6	4.0	9.6	12.0	1.2	3.5	1.3	1.6	0.2	1.4	0.8	100.0
2007-08	14.3	4.1	10.2	11.9	1.1	3.4	1.4	2.4	0.2	2.1	0.8	100.0
2008-09	15.7	4.9	10.8	14.1	1.3	3.4	2.3	1.6	0.3	1.4	0.7	100.0
2009-10	15.9	4.7	11.2	14.1	1.4	3.3	2.2	1.7	0.2	1.5	0.8	100.0
2010-11	15.6	4.9	10.7	13.6	1.2	3.0	2.3	2.0	0.5	1.5	0.8	100.0
2011-12(RE)	14.9	4.8	10.1	13.1	1.2	3.1	2.4	1.8	0.2	1.5	0.7	100.0
2003-12	15.1	4.5	10.6	13.0	1.3	3.4	4.7	2.1	0.4	1.5	0.8	100.0

contd...

...contd...

	Total Exp (Rev+Cap)	of which		Rev Exp	of which			Cap Exp	of which		Defence (Capital Outlay)	GDP at Current
		Plan	Non-Plan		Defense	Interest Payments	Subsidies		Loans & Advances	Capital Outlay		
						Year on Year Growth Rates						
1994-95	13.3	8.5	15.4	12.9	9.7	19.9	2.1	14.7	16.0	13.8	-0.7	17.3
1995-96	10.9	-2.1	16.4	14.5	14.7	13.6	6.9	-0.6	2.4	-5.3	17.5	17.3
1996-97	12.8	15.4	11.8	13.6	11.4	18.8	22.4	9.5	14.6	0.7	6.2	15.7
1997-98	15.4	10.4	17.3	13.5	24.7	10.4	19.6	22.9	22.7	23.5	7.0	10.8
1998-99	20.4	13.1	22.9	20.0	14.1	18.7	27.3	21.6	28.8	7.5	10.2	14.7
1999-00	6.7	14.0	4.4	15.1	17.9	15.9	3.8	-22.1	-43.4	27.6	18.1	11.6
2000-01	9.2	8.5	9.5	11.5	5.7	10.0	9.6	-2.5	-7.7	2.9	4.5	7.8
2001-02	11.3	22.4	7.5	8.5	2.2	8.2	16.3	27.4	49.0	7.3	30.9	8.3
2002-03	14.1	10.2	15.6	12.4	7.0	9.6	39.5	22.5	-7.6	9.6	-7.7	7.8
1993-2003	12.7	11.2	13.4	13.6	11.9	13.9	16.4	10.4	8.3	9.7	9.6	12.4
						Post-FRBM						
2003-04	14.0	9.7	15.6	6.9	6.1	5.3	1.8	46.4	-9.2	17.3	12.8	12.1
2004-05	5.7	8.2	4.9	6.1	1.5	2.3	3.7	4.4	0.5	53.3	89.7	14.2
2005-06	1.5	6.3	-0.2	14.3	9.9	4.5	3.4	-41.7	-60.8	5.1	1.1	13.9
2006-07	15.4	20.8	13.3	17.1	7.2	13.3	20.2	3.6	-24.8	9.5	4.6	16.3
2007-08	22.2	20.7	22.7	15.5	4.9	13.8	24.2	71.9	32.5	77.5	10.7	16.1
2008-09	24.0	34.2	19.9	33.5	35.2	12.4	82.9	-23.7	24.9	-28.9	9.2	12.9
2009-10	15.9	10.2	18.5	14.9	23.7	10.9	9.0	25.0	10.9	27.6	24.9	14.7
2010-11	16.9	24.9	13.5	14.1	1.5	9.8	22.7	39.0	157.0	20.0	21.4	18.8
2011-12(RE)	10.1	12.6	9.0	11.6	13.8	17.8	24.7	0.1	-48.0	16.7	6.6	15.4
2003-12	14.0	16.4	13.0	14.9	11.5	10.0	21.4	13.9	9.2	22.0	20.1	14.9

Source: Trends in Expenditure, Expenditure Budget for Total Expenditure and plan and non-plan expenditure.

Handbook of Statistics 2012, RBI for revenue expenditure, defence interest payments, subsidies, capital expenditure, loans & advances of which capital outlay of which defence.

Handbook of Statistics on the Indian Economy, 2002-03, RBI.

Receipts *Budget 2003-04*, GoI.

Calculated from *Handbook of Statistics on Indian Economy 2012*, RBI.

Annexure Table A-8.4

Gross Devolution of Resources from Centre to States (Accounts)

(₹ crore)

Year	Share in Central Taxes	Plan Loans	Non-Plan Loans	Plan Grants	Non-Plan Grants	Gross Total Transfers
2000-01	50734	16752	2214	24643	13141	107484
2001-02	52215	21218	3443	29295	13787	119958
2002-03	56655	20743	6473	30440	15242	129554
2003-04	67079	24412	1715	37119	14228	144553
2004-05	78550	23754	2404	41960	#14897	161565
2005-06	94024	8062	34	44617	#32133	178870
2006-07	120293	6158	-440	60045	34406	220462
2007-08	151402	7235	17	74314	34309	267277
2008-09	161052	6998	7	92546	37378	297981
2009-10	165014	8210	-110	103886	47087	324086
2010-11	219489	10500	-1020	114588	48909	392466
Year			*Year on Year Growth Rate (%)*			
2001-02	2.9	26.7	55.5	18.9	4.9	11.6
2002-03	8.5	-2.2	88.0	3.9	10.6	8.0
2003-04	18.4	17.7	-73.5	21.9	-6.7	11.6
2004-05	17.1	-2.7	40.2	13.0	4.7	11.8
2005-06	19.7	-66.1	-98.6	6.3	115.7	10.7
2006-07	27.9	-23.6	-1394.1	34.6	7.1	23.3
2007-08	25.9	17.5	-103.9	23.8	-0.3	21.2
2008-09	6.4	-3.3	-58.8	24.5	8.9	11.5
2009-10	2.5	17.3	-1671.4	12.3	26.0	8.8
2010-11	33.0	27.9	827.3	10.3	3.9	21.1

 # Break-up of Central Non-Plan Grants to States

(₹ crore)

Year	Statutory Grants	Grants for Relief on Account of Natural Calamities	Other Grants	Total Non-Plan Grants
2004-05*	7963	2167	4767	14897
2005-06	18049	3272	10812	32133
Year on Year Growth Rate (%)	127	51	127	116
		Composition (%)		
2004-05*	53	15	32	100
2005-06	56	10	34	100

Note: * includes NCT Delhi

Source: Calculated from various issues of *State Finances: A Study of Budgets*, RBI.

Annexure Table A-8.5

Cross Section of Dispute and Undisputed Revenue Raised But Not Realised: (Principal Taxes)

(in %)

Sl. no	*Major Head*	*> 1 yr but < 2 yrs (2009-10)*	*Over 2 yrs but < 5 yrs (2006-07 to 2008-09)*	*Over 5 yrs but < 10 yrs (2001-02 to 2005-06)*	*> 10 years (2000-01)*	*Total*
				As a % of Grand Total		
1	Amounts under dispute	20.0	46.6	7.9	0.8	75.4 (188,010.2)
2	Amounts not under dispute	11.7	6.4	5.5	0.9	24.6 (61,432.7)
3	Total (1+2)	31.8	53.0	13.4	1.8	100.0 (249,443.0)
				Relative Share (%)		
4	Amounts under dispute	26.6	61.8	10.5	1.1	100 (188,010.2)
5	Amounts not under dispute	47.7	26.0	22.5	3.8	100 (61,432.7)

Note: As at the end of Reporting Year 2010-11. Under Rule 6 of the FRBM Rules 2004.

Amount not under disputes include cases pending for adjudication also.

Figures in parenthesis are total amount in ₹ Crore.

Source: Receipts Budget, 2012-13, Government of India.

Annexure Table A-8.6

Share of Total Unrealised Tax Revenues in Centre's Tax Revenue and States' Share in Central Taxes (Principal Taxes)

(₹ crore)

Sl. No.	Major Head	Over 1 yr < 2 yrs 2009-10	Over 2 Yrs < 5 yrs 06-07 to 2008-09	Over 5 yrs < 10 yrs 2001-02 to 2005-06	Total*
1	Amounts under dispute	49,973.2	116,242.8	19,687.8	185,903.8
2	Amounts not under dispute	29,294.5	15,988.6	13,821.4	59,104.4
3	Total 1+2	79,267.6	132,231.3	33,509.2	245,008.2
4	Gross Tax Revenue	624,528.0	1,671,958.0	1,328,783.0	3,625,269.0
5	Net-Centre's Tax Revenue	456,536.0	1,234,049.0	972,797.0	2,663,382.0
6	Sate's Share in Tax	164,832.0	432,309.0	347,710.0	944,851.0
	As % of Centre's Gross Tax Revenue				
1	Amounts under dispute	8.0	7.0	1.5	5.1
2	Amounts not under dispute	4.7	1.0	1.0	1.6
3	Total 1+2	12.7	7.9	2.5	6.8
	As % Centre's Net Tax Revenue				
1	Amounts under dispute	10.9	9.4	2.0	7.0
2	Amounts not under dispute	6.4	1.3	1.4	2.2
3	Total 1+2	17.4	10.7	3.4	9.2
	As % States' Share in Central Taxes				
1	Amounts under dispute	30.3	26.9	5.7	19.7
2	Amounts not under dispute	17.8	3.7	4.0	6.3
3	Total 1+2	48.1	30.6	9.6	25.9

Note: *Total does not include amounts under dispute and not under dispute for over 10 years category.

Source: As per Table A-8.5.

Annexure Table A-8.7

Tax Revenues Raised But Not Realised: Share Accruing to Centre and States (Principal Taxes) (As % of GDP)

Sl. No	Major Head	Over 1 Year But <2 Years 2009-10	Over 2 Years But < 5 Years 20 06-07 - 2008-09	Over 5 Years But < 10 Years 2001-02 - 2005-06	Total*
	Total Amount Under Dispute + Not Under Dispute				
1	Gross Tax Revenue of the Centre	9.67	11.21	9.07	10.06
2	Centre's Net Tax Revenue	7.07	8.28	6.64	7.39
3	Total Uncollected proportion Accruing to the Centre	0.90	0.66	0.17	0.50
4	Estimated Centre's Net Tax Revenue (2+3)	7.97	8.93	6.81	7.90
1	States' Share in Central Taxes	2.55	2.90	2.37	2.62
2	Total Uncollected proportion Accruing to the States	0.33	0.23	0.06	0.18
3	Estimated States' Share in Central Taxes (1+2)	2.88	3.13	2.43	2.80
	Amounts Under Dispute				
1	Gross Tax Revenue of the Centre	9.67	11.21	9.07	10.06
2	Centre's Net Tax Revenue	7.07	8.28	6.64	7.39
3	Total Uncollected proportion Accruing to the Centre	0.57	0.58	0.10	0.38
4	Estimated Centre's Net Tax Revenue (2+3)	7.64	8.85	6.74	7.78
1	States' Share in Central Taxes	2.55	2.90	2.37	2.62
2	Total Uncollected proportion Accruing to the States	0.21	0.20	0.04	0.13
3	Estimated States' Share in Central Taxes (1+2)	2.76	3.10	2.41	2.76

contd...

...contd...

Sl. No	Major Head	Over 1 Year But <2 Years 2009-10	Over 2 Years But < 5 Years 20 06-07 - 2008-09	Over 5 Years But < 10 Years 2001-02 - 2005-06	Total*
	Amounts Not Under Dispute				
1	Gross Tax Revenue of the Centre	9.67	11.21	9.07	10.06
2	Centre's Net Tax Revenue	7.07	8.28	6.64	7.39
3	Total Uncollected proportion Accruing to the Centre	0.33	0.08	0.07	0.12
4	Estimated Centre's Net Tax Revenue (2+3)	7.40	8.36	6.71	7.51
1	States' Share in Central Taxes	2.55	2.90	2.37	2.62
2	Total Uncollected proportion Accruing to the States	0.12	0.03	0.02	0.04
3	Estimated States' Share in Central Taxes (1+2)	2.67	2.93	2.40	2.67

Note: *: Same as Table A-8.6.

Source: Calculated from Budget documents.

Annexure Table A-8.8

Recovery Levels in Indirect Taxes Post Audit Acceptance
(For a duration of 5 years 2006-07 to 2010-11)

(in ₹ crore)

Tax	*Acceptance Value*	*Recovery Value*	*Recovery Level (%)*
Excise	1485.77	195.09	13.13
Customs	335.05	79.59	23.75
Service	759.05	38.26	5.04

Source: Computed from various Reports on Indirect Tax, the *Union Audit Report 2011-12*.

References

Acharya, S. (2001). "High Fiscal Deficits Hurt Growth", *The Economic Times*, November 1.

Bagchi. A (2001). "Perspective on Correcting Fiscal Imbalances in the Indian Economy – Some Comments", *ICRA Bulletin* (January-June).

Comptroller and Auditor General of India (n.d.). *Union Receipts Audit Report 2010-11: Report on Direct Tax.*

——— *(n.d.). Union Receipts Audit Report 2011-12: Report on Direct Tax.*

——— *(n.d.). Union Receipts Audit Report 2010-11: Report on Central Excise.*

——— *(n.d.). Union Receipts Audit Report 2010-11: Report on Customs.*

——— *(n.d.). Union Receipts Audit Report 2010-11: Report on Service Tax.*

——— *(n.d.). Union Rcccipts Audit Report 2011-12: Report on Customs.*

——— *(n.d.). Union Receipts Audit Report 2011-12: Report on Central Excise.*

——— *(n.d.). Union Receipts Audit Report 2011-12: Report on Service Tax.*

Dholakia H. Ravindra, Jeevan K. Khundrakpam, Dhirendra Gajbhiye (2009). *An Outline of Post 2009 FRBM Fiscal Architecture of the Union Government in the Medium Term.* Study no. 31. Mumbai: Department of Economic Analysis and Policy, RBI.

Government of India (2004). *Report of the Task Force on the Implementation of the Fiscal Responsibility and Budget Management Act, 2003.* New Delhi: Ministry of Finance.

———. (2004a). *Report of the Twelfth Finance Commission (2005-10).* New Delhi: Ministry of Finance.

———. (2005). *Budget Speech for 2005-06.* New Delhi: Ministry of Finance. February 28.

———. (2009). *Report of the Thirteenth Finance Commission (2010-15).* New Delhi: Ministry of Finance.

———. (2013). N*otification on 'Terms of Reference' of the Fourteenth Finance Commission.*

Karnik, Ajit (2002). "Fiscal Responsibility and Budget Management Bill: Offering Credible Commitments", *Economic and Political Weekly,* January 19.

Kumar, R., and A. Soumya (2010). "Fiscal Policy Issues for India after the Global Financial Crisis (2008–2010)", *ADBI Working Paper* 249. Tokyo: Asian Development Bank Institute.

Lahiri, A. and R. Kannan (2001). "India's Fiscal Deficits and Their Sustainability", *Discussion Paper* No. 5. NIPFP.

Ministry of Finance (2006). *Economic Survey (2005-06).* New Delhi: Government of India.

———. (2007). *Economic Survey (2006-07).* New Delhi: Government of India.

———. (2009). *Economic Survey (2008-09).* New Delhi: Government of India.

———. (2009a). "Receipts Budget 2009-10", *Union Budget 2009-10.* New Delhi: Government of India.

———. (2010). *Economic Survey (2009-10).* New Delhi: Government of India.

———. (2012). "Receipts Budget 2012-13", *Union Budget 2012-13.* New Delhi: Government of India.

Mohan, R. (2000). "Fiscal Correction for Economic Growth: Data Analysis and Suggestions", *Economic and Political Weekly*, June 10.

Patnaik, P. (2001). "The Humbug of Finance", *www.macroscan.com*

Rakshit, Mihir (2000). "On Correcting Fiscal Imbalances in the Indian Economy: Some Perspectives", *ICRA Bulletin*.

Rangarajan, C. and D.K. Srivastava (2005). "Fiscal Deficits and Government Debt in India: Implications for Growth and Stabilisation", *NIPFP Working Paper* 35.

Reserve Bank of India (2012). *Handbook of Statistics on Indian Economy 2011-12. Mumbai.*

Shetty S.L. (2001). "Reviving the Economy: Some Explorations", *Economic and Political Weekly 36(30). July-August.*

Virmani, Arvind (2001). "India's 1990-91 Crisis: Reforms, Myths and Paradoxes", *Planning Commission, Working Paper* No. 4 /2001-PC. December.

9 Federal Fiscal Sharing and Fiscal Accountability in India

An Integrated Approach

J.V.M. Sarma and Pradeep Kamble

Introduction

India has embarked on fiscal accountability measures for almost a decade now. The approach generally has been to contain fiscal and revenue deficits and debt-GDP (gross domestic product) ratio both at the Central government and the state government levels. However, the issue has been to objectively prescribe the quantitative limits for fiscal and revenue deficits and debt-GSDP (gross state domestic product) ratio as also prescribing the roadmap for attaining the target limits.

The Finance Commission (FC) is entrusted with the task of determining the limits. The 12th Finance Commission (TwFC) while recommending the limits prescribed one for the Centre, and another at the states' level. The state level fiscal targets were uniform for all the states. Later the 13th Finance Commission (ThFC) found that prescribing a uniform limit for all the states is not proper as states differ in their potential fiscal capacity and the resultant fiscal behaviour. Accordingly, the ThFC came out with differential time deadlines for achieving the fiscal deficit limits for different categories of states. Yet, the degree of differentiation does not seem good enough. Ideally, the fiscal targets (the fiscal and revenue deficits and the debt-GDP ratio) need to be state-specific as the fiscal behaviour of each state is conditioned by factors such as its own economic environment and fiscal capacity. There is also a need to derive the state-specific limits more objectively.

The task of prescribing state-specific fiscal targets is similar to the task of determination of state-specific horizontal revenue shares among the states. The FC usually determines the state-wise tax devolution shares on the basis of certain criteria representing the economic environment, fiscal capacity and fiscal management of the states.[1] The primary objective of the Fiscal Responsibility and Budgetary Management Act (FRBMA) is to control the fiscal deficit (as also the revenue deficit and the debt–GSDP ratio). The primary objective of the FC transfers to a state is to reduce its fiscal gap (which we define as 'own revenue–total expenditure' and can be viewed as a variant of fiscal deficit). Given the commonality in the objectives, it is only proper that the criteria should be more or less the same. The suitable strategy appears to be first identifying the factors responsible for the existing fiscal gap across the states. If the revenue sharing is linked to the factors that influence the fiscal gap, then such a mechanism will also be conducive to achieving the fiscal responsibility targets.

This paper critically examines the horizontal sharing methods adopted by the FC and briefly describes a more rational method proposed in an earlier study by Sarma (1997). It illustrates the process of deriving the horizontal shares using the model and methods as given there. It also proposes an extension of the method to derive the norms for the fiscal responsibility targets and gives an empirical example, and concludes with a summary.

Horizontal Federal Fiscal Sharing: A More Rational Method

In an earlier paper Sarma (1997) has critically examined the horizontal sharing mechanisms adopted by the past FCs and proposed a more rational method relevant for India. There it emphasised the need to incorporate more objectivity in the determination of the state-wise revenue shares.

1. In the Indian federal system the powers of taxation as also the expenditure responsibilities are divided vertically between the Central government and the state governments. The division of the powers is such that the Central government ends up with surplus revenue while the states have more expenditure obligations than the Centre resulting in vertical imbalance. The corrective mechanism used by the institution of FC has been only partially successful. Every five years the FC assesses the fiscal gaps of the states and recommends annual transfers from the Centre to states for the next five years. The total transfers allocated to states are then distributed among states with a view to narrowing down the own revenue–expenditure gaps of the states. The horizontal sharing formula aims at encouraging efficient fiscal management, besides taking into account the need factors. Accordingly, the revenue shares are determined on the basis of certain indicators of fiscal efficiency along with factors that indicate the needs of the states.

Till the last FC (ThFC), the formula used for determination of the shares is based on purely the wisdom and experience of the honourable members of the FC. The selection of the indicators, the quantification methods, the weights assigned for each of the criteria etc., however, remain subjective. Successive FCs tended to use similar formula albeit with modifications that made the formula even more subjective and more inconsistent.

It is not that better ways of formulating the revenue sharing criteria are not available. It is only that these better formulations demand more in-depth reasoning, more technical work and above all, more willingness and determination on the part of the FC to keep the revenue sharing apolitical.

The method proposed by Sarma (1997) is much simple, straightforward and leaves very little room for subjectivities. The method conceptually depends on the principle that federal fiscal efficiency requires offsetting of the inequity among the federating units (states) with respect to the NMBF (net marginal benefit due to federating). This is what is emphasised in studies such as Breton, 1965; Gramlich, 1977; Rao and Chelliah, 1991 either directly or indirectly.

The NMBF can be broadly defined as the difference between marginal fiscal benefit and marginal fiscal costs of federation where, fiscal costs of federating can be the tax powers and revenue forgone to the federal government, while the fiscal benefits could be the gains in terms of increases in the state government revenues (owing to a possible rise in the tax base due to lower trade barriers across the states and so on), and economies of scale resulting in increased supply, and/or lower unit costs of providing the public goods (defence, law and order etc.). The NMBF of a state is likely to be reflected in its own revenue–total expenditure gap (which we refer as 'fiscal gap').

The main task of the FC therefore would be firstly, to assess the variations in the fiscal gaps across the states and identify the factors responsible for it. The set of factors consistently influencing the own revenues and the expenditures, and consequently the fiscal gap, might differ among the states. The overall fiscal gap of a state comprises two components: one due to the factors common to all the states, and another attributed to the state-specific factors. Consequently, the norms of fiscal behaviour ultimately can differ among the states. The method recognises the fact that state level fiscal behaviour is conditioned by several factors unique for each state and it is only fair that these natural differences should be kept in view while determining their revenue shares on the basis of fiscal behaviour. As a matter of fact, the division of states into general and special categories in India underlines the fact that these two categories of states operate in two separate fiscal spaces. The method thus argues that each of the states operates in its own fiscal environment, and therefore needs to be judged on its own. In the illustrative example given in Sarma (1997), it is found that the appropriate assessment method would be a 'fixed effects' model, emphasising the fact that the influence of common factors is uniform across the states but that of state-specific factors differs though reasonably stable.

Determining the Norms

To be clearer, let the fiscal gap $G_{it} = R_{it} - E_{it}$ of ith state in t^{th} year represent the shortfall of own revenue (R_{it}) to meet its expenditure needs (E_{it}).

After experimenting with a number of specifications, we find that the following specification yields robust econometric results. The model comprised two simple log-linear equations seeking to explain per capita own revenue and per capita revenue expenditure both in terms of per capita income (GSDP) along with the state-specific fixed effects. The model used is as follows.

$$(R/P)_{it} = (Y/P)_{it}^{\beta}.e^{\alpha+\gamma_j+\varepsilon_{ij}}$$

$$(E/P)_{it} = (Y/P)_{it}^{\xi}.e^{\phi+\psi_j+\upsilon_{ij}}$$

Where the variables are:

R =own revenue; E=revenue expenditure;

Y=GSDP; P=population.

The parameters are:

α, β, γ = constant, coefficient of per capita income and state-specific fixed effect respectively—all relevant for the own revenue function.

ϕ, ξ, ψ = constant, coefficient of per capita income and state-specific fixed effect respectively—all relevant for the revenue expenditure function.

The stochastic terms are: ε, υ in the two functions, respectively.

The subscripts i and t represent the state and time dimensions respectively.

After considerable experimentations, we find this simple two-equation model could sufficiently explain the variations in the state-wise fiscal gaps. We tried to include several other explanatory factors such as urbanisation, backwardness, poverty, literacy, level of infrastructure development, structure of GSDP etc., but the influence of most of these factors appear to be subsumed in the two primary grassroot factors, GSDP and population as indicated by their multicollinearity with these primary factors. For example, poverty, backwardness or infrastructure, are reflected in the level of per capita GSDP and therefore there is no need to include them.

An Illustration of the Method

In this section, an attempt is made to illustrate the method of: (i) determining the horizontal tax devolution shares; and (ii) derive fiscal responsibility targets for Indian states. To simplify the illustration, we make the following assumptions:

(i) The fiscal responsibility target is basically to achieve revenue deficit to GSDP ratio to be zero. The same logic can be applied for other parameters of fiscal responsibility, such as the fiscal deficit, and debt-GSDP ratio.

(ii) All revenue transfers are from the FC only and that the fiscal gap on revenue account of a state is the difference between its own revenue and its total revenue expenditure. Accordingly, we tried to identify the factors responsible for the variation in the own revenue and those in respect of the revenue expenditure.

(iii) The period for which the revenue shares and fiscal targets are to be determined is, 2010-2015 and the states are 28 in number.

The revenue share (average for five years, 2010-2015) of a state *i* would be

$$(R/P)_{it} = (Y/P)_{it}^{\beta}.e^{\alpha+\gamma_j+\varepsilon_{ij}} \quad (1)$$

$$(E/P)_{it} = (Y/P)_{it}^{\xi}.e^{\phi+\psi_j+\upsilon_{ij}} \quad (2)$$

$$\hat{s}_i = G_{it} / \sum_{i}^{N} G_{it} \quad (3)$$

$$RD_{it} = \hat{G}_{it} + \hat{s}_i T_t \quad (4)$$

$$(R/P)_{it} = (Y/P)_{it}^{0.836435638} . e^{-0.788152134 + \gamma_i} \quad (5)$$

$$(E/P)_{it} = (Y/P)_{it}^{0.892522968} . e^{-0.511111485 + \psi_i} \quad (6)$$

$$g_i = G_{it} / \sum_{i}^{N} G_{it} \quad (7)$$

The revenue deficit forecasts for each state would be

$$RD_{it} = G_{it} + s_i T_t \quad (8)$$

Where T_t represents the total transfers to the states, and g_i is the share of ith state. Given that the revenue deficits of each of the states derived from the above method are normative, the efforts of the states are called for containing the future revenue deficits first to be within that limit in the first stage, and second to reduce it further to zero. Thus for example, if a state's future revenue deficit is eight per cent and its normative revenue deficit is five per cent, the attempt of the state in the first stage should be to bring down the future revenue deficit from eight per cent to five per cent, and then further to bring down from five per cent to zero per cent.

As regards providing incentives for reduction of the deficit, the reduction of the actual deficit up to the normative level need not qualify for any incentive, while some incentive can be built for reducing the normative level of revenue deficit to the desired level of zero.

Empirical Illustration

The following results of the illustrative empirical exercise comprise the estimated own revenue and expenditure equations, the derived revenue shares, and the forecasts of the normative revenue deficits for each of the 28 states. The fiscal data used are culled out from the Reserve Bank of India (RBI) publications, the GSDP data from Ministry of Statistics and Programme Implementation (MoSPI) and population data from Census 2001 and Census 2011, Ministry of Home Affairs, Government of India (GoI).

$$(R/P)_{it} = (Y/P)_{it}^{0.836435638} .e^{-0.788152134+\gamma_i}$$

$$(E/P)_{it} = (Y/P)_{it}^{0.892522968} .e^{-0.511111485+\psi_i}$$

The detailed regression results are as in Annexure A-9.1.

It should be noted that as our aim is just to illustrate the methods described above, we have not paid sufficient attention to the validity of the empirical results and therefore cannot be depended upon. Considerable further efforts are needed in this respect by way of inclusion or exclusion of factors in the functions, choosing the right specification of the functions, obtaining robust results, as well as building other policy variables and policy conventions to obtain authentic results. State-wise illustrative shares of fiscal transfers derived from the model are given in Table 9.1.

Table 9.1

State-wise Share of Fiscal Transfers Recommended by 13th Finance Commission and Derived from the Model

	State	*Shares for Commission Period*	
		Recommended by the 13th Finance Commission	*Derived from Our Model*
1	Andhra Pradesh	6.94	7.16
2	Arunachal Pradesh	0.33	0.37
3	Assam	3.63	3.36
4	Bihar	10.92	7.74
5	Chhattisgarh	2.47	1.68
6	Goa	0.27	0.22
7	Gujarat	3.04	4.12
8	Haryana	1.05	1.65
9	Himachal Pradesh	0.78	1.06
10	Jammu and Kashmir	1.55	1.68
11	Jharkhand	2.80	3.18
12	Karnataka	4.33	4.07
13	Kerala	2.34	4.29
14	Madhya Pradesh	7.12	4.84
15	Maharashtra	5.20	6.63
16	Manipur	0.45	0.42
17	Meghalaya	0.41	0.35
18	Mizoram	0.27	0.35
19	Nagaland	0.31	0.43
20	Orissa	4.78	3.97
21	Punjab	1.39	3.20
22	Rajasthan	5.85	5.58
23	Sikkim	0.24	0.18
24	Tamil Nadu	4.97	4.95
25	Tripura	0.51	0.49
26	Uttaranchal	1.12	1.86
27	Uttar Pradesh	19.68	14.42
28	West Bengal	7.26	11.41

State-wise Illustrative Normative Pre- and Post-Devolution Revenue Gap/Deficit Forecast Derived from the Model

The normative pre-devolution revenue gap forecast for the year 2011 to 2015 derived from the model is shown in Table 9.2. As can be noted

Table 9.2

State-wise Projections of Pre-Devolution Revenue Gap for the Years 2011 to 2015: Derived from the Model

(in ₹ crore)

State	*2011*	*2012*	*2013*	*2014*	*2015*
Andhra Pradesh	-23,773	-26,669	-29,911	-33,540	-37,603
Arunachalpradesh	-2,857	-3,197	-3,577	-4,002	-4,478
Assam	-10,579	-11,501	-12,503	-13,592	-14,775
Bihar	-29,428	-32,666	-36,260	-40,248	-44,675
Chhattisgarh	-5,275	-5,955	-6,722	-7,586	-8,560
Goa	-776	-915	-1,078	-1,268	-1,489
Gujarat	-13,186	-14,998	-17,055	-19,386	-22,029
Haryana	-5,491	-6,281	-7,180	-8,202	-9,363
Himachal Pradesh	-7,282	-8,002	-8,794	-9,665	-10,620
Jammu & Kashmir	-11,668	-12,787	-14,013	-15,357	-16,830
Jharkhand	-9,773	-10,756	-11,837	-13,027	-14,336
Karnataka	-12,751	-14,349	-16,143	-18,153	-20,408
Kerala	-13,780	-15,330	-17,053	-18,968	-21,094
Madhya Pradesh	-15,989	-17,560	-19,285	-21,177	-23,254
Maharashtra	-21,227	-24,166	-27,496	-31,267	-35,538
Manipur	-2,789	-3,030	-3,293	-3,578	-3,888
Meghalaya	-2,546	-2,816	-3,114	-3,443	-3,808
Mizoram	-2,595	-2,844	-3,118	-3,418	-3,747
Nagaland	-3,058	-3,331	-3,627	-3,950	-4,302
Orissa	-13,235	-14,917	-16,810	-18,943	-21,345
Punjab	-10,284	-11,285	-12,381	-13,583	-14,900
Rajasthan	-18,563	-20,561	-22,773	-25,221	-27,931
Sikkim	-1,478	-1,701	-1,957	-2,251	-2,588
Tamil Nadu	-16,116	-18,198	-20,543	-23,181	-26,149
Tripura	-3,281	-3,557	-3,856	-4,181	-4,533
Uttar Pradesh	-48,107	-52,973	-58,328	-64,222	-70,709
Uttaranchal	-6,762	-7,741	-8,862	-10,144	-11,610
West Bengal	-37,963	-41,479	-45,319	-49,515	-54,098

from the table, all the states will be in revenue deficit for the period 2011 to 2015. Table 9.3 shows the state-wise post-devolution normative revenue deficit derived from the model. The post-devolution normative revenue deficit derived from the model indicates minimum revenue deficit the states can achieve given their efficiency level of fiscal management. If a

Table 9.3

State-wise Projections of Post-Devolution Revenue Deficit for the Years 2011-2015: Derived from the Model

(in ₹ crore)

State	*2011*	*2012*	*2013*	*2014*	*2015*
Andhra Pradesh	-9,198	-9,574	-9,881	-9,755	-9,547
Arunachal Pradesh	-2,114	-2,325	-2,556	-2,789	-3,048
Assam	-3,736	-3,475	-3,099	-2,425	-1,604
Bihar	-13,670	-14,183	-14,604	-14,533	-14,342
Chhattisgarh	-1,861	-1,951	-2,030	-2,015	-1,989
Goa	-329	-391	-464	-539	-629
Gujarat	-4,806	-5,171	-5,539	-5,712	-5,900
Haryana	-2,141	-2,352	-2,576	-2,735	-2,915
Himachal Pradesh	-5,133	-5,483	-5,842	-6,159	-6,485
Jammu and Kashmir	-8,243	-8,770	-9,307	-9,769	-10,238
Jharkhand	-3,299	-3,163	-2,940	-2,462	-1,874
Karnataka	-4,464	-4,630	-4,754	-4,630	-4,457
Kerala	-5,037	-5,076	-5,038	-4,700	-4,265
Madhya Pradesh	-6,140	-6,009	-5,750	-5,105	-4,296
Maharashtra	-7,739	-8,346	-8,959	-9,255	-9,573
Manipur	-1,934	-2,027	-2,118	-2,182	-2,242
Meghalaya	-1,843	-1,991	-2,148	-2,296	-2,455
Mizoram	-1,888	-2,015	-2,147	-2,265	-2,386
Nagaland	-2,175	-2,295	-2,414	-2,509	-2,602
Orissa	-5,145	-5,428	-5,692	-5,741	-5,772
Punjab	-3,764	-3,638	-3,421	-2,943	-2,349
Rajasthan	-7,196	-7,229	-7,152	-6,672	-6,050
Sikkim	-1,107	-1,266	-1,447	-1,645	-1,874
Tamil Nadu	-6,036	-6,376	-6,691	-6,732	-6,747
Tripura	-2,292	-2,397	-2,497	-2,567	-2,629
Uttar Pradesh	-18,744	-18,533	-17,976	-16,305	-14,188
Uttaranchal	-2,981	-3,307	-3,666	-3,974	-4,333
West Bengal	-14,725	-14,224	-13,386	-11,594	-9,368

particular state further improves its efficiency in revenue collection and revenue expenditure, then it would achieve higher revenue surplus or lower revenue deficit.

A Model for Determining the Fiscal Responsibility Mechanism

As regards the fiscal responsibility targeting, once we recognise that each state operates under different economic circumstances, it is not fair to specify uniform fiscal and revenue deficit targets for all states. Perhaps realising this, the latest FC accordingly recommended differential time deadlines to attain the fiscal deficit and revenue deficit targets, which in effect means differential targets. The only problem however is that the differentiation is purely intuitive and bears no relation to the fiscal efficiency indicators used for horizontal revenue sharing.

More prudent would be to specify the fiscal and revenue deficit targets for each state separately. Thus, if the FC believes that a set of factors are responsible for the variation in fiscal behaviour among the states, consistency requires that the same set of factors should be used to specify differential fiscal responsibility targets. In general, if certain factors are identified and used as guiding factors for determining the horizontal shares, there is no reason why some other set of factors should be used for specifying fiscal accountability targets. The FC while recommending the horizontal revenue shares can simultaneously derive the fiscal and revenue deficit targets for each state.

Issue of Target Fixation

We strongly believe that targets should differ from state to state because of differences in stage of development fiscal efficiency among the states. Therefore we emphasised that each state should be asked to attain its revenue deficit and fiscal deficit target. The past FCs did not pay much attention to this aspect. Both the TwFC and ThFC have prescribed a uniform target for all states. The ThFC although it recognised the need for a separate target for each state, however, has not carried the analysis to the logical end. They have simply prescribed different ranges for different groups of states on purely unintuitive basis.

Keeping in view this argument our endeavour of the study is to design state specific accountability target, to the extent permitted by the data. We could derive the state-wise revenue deficit/surplus target as shown in Table 9.4.

Table 9.4

State-wise Estimated Post-Devolution Revenue Deficit/Surplus as a Percentage of GSDP for the Year 2011-2015: Derived from the Model

State	*2011*	*2012*	*2013*	*2014*	*2015*
Andhra Pradesh	-1.67	-1.55	-1.43	-1.26	-1.10
Arunachal Pradesh	-26.42	-25.74	-25.06	-24.23	-23.44
Assam	-3.69	-3.14	-2.56	-1.84	-1.11
Bihar	-6.88	-6.38	-5.87	-5.22	-4.60
Chhattisgarh	-1.66	-1.54	-1.42	-1.25	-1.09
Goa	-0.97	-1.00	-1.02	-1.03	-1.04
Gujarat	-0.99	-0.94	-0.89	-0.81	-0.74
Haryana	-0.85	-0.83	-0.80	-0.76	-0.71
Himachal Pradesh	-9.88	-9.54	-9.19	-8.76	-8.34
Jammu & Kashmir	-15.50	-14.95	-14.38	-13.68	-13.00
Jharkhand	-3.10	-2.68	-2.25	-1.71	-1.17
Karnataka	-1.16	-1.07	-0.98	-0.86	-0.74
Kerala	-1.94	-1.76	-1.56	-1.31	-1.06
Madhya Pradesh	-2.46	-2.18	-1.90	-1.53	-1.17
Maharashtra	-0.76	-0.73	-0.69	-0.64	-0.58
Manipur	-21.25	-20.35	-19.42	-18.29	-17.16
Meghalaya	-12.52	-12.13	-11.75	-11.27	-10.81
Mizoram	-32.34	-31.24	-30.11	-28.75	-27.41
Nagaland	-19.25	-18.47	-17.67	-16.70	-15.75
Orissa	-2.77	-2.58	-2.39	-2.12	-1.88
Punjab	-1.71	-1.51	-1.29	-1.02	-0.74
Rajasthan	-2.46	-2.22	-1.98	-1.66	-1.36
Sikkim	-20.25	-20.07	-19.88	-19.60	-19.35
Tamil Nadu	-1.14	-1.07	-1.00	-0.89	-0.80
Tripura	-13.68	-13.10	-12.50	-11.77	-11.04
Uttar Pradesh	-3.25	-2.90	-2.54	-2.09	-1.64
Uttaranchal	-3.89	-3.74	-3.59	-3.37	-3.19
West Bengal	-3.30	-2.90	-2.48	-1.96	-1.44

Note: GSDP for the years 2011 to 2015 is extrapolated using exponential growth rate.

The ThFC has recommended those states to achieve zero revenue deficit by 2011-12 which reported zero revenue deficit or revenue surplus in 2007-08 and that the rest of the states should achieve the target of zero revenue deficit by 2014-15. States like Kerala, Punjab and West Bengal incurred a revenue deficit in the year 2007-08, therefore the ThFC has recommended revenue deficit correction path as shown in Table 9.5; while all the other states were asked to attain the target of zero revenue deficit by 2011-12. However, we are of the view that the revenue deficit targets recommended by the ThFC are difficult to attain by the states. This is because our normative assessment of revenue deficits is a reflection of state specific constraints on revenue collection and expenditure need. Therefore, it is difficult for those states to achieve zero revenue deficit targets by 2014-15 that have normative revenue deficit greater than zero (Table 9.4).

Such revenue deficit targets derived from above-mentioned method are the best target achievable by a particular state as these targets are derived from the model that takes into account state specific economic environment, fiscal capacity and therefore, these targets are the best we can expect from the states.

Table 9.5

Revenue Deficit Path Recommended by 13th Finance Commission

(Per cent of GSDP)

State	*2007-08*	*2011-12*	*2012-13*	*2013-14*	*2014-15*
Kerala	2.3	1.4	0.9	0.5	0.0
Punjab	2.9	1.8	1.2	0.6	0.0
West Bengal	2.7	1.6	1.1	0.5	0.0

Note: ThFC recommends all other states to attain target of zero revenue deficit by 2011-12.

Summary and Conclusion

Ever since India has embarked on fiscal accountability measures, the issue has been to objectively prescribe the quantitative limits for fiscal and revenue deficits, and debt-GSDP ratio as also prescribing the roadmap for attaining the target limits. The TwFC prescribed more or less uniform limits for all the states. Later the ThFC realised that prescribing uniform limits for all the states is not appropriate as states differ in their potential fiscal capacity and the resultant behaviour. Accordingly, the ThFC came out with differential time deadlines for achieving the fiscal deficit and revenue deficit limits for different categories of states. However, the degree of differentiation does not seem good enough.

Integrated Approach

In our proposed integrated approach, we have dealt with the issue of fiscal transfers and fiscal accountability targets simultaneously from the same model. Firstly, we derived state specific shares in fiscal transfers from the model that takes into account fiscal capacity and expenditure needs of a particular state. Secondly, we derived state specific revenue deficit targets from the same model. The revenue deficit of the states derived from the model is that level of revenue deficit which reflects state specific revenue rising capacity and expenditure needs and therefore, it is difficult for a particular state to reduce it further. Therefore, these normatively accessed state specific revenue deficits should be used as the fiscal accountability target.

The Fiscal Accountability Targets

This paper argues that ideally, the fiscal targets (the fiscal and revenue deficits and the debt-GDP ratio) need to be state-specific as the fiscal behaviour of each state is conditioned by factors such as its own economic environment and fiscal capacity. There is also a need to derive the state-specific limits more objectively. The task of prescribing state-specific fiscal targets is similar to the task of determination of state-specific horizontal revenue shares among the states. The primary objective of FC transfers to a state is to reduce its fiscal gap (own revenue–expenditure). The primary objective of the fiscal responsibility act is to reduce the fiscal deficit (revenue deficit and debt–GSDP ratio). Given the commonality in the objectives, it is only proper that the criteria should be more or less the same. The suitable strategy appears to be first identifying the factors responsible for the existing fiscal gap across the states. If the revenue sharing is linked to the factors that influence the fiscal gap, then such a mechanism will also be conducive to achieving the fiscal responsibility targets.

The fiscal accountability indicators are basically derived from the revenue sharing model suggested by Sarma (1997). As shown there, such a model has several advantages over the conventional intuitive formula-based determination of the horizontal shares. The transfer shares are determined on the basis of rational fiscal behavioural framework keeping in view the basic motivations of the federating units for coming together. The criteria and the weights for horizontal distribution of transfers are derived from factors responsible for variations in the basic NMBF and not imposed from outside as has been the case so far. Deriving the state-specific fiscal accountability targets using such a model is preferable.

References

Breton, A. (1965). "A Theory of Government Grants", *Canadian Journal of Economic and Political Science* 31(2).

Gramlich, E.M. (1977). "Intergovernmental Grants: A Review of Exmpirical Literature", in W. E. Dates, *The Political Economy of Fiscal Federalism*. Lexington, Mass.: Lexington Books.

Rao, M.G. and R.J. Chelliah (1991). *Survey of Research on Fiscal Federalism in India*. New Delhi: National Institute of Public Finance and Policy.

Sarma, J.V.M. (1997). "Federal Fiscal Relations in India: The Issue of Horizontal Transfers", *Economic & Political Weekly* 1719-23.

Annexure Table A-9.1

Detailed Estimates of the Revenue and Expenditure Functions

	Dependent Variable: LOG(OWNREV/POPN) Method: Pooled Least Squares Date: 07/26/13 Time:19:27 Sample: 2006 2010 Included observations: 5 Cross-sections included: 28 Total pool (balanced) observations: 140			Dependent Variable: LOG(OWNREV/POPN) Method: Pooled Least Squares Date: 07/26/13 Time:19:27 Sample: 2006 2010 Included observations: 5 Cross-sections included: 28 Total pool (balanced) observations: 140		
	Variable	*Coefficient*	*Std. Error*	*Variable*	*Coefficient*	*Std. Error*
	C	-0.788152134	0.603113104	C	-0.511111485	0.34606385
	LOG(GSDP/POPN) Fixed Effects (Cross)	0.836435638	0.057077373	LOG(GSDP/POPN) Fixed Effects (Cross)	0.892522968	0.032750765
Fixed Effects (Cross)						
1 Andhra Pradesh	_AP–C	0.193265026		_AP–C	-0.313065839	
2 Arunachal Pradesh	_AR–C	0.299007296		_AR–C	0.911193665	
3 Assam	_AM–C	-0.081077746		_AM–C	-0.0881171691	
4 Bihar	_BH–C	-0.654628969		_BH–C	-0.062814226	
5 Chhattisgarh	_CH–C	0.150514096		_CH–C	-0.312832884	
6 Goa	_GO–C	0.642210975		_GO–C	-0.146463574	
7 Gujarat	_GJ–C	0.036969646		_GJ–C	-0.561469284	
8 Haryana	_HY–C	0.25653054		_HY–C	-0.446955623	
9 Himachal Pradesh	_HP–C	0.214739026		_HP–C	0.248476103	
10 Jammu & Kashmir	_JK–C	0.017353777		_JK–C	0.453617933	
11 Jharkhand	_JH–C	-0.170299327		_JH–C	-0.193791041	
12 Karnataka	_KN–C	0.318788632		_KN–C	-0.299050951	

contd...

...contd...

	Dependent Variable: LOG(OWNREV/POPN) Method: Pooled Least Squares Date: 07/26/13 Time:19:27 Sample: 2006 2010 Included observations: 5 Cross-sections included: 28 Total pool (balanced) observations: 140			Dependent Variable: LOG(OWNREV/POPN) Method: Pooled Least Squares Date: 07/26/13 Time:19:27 Sample: 2006 2010 Included observations: 5 Cross-sections included: 28 Total pool (balanced) observations: 140		
	Variable	*Coefficient*	*Std. Error*	*Variable*	*Coefficient*	*Std. Error*
	C	-0.788152134	0.603113104	C	-0.511111485	0.34606385
	LOG(GSDP/POPN) Fixed Effects (Cross)	0.836435638	0.057077373	LOG(GSDP/POPN) Fixed Effects (Cross)	0.892522968	0.032750765
13 Kerala	_KR–C	0.08602547		_KR–C	-0.3057552	
14 Madhya Pradesh	_MP–C	0.058700437		_MP–C	-0.254483204	
15 Maharashtra	_MH–C	0.101035559		_MH–C	-0.578092482	
16 Manipur	_MN–C	-0.623755646		_MN–C	0.583210604	
17 Meghalaya	_MG–C	-0.407795		_MG–C	0.179283893	
18 Mizoram	_MZ–C	-0.390155535		_MZ–C	0.980674567	
19 Nagaland	_NG–C	-0.94275493		_NG–C	0.484966301	
20 Orissa	_OR–C	-0.089396756		_OR–C	-0.279948259	
21 Punjab	_PJ–C	0.291957387		_PJ–C	-0.221401062	
22 Rajasthan	_RJ–C	0.013692876		_RJ–C	-0.280593083	
23 Sikkim	_SK–C	1.808792816		_SK–C	1.380190716	
24 Tamil Nadu	_TN–C	0.215448703		_TN–C	-0.400417287	
25 Tripura	_TR–C	-0.701558192		_TR–C	0.215033059	
26 Uttaranchal	_UL–C	-0.069473794		_UL–C	-0.1408432	
27 Uttar Pradesh	_UP–C	-0.084268995		_UP–C	-0.209931372	
28 West Bengal	_WB–C	-0.48990287		_WB–C	-0.347566578	

contd...

...contd...

Effects Specification *Cross-section fixed (dummy variables)*			*Effects Specification* *Cross-section fixed (dummy variables)*		
R-squared	0.976319905		R-squared	0.987907616	
Adjusted R-squared	0.970346547		Adjusted R-squared	0.984857285	
S.E. of regression	0.135507939		S.E. of regression	0.077753905	
Sum squared resid	2.038226565		Sum squared resid	0.67106934	
Log likelihood	97.41796801		Log likelihood	175.1853716	
F-statistic	163.4457557		F-statistic	323.8689796	
Prob (F-statistic)	1.54E-77		Prob (F-statistic)	1.13E-93	
Mean dependent var		8.048525298	Mean dependent var		8.918110808
S.D. dependent var		0.786913701	S.D. dependent var		0.631859231
Akaike info criterion		-0.977399543	Akaike info criterion		-2.088362451
Schwarz criterion		-0.368059327	Schwarz criterion		-1.479022235
Hannan-Quinn criterion		-0.729781904	Hannan-Quinn criterion		-1.840744811
Durbin-Watson stat		1.344107513	Durbin-Watson stat		1.31529012

Annexure Table A-9.2

State-wise Share of Fiscal Transfers: Derived from the Model

(in ₹ crore)

State	*2011*	*2012*	*2013*	*2014*	*2015*
Andhra Pradesh	14,575	17,095	20,030	23,785	28,056
Arunachal Pradesh	743	872	1,021	1,213	1,430
Assam	6,843	8,026	9,404	11,167	13,172
Bihar	15,758	18,483	21,656	25,716	30,333
Chhattisgarh	3,414	4,004	4,691	5,571	6,571
Goa	447	524	614	729	860
Gujarat	8,379	9,828	11,515	13,674	16,129
Haryana	3,350	3,929	4,604	5,467	6,449
Himachal Pradesh	2,148	2,520	2,952	3,506	4,135
Jammu & Kashmir	3,425	4,017	4,706	5,589	6,592
Jharkhand	6,474	7,593	8,897	10,565	12,462
Karnataka	8,287	9,719	11,388	13,523	15,951
Kerala	8,743	10,255	12,015	14,268	16,830
Madhya Pradesh	9,849	11,552	13,535	16,073	18,959
Maharashtra	13,489	15,821	18,537	22,012	25,964
Manipur	855	1,003	1,175	1,395	1,646
Meghalaya	703	824	966	1,147	1,353
Mizoram	707	829	971	1,153	1,361
Nagaland	883	1,036	1,214	1,441	1,700
Orissa	8,090	9,489	11,118	13,202	15,573
Punjab	6,520	7,647	8,960	10,640	12,550
Rajasthan	11,367	13,332	15,621	18,549	21,880
Sikkim	371	435	510	606	714
Tamil Nadu	10,080	11,822	13,852	16,449	19,402
Tripura	989	1,160	1,359	1,614	1,903
Uttar Pradesh	29,363	34,440	40,353	47,918	56,522
Uttaranchal	3,780	4,434	5,195	6,169	7,277
West Bengal	23,237	27,255	31,934	37,921	44,730

Section III: State Finances: Specific Issues

10 Fiscal Transfers to Andhra Pradesh in the Post-Fiscal Reform Period of the State

R. Sudarsana Rao and
G. Pavan Kumar

Introduction

Andhra Pradesh (AP) is one of the major states considered as a NSC (non-special category) state for providing central assistance for plan purposes. It has been receiving fiscal transfers both by the Finance Commission (FC) and Planning Commission. The fiscal transfers to AP have increased from ₹ 7 crore during 1956-57 to ₹ 34,067 crore in 2011-12. Besides substantial growth of fiscal transfers from Centre to AP, the size, nature and criteria of fiscal transfers from Centre to states have undergone substantial changes in the last few decades. AP has launched fiscal reforms since 1995-96. During the reform period a Medium-Term Fiscal Framework (MTFF) covering the period 2001-2006 was prepared. Therefore, the state was covered by Fiscal Reform Facility (FRF) as recommended by the 11th Finance Commission (EFC). Within the framework of fiscal reforms the state has undertaken a number of measures relating to revenue mobilisation, expenditure restructuring, debt and deficits and several sectoral reforms with a view to achieve the set goals. All these initiatives have their own impact on state finances. As central fiscal transfers are an important component of state finances, an attempt is made to analyse the growth of fiscal transfers and their bearing on state finances of AP. Moreover, the Twelfth Five Year Plan was launched from 1 April 2012 and the 14th Finance Commission (FFC) was constituted in 2013. Therefore, it is pertinent to make an attempt to analyse various aspects of central fiscal transfers to AP during 1995-96 to 2011-12.

Objectives

Following are the specific objectives of the paper:

(i) To make an analysis of FC transfers to AP during 1995-96 to 2011-12.

(ii) To study various types of plan transfers from the centre to AP.

(iii) To examine the trends in fiscal dependence of the state on fiscal transfers in the post-fiscal reform period.

Methodology and Data Sources

The paper is based on secondary sources of data and information and pertains to the period 1995-96 to 2011-12. The chosen period covers the post reform period and EFC (2002-03 to 2004-05), the 12th Finance Commission (TwFC) (2005-06 to 2009-10) and first two years of the 13th Finance Commission (ThFC) (2010-11 to 2011-12).

Required data and information have been obtained from various *Reports of the Union Finance Commission*, *Socio-Economic Survey* and *Budget Documents*, Government of Andhra Pradesh (GoAP), documents of Planning Commission and publications of Reserve Bank of India (RBI) such as *Annual Reports on the Study of State Finances* and *Monthly Bulletins*. Simple statistical tools like percentages, exponential growth rates, trend lines and bar diagrams have been used to analyse various aspects of fiscal transfers. The GSDP (gross state domestic product) data of Revised (RE), Provisional (PE), Quick (QE) and Advance Estimates (AE) have been used for the years 2007-08, 2008-09, 2009-2010 and 2010-11 respectively. With regard to fiscal variables, RE for 2011-12 have been used.

The paper presents an analysis of FC transfers and deals with an analysis relating to central plan assistance to State Plan Schemes and Centrally Sponsored Schemes (CSS). Finally, trends in fiscal dependence of the state and important conclusions are presented.

Fiscal Transfers to Andhra Pradesh

Like any other state in the Indian federation, AP also has been receiving shared tax revenue, grants-in-aid and loans for plan and non-plan purposes through the FC, Planning Commission and from different Union ministries during the period under reference. What follows is an analysis of the nature and growth of fiscal transfers to AP during 1995-96 to 2011-12. A critical analysis of the FC transfers to AP is presented followed by plan transfers during the chosen period.

Finance Commission Transfers

The 10th Fiance Commission (TFC) was constituted in June 1992 and submitted its report in November 1994. The Commission made a remarkable departure by recommending an alternative scheme of devolution along with the traditional scheme of devolution.

The Commission recommended that the share of states in the gross receipts of central taxes except taxes and duties referred to in Articles 268 and 269, surcharges and cesses shall be 26 per cent and another 3 per cent in the gross tax receipts of the Centre in lieu of Additional Excise Duties (AED) to those states which do not levy Sales Tax on the three commodities of textiles, tobacco and sugar. This recommendation has been accepted by changing the word, 'gross receipts as net receipts' and subsequently made a Constitutional Amendment. This is a recommendation which has solved several irritants between the centre and states.

The EFC was constituted in July 1998 and submitted its report in June 2000. The Commission, while taking stock of the deteriorating financial situation of the states and the centre, observed that both the centre and states were struggling with fiscal problems like rising revenue and fiscal deficits, mounting debt and interest burden, declining tax-GDP and GSDP ratios at the centre and states respectively. Taking into consideration the resource position and the needs of the centre as well as the states, it increased the percentage of tax devolution to 28 per cent of the net proceeds of all taxes and duties of the Union government, except the taxes and duties referred to in Articles 268 and 269 the surcharges and cesses for each of the five years. It also recommended that 1.5 per cent of all shareable Union taxes and duties in lieu of the erstwhile AED. Hence, the states' total tax share effectively comes to 29.5 per cent of the net proceeds of all shareable central taxes and duties. As AP government has not imposed Sales Tax on the three commodities, it was entitled to 29.5 per cent share. The TwFC has increased this share by one percentage point by fixing it at 30.5. The Commission has treated the AED in lieu of Sales Tax on textiles, tobacco and sugar as part of the general pool of central taxes. The TwFC has not accepted the suggestion of the Government of AP for a further hike in the aggregate share of states. However, it has increased the indicative ceiling on overall central revenue transfers from 37.5 per cent as fixed by the EFC to 38 per cent. The states' share has been further raised to 32 per cent by the ThFC. Though the aggregate states' share in central taxes and duties has been increased by the successive Finance Commissions, the share in central tax revenue of AP has been declining from EFC onwards.

Table 10.1

Share in Central Taxes to Andhra Pradesh

Item/Finance Commission	*TFC 1995-2000*	*EFC 2000-2005*	*TwFC 2005-2010*	*ThFC 2010-2012*
Percentage of Tax Share to All States from the Union Taxes	28.0	29.5	30.5	32.0
Andhra Pradesh Share in the Total Shared Tax Revenue	7.910	7.701 (-0.209)	7.356 (-0.345)	6.937 (-0.419)

Source: Reports of the Union Finance Commission (UFC), GoI.

It may be seen in Table 10.1 that the share in central tax revenue as recommended by the EFC is 7.701 which has declined by 0.209 per cent compared to the TFC.[1] It has further declined to 7.356 and 6.937 during TwFC and ThFC. The decline in the states share is by 0.345 percentages between EFC and ThFC while the decline is 0.419 between the TwFC and ThFC. It is also pertinent to note that the decline in percentage of AP tax share is increasing, causing a reduction in the tax devolution from the divisible pool. This is mainly due to the criteria evolved, factors incorporated and the weights given by successive FCs for *inter se* distribution.

1. Report of the Finance Commission, December 1994, GoI.

Criteria for inter se Distribution

Successive FC have been suggesting different criteria and also have been tinkering with the weights given to different factors. Table 10.2 shows the criteria and weights given to different factors by different FCs. Recognising that population is a basic indicator of need for the provision of goods and services and ensures equal per capita fiscal transfers, the weightage given to this factor has been reduced by the EFC to 10 per cent from the existing 20 per cent as recommended by the TFC. Similarly the weightage given to tax effort has been reduced from the 10 per cent to 5 per cent by the EFC. Also, it has increased the weightage given to income distance to 62.5 per cent from the existing 60 per cent. All these changes in the weights given to the above factors caused a decline in the relative share of AP during the EFC period.

Table 10.2

Criteria and Weights Adopted by Finance Commissions

(%)

	Finance Commission			
Criteria/Weights	*TFC*	*EFC*	*TwFC*	*ThFC*
Population	20	10	25	25
Income Distance	60	62.5	50	
Area	5	7.5	10	10
Tax Effort	10	5.0	7.5	
Fiscal Discipline		7.5	7.5	17.5
Fiscal Capacity Distance				47.5
Index of Infrastructure	5	7.5		
Total	100	100	100	100

Source: Reports of the UFC, GoI.

The share of AP in the share of central taxes has further declined to 7.356 per cent as recommended by the TwFC from 7.701 per cent of EFC registering a decline of 0.345 per cent in between the two Commissions as shown in Table 10.1. This is again due to the changes effected by the Commission with regard to income and other factors. Though the increase in the weightage given to population, area and tax effort are in favor of the state, the upper ceiling imposed with regard to area factor reduced the relative share of AP.

The ThFC which was appointed in November 2007 under the chairmanship of Dr Vijay Kelkar submitted its recommendations in December 2009 which have become effective from April 2010 to March 2015. The ThFC has used four indicators—population, area, index of fiscal discipline and (FCD) fiscal capacity distance—in its horizontal distribution formula. While it has retained the same weightage to population (25%) and geographical area (10%) as given in the TFC, it has increased the weightage given to fiscal discipline factor from the existing 7.5 per cent to 17.5 per cent and introduced a new factor FCD with a weightage of 47.5 per cent in the place of income factor. The FCD factor benchmarks the states according to their respective tax capacities with a prescriptive tax effort. The Commission has worked out the average tax-GSDP ratios separately for each and every state in the general category as well as special category. Also, it has calculated the group-specific average of tax-GSDP ratio to obtain the potential tax effort of the state concerned. This has been used to estimate the per capita fiscal capacity at comparable levels of taxation. The fiscal distance of each state has been computed by the distance of its estimated per capita revenue from that of Haryana. Then the ThFC has estimated the per capita revenue entitlement of each state on the basis of its fiscal distance (Chakraborty, 2010). AP would have fared better in its tax share entitlement had the ThFC given higher weightage to population (30%) and area (15%) as suggested by it in its memorandum[2] as the state is the fifth largest in population among all the states in the country. Also, the state would have got higher tax share, had the ThFC taken the original share of geographical area (8.395) instead of the adjusted share (7.134). However, the average devolution as percentage of GSDP has increased slightly from 2.80 to 3.34 registering an increase of 0.54 per cent.[3] This percentage increase of the state is more when compared with the other southern middle income states of Karnataka (0.48), Kerala (0.19) and Tamil Nadu (0.51).

2. Report of the Finance Commission, 2009, Vol.II, Annexure, p.401.
3. Ibid., Vol.I, p.123.

Grants-in-Aid

The FC is required to make recommendations and the principles that should govern grants-in-aid of revenues of states out of the Consolidated Fund of India (CFI). It also recommends the sums to be paid to states which are in need of revenues under Article 275 of the Constitution, for purposes other than those specified in the provisos to clause (1) of that Article. Using these provisions successive FC recommended grants-in-aid for non-plan purposes (except the 3rd and 9th Finance Commissions) like revenue deficit grants, and grants for up-gradation of essential social and administrative services. The quantum as well as the types of grants varied across successive FCs. The size of the grants has increased over successive FCs though the increase is not consistent. For instance, they vary from 7.7 per cent of the total transfers under the 7th FC, 26.1 per cent under the 6th Commission and 6.65 per cent and 8.48 per cent under 8th and 9th Commissions, respectively.[4] Figure 10.1 shows the relative size of grants and shared tax revenue in the total transfers to AP recommended by the TFC, EFC, TwFC and ThFC.

The credit goes to the TFC which recommended for the first time in the history of fiscal federalism in India grants-in-aid for local bodies consequent upon the 73rd and 74th amendments of the Constitution besides other types of grants. It has recommended a total amount of ₹ 21,750 crore for the five year period and ₹ 483 crore and ₹ 203 crore as revenue deficit grants to Andhra Pradesh during 1995-96 and 1996-97 respectively.[5]

The EFC recommended an amount of ₹ 58,587 crore to all the states of which AP got an amount of ₹ 2,031 crore. As the state has been assessed to have revenue surplus on its non-plan revenue account, it was not eligible to get any non-plan revenue deficit grants. However, it is surprising that relatively richer states like Punjab and West Bengal were awarded deficit grants though AP was not eligible for such grants. Besides these grants, the FC awarded grants for other purposes like upgradation and special problems, local bodies and calamity relief expenditure etc. The Government

4. Report of the Finance Commission, 2009. Vol.I ch.12, p.203 and Vol.II, Annexure 4.1 p.375.
5. Report of the Finance Commission, 1994, *op.cit.* no.1.

Figure 10.1

Shared Tax Revenue and Grants-in-Aid of Andhra Pradesh

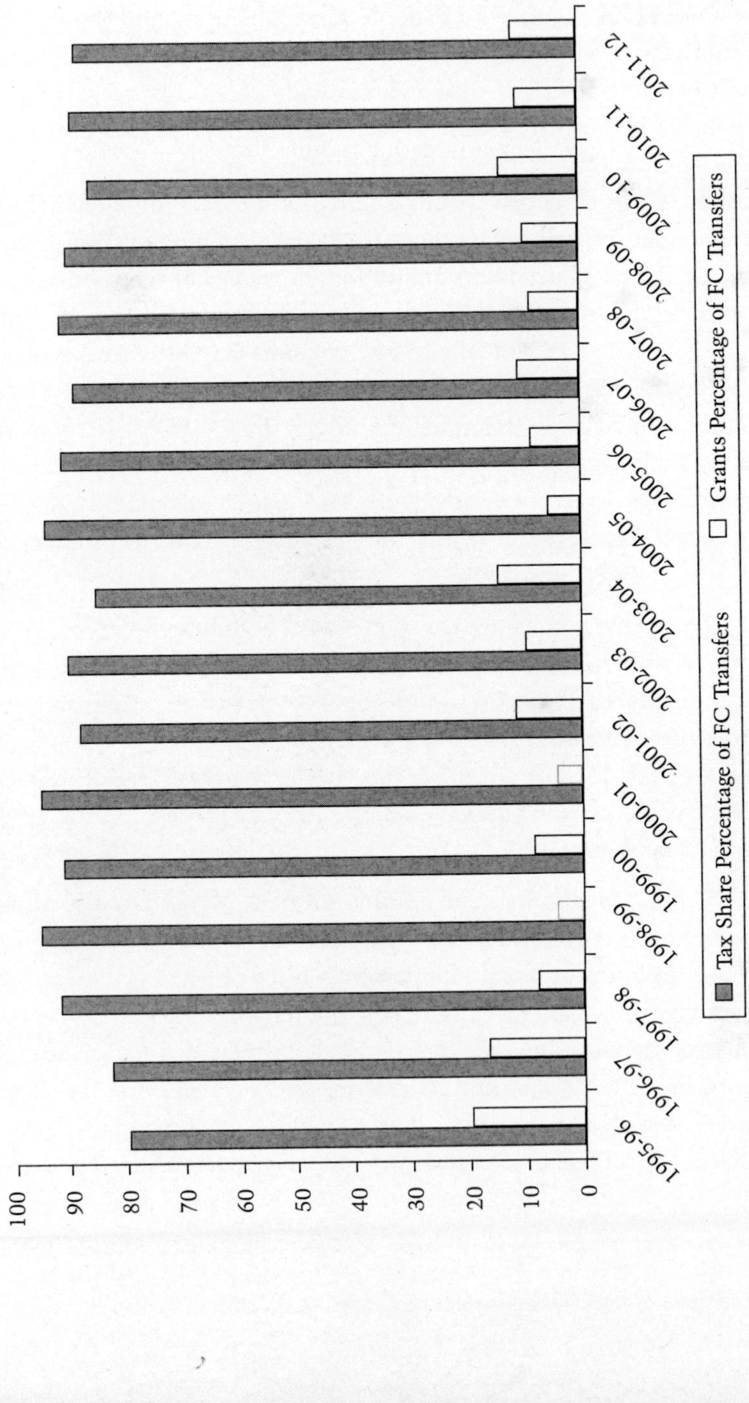

Source: Government of Andhra Pradesh, *Socio-Economic Survey*, various issues.

of AP got ₹ 285.23 crore for upgrading the essential public services and for special problems of the state. It has recommended an amount of ₹ 760.24 crore to panchayati raj institutions (PRIs) and ₹ 164.6 crore for Municipal governments for the five year period 2000-05. Further, it recommended ₹ 820.80 crore to the state to meet the relief expenditure that arises due to natural calamities. It is interesting to note that the state obtained only 3.47 per cent of the total grants-in-aid awarded to all the states.

The TwFC followed a normative basis encompassing both the revenue and expenditure heads taking 2003-04 as the base year. Taking adequate care to improve the tax-GDP and tax-GSDP ratios of the centre and states respectively, it recommended both general (unconditional) and conditional grants. While awarding the conditional grants care was taken to see that the gap pertained only to the deficiency in fiscal capacity and not due to other factors or priorities (Sarma, 2008).

The commission recommended a total amount of ₹ 142,640 crore for the five year period of which ₹ 56,856 crore were grants for filling the non-plan revenue gap of Kerala, Orissa (2005-06), Punjab (3 years) and West Bengal (2 years) besides the special category and newly formed states. AP was not eligible to get these grants having a surplus of ₹ 37,779.30 crore during 2005-2010 on its non-plan revenue account. Besides these grants, the TwFC recommended an amount of ₹ 15,000 crore for maintenance of roads and bridges, ₹ 5,000 crore for maintenance of public buildings, ₹ 1,000 crore for maintenance of forests and ₹ 625 crore for heritage conservation. It also recommended conditional grants to health (₹ 5,887 crore) and education sectors (₹ 10,172 crore).

AP has been awarded only 3.66 per cent in the total grants-in-aid to all states. This is mainly due to non-eligibility of the state for revenue-gap grants and for education and health. TwFC recommended an amount of ₹ 10,172 crore to eight states—Assam, Bihar, Jharkhand, Madhya Pradesh, Orissa, Rajasthan, Uttar Pradesh, and West Bengal for the development of education and seven states—Assam, Bihar, Jharkhand, Madhya Pradesh, Orissa, Rajasthan and Uttar Pradesh, for the development of health. AP did not receive upgradation grants for these two important social services though the rank of AP in Human Development Index (HDI) had declined from 9th to 10th between 1991 and 2001. Similarly the rank of AP in the HDI regarding health sector also declined from 11th to 12th.

The Commission has taken per capita expenditure on education and health of the states and recommended grants to states which have fallen below the national average. Had it considered the physical indicators like literacy levels and health indicators, AP would have got grants-in-aid under this head. For instance, the literacy level of AP (61.11% in 2011) is less than some of the states like Assam (64.28%), Madhya Pradesh (64.11%) Orissa (63.61%) and West Bengal (69.22%). Of course, all these states are relatively backward states compared to AP.

Regarding grants for relief expenditure, the Commission followed more or less the methodology adopted by its immediate predecessors. In spite of the requests made by some states including AP, it has not made any changes either in the method of determining the size of the Calamity Relief Fund (CRF), or its composition of sharing between the centre and states. In fact this demand of states merits consideration in view of the hiatus between the central grant and the actual expenditure for calamity relief operations. For instance, the central grant, accounts for less than 50 per cent of actual expenditure incurred by AP during the period 2000-01 to 2004-05 (Rao *et al.*, 2008). This suggests a change in the criteria adopted by the FC in determining the size of CRF as well as an increase in the grant component. AP along with Punjab, Uttar Pradesh and Himachal Pradesh urged for an increase of CRF at least by 10 per cent per annum and for a reduction of states share by 10 per cent to the CRF. Neither of the suggestions has been accepted by the Commission. It would be better if Commissions considered physical factors like length of coastal line, rainfall etc., and proneness to calamities instead of average expenditure on calamity relief in the preceding years.

The ThFC has recommended 10 broad types of grants-in-aid surpassing its predecessors with regard to the coverage and conditionality of grants-in-aid following more or less, the same approach of the past FC. Considering grants-in-aid as an important instrument, the Commission has made the whole scheme of transfers by using grants to correct the cost disabilities faced by many states. Accordingly it recommended an amount of ₹ 318,581 crore as grants-in-aid constituting 18.03 per cent in the total transfers for a variety of purposes, like non-plan deficit grants, local bodies, disaster relief, up-gradation of services etc., for the period 2010-11 to 2014-15.

Besides grants-in-aid to local bodies, disaster relief, revenue gap grants, grants for upgradation of services, protection of environment, it has recommended ₹ 27,945 crore for implementation of state-specific needs and an amount of ₹ 50,000 crore for implementation of the impending model goods and services tax (GST). Especially making grants for improving outputs and outcomes, to increase the public expenditure efficiency and the attempts, though modest, to incentivise performance for better governance and delivery of public services is a good beginning. Similarly making the grants 'forward looking and linking them with the attainment of goals' with regard to purposes like renewable energy, water sector management and reduction of infant mortality is appreciable. Of course, the large scale use of grants for a variety of purposes, the conditionality imposed, the inadequacy of monitoring mechanism for several purposes of grants-in-aid have been criticised (Rao, 2010). But it is pertinent to note that the award of the specific purpose grants by the Commission is quite in conformity with the constitutional propriety of the UFC and absence of conditions does lead to substitution or diversion effects as the past experience shows. Of the total grants-in-aid, AP has been recommended an amount of ₹ 13,532 crore (excluding the grants relating to GST implementation, IMR [infant mortality rate] and renewable energy) constituting 5.23 per cent in the total grants given to all the states. This is much higher than that of its immediate predecessors. The state has been awarded grants-in-aid of all types except the post devolution non-plan revenue deficit grants and grants for performance incentive.

The Commission has awarded about eight per cent of the total grant amount awarded to local bodies and disaster relief to AP, besides grants for upgradation and improving of services and for environmental protection. An amount of ₹ 1,270 crore has been awarded to state specific needs like provision of drinking water in the rural areas (₹ 550 crore), SBS (Seed Bank Scheme) (₹ 100 crore), police training (₹ 113 crore), construction of prisons (₹ 90 crore), development of culture (₹ 60 crore), fire and emergency services (₹ 17 crore), heritage conservation (₹ 100 crore), establishments of primary health centers

(₹ 200 crore), strengthening the pollution control board and establishment of a centre for innovations in public systems (₹ 20 crore each). This shows the coverage and improvement of the public services, their delivery mechanisms and governance.

Figure 10.2 reveals the increasing role of grants-in-aid in the total transfers made by the FCs both at the All-India level as well as in the case of AP. For instance the proportion of grants-in-aid in the total transfers of FC has increased since the TFC onwards though there is a marginal decline during the ThFC. The proportion of grants-in-aid in the total FC transfers for AP has declined during the EFC compared to TFC but since than they are on the increase. Though considerable increase in the quantam of grants-in-aid is found during the period of ThFC, it has not recommended grants to AP under the category of specific purposes like coastal area development (in view of its long coast line of about 1000 kms) and for the development of tourism in view of the state's large potential for eco-tourism and temple tourism.

Transfers through the Planning Commission

The Government of India constituted the Planning Commission, a non-statutory body, in March 1950, by an executive order. Though originally aimed to formulate and evaluate the Five Year Plans for economic development, the Planning Commission transferred fiscal resources under Article 282 of the Constitution by providing grants and loans in the form of central assistance for State Plan Schemes. In fact, the overwhelming influence of the Planning Commission in the sphere of centre-state financial relations has downgraded the FCs role in the process of fiscal adjustment (Rao, 1999). The Planning Commission provides financial resources in the form of grants and loans to State Plan Schemes, Centrally Sponsored Schemes (CSS), Central Sector Schemes, Additional Central Assistance and Externally Aided Projects (EAP). Figure 10.3 shows the amount of grants recommended by the Planning Commission besides the loan component

Figure 10.2

Statutory Grants in Finance Commission Transfers

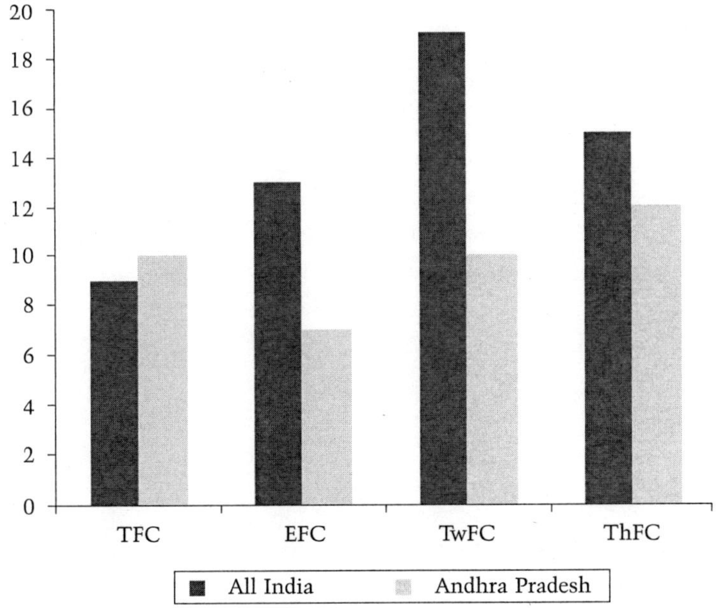

Source: Government of Andhra Pradesh, *Socio-Economic Survey*, various issues.

It may be noted that the plan grants are considerable in size in comparison with other forms of grants. AP being a major state under the general category has been provided loans and grants for all the above mentioned plan programmes during the last 11 Five Year Plans. What follows is an analysis of fiscal transfers for plan purposes from Centre to AP during the period 1995-96 to 2011-12.

Gadgil-Mukherjee Formula

(i) Set apart funds required for EAP from the total central assistance.

(ii) Provide reasonable amounts for special area programmes such as hill areas, tribal areas, border areas, NEC (North Eastern Council) and other programmes.

(iii) Thirty per cent for the special category states from the balance.

(iv) Balance amount to be distributed among the non-special category states as per the following criteria and weights.

Figure 10.3

Different Types of Grant-in-Aid to Andhra Pradesh

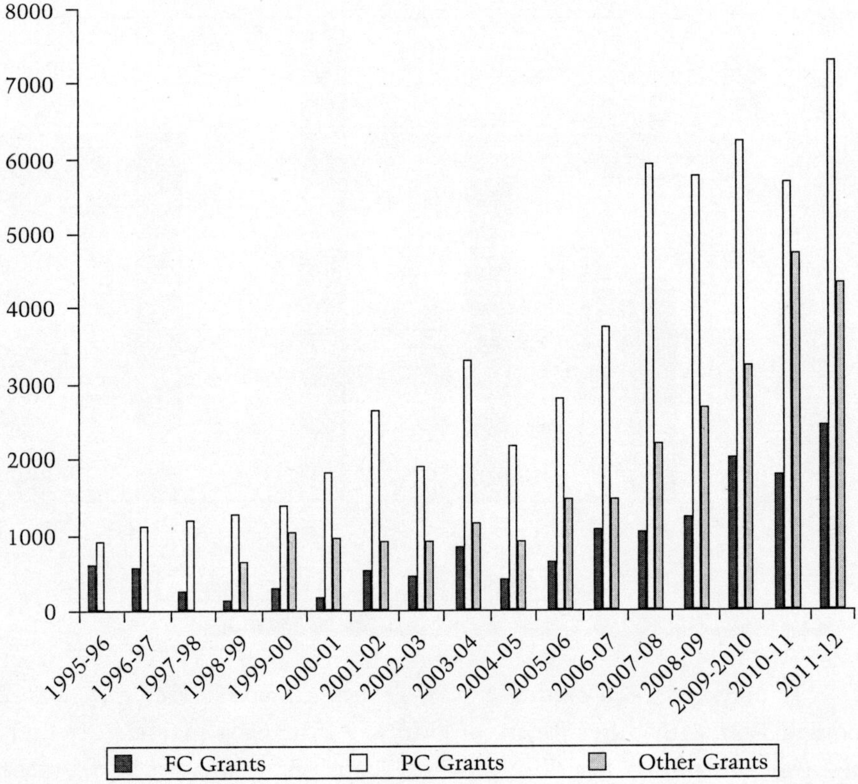

Table 10.3

Types of Grants-in-a-Aid

Sl.No	*Criteria*	*Weights %*
1	Population (1971)	60
2	Per Capita Income	
	(a) Deviation Method 20%	
	(b) Distance Method 5%	25
3	Performance	
	(a) Tax Effort	
	(b) Fiscal Management	
	(c) Progress in Respect of National Objectives	7.5
4	Special Problems	7.5

Source: Department of Planning, Govt. of A.P.

The GoAP received central assistance for state plan schemes during 1995-96 to 2011-12 under the Gadgil-Mukherjee (G-M) formula as detailed above. The Planning Commission transferred ₹ 1,308 crore in 1995-96 which increased to ₹ 8,328 crore in 2011-12 (RE). During 2002-03, ₹ 1,612 crore was provided under normal plan assistance using G-M formula, which increased to ₹ 5,775 crore during 2011-12 (RE). It may be noted that the loan component of the normal plan assistance has been discontinued on the basis of the recommendations of the TwFC since 2005-06. The TwFC recommended "that the system of imposing a 70:30 between loans and grants for extending plan assistance to general category states should be done away with."[6] Subsequently the Planning Commission is confined to extend plan grants and the states have been given the liberty to decide how much and from whom they would like to borrow.

This important change is expected to ensure greater fiscal discipline and also removes the structural obligation to borrow from the Centre. Hence, the non-existence of the central plan loan component since 2005-06. Besides the normal plan assistance, the Planning Commission extends assistance for EAP. This assistance is also given in the form of loans and grants which differ across projects. The assistance extended to AP was ₹ 1,928 crore in 2002-03 which increased to ₹ 2,553 crore in 2011-12 (RE). Of the total assistance for EAP provided to the state, a larger proportion is in the form of loans, contributing to the states mounting indebtedness. The other important part of central assistance for plan purposes is the assistance for Central Sector and Centrally Sponsored Schemes.

Centrally Sponsored Schemes

The Central government ministries provide assistance, generally on the basis of recommendation of the Planning Commission, to states for CSS in the form of specific purpose grants under Article 282 of the Constitution. The objective of CSS is to provide additional resources to states for expenditure which the centre considers to be of national priority, though the schemes are implemented in the states domain. For CSS, the outlay, objectives, and the nature of the schemes are determined by the centre and states cannot alter them. In view of the possible erosion of

6. Report of the Finance Commission, 2004, p.174.

fiscal autonomy of the states, the National Development Council (NDC) decided that the total allocation for CSS should not exceed 1/6 of the block assistance given for State Plan Schemes. But since then, the CSS have grown in number as well as in the size of allocations. The states are also required to make matching contribution which was as much as 50 per cent during 80s but later has been reduced to 25 per cent in the 90s. Some of the important CSS are like the Pradhan Mantri Gram Sadak Yojana (PMGSY), Sarva Siksha Abhiyan (SSA), Mid-Day Meals (MDD) and Mahatma Gandhi National Rural Employment Guarantee Scheme (MGNREGS), which are provided 100 per cent grant from the centre. Table 10.4 shows the enormous growth of these schemes both in number and allocations.

Table 10.4 shows the number of schemes and the amount of allocation, and its percentage in Gross Budgetary Support (GBS) and in the central assistance to states and Union Territories during the Ninth, Tenth and Eleventh Five Year Plans. It may be noted that the number was as high as 360 during the Ninth Plan which declined to 147 during the Eleventh Plan. Similarly their proportion in the GBS has increased from 31.30 per cent during the Ninth Plan to 41.59 per cent during the Eleventh Plan. A higher growth rate of allocation of expenditure under CSS is evident by a higher exponential growth rate compared to the growth rate of allocation for State Plan Schemes as presented in Table 10.5.

Table 10.4

Number and Allocation of Centrally Sponsored Schemes

(₹ crore)

Plan	*GBS*	*No. of Schemes*	*CSS*	*% of CSS to GBS*	*Central Assistance to States and UTs*	*% of Central Assistance to GBS*
1	*2*	*3*	*4*	*5*	*6*	*7*
Ninth Plan* (1997–2002)	3,16,286	360	99,001.68	31.30	1,38,394	43.75
Tenth Plan* (2002–2007)	594,649.00	155	229,763.14	38.64	2,03,117.00	34.15
Eleventh Plan (2007–2012)	15,88,273.24	147	660,506.00	41.59	3,97,418.93	25.02

Note: * At Constant Prices.

Source: Planning Commission, Government of India.

Table 10.5

Growth Rates of Allocation on CSS and Central Assistance for State Plan Schemes

Items	R^2	*b*	*T-value*	*N*
CSS	0.747	0.337	4.859*	10
State Plan Schemes	0.755	0.107	4.963*	10

Note: *Indicates 1% level of Significance

Source: Basic Data from Planning Commission, Government of India.

GoAP has been getting a large number of these schemes and the state's implementation performance is also comparatively better among the states. The total amount of assistance for CSS has increased from ₹ 480 crore in 1995-96 to ₹ 4,016 crore in 2011-12 (RE). It may also be observed that the loan component of these schemes is rather negligible. No doubt, there are problems associated with these schemes like lack of freedom and flexibility in both design and implementation, requirement of matching contributions etc. But the amount of funds devolved to the state for CSS is considerably large. As has been demanded by several states including AP, there is a need to restrict the number of these schemes in such a way that the states enjoy more flexibility and freedom to the extent that the funds are not diverted or misutilised. The resources thus saved need to be pooled in the normal central assistance to be distributed on the basis of the G-M formula during the Twelfth Five Year Plan. In view of the fact that at least 80-90 CSS would be continued in the Twelfth Five Year Plan, the state needs to take adequate initiative to bag as much as possible of these schemes. Of course, an increased share in the flagship programmes (CSS) where the grant component is 100 per cent will provide financial flexibility to the state.

Growth and Fiscal Dependence

The total fiscal transfers—shared tax revenue, grants and loans—have increased from ₹ 5,777 crore in 1995-96 to ₹ 33,062 crore in 2011-12 (RE). In order to analyse the relative importance in terms of growth of fiscal transfers, exponential growth rates for different components of fiscal transfers to AP for the period 1995-96 to 2011-12 have been calculated. Table 10.6 shows the growth rates and their significance levels for shared tax revenue and different types of grants. It may be seen in the table that shared tax revenue and all types of grants put together have increased by 13.9 per cent while shared tax revenue recorded a growth rate of 12.3 per cent. It may be noted that the growth rate of total grants-in-aid is greater than the growth rate of shared tax revenue.

Table 10.6

Growth Rates of Shared Tax and Grants During 1995-96 to 2011-12

Items	R^2	*b*	*t-value*	*N*
1. Shared Tax	0.98	0.123	19.73*	17
2. Grants	0.925	0.139	13.57*	17
a) FC Grants	0.676	0.138	5.59*	17
b) PC Grants	0.844	0.133	9.007*	17
3. CSS Grants	0.924	0.119	13.46*	17
4. NP Grants	0.185	0.149	1.84**	17
Total Transfers	0.945	0.104	16.07*	17

Note: * Denotes 1% level of significance. ** Denotes 5% level of significance.

Source: Basic Data from Reserve Bank of India, *Database on Indian Economy*.

This may be due to the fast growth of non-plan grants. The growth rate of plan grants (13.3%) is lower than the FC grants. Though the total fiscal transfers to the state and their components recorded good growth during the Tenth and Eleventh Five Year Plans, their proportion as GSDP of the state is not encouraging. It may be noted from Figure 10.4 that the central fiscal transfers as a proportion of GSDP were 7.10 in 1997-98 and 7.03 in 1995-96 which had declined to 5.63 per cent in 2002-03. Though the percentage increased to 6.62 in 2003-04, it further declined to 4.71 in 2004-05.

Since then it has hovered around 4-5 per cent. The decline in many of the years is mainly due to a decline in the states' share in the total shareable taxes. It may be noted that fiscal transfers as a per cent of GSDP between 2007-08 and 2010-11 was just above or lower than 5 per cent though it exceeded 5 per cent in 2011-12 (RE). The share of AP in central tax and grants was only 4.3 per cent in the 1st Finance Commission and increased to as high as 9.4 per cent under the 3rd Finance Commission and declined later. It may also be noted that this kind of decline in shared tax revenue is not only in the case of AP but also in the case of other

Figure 10.4

Fiscal Transfers as Per cent of GSDP of Andhra Pradesh

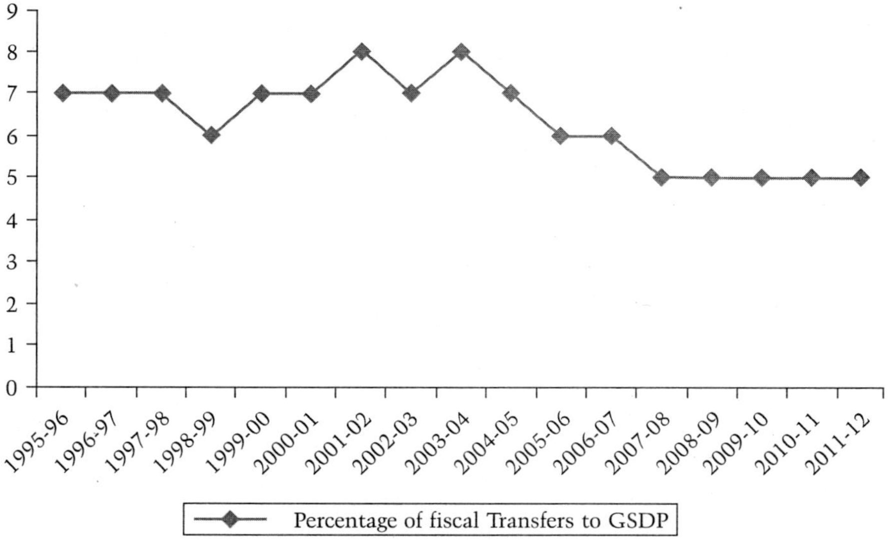

Source: Government of Andhra Pradesh, *Socio-Economic Survey*, various issues.

middle income states like Karnataka, Kerala, Tamil Nadu and West Bengal (Srivastava and Rao, 2009). A comparison of percentage of total transfers under the three FCs of southern states reveals that the mean percentage of share of AP is slightly higher, as shown in Table 10.7, compared to other southern states of Karnataka, Kerala and Tamil Nadu.

Table 10.7

Share in Total Transfers as Recommended by Successive Finance Commissions

State	*Finance Commission*				
	TFC	*EFC*	*TwFC*	*ThFC*	*Mean*
Andhra Pradesh	7.98	7.13	6.66	6.94	7.18
Karnataka	4.64	4.53	4.16	4.33	4.42
Kerala	3.41	2.83	2.59	2.34	2.79
Tamil Nadu	5.89	4.97	4.85	4.96	5.17

Source: Report of the Thirteenth Finance Commission, Vol-1, p.28.

The central transfers, both shared tax revenue and grants-in-aid are important characteristic in that they have an impact on the revenue receipts and revenue expenditure of the receiving state. The share of these transfers in revenue receipts and expenditure indicates the dependence of the state on fiscal transfers from the Centre. This dependency may differ over time. So an analysis has been made to observe trends in the dependence of the state during the post fiscal reform period. Figure 10.5 shows that the percentage of fiscal revenue transfers in revenue receipts of Andhra Pradesh was the highest in 1995-96 and lowest in the year 2002-03. In the rest of the years, it has been oscillating between 30-33 per cent, the annual average being 32.07 per cent over the period. It may be noticed that it marginally increased between the years covered under EFC period and TwFC period. Similarly central grants and shared tax revenue as a percentage of revenue expenditure as shown in Figure 10.5, indicate an increase over the period. The percentage of central tax share and grants in revenue expenditure of the state was as high as 39.09 per cent in 1995-96. Since then, it has declined gradually to 26 and 25 per cent by 2001-02 and 2002-03 respectively. The percentage share has later increased slowly only to reach 31.71 in 2003-04 and again to 34.20 per cent by 2009-10. The percentage has declined over the years consistently implying reduced importance of fiscal transfers in state finances during the post-reform period. It follows that the percentage of fiscal transfers in revenue receipts and the dependence on these transfers to finance revenue expenditure of Andhra Pradesh declined during the study period compared to the period of earlier FCs. This is partly due to the declining share of the state in the all-states share of central taxes and also due to better revenue efforts of the state in the post-fiscal reform period. It is pertinent to note that equalisation efforts of the recent FCs by adopting more progressive criteria for *inter se* distribution placed AP at a relatively disadvantaged position as far as the central fiscal transfers are concerned.

Conclusions

There exist both vertical and horizontal federal fiscal imbalances in India right from the adoption of fiscal federalism. AP being a major state has been getting fiscal transfers through successive FCs and also through the Planning Commission. Analysis of aggregate fiscal transfers as a

Figure 10.5

The Proportion of Transfers in Revneue Receipts and Revenue Expenditure: Andhra Pradesh

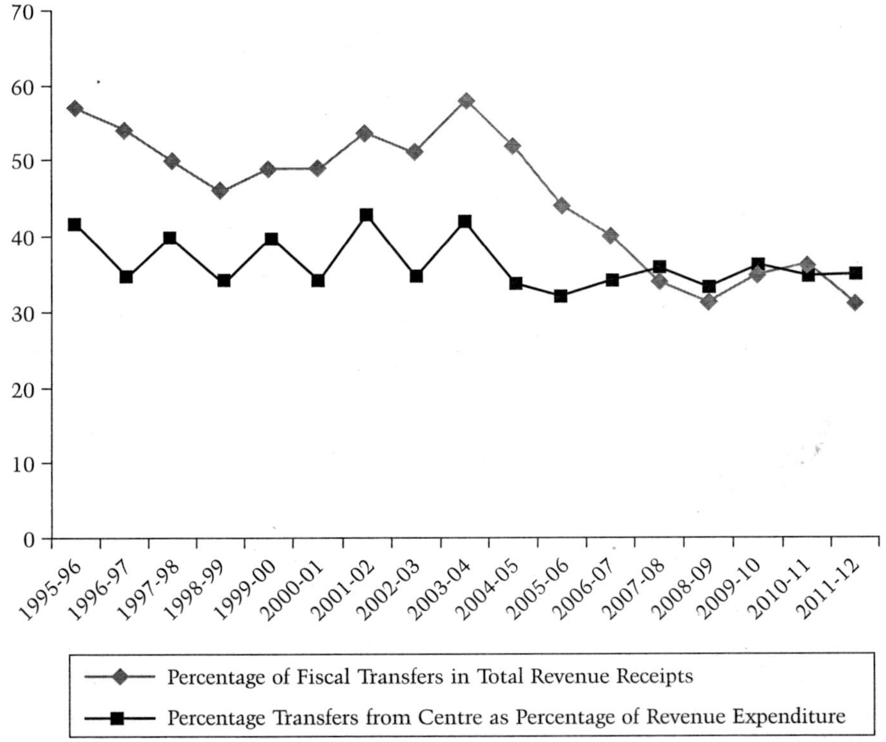

Source: Government of Andhra Pradesh, *Socio-Economic Survey*, various issues.

proportion of GDP (gross domestic product) reveals that it has hovered around 4.5 per cent during the EFC and TwFC periods through it was much higher earlier, except in the year 2011-12 when it has exceeded 5 per cent.

The states' share from central tax revenue has increased from 29 per cent under the TFC period to 32 per cent during the ThFC period. Though the aggregate sates' share in central taxes and duties has been increased by the successive FCs, the share in central tax revenue of AP has been declining from the EFC onwards. This is mainly due to the criteria adopted, factors incorporated and weights given by successive FCs for *inter se* distribution. Though the increase in weightage given to population, area and tax effort are in favour of the state, the upper ceiling imposed with regard to area factor has reduced its share. The criteria and methodology followed by the ThFC have led to a decline in the state's share. The state would have fared better in its tax share entitlement had the ThFC given higher weightage to population and area as suggested by Andhra Pradesh in its memorandum. Also the state would have got higher tax share, had the ThFC taken the original share of geographical area instead of the adjusted share. Of course the state fared better compared with other southern and middle income states of Karnataka, Kerala and Tamil Nadu.

As far as Article 275(1) grants-in-aid are concerned, the state was not eligible to get non-plan revenue deficit grants under the EFC, TwFC and ThFC. However, the state has been awarded grants-in-aid for upgradation of essential social and administrative services, local governments, and special problems and to meet calamity relief expenditure. The state was not eligible for grants-in-aid for education and health under the TwFC mainly due to the criteria adopted by the Commission. Had the Commission considered physical indicators like literacy levels and health, AP would have got grants-in-aid for these two services. With regard to grants for relief expenditure, there has been a wide gap between the central grants and the actual expenditure of calamity relief operations. The state would have benefited, had the Commission considered physical factors like length of coastal line, rainfall etc., and proneness to calamities instead of average expenditure on calamity relief in the preceding years of the states. The innovative practices of the ThFC for awarding grants-in-aid are laudable. Though ThFC has recommended grants-in-aid for a variety of specific purposes, its non-awarding of grants to AP for specific purposes like coastal area development in view of its long coast line of about 1000 kms and for the development of tourism in view of the state's large potential for eco and temple tourism is conspicuous.

The Planning Commission provides financial resources in the form of grants and loans to State Plan Schemes, CSSs, Central Sector Schemes, Additional Central Assistance and EAP. AP has been getting financial resources in terms of loans and grants to all the programmes mentioned above. The state has been getting considerable amount of resources under the EAP of which a large proportion is in the form of loans, contributing to the state's mounting indebtedness. Similarly the state is getting several CSSs. In spite of the ceiling imposed on the total assistance of CSSs by the

NDC, the number as well as the size of allocation has increased over the plan period. In view of the fact that 80-90 CSSs would be continued in the Twelfth Five Year Plan, the state needs to take necessary initiative to bag as much as possible of these schemes. It is pertinent to note that an increased share in flagship programmes with 100 per cent grant component will provide financial flexibility to the state.

An analysis of growth rates of different components of fiscal transfers reveals that shared tax revenue recorded a growth rate of 12.3 per cent while total grants-in-aid obtained a growth rate of 13.9 per cent during the period 1995-96 to 2011-12 (RE). This is mainly due to the fast growth of grants-in-aid for CSS and non-plan grants. It is interesting to note that the growth rate of FC grants is greater than the plan grants. A comparison of percentage of total transfers under the three FCs (EFC, TwFC, and ThFC) of southern states reveals that the mean percentage share of AP is slightly higher than the other southern states of Karnataka, Kerala and Tamil Nadu. The fiscal dependency in terms of percentage of tax shared and grants-in-aid in revenue expenditure of the state was the lowest in 2001-02 implying the lowest dependence on central revenue transfers. This may be due to its declining share in all states' share of Central tax revenue and also due to the better fiscal performance of the state during the post-reform period. Also more progressive criteria followed by *inter se* distribution by successive Commissions placed the state of AP at disadvantaged position as far as central fiscal transfers are concerned.

References

Chakraborty, Pinaki (2010). "Deficit Fundamentalism vs. Fiscal Federalism: Implications of 13th Finance Commission's Recommendations", *Economic and Political Weekly*, Nov-27.

Rao, M. Govinda (2010). "The 13th Finance Commission's Report: Conundrum in Conditionalities", *Economic and Political Weekly*, Nov-27.

Rao, M.N., R. Sudarsana Rao and K. Radha Pushpavathi (2008). "Financing of Calamity Relief Expenditure of the States and Recommendation of the Twelfth Finance Commission", in R. Sudarsana Rao (ed.), *Issues and Recommendations of Twelfth Finance Commission*. New Delhi: Serials Publications. pp.212-21.

Rao, S. Rokkam (1999). "Federalism and Fiscal Autonomy of States: The Indian Experience", in Ian Copland and John Rickard (eds.), *Federalism Comparative Perspectives from India and Australia*. New Delhi: Manohar. p.273.

Sarma, J.V.M. (2008). "Issues and Approach: An Appraisal", in R. Sudarsana Rao (ed.), *Issues and Recommendations of Twelfth Finance Commission*. New Delhi: Serials Publications.

Srivastava, D.K. and C. Bhujanga Rao (2009). *Review of Trends in Fiscal Transfers in India*. Madras School of Economics. Chapter 3. p.67.

11

Plan Financing in Andhra Pradesh

Trends and Concerns

G.R. Reddy

Introduction

With the introduction of planned economic development and the launching of the First Five Year Plan in 1951, public expenditure in India is being categorised as plan and non-plan in addition to the constitutionally mandated categorisation into revenue and capital. Plan expenditure arises out of new schemes introduced in a Five Year Plan. Plan expenditure adds to the productive capacity of a state economy and denotes the state government's investment in enhancing productive capacity. Non-plan expenditure refers to the expenditure on the existing schemes of the government. While non-plan expenditure maintains the existing capacities, plan expenditure denotes government's investment in enhancing productive capacity.[1]

The distinction between plan and non-plan expenditure is not so watertight. Maintenance expenditure in respect of the completed plan schemes is shifted to non-plan in the following Five Year Plan. Thus, plan expenditure in a Five Year Plan adds to the non-plan expenditure in the succeeding Five Year Plan. There is another way in which the plan expenditure creates additional commitment on the non-plan expenditure. A large part of the plan investment financed through borrowings creates additional liability in the form of interest payments and repayments, thus adding to non-plan expenditure.

This paper gives a broad categorisation of plan financing at state level, fiscal situation in 1980s. Subsequently, it reviews the plan financing in

1. Government of India (GoI), Planning Commission, *Eleventh Five Year Plan 2007-2012*.

Andhra Pradesh (AP) during Tenth and Eleventh plan periods and estimates of Twelfth plan period. This paper gives an inter-state comparison of plan financing and sector-wise plan allocation in AP, and concludes with a way forward.

Resources for financing the plan expenditure of a state are broadly categorised into three components, *viz.*, state's own resources, borrowings and central assistance for state plans. States' own resources are non-debt, comprising balance from current revenues (BCR), miscellaneous capital receipts (MCR) and additional resources envisaged to be raised during a plan period. The opening cash balance of the state government at the beginning of a financial year, though insignificant, is also a component of the state's own resources in addition to the above components. BCR, one of the main components of state's own resources represents the balance from the current non-plan revenues after meeting all the non-plan expenditure commitments on the revenue account. Non-plan revenues include state's own tax and non-tax revenue, state's share in central taxes, non-plan grants from the Centre, grants recommended by the Finance Commissions (FCs), such as, non-plan revenue gap grants, grants for local bodies, Centre's share of Calamity Relief Fund (CRF) and other non-plan grants including those for upgradation of standards of administration. MCR mainly comprise recovery of loans and advances, receipts from sale of capital assets and net public account. Non-plan capital outlay and disbursements of non-plan loans and advances are subtracted from these receipts to arrive at net MCR.

State's borrowings consist of market borrowings allocated by the Centre, loans from financial institutions, net accretion to State Provident Fund (SPF), loans from the National Small Savings Fund (NSSF) and other loans. Borrowings from these sources, net of repayments, constitute the resource available for plan financing.

The third component of plan financing is central assistance comprising normal central assistance, additional central assistance for EAP (externally aided projects) and assistance for certain flagship programmes and other additional assistance for the implementation of programmes initiated by the Central government. Normal central assistance is dispensed to states based on the revised Gadgil-Mukherjee (G-M) formula. Currently, out of the money earmarked for normal plan assistance, 30 per cent is earmarked for special category states and the remaining amount is distributed among the non-special category states based on the G-M formula. Under the formula, 60 per cent weightage is assigned to population, 25 per cent to per capita income, 7.5 per cent each to certain performance indicators and special problems. The 25 per cent weightage assigned to per capita income has two components: 20 per cent weight covering only those states whose per capita income is below the national average and 5 per cent weight covering all the states. The 7.5 weightage assigned to performance indicators is distributed among tax policy (2.5%), fiscal management (2.0%) and fulfilment of national objectives of population control (1.0%), elimination of illiteracy, (1.0%), timely completion of EAP (0.5%) and land reforms (0.5%). The assistance under 7.5 per cent weightage assigned to special problems is entirely discretionary. Until 2004-05, central assistance for state plans was dispensed in the grant-loan ratio of 30:70 in the case of general category states and in the ratio of 90:10 for special category states. The grant-loan ratio was based on the revenue component of plan expenditure which was about 30 per cent in the first two decades of planned development. Though the revenue component of the plan increased to over 60 per cent with the focus of planning shifting to social sectors, the grant-loan component remained unchanged till the loan component of central assistance was dispensed with beginning 2005-06, following the recommendations of the 12th FC. Now the entire central assistance for state plans consists of only grants. Issues relating to normal central assistance are discussed later in this paper.

Till the early eighties, with the exception of a few years, the states as a whole enjoyed a surplus on the revenue account. This enabled the states to have a surplus balance from current revenues enabling them to meet over one-third of plan financing through non-debt means. An idea of the plan financing pattern before the deterioration in state finances set in is presented in Table 11.1.

Table 11.1

Pattern of Plan Financing in the Sixth Five Year Plan (1980-1985)

(₹ crore)

Source	*Andhra Pradesh*	*% to Total*	*General Category States*	*% to Total*
1. States' Own Resources (a to e)	1007.02	34.77	12548.02	31.95
a) Balance from Current Revenues	568.93	19.65	7859.72	20.01
b) Miscellaneous Capital Receipts	-311.24	-10.75	-3295.26	-8.39
c) Contribution of Public Enterprises	-193.48	-6.68	-6202.06	-15.79
d) Additional Resource Mobilisation (ARM)	758.79	26.20	13327.28	33.94
e) Others	184.02	6.35	858.34	2.14
2. Net Borrowings	881.38	30.44	14597.46	33.94
3. Central Assistance	1007.51	34.79	12125.57	30.88
a) Normal	898.06	31.01	10599.80	26.99
b) Externally Aided Projects	109.45	3.78	1525.77	3.89
Total Resources	2895.91	100.00	39271.05	100.00

Source: GoI, Planning Commission.

During the Sixth Plan, in AP, own revenue resources contributed nearly 35 per cent of the total resources of the plan followed by central assistance and net borrowings, whose respective contributions were 34.79 per cent and 30.44 per cent. The performance of AP exceeded both in terms of contribution of own resources and lower dependence on borrowings as compared with the general category states. As 70 per cent of the central assistance was in the form of loan, debt funding of the plan would be higher than that suggested by net borrowings. Thus, nearly 55 per cent of the plan funding was done through borrowings in AP (30.44% through net borrowings and 24.35% being the loan component of central assistance).

Fiscal Deterioration in the Eighties

States as a whole started witnessing a deficit on their revenue accounts beginning 1987-88 almost continuously. In AP, the revenue account went into a deficit for the first time in 1983-84 and remained in deficit till 1986-87. After posting a marginal surplus in the years 1987-88 and 1988-89, the revenue account of the state again went into a deficit in 1989-90 and remained so till 2005-06. The deficit on revenue account not only persisted but deepened with every passing year. The revenue deficit of all states worsened from 0.29 per cent of GDP (gross domestic product) in 1987-88 to 2.70 per cent of GDP in 2001-02. The revenue account of AP worsened from a small surplus to a deficit of 1.84 of GSDP (gross state domestic product) in the same period. States resorted to higher borrowings not only to meet their higher plan outlays but also to meet the deficits on their revenue accounts. This was a recipe for fiscal unsustainability resulting in mounting debt and higher interest payments putting further pressure on the revenue accounts of states. By 2002-03, the revenue and fiscal deficits of states assumed alarming proportions. While the revenue deficit of all states worsened from 0.9 per cent of GDP in 1997-98 to 2.3 per cent of GDP in 2002-03, the revenue deficit of AP worsened from 0.73 per cent of GSDP to 1.83 per cent of GSDP in the same period. During the same period, the fiscal deficit of all states worsened from 2.8 per cent of GDP to 4.1 per cent of GDP. The deterioration in the fiscal deficit of AP was much sharper from 2.51 per cent of GSDP to 4.56 per cent of GSDP in the same period.

Three important developments have prevented the state finances from further deterioration. The first was the introduction of economic reforms in the early nineties aimed at liberalising the economy and making the public finances sustainable. Following the higher growth trajectory in the post 2003-04 period, improvement in state finances started around 2004-05 facilitated by a higher growth of the economy and the resultant increase in the buoyancy of state taxes. The second major development was the introduction of Value Added Tax (VAT) by most states in 2005-06 which enhanced their tax base considerably. The third major development was the boost the state finances received following the recommendations of the 12th FC. The 12th FC recommended an increase in the states' share in central taxes from 29.5 per cent to 30.5 per cent. The 12th FC also recommended the debt consolidation and relief facility (DCRF) linked to reduction in the revenue deficit and containment of fiscal deficit at 2004-05 level. The benefits of DCRF were conditional on states enacting fiscal responsibility and budget management legislations (FRBMA) mandating elimination of revenue deficit by 2008-09 and containing fiscal deficit at three per cent of GSDP. The enactment of FRBMA in 2005-06 ushered in an era of rule based management of public finances in the state.

Following these developments, there was considerable improvement in state finances. The revenue account of the state turned into a surplus in 2006-07 after remaining in deficit for close to 17 years and the fiscal deficit moderated to 1.9 per cent of GSDP in the same year.

The improvement in state finances continued till 2007-08. The global downturn witnessed following the collapse of Lehman Brothers had its effect on the growth outcomes in India. The decline in growth had its adverse impact on public finances in terms of fall in the growth of revenue and additional commitments on account of the stimulus package put in place to minimise the impact of the global downturn on the Indian economy. While the GDP growth of the country declined from 9.3 per cent in 2007-08 to 6.8 per cent in 2008-09, the GSDP growth in AP declined from 12.0 per cent in 2007-08 to 6.9 per cent in 2008-09. Though the GSDP growth improved to 10.0 per cent in 2010-11, it slipped again to 6.9 per cent in 2011-12. Following the deceleration in the growth of the economy, the fiscal deficit of the state deteriorated to 2.91 per cent of GSDP in 2008-09. Since then, there has been a marginal moderation in the fiscal deficit and improvement in the revenue surplus of the state. In the Budget for 2012-13, the fiscal deficit and the revenue surplus of the state were budgeted at 2.6 per cent and 0.57 per cent of the GSDP, respectively.

In the above backdrop, the trends in the pattern of plan financing in AP are analysed below. The trends are analysed for the period commencing from the Tenth Five Year Plan (2002-2007).

Review of Plan Financing in Andhra Pradesh

Tenth Plan (2002-2007)

The Tenth Plan period represents a distinct shift from the past trends in terms of economic growth as well as the health of state finances. During the Tenth Plan, AP clocked average GSDP growth of 9.5 per cent per annum as compared with the average annual growth of 5.5 per cent achieved in the Eighth Plan period. The year 2003-04 marks a distinct shift from past trends. The trigger for this shift was the higher growth trajectory witnessed at the national as well as the state level. While the GDP growth of the country improved from 3.84 per cent in 2002-03 to 8.52 per cent in 2003-04, the GSDP growth of AP jumped from 2.9 per cent to 9.1 per cent. The total revenue-GSDP ratio in AP witnessed an improvement from 13.68 in 2002-03 to 14.08 in 2003-04 and further to 18.00 in 2007-08. The Tenth Plan period also witnessed game changing developments, such as, enactment of FRBM legislation, introduction of VAT and DRCF and higher transfers recommended by the 12th FC. All these development resulted in fiscal consolidation and an improvement in plan financing. The position with regard to plan financing in the state during the Tenth Plan period is presented in Table 11.2.

The actual mobilisation of resources for the Tenth Plan in AP exceeded the initial estimates by 27.22 per cent. The sole contributory to this improvement was state's own resources, the contribution of which exceeded the initial estimates by nearly 256 per cent. Among the components, the resources from BCR and MCR exceeded the estimates. While the improvement in BCR was on account of better revenue performance, the improvement in MCR mainly came from the proceeds of sale of government lands. Despite less than estimated central assistance and net borrowings, the better performance of BCR and MCR more than made up their shortfall. The redeeming feature of plan financing in the Tenth Plan was the reduced dependence on borrowings as a means of plan financing. Though, net borrowings constituted only 17.78 of the total resources, the actual share of borrowings in total financing was higher at about 33 per cent taking into account 70 per cent of normal central assistance and assistance for EAP which was in the form of loans till 2004-05. The fall in the share of central assistance in the last two years of the Plan was on account of the dispensation of the practice of lending of 70 per cent of the normal plan assistance to states by the Centre from 2005-06 onwards. To the extent of this fall, there was a corresponding increase in the market borrowings of the state in the last two years of the Tenth Five Year Plan.

Eleventh Plan (2007-2012)

Eleventh Plan was formulated in the backdrop of a turnaround in the state finances as well as in the growth of the economy. Therefore, much emphasis was placed on the contribution of state's own resources. The contribution of state's own resources was envisaged at 67.51 per cent as

Table 11.2

Pattern of Plan Financing in Andhra Pradesh: Tenth Five Year Plan (2002-2007)

(₹ crore)

Source of Financing	Tenth Plan Projection	Actual Realisation						Actual Realisation as % of Projection
		2002-03	2003-04	2004-05	2005-06	2006-07	Total 2002-2007	
1. State's Own Resources	9837.45	2026.89	7356.74	6512.11	8043.83	11080.65	35020.22	355.99
a) BCR	9192.53	30.17	474.07	1860.92	3988.05	8517.90	14871.11	161.77
b) MCR	-558.04	1701.24	6821.63	5101.26	3674.23	2216.32	19514.68	3497.00
c) Finance Commission Grants	986.41	58.65	62.40	7.15	6.50	154.60	161.00	16.32
d) ARM	152.45	152.45						
e) Opening Balance	64.1	236.83	-1.36	-457.22	375.05	191.93	345.23	538.58
2. Net Borrowing	19570.33	2830.24	-581.17	1706.93	3986.84	4759.44	10730.42	54.83
3. Central Assistance.	18037.93	3540.67	4001.03	3247.52	1448.74	2372.37	14610.33	81.00
a) Normal	5764.12	1131.79	1148.48	1267.57	448.58	356.23	4352.65	75.51
b) EAP	7861.77	1905.69	1546.69	1305.83	294.92	310.68	5363.81	68.23
c) Others	4412.04	503.19	1305.86	674.12	705.24	1705.46	4893.87	110.92
Net Total Resources	47445.71	8397.80	10776.60	11466.56	13479.41	18212.46	60360.97	127.22

contd...

...contd...

Source of Financing	*Tenth Plan Projection*	*Actual Realisation*						*Actual Realisation as % of Projection*
		2002-03	*2003-04*	*2004-05*	*2005-06*	*2006-07*	*Total 2002-2007*	
		As Percentage of Total Resources for the Plan						
1. State's Own Resources	20.73	24.14	68.27	56.79	59.67	60.84	58.02	
a) BCR	19.37	0.36	4.40	16.23	29.59	46.77	24.64	
b) MCR	-1.18	20.26	63.30	44.49	27.26	12.17	32.33	
c) Finance Commission Grants	2.08	0.70	0.58	0.06	0.05	0.85	0.27	
d) ARM	0.32							
e) Opening Balance	0.14	2.82	-0.01	-3.99	2.78	1.05	0.57	
2. Net Borrowing	41.25	33.70	-5.39	14.89	29.58	26.13	17.78	
3. Central Assistance.	38.02	42.16	37.13	28.32	10.75	13.03	24.20	
a) Normal	12.15	13.48	10.66	11.05	3.33	1.96	7.21	
b) EAP	16.57	22.69	14.35	11.39	2.19	1.71	8.89	
c) Others	9.30	5.99	12.12	5.88	5.23	9.36	8.11	
Net Total Resources	100.00	100.00	100.00	100.00	100.00	100.00	100.00	

Note: BCR=Balance from Current Revenues; MCR=Miscellaneous Capital Receipts; ARM= Additional Resource Mobilisation.

Source: Government of Andhra Pradesh, Finance Department.

compared with 20.73 per cent in the Tenth Plan period. The developments unfolding in the wake of the global downturn cast their shadow on the performance of the state economy too. As indicated earlier, the growth of GSDP witnessed a sharp fall in the year 2008-09. It was only in 2010-11 that the economy recovered to 10.0 per cent of GSDP growth. The pattern of plan financing during the Eleventh Plan period is presented in Table 11.3.

During the Eleventh Plan, the contribution of state's own revenue fell sharply to 54.21 per cent of the original estimate. This is mainly on account of the deceleration in the growth of own revenues as well as a decline in the MCR. In 2009-10, while the growth of tax revenue declined to 5.45 per cent from over 25 per cent in the previous year, non-tax revenues recorded a negative growth as compared with the growth of 37.08 per cent in 2008-09. As the sale of government land was resorted to only in the first year of the Plan, the realisation of MCR was much lower than the estimate. The actual realisation of total resources in the entire five-year period was expected to be only 77.56 per cent of the estimate. As the projections of resources for the Eleventh Plan were made against the overall improvement in the state finances witnessed since 2003-04, there was an element of overestimation as compared with the estimates for the Tenth Plan. This also partly explains the underperformance of the BCR and MCR as compared with the estimates in the Eleventh Plan period. The shortfall in the realisation of resources would have been much sharper but for the increase in the central assistance and borrowings. There was also a substantial increase in the grants from the FC. Because of a significant shortfall in the share of BCR and MCR in plan financing as compared with the original estimates, there was increased dependence on borrowings in the Eleventh Plan as compared with the Tenth Plan. The dependence on borrowings was likely to be 39.46 per cent of the total resources in the Eleventh Plan as compared with 33 per cent in the Tenth Plan. But for the limits on borrowings following the enactment of FRBMA, higher FC transfers and higher than estimated central assistance, the dependence on borrowings as a source of plan financing would have been much higher.

Estimates of Plan Financing in the Twelfth Plan (2012-2017)

Preliminary estimates with regard to the pattern of plan financing for the Twelfth Five Year Plan are available (Table 11.4). It may be interesting to compare these with the actual pattern of plan financing in the state during the Eleventh Plan period.

Though the pattern of resources projected for the Twelfth Plan broadly corresponds with that realised during the Eleventh Plan period, there is higher reliance on BCR. In the projection of resources for the Twelfth Plan, the share of BCR is placed at 48.40 per cent as compared with the share of 40.94 realised during the Eleventh Plan period. This is in line with the increasing share of BCR in total resources being witnessed since the Tenth Plan period. The contribution of MCR as projected for the Twelfth Plan is (-) 0.02 as compared with the share of 5.46 per cent realised in the previous plan period. This is because, proceeds from government land sale as a source of plan financing has dried up. Net borrowings and central assistance are projected at a marginally lower level than that realised in the Eleventh Plan. The projected decline in the share of central assistance can be mainly attributed to a lower share of assistance in respect of EAP. Higher FC grants projected for the Twelfth plan make up for the marginally lower share of normal central assistance. Realising the share of BCR in total resources for the Plan projected at 48.40 per cent, involving a higher growth of tax and non-tax revenue and a moderate growth of non-plan expenditure, will be the main challenge in the Twelfth Plan.

Plan Financing: Inter-State Comparison

The actual outcomes of source-wise plan financing are not available for all the states. The Planning Commission's website has information regarding the approved financing pattern for the annual plans and the latest estimates for only a few years of the Eleventh Plan period. In contrast, information regarding actual plan outlays is available from the study of State finances by the Reserve Bank of India (RBI). Constrained by the information availability, the inter-state analysis of plan performance is restricted to annual plan expenditure by the states in the Tenth and Eleventh Plan periods. A summary of the plan outlays is presented in the Table 11.5. The analysis is restricted to general category states as the plan

Table 11.3

Pattern of Plan Financing in Andhra Pradesh: Eleventh Five Year Plan

(₹ crore)

Source of Financing	Eleventh Plan Projection	Realisation						Actual Realisation as % of Projection
		2007-08	2008-09	2009-10	2010-11	2011-12 (LE)	Total 2007-2012	
1. State's Own Resources	138397.44	16413.43	15564.05	10756.40	15870.36	16422.19	75026.43	54.21
a) BCR	108148.48	8401.92	13829.00	10750.79	16163.33	15953.16	65098.20	60.19
b) MCR	29508.96	7938.44	1463.33	124.63	-855.74	2.67	8673.33	29.39
c) Finance Commission Grants	740.00	146.00	191.66	199.16	298.83	561.80	1397.45	188.84
d) Opening Balance		-74.93	80.06	-318.18	263.94	-95.44	-144.55	
2. Net Borrowing	50703.23	6987.28	11028.79	14394.47	12403.96	17924.00	62738.50	123.74
3. Central Assistance.	15899.73	3792.42	4039.44	4254.38	3318.59	5825.33	21230.16	133.53
a) Normal	2605.85	368.07	512.48	496.57	439.57	620.76	2437.45	93.54
b) EAP	955.75	484.58	166.05	90.50	72.08	50.00	863.21	90.32
c) Others	12337.73	2939.77	3360.91	3667.31	2806.94	5154.57	17929.50	145.32
Net Total Resources	205000.00	27193.13	30632.28	29405.26	31592.91	40171.52	158995.10	77.56

contd...

...contd...

(₹ crore)

Source of Financing	*Eleventh Plan Projection*	*Realisation*						*Actual Realisation as % of Projection*
		2007-08	*2008-09*	*2009-10*	*2010-11*	*2011-12 (LE)*	Total 2007-2012	
		As Percentage of Total Resources						
1.State's Own Resources	67.51	60.36	50.81	36.58	50.23	40.88	47.19	
a) BCR	52.76	30.90	45.15	36.56	51.16	39.71	40.94	
b) MCR	14.39	29.19	4.78	0.42	-2.71	0.01	5.46	
c) Finance Commission Grants	0.36	0.54	0.63	0.68	0.95	1.40	0.88	
d) Opening Balance		-0.28	0.26	-1.08	0.84	-0.24	-0.09	
2. Net Borrowing	24.73	25.70	36.00	48.95	39.26	44.62	39.46	
3. Central Assistance.	7.76	13.95	13.19	14.47	10.50	14.50	13.35	
a) Normal	1.27	1.35	1.67	1.69	1.39	1.55	1.53	
b) EAP	0.47	1.78	0.54	0.31	0.23	0.12	0.54	
c) Others	6.02	10.81	10.97	12.47	8.88	12.83	11.28	
Net Total Resources	100.00	100.00	100.00	100.00	100.00	100.00	100.00	

Source: Government of Andhra Pradesh, Finance Department.

Table 11.4

Pattern of Plan Financing in Andhra Pradesh: Twelfth Five Year Plan

(₹ crore)

Source of Financing	Eleventh Plan Latest Estimates	Twelfth Plan Projections	Annual Plan 2012-13 Estimates	As Per cent of Total Resources		
				Eleventh Plan Latest Estimates	Twelfth Plan Projections	2012-13 (BE)
1. State's Own Resources	75026.43	179363.51	22548.16	47.19	49.54	46.08
a) BCR	65098.20	175237.45	23010.13	40.94	48.40	47.02
b) MCR	8673.33	-77.87	-643.95	5.46	-0.02	-1.32
c) FC Grants	1397.45	4203.93	592.88	0.88	1.16	1.21
d) Opening Balance	-144.55	-	-410.90	-0.09	0.00	-0.84
2. Net Borrowing	62738.50	137012.16	20523.30	39.46	37.84	41.94
3. Central Assistance.	21230.16	45699.96	5863.44	13.35	12.62	11.98
a) Normal	2437.45	4950.54	713.87	1.53	1.37	1.46
b) EAP	863.21	120.00	55.00	0.54	0.03	0.11
c) Others	17929.50	40629.42	5094.57	11.28	11.22	10.41
Net Total Resources	158995.10	362075.63	48934.90	100.00	100.00	100.00

Source: Government of Andhra Pradesh, Finance Department.

Table 11.5

State-wise Plan Outlays: Tenth and Eleventh Five Year Plans

States	*Total Tenth Plan (2002-07)*		*Eleventh Plan Outlays (2007-12) (₹ billion)*						
	Plan Outlay (₹ crore)	*Plan Outlay as Per cent of GSDP*	*2007-08 (Actual)*	*2008-09 (Actual)*	*2009-10 (Actual)*	*2010-11 (RE)*	*2011-12 (Approved)*	*Total Eleventh Plan Outlay 2002-2007*	*Eleventh Plan Outlays as Per cent of GSDP*
1. Andhra Pradesh	62177	5.46	271.7	306.2	293.9	322.5	430.0	1624.3	6.53
2. Bihar	21045	5.32	96.5	125.1	141.8	132.3	240.0	735.7	8.07
3. Chhattisgarh	15576	6.51	62.0	81.4	102.8	183.5	167.1	596.8	10.46
4. Goa	3786	6.22	12.2	15.7	19.7	27.1	33.2	107.9	8.17
5. Gujarat	45976	4.41	156.5	217.6	226.3	300.0	380.0	1280.4	5.83
6. Haryana	12980	2.65	57.5	71.1	96.2	182.6	203.6	611.0	5.47
7. Jharkhand	15523	5.79	57.1	68.7	65.3	92.4	153.2	436.7	8.86
8. Karnataka	59659	7.10	172.3	221.2	259.7	310.5	380.7	1344.4	7.54
9. Kerala	19543	3.29	50.9	62.4	77.7	100.3	120.1	411.4	3.52
10. Madhya Pradesh	34003	5.95	120.5	130.8	146.1	190.0	230.0	817.4	7.47
11. Maharastra	56100	2.65	141.5	228.7	277.3	379.2	420.0	1446.7	3.17
12. Odisha	14099	3.79	60.3	75.7	77.3	100.0	152.0	465.3	5.56
13. Punjab	14885	2.95	50.2	69.3	49.7	89.3	115.2	373.7	3.75
14. Rajastan	33735	5.26	137.9	149.2	180.2	212.2	275.0	954.5	7.18
15. Tamil Nadu	42676	3.81	142.2	162.5	178.3	200.7	235.3	919.0	3.81
16. Uttar Pradesh	49338	3.76	243.0	342.9	372.1	384.3	470.0	1812.3	6.95
17. West Bengal	22396	2.12	88.6	104.0	121.2	179.9	222.1	715.8	3.56
Total 17 Major States	523497	4.10	1921.0	2432.4	2685.58	3386.7	4227.6	14653.3	5.49

Source: Reserve Bank of India, *Study of State Finances*, various issues.

outlays of special category states are mainly funded by central transfers and tend to be higher as a proportion of GSDP making them non-comparable.

During the Tenth Plan, Karnataka with a ratio of plan outlays to GSDP at 7.10 stood at the first place among 17 major states, while West Bengal with a ratio of 2.12 stood at the last place as compared with the average ratio of 4.10 for 17 general category states. Though the performance of AP with a plan outlay-GSDP ratio of 5.46 was above the average, it lagged behind Chhattisgarh, Goa, Jharkhand, Karnataka and Madhya Pradesh. Among the states performing better than Andhra Pradesh, the performance of Chhattisgarh, Jharkhand and Madhya Pradesh can be explained in terms of higher central transfers. Goa, with a higher per capita income, is an outlier. In recent years, Karnataka has been doing extremely well in terms of tax-GSDP ratios. Its own tax-GSDP ratio of 12.6 per cent in 2007-08 was the highest among all the states. Karnataka was the first state in the country to have enacted the fiscal responsibility legislation and among the first to achieve the targets laid down under the legislation. Its performance stands out relative to all other states.

The performance of AP in terms of plan outlays in the Eleventh Plan was much better than that in the Tenth Plan. The ratio of plan outlay-GSDP stood at 6.53 as compared with the average ratio of 5.49 for 17 general category states. The performance of AP exceeded that of Kerala and Tamil Nadu but lagged behind Karnataka. The states of Bihar, Chhattisgarh, Goa, Jharkhand, Madhya Pradesh, Rajasthan, and Uttar Pradesh fared better than AP.

Sector-wise Allocation of Plan Outlays in Andhra Pradesh

Allocation of plan outlays by sectors during the Tenth and Eleventh Five Year Plans are presented in Table 11.6.

Distribution of plan outlays by sectors in the Tenth Plan period reveals the priority accorded to the irrigation sector by the AP Government. The irrigation sector accounted for 36.14 per cent of the total outlay during the plan followed by the social sector (26.53%), power sector (11.82%) and rural development (6.99%). These four sectors accounted for over 80 per cent of the total plan outlay during the Tenth Plan. While the irrigation sector more or less retained its predominant share of over 34 per cent in

Table 11.6

Sector-wise Allocation of Plan Outlays During the Tenth and Eleventh Plan

Sector	*Tenth Plan Outlay (2002-2007) Actual*		*Eleventh Plan Outlay (2007-2012) Actuals for 2007-2011 and RE for 2011-12*	
	Outlay (₹ crore)	*Percentage to Total*	*Outlay (₹ crore)*	*Percentage to Total*
1. Agriculture & Allied Sectors	2373.09	3.82	9510.44	6.02
2. Rural Development	4345.44	6.99	15525.90	9.83
3. Irrigation	22473.58	36.14	54384.81	34.44
4. Power	7374.67	11.82	1301.24	0.82
5. Industry & Minerals	1298.13	2.09	1976.78	1.25
6. Transport & Communications	5168.26	8.31	10883.44	6.89
7. Social & Community Services	16492.79	26.53	57943.01	36.69
8. Special Area Development	1898.97	3.05	5550.62	3.51
9. General Services	778.88	1.25	836.80	0.53
Total	62176.82	100.00	157913.00	100.00

Source: Government of Andhra Pradesh, *Annual Plan 2012-13*.

the Eleventh Plan, the share of the social sector witnessed improvement from 26.53 per cent in the Tenth Plan to 36.69 per cent. The power sector lost out heavily in the allocation/plan expenditure during the Eleventh Plan. There has been some improvement in the shares of agriculture and rural development sectors during the Eleventh Plan. The distribution of plan outlays clearly reveals a distinct shift in plan expenditure towards the social sectors. This shift comes out much sharper when the distribution of the current plan outlays by sectors is compared with that in the Fourth Plan period. During the Fourth Plan, power sector accounted for 42.46 per cent of the total outlay followed by irrigation (27.84%), social sector (12.41%), transport (12.41%) and agriculture (6.11%).

Issues in Plan Financing: Way Forward

There are several issues in plan financing which need to be resolved. Of late, there has been a tendency to budget higher annual plan outlays than can be supported by state's resources and borrowing limits. The practice of budgeting higher plan outlays has set in around 1999-2000. Till 1998-99, actual plan expenditure exceeded the budget estimates as well as the approved outlays broadly indicating prudence in budgeting the plan outlays. Since 1999-2000, actual Plan expenditure tended to fall short of the budgeted as well as approved outlays by a huge margin. While the actual expenditure in the Tenth plan fell short of the budgeted outlays and approved outlays by 8.38 per cent and 4.58 per cent, respectively, the shortfall in the Eleventh Plan is expected to be 16.31 per cent and 15.56 per cent, respectively. Table 11.7 presents the trends relating to budgeted plan outlays, approved plan outlays and actual expenditure.

There are a number of adverse impacts of budgeting higher plan outlays than that can be supported by state finances and including innumerable schemes in the plan. Firstly, such practices result in spreading resources too thinly across a number of schemes leading to cost and time overruns. Secondly, higher plan outlays often come at the expense of proper maintenance of assets already created. This results in running down of service delivery capacity already created. Higher expenditure commitments necessitate economy measures banning the creation and filling up of vacancies, hampering service delivery even in social sectors such as education and health. Many minor irrigation works going into

Table 11.7

Budgeted, Approved and Actual Plan Outlays in Andhra Pradesh

(₹ crore)

Five Year/Annual Plan	*Budgeted Outlay*	*Approved Outlay*	*Actual Outlay/ Expenditure*	*Actual Expenditure as Per cent of*	
				Budgeted Outlay	*Approved Outlay*
Total Eighth Plan (1992-1997)	12629.00	11845.00	13606.61	107.74	114.87
1992-93	1995.80	1675.00	2364.04	118.45	141.14
1993-94	2075.55	1851.00	2867.46	138.15	154.91
1994-95	2409.88	2170.00	2453.47	101.81	113.06
1995-96	3159.00	3159.00	2869.38	90.83	90.83
1996-97	2988.77	2990.00	3052.26	102.12	102.08
Total Ninth Plan (1997-2002)	31187.18	29943.51	28572.41	91.62	95.42
1997-98	3809.60	3585.05	3980.57	104.49	111.03
1998-99	4678.95	4780.95	5141.33	109.88	107.54
1999-2000	5479.50	5491.51	4748.31	86.66	86.47
2000-01	8228.12	7708.00	6531.10	79.38	84.73
2001-02	8994.02	8378.00	8171.10	90.85	97.53
Total Tenth Plan (2002-2007)	68547.08	69511.65	62176.83	89.40	89.45
2002-03	10082.75	10100.00	8315.09	82.47	82.33
2003-04	10970.46	10970.46	10758.80	98.07	98.07
2004-05	13291.20	12790.43	11456.54	86.20	89.57
2005-06	15650.77	15650.77	19551.91	124.93	124.93
2006-07	19551.90	20000.00	18206.99	93.12	91.03
Total Eleventh Plan (2007-12)	189484.07	187796.75	158585.42	83.69	84.44
2007-08	30013.54	30500.00	27170.80	90.53	89.08
2008-09	43191.61	44000.00	30617.68	70.89	69.57
2009-10	36635.58	33496.75	29390.97	80.23	87.74
2010-11	36727.97	36800.00	32248.71	87.80	87.63
2011-12 (RE)	42915.37	43000.00	39157.26	91.25	91.06

Source: Government of Andhra Pradesh, Finance Department, *Annual Plan-2011-12*.

disuse is an example of the neglect of maintenance of existing facilities in a rush to create new and additional irrigation capacity. Besides, inclusion of too many schemes beyond what can be supported by the availability of resources had the undesirable consequence of building up of cost of unproductive administrative establishment. There is a tendency to create new jobs to run the new schemes. This ultimately becomes a committed liability for the state. Implementation of too many schemes stretches the ability of the administration to ensure their proper implementation. This results in inefficient implementation of the plan schemes.

With the borrowing limits in place with the enactment of the FRBMA, there has been a tendency to overestimate BCR and MCR in order to project higher plan outlays. Higher estimates of BCR are often the result of underestimating the non-plan commitments. This is a double whammy for the states. Firstly, they lose out in the assessment of non-plan revenue expenditure needs done by the Central Finance Commissions (CFC) every five years. Secondly, the perceived benefits of overestimation of BCR to project higher plan outlays is negated by a running down of service delivery capacity already created as indicated earlier.[2]

Of late, there have been considerable delays on the part of the PC in communicating the approved outlays to states. The approved outlays are communicated as late as July and August by which time the state budgets would have been passed by the Legislatures. These delays indirectly lead to budgeting of higher plan outlays by states and subsequent disruption in the allocation of funds to schemes included in the Annual Plan. There is a need to synchronise approved outlays with those budgeted by states.

There is a tendency to continue schemes under the plan instead of shifting them to the non-plan in order to show a higher plan outlay. Sometimes schemes not allowed under the non-plan are included in the plan. If a scheme is not found useful under the non-plan, it should be equally unacceptable under the plan. Often such issues are overlooked to increase the number of schemes under the plan.

In the initial years of planning, schemes were mostly capital in nature and the plan resources could be allocated to new schemes after the completion of on-going schemes. Such flexibility is no longer available as, the focus of the plan has shifted to revenue expenditure based schemes. Consequently, a major proportion of plan expenditure has become committed as observed by the Rangarajan Committee.[3] When the revenue component of the plan was negligible there was some sort of a link

2. Planning Commission, Eleventh Five Year Plan, Vol.I.
3. GoI, Planning Commission, *Report of the Expert Committee on Efficient Management of Public Expenditure 2011*.

between the plan expenditure and additional revenue to the government on completion of the schemes such as irrigation and power projects. With the revenue component of the plan becoming sizeable, the link between plan expenditure and additional revenue is broken. The impact of the revenue expenditure on social sectors is indirect through better education and health of the population and the resultant increase in productivity. This is all the more reason for reducing the dependence on borrowings and to improve the BCR over the years through better tax administration and curtailing unproductive expenditure and cutting short delays in project implementation by adequately funding the schemes included in the plan. This requires a focused approach to planning instead of the current practice of spreading resources too thinly across a number of schemes.

With the increase in the revenue component of the plan, there will be a severe restriction on the manoeuvrability of the states in plan financing. With the bulk of the plan expenditure becoming committed effectively, there are likely to be constraints in further increasing the revenue component of the plan and taking up new projects to any significant effect. With the FRBMA stipulating zero revenue deficit, revenue component of the plan cannot exceed the BCR and the plan grants from the Centre.

With a major component of plan expenditure becoming committed, there is a far greater need today to involve the private sector in infrastructure development and other capital intensive projects. The Second Plan assumed that nearly 46 per cent of the investment required for realising the targets would come from the private sector. During this Plan period, gross capital formation by the private and public sector was estimated at 7.22 per cent of GDP and 6.36 per cent of GDP, respectively. The situation has drastically changed over the years. Private sector has emerged as a significant contributor to the total investment in the country. In 2008-09, gross capital formation of the private sector amounted to 24.6 per cent of GDP while that of the public sector to 9.5 per cent of GDP. The *Approach Paper to the Twelfth Five Year Plan (2012-2017)* has assumed that nearly 73 per cent of the fixed investment required for realising the growth target of 9 per cent per annum would come from the private sector including the household sector.

In the context of the reduced manoeuvrability of the state government to mobilise resources for financing new projects, it is imperative that the private sector is involved more intensively to realise the plan targets by way of proactive policies and creating suitable environment for the private sector to thrive in the state. The possibilities of involving the private sector through PPP (public-private partnership) and viability gap funding in a transparent manner should be explored seriously by the state government. The state can draw upon the experience of the Central government in this regard. Leveraging the limited resources of the state will be crucial in the Twelfth Plan and subsequent plans. The Partnership Summit jointly hosted by the Government of Andhra Pradesh, Department of Industrial Policy and Promotion of the GoI and the Confederation of Indian Industry in January 2012 was a good beginning. Investment proposals worth over 6 lakh crore are reported to have been committed at this Summit. The state government should ensure that the bulk of this investment is realised in the Twelfth Plan period.

There are likely to be concerns with regard to redemption of past debt and the possible reduction in the repayment period of the loans contracted from the National Social Security Fund (NSSF) during the period of the Twelfth Five Year Plan. In the outstanding debt of the state government, market loans, loans from the NSSF and provident funds are predominant accounting for over 80 per cent of the total. The profile of the market loans (Table 11.8) and the loans from the NSSF (Table 11.9) are analysed to assess the kind of redemption pressure that is likely to arise during the course of the Twelfth Plan period.

In the case of the market loans, debt servicing (repayments and interest payments) accounted for 49.39 per cent of the gross market loans in 2010-11. As can be seen from the Table 11.8, the reduction in the debt servicing burden from 122.74 in 2005-06 per cent to 49.39 per cent in 2010-11 and further to 38.24 per cent of gross loans in 2011-12 is mainly on account of the increase in the level of borrowings. As the higher level of borrowings is likely to be maintained in the Twelfth Plan, it is likely that there may not be a redemption pressure immediately. The pressure is likely to arise immediately after the Plan period as there will be bunching of repayments in 2018-19 and 2019-20 because of higher level of market borrowings in 2008-09 and 2009-10. But the scenario is likely to be totally different in the case of loans from the NSSF.

Table 11.8

Profile of Market Loans: Andhra Pradesh

(₹ crore)

Year	*Gross Market Loans*	*Repayment of Market Loans*	*Interest Payments*	*Total Outgo (Col.3+4)*	*Debt Servicing as % of Gross Loans*
1	*2*	*3*	*4*	*5*	*6*
2005-06	1956.37	573.00	1828.32	2401.32	122.74
2006-07	2725.94	529.54	1915.72	2445.26	89.70
2007-08	6650.00	1007.64	2044.03	3051.67	45.89
2008-09	10933.57	1782.69	2504.68	4287.37	39.21
2009-10	15383.11	2097.26	3397.08	5494.34	35.72
2010-11	12000.00	1639.06	4287.28	5926.34	49.39
2011-12(RE)	19867.92	2394.74	5202.25	7596.99	38.24
2012-13(BE)	23164.17	3401.71	6665.60	10067.31	43.46

Source: Government of Andhra Pradesh, Budget Documents, various years.

Table 11.9

Profile of Loans from NSSF: Andhra Pradesh

(₹ crore)

Year	*Loan from NSSF*	*Repayment to NSSF*	*Interest Payment to NSSF*	*Total Outgo (Col 3+4)*	*Debt Servicing as Percentage of Loans from NSSF*
1	*2*	*3*	*4*	*5*	*6*
2005-06	4534.64	322.34	1585.54	1907.88	42.07
2006-07	4143.77	146.41	2044.67	2191.08	52.88
2007-08	387.44	203.68	2380.61	2584.29	667.02
2008-09	323.20	336.73	2364.39	2701.12	835.74
2009-10	1531.19	515.61	2359.74	2875.35	187.78
2010-11	3005.75	759.21	2452.94	3212.13	106.87
2011-12(RE)		1004.91	2659.16	3664.07	
2012-13(BE)		1212.10	2560.42	3772.52	

Source: Government of Andhra Pradesh, Budget Documents, various years.

The debt servicing of NSSF loans is much higher than fresh borrowings in recent years because of the steep fall in small saving collections. The state had not taken any loan from the NSSF in 2011-12 because of negative net small saving collections in the state. For the year 2012-13, the State opted for 50 per cent of net small saving collections but did not budget for any loan from the NSSF. The state had to finance the debt servicing through borrowings from other sources. The collection of small saving collections may improve somewhat with the recent alignment of interest rates on small saving instruments with the market rates of interest. But, it may not matter much whether small saving collections in the state improve or not as the borrowing limits are fixed every year keeping in view the FRBMA targets and the state can access market loans to the extent of the limits. However, there are likely to be concerns with regard to the shortening of the duration of loans from NSSF from the current 25 years to 10 years and doing away with the moratorium of five years in the repayment of NSSF loans. These developments are likely to add to the debt servicing burden in the Twelfth Plan period and need to be factored in.

There are other broader issues relating to the growing expenditure commitments of states, size of the state plan, channelling of central assistance, direct transfers to implementing agencies bypassing the state governments and the mushroom growth of CSS (centrally sponsored schemes). As observed by the 13th FC, there are a number of Central and state legislations, the compliance cost of which mostly falls on the states. The benefits of activities like mining are not so significant to states as compared with the costs in terms of displacement of people, degradation of land, loss of agricultural output, damage to roads and air and water pollution. Macroeconomic benefits of mining are much greater as compared with the benefit accruing to a mining state.

There are also other developments which have greatly increased the expenditure commitments of states. Central enactments with regard to right to education, food security and land acquisitions are likely to add to the expenditure commitments of states. While the states are willing and prepared to play a crucial role in fulfilling the objective of faster, sustainable and inclusive growth, they are constrained by the lack of resources at their command.

Contrary to the imperative of empowering states with more resources, the developments over the last few decades have resulted, though unwittingly, in the centralisation of resources. Centralisation of resources is multi-faceted and has taken place in a number of areas. A few of these areas merit a mention here. The most glaring area is the declining share of states in the plan outlays. The share of states in plan outlays declined from over 63 per cent in the First Plan period (1951-1956) to less than 42 per cent in the period covered by the Tenth Plan. For the Eleventh, the share envisaged for the states was only 39 per cent.

The decline in the share of the states in plan outlays is mainly on account of the increase in the internal and extra budgetary resources (IEBR) of central public sector undertakings (CPSUs) and partly on account of the reduction in the gross budgetary support (GBS) to state plans. The share of the IEBR in total Central plan outlay had witnessed a substantial increase from about 16 per cent in the First Plan to nearly 56 per cent in the Ninth Plan. In the Eleventh Plan, IEBR were estimated to contribute nearly 45 per cent of the Central plan outlay. The CPSUs, particularly in the oil and coal sectors have been generating huge surpluses because of their size and near monopoly position. With the aid of tax free bonds, other PSUs of the Central government are able to raise borrowings to finance the Central plan. In contrast, the PSUs of states are mostly loss making and have failed to generate resources for funding the state plan.

Added to this, the reduction in the GBS of the Centre to state plan has also partly resulted in the declining share of states in total plan outlays as indicated above. In the original Tenth Plan, Centre's budgetary support to the plan was distributed between the Central plan and state plan in the ratio of 58:42. The actual ratio turned out to be 66:34. For the Eleventh Plan, Centre's budgetary support to the state plan was only 23 per cent of the total support for the plan. It is a matter of concern that this issue of declining state share has not been addressed in the *Approach Paper to the Twelfth Plan*. The Approach Paper has envisaged only a marginal increase in the central assistance to State and Union Territory (UT) Plans from the current 1.18 per cent of GDP to 1.23 per cent of GDP in the Twelfth Plan period. Given the imperative of greater role of states, there is a need to improve the transfers to states substantially.

Apart from the declining central assistance for state plans, there has been a change in the composition of reduced level of central assistance to the disadvantage of states. Central assistance for state plans was agreed to be given to states entirely in the form of normal Central assistance on the basis of Gadgil formula in 1969. The block grant character of normal central assistance was diluted with the introduction of specific purpose schemes, the assistance in respect of which is given in the form of additional central assistance. Another development that has diluted normal central assistance to states is the mushroom growth of CSS. A third development is the budgeting of schematic outlays in the budgets of Central ministries as state plan outlays. Another development is the direct transfer of resources to the implementing agencies bypassing the states at the expense of accountability. In the Central Budget for 2012-13, an amount of ₹ 1,33,359 crore was provided for direct transfer to implementing agencies bypassing the state governments. As observed by the 13th FC, large amounts are lying in the bank accounts of a few implementing agencies unutilised. As a result of the above developments, the share of normal central assistance has gradually come down to the present insignificant level of less than 20 per cent. For the Eleventh Plan period, normal plan assistance is estimated to be only 6.74 per cent of the GBS to the Plan. The Chaturvedi Committee on CSS in its report (2011) has recommended that normal central assistance should be at least 10 per cent of GBS so as to provide more freedom to states in the use of resources for the plan. In the context of the greater role of states for achieving the objective of inclusive and sustainable growth, these developments in the dispensation of central assistance need to be reversed and the primacy of normal central assistance as the predominant channel needs to be restored.

Though a number of Committees have recommended reduction in the size and number of CSS, there has been no progress in this direction. At least for the Twelfth Plan, the number of CSS may be reduced and restricted to those schemes serving national objectives and the money thus saved may be passed on to states in the form of normal central assistance. The Chaturvedi Committee[4] has recommended reduction in the number of CSS from the present 147 to 59. The Committee has recommended consolidation and merger of a number of schemes. Even if this recommendation is acted upon, it is unlikely that there will be reduction in the allocations to CSS as the flagship schemes account for

4. GoI, Planning Commission, *Report of the Committee on Restructuring of CSS. 2011.*

the bulk of the allocations under the CSS and the Committee has not recommended any reduction in their number. For an effective change in the present regime, the reduction in the number of CSS should be accompanied by a reduction in their outlays and the money thus released should be transferred as normal central assistance so as to restore its primacy as a predominant channel of central plan transfers to states.

Another development in the context of the financing of the Twelfth Plan is the increasing reliance placed by the Central government on the levy of cesses and surcharges. Surcharges, which are supposed to be levied for meeting an exigency and abolished after the exigency is met, are being continued indefinitely. There has also been a greater recourse to the levy of cesses for specific purposes. Cesses and surcharges now constitute over 15 per cent of the gross tax revenue of the Centre. These levies have reduced the size of the divisible pool of central taxes, thus depriving the states of their legitimate share in central taxes. In the interest of state finances and maintaining the sanctity of FC recommended states' share in central taxes, there is a need to review the levy of cesses and surcharges and to keep them at a minimum level.

The levy of royalty rates on major minerals vests with the Central government and these rates are supposed to be revised every three years. In the past, there have been undue delays in the revision of rates for macroeconomic considerations. These rates need to be revised without any delays in the interest of augmenting state finances.

In the Gadgil formula governing the distribution of central assistance for State Plans, a weightage of 7.5 per cent is assigned for special problems. There are no specific guidelines determining the special problems. In effect, the assistance attributable to special problems is distributed to certain states as special packages in a highly discretionary and arbitrary manner. The weightage assigned to special problems may be deleted and the weightage distributed to other parameters after due consultations with states. With the per capita income of AP becoming above average, the state is deprived of a share in the 20 per cent allocation earmarked for states with lower than average per capita income. Revision of the Gadgil formula is overdue and needs to be pursued vigorously at least to do away with the discretionary component in the formula.

The focus of the Twelfth Five Year Plan as articulated in the Approach Paper is faster, sustainable and more inclusive growth. As sectors, such as agriculture, education, skill development, provision of health services, welfare of weaker sections, etc., which are at the core of an inclusive social and economic order come within the purview of the states under the Constitution, there is an urgent need to realign resources in favour of states. Over the years, plan outlays have become synonymous with borrowings, incomplete projects, continuing salary liabilities, mounting interest liabilities, spreading of resources too thinly resulting in cost and time over runs and locking up valuable resources in the creation of low yielding assets. These concerns needs be addressed with earnestness in the Twelfth Five Year Plan.

12 Fiscal Imbalances and Indebtedness across Indian States

Recent Trends

Tapas K. Sen and Santosh K. Dash[1]

Introduction

By the end of the last century, fiscal imbalances and indicators thereof in most of the Indian states had reached disturbing levels with respect to deficit indicators and debt level (Rao, 2002; Gurumurthi, 2002). The fiscal health of Central government was not any better. The link between the deficits and indebtedness at the sub-national level in India is well-known (Sen, 2012); all the same, it was at that point felt necessary to not only correct the fiscal imbalances to reduce the level of indebtedness eventually, but to directly target sub-national debt (Rajaraman *et al.*, 2005). In an effort to restore fiscal discipline, fiscal rules were mooted, and the Fiscal Responsibility and Budget Management Act (FRBMA) was passed in the Parliament in 2003. Thus, the Central government agreed to abide by fiscal rules first. A few states followed suit quickly with their own Acts, while several others also passed their version of the FRBMA after the 12th Finance Commission (TwFC) provided some incentives for the states to do so. The main objectives of the legislations were to eliminate revenue deficits and reduce fiscal deficit to or below three per cent of GDP (gross domestic product).[2]

Fiscal rules have been in operation for a long time now in other countries, and are not universally accepted as effective in bringing about

1. The views expressed here reflect those of the authors, not of the organisation they belong to. Errors, if any, are the responsibility of the authors. They, however, wish to thank Diwan Chand and Gita Bhatnagar for help with the data.

2. For more details regarding the context and contents of fiscal reforms, see Rangarajan and Prasad (2013).

fiscal correction. In fact, they are considered to be neither necessary nor sufficient for the purpose, but in combination with certain other complementary factors, they can make a useful contribution to the achievement of fiscal balance (Kennedy and Robbins, 2001; Balassone *et al.*, 2003). Sub-national borrowing is sometimes viewed with suspicion in the context of macroeconomic management in a federal system (Drummond and Mansoor, 2002; Ahmad *et al.*, 2005), and is seen to require some kind of control, although its utility as a tool for developmental efforts is recognised. In contrast, some studies actually find a virtue in decentralisation in terms of controlling public debt (Baskaran, 2010), and leviathan theorists would certainly agree to such reasoning. Further, there are possible variations in fiscal rules, and what has been adopted in India—the fixed target rule—is only one among them (Groneck, 2010). The question of whether this is the best for the Indian sub-national context has not been asked.

This paper examines the extent to which Indian states have been successful in achieving the FRBMA targets in the last decade, and the route through which the necessary fiscal adjustments were undertaken. Since there are alternative ways of achieving fiscal adjustment and since each of them has a different impact on the economy of the state, this issue has some economic importance. Further, if there is a pattern in the method of fiscal adjustment undertaken by different groups of states, it can provide further insights into sub-national fiscal behaviour. In particular, if the burden of adjustment has been heavier on the low-income states as compared to the other states, and if the adjustment has been more through controlling expenditures, then there are possible serious implications on public supply of services that need to be highlighted.

The reference period for this study is 2000-01 through 2010-11 for the 28 states of India, examined in two groups of special category and non-special or general category states. We utilise the method of comparing the simple averages of two 4-year periods at the beginning and at the end of our reference period, namely, 2000-2004 and 2007-2011. This implicitly takes the first period to be the pre-reform period and the second as the post-reform period, with the intervening years as the core reform years. This is based on the assumption of announcement effects of the TwFC recommendations and the fiscal circumstances in most states being most conducive for reforms during these years. The five broad fiscal indicators we have considered are revenue deficit, fiscal deficit, primary deficit, interest payments and fiscal liability. All the indicators are normalised by GSDP (gross state domestic product) of respective states at current prices (Base: 2004-05). All the data except those on GSDP and population are taken from *Finance Accounts* of the respective states, while GSDP and population data have been taken from *National Accounts Statistics (NAS)*. Fiscal liability of a state is used here in the broad sense including public debt as well as public account liabilities, but not including contingent liabilities.

The Pattern of Adjustments

Revenue Deficits

We first focus on the behaviour of deficit indicators. The ratio of revenue deficit over GSDP for general category states for two averages has been depicted in Figure 12.1. It can be seen that almost all the states have reduced revenue deficit in the second period as a percentage of GSDP except Jharkhand and Haryana. However, it can also be seen that the averages of these two states were the lowest in the first period. In contrast, while West Bengal did reduce its revenue deficit, it had the highest average revenue deficit to GSDP ratio among all the general category states in both periods. It appears that Jharkhand and Haryana, with low revenue deficits in the first period itself, were not particularly motivated to undertake revenue account adjustments during the reform period, which resulted in relatively small adjustments seen in the second period as compared to the first. But West Bengal, obviously undergoing serious revenue account imbalance in the first period, did try to achieve some adjustments. However, it was not enough to bring down the revenue deficit ratio substantially in the second period. Oddly enough, West Bengal was one of the two states that did not adopt any fiscal reform legislation as suggested and incentivised by the TwFC, possibly because it was not likely to meet the targets.

Figure 12.1

Revenue Deficit/GSDP (Non-Special Category States)

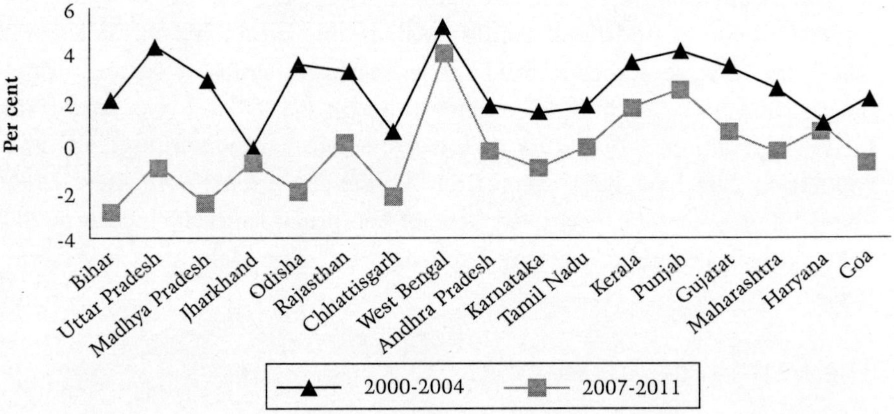

Source: All the data except those on GSDP and population are taken from Finance Accounts of the respective states, while GSDP and population data have been taken from National Accounts Statistics.

While all the general category states except Jharkhand had some amount of revenue deficit in the first period averages, all but four (West Bengal, Punjab, Kerala and Gujarat, in order of the size of the ratio) of them transited to revenue surpluses in the second period. It is clearly no coincidence that the first three have a history of persistent fiscal imbalance since the 1990s. In terms of the extent of reduction in the ratio, Odisha led the states with a reduction of 5.56 percentage points, followed by Madhya Pradesh, Uttar Pradesh and Bihar with adjustments to the extent of 5.46, 5.10 and 4.76 percentage points. The lowest average revenue deficit to GSDP ratio—actually the highest revenue surplus ratio—for the second period was recorded by Bihar, followed by Madhya Pradesh, Chhattisgarh, and Odisha in that order.

The states are deliberately arranged in order of per capita income in Figure 12.1, to reflect the pattern in the adjustments by level of income, if any. As far as the general category states are concerned—the pattern is immediately noticeable (barring Jharkhand)—the extent of reduction in revenue deficits is substantially larger in the low income states as compared to the other states. The reason could possibly lie in the strength of motivation for adjustment; the importance of the incentives mandated by the TwFC could have been the highest for the low income states as compared to others.

Figure 12.2 presents a similar analysis for the special category states, though no clear pattern in their case catches the eye. One common feature with general category states is that all the special category states had either revenue surpluses or revenue deficits close to zero (Uttarakhand and Himachal Pradesh) in the second period; but in general, they did not have average revenue deficit to GSDP ratio higher than 3 per cent even in the first period, the two exceptions being Mizoram and Himachal Pradesh. A standout feature of Figure 12.2 as compared to Figure 12.1 is the large revenue surplus to GSDP ratios that were achieved by some of the states in the second period. Manipur and Arunachal Pradesh had second period averages around as high as 15 per cent. In fact, the extent of adjustment carried out in revenue deficit by all the special category states together as per the four-year averages at 5.6 percentage points was considerably larger than that by the general category states (2.8 percentage points).

Figure 12.2

Revenue Deficit/GSDP (Special Category States)

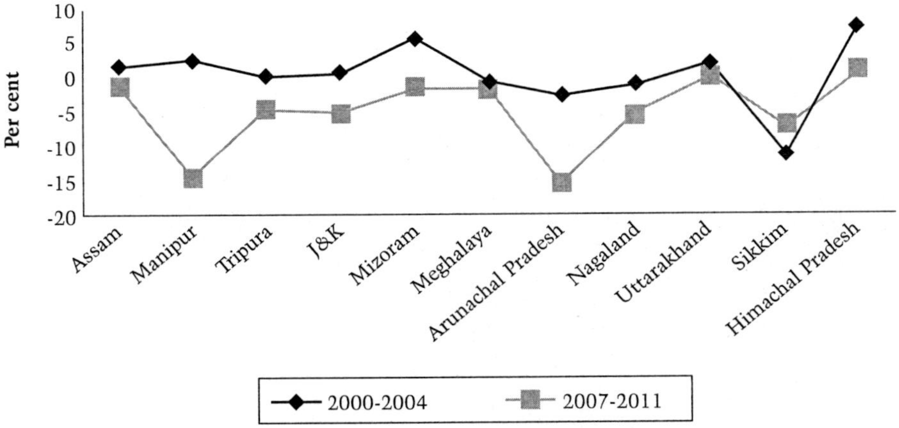

Source: Same as Figure 12.1.

In this category of states, the highest extent of adjustment was recorded by Manipur in terms of the four-year averages, while the lowest was recorded by Meghalaya. Just as Haryana did not carry out much of an adjustment in revenue deficits, Meghalaya, Uttarakhand and Sikkim also did not, perhaps for the same reason, since all three states had either a low fiscal deficit or fiscal surplus in the first period. Of these three states, the case of Sikkim is notable because it is the only state that recorded a decrease in the revenue surplus ratio; simultaneously, it must also be noted that it had the highest revenue surplus ratio in the first period itself which remained at a high level even in the second period after the decrease, and it was the only state in the special category that did not adopt a fiscal responsibility legislation as desired by the TwFC. However, unlike West Bengal, there did not appear to be any need for the same, at least with respect to revenue balance.

Adjustments to reduce deficits in the revenue balance can be achieved through increase in receipts (own tax or non-tax, and transfers from the centre in the form of shared taxes or grants) and/or through expenditure contraction. It is instructive to examine this in some detail to see (i) the role of endogenous and exogenous factors, and (ii) to understand the impact of the adjustment on the citizens. Table 12.1 provides the necessary information for both the categories of states.

In the majority of general category states, the single largest source of adjustment in the revenue account was expenditure contraction, with Chhattisgarh, Jharkhand, Madhya Pradesh, Uttar Pradesh and West Bengal being the exceptions. Jharkhand is a totally different case with a large increase in revenue expenditures. Increases in revenue expenditure can be observed in Chhattisgarh and Uttar Pradesh too, but of a smaller magnitude. Goa had the largest cut in revenue expenditures among these states (more than 8 percentage points), followed by Gujarat (4.17) Odisha and Punjab (3.48 and 3.25 percentage points respectively). For all states together in this category, the reduction was 1.38 percentage points out of the total adjustment (decrease) of 2.81 percentage points in revenue deficit. Total non-tax revenues contributed a little more than equal adjustment (increase) of 1.40 percentage points, states' own and grants contributing equally, for all these states together. The largest increases in both own non-tax revenues and central grants can be seen in Bihar, Chhattisgarh, Jharkhand, Madhya Pradesh and Uttar Pradesh. However in Gujarat and Rajasthan, the central grants actually decreased.

Table 12.1

Sources of Revenue Account Adjustment

(Percentage of GSDP Points)

States	*Reduction in Revenue Deficit*	*Increases in*				*Change in Revenue Expenditure*
		Own Taxes	*Own Non-Tax*	*Central Taxes*	*Grants*	
I. Non-Special Category						
Andhra Pradesh	2.05	0.67	0.20	0.05	0.07	-1.06
Bihar	4.76	0.24	1.14	0.04	2.68	-0.65
Chhattisgarh	3.08	1.69	1.28	0.59	1.63	2.11
Goa	2.93	-0.63	0.31	-4.99	0.13	-8.11
Gujarat	2.86	-0.03	0.35	-1.23	-0.40	-4.17
Haryana	0.08	-0.92	0.15	-0.73	0.39	-1.18
Jharkhand	0.52	1.15	2.51	0.38	1.82	5.34
Karnataka	2.49	0.92	0.09	-0.39	0.51	-1.36
Kerala	1.93	0.26	0.10	-0.01	0.10	-1.48
Madhya Pradesh	5.46	1.42	1.56	0.44	1.47	-0.57
Maharashtra	3.05	-0.18	0.17	-0.18	0.67	-2.57
Odisha	5.56	0.53	0.29	0.60	0.66	-3.48
Punjab	1.88	-0.28	0.36	-1.74	0.29	-3.25
Rajasthan	3.10	0.46	0.88	0.18	-0.15	-1.74
Tamil Nadu	1.83	0.15	0.26	-0.01	0.49	-0.94
Uttar Pradesh	5.10	0.97	1.83	0.98	1.42	0.11
West Bengal	1.16	0.00	0.45	0.24	0.07	-0.40
Average	2.81	0.38	0.70	-0.34	0.70	-1.38
II. Special Category						
Arunachal Pradesh	12.49	1.11	3.32	6.31	7.00	5.25
Assam	3.05	1.15	2.34	1.13	1.73	3.30
Himachal Pradesh	6.18	1.07	0.62	2.87	-0.17	-1.79
Jammu & Kashmir	5.59	2.07	1.60	-1.03	2.13	-0.82
Manipur	17.12	0.92	3.96	1.77	14.33	3.86
Meghalaya	0.76	0.66	1.88	0.09	-0.22	1.64
Mizoram	7.05	1.01	4.09	0.66	1.74	0.44
Nagaland	4.38	0.56	2.72	0.58	1.77	1.26
Sikkim	-2.81	0.28	1.89	-30.34	-15.02	-40.39
Tripura	5.66	1.45	2.59	-0.67	4.14	1.86
Uttarakhand	2.03	0.79	1.36	-0.24	-0.77	-0.90
Average	5.59	1.01	2.40	-1.72	1.51	-2.39
All States	3.90	0.62	1.37	-0.88	1.02	-1.77

Source: Same as Figure 12.1.

States' own tax revenues contributed a smaller increase of 0.38 percentage points, almost fully offset by a fall in shared taxes. While the largest increases in own tax revenues were seen in Chhattisgarh, Madhya Pradesh and Jharkhand (in order of the extent of increase), there were some states where there was no increase but a decrease (Goa, Gujarat, Haryana, and Punjab). It is of interest to note that all these states are among the high income states of India. Shared taxes also decreased for all these states, plus some of the middle income states (Karnataka, Kerala and Tamil Nadu).

The pattern that emerges is that of the low income states carrying out a steeper reduction in revenue deficit in general, with an all-round adjustment effort (increase in both types of own revenues and reduction in revenue expenditure), supported by both types of central transfers. While Jharkhand and Chhattisgarh could not reduce their revenue expenditure despite significant adjustment on the receipts side, the massive adjustment of revenue deficit in Odisha was primarily achieved through expenditure contraction. In Madhya Pradesh, the large adjustment was mainly through own revenues (both tax and non-tax), with only a small degree of expenditure contraction. In Uttar Pradesh too the expenditure contraction was relatively small, but all sources of revenue receipts contributed to the revenue account adjustment. Bihar managed a significant adjustment primarily through increased central grants. Of the states with higher per capita incomes, Goa, Gujarat and Maharashtra exhibit relatively large reductions in revenue deficits, and in all three cases this was achieved primarily by slashing expenditures.

In the case of special category states, their adjustment efforts were by and large heavily dependent on central transfers, which is not surprising given their dependence on the same. Two large adjustments in Arunachal Pradesh and Manipur are obvious examples of this. However, all of them barring Sikkim made significant efforts to raise their own revenues too. Uttarakhand's adjustment could actually be ascribed primarily to own revenues, as also of Jammu & Kashmir. The case of Sikkim is a peculiar one, with huge reductions in central transfers and almost matching reduction in expenditures (probably a case of transfer-financed expenditures), with a net result of increase in revenue deficit. Barring Sikkim, and to a much smaller extent Himachal Pradesh, special category states by and large did not carry out adjustments through expenditure contraction to any significant extent, and in several cases actually increased expenditures.

Fiscal and Primary Deficit

The scenario with respect to fiscal deficits is very similar to that regarding revenue deficits in general category states (Figure 12.3); so much so that the Figure 12.3 looks almost the same as Figure 12.1 but for the scale. This is not particularly surprising since revenue deficits were the overwhelming components of fiscal deficits of states, with capital outlays and net lending relatively small and in some cases insignificant. Turning to adjustment pattern of fiscal deficit, we find that all the states except Jharkhand and Haryana have substantially reduced fiscal deficit in the second period. Not so surprisingly, Jharkhand registered an increase in the fiscal deficit by 0.79 percentage points; having the lowest fiscal deficit ratio in the first period itself (below 2%), it could afford a slight increase since the target ratio was 3 per cent or less for all states. The largest extent of adjustment was again in Odisha (about 6 percentage points) followed by Bihar (3.37) and Rajasthan (3.32). Notice that the four-year average fiscal deficit ratios of two states—Odisha and Chhattisgarh—were reduced to a level of almost zero, considerably below the target level. Most other states stayed close to or inside a band of 2-3 per cent in the second period. Only

Figure 12.3

Fiscal Deficit/GSDP (Non-Special Category States)

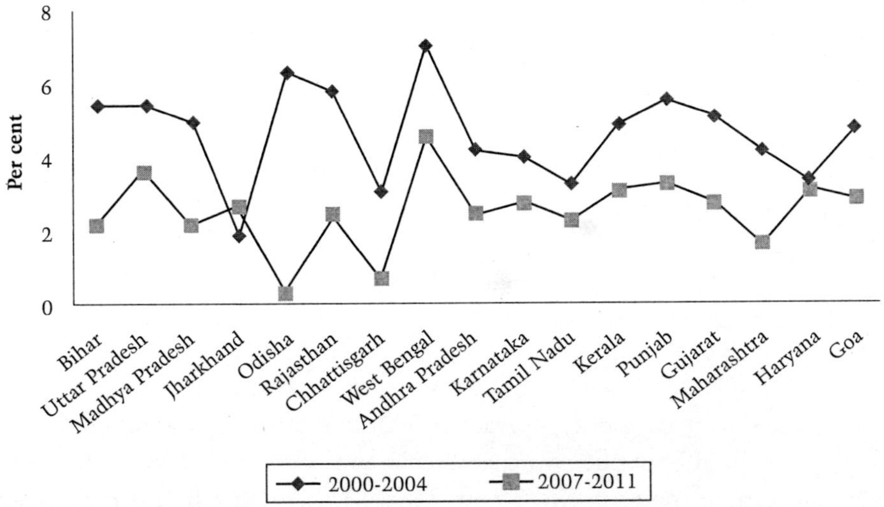

Source: Same as Figure 12.1.

West Bengal had a relatively high fiscal deficit ratio of above 4 per cent even in the second period, despite undertaking visible fiscal adjustment. Taken together, the general category states reduced fiscal deficit ratio by 2.28 percentage points.

With respect to special category states, the picture relating to fiscal deficits is qualitatively different from that relating to revenue deficits. While Arunachal Pradesh and Himachal Pradesh undertook large reductions in fiscal deficit (6.8 and 6.1 percentage points respectively) to get close to the target level of 3 per cent, Mizoram had a very high level of fiscal deficit ratio of around 9 per cent in the second period despite undertaking a sharp reduction in the same by 6.7 percentage points, because its fiscal deficit ratio was extremely high at above 15 per cent in the first period.

Figure 12.4

Fiscal Deficit/GSDP (Special Category States)

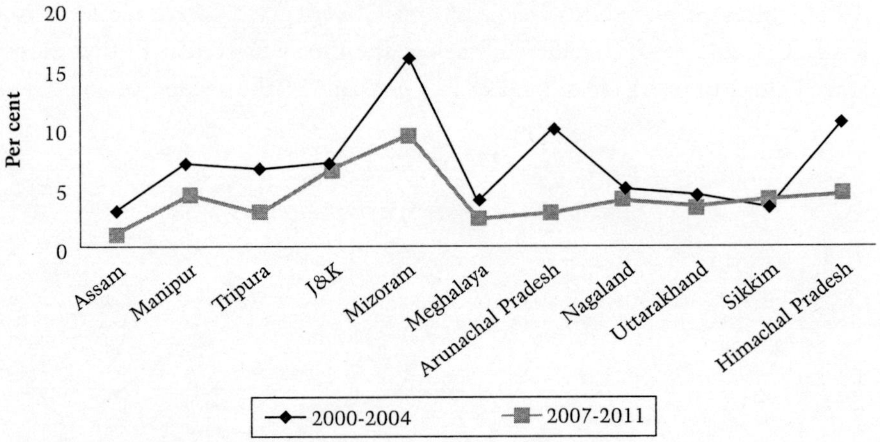

Source: Same as Figure 12.1.

Sikkim was the only state in this category which had a higher ratio in the second period as compared to the first, though by a relatively small 1.5 percentage points, possibly because it did not subject itself to the discipline of a fiscal responsibility legislation. However, it is clear that despite adopting the same, several states in this category missed out on the incentives in at least one year each due to non-fulfilment of the conditions. Taken together, states in this group reduced fiscal deficit by 2.7 percentage points in the second period.

In the case of primary deficit, among the general category states, a large reduction between the two averages is observed in states like Odisha, Madhya Pradesh, Maharashtra, and Rajasthan (2.9, 2.08, 1.94, and 1.93 percentage points respectively). Since Jharkhand showed an increased fiscal deficit in the second period, it is no surprise that the same is seen in primary deficits as well. The same is seen in the case of Haryana too where the smaller interest payments in the second period converts the marginal reduction in fiscal deficits to an increase in primary deficits. While none of these states had a primary surplus (only Jharkhand had a primary deficit close to zero) in the first period, four of them (all of them being low income states—Bihar, Odisha, Rajasthan and Chhattisgarh) had primary surpluses in the second period, with Madhya Pradesh and Maharashtra having average primary surpluses close to zero.

Figure 12.5

Primary Deficit/GSDP (Non-Special Category States)

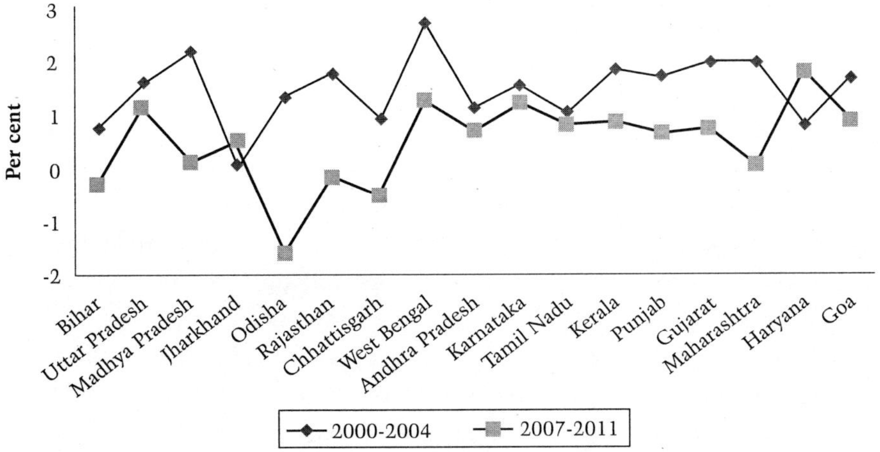

Source: Same as Figure 12.1.

In the case of special category states, all of them except Sikkim (which converted its substantial surplus into deficit) recorded a fall in the average primary deficits. There was a rise of 4.3 percentage points between these two averages in Sikkim, while large reductions came from Arunachal Pradesh, Mizoram and Himachal Pradesh (5.77, 4.57, and 4.39 percentage points respectively). None of these states except Sikkim had a primary surplus in the first period, and only Assam and Arunachal Pradesh had noticeable surpluses in the second. Mizoram had a relatively large primary deficit even after a large reduction, while all other states had primary deficits close to zero, or at least not too large, in the second period.

Figure 12.6

Primary Deficit/GSDP (Special Category States)

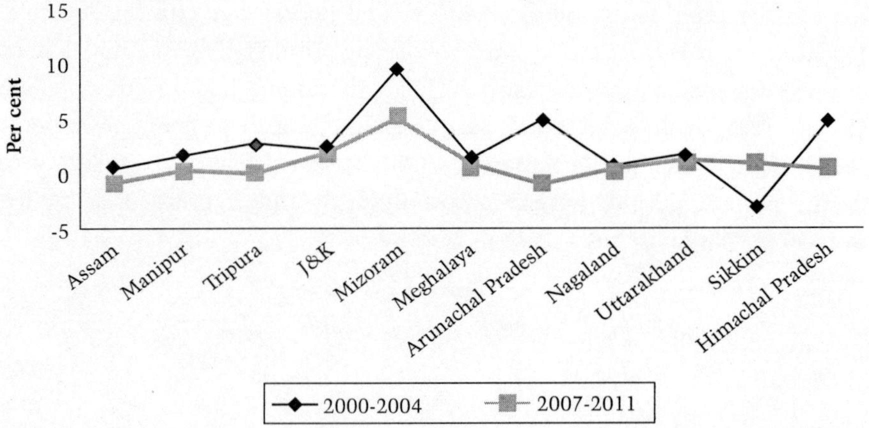

Source: Same as Figure 12.1.

Given the revenue account adjustments, those in fiscal deficits are additionally determined by mainly two components: capital outlay and net lending. The remaining (small) extent of adjustment is traceable to miscellaneous receipts, mostly receipts from disinvestments in state public enterprises (Table 12.2). In general, states did not cut down on capital outlay in the process of adjustment, the only exception being Sikkim, allowing it to post a smaller increase in fiscal deficit as compared to the increase in revenue deficit. Because of the increase in capital outlay, in most states the reduction in fiscal deficit was smaller than that in the revenue deficit, but there were notable exceptions when the cut in net lending exceeded the increase in capital outlay—Haryana, Odisha, Punjab, Rajasthan and West Bengal were in this group.

In the special category states, the most outstanding case was that of Manipur, with a huge reduction in revenue deficit (more than 17 percentage points) neutralised to a large extent by only slightly less huge increase in capital outlay (14.57 percentage points). A similar, but less extreme case was that of Arunachal Pradesh. Jammu & Kashmir and Nagaland

Table 12.2

Sources of Adjustment in Fiscal Deficits

(Percentage of GSDP Points)

States	*Decrease in Fiscal Deficit*	*Decrease in Revenue Deficit*	*Increase in Capital Outlay*	*Decrease in Net Lending*	*Increase in Misc. Receipts*
I. Non-Special Category					
Andhra Pradesh	1.65	2.05	0.58	-0.16	0.35
Bihar	3.37	4.76	2.70	1.31	0.00
Chhattisgarh	2.40	3.08	1.17	0.47	0.01
Goa	1.91	2.93	0.99	-0.02	0.00
Gujarat	2.29	2.86	0.36	-0.21	0.00
Haryana	0.22	0.08	0.79	0.93	0.00
Jharkhand	-0.79	0.52	1.34	0.03	0.04
Karnataka	1.26	2.49	1.32	0.05	0.01
Kerala	1.82	1.93	0.28	0.17	0.05
Madhya Pradesh	2.72	5.46	1.53	-1.25	0.00
Maharashtra	2.50	3.05	0.41	-0.14	0.00
Orissa	5.98	5.56	0.61	1.03	0.00
Punjab	2.54	1.88	0.17	0.83	0.00
Rajasthan	3.32	3.10	0.20	0.42	0.00
Tamil Nadu	0.96	1.83	0.86	-0.01	0.00
Uttar Pradesh	1.86	5.10	1.99	-1.25	0.00
West Bengal	2.47	1.16	0.13	1.45	0.00
Average	2.28	2.99	0.89	0.15	0.03
II. Special Category					
Arunachal Pradesh	6.79	12.49	5.63	-0.06	0.00
Assam	2.05	3.05	1.18	0.19	0.00
Himachal Pradesh	6.09	6.18	0.32	-0.13	0.36
Jammu and Kashmir	0.52	5.59	5.30	0.22	0.02
Manipur	2.55	17.12	14.57	0.00	0.00
Meghalaya	1.54	0.76	0.12	0.89	0.00
Mizoram	6.68	7.05	1.36	0.99	0.00
Nagaland	0.96	4.38	3.42	0.00	0.00
Sikkim	-1.49	-2.81	-1.65	-0.34	0.00
Tripura	3.20	5.66	2.47	0.01	0.00
Uttarakhand	0.88	2.03	1.48	0.34	0.00
Average	2.71	5.59	3.11	0.19	0.03
All States	2.37	3.90	1.77	0.21	0.03

Source: Same as Figure 12.1.

also exhibited similar outcomes of revenue account adjustments being neutralised significantly by relatively large increase in capital outlay, thereby limiting their adjustment of fiscal deficit to a small one.

It is a matter of some comfort that Indian states understand the importance of capital outlays (possibly on social and economic services) *qua* public investment for development, even at a time of strong pressures to cut their fiscal deficits. This behaviour in fact negates some views that capital outlays are the first casualty during times of belt-tightening, as they constitute expenditures that are most discretionary in nature. Many of the states (but not all) have preferred to cut down on net lending instead, which may not necessarily be a bad development; in many cases such lendings were only to perpetuate dysfunctional public enterprises that also had become financial liabilities. The fiscal adjustments could have proved to be the necessary catalyst for public enterprise reforms.

Liabilities

Fiscal sustainability of a state government is also judged by its fiscal liabilities position, apart from its deficits. This is obviously because liabilities provide the stock figure, which annual deficits add to. A small amount of liabilities can allow high levels of deficit for some time without affecting sustainability too much, while a high level of liabilities reduces the tolerance for deficits drastically. It is for this reason that the TwFC had recommended a prudent maximum level of state indebtedness at 25 per cent of GSDP. Since the reference period for the analysis here is a decade, it provides ample scope for substantial changes in fiscal liabilities flowing from fiscal reforms.

The changes in the fiscal liabilities position is shown in Figures 12.7 and 12.8 for the general and special category states respectively. In the general category states, the pattern of fiscal adjustment with respect to fiscal liabilities by and large replicates the adjustment in fiscal deficits with some notable exceptions. Despite significant reductions in fiscal deficit, Andhra Pradesh, Kerala, Madhya Pradesh, Uttar Pradesh and West Bengal managed only a small reduction in the accumulated liabilities. In contrast, Haryana managed a larger reduction in the liabilities in spite of a small adjustment in fiscal deficit. The largest reduction in liabilities occurred again in Odisha (more than 28 percentage points); other states

Figure 12.7

Total Liability/GSDP (Non-Special Category States)

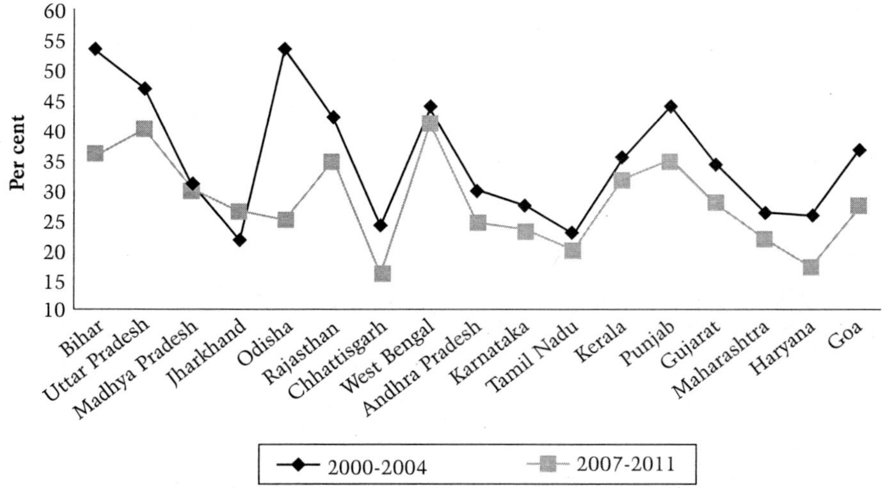

Source: Same as Figure 12.1.

Figure 12.8

Total Liability/GSDP (Special Category States)

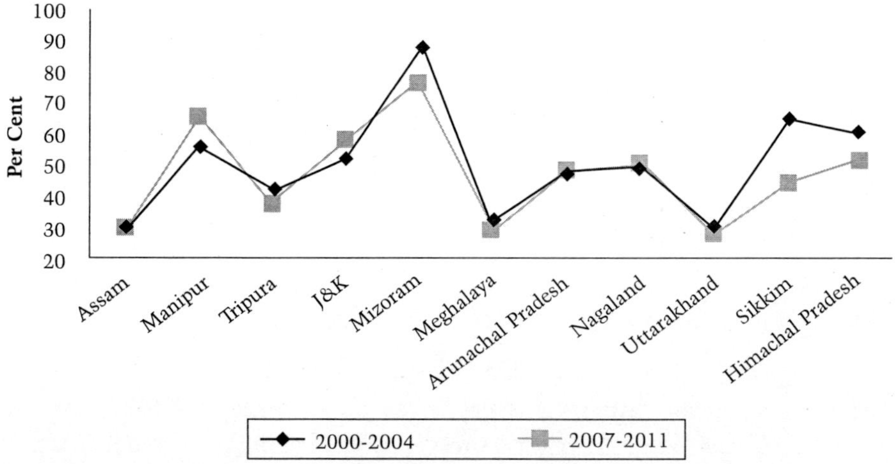

Source: Same as Figure 12.1.

with large reductions were Bihar and Punjab (about 18 and 12 percentage points respectively). The average reduction of all general category states was a substantial 6.6 percentage points. After the reduction, the four-year average for the second period was the lowest in Chhattisgarh (16% of GSDP); other states below the 25 per cent prudent limit were Andhra Pradesh, Karnataka, Tamil Nadu, Maharashtra and Haryana. The figure for Odisha was marginally above 25 per cent; but with progressively declining liabilities, its latest figure was below the prudent limit and likely to decline further. The highest post-adjustment average was in West Bengal (42%).

Special category states reduced their collective fiscal liability by 2.03 percentage point between the first and the second period, a smaller reduction compared to the general category states. Though large reductions occurred in Sikkim, Himachal Pradesh and Uttarakhand (13.85, 11.46 and 7.71 percentage points respectively), states like Jammu & Kashmir, Arunachal Pradesh, Manipur, Meghalaya, Mizoram, Nagaland recorded an increase in outstanding liability. The increase in Jammu & Kashmir was the largest by 6.19 percentage points, but the states that had fairly high levels of liabilities even in the second period averages were Mizoram and Manipur, at 76 and 66 per cent of GSDP respectively. None of these states could pull down their liabilities below the prudent limit of 25 per cent of GSDP, the lowest being in Meghalaya at a little higher than 29 per cent. Uttarakhand and Assam also had similar levels of fiscal liability.

Reduction in Interest Payments

In recent years, interest payments have been one of the major components of revenue expenditure of states, so much so that the TwFC felt obliged to indicate a prudent limit for it. The reasons for rising interest payments have been discussed at length in the relevant literature. Instead of going into that discussion, we examine here the extent of reduction in interest payments for individual states in the background of the prominent role played by expenditure contraction in the adjustment efforts of states.

Figures 12. 9 and 12.10 depict the reduction from the first to second period average of interest payments (as percentages of GSDP) for the general and special category states respectively. Among the general category states, the largest reductions in interest payments are seen in Odisha and Bihar. It may be recalled that the huge deficit reduction in Odisha was

Figure 12.9

Reduction in Interest Payments (General Category States)

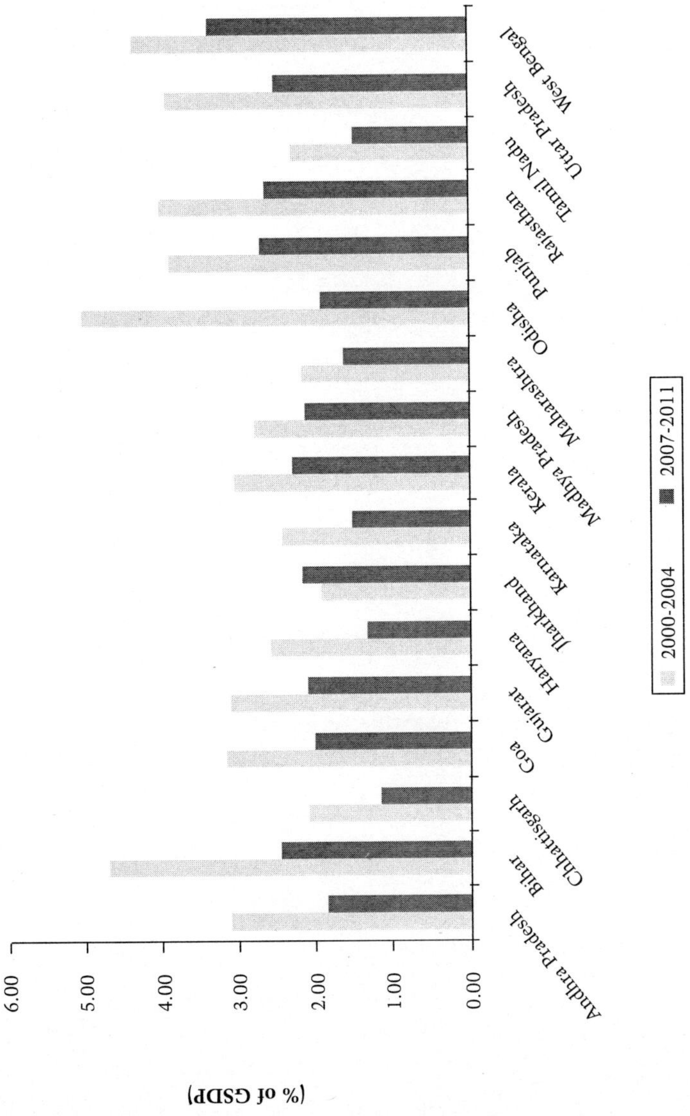

Source: Same as Figure 12.1.

Figure 12.10

Reduction in Interest Payments (Special Category States)

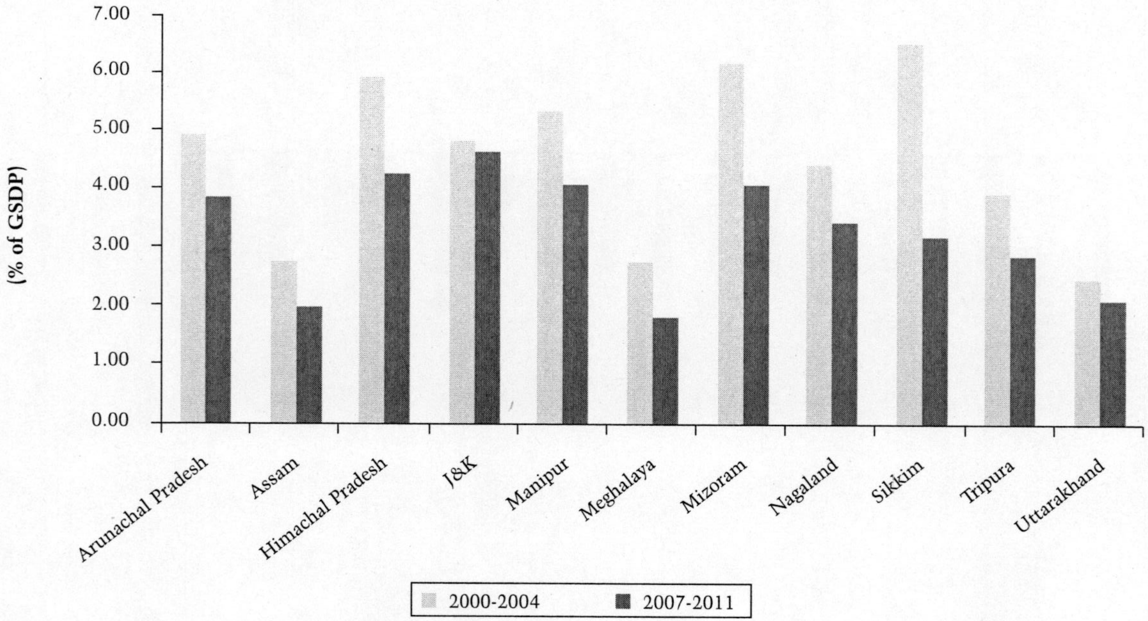

Source: Same as Figure 12.1.

largely ascribable to a large reduction in revenue expenditures; it turns out that it was primarily caused by a large reduction in interest payments, thus removing the possibility of a significant contraction of developmental expenditures. In Bihar, it makes the quality of the adjustment even better—the large reduction in interest payment means that the perceived expenditure contraction was actually increase in expenditures in terms of non-interest revenue expenditures. The only state showing increase in interest payment is Jharkhand, and probably this contributed to lack of fiscal adjustment there. Among other states with relatively high interest outgo were Punjab, Rajasthan, Uttar Pradesh, and West Bengal. Of these, the reduction was the least in West Bengal, coinciding with its inability to cut down its revenue deficit by a large margin that was required to bring its fiscal balance to a comfortable level. Clearly, the importance of being able to reduce interest payments in undertaking fiscal adjustment cannot be minimised.

In the special category states, all of them succeeded in reducing their interest payments. Sikkim, Mizoram, Himachal Pradesh and Manipur had the highest levels of interest-GSDP ratios; despite significant reductions in the ratios, all four continued to have relatively high interest outgo in the second period too. But the highest level of post-adjustment interest payments is seen in Jammu & Kashmir, which could reduce the same from the first to the second period only marginally. The link between reduction in interest payments and the extent of fiscal correction achieved is not seen to be so clear-cut in the case of special category states, because not many of them relied on expenditure contraction to achieve fiscal adjustment.

Fiscal Adjustment by Income Groups of States

We now try to ascertain whether the fiscal adjustment process was more strenuous for the poorer states or not. This presumption has some logical basis: in a normative sense, the revenue base in the poorer states is smaller but the expenditure responsibilities are larger because of lower private capacity to pay for various services and the need for larger investments for development, leading to higher deficits. The fact that this is not seen in the actual numbers for deficits of income categories of states is mainly because per capita expenditures in Indian states are positively correlated with per capita incomes—the affordability factor is much

Table 12.3

Trends in Fiscal Adjustment by Per Capita Income Groups

(Percentage of GSDP)

	Revenue Deficit			*Fiscal Deficit*			*Primary Deficit*			*Total Liability*		
States	*2000-04*	*2007-11*	*Reduction*	*2000-04*	*2007-11*	*Reduction*	*2000-04*	*2007-11*	*Reduction*	*2000-04*	*2007-11*	*Reduction*
High income	2.71	0.56	2.16	4.62	2.72	1.89	1.63	0.81	0.82	34.42	25.40	9.01
Medium income	2.85	0.96	1.89	4.66	3.02	1.63	1.63	0.94	0.69	30.59	28.29	2.29
Low income	2.40	-1.54	3.94	4.69	1.99	2.70	1.22	-0.12	1.34	36.50	28.55	7.95

Source: Same as Figure 12.1.

more important than need. In any case, given the relative compulsion of their fiscal stance, imposition of a uniform level of deficits across the states would be expected to strain the poorer states to a greater extent. Nonetheless, they would also be expected to undertake the strain more enthusiastically, since the payoff in terms of the incentives would be more attractive to them because of paucity of resources. Table 12.3 summarises the actual adjustments by income categories of states.

It can be seen from Table 12.3 that it is indeed the low-income states that have undertaken a greater extent of fiscal adjustment than both high-income and middle-income states in terms of all deficit indicators. To the extent that this was achieved through methods other than contraction of developmental expenditure and capital outlay, it would not be so much a matter of concern. Our discussion regarding the decomposition of revenue account adjustments coupled with the discussion of interest payments shows that there was no serious contraction of developmental expenditure in low income states except in Odisha (to a small extent). This leads to the conclusion that the negative fallout of the fiscal adjustment process should have been minimal, one that contradicts some earlier observations that the process adversely affected social sector expenditures to a significant extent [see Sethi (2009), for example].[3] In the cases where own revenues contributed a large part of fiscal adjustment also, there could possibly be a negative impact in that states' own revenue receipts which are mostly indirect taxes and user charges that may not be progressive in nature, and a higher resource mobilisation by the government could mean a significant reduction in the already limited private disposable income (and therefore consumption) in low-income states. Reverting again to the decomposition of revenue account adjustments, four low-income states are seen to have relied to a significant extent on own revenues—Chhattisgarh, Jharkhand, Madhya Pradesh and Uttar Pradesh. The possibility of increased hardships

3. Possible reasons explaining the opposing conclusions derived from essentially a similar set of budgetary data would be that the present paper uses a longer data set and comparison of averages over two periods of time instead of relying on year-to-year changes. It may be noted in passing that for proper comparison of public expenditure in the social sector at the sub-national level, it is necessary to consider those outside the budget (through various 'societies' set up by centrally sponsored schemes like Sarva Shiksha Abhiyan (SSA) or National Rural Health Mission (NRHM)), because the latter increased significantly after the initial one or two years of the last decade.

for the citizens of these states as a result of the fiscal correction undertaken cannot be dismissed, although a firmer assessment can be made only after a detailed examination of the sources of increased revenues in each of them.

Concluding Observations

Few would dispute the need for fiscal adjustments that was expressed by many observers during the early years of the last decade. Such adjustments had become important for both the central and the state governments in general. Apart from reducing the deficits, reducing the high levels of indebtedness was also considered to be a policy priority. The TwFC and the 13th Finance Commissions took these concerns on board, although their motivation appeared to be more in the context of macroeconomic concerns and not so much the fiscal health and consequent developmental issues relating to the governments concerned. This is relevant to the present discussion because the wrong motivation (considered 'wrong' here because macroeconomic stabilisation is not really a subject in the domain of the states, and it was unfair to make them bear the burden of adjustments to achieve that objective) possibly led to the choice of the fiscal rules that were incentivised, and the choice might not have been the right one. It is possible to think of alternatives like the 'golden rule' that any excess of deficits over the stipulated target must be expended for capital outlay. Such a rule is in operation in Germany for example, and it would be less stifling on the developmental aspirations of the poorer states than the present system. If we consider the objections to the extant system as (i) eroding state autonomy (Ghosh, 2005), and (ii) using a naïve 'one size fits all' approach, perhaps both strands of objections can be largely met using an alternative approach like the 'golden rule'. The objections, and the charge of the Finance Commissions (FCs) playing into the hands of the Central government become even more serious in the light of the allegations by Buiter and Patel (2012) that the 'fiscal room' created by the state level adjustments was usurped by the Centre, leading to little macroeconomic impact. Future FC recommendations may thus do well to consider alternative fiscal rules as a matter of principle, if such rules are to be continued.

During the initial stages of adjustment, as our analysis shows, there was scope for carrying out such adjustment successfully without actually reducing important public expenditures, and thus the impact was probably not felt so much by the ordinary citizens; temporary adjustment of the deficit targets in response to the global recession also helped to mitigate the negative impact of fiscal adjustments to some extent. Both these factors are likely to be absent now, and the objections raised earlier could apply with their full force only in the near future. Thankfully, at least at the sub-national level, fiscal indicators including indebtedness are at levels far less worrisome than before, obviating the need for stringent measures. This opportunity may be utilised to bring in reforms in the system that would reward good fiscal management, which is probably not the case now as Bose *et al.* (2011) indicate in the context of state borrowings and market-determined coupon rates for the same. This would constitute a more durable incentive than anything awarded through specific policy prescriptions. Pointers in the direction of establishing a well-functioning and fair sub-national debt market that can be built upon are available in the literature (Noel, 2000; Sen, 2003 for example). It hardly needs reiterating that the overarching objective of all public agencies, even an essentially arbitrating body like the FC, is to achieve the highest degree of socioeconomic development possible, particularly in the less developed regions, and all policy prescriptions must pass this litmus test.

References

Ahmad, Ehtisham, Maria Albino-War and Raju Singh (2005). "Subnational Public Financial Management: Institutions and Macroeconomic Considerations", *IMF Working Paper No. WP/05/108*. Washington D.C.

Balassone, Fabrizio, Daniele Franco and Stefania Zotteri (2003). "Fiscal Rules for Subnational Governments in the EMU Context", *Societa italiana di economia publica Working Paper* No. 196/2003. Pavia.

Baskaran, Thushyanthan (2010). "On the Link between Fiscal Decentralization and Public Debt in OECD Countries", Online at *http://mpra.ub.uni-muenchen.de/21599/*

Bose, Dhritidyuti, Rajeev Jain and L. Lakshmanan (2011). "Determinants of Primary Yield Spreads of States in India: An Econometric Analysis", *Working Paper* 10/2011. Mumbai: Department of Economic and Policy Research, Reserve Bank of India.

Buiter, Willem H. and Urjit R. Patel (2012). "Fiscal Rules in India: Are they Effective?", in Chetan Ghate (ed.), *Handbook of the Indian Economy.* New Delhi: Oxford University Press. pp. 621-55.

Drummond, Paulo and Ali Mansoor (2002). "Macroeconomic Management and Devolution of Fiscal Powers", *IMF Working Paper* No. WP/02/76. Washington D.C.

Ghosh, Jayati (2005). "Twelfth Finance Commission and Restructuring of State Government Debt: A Note", *Economic and Political Weekly:* 3435-39, July 30.

Groneck, Max (2010). "A Golden Rule of Public Finance or a Fixed Deficit Regime? Growth and Welfare Effects of Budget Rules", *Economic Modelling* 27: 523-34.

Gurumurthi, S. (2002). "Twelfth Finance Commission and States' Debt Burden", *Economic and Political Weekly*: 4135-42, October 05.

Kennedy, Suzanne and Janine Robbins (2001). "The Role of Fiscal Rules in Determining Fiscal Performance", *Department of Finance Working Paper* 2001-16. Government of Canada. Online at *http://www.publications.gc.ca/collections/Collection/F21-8-2001-16E.pdf*

Noel, Michel (2000). "Building Subnational Debt Markets in Developing and Transition Economies", *Policy Research Working Paper* 2339. Washington D.C.: The World Bank.

Rajaraman, Indira, Shashank Bhide and R.K. Pattnaik (2005). *A Study of Debt Sustainability at State Level in India.* Mumbai: Reserve Bank of India.

Rao, M. Govinda (2002). "State Finances in India: Issues and Challenges", *Economic and Political Weekly*: 3261-71, August 03.

Rangarajan, C. and Abha Prasad (2013). "Managing State Debt and Ensuring Solvency: The Indian Experience", in Otaviano Canuto and Lili Liu (eds.), *Until Debt Do Us Part.* Washington D.C.: The World Bank. pp.109-44.

Sen, Tapas K. (2003). "Finances of Governments and their Capacity to Spend", in *India Infrastructure Report 2003: Public Expenditure Allocation and Accountability.* Published for the 3i Network. New Delhi: Oxford University Press. pp.140-50

———. (2012). "Recent Developments in Kerala State Finances", *Working Paper Series* 449. Thiruvananthapuram: Centre for Development Studies.

Sethi, Tanya (2009). "Can Poor States Afford the Fiscal Responsibility Legislation?", *Economic and Political Weekly*: 18-22, October 10.

13 Debt Sustainability in Indian States

N. Srinivasa Rao and Divya Parmar

Introduction

Debt sustainability is defined as the ability of a country to meet its debt obligations without requiring debt relief or accumulating arrears. To assess this type of debt sustainability, three main international methodologies have been developed by the International Monetary Fund (IMF) and World Bank. They are:

(i) Heavily Indebted Poor Countries Debt Relief Analyses,

(ii) The Low Income Countries Debt Sustainability Framework (LIC-DSF).

(iii) The Middle-Income Countries Debt Sustainability Framework (MIC-DSF).

They all involve making projections of intended borrowings and economic variables over a maximum 20-year period, and then using ratios comparing debt stock, present value or debt service with GDP (gross domestic product), exports or budget revenue to assess payment capacity of a country. These assessments are useful from a financial point of view. However, developing countries see debt sustainability as fully positive only if it is providing enough finance to reach their overall national development goals. Therefore, the key aim of assessing debt sustainability should be to reconcile financing needs for development along with sustainable debt levels.

Continuous government borrowing to cover fiscal imbalances results in an ever-rising public debt, the servicing of which must eventually come out of public revenues in subsequent years. As public debt accumulates, there is legitimate concern over whether the borrowing government will be in a position to service its debt. Ultimately, when financial markets perceive the debt stock of any government as unsustainable, further lending to that government will stop. Many state governments in India are precariously close to such a situation. A look at the trends and patterns over the last three decades (1980–2010) in India, which span both the pre- and post-reform period, helps us understand the relationship between fiscal expansion and growth in the Indian economy. The first surge in India's economic growth rate came in the early 1980s, when it increased to above 5 per cent, which was achieved by unsustainable fiscal expansion financed by domestic credit and external borrowing. Growth accelerated to 5.8 per cent during the 1980s, but in the second half of the decade, fiscal and current account deficits widened significantly, causing macroeconomic imbalances and culminating in the BoP (balance of payment) crisis of 1991. Thus initiating the economic reforms. The present paper initiates the discussion with explaining what is state debt and moves ahead with discussing various channels of fiscal transfers, deficit financing, measures taken by the central government in restricting the debt and the problem of sustainability.

What is State Debt?

States' debt consists of all liabilities that require payment of interest and /or principal by the state government at some future date. In India, under Article 293 (3) of the Constitution, a state may not without the consent of the Government of India (GoI) raise any loan if there is any part of a loan still outstanding which has been made to the state by the GoI or by its predecessor government, or in respect of which a guarantee has been given by the GoI or by its predecessor government. The Gadgil formula in 1969 (named after the then deputy chairman of the Planning Commission Dr D.R. Gadgil), was formulated with the formulation of the Fourth Five Year Plan for the distribution of plan transfers amongst the states. Other than giving preference to the special category states, the balance of the central assistance was decided to be distributed among the remaining states on the basis of the following criteria:

(i) Sixty per cent on the basis of population.

(ii) Ten per cent on the basis of tax effort, determined on the basis of individual state's per capita tax receipts as percentage of the state's per capita income.

(iii) Ten per cent on the basis of per capita state income, assistance going only to states whose per capita incomes are below the national average.

(iv) Ten per cent on the basis of spill-over into the Fourth Plan of major continuing irrigation and power projects.

(v) Ten per cent for special problems of individual states.

The 11th Finance Commission (EFC) (for the period 2000-2005), for the first time, introduced the concept of overall ceiling on total central transfers to states from all channels on the revenue account. The indicative ceiling recommended by the Commission was 37.5 per cent of the gross revenue receipts of the Centre. This was raised to 38 per cent by the 12th Finance Commission (TwFC). This indicative ceiling was based on the then prevailing level of transfers on the revenue account. The recommendation of the indicative ceiling seems to have been prompted by considerations relating to macroeconomic and fiscal stability. This has prompted states to demand that the total revenue account transfers might be fixed at 50 per cent of the gross revenue receipts of the Centre on the ground that this was the level reached in the year 1999-2000.

The TwFC (for 2005-2010) recommended a multi-dimensional restructuring aimed at both qualitative and quantitative aspects of managing government finances. The core strategy centred on raising the trend rate of growth by reducing government dis-savings, which in turn required elimination of revenue deficit and reduction of fiscal deficit. Fiscal consolidation suggested by the Commission included elimination of revenue deficit by the Centre and the states by 2008-09, reducing fiscal deficit to 3 per cent of GSDP (gross state domestic product)/GDP by the states and the Centre and bringing down the combined debt-GDP ratio to 75 per cent by 2009-10. The long term goal for the Centre and the states as suggested by the Commission was to bring down and maintain the debt-GDP ratio at no more than 28 per cent each. To achieve these levels, the Commission recommended wide ranging reforms on tax, non-tax and expenditure fronts. The TwFC was also asked to examine the issue whether non-tax income of profit petroleum to the Union, arising out of contractual provisions, should be shared with the states and if so, to what extent.

Definition of Fiscal Transfers

There are four components or channels to the fiscal transfer system with implied associated hierarchical controls.

Finance Commission Transfers

Rules for making transfer awards have varied from Commission to Commission, so that a set of firm principles to guide incoming Commissions has not evolved. Minor debt relief has been extended periodically by the Centre to states on the recommendations of successive Finance Commissions (FCs) but it was seen that when the quantum of debt relief is normalised by the state domestic product of the year in which it was granted, the trend is clearly one of decreased relative commitment to central debt forgiveness over time.

Whereas, the tax shares were allocated to states on the basis of objective criteria such as population and disparities in per capita state income, block grants have been allocated to states on the basis of their projected gap on non-plan account between projected revenues and projected expenditures for a five-year period. Using these projections, the Commission makes recommendations for tax devolution and grants-in-aid as required by the Constitution to achieve a hypothetical balance or surplus on non-plan current account. This gap filling methodology has been a major contributor to softening of originally hard budget constraints of the states by encouraging them to slip from current account surpluses into deficit positions.

Econometric research on the determinants of states own tax effort also indicates that increases in grants from the Central government to the states have reduced the efficiency of tax collections by states and that the poorer states, which benefit most from the gap filling approach, are the least efficient in tax collection. Jha *et al.* (1999) model the determinants of tax effort by major states and find that the higher the ratio of central grants in total expenditures of any government, the lower is its tax effort.

The 10th Finance Commission (TFC) sought to reform the incentive of the transfer system by recommending:

(i) A phased reduction of general grants-in-aid, which had previously been used to fill revenue gaps between current revenues and expenditures; and

(ii) Two new incentive schemes for debt relief of principal owed to the Centre, one tied to improvement in fiscal performance in the current account, and a matching debt relief scheme tied to the amount of state PE (public enterprises) divestment proceeds used to retire state debt.

These two debt reduction schemes might have been expected to provide a powerful incentive for the states to adjust, but in practice the actual fiscal benefits realised by the states from these schemes has not been much. Little privatisation of state-owned enterprises has occurred since the release of the TFC's report, in part because of the political power of state employees, who resist privatisation.

Successive FCs also established a tradition of unconditional debt forgiveness. The 6th, 7th and 8th FCs gave substantial debt relief to the most indebted states in the proportion of their indebtedness relative to the size of their economies.

Planning Commission Transfers

The second channel is provided by the Planning Commission, which has a mandate to coordinate the development plans of the Centre and the states. At its inception, the Planning Commission was enjoined to reduce poverty and to work to minimise inequalities in income, status, facilities, and opportunities among individuals and groups. The states were responsible for preparing their own plans. However, these were assessed and adjudicated by the Planning Commission in terms of national objectives and norms before financial support of a state plan secured.

Most transfers awarded by the Planning Commission to the larger states are block transfers, composed of loans (70%) and grants (30%). The Centre also lends bilateral and multilateral agency lending on the same terms as for regular Plan assistance. A formula based largely on population and deviations in per capita income among the states provides a transparent foundation for most grant and debt financing. However, despite the great reliance on formula-based transfers, the annual bilateral negotiations between the Planning Commission and individual states introduces an element of non-transparency into state debt financing and encourages states to pursue fiscal policies leading to moral hazard problems. Much discretion remains at the margin for the Planning Commission to augment both the grant resources of individual states.

Conditional Grant Transfers

The third channel for transfer is conditional matching grants (usually covering between 50% to 80% of costs) for shared cost programmes for Centrally-Sponsored Schemes (CSS) which are intended to ensure that the Center can influence state priorities so as to achieve national policy goals. Examples of such programmes include: primary education expansion programmes, child nutrition programmes, public works and poverty alleviation schemes. The mushrooming of centrally sponsored or shared cost schemes designed and monitored by the Central government has increased state dependency on central resources to finance marginal expenditures. In 1995-96 there were 182 CSS being supported with central funding equivalent to 1.3 per cent of GDP. The vast number of such schemes, their high administrative overhead costs and rigid eligibility criteria, have undermined effectiveness and distorted state priorities. The Centre intends to streamline the CSS system and convert most of the programmes into block grants, but little progress has been made in this initiative to date. One reason for the lack of progress is that the new block funding which has been offered to the states, as a *quid pro quo,* is less generous than existing funding.

Deficit Financing

The fourth channel is deficit financing. Most of this is provided with implicit central guarantees. In the mid-nineties, about 38 per cent of the aggregate fiscal deficit of all states had been financed with net loans from the Centre. This was a dramatic decline from a 50 per cent contribution in 1991-92, reflecting the increased burden of repaying past loan principal. Most of the remaining components in deficit financing are controlled directly or indirectly by the Central government. 'Market borrowings', which designate resources from captive sources of finance, are state-issued bonds placed with banks (as part of their statutory liquidity ratios [SLR] requirements which these institutions must meet), insurance companies and non-government pension and provident funds. The Central government allocates the SLR securities among states, while states initiate other forms of borrowing. The Central Bank assumes responsibility for marketing or assigning the agreed debt obligations of individual states to financial institutions. This is how most of the state issued debt gets into the financial system and is mostly held by the major financial institutions (FIs) such as banks, provident funds, insurance companies and cooperatives. However, with the stabilisation of state finances the trend in the fiscal indicators such as GFD (gross fiscal deficit), RD (revenue deficit) and PD (primary deficit) as well as interest payments and debt have undergone sharp improvement as shown in Figure 13.1 (A and B).

An analysis on states' fiscal deficit, revenue deficit, primary deficit and debt to GSDP since economic reforms broadly exhibits three distinct phases. In the first phase which begins from the early 1990s to mid-1990s, fiscal deficit fell to 2.8 per cent of GSDP in 1997-98 against 3.2 per cent in 1990-91. Similarly falling trends had been witnessed in revenue and primary deficits, and debt levels. However, interest payment burden as a fraction of revenue receipts registered a modest growth.

In contrast, the second phase from 1998-99 to 2003-04, was characterised by sharp deterioration in state finances with all key deficit indicators, debt levels and interest burden rising. Fiscal deficit as a ratio of GDP hovered in the range of 4 to 4.5 per cent against 2.5 to 3 per cent during first phase; revenue deficit doubled to 2.2 per cent in 2003-04 from 1.1 per cent in 1997-98. Ratio of debt to GDP reached a record high of 31.8 per cent in 2003-04 in comparison to 21 per cent in 1997-98. Interest payment burden rose significantly in the second phase averaging 23.4 per cent against 15.4 per cent in the first phase.

The last phase since 2004-05 onwards witnessed unprecedented improvement in fiscal health of the states. The enactment of Fiscal Responsibility and Budget Management Act (FRBM) in 2004 and recommendations by TwFC helped to contain all key deficit indicators, debt levels and interest burden. Targets of zero revenue deficit and reducing

Figure 13.1

Trends and Composition of States' Deficits, Debts and Interest Payment

A

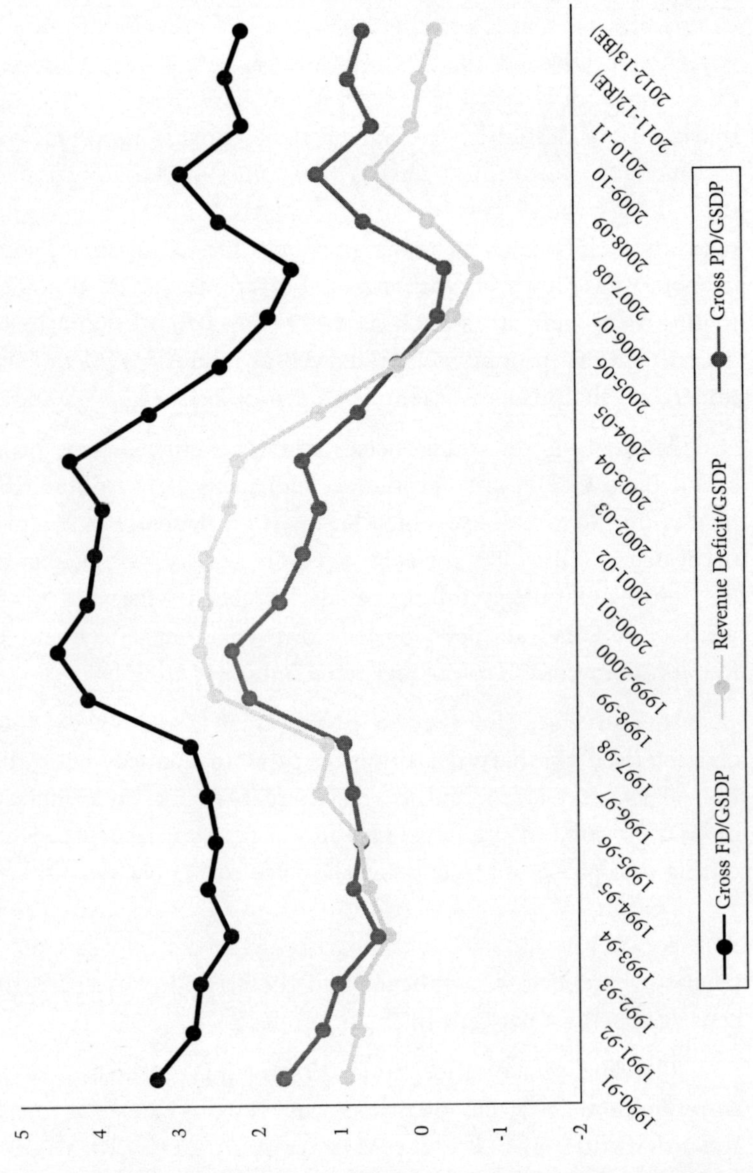

B

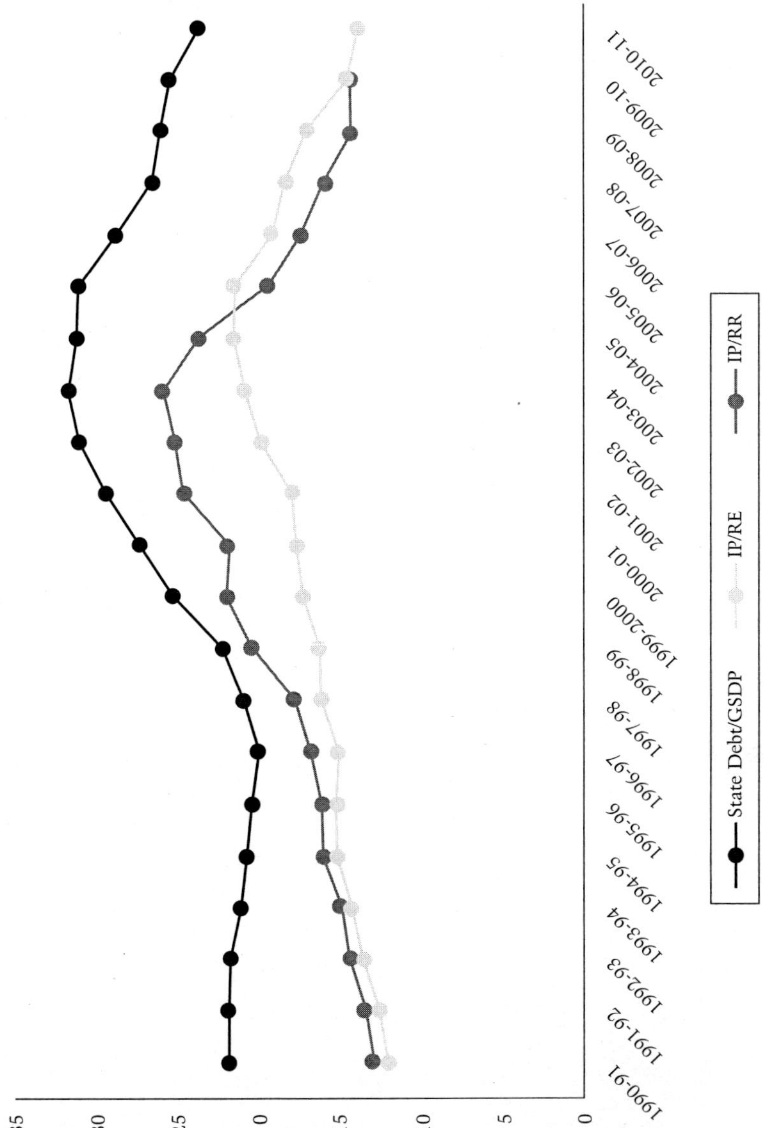

Note: IP= Interest Payment; RR= Revenue Receipts; RE=Revenue Expenditure.

Source: Reserve Bank of India (RBI) Databse and author's calculations.

Figure 13.2

Financing Pattern of State Deficits

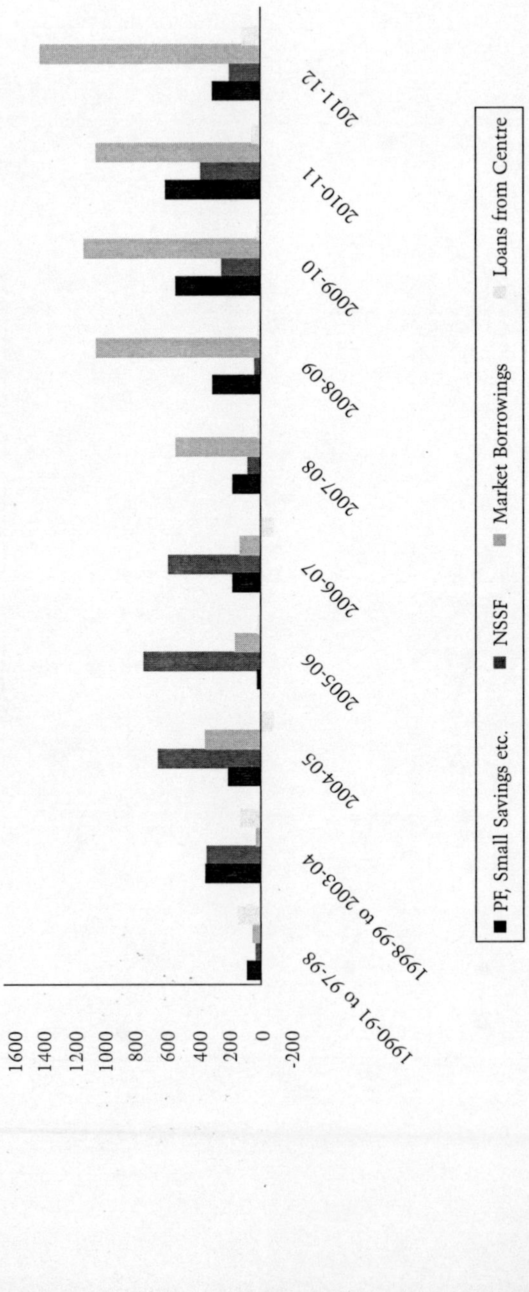

Source: RBI, *A Study of State Budgets.*

fiscal deficit to three per cent by 2008-09 set by TwFC were successfully achieved. Even revenue and primary deficits turned into surplus between 2006-07 and 2008-09.

Figure 13.C illustrates changing pattern in financing of states' deficits. Until the mid-2000s, loans from Central government dominated, amounted to around half of the GFD. While the pattern reversed by the enactment of Fiscal Responsibility Legislation (FRL) by the TwFC. The central assistance to states in the form of grants, loans and transfer of external assistance to states was drastically reduced, reflecting sharp rise in market borrowings. It multiplied to ₹ 1,413 billion in 2011-12 from ₹ 345 billion in 2004-05. Increase in the National Small Savings Fund (NSSF) and small savings borrowings since 2004-05 became evident. In short, the overall trend indicates move towards market-based financing of state deficits since mid-2000.

Measures Taken by Central Government to Restructure Debt

A glance at year-wise states' loans from the Centre since 2002-03 suggests a negative pattern in central loans while there was a sharp rise in market borrowings. After digging deep it was realised that these were the results of measures taken by the Central government to restructure the state debt. These include: (i) Debt Swap Scheme (DSS) in operation from 2002-03 to 2004-05, to mitigate the burden of interest payments on the states, and supplement their efforts towards fiscal management; (ii) Debt Consolidation and Relief Facility (DCRF) introduced during 2005-06, based on recommendations of the TwFC, provided debt relief through debt consolidation and debt write-off.

As the name suggests, under DSS states' loans from the Central government were swapped with low cost market borrowings and their net small savings proceeds at the prevailing interest rates, over a period of three years ending in 2004-05. Total debt swapped between 2002-03 and 2004-05 amounted to ₹ 1,020.3 billion. Half of it was financed through additional market borrowings at interest rates below 6.5 per cent, which was less than half the earlier cost, and the remaining was financed through the issue of special securities to the NSSF at interest rates fixed at 9.5 per cent, earlier rate being 13 per cent. However, it is worth noting that this scheme reduced the interest payment due on outstanding debt, not the amount of outstanding debt.

Under DCRF, cumulative central loans to the states until March 31 2004 and outstanding as on March 31 2005, have been consolidated into fresh loans for 20 years and to be repaid in 20 equal instalments, carrying a lower interest rate of 7.5 per cent.[1] Repayments due from states on these loans during 2005-06 to 2009-10 were eligible for write-off, but only those states can avail the option who have met the condition of enacting FRBM. Therefore, all the states except Sikkim and West Bengal availed debt consolidation during 2005-06 to 2009-10.

Cumulatively central loans amounting to ₹ 1,224 billion were consolidated during 2005-06 to 2009-10, standing at 7.4 per cent[2] of total outstanding debt of states at the end of 2009-10. Further debt consolidation resulted into interest relief and debt relief, amounting to ₹ 186.9 billion and ₹ 197.3 billion respectively during 2005-06 to 2009-10 (Table 13.1). The resultant interest benefit was 3.8 per cent of the cumulative interest payments during 2005-06 to 2009-10. Uttar Pradesh, Andhra Pradesh and Gujarat availed the highest interest and debt reliefs among non-special category (NSC) states while Arunachal Pradesh, Assam and Himachal Pradesh among special category (SC) states (Table 13.1).

The Problem of Sustainability

By 2002-03, the debt of major states stood at 41 per cent of their combined GSDP, higher by 15.7 percentage points than the average for the quinquennium1992-1997. This overall change covers a wide range. Among the major states, the rise in Bihar was 33 per cent, as against a fall in Goa by nearly 1 per cent. The worrying aspect of the trajectory of debt among the major states is that the more indebted states prior to 1997 in general saw larger increases in their debt ratio. Excluding Goa, the rank correlation coefficient between rankings by levels in 1992-1997, and the ranking by change to 2002-03, works out to 0.73, and is statistically significant. The interest rate on state debt crossed the nominal growth rate of GSDP during

1. *State Finances: A Study of Budgets*, Reserve Bank of India.
2. 7.4 per cent is equivalent to the amount of 1,224 billion (in Rupees) as Central loans for the fiscal year 2009-10. It stands for the total outstanding debt proportion..

Table 13.1

Debt Consolidation, Debt Relief and Interest Relief

(₹ Billion)

No.	State	Debt Consolidation	2005-06 to 2009-10	
			Debt Relief	Interest Relief
1	Andhra Pradesh	140.6	25.9	25.2
2	Arunachal Pradesh	4.0	0.4	0.7
3	Assam	21.1	4.2	1.6
4	Bihar	77.0	7.7	12.7
5	Chhattisgarh	18.7	4.7	3.1
6	Goa	4.0	0.4	0.6
7	Gujarat	94.4	17.3	16.7
8	Haryana	19.3	2.9	3.0
9	Himachal Pradesh	9.1	1.2	1.6
10	Jharkhand	21.0	3.1	2.1
11	J&K	15.2	0.0	1.0
12	Karnataka	71.7	14.3	13.1
13	Kerala	41.8	2.5	7.0
14	Madhya Pradesh	72.6	18.2	13.2
15	Maharashtra	68.0	13.6	9.9
16	Manipur	7.5	1.5	0.3
17	Meghalaya	3.0	0.4	0.4
18	Mizoram	2.6	0.3	0.4
19	Nagaland	3.2	0.3	0.6
20	Odisha	76.4	19.1	9.6
21	Punjab	30.7	3.7	6.0
22	Rajasthan	61.7	9.3	8.9
23	Sikkim $	1.1	0.0	0.0
24	Tamil Nadu	52.7	13.2	9.1
25	Tripura	4.4	0.9	0.8
26	Uttarakhand	2.6	0.3	0.3
27	Uttar Pradesh	212.8	31.9	39.1
28	West Bengal $	86.3	0.0	0.0
	Total	1223.5	197.3	186.9

Note: $ Consolidation effective from 2010-11, under recommendations of 13th Finance Commission.

Source: *Indian Public Finance Statistics 2011-12.*

Table 13.2

Trends in Key Fiscal Indicators of Major States in India for the Last Two Decades

	1992-1997 (Average)			1997-2002 (Average)			2002-2007 (Average)			2007-2012 (Average)		
Non Special Category	*RD*	*GFD*	*Debt*	*RD*	*GFD*	*Debt*	*RD*	*GFD*	*Debt*	*RD*	*GFD*	*Debt*
1	2	3	4	5	6	7	8	9	10	11	12	13
Andhra Pradesh	1.1	3.2	22.4	1.7	4.2	27.2	0.7	3.4	32.8	-0.3	2.6	25.2
Bihar	2	3.5	37.8	1.9	3.8	47.3	0.3	4.6	55.9	-2.7	3.2	34.9
Goa	-1.1	2.8	41.6	2.3	4.6	32.8	0.8	4.2	38.2	-0.3	3.4	28.8
Gujarat	0.2	2.2	20.5	3.6	5.5	28.6	1.2	3.7	35.4	0.3	2.5	28.8
Haryana	0.9	2.6	20	2.1	4.2	24.6	-0.2	1.2	25.6	0.4	2.4	18.2
Karnataka	0.3	3.1	20.3	1.8	4	24.1	-0.3	2.8	27.6	-0.7	2.6	23.2
Kerala	1.3	3.4	28	3.9	5.5	34	3.1	4.1	37.1	1.7	3.1	31.7
Madhya Pradesh	0.3	2.3	22	2.1	3.3	23	0.4	4.6	37.4	-2.1	2.4	30.4
Maharashtra	0.4	2.5	17.9	2.3	3.9	24.1	1.7	4.0	29.9	-0.3	1.6	22.9
Odisha	2.1	5.2	41.7	5.5	8.2	53.7	0.7	2.6	51.4	-1.1	1.1	27.6
Punjab	2.3	4.4	36.2	4.2	6	41.5	2.9	4.2	46.4	2.5	3.8	34.4
Rajasthan	1.1	4.4	28.9	3.4	5.9	37.7	1.9	4.9	47.3	-0.1	2.2	34.5
Tamil Nadu	1.3	2.5	19.7	2.4	3.4	22	0.5	2.4	26.0	-0.1	2.3	21.7
Uttar Pradesh	1.7	4.3	34.2	3.7	5.7	37.6	2.5	4.6	52.0	-0.8	3.6	41.8
West Bengal	1.7	3.3	24.2	5	7	33.4	4.1	5.3	47.5	3.6	4.3	42.6
Total (All states)	1.1	3.2	25.3	3.1	5	31.9	1.06	3.14	30.84	-0.14	2.24	24.92

Note: Since Gujarat's GDP for 2011-12 is not available, its 2007-2012 average for RD and GFD consists of first four years.

Source: Directorate of Economics & Statistics of representive State Governments, and for All-India-CSO; State Finances, RBI.

the period 1997-2002. The interest rate on debt of major states, at 10.4 per cent on average in 1997-2002, was higher than the nominal growth rate of GSDP, of 9.9 per cent. This is in contrast to 1992-1997, when the interest rate was at 9.9 per cent, as against nominal GSDP growth of 16.1 per cent.

As can be seen from the Table 13.2, the debt of major states during 1992-1997 which was 25.3 per cent of all states' GSDP increased significantly to 31.9 per cent by the year 2001-02 and remained more or less at the same level, i.e., around 31 per cent by the end of 2006-07. However, the improvement in the state finances in general and revenue buoyancy in particular, and the fiscal measures implemented by the states consequent to the recommendations of TwFC have resulted in considerable progress in the quality of fiscal balances of the above mentioned major states. This is reflected in the ratios of revenue and fiscal deficits apart from the significant improvement in the overall debt position of the states.

Conclusion

In developed countries, the situation of fiscal deficits has been primarily met by reduction of expenditure, especially in respect of wages, transfers and interest payments. The expenditure adjustment was facilitated by reforms in public expenditure management, a larger role of the private sector in the provision of public goods, introduction of user charges, liberalising public procurement and voucher-based distribution of merit goods and services. The declining fiscal deficits have made a perceptible impact on the levels of public debt in advanced countries, and consequently on improving their fundamentals. To draw a parallel with the states in India, they too have significantly improved their revenue bases as well as increased their cash balances for better management of their fiscal deficits, thereby leading to improved debt positions during the past five years (2007-2012, refer Table 13.2) which led to release of resources for the development objectives of the states. This is further corroborated by the fact that almost all the states have enacted the respective FRBM in the years 2005 and 2006 which have clearly delineated the fiscal reform path over a five year horizon. They have also implemented several fiscal and economic reforms spanning several key growth areas which have resulted in the development benefits in most of the major states, for instance Bihar, Madhya Pradesh, Rajasthan and Gujarat have made significant strides in economic growth in recent years. Further, reforms such as VAT (value added tax) and other revenue-oriented measures have led to marked improvement in the revenue earning capacity of the states. A major boost to their revenue earning capacity would be the introduction of GST (goods and services tax) as early as possible, once a consensus is reached amongst the states and centre.

References

Alex, Dony (2009). "Debt Sustainability in India", *ICRIER Think Ink.* New Delhi: ICRIER. January 07.

De, Supriyo (2012). "Fiscal Policy in India: Trends and Trajectory", *Working Paper.* New Delhi: Ministry of Finance. January.

Jadhav, Narendra (n.d.). *Fiscal Sustainability in India: An Assessment and Implications.* Prepared with with inputs from the fiscal team of the the Department of Economic Analysis and Policy (DEAP), Reserve Bank of India.

Rajaraman, Indira, Shashank Bhide and R.K. Pattnaik (2005). *A Study of Debt Sustainability at State Level in India. Mumbai:* Reserve Bank of India. August.

Section IV : Sector Specific Issues

14 Financing of Elementary Education in India by Central Government through Centrally Sponsored Schemes

A Study of Sarva Shiksha Abhiyan

B. Shiva Reddy and K. Anji Reddy

Introduction

Education is important for economic and social development. Though the relative importance of different types and levels of education changes over time, place and level of development, all have their own place and role in their contribution to development. Therefore for overall development of the economy and society, overall development of education is of paramount importance.[1]

In the last six decades Indian education system (IES) has grown in all respects in terms of number of institutions, enrolment, teachers and in all other parameters used to measure the progress. This could not have been possible without earmarking sizeable resources—both financial and physical—and without the active support of the Central government, state governments and local bodies, and also the private sector. Though recent developments indicate an increase in the role of private sector, Government continues to play an important role in the management and financing.[2]

---

1. See Ozturk (2001) for the role of education for social and economic development.
2. The role of private sector increased in all levels and types of education in recent years. Even in elementary education the enrolment in private schools increased significantly in recent years from 18.7 per cent in 2006 to 28.3 per cent in 2012 (ASER, 2012:47). In some states like Kerala and Manipur, it is more than 60 per cent. This is also the period during which the number of schools opened under Sarva Shiksha Abhiyan (SSA) increased.

Among the different levels of education, Elementary Education (EE) accounts for the major share in terms of number of institutions, enrolment, teachers and financial resources. When compared to other levels and types of education, EE is receiving the maximum support from the government.

In the management and financing of EE, all levels of government—Central government, state governments and local bodies—are involved. The Constitution of India clearly specified their role and responsibilities in education. Amendments to the Constitution brought certain changes in their role. The 42nd Amendment shifted education from the State list to the Concurrent list. Through the 73rd and 74th Amendments, local bodies were assigned more role in education. Despite these amendments to the Constitution, the main responsibility in the management and of financing of EE continues to be with the state governments. However, the Central government's role is increasingly felt in the development of EE in recent years, mainly in the form of financing several schemes. The main form of financing EE by Central government is in the form of Centrally Sponsored Schemes (CSS) and at present the important CSS to finance EE is the SSA. Despite the increase in the role of Central government in financing of EE through CSS, not much research is done on different aspects related to it.

Therefore, in this paper an attempt is made to examine the role of Central government in financing of EE in India through SSA, the trends in the Central government expenditure on EE, particularly for the period after economic reforms, and the basic features of and trends in financing SSA. The problems and implications of financing of SSA by Central government for the development of EE are also explained and we conclude with a few possible suggestions.

The paper is based on the information/data collected mainly from the research work done on the related theme and some official publications. Though an attempt was made, authentication of data sources is not done except by acknowledging the sources from which the material is drawn.

Role of Central Government in Elementary Education

There is a controversy on the role of Central government in education. It was a state subject till 1976. The Constitutional Amendment of 1976 shifted education to the Concurrent List. Despite the fact that it was a state subject the Central government intervention in education continued even before 1976. According to Naik (1963) there were three important developments that necessitated the presence of Central government in education. First, there was a growing desire to evolve a national system of education for the country as a whole. Second, was the revival of central grants for education in the financial and administrative set-up created by the Constitution which vests all the best resources in the Centre and makes the states responsible for all the expensive social services. Third, development and adoption of centralised planning, and the creation of the Planning Commission, gave more responsibility of taking decisions to the Centre than to the States with regard to national targets, the fixation of priorities, the allocation of resources to different sectors including education (Naik, 1963).

All these developments have necessitated the amendment to the Constitution through which education was shifted from the State List to the Concurrent List. This had both legalised and also legitimised the involvement and dominance of the Central government in education sector. Many state governments have opposed this shifting of education to the Concurrent List. Though education was put under the Concurrent List, it did not show any difference in terms of organisation and financing of education in India till recently (Varghese and Tilak, 1991). After economic reforms, there were significant changes in the management and financing of all levels and types of education, including EE in the country. The most important change was the dominance of Central government in financing of EE through sponsoring different programmes.

The Central government intervenes in education in three main ways. The Central government has its own sector in education[3] besides the sectors listed in the Union List. Management as well as financial functions of this sector are the total responsibility of the Central government. These activities are planned, implemented and financed exclusively by the

3. The list includes Central Schools, the Regional Colleges of Education, National Scholarships, the programmes of the University Grants Commission (UGC) such as the creation of Centres for Advanced Study, etc.

Centre. Secondly, there is a sector[4] which is completely funded by Central government but implemented by the state government. They constitute a part of the central plan in respect of which the states act as executive agencies. Normally the states do not accept responsibility on their own for such activities. The Central government could, however, persuade the state governments to accept the responsibility of implementation of such activities. Thirdly, there is a sector[5] which includes activities in the promotion of which the Centre is actively interested though they are embodied in the state plans. The states only partially accept the financial responsibilities of this sector. The financial contribution of the Centre to such activities might vary according to the activity and the place of its implementation. But in a majority of the cases, the Central Government bears more burden than the states in the total cost of these activities. These activities which have become the dominant mode of financing by the Central government are referred to as CSS. The central grants for these three categories often lead to the decision-making at the state level being replaced by central decisions and to that extent such grants erode state autonomy (Chelliah *et al.*, 1981).

The role of Central government in education before the Constitutional Amendment of 1976 was explained by Naik (1963). Of the 18 functions of Central government in education there was one aspect dealing with EE. According to the Article 45 (read with Article 22) EE is the joint responsibility of both Central and state governments though it was part of the State list. According to Naik (1963: 25) "The role of the Government of India would obviously be restricted to the formulation of national targets to be reached, to the grant of financial assistance to State Governments for implementing this programme and to the maintenance of an equal standard of attainment, both in quantity and quality, in all parts of the country."

Naik also made a reference to the financing of education by Central government for the development of education in the states. According to him there are three forms of grants to states for financing education.

4. The activities in this sector include promotion of Sanskrit, Hindi in non-Hindi speaking states, promotion of students' tours, etc.
5. The opening of non-formal education centres, enrolment of handicapped students in the integrated schools, etc., are some of such activities. At present, all the major schemes in education fall under this category.

> The first is a transfer of additional revenues in order to enable the State Governments to plan their programs in all welfare services with greater confidence and self-reliance; the second is the institution of a general grant for educational purposes but not earmarked for any specific program; and the third is a specific purpose grant which is intended for a program organised and implemented with the approval of the Centre. It is obvious that if the autonomy and independence of the States is to be respected in the educational field, greater reliance will have to be placed on the first two of these grants (Naik 1963: 26).

But contrary to what Naik preferred, the third form i.e., the specific purpose grant has become the dominant mode of funding EE by Central government. Under this mode there are two forms: Central Schemes (CS) and CSS. The former are totally financed by the Centre while the latter are financed by both the Central and state governments together. The rationale for CSS is to enable state governments to undertake programmes that are considered to be in the wider national interest, which the state governments may not be able or willing to undertake on their own. Provision of EE, though considered a state subject, has considerable national importance and hence the need for the intervention and support by the Central government through CSS.

At present the specific purpose grant to State governments is provided mainly through CSS. There are several reasons for financing EE by Central government through CSS. Due to fiscal problems many state governments could not allocate required funds for EE. As a result of the fiscal crisis of 1991, India had to go in for economic reforms that had implications for budget allocation to social sectors like education. International funding to education was sought to minimise adverse effects of economic reforms on EE budget. At present, for many CSS in education international funding is available.

CSS are formulated by the Centre which also funds a major part of the implementing costs. States, which are the implementing agencies, fund the remaining portion. The sharing arrangement between the Centre and states vary according to the scheme and the phase of its implementation. In all CSSs, the major share of the burden is borne by the Central Government while the state governments have to bear the remaining costs. The states have shown preference for CSS as it is given as grants and not loans which reduce their fiscal burden.

Centre's grants-in-aid assistance to states took the shape of CSS and there were several of them to finance EE during the late 1980s and early 1990s. There were many CSS in EE covering several dimensions. Important among them which have made some impact are Operation Blackboard (OBB) and District Primary Education Programme (DPEP). However, many CSS in EE which existed in the late 1980s and early 1990s were mainly aimed at infrastructure provision and teacher training. The funds received by the state governments under CSS cannot be reallocated in favour of any other sector. Earlier funding through CSS was not significant as it formed very insignificant part of total education finance in India.

Now CSS have become critical players in education finance. According to Saxena (2006) as a consequence of liberalisation, Central government's involvement with industry and energy sector was reduced, and so more plan resources were left in its hands for state subjects. These plan resources are usually allocated through CSS, and education being a concurrent subject, CSS has been one of the key resource transfer mechanisms for education.

A common trend noted in the earlier years was that while many new CSS were launched during the eighties and nineties, their share in the total expenditure usually declined after the few initial years following their launch. Saxena (2006) explained how these schemes give political mileage to the party which initiates them as their benefits can be identified easily. So it is to the Central government's advantage to increase resources through CSS rather than increase aggregate expenditure. But when the political party in power undergoes a change, the new government loses interest in their implementation for the success will be credited to the earlier government. Therefore, rather than putting in more efforts and resources for continuing the earlier schemes, new schemes are announced periodically. DPEP however was an exception. Except for a couple of years, it has maintained a fairly stable share of 20-25 per cent of the total expenditure. But an adverse side effect of introducing these schemes in selected areas has been creation of islands of excellence without proper integration into the mainstream. Accordingly, their positive effects tend to fade away once they are over.

It is interesting to note that the *National Policy on Education* (GoI, 1986) puts emphasis on decentralised planning and management of education even though education continues to be in the Concurrent List. In many states the local bodies manage the majority of the schools though funds for them mainly come from the state government and to some extent from Central government. The CSS in EE like DPEP and SSA have also emphasised decentralisation. However, the decentralisation in EE has been confined to certain aspects only and Central government's dominance is felt in the form of norms and conditions laid down in the implementation of these programmes.

Trends in the Central Government Expenditure on Elementary Education

With regard to public expenditure on education the Central government allocation has steadily increased since 2001-02. In the last decade there has been a five-fold increase in Central government's budget allocation for education. As a percentage of GDP (gross domestic product), it increased significantly and was almost one per cent in 2008-09 (Table 14.1). However, the total education budget (both Centre and States together) did not exceed four per cent of GDP compared to six per cent as suggested by the Kothari Commission.[6]

As a per cent of total budget also Central government expenditure on education increased from 2.3 per cent in 2001-02 to 5.3 per cent in 2009-10. As a result of this the share of Central government in financing of education in India increased significantly. From 12.8 per cent in 1993-94 it increased to 24.3 per cent by 2005-06 and that of state governments declined from 87.2 per cent to 75.7 per cent during the same period (Table 14.2). The share of Central government has further increased in recent years due to introduction of new and continuation of the existing CSS in education.

6. Kothari Education Commission, 1964-1966.

Table 14.1

Public Expenditure on Education in India by Union Government

Year	*Central Government (₹ in crore)*	*Central Government as % of GDP*	*Pelementary Education as % of GDP*	*As % Total Budget*
2001-02	14120	0.67	3.81	2.22
2002-03	16157	0.71	3.78	2.20
2003-04	17101	0.67	3.51	2.16
2004-05	18026	0.63	3.36	2.66
2005-06	23210	0.71	3.45	3.52
2006-07	34018	0.91	3.64	4.09
2007-08(RE)	38107	0.88	3.74	5.35
2008-09(BE)	46328	0.94	3.78	5.15
2012-13(BE)	74056	-	-	5.13*

Note: *2009-10.

Source: Planning Commission (2011) (Chapter-6: Table 6.1) and Kapur and Chowdhury (2012) for 2012-13.

Table 14.2

Share of Central and State Governments in Total Public Expenditure on Education

Year	*Central Government*	*State Governments*	*Total*
1993-94	12.77	87.23	100
1994-95	11.74	88.64	100
1995-96	14.54	85.46	100
1996-97	14.38	85.62	100
1997-98	14.67	85,33	100
1998-99	15.71	84.29	100
1999-2000	14.58	85.42	100
2000-01	12.36	87.64	100
2001-02	17.70	82.30	100
2002-03	18.90	81.10	100
2003-04	19.20	80.80	100
2004-05	20.22	79.78	100
2005-06	24.30	75.70	100

Source: De and Endow, 2008: Table-A2:.39.

The expenditure on EE (plan+non-plan) has increased steadily in the last six decades. The share of Central government in financing of EE was negligible till the 1980s. The funds provided by the Central government increased steadily since the 1990s. The share of Central government in total budget for EE was less than 1 per cent till early 1980s, less than 5 per cent till mid-1990s, less than 15 per cent till early 2000s, and more than one-fourth in the last half decade. Thus, the major share of increased education budget of Central government is earmarked for EE. The share of EE continues to be more than half of the education budget of Central government.

The increase in Central budget for EE from ₹ 12,244 crore in 2005-06 to ₹ 38,298 in 2012-13 was mainly in the form of plan expenditure. Plan expenditure is by and large considered to be development expenditure financed by the Planning Commission. Part of the non-plan expenditure is met from Finance Commission (FC) transfers and considered to be non-developmental in nature and aimed at meeting the committed expenditure. The role of Central government is more in financing plan expenditure than non-plan expenditure and has increased significantly in recent years. The Central government's share in total plan expenditure on EE was less than 10 per cent in the mid-1990s but increased significantly thereafter accounting for more than half of the plan expenditure on EE in the last eight years. Correspondingly the state Governments' share declined considerably (Table 14.3).

The increase in the Central government's share is due to launching of several programmes in the last two decades. The important programmes for development of EE include OBB (1980s), DPEP (1990s) and SSA (from 2002 onwards). In the last decade, SSA was in vogue and has been playing an important role in the development of EE in India. The Right to Education (RTE) Act of 2009 further increased the responsibility of Central government in financing of EE through SSA.

Financing of Elementary Education under SSA

SSA is a comprehensive and integrated flagship programme to attain universalisation of EE in the country in a mission mode and in a time bound manner. It is being implemented in partnership with the state governments. The stated goals of SSA are: (i) enrolling all children in the age-group of 6-14 years in school, (ii) bridging gender and social gaps, (iii)

Table 14.3

Plan Expenditure on Elementary Education

(₹ '0,000,000)

Year	Central Government					State Governments	
	Total Allocation on Education	Allocation on Elementary Education	% Allocation on Elementary Education	% Increase Elementary Education	% Allocation on Mid-day Meal to Total Elementary Education Allocation	% Budget to Education	% Budget to Elementary Education
2000-01	4858.8	3117.4	64.2		42	20.1	9.8
2001-02	5560.1	3569.2	64.2	15	29	18.2	9.7
2002-03	6380.0	4257.6	66.7	19	24	18.0	9.7
2003-04	7371.1	5201.0	70.6	22	26	16.3	9.6
2004-05	10133.2	7710.2	76.1	48	21	16.4	9.5
2005-06	14552.5	11749.3	80.7	52	27	17.0	10.2
2006-07	20213.8	16560.0	81.9	41	32	17.1	10.3
2007-08	25452.4	20304	79.8	23	37	17.4	10.4
2008-09	34393.5	21795	63.4	7	37	17.6	10.4
2009-10	42000	25000	59.2	15	35	17.8	10.3

Sectors such as department of languages, scholarships, book promotion, planning and administration are included in the total.

Source: Union Budget 2008-09: Expenditure Budget Vol II and earlier years and documents; and Financial Statistics of Education during the Eighth, Ninth (1997-2002) and the Tenth (2002-2007) Five-Year Plans. MHRD Budget Statistics 2000-2009.

retaining all children in school till they complete EE, and (iv) providing education of satisfactory quality. Thus, the focus of SSA is on providing access to quality education for all children of the relevant age group (6-14 years) by ensuring norm-based supply, provision of school infrastructure including buildings, boundary walls, regular teachers' training, use of teaching-learning material and such other educational inputs, leaving scope for innovative activities as well (See Annexure A-14.1).

The implementation process of SSA programme starts with the preparation of Annual Work Plans and Budgets (AWPB). An autonomous state level implementation agency (state project office or SPO) is set up for this purpose, with counterparts at the district level. It is the SPO that receives the funds from the Central government and accounts for them, with the state governments playing an active role through deputation of staff, supervision, regular monitoring and financial contribution.

Table 14.4

Centre-State Sharing of SSA Costs

Year/Plan	*All States (Excluding North-Eastern States)*			*Remarks*
	Proposed	*Revised*	*North-Eastern States*	
Tenth Plan (2002-03 to 2006-07)	75:25	75:25	90:10	There is demand from the state governments to increase the Central government's share further to reach 90:10.
Eleventh Plan (2007-08 to 2011-12)	50:50	65:35 for first two years		
		60:40 third year (2009/10)		
		55:45 fourth year (2010/11)		
		50:50 last year (2011/12)	90:10	
		65:35 (Proposed Under RTE) and 68:32	90:10	

Source: SSA.

SSA is a cost-shared programme with state contribution required in the mandated ratio to match the central contribution (Table 14.4). There are some broad factors specified along with weights to determine the overall state shares, but the system is intrinsically a demand-driven one with the AWPB playing a crucial role. Before the beginning of each financial year, states are expected to send their AWPB prepared as per programme guidelines for approval to the concerned department of the Ministry. The plans are expected to be prepared in a bottom-up fashion with the full involvement of the local body and the community. Detailed budgets have to be prepared for schools and other bodies like the mandal/block/cluster resource centres and administrative offices.

SSA is based on the premise that financing of EE is sustainable and the state governments have to maintain the funding of EE at the level of 1999-2000 in real terms. As per the SSA provisions the Central government has to release the project funds in two instalments every year. The release of the first instalment should take place in the month of April and the second in the month of September subject to the fulfilment of certain conditions. The first condition is that state governments have to maintain the EE budget at a level not less than the level during 1999-2000. Second, the state governments have to release their share to the SSA implementing agency within a month of the release of the Central government share. Further, various provisions and checks have been incorporated with an objective to ensure the timely availability and utilisation of funds.

The AWPB is examined and approved by the designated central level committee. The first instalment is then released at the beginning of the financial year on the basis of the approved budget and balance carried forward from the previous year. The second instalment is to be released normally in September on the basis of demand supported by all the necessary accounts, certificates and other documentary requirements as per guidelines.

The major part of the Central government budget on EE is allocated to finance SSA (Table 14.5). Funds to SSA increased from ₹ 2,732 crore in 2003-04 to ₹ 25,555 crore in the current (2012-13) budget of Central government. It accounts for about two-third of the EE budget of the Central government. Part of the SSA budget is financed through the 2 per cent cess levied by Central government on all the central taxes which increased from ₹ 83,160 crore in 2007-08 to ₹ 119,920 in 2011-12. The SSA received 74.7 per cent of the revenue generated through the cess in 2007-08 but it declined to 65.4 per cent by 2011-12. The percentage of SSA expenditure met from the cess declined from 63.1 to 57.1 during the same year (Mukherjee and Sikdar, 2012: Table 2.1, p.19).

Table 14.5

Central Government Budget to SSA

(₹ in crore)

Year	*Amount*
2003-04	2732.3
2004-05	4753.6
2005-06	7166.3
2006-07	10145.7
2007-08	12020.2
2008-09	11940.0
2012-13(BE)	25555.0

Note: For the year 2009-10, 2010-11 and 2011-12, data not collected.

Source: Mukherji and Sikdar (2012).

As per the SSA sharing arrangement the Centre-State Ratio (CSR) was fixed at 75:25 for all the states except for Special Category States (North Eastern States) where it was 90:10. Central government has to bear 75 per cent of the costs while the rest is borne by the state governments. Some states have either contributed less (Orissa, Karnataka and Gujarat, Himachal Pradesh) or more (Andhra Pradesh, Kerala, Maharashtra, Punjab, Rajasthan) than the state share stipulated (Table 14.6). Some states do, however, conform to the sharing ratio of 75:25. In 2009-10, CSR was fixed at 60:40 for non-special category states. Rajasthan, Madhya Pradesh and West Bengal have contributed less while others (Punjab, Gujarat and Bihar) have contributed more than the stipulated state share. Most states do, however, conform to the sharing ratio of 60:40. It was observed that at 2009-10 sharing levels of 60:40 for the SSA, as many as 14 states defaulted on their shares. Andhra Pradesh, Maharashtra, Rajasthan, Chhattisgarh, Himachal Pradesh, Odisha are among the defaulters.

Problems and Implications of Financing of SSA

The evaluation of CSS is done using several parameters. First, whether objectives for which the scheme is introduced are realised or not? If not, the factors responsible for it. There have been evaluation studies which claim that the CSS have not only eased the resource constraint, but have had a positive impact on the outcomes in the education sector. The OBB and DPEP had led to a decline in the number of single-classroom primary

Table 14.6

Central Government Contribution as % of Total Release to SSA and Expenditure as % of Assistance to SSA

State/UT	Central Government Contribution as % of Total Release to SSA		Expenditure as % Assistance to SSA(Centre+States)	
	2003-04	2006-07	2003-04	2006-07
Andhra Pradesh	69	75	116	93
Andaman Islands	57	75	75	79
Arunachal Pradesh	59	96	116	92
Assam	83	73	171	62
Bihar	75	66	95	99
Chandigarh	82	51	61	120
Chhattisgarh	75	76	74	96
Daman&Diu	0	0	16	89
Delhi	90	78	29	91
Goa	0	59	0	145
Gujarat	84	65	106	122
Haryana	75	74	99	87
Himachal Pradesh	85	75	98	122
Jammu & Kashmir	73	79	50	708
Jharkhand	75	85	73	108
Karnataka	90	77	116	101
Kerala	69	55	84	130
Lakshdweep	0	80	0	69
Madhya Pradesh	73	62	78	84
Maharashtra	72	65	114	127
Manipur	100	73	0	86
Meghalaya	80	79	53	121
Mizoram	88	90	88	98
Nagaland	0	60	203	101
Odisha	88	73	102	104
Puducherry	38	0	46	410
Punjab	68	83	47	102
Rajasthan	71	72	102	106
Sikkim	66	58	164	106
Tamilnadu	75	69	165	98
Tripura	83	71	139	116
Dadra & Nagar Haveli	100	100	0.3	310
Uttar Pradesh	75	75	105	101
Uttarkhand	75	76	89	71
West Bengal	75	76	65	110
All India	76	70	97.7	110.0

Source: Planning Commission, 2010: Annexure 5.1 and 5.2, pp.87-88.

schools, improvement in average number of teachers and availability of teaching learning material in primary schools.

However, there is some scepticism about the impact financing of EE by Central government through CSS. Whether these schemes have added to available resources or substituted other sources? There are some in-built constraints in the design of CSS like SSA which have limited their usefulness of them in the development of EE in India.

Inadequacy of Funds

Adequacy of funds can be judged from the release of approved outlay for SSA by Central government to the MHRD (Table 14.7). However, the funds released as per cent of approved outlay ranged between 50 to 75 per cent in the last decade. Releasing less than the approved outlay indicates that adequate funds for the scheme are not allocated. The required outlays arrived at by following the SSA norms at the district and the state level are considered to be conservative (Geetha Rani, 2010). Needless to say, the inadequacy of funding has its negative effect in the achievement of SSA objectives.

Table 14.7

Central Government Budget to SSA

(₹ in crore)

Year	*Approved Outlay by MHRD under SSA*	*Central Government Allocation*	*Funds Released by MHRD under SSA*
2000-01	----	325	----
2001-02	1138	500	500
2002-03	3080	1567	1569
2003-04	8335	2732	2733
2004-05	11019	4754*	11015
2005-06	12931	7156	8741
2006-07	20085	10041	13318
2007-08	20060	10671	15039
2008-09	22321	13100	12612
2009-10	27235	13100	13637
2010-11	27588	15000	----

Source: Geetha Rani (2011: Table -1).

Delay in the Fund Flow

As per the norm, the first instalment is to be released in April and the second and the last instalment in September every year. This is rarely adhered to in many states. According to Geetha Rani (2010), in a majority of the states the first instalment was released in September or later and the last instalment in the last month of the financial year (Table 14.8).

Table 14.8

Timing of Release of SSA Funds by Central Government to States

Year	*No of States Who Received Ist Instalment in/or After September*	*No of States Who Received IInd Instalment in March*
2001-02	19	5
2002-03	22	10
2003-04	13	5
2004-05	12	11

Source: Report of the Comptroller and Auditor General (CAG) (2006).

For example in Andhra Pradesh, Centre and state shares were not received as per the norm in the last 10 years (Table 14.9). There was a delay not only in the release by Central government and state governments but also a time lag between the release and the receipt by the implementing society.

The proportion of funds utilised from those released varies for different states and is usually lower for the poorer states. The need to obtain matching grants and approval of the annual work plan and budget is useful for efficient resource utilisation. However, this puts the poorer states at a disadvantage for their resource base is smaller and they also have lower institutional capacity (De and Endow, 2008: 28).

From the information provided on quarterly release of central funds for SSA during 2009-10, it can be seen that the average quarterly release is around 30 and 50 per cent for Q1 and Q3 respectively, while Q2 and Q4 together account for around 20 per cent. In general, this is what we would expect to happen if states follow the financial management and reporting norms under SSA.

Table 14.9

Date-wise Release of Centre and State Shares in Andhra Pradesh

Year	Central Government		State Government	
	Date of Release	Date of Receipt by Society	Date of Release	Date of Receipt by Society
2001-02	22-08-2001	24-11-2001	16-10-2001	12-12-2001
	19-09-2001	12-12-2001		
2002-03	14-03-2002	19-12-2002	15-07-2002	19-12-2002
	03-09-2002	16-10-2002		
	20-01-2003	14-02-2003	28-12-2002	04-06-2003
2003-04	27-08-2003	17-09-2003	11-03-2003	04-06-2003
	23-03-2004		19-12-2003	31-03-2004
			23-10-2004	16-12-2004
2004-05	18-05-2004	16-06-2004	01-01-2005	22-01-2005
	09-08-2004	08-09-2004	19-02-2005	
	18-01-2005	11-02-2005	22.03.2005	
2005-06	26-05-2005	23-06-2005	27-09-2005	17-02-2006
	07-06-2005	29-06-2005	22-03-2006	31-03-2006
	05-09-2005	24-10-2005		
	23-12-2005	16-01-2006	20-12-2006	07-03-2007
2006-07	14-06-2006	27-07-2006	20-01-2007	19-02-2007
	21-08-2006	06-11-2006	10-08-2007	06-12-2007
	29-03-2007	04-04-2007	12-10-2007	17-12-2007
2007-08	07-08-2007	29-08-2007	22-10-2007	04-03-2008
	25-02-2008	28-02-2008	15-03-2008	03-04-2008
			07-07-2008	17-09-2008
2008-09	23-05-2008	27-06-2008	17-10-2008	23-03-2009
	02-11-2008	25-02-2009		
2009-10	02-06-2009	06-06-2009	08-10-2009	04-12-2009

Source: SSA unpublished records.

However, the low average figure for Q4 masks the fact that for three states—Andhra Pradesh, Bihar and Jharkhand—the fourth quarter releases are still substantial. As per the SSA financial management guidelines, the centre is supposed to release funds in Q1 and Q3 depending on the state fulfilling its obligations. For five states—Himachal Pradesh, Karnataka, Kerala, Punjab and Tamil Nadu—the whole tranche was released in Q1 and Q3 combined. For eight other states, the ratio of release of funds was between 80 and 90 per cent, which is also very good considering the conditionalities of the release. The states which are of concern as far as fund flow is concerned are those where Q1 and Q3 releases taken together fall below 70 per cent (Gupta *et al.*, 2011: 50).

The timing of release, however, reveals some problems with the system of flow of funds. There are five states for which there was no release in the first quarter at all. Clearly, these were states where the necessary documentation was delayed, or did not meet with quick approval. Similarly, there were two states (Andhra Pradesh and Jharkhand) where releases in the fourth quarter were unduly large; in particular, Andhra Pradesh received more than 60 per cent of its releases only in the last quarter. While the consequent ill-effects of such a pattern of releases are well-known, the state-specific nature of the problem indicates that it was not systemic (Gupta *et al.*, 2011: 51).

According to De and Endow (2008: 25-26) there are two important reasons for inefficiency in the utilisation of SSA funding. They are: (i) asymmetry in allocation within the sector, and (ii) lack of coordination among the three tiers of government.

Inequality

One of the objectives of SSA is to reduce the inequalities in the development of EE through the provision of basic inputs. For a country that still has a significant number of out-of-school children especially from marginalised communities, the most pressing need is equitable financial allocations across all regions. For long, EE was a state subject and a 'protected' sector and was not open for central/any external aid. The financial allocations for education sector varied among the states depending upon their fiscal capacities and priorities. The capacities of mobilisation of resources by the states differed considerably leading to vertical and horizontal disparities in education financing and resultant outcomes. To correct the vertical and horizontal imbalances, education sector was transferred from State List to Concurrent List in 1997, paving the way for the much needed transfer of funds to the states from the Centre's pool. It is essential that policy and programme designs in the crucial educational social sector should promote a strong equity-oriented approach that ensures that regions and population groups that have EE lagging behind receive much higher attention and resources. Providing a more equitable distribution of public resources and effort would be a pre-requisite for bridging gaps in education.

CSS are a channel through which the Central government has been adding resources to the state education sector. However, their coverage has varied over time and there has been no uniformity in its distribution over different states. Maharashtra and Karnataka, two of the educationally better developed states, have received a major share of OBB funds (17.4 and 10.9%) while Madhya Pradesh and West Bengal received very little (4.5 and 2.1%). This brings us to an important aspect in the education scenario—regional imbalances in state education indicators and failure of budgetary mechanisms to compensate for it. Similar imbalances are also felt in the regional distribution of SSA funds.

> The disbursements to the districts was not based on any criteria of educational backwardness/low female literacy or high percentage of socially disadvantaged groups (tribal areas) but on the number of schools, unspent balances, utilization. In Andhra Pradesh, Uttar Pradesh and West Bengal, districts with more number of educationally backward blocks were disbursed less funds than other districts. In 2003-04, East Godavari district (Andhra Pradesh) which has only one backward block received Rs.29.5 crores as compared to Chittoor with 20 backward blocks which received Rs.15.09 crores (Planning Commission, 2010: 40).

According to Jingran and Sankar (2009):

> There is an apparent disconnect between the 'real investment needs' of the districts, reflected in their level of educational development and the actual allocations made on an annual basis. The analysis shows that although all districts received more funds for investing in Elementary Education programs, the most disadvantaged and needy districts received proportionately more funds, which helped these districts to bridge access and infrastructure gaps and appoint more teachers. Benchmarking sector development by spatial entities helps not only in monitoring the outcomes, but also in targeting planning and funding to reduce disparities.

According to Jingran and Sankar (2009: 17) SSA financial allocations were not strongly linked to educational disadvantage because of two reasons:

(i) The normative framework of planning in SSA and the financial guidelines did not actively encourage an equity-oriented approach. The programme supported a uniform budgeting approach that was not able to specifically provide for differentiated allocations for different situations. Almost 67 per cent of the total AWPB allocations of SSA are linked to the size of the district i.e., the number of schools and teachers in a district, and therefore not linked to any specific situation of a particular district.

(ii) Several states and districts did not undertake evidence and need based planning processes that reflect real requirements of each district. Thus, AWPB were usually a summation of the costs allowed under each component of SSA without an in-depth and real analysis of the needs of each district. The revised norms to reduce the inter-state and inter district differences have met with partial success

Under-Utilisation and Misappropriation of SSA Funds

Despite all the crystal clear framework of funding, responsibilities, commitments and monitoring the SSA funds have remained under-utilised in many states. The released amount is much lower than the approved outlay in almost every case. Clearly, this is either because of problems in actually carrying out the planned activities (this could happen in the previous year also, in which case there would be unduly large opening balances that would reduce releases in the current year), or inability to meet the documentary requirements like utilisation certificates.

Under-utilisation of SSA funds is common across many states and districts within a state, and many activities with a district. There is a provision in SSA that funds not spent in the previous year are carried forward to the next year. Under-utilisation of SSA funds have thus given scope for the misappropriation in many states including Andhra Pradesh.

Though certain irregularities are reported in utilising the funds under different schemes, the misappropriation of funds under DPEP/SSA is worth noting. It reached such proportions that Government had to appoint a Commission (GoAP, 2008) to look into the irregularities. Though official sources say the amount of misappropriation is about ₹ 15 crore unofficial sources say it is several times more. The Commission in its Report has come out with interesting and useful findings about the lapses in the monitoring of fund flows and mechanisms by which funds are misappropriated. The funds from many districts were diverted when the district officials refunded the unutilised amount through demand drafts/cheques to the head office at Hyderabad.

Andhra Pradesh is not the only state where irregularities in the utilisation of SSA funds occurred. CAG Report (GoI, 2006) gave details about the financial irregularities, underutilisation of funds and under-achievement of targets and funds released to non-existing schools in different states.

Reasons for under-utilisation and misappropriation of DPEP/SSA funds, include among others, the appointment of non-education cadre officials, delay in release of funds and lack of proper maintenance of records.

Dependency Syndrome

Central grants for education has created a situation in which a very large part of the funds needed for educational development came from the Centre through grant-in-aid. Consequently, the states have tended to lose their spirit of self-reliance and self-confidence, and are developing a habit of looking up to the Centre for almost everything. It may be noted that almost all the CSS in EE in the last three-to-four decades made state governments depend on the Centre and the RTE Act of 2009 further increased their dependency.

There is also a fear that increase in expenditure by the Union government is 'crowding out' expenditure by the states. According to Mukherjee and Sikdar (2012: 23)

> The initial evidence seems to indicate that the state governments have not increased their education expenditure commensurately. They are becoming increasingly more reliant on the union government to augment their resource base for education. Consequently, education policy is increasingly being determined at the national, rather than the state level, as was originally envisaged in the Constitution. The implementation framework of the RTE and the proliferation of centrally-sponsored schemes would essentially guarantee the pre-eminence of the union government in the financing of education in the near future.

Implementation Problems

As in the case of any programme there are also implementation problems in SSA. There is a lack of authority of Central government and a lack of a proper monitoring system at the state level. As a result there is corruption, patronage and mediocre implementation. According to Ramachandran and Sharma (2009: 2), "Yet all these programmes, from the simplest to the relatively more complex, from the most rigid to the flexible, have been bogged down by a common problem of 'poor implementation'." Some states have done better than others due to effective implementation of SSA.

Resources But Not Outcomes

Under SSA many initiatives to expand access and improve quality of EE were taken up. They include opening of new schools in unserved and under-served habitations. Under SSA 2,05,294 new primary and 1,76,764 new upper primary schools were sanctioned upto 2012-13 and of these 1,94,717 new primary and 1,48,991 new upper primary schools were opened till 2011-12. As a result 99 per cent of the habitations have access to primary school/section within one kilometre and 92 per cent have access to upper primary school/section within three kilometres. Alternative and innovative education centres were opened in habitations having less than 25 out-of-school children. To promote girls' education Kasturba Gandhi Balika Vidyalayas were opened for girls from Scheduled Castes (SC), Scheduled Tribe (ST), Other Backward Classes (OBC) and Muslim minorities. National Programme for Girls education at EE level was also launched in educationally backward districts.

These initiatives have helped in reducing the percentage of out-of-school children of 6-14 years from 6.9 per cent in 2005 to 4.2 per cent in 2009 (Figure 14.1). In this respect it is not far off to realise the objective of Universalisation of EE shortly. However, the out-of-school children proportion is more among girls, SCs, STs and Muslims. Further, the data presented indicates STs are better than SCs and SCs are better than Muslims. As per RTE all these out-of-school children have to be enrolled in schools.

Along with the decline in out-of-school children, the drop-out rates[7] also have declined significantly in the last decade (Figure 14.2). There was

7. Drop-out rate is calculated by dividing the number of students who discontinued before completing the given class by the total number of students in the beginning of the year. Drop-out rate in EE is the number of students in class VIII divided by the number of children in class I and is expressed in percentage.

a more than 10 percentage points decline in drop-out rates during 2001-2008. Unless the drop-out rate is reduced to zero, it is not possible to achieve Universalisation of EE in India. At this rate of decline, India needs many more years to achieve it.

Figure 14.1

Percentage of Out-of-School Children in the Corresponding Age Group 6-14 Years

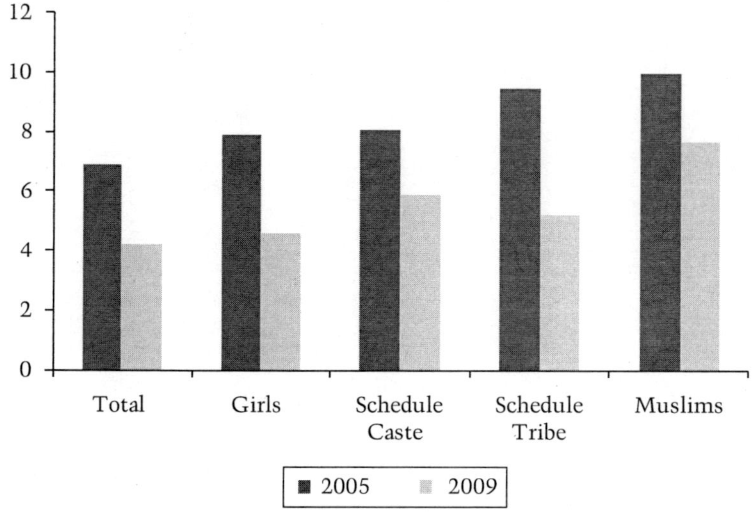

Source: NUEPA (2012): Table 3.9, p.43.

The decline in drop-out rate is associated with increase in the transition rate[8] (Figure 14.3). More than 80 per cent of the students who completed class V were able to enrol in class VI. The increase is partly due to upgrading of primary schools (classes I-V) in to upper primary schools (classes I-VIII). As per the requirement, an upper primary school for every two primary schools can be provided under SSA.

Compared to resources spent, there is little to show at EE level in terms of learning achievement. While the GoI has significantly expanded outlays for education in recent years, outcomes continue to be poor.

The most important objective of SSA is to provide education of satisfactory quality to all the children. Whether this is achieved or not

8. Transition rate is calculated by dividing the number of students in class VI by number of students in class V and expressed in percentage.

Figure 14.2

Drop-out Rates (%) in Elementary Education (Classes I-VIII)

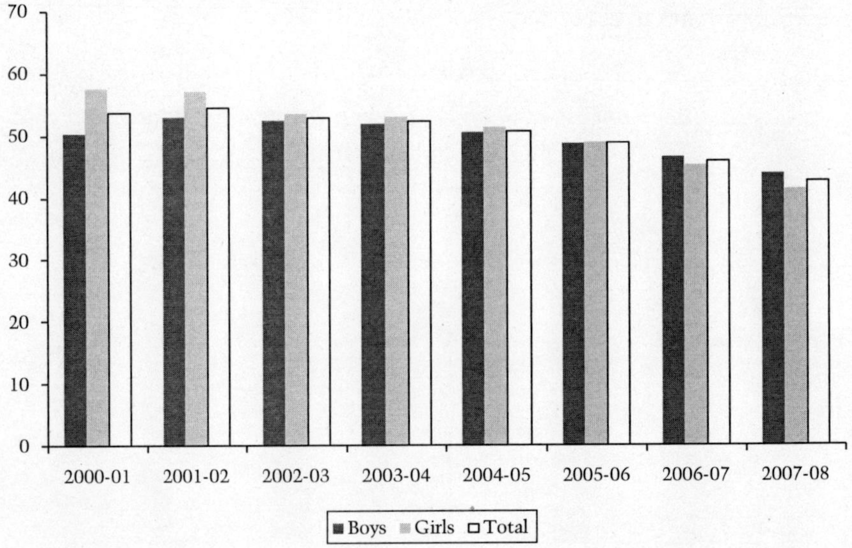

Source: NUEPA (2012): 103.

Figure 14.3

Transition Rates (%) from Primary to Upper Primary Level

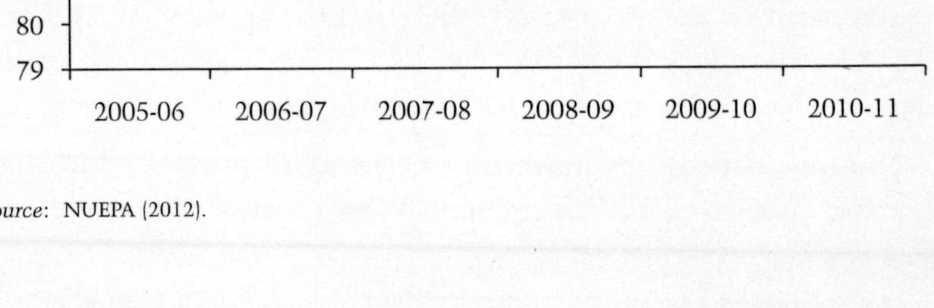

Source: NUEPA (2012).

can be seen by the achievement levels of the children. As per National Achievement Survey (NAS) of National Council of Educational Research and Training (NCERT) the mean score[9] of children in Class V in language (Figure 14.4) and mathematics (Figure 14.5) show that learning levels are poor. In 2010, the mean scores were 56 in Language, 53 in Mathematics and 53 in Environmental Studies. In fact there is some decline in the mean achievement score in language during the period 2000-2010. In addition there are differences in the achievement levels between rural and urban areas and between boys and girls. (National University of Educational Planning and Administration (NUEPA), 2012).

As per the Annual Status of Education Report (ASER) (2012), the percentage of children in standard V in government schools who could not read a standard II level text increased from 49.3 per cent in 2010 to 58.3 per cent in 2012. The percentage of children in Standard III in government schools who could not read a standard I level text increased steeply from 53.4 per cent in 2009 to 67.7 per cent in 2012. All these schools received SSA grants. Further, ASER (2012) results show that the percentage of children in standard V who could not solve simple two-digit subtraction problem with borrowing increased from 29.1 per cent in 2010 to 46.5 per cent in 2012. The percentage of children in standard V who could not do division problems increased from 63.8 per cent in 2010 to 75.2 per cent in 2012.

Summary and Conclusion

The quantum of public expenditure on education by the Central government has gone up significantly in the last decade. The bulk of this expenditure is earmarked for the key flagship programme of SSA (the vehicle for implementation of the RTE). The Central government funding in India did contribute to the development of EE in terms of increasing access and reducing social and gender disparities. However, the concerns related to the quality still remain. The SSA norms were found to be rigid in certain respects and have not been able to take into account the recent developments. There appears to be both education and economic inefficiency in the delivery of quality EE.

9. Mean score is the average number marks obtained out of a total of 100. There are extreme situations with majority scoring less than the average marks

Figure 14.4

Language Achievement Mean Score (%) Class V

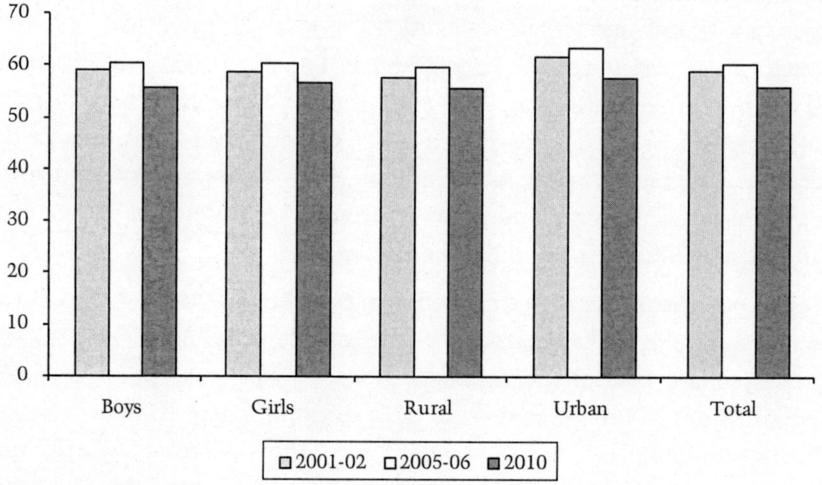

Source: NUEPA (2012).

Figure 14.5

Mathematics National Achievement Mean Score (%) Class V

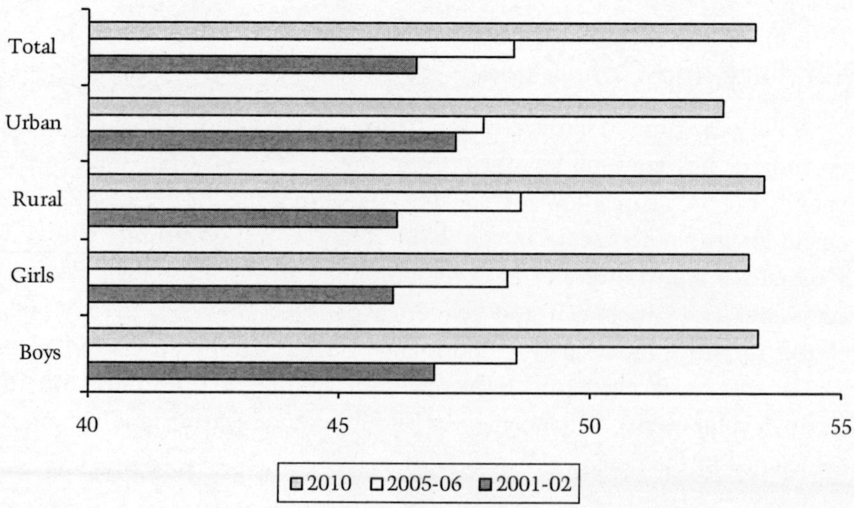

Source: NUEPA (2012), Table 7.9, p.107 and Table 7.11, p.108.

One of the key issues that need the attention of policy makers is the decline in the number of children in many habitations in recent years. Due to decline in fertility rate, the number of children to be enrolled has come down drastically. This is a positive indication from the demographic point of view, but is a cause of concern from education point of view. From 1990s onwards there has been witnessed a decline in the number of children on the one hand, and increase in the number of primary schools, on the other. This has resulted in unviability of many schools. The increase in access in terms of decline of physical distance has followed by decline in quality and effectiveness of primary education in many schools located, particularly, in remote areas. In many schools, the number of students in each class rarely exceed single digit. Two teachers, one regular and the other a para teacher, have to attend to all the five classes. On many occasions one may find only one teacher to manage the entire school. Hardly anything worthwhile learning takes place.

In this context, it is necessary to look at the relevance of SSA norms—primary section within one kilometer and 1:40 teacher pupil ratio (TPR) with a minimum of two teachers. The distance norm was specified when the transport and communication system was not developed. Further, the 1:40 TPR norm was specified when there are enough number of children in each age group such that number of students in each class are about 40. Now many remote areas are connected. Transport facility—private or public—is available. Many parents do not hesitate to send their children to nearby schools. Therefore instead of having unviable schools—educationally and economically—in each small habitation, it is better to have a full-fledged school within a few kilometers. A full-fledged school should have one class room for each class and one teacher for each class. Additional sections can be added if the number of students exceeds 40. The students from nearby habitations can be provided transport facility. If public transport is not possible, the school should make alternative arrangement. The existing schools in small habitations can be used both as Integrated Child Development Services (ICDS) centers and also for school readiness programmes. Of the two teachers, one can be sent to full-fledged school. This alternative proposal may not add to the financial burden.

The main concern of the authorities is this proposal may violate the RTE Act of providing school facility within one kilometer. A carefully planned initiative taking the norm into account is possible. The existing schools in the habitations can continue to function both as ICDS center and school. But there should be a full-fledged school within few kilometers which should be connected by proper transport. If the full-fledged school ensures teaching learning environment and proves to be a better place for learning than the school located in the small habitation, within a few years many parents from these habitations will prefer to send their children to this school.

Therefore, SSA funds should be utilised to create such a teaching-learning environment in schools that universalisation of EE become a reality in true sense.

References

ASER (2012). *Annual Status of Education Report*. Mumbai: Pratham.

Chelliah, R.J., P.K. Aggarwal, R. Goshal, A. Gupta and M.G. Rao (1981). *Trends and Issues in India Federal Finance*. New Delhi, Allied.

De, Anuradha and Tanuka Endow (2008). "Public Expenditure on Education in India: Recent Trends and Outcomes", *Research Consortium on Educational Outcomes and Poverty* WP08/18. India: Collaborative Research and Dissemination (CORD).

Geetha Rani (2010). "Fund Flow Pattern and Utilisation of Resources under SSA in India", Paper presented in National Seminar on *Financing Elementary Education in States: Fund Flow Pattern and Utilisation of Resources under Sarva Shiksha Abhiyan*. Organised by National University of Educational Planning and Administration, New Delhi. March 18-20.

GoAP (2008). *Report of Sri Justice A.Venkat Ram Reddy Commission of Enquiry (To Inquire into Misappropriation of DPEP and SSA Funds)*. Hyderabad.

GoI (1986). *National Policy on Education*. New Delhi: Department of Education.

———. (2006). *Report of the Controller and Auditor General of India*.

Gupta, Manish, Anit Mukherji, Tapas K. Sen and R. Srinivasan (2011). *Improving Effectiveness and Utilisation of Funds for Selected Schemes through Suitable Changes in Timing and Pattern of Releases by the Centre*. Report of research project sponsored by Planning Commission of India and National Institute of Public Finance and Policy, New Delhi. October.

Jingran, D. and Deepa Sankar (2009). "Addressing Educational Disparity Using District Level Education Development Indices for Equitable Resource Allocation in India", *World Bank Policy Research Working Paper* 4955.

Kapur, Avani and Anirvan Chowdhury (2012). *Budget Briefs: Sarva Shikha Abhayan, GoI 2012–13*. New Delhi: Accountability Initiative, Centre for Policy Research. *http://www.accountabilityindia.in/sites/default/files/sarva_shiksha_abhiyan_2012-13.pdf*

Mukherji, Anit N. and Satadru Sikdar (2012). *Public Expenditure on Education in India by the Union Government and Roadmap for the Future: India Infrastructure Report*. New Delhi: Oxford University Press.

Mukherjee, Anit N. and Angela W. Little (2010). "Access to Elementary Education in India: Policies, Politics and Progress, Create Pathways to Success Research", *Monograph No. 44.* September.

Naik, J.P. (1963). *The Role of Government of India in Education.* New Delhi: Ministry of Education, Government of India. *www.vidyaonline.org/dl/JPNAik_0.1pdf*

NUEPA (2012). *Education for All: Status and Trends.* New Delhi: National University of Educational Planning and Administration.

Ozturk, Ilhan (2001). "*The Role of Education in Economic Development*", *Journal of Rural Development and Administration* XXXIII(1) (Winter): 39-47.

Planning Commission (2010). *Evaluation Report on Sarva Shiksha Abhiyan*. PEO Report No.203. New Delhi.

————. (2011). *Mid Term Appraisal of Eleventh Five Year Plan*. New Delhi.

Ramachandran, V. and R. Sharma (2009). "Introduction", in R. Sharma and V. Ramachandran (eds.), *The Elementary Education System in India: Exploring Institutional Structures, Processes and Dynamics.* New Delhi: Routledge. pp.1-32.

Sankar, Deepa (2007). *Financing Elementary Education in India through SSA: Challenges in Recent Times.* South Asia Human Development, The World Bank.

Saxena, Naresh C. (2006). *Central Transfers to States and Centrally Sponsored Schemes.* Draft paper for National Advisory Council. *http://pmindia.gov.in/nac/concept.htm*

Sharma, R. and V. Ramachandran (2009). "State Education Policy and Institutions", in R.V. Sharma and V. Ramachandran (eds.), *The Elementary Education System in India: Exploring Institutional Structures, Processes and Dynamics.* New Delhi: Routledge. pp.33-69

Shiva Reddy, B. (2011). "Fund Flow Pattern and Utilisation of Resources under SSA in Andhra Pradesh", Paper presented in National Seminar on *Financing Elementary Education in States: Fund Flow Pattern and Utilisation of Resources under Sarva Shiksha Abhiyan.* Organised by NUEPA, New Delhi. March 18-20.

Varghese, N.V. and J.B.G. Tilak (1991). *Financing of Education in India.* Paris: International Institute for Educational Planning.

Annexure Table A-14.1

SSA Norms

Sl. No	*Intervention*	*Norm*
1	Teachers	• One teacher for every 40 children in primary and Upper Primary School (UPS). • At least two teachers in Primary School.
2	School/Alternative Schooling Facility	Within one kilometre of every habitation.
3	UPS/Section	As per requirement based on the children completing primary education up to a ceiling of one UPS/section for every two primary schools.
4	Class Rooms	A room for every teacher in primary and upper primary (UP). A room for Head Master in UPS/section.
5	Free Education Text Books	To all girls/SC/ST children at primary and UP level within an upper ceiling of ₹ 150 per child.
6	Civil Works	Ceiling of 33 per cent SSA programme funds. For improvement of school facilities construction of Block Resource Centre/Cluster Resource Centre (BRC/CRC).
7	Maintenance and Repair of School Buildings	• Only through School Management Committee. • Upto ₹ 5000 per year as per a specific proposal by the school committee. • Must involve elements of community contribution.
8	Up gradation of Education Guarantee Centre to regular school	• Provision of Teaching Learning Equipment (TLE) ₹ 10,000 at per school. • Provision for teacher and class rooms.
9	TLE for UPS	₹ 50,000 per school for uncovered schools.

contd...

...contd...

Sl. No	*Intervention*	*Norm*
10	School Grant	₹ 2,000 per year per primary/UPS for replacement.
11	Teacher Grant	₹ 500 per teacher per year in primary/UPS.
12	Teacher Training	Provision of 20 days in service training for all teachers, 60 days refresher courses for untrained teachers and 30 day orientation for freshly trained recruits.
13	State Institute of Educational Management Administration and Training (SIEMAT)	One time assistance upto ₹ 3 crore.
14	Training of Community Leaders	For a maximum of 8 persons in a village for two days at ₹ 30 per day.
15	Provision for Disabled Children	Upto ₹ 1,200 per child for integration of disabled children, as per specific proposal.
16	Research, Evaluation, Supervision and Monitoring	• Up to ₹ 1,500 per school per year. • By creating pool of resource persons, providing travel grant and honorarium for monitoring, generation of community based data, research studies, cost of assessment and appraisal teams and their fileld activities.
17	Management Cost	Not to exceed Educationd 6 per cent of the budget of District Plan.
18	Innovative Activity for girls' education, early childhood care and education, interventions for children belonging to SC/ST community, computer education especially for UPS	Up to ₹ 15 lakh for each innovative project and ₹ 50 lakh for a district.

contd...

...contd...

Sl. No	*Intervention*	*Norm*	*Remarks*
19	BRC/CRC	• ₹ 6 lakh ceiling for BRC wherever required. • ₹ 2 lakh for CRC wherever required. • Deployment of upto 20 teachers in a block with more than 100 schools. • Provision of furniture etc @₹ 1 lakh for BRC and ₹ 10,000 for CRC. • Contingency Grant of ₹ 12,500 for a BRC and ₹ 2,500 for CRC per year.	
20	Interventions for Out-of-School Children	As per norms approved under Education Guarantee Scheme & alternative and innovative education providing for: a. Setting up Education Guarantee Education Centre in unserved habitations, b Setting other alternative schooling models, c. Bridge courses, remedial courses, back-to-school camps with a focus on mainstreaming out of school children into regular schools.	
21	Preparatory activities for micro planning, household surveys, studies, community mobilisation school based activities, office equipment etc	As per specific proposals.	

Source: www.educationforallinindia.com/ssa.htm

15 Why Government Should Prioritise Spending on Health?

Exploring the Health Expenditure, Health Outcome and Output Relationship in Indian States

Biswa Swarup Misra

Introduction

India aspires to be a developed cconomy making full use of its demographic advantage as 31 per cent of the population is under the age of 15. However, a key worry in this context is the poor health status of its population and especially that of the children. This is evident from the worrisome health indicators like infant mortality rate (IMR) of 47, under five mortality rate of 59, and percentage of 1 year children immunised against measles at 70, which are far below the millennium development goals (MDGs).

The poor record on the health front is due to of the inadequacy in health care service provided by the government. The shortage is both in terms of physical infrastructure and qualified manpower. According to the Rural Health Statistics (RHS) 2010, there is shortage of 19,590 Sub-centres (SCs); 4,252 Primary Health Centres (PHCs) and 2,115 Community Health Centres (CHCs) in the country. The shortage of doctors at PHCs, specialists at CHCs and nurses at both PHCs and CHCs is 10.27 per cent, 62.6 per cent and 24.69 per cent respectively. In addition, there is shortage of 27.13 per cent pharmacists and 50.42 per cent laboratory technicians at PHCs and CHCs in the country.

Part of the reason for the poor state of health infrastructure and hence health outcome is the low priority given to public spending on health. Between 1996-97 and 2005-06, government spending as proportion of GDP (gross domestic products) was stagnant at about 1 per cent of GDP

(Rao and Choudhary, 2012). Notwithstanding the introduction of National Rural Health Mission (NRHM) in 2005 to improve health infrastructure in the rural areas, public spending on health accounted for a meagre 1.3 per cent of GDP in 2010. The low level of public spending has led to greater dependence on the private sector for health care delivery at one end and relatively higher private sector spending to access health care facilities on the other. Thus one finds that compared to spending of 1.3 per cent of GDP by different levels of government, private spending accounted for 2.9 per cent in 2010. The higher private spending on health is reflected in the fact that 80 per cent of doctors, 26 per cent of nurses, 49 per cent of beds and 78 per cent of ambulatory services and 60 per cent of in-patient care are sourced from the private sector (Sen, 2012).

To implement Universal Health Coverage (UHC), the High Level Expert Group (HLEG) (2011) had recommended that public spending on health should reach 2.5 per cent by the end of the Twelfth Five Year Plan and 3.0 per cent by 2022 or by the end of the Thirteenth Five Year Plan. Public health expenditure is likely to reach 1.4 per cent of GDP (including drinking water and sanitation to 1.8% of GDP) by the end of Eleventh Plan. Though the Draft Approach Paper of the Twelfth Five Year Plan sought to raise total health expenditure to 2.5 per cent of GDP by the end of the Twelfth Plan, the actual public spending on health has been pegged at 1.58 per cent of GDP. The projected government spending on health at the end of the Twelfth Five Year Plan is less than the proposed spending of 2.0 per cent of GDP made in the Eleventh Five Year Plan. The intent to spend on public health is not only lower than previous commitments made by the government, but much lower than a minimum of 5.0 per cent of GDP as recommended by the World Health Organization (WHO).

The 12th Finance Commission (TwFC) had taken a positive step towards equalisation of health expenditure across states. TwFC had provided grants on health to those states whose per capita expenditure on health was below the all-states average. The Commission had provided 30 per cent of the gap between the states' per capita health spending and all states' per capita health spending. Seven states i.e., Assam, Bihar, Jharkhand, Madhya Pradesh, Odisha, Uttar Pradesh and Uttarakhand were eligible to receive grants under this classification. The 13th Finance Commission (ThFC) has moved away from the equalisation grant to an incentive grant of ₹ 5,000 crore to states over a three year period between 2012 and 2015 for improvement in IMR. The incentive grant recognises that bringing about improvement from a higher base is often more difficult and requires more effort than bringing about improvement from a lower base. As such the incentive grant has two components. The first component rewards reduction in IMR and the second component provides a premium if the improvement is made above the median value of IMR for all states. Thus, states are rewarded both for improvement in the parameter as well as the level at which the improvement is made. Besides, the ThFC recommended state-specific grants to 12 states on the basis of requests made by them to bridge gaps in critical infrastructure for health including care for children. IMR undoubtedly is a key indicator of health but there are other important indicators like immunisation of children, MMR (measles, mumps and rubella) vaccination etc., which deserve attention in terms of prioritisation of public spending. In short, the interventions though have been positive but are inadequate.

Making progress towards a healthier economy is incumbent on intent and outcome. While the intent of policy is captured through allocation of spending, the outcome of the increased outlay should be reflected in better health outcome. Improved health status should positively influence the national output for the people to enjoy a better living standard. In this backdrop, we study the impact of public spending on one of the basic health indicators i.e., IMR and how improvements in IMR affect output. We also examine the growth dependency of public expenditure on health. The paper examines the historical relationship between output, health expenditure and IMR for 17 general category states of India for the period 2000-2012. The rest of the paper is schematised along the following lines. It provides a brief review of literature on the relationship between economic growth, health care expenditure and health outcomes followed by some stylised facts about the behaviour of output, health expenditure and IMR in the Indian states. Then it explains the methodology used to study the relation between output and health expenditure, between health expenditure and IMR, and between IMR and output followed by a description of the data. After that, the results from the empirical estimates are outlined followed by concluding observations.

Review of Literature

Health status of the population can make a difference to the growth prospects of a nation. This can be seen from a number of dimensions. First, a healthy workforce ensures less absenteeism and thus higher productivity. Second, there are increased incentives to invest in human and physical capital as life expectancy increases. Third, better health status has the potential to augment the savings rates in the economy as workers have an incentive to save for retirement and lastly, better health status improves labour force participation rate as serious illness forces people to drop out of the labour market. Health is also important from the perspective of 'demographic transformation'. As health awareness improves, IMR drops and people are motivated to have smaller families. Seen from another angle, to the extent health expenditure can be treated as an investment in human capital, it has the scope to act as an engine of growth (Lucas, 1988).

The impact of economic growth on health status of the population can be discerned by looking at the behaviour of health care spending. This is because health expenditure is a function of total resources available (income or wealth) in the system. When incomes are rising, there is scope for a rise in both private and public health expenditure. As we have discussed, a rise in health expenditure augments labour supply and productivity, eventually leading to higher income. Thus runs the virtuous cycle. Barro (1997) has found that a 10 per cent increase in life expectancy leads to half a per cent increase in income growth for the developed countries. In the case of Britain, Fogel (1994) found that 30 per cent of British economic growth over last 200 years could be attributed to improvements in nutrition. Several other longitudinal studies also support this conclusion (Heshmati, 2001). Thus from a policy perspective, health is as much an input to economic development as an outcome.

There have been several attempts to study how growth impacts health outcome at the empirical plane. Some prominent ones are Newhouse (1977), Parkin *et al.* (1987), Posnett and Hitris (1992), Pritchett and Summers (1996), Hansen and King (1996) and Barros (1998). All these studies bring out the consistently strong effect that income has on health differences. Bhalotra (2006), however, observed a positive association of health and income but limited evidence of an impact of aggregate income (GDP [gross domestic product]) on health, from a study of macroeconomic evidence from rich and poor countries. Anand and Ravallion (1993) in a cross-country analysis of developing country data found no evidence of GDP having effect on health outcomes, if poverty and public expenditure are held constant. Pritchett and Summers (1996) using panel data for 58 developing countries identify a robust impact of aggregate income on health with elasticity estimated to range between (-)0.12 and (-)0.3 depending on the estimates used and on whether or not education is held constant. Bhalotra (2006) found unconditional growth elasticity of 'under 5' mortality in India at about (-)0.7. Controlling for state 'fixed effects', raised the elasticity up to (-) 1.0. But inclusion of 'year effects' reduced it to (-)0.6. Malik (2006) observed that health indicators do not have a significant effect on GNI (gross national income). The estimates based on two-stage least squares reduced form equation shows no significant effect of health indicators, such as life expectancy, IMR and total fertility rates on growth in income.

As regards developed countries, Deaton and Paxson (2004) find no effect of income on mortality in the UK and a small effect in the US. The effect is considerably diminished when time dummies and education are built into the model. Effect of income on health may not find full reflection when mortality risk is concentrated (such as in pockets of poverty) and income distribution is very much skewed. Apart from this variation in evidence, there are differences in the evidence depending on whether it is based on microeconomic data on health and income or aggregated data. Deaton and Paxson (2001; 2004) conclude that understanding the effect of income on mortality presents many puzzles, between countries, and between analyses at different levels of aggregation.

The interest in health expenditure ultimately lies in its potentiality to improve the health outcomes of a nation. A number of studies including that of Poullier *et al.* (2002) and Bokhari *et al.* (2007) bring out the importance of government spending on health in determining health outcomes. Bokhari *et al.* (2007) find that for developing countries, while economic growth is an important contributor to health outcomes, government spending on health is an equally important factor. Though government spending is important in general, it is very possible that the scope of health expenditure may expand in an economy without significant improvement in health outcomes. This point of view is substantiated by an analysis of data on health expenditure and health outcome for 150 countries including both developed and developing, and underdeveloped countries by Poullier *et al.* (2002) who find that health spending does determine health outcomes but the relationship is not linear. Poullier *et al.* (2002) in their study find three broad patterns that explain the relationship between health spending and health outcome. First, in countries that, to begin with, spent less on health care, higher spending has a significant impact on health status. Second, public policy makes a difference in the effectiveness of health spending in determining health outcomes in the low spending countries. Third, among high spending countries, additional spending bears little relationship to improvements in health adjusted life expectancy.

In the light of the cross-country empirical findings, it would be of interest to examine how public health expenditure, growth and health outcomes interact in the case of India. As the aggregate picture often conceals more than what it reveals, we try to explore the direction of causation, the strength of the relationship between economic growth, public health expenditure and health outcomes for India at the disaggregated state level. What follows is a discussion on the broad behaviour of output, public health expenditure and IMR in the post-reform period before we study the causality.

Stylised Facts

The low public spending on health is on account of a couple of factors. Broadly, it was a consequence of fiscal profligacy coupled with misplaced fiscal priorities in the 1980s and the 1990s. Subsequently, there have been attempts to enforce fiscal discipline both at the level of the Central and state governments through the promulgation of the fiscal responsibility legislation (FRL), in the year 2003, which prescribes outer limits for government's fiscal deficit. In light of constraints posed by the FRL at one end and government's committed administrative expenditure at the other, there is grave concern that public spending on health in India may not be able to meet the growing needs of the population, not even in the foreseeable future (Panda, 2006).

Health care facilities in India have always lagged behind demand for such services including the availability of health care professionals in the country. Just before India's Independence, Sir Joseph Bhore Committee (1946) prescribed the norm of one doctor per 1,500 population and one nurse per 500 populations. Instead, the doctor-population ratio was 1:1800 in as late as the year 2001. Like the doctor-population ratio, progress in the provision of important health care infrastructure has also been tardy. This is brought out in Table 15.1. Further, the deficiency in health care infrastructure has been acute in the rural areas.

Table 15.1

Progress in Health Care Availability (1951-2010)

(Per lakh population)

Health Infrastructure	*1951*	*1981*	*1991*	*2000*	*2004*	*2005*	*2011*
SC/PHC/CHC	0.20	8.45	6.73	16.08	15.57	15.56	14.90
Hospitals	2.57	3.47	2.77	4.27	3.50	2.52	1.01
Beds (Pvt & Public)	32.65	83.87	95	88	84.24	42.8	46.5*
Doctors (Modern System)	17.21	39.57	31.55	49.66	57.58	59.50	69
Nursing Personnel	5.03	21.19	16.89	72.63	77.01	78.45	92*
Health Outcome							
Life Expectancy	36.7	54	57**	64.6	63.3	64	-
IMR	146	110	80	68	60*	58	47

Note: 2011 figures for hospitals refers to only government hospitals.
*refers to as of 2009,** for male.

Source: *National Health Policy 2002; Socioeconomic Statistics, India, 2011.*

Notwithstanding the deficiency in health care infrastructure, India has made significant strides in health outcomes. This has been made possible by the health care facilities provided by the private sector and people's willingness to pay for private medical facilities. The all India picture subsumes the details and regional variations in the health expenditure and health outcomes. Federating states of the Indian Union are in different places of the income spectrum and have varied achievement in social parameters. As health is a state subject, much would depend on the initiative of the state concerned in putting health as a priority in its scheme of resource commitment. Here, we look at the changing pattern of health care spending across states in the past 13 years and the growth in health care spending *versus* spending on other heads across the 17 states.

As far as health expenditure in the GCS (general category states) is concerned, we find Maharashtra had the highest health expenditure and Goa had the lowest in absolute amounts in 2000. If we exclude Goa, Chhattisgarh had the lowest health expenditure in absolute amounts. However, in per capita terms, Goa had the highest health expenditure at ₹ 651 followed by Punjab ₹ 215 and Bihar had the lowest at ₹ 62. By 2012, Uttar Pradesh had relegated Maharashtra to the second position and has emerged as the state having the highest health expenditure. Goa had the lowest absolute amounts of expenditure on health across states. If we exclude Goa, Jharkhand has replaced Chhattisgarh at the bottom position. In per capita terms, Goa (₹ 2,258) again had the highest expenditure on health followed by Kerala (₹ 710) and Bihar had the lowest ₹ 183.10

In these 13 years both Bihar and Goa have retained positions at the bottom and the top. However, the per capita expenditure has grown by 3.8 times for Bihar and only 3.5 times for Goa. For Punjab which had the second highest per capita health expenditure, the growth has been only 2.7 times and for Maharashtra, the growth has been only 3.1 times. When we look at the absolute health expenditure, for Bihar the growth has been 4.7 times whereas for Punjab and Maharashtra the growth has been only 3.4 times and 3.7 times. Only in case of Goa, the growth in total health expenditure has been 5.1 times.

During the entire period under study, health expenditure as a proportion of SDP (state domestic product), was observed at 0.6 per cent. Goa had the highest share at 1.0 per cent followed by Bihar (0.9%) and Jharkhand and Uttar Pradesh (0.8%). Maharashtra and Haryana had the lowest share at 0.4 per cent. Health expenditure falls under developmental expenditure. Development expenditure accounted for 62 per cent of total expenditure in the states with Chhattisgarh having the highest share at 70.5 per cent and Jharkhand at 70.3 per cent and Andhra Pradesh at 68.2 per cent. Punjab had the lowest share of development expenditure in total expenditure at 46.3 per cent followed by Kerala (52.7%) and West Bengal (53.5%). Health expenditure as proportion of developmental expenditure was 6.1 per cent for these 17 states. This ratio was the highest for Kerala at 9.0 per cent followed by West Bengal at 8.7 per cent and Punjab at 7.7 per cent. Haryana had the lowest share at 4.5 per cent followed by Gujarat at 4.7 per cent.

Total expenditure as proportion of SDP was the highest for Bihar (23.4%) followed by Goa (20.6%), Uttar Pradesh (20%) and Jharkhand (19.4%). Maharashtra had the lowest share (13%). Health expenditure falls under social services in the budgetary classification of states. Social services accounted for 54 per cent of the combined expenditure on social and economic services. West Bengal (66.1%) had the highest share of social services in the combined expenditure followed by Kerala (62.6%) and Rajasthan (61.7%). Goa (45.4%) had the lowest share followed by Karnataka (48.1%). Health expenditure as proportion of social services expenditure amounted to 11.3 per cent for all the GCS. This share has been highest for Goa (16.2%) followed by Odisha (15.5%) and Kerala (14.4%). Haryana (9.1%) had the lowest share followed by Gujarat (9.3%) and Chhattisgarh (9.6%). The proportion of plan and non-plan expenditure on health has been in the ratio of 76:24.

Growth in per capita total expenditure for these 17 states has been at the same pace as the per capita SDP. However, this pattern was not uniform for all the 17 states. We find, 9 states had a per capita expenditure growth higher than the growth in per capita SDP and for the rest 8, it was lower. However, growth of per capita health expenditure at 11 per cent has fallen short of per capita SDP growth of 12 per cent during 2000-2012 for the 17 states taken together. During this period, population growth has been 1.5 per cent. There are a number of states like Jharkhand, Madhya Pradesh, Chhattisgarh and Uttar Pradesh where per capita health expenditure has grown at a faster pace than the per capita SDP growth. However, Chhattisgarh is the only state where not only per capita health expenditure has grown at a faster pace than per capita SDP growth but the per capita SDP growth has been higher than that for all states taken together. Uttar Pradesh had the highest per capita growth in health expenditure at 16.1 per cent followed by Chhattisgarh at 13.9 per cent and Haryana at 13.8 per cent. Punjab had the least growth at 6.5 per cent followed by Maharastra at 9.5 per cent and Rajasthan at 9.7 per cent.

While developmental expenditure has grown at a faster pace than that of output in per capita terms, non-developmental expenditure has grown at a much lower pace for all states taken together. At the level of individual states, per capita development expenditure grew at a slower pace than per capita SDP only in case of Goa, Gujarat and Kerala. As far as non-

Table 15.2

Share of Health Related Expenditure in SDP

(Per cent)

	Share of Total Expenditure to SDP	Share of Developmental Expenditure to Total Expenditure	Share of Non-Developmental Expenditure to Total Expenditure	Share of Health Expenditure to Developmental Expenditure	Share of Health Expenditure to SDP	Share of Non-plan Component in Health Expenditure	Share of Plan Component in Health Expenditure	Share of Social Services Expenditure in Combined Social and Economic Services	Share of Economic Services Expenditure in Combined Social and Economic Services	Share of Health Expenditure to Social Services Expenditure
Andhra Pradesh	16.7	68.2	31.3	5.3	0.6	76.9	23.1	48.3	51.7	10.9
Bihar	23.4	60.7	39.2	6.4	0.9	85.3	14.8	58.0	42.1	10.9
Chhattisgarh	17.7	70.5	26.4	5.3	0.7	52.3	47.4	55.3	45.2	9.6
Goa	20.6	67.1	32.9	7.3	1.0	69.6	30.4	45.4	54.6	16.2
Gujarat	14.7	67.9	31.7	4.7	0.5	65.1	34.9	50.8	49.2	9.3
Haryana	13.7	66.8	32.6	4.5	0.4	73.7	26.3	48.8	51.2	9.1
Jharkhand	19.4	70.3	29.8	6.1	0.8	65.1	34.7	54.0	45.9	11.3
Karnataka	17.1	68.0	28.5	5.4	0.6	67.4	32.6	48.1	51.9	11.1
Kerala	15.0	52.7	43.6	9.0	0.7	88.5	11.5	62.6	37.4	14.4
Maharashtra	13.0	63.6	35.0	5.4	0.4	78.3	21.7	55.4	44.6	9.7
Madhya Pradesh	18.9	65.6	30.3	5.6	0.7	76.5	23.6	47.7	52.1	11.8
Odisha	18.4	59.6	39.1	5.9	0.6	81.5	18.5	58.3	41.7	10.1
Punjab	17.0	46.3	52.2	7.7	0.6	89.8	10.2	49.7	50.3	15.5
Rajasthan	17.7	63.8	36.1	6.5	0.7	83.6	16.4	61.7	38.3	10.5
Tamil Nadu	15.0	60.1	34.3	6.3	0.6	74.8	25.2	59.5	40.5	10.7
Uttar Pradesh	20.0	57.8	38.9	6.8	0.8	75.5	24.4	51.3	48.7	13.4
West Bengal	14.9	53.5	45.6	8.7	0.7	78.0	22.0	66.1	33.9	13.1
GCS	16.3	62.1	35.9	6.1	0.6	75.8	24.2	53.9	46.1	11.3
India	15.6	62.3	35.8	6.2	0.6	74.4	25.7	53.6	46.4	11.5

Note: SDP refers to gross SDP at current market prices with 2004-05 as the base year.

Source: Author's calculations based on data obtained from Budget Documents.

Table 15.3

CAGR (Compound Annual Growth Rate) of Health Expenditure and SDP

State	*Growth of Per Capita SDP*	*Growth of Population*	*Growth of Per Capita Health Care Expenditure*	*Growth of Per Capita Health Care Expenditure Plan Component*	*Growth of Per Capita Health Care Expenditure Non-plan Component*	*Growth of Per Capita Total Expenditure*	*Growth of Per Capita Develop-mental Expenditure*	*Growth of Per Capita Non-Develop-mental Expenditure*	*Growth of Per Capita Expenditure on Social Services*	*Growth of Per Capita Expenditure on Economic Services*
Andhra Pradesh	13.4	1.1	12.1	15.2	11	13.9	15.4	10.8	14.7	16.2
Bihar	11.4	1.7	12	16.1	11.4	13.9	16.9	9.2	14.6	20.2
Chhattisgarh	12.7	1.9	13.9	20.8	8.1	15.8	17.8	11.1	16.9	18.7
Goa	13.2	3.2	11.7	17.5	9.4	9.5	11.9	5	12.1	11.8
Gujarat	13.4	1.6	10.5	22.5	4.1	9.6	9.4	10.1	10.6	8.1
Haryana	13.9	1.8	13.8	21	11.2	13.2	15.3	8.7	15.8	14.7
Jharkhand	9.6	1.6	13	17.8	10.3	12.9	13.2	11.9	13.5	12.9
Karnataka	12.3	1.2	10.6	15.9	8	12.8	14.1	8.9	13.8	14.4
Kerala	12.3	0.9	11	13.6	10.7	11.3	10.3	10.6	11.2	8.8
Maharashtra	12.7	1.5	9.5	12.3	8.7	11	12.8	8	12.8	12.8
Madhya Pradesh	9.9	1.8	10.5	7.8	11.2	12.5	12.8	11	12.6	13.2
Odisha	13.9	1.3	10.3	7.1	11.2	12.4	14.1	9.7	12.7	16.1
Punjab	10	1.8	6.1	-4.6	7.3	9.2	10.4	7.6	10.4	10.4
Rajasthan	11.1	1.9	9.7	10.9	9.4	10.4	11.9	7.9	10.6	14
Tamil Nadu	13	0.8	11.7	13.8	11.9	13.3	14.4	10.6	14.1	14.8
Uttar Pradesh	10.1	1.9	16.1	35.8	12.4	13.1	14.9	10.3	16.4	13.5
West Bengal	11.2	1.1	8.5	7.9	13.3	11	12.1	9.8	12.2	11.5
GCS	12	1.5	11.1	15.1	9.9	12	13.3	9.5	13.3	13.3
India	12	1.5	11.3	14.6	10.2	12.1	13.2	9.7	13.2	13.3

Note: GSDP refers to per capita gross SDP at current market prices with 2004-05 as the base year.

Source: Author's calculations based on data obtained from Budget Documents.

developmental expenditure is concerned, only in the case of Jharkhand, Madhya Pradesh and Uttar Pradesh the growth was higher than growth in per capita SDP. Further, except Kerala in all other states, the growth in planned development expenditure was higher than that of the non-plan component in per capita terms.

Both social and economic services in per capita terms have grown at a faster pace than output for all the 17 states taken together. In the case of Gujarat, Goa and Kerala, growth in expenditure on both social and economic services have been lower than that of output. Further, in Odisha and Rajasthan, growth in per capita expenditure on social services has been lower than that of per capita SDP. In all other states, growth in expenditure on economic and social services has outpaced that of output.

Except Madhya Pradesh, Odisha, Punjab and West Bengal, in all other states the growth in planned health expenditure was higher than that of non-plan health expenditure in per capita terms. Within social sector expenditure, the growth in the plan component was much higher than the non-plan component for all the states taken together as well for the individual states. Within expenditure on economic services, the growth in plan component was much higher than that for the non-plan component for all states taken together and seen individually except for Kerala. The more important question is does the health expenditure influence the health outcome?

Seen from a different perspective, the standard deviation of log of per capita SDP has increased to 0.45 in 2010 from 0.39 in 2000. However, the standard deviation of log of per capita health expenditure has declined from 0.36 in 2000 to 0.29 in 2010. This suggests that states which were earlier spending less on health have relatively increased their spending over time compared to states having higher per capita health expenditure to begin with. This is a welcome trend. This broad trend is also noticed for per capita total expenditure, per capita development expenditure, per capita social sector expenditure and per capita expenditure on economic services. Between 2001 and 2010, the standard deviation in log of IMR has also shown a marginal decline suggesting that the achievement in reduction in IMR has been relatively better in the states having very high IMR to begin with. The decline however, has not been steady. Odisha had the highest IMR in 2000 at 95 and

Kerala the lowest at 14. By 2010, Goa had the lowest IMR at 10 but the IMR of Odisha had reduced to 61. Uttar Pradesh and Madhya Pradesh had the highest IMR at 62 in 2010. Kerala's IMR was 13.

India experienced high growth during 2004-05 to 2007-08. This was a good opportunity to devote a larger share of government spending on health so as to increase the share of public spending as a share of GDP. However, India has missed that opportunity. India has witnessed a significant slowdown in growth in the recent times. As overall growth for the Twelfth Five Year Plan has been scaled down from 9 per cent in the Approach Paper to 8.2 per cent in the best case scenario, it naturally follows that the government would face a resource crunch. As social sector spending is a soft target for expenditure compression, there is every possibility of public spending on health sharing a larger burden of this squeeze.

Empirical Methodology

In this section, we decipher the relationship between output, health expenditure and IMR, in a causality framework employing panel Fully Modified Ordinary Least Squares (FMOLS) tests. The standard approach to test for causality amongst economic variables is the Granger causality. As we have information both in the time series and the cross-section dimension, test of cointegration in a panel context becomes more useful.

We employ a battery of panel unit root tests, and the results indicate that the three variables—log of per capita SDP (LPSDP), log of per capita health expenditure (LPHE) and log of infant mortality rate (LIMR)—are I(1). As they are I(1), we have examined for cointegration between LPSDP and LPHE, LPHE and LIMR, and between LSDP and LIMR, and found them to be cointegrated. Given the cointegration between the variables under study we discuss the appropriate methods that can be employed to study causality. We use efficient estimation method, FMOLS, to get estimates of the cointegration relationship. FMOLS makes corrections for endogeneity of the regressors and serial correlation in the error term. Due to the corrections, the estimators are asymptotically unbiased to study the causality between output and health expenditure and also between health expenditure and SDP.

Panel Causality in Error Correction Model Framework

As we find evidence of cointegration, a moot issue is determination of the direction of causality. For this, a panel error correction model (ECM) is estimated. Many authors use panel OLS to construct the error correction terms in the ECM set up. However, as FMOLS is the appropriate estimation technique when there is evidence of panel cointegration, constructing the ECM-term based on the residuals from an OLS may not be appropriate. As such, we use residuals from the panel FMOLS estimate to construct the ECM-term in the test for Granger causality.

$$\Delta X_{it} = a_{1j} + \sum_{j=1}^{k} \alpha_{1j} \Delta X_{i,t-j} + \sum_{j=1}^{k} \beta_{1j} \Delta Y_{i,t-j} + \lambda_{1i} ecm_{t-1} + \mu_{1t} \quad (1)$$

$$\Delta Y_{it} = a_{1j} + \sum_{j=1}^{k} \alpha_{2j} \Delta X_{i,t-j} + \sum_{j=1}^{k} \beta_{2j} \Delta Y_{i,t-j} + \lambda_{2i} ecm_{t-1} + \mu_{1t} \quad (2)$$

The lag of the residual so obtained constitutes the ECM-term in the estimation of (1) and (2). The estimated coefficients of β_{1ij} and λ_{1i} in (1) and α_{2ij} and λ_{2i} in (2) is used to infer about short run and long run causality. Pedroni (2004) has established that if X and Y are truly cointegrated, then both λ_{1i} and λ_{2i} will not be simultaneously zero. More specifically, if the hypothesis that β_{1ij} is zero is rejected, we infer that there is causality running from Y to X in the short run. Further, if the hypothesis that λ_{1i} is zero, is rejected, there is long run causality from Y to X. Similarly in equation (2), a non zero α_{2ij} would suggest short run causality running from X to Y and a non zero λ_{2i} would imply long run causality running from X to Y.

We consider per capita SDP, per capita health expenditure and the IMR as the variables of interest for this study. While information on SDP and health expenditure for the period 2000 to 2012 is available for all the states, information on IMR is available only for the period 2000-2010. As such, we have used the period for which consistent information on all the three parameters of interest for our study. We use three alternative tests to study the unit root character of the variables in a panel context. Pedroni's method has been applied to study cointegrating relationship between LPSDP and LPHE and also between LPHE and IMR. Panel FMOLS estimates are employed to decipher the pattern of elasticity amongst the two set of variables. Subsequently, we look into the causality between LPSDP and LPHE and between LPHE and IMR from the panel data perspective

Results

We first test the stationary property of the variables under consideration in the panel context. We employ three different panel unit root tests to draw robust inferences. The results of the panel unit root tests for each of our variables are shown in Table 15.4. In no case the null hypothesis that every state has a unit root for the series in log levels is rejected. However, the series are stationary in their first differences. Hence, the variables considered are I(1). Once ascertained that all the three variables are I(1), we turn to the question of possible co-integration between them.

Table 15.4

Panel Unit Root Tests

Series	*LLC*	*tips*	*ADF-Fisher Chi-square*	*PP-Fisher Chi Square*
LPSDP	12.096 (1.000)	13.401 (1.000)	0.749 (1.000)	0.087 (1.000)
LPHE	10.285 (1.000)	11.374 (1.000)	1.436 (1.000)	1.041 (1.000)
LIMR	4.153 (1.000)	7.536 (0.000)	14.212 (0.998)	9.376 (1.000)
Δ LPSDP	-4.993 (0.000)	-1.528 (0.063)	55.475 (0.011)	95.821 (0.000)
Δ LPHE	-4.349 (0.000)	-1.247 (0.106)	51.395 (0.028)	56.223 (0.009)
Δ LIMR	-6.980 (0.000)	-3.305 (0.000)	71.586 (0.000)	83.079 (0.000)

Note: Figures in brackets indicate p- values.
Assumption: Individual intercept included in test equation.
Schwarz criterion for Automatic Lag Selection.

Table 15.5 reveals the evidence regarding the co-integration property between output and health expenditure, between health expenditure and IMR, and also between SDP and IMR for the Indian states. Pedroni (1999) shows that in small samples of N and moderate samples of T, the group-ADF statistics has the best power. Though we get mixed results, the group-ADF statistics suggest that the null hypothesis of no co-integration between the three set of variables under consideration is rejected. Having found evidence of panel cointegartion, we obtain the FMOLS estimates (Annexure Table A-15.1). We also compute the estimates obtained from standard OLS and fixed effect estimates to compare and contrast the elasticities. We find that elasticity of output to health expenditure is much higher than elasticity of health expenditure to output. More importantly, the elasticity of IMR to health expenditure is higher than that of SDP. Health expenditure has direct connotation for improving health outcome. However, growth affects IMR indirectly by creating fiscal space for higher public spending on health and indirectly by enabling people to spend from their purse on health care facilities. The results points to the need for prioritising public spending on health rather than relying on the percolation effect of growth to improve health outcome. We also find that elasticity of SDP to IMR is much higher than elasticity of IMR to SDP. This suggests that response of output is much higher to improved health outcome than output influencing health outcome through the direct and indirect channel. Because health expenditure has a larger impact on health outcome and better health outcome in turn having a larger impact on output, we find that the elasticity of output to health expenditure is much higher than that of elasticity of health expenditure to output.

Table 15.5

Panel Co-integration Test

	LPHE and LPSDP	*LPHE and LIMR*	*LPSDP and LIMR*
Panel - v	13.208 (0.000)	6.078 (0.000)	0.948 (0.171)
Panel - rho	1.086 (0.861)	2.126 (0.983)	-0.45 (0.326)
Panel - pp	-3.103 (0.001)	-0.489 (0.312)	-2.921 (0.001)
Panel - ADF	-4.289 (0.000)	-3.986 (0.000)	-5.475 (0.000)
Group - rho	2.742 (0.997)	3.241 (0.999)	1.183 (0.881)
Group - pp	-2.937 (0.001)	-0.205 (0.418)	-2.389 (0.008)
Group - ADF	-3.288 (0.000)	-3.122 (0.000)	-4.912 (0.000)

Note: Assumption: Deterministic Trend and Intercept.

The causality tests indicate the presence of short run causality only from health expenditure to SDP. In no other case, we find evidence of short run causality (Table 15.6). Health expenditure is endogenous to the system as it forms a part of the total government expenditure and hence the short run causality running from health expenditure to SDP is not a very surprising result. We find absence of short run causality from SDP to health expenditure. Thus, the results indicate that competing claims on expenditure at one end and lack of fiscal space might be preventing an increase in health expenditure when SDP grows in the short run.

Table 15.6

Panel Causality Tests

	Short Run	Long Run
LPSDP ® LPHE	No	Yes
LPHE ® LPSDP	Yes	Yes
LPHE ® LIMR	No	Yes
LIMR® LPSDP	No	Yes
LPSDP® LIMR	No	Yes

Note: Based on 10 per cent level of significance.

However, the long run causality results indicate that over time, an increase in SDP leads to increased allocation for health. The more significant finding is that all the causality results hold in the long run.

Table 15.7

Responsiveness of Health Expenditure and IMR to SDP

RHS Variable	OLS	FE	FMOLS
		LHS Variable-LIMR	
LPHE	-0.676 (-15.101)	-0.334 -0.02	-0.4 (-123.544)
LPSDP	-0.56 (-11.464)	-0.351 (-20.978)	-0.344 (-181.496)
		LHS Variable-LPSDP	
LPHE	0.928 -25.97	0.963 -25.165	1.134 (-0.288)
LIMR	-0.741 (-11.464)	-2.045 (-20.798)	-2.566 (-57.101)
		LHS Variable-LPHE	
LPSDP	0.845 -25.976	0.819 -25.165	0.910 (-6.765)

This is also along the expected lines as there is a lag between health expenditure and health outcome, and between health outcome and its impact on output. We find that increase in SDP affects health outcome in the long run (Table 15.7). This could be possible because of the combined impact of increased public expenditure on health made possible from the rising output and higher capability of people to spend from their pocket as incomes are rising. An improvement in health status reflected through a decline in IMR also positively impacts SDP in the long run. This could be again on account of a number of reasons such as improved labour productivity, lower health related absenteeism and higher savings rate because of greater incentive to save. The key take away from the causality results for the policy makers is that public spending on health is pro-growth through its impact on health outcome.

Concluding Observations

One of the chief concerns of a modern day welfare state, providing health care for all, has all along been a challenging task in India. India however, missed out a good chance to reprioritise its spending towards health care during the high growth phase of 2003-04 to 2007-08. Now that growth prospects have slowed down, there is a possibility that health care spending by the government sector will be squeezed. The Twelfth Five Year Plan has already scaled down public spending on health to 1.58 per cent from 2.5 per cent enunciated in the Approach Paper. In this backdrop, the present study analysed if there is good enough reason to have a bias in public spending towards health. The study considered the relationship between SDP, public health expenditure and IMR for 17 states of India using panel estimates for the period 2000-2012. The broad finding of the empirical estimation is that public spending on health influences health outcome more than economic growth. The implication of this finding from a public policy perspective is that instead of leaving it to growth, intervention in the form of public spending on health has a larger impact on health outcome. Further, it was found that the health status of the population significantly affects output. Thus, higher public spending on health is not only pro-people but also pro-growth.

The ThFC introduced an incentive grant for improving IMR apart from providing state specific grants to 11 states for closing gaps in critical health infrastructure. The incentive approach has replaced the equalisation grants recommended by the TwFC. The interventions though have been positive but inadequate. In view of the results obtained, the 14th Finance Commission needs to adopt a more broad-based approach giving due emphasis on equalisation and incentives while allocating funds for the health sector.

References

Anand, Sudhir and Martin Ravallion (1993). "Human Development in Poor Countries: On the Role of Private Incomes and Public Services", *The Journal of Economic Perspectives* 7(1): 133-50.

Ahuja, Rajeev and Johannes Jutting (2003). "Design of Incentives in Community Based Health Insurance Schemes", *ICRIER Working Paper* No. 95, February.

Banerjee, A. (1999). "Panel Data Unit Root Tests and Cointegration: An Overview", *Oxford Bulletin of Economics and Statistics (*Special Issue) 61: 607-29.

Barro, R.J. (1997). *Determinants of Economic Growth: A Cross-county Empirical Study*. Cambridge, MA: MIT Press.

Barro, Robert J. (1996). *Health, Human Capital and Economic Growth.* Program on Public Policy and Health, Division of Health and Human Development. Paper Prepared for the American Health Organization. November.

Barro, Robert J. and X. Sala-I-Martin (1995). *Economic Growth.* New York: McGraw- Hill.

Barros, P.P. (1998). "The Black Box of Health Care Expenditure Growth Determinants", *Health Economics* 7: 538-44.

Becker, Gary Stanley (1964). *Human Capital: A Theoretical and Empirical Analysis, with reference to Education.* New York: NBER, Columbia University Press.

Bennedsen, Morten, Nikolaj Malchow-Moller and Frederik Vinten (2005). *Institutions And Growth-A Literature Survey.* Report prepared for the Danish International Development Agency, Centre for Economic and Business Research. May 3.

Benz, U. and S. Fetzer (2004). "Indicators for Measuring Fiscal Sustainability: A Comparative Application of the OECD-Method and Generational Accounting," *Working Paper Series* 118/04, Freiburg: Institute of Public Finance Albert-Ludwigs, University of Freiburg.

Bhadra, Kaushik K. and Jayeeta Bhadra (2012). "Public Expenditure on Health Across States in India: An Evaluation of Selected Issues and Evidences", *International Journal of Research in Finance and Marketing* 2(6).

Bhalotra, Sonia (2006). "Health and Growth in India: Panel Data Estimates", *Working Paper.* UK: University of Bristol.

Bloom, David E., David Canning and Jaypee Sevilla (2001). "The Effect of Health on Economic Growth: Theory and Evidence", *NBER Working Paper* 8587, November.

Bokhari, F.A.S, Y. Gai and P. Gottret (2005). "Government Health Expenditures and Health Outcomes", *Working Paper*. Department of Economics, Florida State University. Revised May 2006.

————. (2007) "Government Health Expenditures and Health Outcomes", *Health Economics* 16: 257-73.

Bonin, H. (2001). *Generational Accounting: Theory and Application.* Berlin.

Breyer, F. and S. Felder (2004). "Life Expectancy and Healthcare Expenditures: A New Calculation for Germany Using the Costs of Dying", *DIW Discussion Paper* No. 452.

Buchner, F. and J. Wasem (2004). "Steeping of Health Expenditure Profiles", *Discussion Paper Series Essex University* No. 139. Brundtland.

Cole, Mathew A. and Eric Neumayer (2005). "The Impact of Poor Health on Total Factor Productivity", *Working Paper*, March.

Deaton, Angus (2001). "Health, Inequality and Economic Development", *NBER Working Paper* 8318, June.

———. (2004). "Health in an Age of Globalization", *NBER Working Paper* 10669, August.

Deaton, A. and C. Paxson (2004). "Mortality, Income and Income Inequality Over Time in Britain and the United States", in D. Wise (ed.), *Perspectives on Economics of Ageing*. Chicago: University of Chicago Press.

Dickey, D. and W. Fuller (1979). *Distribution of the Estimators for Autoregressive Time Global Forum for Health Research, 2001-2002*. The 10/90 Report on Health Research.

Engle, R.F. and C.W.J. Granger (1987). "Cointegration and Error Correction: Representation, Estimation, and Testing", *Econometrica* 55(2): 251-76.

Fogel, R.W. (1994). "Economic Growth, Population Theory and Physiology: The Bearing of Long-Term Processes on the Making of Economic Policy",*The American Economic Review* 84(3): 369-95.

Gopalan, Sarala and Mira Shiva (eds.) (2000). *National Profile on Women, Health and Development*. World Health Organisation. April.

Government of India (2005). *Report of the National Commission on Macroeconomics and Health*. New Delhi: Ministry of Health and Family Welfare.

———. (2005a). *NCMH Background Papers-Burden of Disease in India*. New Delhi: Ministry of Health and Family Welfare.

———. (2011). *Faster, Sustainable and more Inclusive Growth: An Approach to the Twelfth Five Year Plan*. New Delhi: Planning Commission.

———. (2011a). *High Level Expert Group Report on Universal Health Coverage for India*. New Delhi: Planning Commission.

———. (2011b). *National Health Profile*. New Delhi: Directorate General of Health Services, Ministry of Health and Family Welfare.

———. (2012). *Report of the Steering Committee on Helath for the 12th Five Year Plan*. New Delhi: Planning Commission of India.

Gro, Harlem (2002). *Health and the International Economy*. Report of Working Group 4 of the Commission on Macroeconomics and Health. August.

Hagist, Christian and Laurence J. Kotlikoff (2005). " Who's Going Broke? Comparing Health Care Costs in Ten OECD Countries", *Working Paper* 11833. NEBR. December.

Hall, Robert E. and Charles I. Jones (2005). "The Value of Life and the Rise in Health Spending", UC Berkeley *mimeo*. 18 October.

Hansen, P. and A. King (1996). "The Determinants of Health Care Expenditure: A Cointegration Approach", *Journal of Health Economics* 15: 127-37.

Hasley, Rogers (2005). "Missing in Action: Teacher and Health Worker Absence in Developing Countries", *Journal of Economic Perspectives* 19(4), Fall.

Heshmati, A. (2001). *On the Causality between GDP and Health Care Expenditure in Augmented Solow Growth Model*. Department of Economic Statistics Stockholm School of Economics.

High Level Expert Group (HLEG) (2011). *Report on Universal Health Coverage for India* (Chairperson: K. Srinath Reddy). Instituted by Planning Commission. Submitted to the Planning Commission, New Delhi. November.

Hitiris, T. and J. Posnett (1992). "The Determinants and Effects of Health Expenditure in Developed Countries", *Journal of Health Economics* 11: 173-81.

Hofmarcher, M. and M. Riedel (2002). "Age Structure and Health Expenditure in the EU: Costs Increase, but Do Not Explode," *Health System Watch* 3: 1-23.

Im, K.S., M.H. Pesaran and S. Shin (1995). "Testing for Unit Roots in Heterogeneous Panels"" *Mimeo. Department of Applied Economics.* University of Cambridge.

Im, K.S., M.H. Pesaran and Y. Shin (1997). "Testing for Unit Roots in Heterogeneous Panels". *Mimeo.* Department of Applied Economics, University of Cambridge.

Jean-Pierre Poullier, Patricia Hernandez, Kei Kawabata and William D. Savedoff (2002). "Patterns of Global Health Expenditures: Results of 191 Countries", *Discussion Paper* No. 51. World Health Organisation.

Jones, Charles I. (2004). *Why Have Health Expenditures as a Share of GDP Risen So Much.* Department of Economics, U.C. Berkeley. May 5.

Lucas, R. (1988). "On the Mechanics of Economic Development", *Journal of Monetary Economics* 22(1): 3-42.

Mahal, Ajay and Peter Berman (2001). *Health Expenditures and the Elderly: A Survey of Issues in Forecasting, Methods Used, and Relevance for Developing Countries.* Department of Population and International Health, Harvard School of Public Health. December.

Malik, Garima (2006). "An Examination of the Relationship between Health and Economic Growth", *Working Paper* No. 185. New Delhi: Indian Council for Research in International Economic Relations.

McCarthy, Wolf H. and Y. Wu (2000). "The Growth Costs of Malaria", *Working Paper* No. 7541. National Bureau of Economic Research.

Miller, T. (2001). "Increasing Longevity and Medicare Expenditures", *Demography* 38(2): 215-26.

Misra, Rajiv, Rachel Chatterjee and Sujata Rao (2003). *India Health Report.* Oxford University Press.

Newhouse, J. (1977). "Medical-care Expenditures: A Cross-national Survey", *Journal of Human Resources* 12(1): 115-25. *http://dx.doi.org/10.2307/145602*

Newhouse, J.P. (1992). "Medical Care Costs: How Much Welfare Loss?", *Journal of Economic Perspectives* 6 (3): 3-21.

Observer Research Foundation (2004). *Decentralised Delivery of Health Care: International and Indian Experiences.* Conference Report. Forum of Federations.

Panda, A. K. (2006). "Health Care " *Yojana*, October.

Parkin, D., A. McGuire, and B. Yule (1987). "Aggregate Health Care Expenditures and National Income: Is Health Care a Luxury Good?", *Journal of Health Economics* 6.

Pedroni, Peter (1999). "Critical Values for Cointegration Tests in Heterogeneous Panels with Multiple Regressors", *Oxford Bulletin of Economics and Statistics* 61: 653-70, Special Issue.

————. (2001). "Purchasing Power Parity Tests in Cointegrated Panels", *Review of Economics and Statistics* 83: 727-31.

————. (2004). "Panel Cointegration; Asymptotic and Finite Sample Properties of Pooled Time Series Tests with an Application to the Purchasing Power Parity Hypothesis", *Econometric Theory* 20: 597-625.

Phillips, P. and P. Perron (1988). "Testing for a Unit Root in Time Series Regression", *Biometrika* 75: 335-46.

Poullier, Jean-Pierre, Patricia Hernandez, Kei Kawabata and William D. Savedoff (2002). "Patterns of Global Health Expenditures: Results of 191 Countries", *Discussion Paper* No. 51. World Health Organisation.

Pritchett, L. and L.H. Summers (1996). "Wealthier is Healthier", *The Journal of Human Resources* 31: 841-68.

Rao, M. Govinda and Mita Choudhury (2012). "Health Care Financing Reforms in India", *Working Paper* No. 2012-100. New Delhi: National Institute of Public Finance and Policy.

Rao, Vijayendra, Indrani Gupta and Samarjit Jana (2001). "Sex Workers and the Cost of Safe Sex: The Compensating Differential for Condom Use in Calcutta", *Working Paper Series*. Population Studies and Training Centre, Brown University.

Schultz, T. Paul (2005), "Productive Benefits of Health: Evidence from Low-Income Countries", *Economic Growth Centre Discussion Paper* No. 903. Yale University. January.

Sen, G. (2012). "Universal Health Coverage in India: A Long Winding Road", *Econoimc and Political Weekly* XIVII(8): 45-52.

Singh, S.K. Ravi K. Verma and Rajiv Prasad (2003). *The Impact of HIV/AIDS-related Deaths on Households and their Coping Strategies: A Study with Special Reference to Children*. Research Report. Deonar, Mumbai: International Institute for Population Sciences.

Sloss, Christine M. and Gary W. Hrper (2004). "When Street Sex Workers are Mothers", *Archives of Sexual Behaviour* 33(4): 329-41, August.

Solow, Robert M. (1966). "Review of Capital and Growth", *American Economic Review* 56: 1257-60.

UNDP (2004). *Human Development Report*. Oxford University Press.

Weil, David N. (2005). "Accounting for the Effect of Health on Economic Growth", *NBER Working Paper* 11455, June.

World Helth Organisation (2012). *World Health Statistics*. Geneva.

Wilson, R. Mark (1999). "Medical Care Expenditures and GDP Growth in OECD Nations", *American Association of Social and Behavioural Sciences Journal* 2, Fall.

World Bank (2005). *World Development Report*. Oxford University Press.

Zweifel, P. (2003). "Medical Innovation. A Challenge to Society and Insurance," *Geneva Papers on Risk and Insurance: Issues and Practice* 28(20): 194-202.

Zweifel, P., S. Felder and A. Werblow (2004). "Population Ageing and Healthcare Expenditure: New Evidence on the Red Herring", *Geneva Papers on Risk and Insurance: Issues and Practice* 29(4): 652-66.

Zweifel, P., S. Felder and M. Meiers (1999). "Ageing of Population and Healthcare Expenditure: A Red Herring?", *Health Economics* 8: 485-96.

Annexure Table A-15.1

FMOLS Estimates

State	*Response of Health Expenditure to Changes in SDP*	*Response of SDP to Changes in Health Expenditure*	*Response of Health Expenditure to Changes in IMR*	*Response of IMR to Changes in Health Expenditure*	*Response of IMR to Changes in SDP*	*Response of SDP to Changes in IMR*
GCS	Dep Var - lphe	Dep Var - lpsdp	Dep Var - HE	Dep Var - limr	Dep Var - LIMR	Dep Var - LPSDP
Andhra Pradesh	0.874 (-1.234)	1.125 (0.903)	-2.577 (-9.661)	-0.339 (-32.000)	-0.303 (-89.381)	-3.413 (-18.668)
Bihar	1.006 (0.042)	0.907 (-1.017)	-3.155 (-4.407)	-0.239 (-35.100)	-0.278 (-42.699)	-3.387 (-10.196)
Chhattisgarh	0.924 (-1.263)	1.068 (0.563)	-2.5785 (-9.003)	-0.362 (-24.197)	-0.314 (-37.760)	-3.015 (-12.119)
Goa	0.862 (-2.208)	1.160 (1.568)	-1.346 (-16.956)	-0.660 (-17.715)	-0.606 (-25.682)	-1.665 (-17.159)
Gujarat	0.787 (-2.563)	1.076 (0.390)	-2.688 (-9.300)	-0.279 (-32.703)	-0.240 (-54.187)	-4.337 (-13.538)
Haryana	0.950 (-0.515)	0.979 (-0.207)	-3.761 (-16.441)	-0.247 (-62.986)	-0.249 (-93.172)	-4.129 (-19.804)
Jharkhand	1.468 (1.932)	0.630 (-4.554)	-3.808 (-4.155)	-0.194 (-28.159)	-0.295 (-29.367)	-2.721 (-7.882)
Karnataka	0.901 (-1.044)	1.061 (0.405)	-2.072 (-6.900)	-0.388 (-19.815)	-0.357 (-38.121)	-2.897 (-10.926)
Kerala	0.867 (-3.247)	1.166 (2.624)	1.344 (0.350)	0.164 (-5.376)	0.089 (-7.988)	1.877 (0.792)
Maharashtra	0.716 (-4.807)	1.517 (2.702)	-1.474 (-10.090)	-0.667 (-17.166)	-0.392 (-32.051)	-2.414 (-13.811)
Madhya Pradesh	0.905 (-1.754)	1.101 (1.631)	-2.551 (-41.643)	-0.396 (-100.736)	-0.365 (-56.628)	-2.659 (-20.594)
Orissa	0.731 (-2.604)	1.319 (1.177)	-1.989 (-9.760)	-0.411 (-16.260)	-0.292 (-58.382)	-3.276 (-16.418)
Punjab	0.325 (-7.629)	2.366 (2.104)	-0.572 (-6.759)	-1.070 (-6.293)	-0.470 (-34.373)	-2.216 (-12.550)
Rajasthan	0.924 (-1.296)	1.067 (0.831)	-2.370 (-9.204)	-0.379 (-22.909)	-0.351 (-37.092)	-2.777 (-13.534)
Tamil Nadu	0.900 (-1.134)	1.064 (0.441)	-1.327 (-18.979)	-0.635 (-27.213)	-0.602 (-39.398)	-1.692 (-19.192)
Uttar Pradesh	1.616 (3.306)	0.576 (-11.128)	-5.527 (-9.494)	-0.187 (-53.280)	-0.324 (-46.327)	-2.994 (-15.066)
West Bengal	0.708 (-1.877)	1.108 (0.379)	-1.146 (-5.421)	-0.521 (-7.478)	-0.509 (-25.419)	-1.912 (-14.770)
Group	0.910 (-6.765)	1.135 (-0.288)	-2.212 (-45.554)	-0.400 (-123.544)	-0.344 (-181.496)	-2.566 (-57.101)

Note: Figures in parentheses indicate t-values.

16

Role of Central Government Finances in Improving Health Services in India

Special Focus on Andhra Pradesh

K.S. Babu

Introduction

Despite spending on various developmental programmes, the progress in India is being overshadowed by growing population. The population of India as on 1 March 2011 (as per the provisional total of Census 2011) was 1,210 million compared to a 1,029 million in 2001. In absolute terms, the population of India has increased by more than 181 million during the decade 2001-2011. The absolute addition to the population during the decade 2001-2011 was slightly lower than the population of Brazil (the fifth most populous country) in the world. At present, a little more than one out of every six persons in the world is from India (Census of India, 2011). The decadal growth of population was below 15 per cent until 1961; it rose till 1991 and the growth rate (24.2%) during 1981-1991 was highest ever recorded during 20th century. Later it dramatically declined by 14.59 per cent during 1991-2001 and 11.1 per cent during 2001-2011(GoAP and CESS, 2008).

The total number of children in the age group 0-6 years during 2001 was about 163.8 million, about 5 million more than the number recorded in 2011. This reduction, is indicative of a fall in fertility and is a positive sign. A comparison with the figures of Census 2001 reveals that the maximum decline in absolute numbers of children has been in Uttar Pradesh. This is followed by Andhra Pradesh, West Bengal, Maharastra and Kerala (Census of India, 2011).

The changing Indian demographic structure has a direct impact on the health scenario of the population. The overall sex ratio was encouraging across the country but the same is not true in the case of the girl child in the age group 0-6 years. After 1991, there has been a consistent rise in overall sex ratio. On the other hand, the fall in child sex ratio has been unabated since 1961. As per the provisional population totals of Census 2011, it has declined to reach an all-time low of 914 as there is a rise in misuse of medical technology (Census of India, 2011; Banerjee, 1999). The proportion of the aged is also increasing. This growing imbalance in child sex ratio and proportion of aged population in recent years may cause social tensions.

Andhra Pradesh accounts for about 7 per cent of the total population in India but this share had declined from 8.3 per cent in 1961 to 7 per cent in 2011 (GoAP and CESS, 2008).

Health Sector

Higher health budgets in various countries have helped in achieving good health outcomes. For instance, the government expenditure on health in Sri Lanka, Malaysia, Thailand, Cuba, Chile and Costa Rica accounts for between 46 per cent and 88 per cent of total health spending, and this leads to reasonably good health outcomes. In India, however, public health expenditure accounts for just about one-sixth of total health expenditure. In terms of GDP (gross domestic product) it accounts for nearly 1 per cent of GDP and private health expenditure accounts for 5 per cent of GDP. The United Progressive Alliance (UPA) government had promised to enhance public health spending to 3 per cent of GDP. Though the share of the Central Government expenditure on health has increased, overall public health spending continues to stagnate at about 1 per cent of GDP. Since 2004-05, the share of the central government in the total public health budget has improved from 15.84 per cent (2004-05) to 27.91 per cent (2009-10). But the share of the state governments in the health budget has declined substantially from 21.4 per cent to 14.5 per cent (Duggal, 2009).

In India, the majority of the population is still living in rural areas and most of the working population is concentrated in the informal sector with low incomes. It is a tough task for the government to provide quality medical care. Moreover, majority of the population is living under conditions susceptible to diseases. Due to the rising medical costs, certain illness episodes push some families to below poverty line (Bhat and Bhat, 2003). Particularly from 1990s, public health facilities are not adequately addressing health needs of the rural population as the government had to adopt structural adjust programme (SAP) during that period.

The public health services are generally underutilised in rural areas due to poor quality and lack of medicines. On the other hand, there is overutilisation of specialised services at secondary and tertiary level in government public services. Moreover, these are mostly used by the rich and are normally accessible to them due to their location and ability to travel to those access points. This results in the poor depending more on private services. Obviously it is a herculean task for the government alone to tackle the health sector (Misra *et al.*, 2003).

For the reasons cited above, majority of the people in India depend on private health facilities (for both in-patient and out-patient care). According to some estimates, there are around 12 lakh practitioners registered with the authorised bodies of various systems. About 85 per cent of them are in private sector. The number of unqualified practitioners is also large. According to a study conducted by United Nations Children's fund (UNICEF)/Social and Rural Research Institute-Indian Market Research Bureau (RRI-IMRB) in Uttar Pradesh, their number is almost equal to the registered medical practitioners (Misra *et al.*, 2003).

Large section of the population is under severe pressure due to unaffordability of medical care, increase in health care costs and increasing burden of new disease patterns. To make private hospitals accessible to the poor, government gives various subsidies such as duty exemption on importing new medical technologies. In return, these hospitals should provide free treatment for some poor patients. In practice, it is not done due to poor monitoring system.

Health sector has undergone number of changes during the liberalisation process. Private hospitals acquired new technologies with less cost due to reduction in import duties. This period has also seen joint ventures and entry of corporate sector. Thus, private capital entered health care sector. The state governments like Punjab, Rajasthan and Delhi have taken some policy initiatives to invite private finance in health sector (Bhat, 1999).

Objectives

The following issues will be examined in the paper:

(i) Finance Commission's Recommendations on Health Sector Funding.

(ii) National Rural Health Mission (NRHM) funding in improving physical infrastructure and human resources in hospitals of Andhra Pradesh compared to Karnataka, Tamil Nadu and Kerala.

(iii) Details of NRHM funds received by Andhra Pradesh and states' matching contribution to NRHM fund, and

(iv) The pattern of NRHM funds disbursed to districts in Andhra Pradesh.

India's health indicators are discouraging compared to other countries. According to United Nations Development Programmes (UNDP's) *Human Development Report 2010*, out of 193 countries, India ranked 143rd in infant mortality rate (IMR), 124th in maternal mortality rate (MMR), 132nd in life expectancy at birth, and 145th in under-five mortality rate. India's performance is just better than that of sub-Saharan Africa. Within the country, large variations exist in IMR among states. In 2008, the difference in IMR between the best state in India (Kerala) and the worst state (Madhya Pradesh) was nearly six fold (12 in Kerala and 70 in Madhya Pradesh) (Govinda Rao and Mita Choudhury, 2012).

This analysis is done based on various secondary data sources such as data from department of health and family welfare, Andhra Pradesh budget documents, Rural Health Statistics (RHS), Census documents etc.

The paper discusses how Finance Commission (FC) grants (12th [ThFC] and 13th [ThFC] Finance Commission) are useful in addressing the gaps in critical infrastructure for health in many states (including Andhra Pradesh) and in reducing IMR. Recently launched Rashtriya Swasthya Bima Yojana (RSBY) is also discussed in this context. The discussion then moves on to the Central government's contribution to state health infrastructure since its launch in 2005. An attempt is made to discuss improvements of health infrastructure (both physical and human) in Andhra Pradesh in comparison to other southern states and how the state budget for health has declined during 2000-2007 and then improved since 2007-08 with the launch of Aarogyasri health insurance scheme. It also explains how the share of plan expenditure on health and family welfare in terms of GSDP (gross state domestic product) showed a continuous decline during 2000-2007. Then the details of NRHM funding to Andhra Pradesh, its budget allocations at district level and expenditure pattern are discussed. Finally the broad conclusion and policy implications are discussed.

Finance Commission's Recommendations on Health Funding

Many Indian states are finding it difficult to provide good health care due to lack of adequate funds. In India, the Constitution assigns states the predominant responsibility for provision of social services and Central government the responsibility for the provision of economic services. There is a high degree of vertical fiscal imbalance as all broad-based taxes are assigned to the Central government (except general sales tax). To resolve these vertical and horizontal imbalances among states, it is necessary to share central taxes with the states and provide grants in aid to the states based on the recommendation of an independent body, the FC, appointed every five years.

Financial resources of the states are used to meet their committed liabilities toward wages, salaries, interest payments and pensions, leaving little scope for spending on health sector. Many states do not have good health infrastructure. Hence, Central government introduced specific-purpose transfers to the states to ensure minimum standard of basic health services. Accordingly, the TwFC provided grants to selected states for improving health indicators. In addition to the general purpose transfers, specific-purpose grants are given by the central ministries for various central schemes formulated within each ministry. The Ministry of Health and Family Welfare (MoHFW) transfer funds under the NRHM. The Prime Minister of India had launched the NRHM on 12 April 2005. The Mission is also an articulation of the government's commitment to increase public spending on health from 0.9 per cent of India's GDP to 2.3 per cent.

The rapid increase in states' committed expenditure could be attributable to a number of factors which include: (i) increase in salaries/wages due to implementation of Sixth Pay Commission award in many states, and (ii) expenditure on pensions has continued to spiral. Improvement in expectation of life against unchanging age of superannuation have resulted in steady increase in expenditure relating to the pension and other retirement benefits (Anand and Chaudhury, 2008).

Poor states are not able to spend adequately on development segment particularly on the health sector. In addition, the majority of the states have approved the Fiscal Responsibility and Budget Management (FRBM) Act which proposed to attain revenue surplus and maintain it thereafter, and also to bring down their fiscal deficit to three per cent of their GSDP by 2007-08. However, the states have more expenditure responsibilities *vis-à-vis* Centre for the provision of various entitlement programmes of public services. Moreover, they do not have alternative sources of finance like monetisation of deficit, external sources of borrowing or unlimited internal borrowing. Therefore, due to commitment towards FRBM Act, the limited capacity to generate additional revenue and high share of committed expenditure out of own revenue, the states are not in a position to spend the required extra amount for health sector towards meeting the target level of health expenditure (Bhadra and Bhadra, 2012).

In view of the factors cited above and the poor health indicators in the states, especially IMR, the TwFC recommended grants amounting to ₹ 5,887 crore for the health sector for seven states (Assam, Bihar, Jharkhand, Madhya Pradesh, Odisha, Uttar Pradesh and Uttarakhand). Similarly the incentive grant (₹ 5,000 crore) for reduction in IMR, recommended by ThFC, is available during 2012-2015. This grant is to be released over 2012-2015, ₹ 1,500 crore each in 2012-13 and 2013-14 and ₹ 2,000 crore in 2014-15. The grant is linked to actual progress in reduction of infant mortality. The Sample Registration System (SRS) conducted annually by the Registrar General of India (RGI) will form the basis to determine eligibility of states for the grant during a particular year.

It is apparent from Figure 16.1 that Andhra Pradesh and other southern states (except Kerala) will be very slow in achieving IMR and MMR goals set by the millennium development goals (MGDs) by 2015.

ThFC has recommended state specific grants to address the gaps in critical infrastructure for health, including care for children. Andhra

Figure 16.1

Status of IMR and MMR against MDG Targets

IMR against MGD Targets

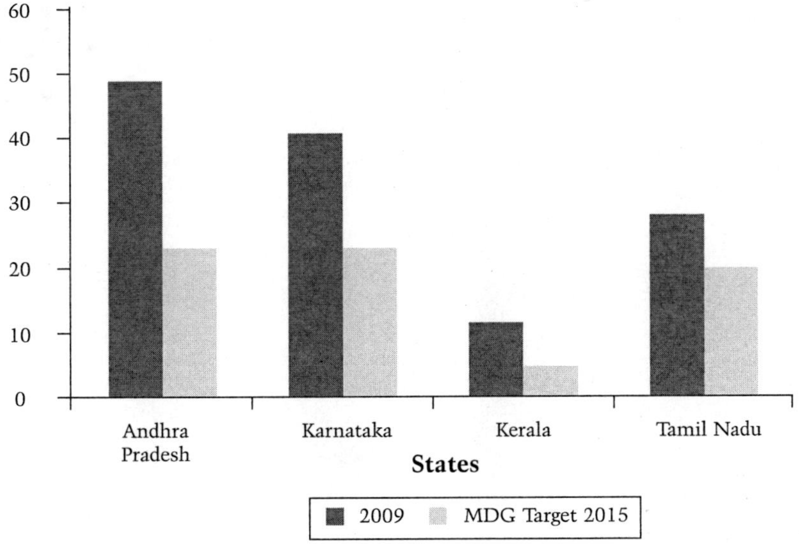

MMR against MDG Target (Per Hundred Thousand)

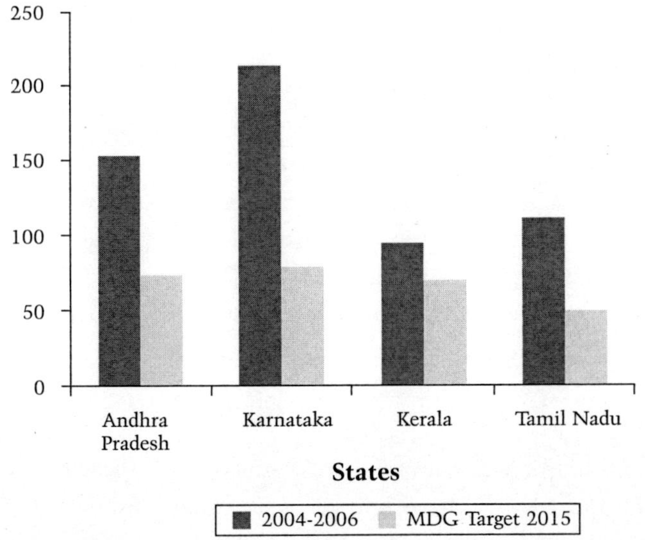

Source: *Millenium Development Goals: States of India Report 2010*, Ministry of Statistics and Programme Implementation, Government of India.

Pradesh, Arunachal Pradesh, Chhattissgarh, Haryana, Mizoram and West Bengal have indicated vast gaps and requested grants for improving physical infrastructure relating to Primary Health Centres (PHCs) and Community Health Centres (CHCs) in rural areas, and sub-divisional and district hospitals and ThFC has recommended grants as per their demand or requirements (Figure 16.2).

Figure 16.2

Thirteenth Finance Commission Recommended Grants

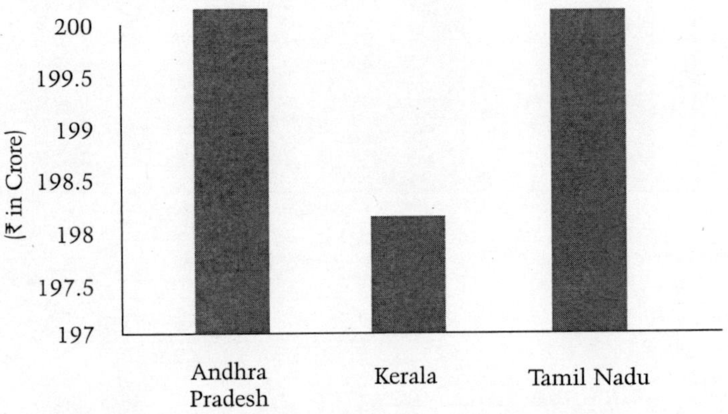

Source: Bhadra and Bhadra, 2012.

The FC transfers are not adequate enough for meetings states' targets on health segment but this is a necessary step to put the states on track. Especially for some states like Madhya Pradesh and Odisha, the requirements for central transfers in terms of grants are very high. Therefore since 2004-05, these transfers have also been supplemented by Centrally Sponsored Schemes (CSS) like NRHM that, in turn, increases public spending on health by the Centre while a gradually declining trend has been observed in the states' spending.

Rashtriya Swasthya Bima Yojana (RSBY)

Ministry of Labour, Government of India (GoI), is also allocating some funds for a health initiative known as Rashtriya Swasthya Bima Yojana (RSBY), which provides insurance coverage for selected hospitalisation expenses and day care procedures (upto ₹ 30,000 per annum) to people below the poverty line. A maximum of five members of a family can be covered under the scheme on a floater basis. A transportation allowance of ₹ 1,000 (with a maximum of ₹ 100 per visit) and the cost of the smart cards (at the rate of ₹ 60 per card) is also extended to these families under the scheme. The premium for the scheme is shared between the central government and the state in the ratio of 75:25 (The beneficiary family has to pay ₹ 30 per annum as a registration fee). As of July 2011, the scheme was being operated in 385 (of the 640) districts of 26 states. About 27 per cent of all poor families in the country were enrolled under the scheme. Some states like Andhra Pradesh, have chosen to implement their own state insurance scheme (*Aarogyasri*) and Karnataka has implemented RSBY in selected districts along with state-level health insurance scheme (*Vajpayee Aarogyasri*). In Andhra Pradesh, on pilot basis, the RSBY scheme was started (in 2012) in Hyderabad, Ranga Reddy, Chittoor and Visakhapatnam districts for construction workers.

National Rural Health Mission (NRHM)

The Prime Minister of India launched the NRHM on 12 April 2005. The NRHM is also an articulation of the government's commitment to increase public spending on health from 0.9 per cent of India's GDP to 2-3 per cent of GDP. The main focus of this programme is to make all health facilities a fully functional, community owned, decentralised health delivery system, with an emphasis on inter-sectoral convergence with sanitation, water, education, nutrition, social and gender equality besides strengthening all health facilities according to Indian Public Health Standards (IPHS). Though the programme covers all the states, the special focus is on eight states identified by the Empowered Action Group (EAG) as having weak public health indicators and health infrastructure facilities. Andhra Pradesh is not one of these EAG states and is categorised as one of the high performing states.

The main components of the NRHM are: (i) Accredited Social Health Activists (ASHAs), (ii) Mission flexible pool untied funding, (iii) Village Health and Sanitation Committees (VHSCs), (iv) Hospital Development Societies (HDS) or Rogi Kalyan Samithis (RKS), (v) Janani Suraksha Yojana, (vi) Revitalising and mainstreaming Ayurveda, Yoga, Unani, Siddha and Homeopathy (AYUSH), (vii) Creation and upgradation of Sub-centres (SCs),

PHCs and CHCs, (viii) Integration of national health programmes (vertical health and family welfare programmes) with state health programmes at state, district and mandal level, and (ix) Public-private partnership—instituting Indian Public Health Standards (Gill, 2009).

For allocating NRHM funds, the states are divided into high-focus states and non-focus states. The states with poor health status are categorised into focus states. The focus states get more funds with 30 per cent higher weight. This programme began as a fully grants-based assistance system, changing into 85:15 (centre:state) cost sharing during the Eleventh Plan and then to 75:25 during the Twelfth Plan. Safeguards are in place to ensure proper utilisation of funds. In order to avoid delay, the transfers were made directly to the state-level societies, bypassing the budgets. Due to the conditionalities attached with NRHM, entire sanctioned amount under NRHM was not being utilised. In 2005-06 ₹ 6,730 crore was the outlay for NRHM against which ₹ 5,703 crore (87.7%) was released. In 2006-07 the NRHM outlay was ₹ 9,000 crore against which ₹ 7,486 crore (83.2%) was released. In 2007-08 ₹ 10,890 crore was allotted to NRHM. The expenditure was ₹ 10,310 crore (94.7%). In 2008-09, ₹ 11,930 crore was allotted and expenditure was ₹ 11,260 (94.4%). In 2009-10, ₹ 14,050 crore was allotted and the expenditure was ₹ 11,260 crore (till 31st January 2010). This clearly shows how the absorptive capacity in the states has considerably increased over years.

Health System in Andhra Pradesh

In this section, an attempt is made to examine the impact of NRHM funding in improving health facilities in Andhra Pradesh compared to three southern states Karnataka, Tamil Nadu and Kerala. In Andhra Pradesh, the process of restructuring the health system started along with the economic reforms in early nineties. In 2005, the governance reform programme 'Delivery of Improved Services in Administration' of Department of International Development (DFID) had provided a strong platform for health sector reform measures, undertaken from 2007 onwards. In 2006, the Centre for Good Governance (CGG) (with the support of DFID) had identified the gaps in state public health system.

This led the Government of Andhra Pradesh (GoAP) to developing a comprehensive Health Sector Reform Strategy (2006-2011) setting out its vision for the sector. The strategy was closely aligned with key provisions of the NRHM. These include increase in public funding in health sector, the need for capacity building for service delivery and gradual convergence of all vertical health programmes for a unified primary health care system (DFID and GoAP, 2010).

NRHM funds were useful in filling health manpower gap by recruiting specialists and doctors in Karnataka, Tamil Nadu and Kerala. In these states a good number of staff nurses were recruited. As it is evident from Figure 16.3, Andhra Pradesh did not pay much attention to recruit specialists and doctors compared to other three states.

In Andhra Pradesh, NRHM funds were used for recruiting ANMs (auxiliary nurse midwife) and ASHAs (Figure 16.4). Compared to other states, Andhra Pradesh utilised the funds for adding many of these health workers. All newly recruited ASHAs in Andhra Pradesh and Karnataka were trained up to IV module and supplied with drugs kit. Tamil Nadu did not pay much attention towards recruiting ASHAs.

Improvement in bed strength in hospitals may indicate the overall improvement in hospital infrastructure. Data on bed strength is available for two years—2005 and 2009. As shown in the Figure 16.5, in Karnataka, Tamil Nadu and Kerala more numbers of beds were added in 2009 compared to the status in 2005 in respective states. Surprisingly only in Andhra Pradesh, the bed strength slightly declined in 2009 compared to the numbers in 2005. Bed strength in Andhra Pradesh hospitals has been stagnant at around 35,000 for the last five years (Figure 16.5).

Figure 16.3

Human Resources Added under NRHM: Doctors and Staff Nurses

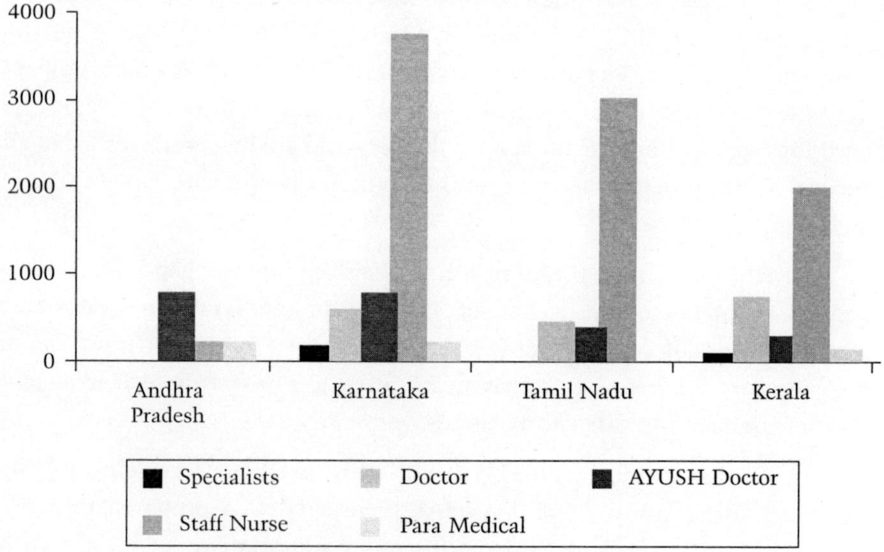

Source: Ministry of Health and Family Welfare, 2010.

Figure 16.4

Human Resources Added under NRHM: ANMs and ASHAs

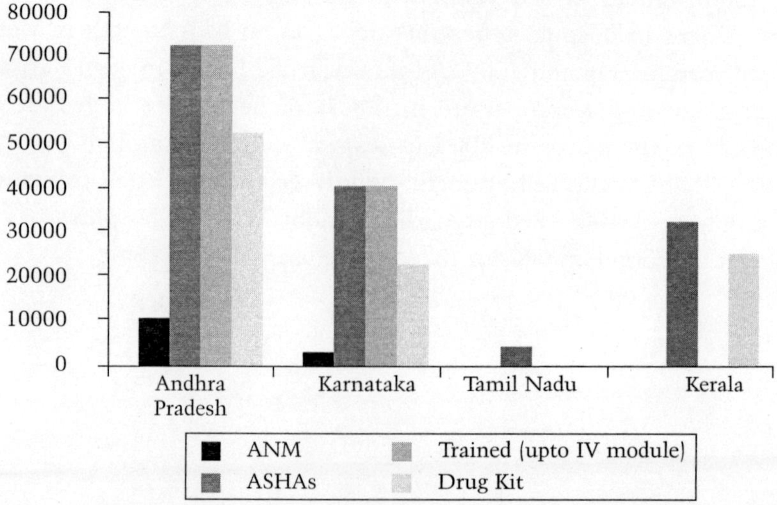

Source: Ministry of Health and Family Welfare, 2010.

Figure 16.5

Bed Strength in Government Institutions (Upto CHC Level)

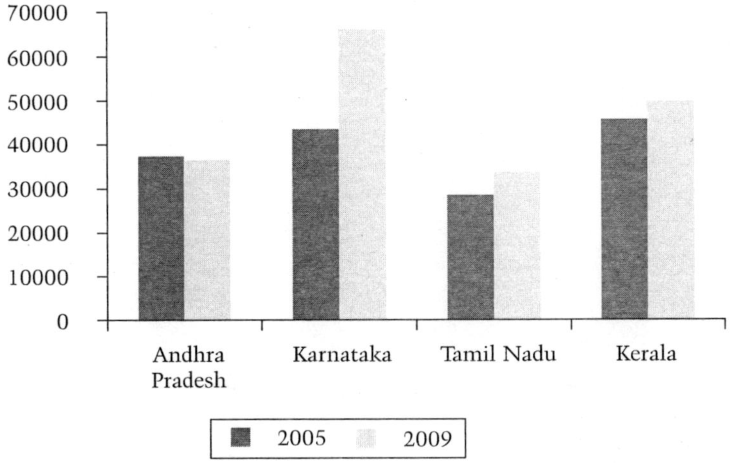

Source: Ministry of Health and Family Welfare, 2010.

The status of number of SCs at the end of Tenth Five Year Plan and as on March 2010 is same in Andhra Pradesh, Karnataka and Tamil Nadu. In Andhra Pradesh, there is no addition in case of SCs, PHCs and CHCs though there were a few additions in other states (Figure 16.6).

As shown in the Table 16.1, adequate number of SCs were reported in Andhra Pradesh, Karnataka and Tamil Nadu. Only in Kerala, there was shortage of 186 SCs. In Andhra Pradesh only one-third of the sub centres were functioning in government buildings. In other three southern states more than half of the centres were functioning in government buildings. Andhra Pradesh is lagging behind even in case of human resources in SCs. More than 10 per cent of the centres in Andhra Pradesh do not have female health worker or ANM. Whereas in other states, the SCs had adequate ANMs or female health workers. Though there is shortage of male health workers in all the states, the situation is bad in the case of Andhra Pradesh and Karnataka as there was a shortage of 50 per cent.

Figure 16.6

Addition of SCs, PHCs and CHCs since Tenth Five Year Plan

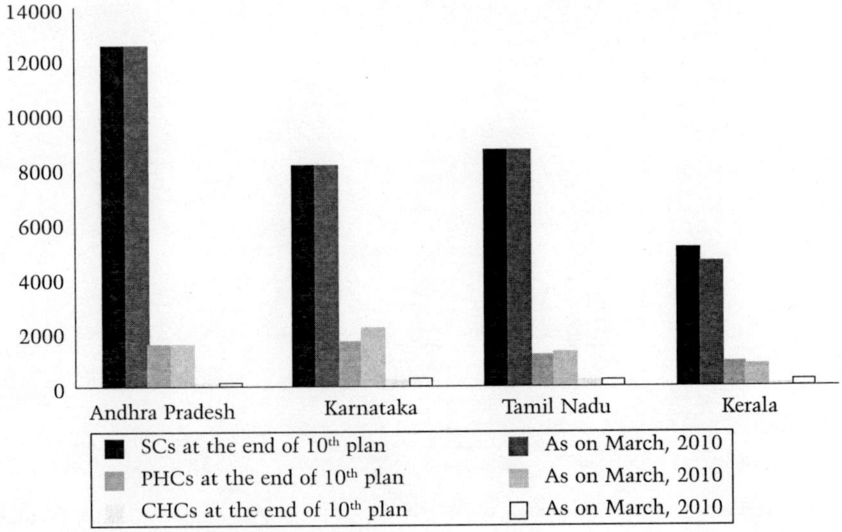

Source: *Rural Health Statistics, 2010.*

Table 16.1

Health Infrastructure and Human Resources at Sub-Centre Level

No.	*Health Infrastructure and Human Resources*	*Andhra Pradesh*	*Karnataka*	*Tamil Nadu*	*Kerala*	*India*
1	SCs Funtional	12522	8143	8706	4575	147069
2	SCs Gap				186	19590
3	In Govt Building	4221	4493	6510	2128	84957
4	In Rented Building	8301	2585	1860	981	46992
5	SCs without HW(F)/ANM	1319		71		6127
6	Without HW(M)	6438	4955	2133	151	76185

Source: *Rural Health Statistics, 2010.*

There was no shortage of PHCs in other three states. In Andhra Pradesh there was a shortage of 354 PHCs. One-fourth of the existing PHCs did not have government buildings and these were functioning from rented accommodation. However, majority of the PHCs in other states were functioning from government buildings. Interestingly, majority of the existing PHCs in Andhra Pradesh had female health assistants/LHVs (lady health visitor), whereas in other states there was shortage of this category of health workers. Comparatively shortage of doctors and referral transport in PHCs was more in Andhra Pradesh and Kerala (Table 16.2).

Table 16.2

Health Infrastructure and Human Resources at PHC Level

No.	*Health Infrastructure and Human Resources*	*Andhra Pradesh*	*Karnataka*	*Tamil Nadu*	*Kerala*	*India*
1	PHC Functional	1570	2193	1283	813	23673
2	PHCs Gap	354				4252
3	In Govt Building	1281	2154	1267	794	19317
4	In Rented Building	289		7	12	1447
5	Vacancy of Health Assistant (F)/ LHV in PHCs	50	1558	415	18	5070
6	Shortfall of Health Assistant (F)/ LHV in PHCs	6		415	18	7275
7	Vacancy of Doctors in PHCs	283	330	301	82	6148
8	Shortfall of Doctors in PHCs					2433
9	Availability of Referral Transport in PHCs	800	1744	1210	10	9720

Source: Rural Health Statistics, 2010.

Table 16.3

Health Infrastructure and Human Resources at CHC Level

No.	*Health Infrastructure and Human Resources*	*Andhra Pradesh*	*Karnataka*	*Tamil Nadu*	*Kerala*	*India*
	Community Health Centres (CHCs)					
1	CHCs Functional	167	325	256	233	4535
2	CHCs gap	314		4		2115
3	In Govt building	167	299	256	233	4236
4	Vacancy of specialists in CHCs	188	574	1024	158	11361
5	CHCs with functional X-ray	167	254		29	3119
6	Quarters for specialists	100	180			2251
7	Specialists living in quarters		180			1853
8	Availability of referral transport	167	254		38	3477

Source: Rural Health Statistics, 2010.

At CHCs level also, Andhra Pradesh had heavy shortage of 314 CHCs and only 167 CHCs were functioning. Other states had adequate number of CHCs which were functioning from government buildings in all the four states and vacancy of specialists was reported in all the states. In Andhra Pradesh and Karnataka referral transport was available whereas this facility was mostly not available in Tamil Nadu and Kerala (Table 16.3).

It is evident from Table 16.3, the NRHM funds are mainly used to improve physical infrastructure and recruitment of health man power in Karnataka, Tamil Nadu and Kerala. However in Andhra Pradesh the number of SCs, PHCs and CHCs is stagnant (Figure 16.6) as there was no new addition of these facilities after the end of Tenth Five Year Plan (till 2007).

Andhra Pradesh State's Contribution for its Health Sector

The overall decline in the share of the health sector in the government budget, particularly after introduction of the SAP, has further worsened the scarcity of resources for the health sector. The share of the health sector in the state budget was highest (6.5%) in the Fifth Five Year Plan period. Thereafter, it declined continuously and fell to 5.2 per cent in the Eight Five Year Plan. It was marginally higher (5.4%) in the Ninth Plan due to added resources of World Bank projects, but declined to 4.5 per cent by 2005-06. The proportion of public expenditure on the health sector to GSDP declined from 1.29 per cent in the Seventh Five Year Plan to 0.94 per cent in the Eight Five Year Plan. Thus, after SAP, there was a decline in the allocations to health services (GoAP and CESS, 2008).

Based on Sreedevi's (2014) computations, the share of medical and public health in GSDP was marginal at 0.92 per cent in the 2000-01 which further declined to 0.7 per cent during 2009-2011. The average expenditure ratio on health and family welfare was 0.85 in 2000-2004 and declined to 0.66 per cent and 0.71 per cent in 2004-2007 and 2007-2011 respectively (Figure 16.7).

Similarly the trends of health and family welfare showed a consistent decline during first seven years of the decade i.e., during 2000-2007 and then started increasing probably due to the introduction of Assistance to the Children Suffering from Heart Diseases (2007-08) which was later renamed as Arogyasri Scheme (2008-09) (assistance to this scheme was ₹ 7.53 crore in 2007-08, ₹ 493 crore in 2008-09 and ₹ 818.647 crore in 2009-10 crore. The revised and budget estimates of 2010-11 and 2011-12 for this scheme was ₹ 925 crore)

Figure 16.7

Health and Family Welfare: Andhra Pradesh

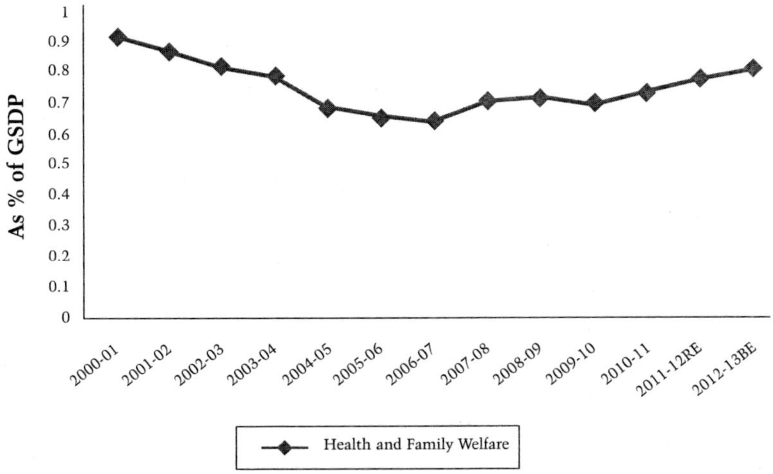

Source: Computed (by N.Sreedevi, CESS, Hyderabad) based on Budget Documents of Andhra Pradesh (various years).

Plan Expenditures on Social Sector: Health

The share of the plan expenditure on health and family welfare (including expenditure on water supply and sanitation) in terms of GSDP showed a continuous decline during 2000-2007—year wise and phase wise—and showed an increase in the third phase because of the schemes life Aarogyasri which offer medical facility. The share of water supply and sanitation also did not increase in the 2000s ranging between 0.23 per cent (2000-01) to 0.17 per cent (2010-11)—averaging 0.31 per cent, 0.30 per cent and 0.24 per cent in phases one, two and three respectively (Figure 16.8).

The trends of health and family welfare in terms of total plan expenditure showed a consistent decline during first eight years of the decade i.e., during 2000-2008 and then started increasing but remained lower than the bench mark year of 2000-01.

The per capita real expenditure on health and family welfare was lower during 2004-2008 when compared to other years.

In general, the share of social sector expenditure either in total expenditure or in the state income shows the main concern of government

Figure 16.8

Plan Expenditure Trends under Social Services of Andhra Pradesh

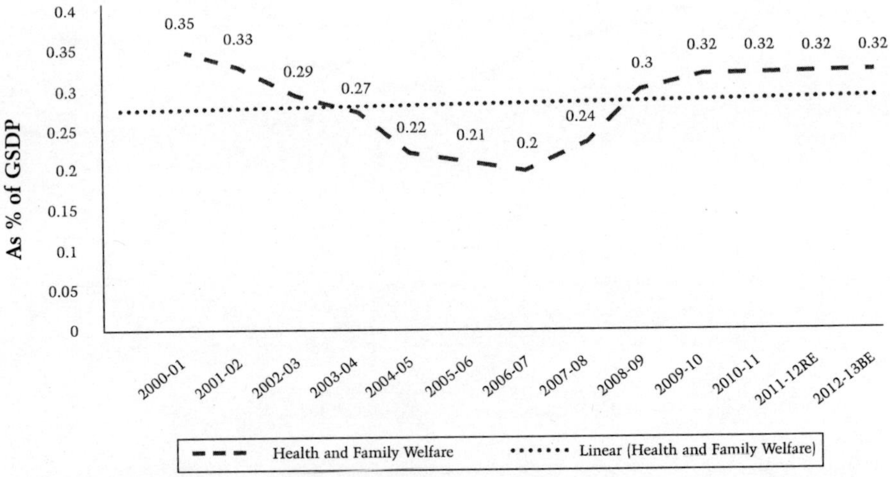

Source: Computed (by N.Sreedevi, CESS, Hyderabad) based on Budget Documents of Andhra Pradesh (various years).

finances/objectives. Low and indistinct distribution of resources/ expenditures and their inconsistent trends may not help either in accomplishing the set objectives of social development or in justifying the claims of the government on human development or in making the best use of limited means. Generally in the reform process, expenditure often undergoes changes in its composition in order to reprioritise the heads of expenditure. But this process should not weaken the very objective of social development.

Though the basic reason for the low share of social sector expenditure either in GSDP or in total expenditure may be attributed to the fiscal crisis which the state experienced in the 1990s (Sarma, 2003; Sreedevi, 2003; 2006), existence of irregularities in revenue collections (Sreedevi, 2011) and expenditure management also contributed to the lower level of social sector expenditure.

Physical and Financial Targets and Achievements

Under NRHM programme, every district in the state prepares its Project Implementation Plan (PIP) which is subsequently approved by the state health authority. The priority for resource allocation is inherent in the PIP, which varies from district to district. Hence, the budget allocation across districts was not uniform. The total outlay for NRHM during 2006-07 (including state normal plan and non-plan) was ₹ 381 crore. During 2009-10, the budget allocation was ₹ 579 crore (Table 16.4) (*Outcome Budget, 2009-10*).

Table 16.4

Budget Allocation and Expenditure under NRHM

(₹ in lakh)

Name of the Scheme	*2006-07*		*2007-08*		*2008-09*		*2009-10*
	BE	*Expr*	*BE*	*Expr*	*BE*	*Expr*	*BE*
	1	2	3	4	5	6	7
Plan							
Centrally sponsored schemes	21153	18652	21066	18570	21176	20840	26009
Normal state plan	15896	17013	19996	19299	25979	21160	18301
Externally aided projects					11700	7456	12700
Non-plan	1114	487	393		908	302	908
Total	38163	36152	41455	37869	59763	49758	57918

Source: *Outcome Budget 2009-10: Health, Medical and Family Welfare*, Government of Andhra Pradesh.

Table 16.5

Budget Provision for Health and Details of Release under NRHM

(₹ in crore)

No	*Year*	*Budget Provision for the Health Sector in the State Budget*	*% of Increase*	*Actual Funds Released*	*Budget Provision under NRHM*	*Amount to be Released to the State Health Society as State's Contribution*	*Amount Actually Provided*
1	2005-06	1587.54	11.89	1436.18	169.33	25	49.56
2	2006-07	1895.34	19.39	1676.32	341.82	50	49.18
3	2007-08	2509.1	32.38	2332.62	472.22	55	86.75
4	2008-09	3150.84	25.58	2793.87	756.51	90	78.64
5	2009-10	3542.5	12.43	2806.45	860.63	113.33	60.79
6	2010-11	3982.78	12.43		1154.8	107	

Source: Department of Health and Family Welfare, Government of Andhra Pradesh.

Table 16.6

Budget Allocation for Various Districts Since 2005-06 to 2008-09, Expenditure Per Lakh Population and Expenditure Pattern During 2008-09

District	*2005-06 (₹ in crore)*	*2006-07 (₹ in crore)*	*2007-08 (₹ in crore)*	*2008-09 (₹ in crore)*	*Total (₹ in crore)*	*₹ crore per 1 lakh Population*	*Expenditure in 2008-09*	
							% of the Fund Available	*% Annual Target Amount*
West Godavari	2.54	8.82	9.51	8.8	29.67	0.78	76.06	80.77
Guntur	2.54	9.83	11.56	11.4	35.33	0.80	80.89	93.99
East Godavari	3.2	13.02	11.98	11.36	39.56	0.81	70.15	78.37
Nellore	1.96	7.97	7.1	6.68	23.71	0.89	73.86	85.2
Visakhapatnam	3.12	10.4	11.18	11.15	35.85	0.95	80.94	88.58
Prakasam	2.23	8.4	13.26	11.1	34.99	1.15	91.36	116.58
Srikakulam	2.14	8.2	10.54	9.39	30.27	1.20	82.93	97.84
Krishna	2.58	8.9	9.3	9.26	30.04	0.86	91.67	93.61
Vizianagaram	2.27	8.7	9.7	7.9	28.57	1.27	92.73	121.17
Andhra	22.58	84.24	94.13	87.04	287.99	0.93		
Hyderabad	1.3	2.03	5.5	6.46	15.29	0.41	72.89	79.57
Ranga Reddy	2.0	6.02	7.9	7.75	23.67	0.67	82.38	86.53
Karimnagar	2.34	9.01	7.6	7.36	26.31	0.76	96.83	88.46
Nalgonda	2.32	9.07	6.5	7.72	25.61	0.79	9144	101.49
Warangal	2.36	9.33	8.8	7.84	28.33	0.88	57.5	67.93
Nizamabad	1.77	5.99	6.5	6.92	21.18	0.90	77.57	86.64

contd...

...contd...

District	*2005-06 (₹ in crore)*	*2006-07 (₹ in crore)*	*2007-08 (₹ in crore)*	*2008-09 (₹ in crore)*	*Total (₹ in crore)*	*₹ crore per 1 lakh Population*	*Expenditure in 2008-09*	
							% of the Fund Available	*% Annual Target Amount*
Mahabubnagar	2.86	10.88	7.94	11.52	33.2	0.95	60.6	69.25
Medak	2.15	7.3	8.1	7.66	25.21	0.95	81.47	87.51
Adilabad	2.2	7.75	8.8	6.73	25.48	1.03	86.62	85.96
Khammam	2.2	8.45	9.6	7.05	27.3	1.06	61.13	65.55
Telengana	21.5	75.83	77.24	77.01	251.58	0.82		
Karnool	2.55	10.42	7.4	10.69	31.06	0.88	65.58	85.91
Chittoor	2.9	10.24	10.64	9.49	33.27	0.89	80.78	93.52
Anantapur	2.87	10.05	10.96	10.62	34.5	0.95	81.49	89.38
Kadapa	2.21	8.88	6.86	8.54	26.49	1.03	66.07	86.84
Rayalaseema	10.53	39.59	35.86	39.34	125.32	0.93		

Source: Department of Family Welfare, Government of Andhra Pradesh; *http://www.educationforallinindia.com/page163.htm*

As shown in the Table 16.5, there was an increase in allocation of budget for health from 2005-06 to 2010-11. But the actual funds released were always less than the allocation. State government has to contribute 15 per cent of matching grant under NRHM. The state government's actual contribution was more than 15 per cent during 2005-06 to 2007-08.

Under NRHM, the amount of ₹ 222 crore was released during 2007-08 for all the districts in Andhra Pradesh. During this period, the expenditure was ₹ 197 crore and the unspent money was ₹ 143 crore. Though allocations had been made during 2006-07 (based on PIPs) for certain activities like regional workshops on RCH II (Reproductive and Child Health Programme), 2-day refreshment training to ASHAs, financial training etc., and minilap training, there was no expenditure at all. The Financial Monitoring Report (FMR) for the financial year 2008-09 made similar observations. The report observed that there was no synchronisation between PIP *versus* utilisation as the expenditure reported under the training head was very high and the expenditure under Behavioural Change Communication (BCC) or Information, Education and Communication (IEC) and procurement was reported with no allocation in PIP. Moreover, deviations from accepted norms were often noticed while reporting was per the format of FMR. Similar pattern was observed in other states also due to the conditionalities attached with funding.

As shown in the Table 16.6, during 2005-06, there were variations in the amounts released to districts (as the allocation was based on PIP approvals). The majority of the districts received ₹ 2-3 crore. Hyderabad district received just ₹ 1.3 crore. East Godavari district (₹ 3.20 crore) and Visakhapatnam district (₹ 3.12 crore) were the major recipients. Prakasam district (₹ 13.26 crore) in 2007-08 and Mahabubnagar (₹ 11.52 crore) in 2008-09 received the highest amounts. From 2005-06 to 2008-09, Vizianagaram, Srikakulam, Prakasam, Khammam, Kadapa and Adilabad districts had received more than a crore rupees per one lakh population, and a higher amount in proportion to their population share. Unspent balance was reported across most districts. During 2008-09, Khammam district could utilise only 65.55 per cent of the target amount (or 61.13% of funds available). Similarly Mahabubnagar district could spend only 69.25 per cent of the targeted amount (60.60% of the funds available). However, Vizianagaram, Prakasam and Nalgonda districts have spent a little more than their target amount but less than the funds available with them. Since 2005-06, East Godavari district was the major recipient with ₹ 39.56 crore followed by Visakhapatnam district (₹ 35.85 crore), Guntur district (₹ 35.33 crore) and Prakasam district (₹ 34.99 crore). Across the three regions, Coastal Andhra was allocated more money, followed by Telangana and Rayalaseema. Coastal Andhra and Rayalaseema regions were the major recipients of money in terms of allocation per lakh population (₹ 0.93 crore) compared to Telengana region (₹ 0.82 crore).

Conclusions

Higher health budgets in various countries have helped in achieving good health outcomes. In India, however, public health expenditure accounts for just about one-sixth of total health expenditure. It accounts for nearly one per cent of GDP and private health expenditure accounts for five per cent of GDP. India's health indicators are very discouraging compared to other countries. According to UNDP's *Human Development Report 2010*, out of 193 countries, India ranked 143rd in IMR. Limited financial resources of the states are mainly used to meet their committed liabilities toward wages, salaries, interest payments and pensions, leaving little scope for spending on health sector. Many states do not have good health infrastructure. Hence, it is necessary for the Central government to introduce specific-purpose transfers to the states to ensure minimum standard of basic health services.

In Andhra Pradesh, the overall decline in the share of the health sector in the government budget, particularly after introduction of the SAP has further worsened the scarcity of resources for the health sector. In general, the low share of social sector expenditure either in total expenditure or in the state income is a matter of concern for health sector. Central government finances such as grants recommended by FC, CSS such as NRHM and RSBY are helping the state health systems in improving the physical infrastructure and health manpower, particularly in the other southern states, Karnataka, Tamil Nadu and Kerala. However, the health infrastructure in Andhra Pradesh is neglected when compared to Karnataka and Tamil Nadu and Kerala. We have sufficient number of SCs, but there is acute shortage of PHCs and CHCs and also health manpower. The situation is however better in other three states. Proper attention is needed in spending the NRHM funds to fill gap of health infrastructure (both physical and human resources) for better health outcomes.

References

Anand, M. and S. Chaudhury (2008). "Demographic and Social Changes: Some Issues for the Sixth Central Pay Commission", *Economic and Political Weekly* 43(7): 54–58.

Banerjee, K. (1999). "Gender Stratification and the Contemporary Marriage Market in India", *Journal of Family Issues* 20(5): 648–76.

Bhadra, K.K. and J. Bhadra (2012). "Public Expenditure on Health Across States in India: An Evaluation on Selected Issues and Evidences", *International Journal of Research in Finance & Marketing* 2(6): 25–39. Retrieved from *http://www.mairec.org/IJRFM/June2012/3.pdf*

Bhat, R. (1999). *A Note on Policy Initiatives to Protect the Poor from High Medical Costs.* Ahmedabad: Indian Institute of Management.

Bhat, R. and S.K. Bhat (2003). *Health Insurance and Third Party Administrators: Issues and Challenges.* Ahmedabad: Indian Institute of Management.

Census of India (2011). *Provisional Population Totals India: Paper 1*. Retrieved from *http://www.censusindia.gov.in/2011-prov-results/prov_results_paper1_india.html*

Chandra, P. (2006). "Globalisation: Malnutrion and Medical Care", *Bharatiya Samajik Chintan* 5(3): 141–50.

DFID and GoAP (2010). *Andhra Pradesh Health Sector Reform Program.* Government of Andhra Pradesh and DFID.

Duggal, R. (2009). "Sinking Flagships and Health Budgets in India", *Economic and Political Weekly* XLIV(33): 14–17.

Gill, K. (2009). *A Primary Evaluation of Service Delivery under the National Rural Health Mission (NIRHM): Findings from a Study in Andhra Pradesh, Uttar Pradesh, Bihar and Rajasthan.* New Delhi: Planning Commission.

GoAP and CESS (2008). *Human Development Report 2007: Andhra Pradesh.* Hyderabad: Centre for Economic and Social Studies. Retrieved from *http://www.aponline.gov.in/Apportal/HumanDevelopmentReport2007/APHDR_2007_Chapter2.pdf*

Govinda Rao, M. and Mita Choudhury. (2012). *Health Care Financing Reforms in India.* Retrieved from *http://www.nipfp.org.in/newweb/sites/default/files/ wp_2012_100.pdf*

Misra, Rajiv, R. Chatterjee and Sujatha Rao (eds.) (2003). *India Health Report.* Oxford University Press.

Sarma, J.V.M. (2003)."Fiscal Management: A Review", C.H. in Hanumantha Rao and S. Mahendra Dev (eds.), *Andhra Pradesh Development: Economic Reforms and Challenges Ahead.* Hyderabad: Centre for Economic and Social Studies.

Sreedevi, N. (2003). "State Finances: Comparative Scenario and Reforms Required", in C.H. in Hanumantha Rao and S. Mahendra Dev (eds.), *Andhra Pradesh Development: Economic Reforms and Challenges Ahead.* Hyderabad: Centre for Economic and Social Studies.

———. (2006). "State Finances of Andhra Pradesh: An Overview", in R.S. Rao, V. Hanumantha Rao and N. Venugopal (eds.), *Fifty Years of Andhra Pradesh 1956-2006*. Hyderabad: CDRC.

———. (2011). *Blockage Confiscation: A Way to Revenue Augmentation: A Case of Andhra Pradesh*. A Study Prepared for Planning Department, Andhra Pradesh. May.

———. (2014). "Financing Human Development" in Second *Human Development Report of Andhra Pradesh* (draft).

Annexure

Table A-16.1

Trends in Health and Family Welfare Expenditure in Andhra Pradesh (Plan+Non-plan)

Health and Family Welfare	*As % of GSDP at Current Prices*	*As % of Total Expenditure*	*Per Capita Real Expenditure at 2004-05 Prices*
1	2	3	4
2000-01	0.92	4.98	256
2001-02	0.87	4.79	250
2002-03	0.82	4.5	230
2003-04	0.79	4.39	222
2004-05	0.69	4.2	195
2005-06	0.66	3.91	202
2006-07	0.64	3.71	215
2007-08	0.71	3.72	265
2008-09	0.72	4.08	284
2009-10	0.7	4.33	289
2010-11	0.73	4.23	328
2011-12RE	0.78	4.43	372
2012-13BE	0.81	4.41	
2000-2004	0.85	4.65	239
2004-2007	0.66	3.91	205
2007-2011	0.71	4.11	294

Source: Computed (by N. Sreedevi, CESS, Hyderabad) based on Budget Documents (various years).

Table A-16.2

Plan Expenditure Trends in Andhra Pradesh: Health and Family Welfare

Year	*As Percentage of GSDP (%)*	*As Percentage of Total Plan Expenditure (%)*	*Real Per capita Plan Expenditure At 2004-05 Prices*
2000-01	0.35	6.71	98
2001-02	0.33	5.64	93
2002-03	0.29	5.13	81
2003-04	0.27	4.33	75
2004-05	0.22	3.97	62
2005-06	0.21	3.66	64
2006-07	0.2	3.02	66
2007-08	0.24	2.99	89
2008-09	0.3	3.95	120
2009-10	0.32	5.11	134
2010-11	0.32	5.55	145
2011-12RE	0.32	4.89	151
2012-13BE	0.32	4.41	
2000-2004	0.31	5.32	86
2004-2007	0.21	3.48	64
2007-2011	0.3	4.44	124

Source: Computed (by N. Sreedevi, CESS, Hyderabad) based on Budget Documents (various years).

17 Financing of Flagship Programmes in Andhra Pradesh

P. Padmanabha Rao

Introduction

The Central government ministries provide assistance to states on the basis of the recommendations of the Planning Commission, on Centrally Sponsored Schemes (CSS). The assistance is given to the states in the form of specific grants under Article 282 of the Constitution. The flagship programmes were launched by Government of India (GoI) to bridge the gaps in education, health, employment and infrastructure. These have been complemented by specific policies for inclusion of Scheduled Castes (SCs), Scheduled Tribes (STs), minorities and women. The ultimate objective behind the flagship programmes is to achieve broad-based improvement in the living standards of all our people and to ensure that growth is widely spread so that its benefits, in terms of income and employment, are adequately shared by the poor and weaker sections of the society, especially the SCs, STs, Other Backward Classes (OBCs) and minorities.

Improving the human development indicators of the state requires considerable allocation of resources in the relevant sectors. Keeping the effective implementation part aside, examining the trends and patterns of government expenditure towards the social sector is very important in the framework of human development. It analyses the conversion of public policies into allocations/expenditures which depends on the sound fiscal health of the economy.

A well-known fact is that the programmes which are included under the CSS fall basically in the constitutionally provided domain of the state governments. Hence, the state governments also provide budgetary allocations towards social development. This paper discusses the financial aspects of some of the flagship programmes in the state of Andhra Pradesh.

The assessment is made in the case of Mahatma Gandhi National Rural Employment Guarantee Scheme (MGNREGS), Indira Awas Yojana (IAY), National Social Assistance Programmes (NSAP), Pradhan Mantri Gram Sadak Yojana (PMGSY), National Rural Drinking Water Supply Programme (NRDWP), Total Sanitation Campaign (TSC) and Jawaharlal Nehru National Urban Renewal Mission (JNNURM).

The paper discusses the social sector expenditure in Andhra Pradesh and some of the flagship programmes mentioned above.

Social Sector Expenditure in Andhra Pradesh

Major heads of social sector expenditure such as education, health, water supply, housing, urban development show that the share of water supply and sanitation had not increased during the 2000s ranging between 0.31 per cent (2001-02) to 0.38 per cent (2002-03)—averaging 0.34 per cent, 0.35 per cent and 0.28 per cent in phases one, two and three respectively. Expenditure towards housing and urban development has increased considerably during 2007-2009. Expenditure towards housing, in terms of GSDP (gross state domestic product) as well as total expenditure has increased considerably, particularly during 2003-04, 2007-08 and 2008-2009.

The share of social sector expenditure in total expenditure or in the state income shows the priorities of government. The inconsistent trend of these ratios—decline in one period and increase in another period and again fall in the subsequent period—may not help in achieving the objectives of social development.

Social sector expenditure in the case of water supply, housing, urban development show that the average plan expenditure on water supply and sanitation had not increased during the 2000s ranging between 0.23 per cent (2000-01) to 0.17 per cent (2010-11). The share of water supply and sanitation in total plan expenditure declined significantly in the last three years of the decade (3.51%) when compared to the earlier period. Expenditure towards housing and urban development, showed an uptrend and has increased considerably since 2007-08.

Figure 17.1

Components of Social Services as Per cent of Total Expenditure of Andhra Pradesh

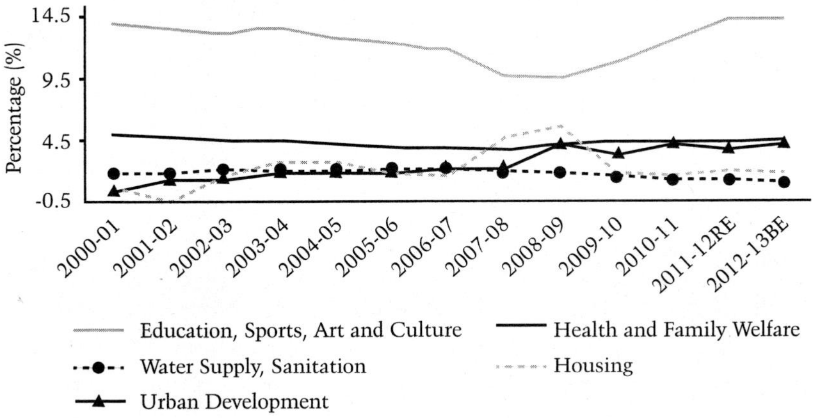

Source: Computed based on Budget Documents of Andhra Pradesh (various years).

Figure 17.2

Plan Expenditure Trends under Social Services of Andhra Pradesh

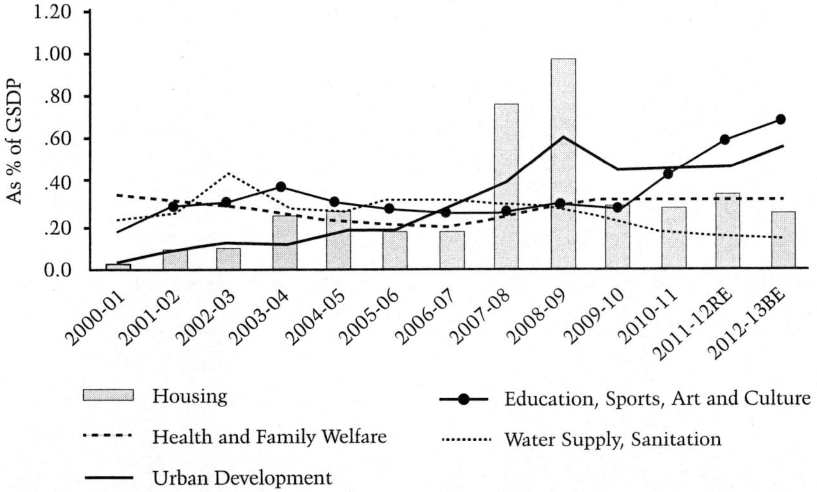

Source: Computed based on Budget Documents of Andhra Pradesh (various years).

Overall, the result was that social development was not achieved to the required levels, and instead it has deteriorated. This resulted in decline of the rank of Andhra Pradesh in the human development index among the major states from 8th in 1981 to 9th in 1991 and 10th in 2001. It would be difficult to achieve the targets if the existing irregularities are not rectified and existing checks over public finance are not effectively implemented (Sreedevi, 2004; 2005). Innovations in flagship programmes and social sector—institutional capacity to spend, maintain the assets and quality of outcomes—need to be addressed.

Analysis of Flagship Programmes

This section discusses financial allocations and releases for some of the flagship programmes as mentioned earlier and their physical performance in Andhra Pradesh. In the 1st year of Twelfth plan, a lot of changes had been envisaged: 21 per cent increase in outlay for social sector and substantial increase in outlay for primary sector.

Dr Chaturvedi committee on restructuring of CSS,[1] suggested that 20 per cent of the budget allocation in all the CSS (10% in flagship schemes) to be called flexi funds should be earmarked in each scheme for this purpose.

During 2011-12, the state had received ₹ 26,000 crore which was almost double the amount received in the 1st year of the Eleventh plan. Of the total allocation of ₹ 26,320.43 crore (₹ 18,757.10 crore as Central share and ₹ 7,563.33 crore as state share), an amount of ₹ 9,782.89 crore (₹ 6,655.37 crore as Centre share and 3,127.52 crore as state share) was released. An amount of ₹ 8,143.14 crore (6,627.59 crore as Central share and ₹ 1,515.55 crore as state share) was spent (83.24%).

All the 15 flagship programmes of Government of India (GoI) are being implemented in Andhra Pradesh. The total allocation under flagship programmes for the year 2012-13 was ₹ 27,616 crore out of which the Central share was ₹ 20,143 crore and the state matching share was about ₹ 7,474 crore. So far, an amount of ₹ 6,340 crore under Central share and ₹ 3,474 crore under the state share has been released for the flagship programmes upto October 2012.

1. Report of the Committee on Restructuring of Centrally Sponsored Schemes (CSS) (Chairman: Dr B.K. Chaturvedi), September 2011, Planning Commission.

Table 17.1

Financial Performance of Flagship Programmes

(₹ in crore)

No	Year	Releases			Expenditure
		Centre	State	Total	
1	2007-08	6,307.65	3,727.57	10,035.22	9,224.75
2	2008-09	8,707.00	5,328.02	14,035.02	11,890.86
3	2009-10	11,053.71	7,099.63	18,153.34	15,788.53
4	2010-11	14,038.50	5,812.08	19,850.58	15,942.73
5	2011-12	9,567.30	8,038.00	17,605.30	17,480.82
Total (2007-08 to 2011-12)		49,674.16	30,005.30	79,679.46	70,327.69
2012-13 Total		6,655.37	3,127.52	9,782.89	8,143.14

Source: Socio Economic Survey of Andhra Pradesh and Outcome Budget, 2012-13.

Figure 17.3

Financial Performance of Flagship Programmes for 2012-13

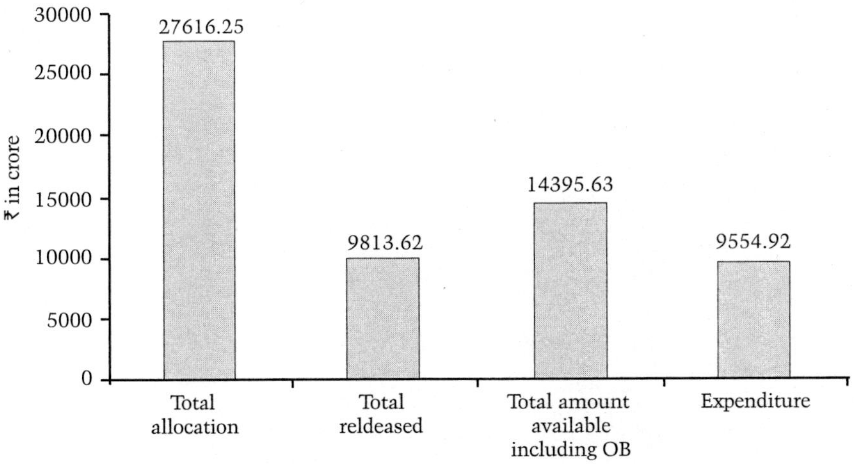

Figure 17.4

Flagship Programmes: Schemes with Financial Performance <50 Per cent 2012-13

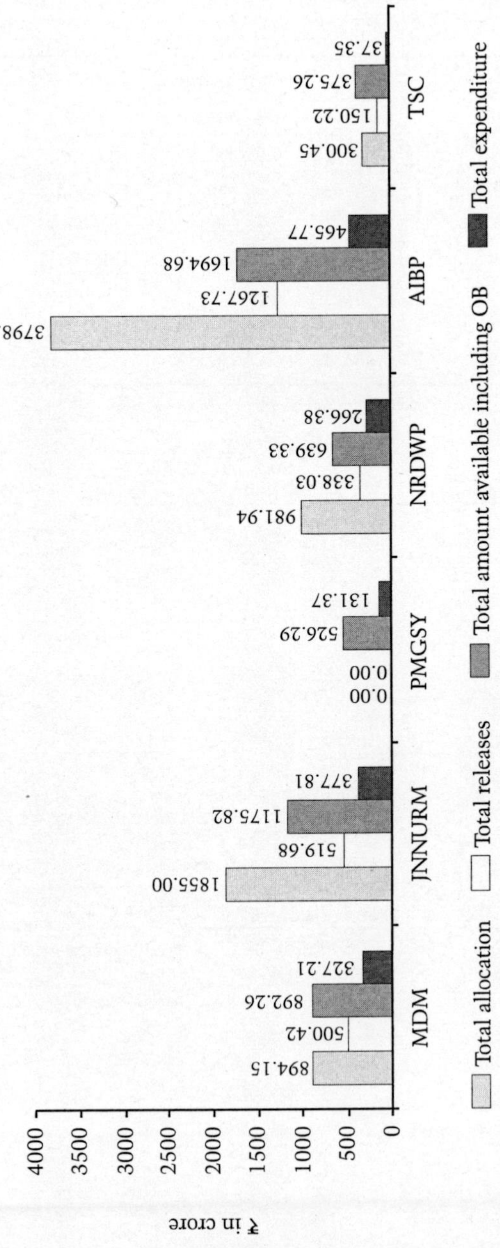

Table 17.2

Flagship Programmes: Eleventh Plan Performance

No.	Name of the Programme	GoI Eleventh Plan Allocation		Eleventh Five Year Plan Performance	
		GoI 11th Plan Expenditure	GoI Allocation 2012-13	Total Expenditure	Allocation 2011-12
1	MGNREGS	1,56,301	33,000	18,981	8,272
2	IAY	41,486	11,075	4,706	1,130
3	JNNURM	48,485	1,100	5,944	1,750
4	PMGSY	65,002	24,000	2,562	607
5	NRDWP	40,162	14,000	4,119	1,044
6	TSC	6,560	0	403	197
7	NSAP	23,536	0	1,663	525
	Total	3,81,532	83,175	38,378	13,525

Total Sanitation Campaign (TSC)

Total Sanitation Campaign (TSC) has been proposed by GoI to ensure sanitation facilities in rural areas with a broader goal to eradicate the practice of open defecation by bringing about behaviour change. TSC programme is being implemented in all 22 districts of Andhra Pradesh with support from the GoI and the state government to ensure sanitation facilities in rural areas. The total cumulative project cost sanctioned for Andhra Pradesh (since inception) is ₹ 1,781.88 crore.

In Andhra Pradesh, 57 per cent of individual households (IHHs) who are below poverty level (BPL) are provided with sanitation, while 44 per cent of above poverty level (ABPL) households are covered under this programme. Sixty-six per cent are covered by individual sanitary latrines (ISL) of which 48 per cent are being used and the balance 18 per cent are being used for other purposes. About 36 per cent of habitations have drainage facilities. However the drains are constructed in a haphazard way, resulting in water stagnation in many habitations and causing problems. Forty per cent of habitations have solid waste management facilities, but in an unscientific way. Thirty-two (32) per cent of people are dumping solid wastes in front of houses and 44 per cent are dumping them on the road side. Although the concept of sanitation has undergone qualitative changes over the years, there has been slow progress in sanitary conditions compared to rural water supply.

During 2009-10, an expenditure of 43.63 crore was incurred under TSC which was 40.20 per cent of the total available funds. A total

Table 17.3

Fund Allocation, Released and Utilisation by Central and State Government Under Total Sanitation Campaign (TSC) Programme in Andhra Pradesh (2003-2004 to 2011-12)

Scheme	*Approved Amount ₹ in Crore*				*Amount Released*		*Beneficiary Contribution*	*Total*	*Expenditure (₹ in Crore)*			
	Centre	*State*	*Beneficiary*	*Total*	*Centre*	*State*			*Centre*	*State*	*Beneficiary*	*Total*
2003-04	133.12	47.90	31.16	212.19	47.83	166.28	22.88	237.00	71.91	75.05	26.71	173.68
2004-05	0.00	0.00	0.00	0.00	33.62	8.60	12.69	54.92	32.77	70.46	13.86	117.10
2005-06	0.00	0.00	0.00	0.00	43.00	54.40	11.92	109.32	18.35	33.59	28.88	80.83
2012-13	225.06	300.45	0.00	300.45	150.23	0.00	150.23	375.29	43.78	30.93		74.71

Source: Socio Economic Survey of Andhra Pradesh and Outcome Budget, 2012-13.

provision of 340 crore had been kept for the year 2011-12 against which ₹ 84.94 crore were released.

To give benefit to the poor, BPL families were identified based on income and expenditure indicators. Total number of BPL households in the state is 1,41,80,703. The total project outlay was ₹ 1,258.04 crore. The state government is extending back-ended support as total subsidy at the rate of ₹ 1,550 per ISL for construction of superstructure and also promoting a bathroom. Thus, the additional state share amount is ₹ 1,207.38 crore.

In all 53,07,927 (about 80%) of BPL Individual households and 72 per cent of APL Individual households (26,28,840) were provided with ISLs. About 1,09,691 schools and 7,355 Anganwadi's were provided with sanitation facilities under TSC programme.

Table 17.4

Achievements under TSC Programme (As on March 31, 2012)

S.No	*Description*	*TSC Targets*	*Provided with Sanitation*	*% Achieved*
1	BPL Individual Households (IHH)	66,36,229	53,01,921	79.89
2	ABL IHH	36,29,688	26,28,840	72.42
3	Latrines for Schools	115,908	10,969	94.63
4	Latrines for Anganwadis	15,040	7,355	49.06
5	Sanitary Complex	575	962	167.03
6	RSM/PCs	221	441	199%

As per guidelines of GoI, ISL are required to the constructed along with each IAY house. The GoI may integrate ISL sanction to the IAY houses and funds may be released along with IAY. Further, the unit cost of ISL may be increased from ₹ 3,050 to ₹ 7,500 with IAY sharing pattern of 75:25 (Central share ₹ 5,625 and state share ₹ 1,875). Similarly, for urban areas it was proposed to increase the unit cost to ₹ 10,000.

Information, Education and Communication (IEC) and Capacity Building

A variety of IEC interventions were made in several districts over a reasonably long period (e.g., Kalajata, wall paintings on hygiene messages, etc.). This created a positive response to the TSC in the rural areas and brought visibility to the programme. IEC interventions largely highlighted toilets and did not adequately focus on aspects related to hygiene, *viz.*, hand washing practices, safe handling of water and disposal of waste water, which need to be promoted.

Children are yet to use these toilets in many villages. Promotion of health and hygiene is missing, especially handling of safe drinking water. The IEC interventions and community mobilisation attempts were not coordinated well. As a result, the villagers were poorly informed about their role in operation and maintenance (O&M) related issues. Convergence among various implementing agencies, as well as convergence of TSC with MGNREGS for the construction of ISLs, institutional toilets and community toilets, have been brought in.

National Rural Drinking Water Programme (NRDWP)

The goal under Bharat Nirman Project was to provide every habitation with safe drinking water. All habitations which have slipped back from full coverage to partial coverage and have water quality problems are to be addressed. The programme intends to provide safe and adequate drinking water facilities to quality affected habitations, not covered habitations and partially covered habitations in rural areas. The programme provides special thrust on sustainability of drinking water sources and funds recharge structures with 100 per cent grant.

Only about 40 per cent of rural households in Andhra Pradesh have access to piped water to meet drinking and domestic water needs. The others use water from tube wells or open wells, while a small minority uses village tanks and springs. There is a high dependence on groundwater for drinking and other domestic purposes. In most of the villages, water is distributed through Public Stand Posts (PSPs). At present, about 72 per cent of water supply schemes are based on groundwater as the source and 28 per cent are covered by surface sources. Further, there is no safe source in about 1,647 habitations, of which 1,064 are fluoride affected. Apart from providing treated surface water to fluoride affected habitations, Rural Water Supply (RWS) department has tried various options for de-fluoridation including reverse osmosis for supplying safe drinking water.

Of the 71,710 habitations in the state, 33,098 were fully covered (FC); 31,910 were partially covered (PC); 5,111 habitations were not covered (NC) and 1,591 habitations have no safe source (NSS) of water supply for drinking purpose. In terms of coverage, of the total 71,710 habitations, 80 per cent (57,368 habitations) are covered through Single Village Scheme (SVS) and 7,888 habitations (11%) through Multi Village Scheme (MVS). This has been achieved by creating infrastructure like 3,20,545 hand pumps, 52,457 SVS schemes and 490 MVS schemes.

About ₹ 658.30 million were spent since inception up to 2007 on creation of drinking water assets. Of the above schemes, surface water schemes constitute about 22.5 per cent while groundwater schemes account for about 71.75 per cent. The approximate amount spent in creating rural water supply and sanitation infrastructure including rehabilitation and extension during the last four years is over ₹ 200 million.

Table 17.5

Coverage of Habitations under Rural Water Supply Schemes

Hand pumps to bore wells	*3,43,376*	*Drinking water to Schools*	*67966*
PWS Schemes	57,038	Fully Covered Habitations	44720
CPWS Schemes	547	Partially Covered Habitations	27276
Water testing labs	171	Quality Affected Habitations	391
Fluoride affected	332	Brackish affected	59
Total Habitations	72387		

Source: Department of Rural Water Supply and Sanitation, Govt. of Andhra Pradesh.

The workload for the year 2012-13 comprises 2209 (SVS and MVS) schemes at a value of ₹ 1,350.87 crore to cover 7,183 habitations. An expenditure of ₹ 170.32 crore was incurred up to August 2012 out of ₹ 982 crore. Out of total 5,266 (PC & QA [Quality Affected]) habitations targeted for coverage, 628 habitations were covered.

Of the total habitations of 71,928 in terms of water supply coverage 15,523 were quality affected habitations. 13,492 of 15,523 QA habitations were brought to FC status under Accelerated Rural Water Supply Programme (ARWSP). An amount of ₹ 689.88 crore was spent under the Bharat Nirman programme for providing drinking water to 15,562 habitations, of which 1,707 were QA habitations.

Potable drinking water was provided to 20,863 schools against the target of 32838 schools at an expenditure of ₹ 71.78 crore. Sanitation facilities were provided in 65,916 schools.

National Social Assistance Programme

NSAP aims at improving the quality of life of the rural poor, aims to provide human security to the poor and the destitute. This is a 100 per cent centrally funded programme which gives financial assistance to those families with little or no regular means of subsistence, living below the poverty line. The NSAP envisages the pension schemes to provide a certain sum as pension to aged, widowed and disabled. During the Eleventh Plan, the Indira Gandhi National Old Age Pension Scheme (IGNOAPS) was extended to all old people above the age of 60 years (from the present 65 years) among the BPL families with a minimum pension of ₹ 400 per month funded by the Centre and the states. The National Family Benefit Scheme (NFBS) continued during the Eleventh Five Year Plan with the support enhanced from ₹ 10,000 to ₹ 25,000.

Out of the 16,19,842 allotment of pensions, Government of Andhra Pradesh (GoAP) disbursed 15,87,813 IGNOAPS, 303945 Indira Gandhi National Widow Pension Scheme (IGNWPS) and 64,595 Indira Gandhi National Disable Pension Scheme (IWNDPS), cumulatively 19,56,353 pensions in 2011-12 and in 2012-13. GoI released funds to a tune of ₹ 388.76 crore per annum at ₹ 200 per month per pensioner. GoAP followed the principle of saturation in Social Security Pensions (SSP) by granting pension to all eligible persons: aged, weavers, widows, toddy tappers and disabled.

Under Old Age, Weavers, Widows and Disabled Pensions Scheme destitute old persons of the age 65 and above are extended support at the rate of ₹ 200 per month. The amount was ₹ 75 per month till 2005-06, which was increased to ₹ 100 per month from 2005-06 and further to ₹ 200 from 2006-07. The GoAP has increased the pension amount for all disabled pensioners from ₹ 200 to ₹ 500 per month. There has been an enormous increase in the number of old age pensions during 2005-06 to 2008-09 under regular pensions and Indiramma programme. The total number of pensions has doubled but the number of regular IGNOAP pensions has come down a little. The Government is also giving more importance to widow and disabled pension schemes, indicating a shift in the priorities of the Government.

Widow Pensions is being implemented by the rural development department in the state since 2006 under which ₹ 200 per pensioner is provided to destitute widows. 4,21,212 widow pensions were given in 2005-06, and the number increased to 1,712,447 in 2008-09, an increase of 307 per cent in the number of widow pensions disbursed during 2005-2009. The increase in the number of widow pensions is higher compared to all other pension schemes. This may indicate the priority given by the Government to destitute women in the state.

Disabled Pensions Scheme is also being implemented by the Rural Development Department. At present ₹ 500 per month is being provided to each disabled person. 246,990 disabled pensions were given in 2005-06, which increased to 779,482 during 2008-09 at a growth rate of 216 per cent during 2005-2009. The growth rate in the number of disabled pensions disbursed is higher than the average growth rate of all the pension schemes being implemented by the Government.

Old Age Pensions	-	33,17,907
Weavers Pensions	-	1,44,514
Widow Pensions	-	15,01,344
Toddy Tappers Pensions	-	1,00,000
Disabled Pensions	-	8,25,523
Total	-	58,89,288

Weavers Pensions Scheme provides ₹ 200 per month to weavers who are 50 years or older and are destitute. 71,838 weavers pensions were given in 2005-06, and the number increased to 133,380 during 2008-09 showing a growth rate of 86 per cent in the number of weavers pensions disbursed during 2005-2009.

Under the National Family Benefit Scheme (NFBS) a lump sum family benefit for households below the poverty line on the death of the primary wage earner in the family (whose age is between 18 to 65) is provided. The primary wage earner is the male or female member of the household whose earnings contribute the largest proportion to the total household income. An amount of ₹ 5,000 is provided as a one-time grant to the bereaved family. GoAP is providing an additional amount of ₹ 300 per month per pensioner from its own funds to all the disabled pensioners (58,723) covered by GoI. GoAP is allocating an amount of ₹ 1,731.76 crore per annum.

Under NSAP scheme for the year 2011-12 an amount of 524.66 crore was released and an amount of 514.72 crore was distributed. During the year 2012-13, an amount of ₹ 216.22 crore was distributed.

Indira Awas Yojana (IAY)

Housing is one of the basic needs along with food and clothing for mankind to provide safety, security, social status, cultural identity, satisfaction and a sense of achievement. The Government has succeeded in reaching the poor through IAY and other schemes to provide *pucca houses*. IAY is a CSS being implemented in the state with a unit cost of ₹ 35,000 and with sharing pattern of 75:25 between the Centre and the state. The target group comprises people below the poverty line living in rural areas belonging to SCs/STs, and freed bonded labourers. The IAY scheme also lays emphasis on individual sanitation and health by incorporating the cost of a sanitary latrine and smokeless *chullah* into the grant. About 3.72 lakh houses had been taken up during 2009-10. The unit cost was ₹ 25,000 till 2005-06 and it increased to ₹ 28,000 in 2006-07, and further to ₹ 35,000 in 2009-10. 2.95 lakh houses were completed under the programme in 2009-10.

Table 17.6

Central Government Allocation to Andhra Pradesh under Indira Awas Yojana, Number of Houses Constructed During the Period 2003-2009

Year	*Central Allocation (in ₹ Crore)*	*Number of Houses Constructed*	*No. of Houses Constructed per lakh People*
2003-04	136.69	105295	139
2004-05	179.82	126039	166
2005-06	243.99	132521	175
2006-07	259.39	146403	193
2007-08	360.28	192148	254
2008-09	375.00	192128	252
2009-10	976.45	295540	388

Source: *Outcome Budgets*, Housing Department, 2008-09 and 2009-10.

Andhra Pradesh spent a total amount of ₹ 1,059.01 crore against central allocations as well as its own state government share under this scheme as on 2009. Since its inception 6,51,465 houses were constructed indicating that 860 houses were built in the state per lakh population as compared to as the national average of 757.

Andhra Pradesh was in fifth place with respect to funds allocated under this programme, after Uttarakhand, Bihar, Odisha and Madhya Pradesh since the inception of the programme in the state. Among the bigger states Odisha, Bihar, Madhya Pradesh and Tamil Nadu are above Andhra Pradesh in terms of number of houses constructed per lakh population. The Central government plan allocation to Andhra Pradesh increased significantly from ₹ 136.69 crore in 2003-04 to 976.45 crore in 2009-10, an increase of 614 per cent. The budget outlays increased by almost three times from ₹ 500 crore in 2008-09 to ₹ 1370 crore in 2009-10, of which the state plan budget was ₹ 394 crore and central plan allocation was ₹ 976.45 crore. There was a steady increase in the number of houses constructed per lakh population from 139 in 2003-04 to 252 in 2008-09 and 388 in 2009-10.

The number of houses constructed per lakh population under IAY in Andhra Pradesh has always been higher than the national figure for the reference period. The position of the state improved from 13 to 7 at the national level with respect to this indicator. This is a positive indication that the programme is progressing well in the state.

In 2003-04, 1,05,295 houses were constructed which came to 139 houses per lakh population. The number increased to 1,34,180 and 176 in 2006-07, which was the first year of the Eleventh Plan. There has been a notable growth in the number of houses constructed under this scheme to 1,92,128 houses in 2008-09, showing an improvement at 252 houses per lakh people in the state. Looking at the trends and growth in the number of houses being constructed, we may infer that this programme has progressed well in recent years in the state.

One major observation is that in many places SC/ST beneficiaries are not coming forward to take up construction. Among those who have started construction, most of the SC/ST beneficiaries are not able to complete the houses due to the lack of additional financial resources that they require to complete construction.

Table 17.7

Physical and Financial Achievement Over 2007-08 and 2009-10: IAY Scheme

Year	Physical Performance (No.)			Financial Performance (₹ Lakh)		
	Target	Ach.	% Ach	Avail Funds	Exp.	% Ach
2007-08	1,92,148	1,94,861	101.41	50,217.17	46,838.96	93.27
2008-09	1,92,132	2,66,654	138.79	1,12,251.50	89,937.81	80.12
2009-10*	3,71,982	89,686	24.11	56,235.17	37,426.13	66.55

Note: * Upto June, 2009.

Source: *Outcome Budget, 2009-10*, A.P. Housing Department, Govt. of Andhra Pradesh.

Under IAY 2011-12 programme, the GoI had communicated an allocation of ₹ 1,130.16 crore to the state. The financial assistance provided under IAY for new construction in plain areas is ₹ 45,000 and difficult areas i.e., Khammam and Adilabad districts is ₹ 48,500.

Table 17.8

Indira Awas Yojana: Physical and Financial Performance

(₹ in crore)

Financial Performance	2011-12	2012-13
Opening Balance	30.91	98.13
Funds Allocated to the State	1,130.16	1,252.21
Funds Released	1,130.16	626.11
Total Available Funds (incl OB & S.S)	1,161.06	724.24
Funds Utilised during the Year	1,113.01	643.39
Physical Performance		
Annual Physical Target	2,49,013	2,70,399
Admn. Sanction Accorded	2,64,098	

Category	Sanctioned 2011-12	Completed 2011-12	Sanctioned 2012-13	Completed 2012-13
SC/ST	1,49,632 (60%)	1,42,565 (58%)	1,62,239 (60%)	65,740
Minorities	36,139 (15%)	28,121 (11%)	40,560 (15%)	8826
Others	78,327 (31%)	78,327 (31%)	67,600 (25%)	63,784
Total	2,64,098 (106%)	2,49,013 (100 %)	2,70,399 (100%)	1,38,350 (51%)

Source: *Outcome Budget, 2009-10*, A.P. Housing Department, Govt. of Andhra Pradesh.

Physical and Financial Allocations and Performance during 2012-13

Under IAY 2012-13 programmes, the GoI had communicated an allocation of ₹ 1,252.215 crore to the state for taking up construction of 2,70,399 houses. There has been a steep escalation in the cost of building materials and labour charges; with the present prevailing market rates, the actual cost for completion of a house is about ₹ 1.20 lakh. Thus, there is a gap of ₹ 75,000 between the actual cost of construction and the unit cost of ₹ 45,000 provided by GoI. Beneficiaries are facing difficulty in mobilising additional funds and thereby there is delay in completion of houses. Wage component of the MGNREGS may also be utilised for completion of the houses in addition to the unit cost which is insufficient.

ISLs are required to be constructed along with each IAY house. The unit cost of ISL may be increased from ₹ 3,050 to ₹ 7,500 with IAY sharing pattern of 75:25. Similarly, for urban areas it is suggested that for new toilets the unit cost of ₹ 10,000 each for flush latrines may be allowed.

Pradhan Mantri Gram Sadak Yojana (PMGSY)

Rural roads are the most essential infrastructure for socioeconomic uplift of the rural community. These create a congenial environment for economic prosperity thereby ensuring healthy living conditions for the rural inhabitants. The rural sector needs attention for balanced growth and physical infrastructure plays a critical role in growth and development. Infrastructure like rural roads can enhance connectivity and offer better marketing possibilities.

PMGSY is a 100 per cent CSS which primarily aims to provide all-weather road connectivity to unconnected habitations. All unconnected habitations with a population of 500 persons (or more) were supposed to be provided connectivity. The works are executed by state governments and monitored by GoI. The responsibility for the maintenance of roads lies with state governments.

According to the state-wise target and achievement in completing the roads, in 2007-08 the target length of roads to be completed in Andhra Pradesh was 2,551 km and the state government laid 2,974 km roads which was 17 per cent in excess of the target. Similarly in 2008-09, the target was 2,500 km whereas 3,042 km of roads were laid, again 22 per cent more than the target. Hence, it is evident that state is implementing the programme successfully and even exceeding its targets.

Andhra Pradesh has shown considerable growth in the release of funds under this programme. During 2006-07 to 2008-09, ₹ 2,155.09 crore was released. In 2006-07 ₹ 316.57 crore was released, in 2007-08 ₹ 470.60 crore was released and in 2008-09 there was an increase of 203.44 per cent in the release of funds over the previous year.

During 2009-10, an expenditure of 795.03 crore was incurred under PMGSY against the available funds of 903.57 crore and release of 727.41 crore by Central and state governments which was 87.99 per cent of the total available funds and 109.30 per cent of the release.

A total provision of ₹ 700 crore was kept for the year 2010-11 under PMGSY. Against which, ₹ 599 crore was released up to November, 2010 from Central and state government. An expenditure of ₹ 431.55 crore was incurred up to November 2010 against the total available funds of ₹ 933.84 crore (including interest and the money deposited by contractors) which is 46.21 per cent of the total available funds and 72.05 per cent of the released.

It is noticed that construction of PMGSY roads has considerably benefitted farmers by providing access to nearby towns during all seasons. People are able to go to nearby towns for daily employment leading to improved job opportunities. The overall field observation is that roads have been laid in the rural areas under this programme in all the study mandals and people have beneffited from this programme.

So far 6,680 works costing ₹ 4,726.32 crore have been sanctioned in nine phases since 2000. Out of these 66,314 works have been completed covering a length of 20,431.09 km as on 31 October 2012 incurring an expenditure of ₹ 3,810.56 crore. The spillover programme is 440 works (183 roads+257 bridges) costing ₹ 787.23 crore to cover a length of 490.15 km. The physical and financial achievement for the year 2012-13 up to the end of August 12 was 100 works completed and an amount of ₹ 109.18 crore spent covering a length of 230.94 km.

During the year 2009-10 the release of funds under PMGSY for Andhra Pradesh was ₹ 200 crore. In terms of upgradation of length (in km), the target for the year 2009-10 was 2,990 km and the achievement was

3,042.31 km. The cumulative achievement (2005-2009) at 102 per cent was higher than the country average of 80 per cent. Major issues affecting the pace of implementation are inadequate institutional and contracting capacity, forest and environment clearance, and making land available for road construction.

Table 17.9

PMGSY Targets and Achievements (2001-2011)

(₹ in crore)

Phase	Year of Sanction	Sanctions			Achievements as on August 2012			%age of Works Completed
		No. of Works	Length (km)	Est. Cost	No. of Works	Length (km)	Exp.	
I	00-01	1479	3383.93	253.28	1479	3384.33	253.69	100%
II	01-02	1569	3497.10	433.96	1569	3483.76	420.95	100%
III	03-04	584	2077.97	266.25	584	2074.69	224.07	100%
IV	04-05	597	2558.74	429.54	596	2556.60	389.85	100%
V	05-06	318	1689.35	402.91	314	1660.93	346.77	99%
VI	06-07	388	2211.65	556.99	373	2059.59	513.07	96%
VII	07-08	829	3363.13	1177.81	821	3312.21	1039.69	99%
VIII	08-09	431	1702.54	579.17	395	1465.87	475.82	92%
X	10-11 Khammam	187	639.01	197.26	85	433.11	76.17	45%
X	10-11 bridges	298	0.00	429.15	98	0.00	70.51	33%
Total		6680	21123.42	4726.32	6314	20431.09	3810.56	95%

Source: *Socio Economic Survey and Outcome Budget of Andhra Pradesh, 2012-13.*

Mahatma Gandhi National Rural Employment Guarantee Act (MGNREGA)

The National Rural Employment Guarantee Act (NREGA) 2005 envisages securing the livelihood of people in rural areas by guaranteeing 100 days of employment in a financial year. The Act provides a social safety net for the vulnerable households and an opportunity to combine growth with equity. The innovations in the implementation process are: payment of wages through banks, IT driven implementation and the social audit system for public vigilance. Andhra Pradesh is in the forefront at the national level in implementation. Under NREGA, 19 districts in the State have been identified for implementing this programme.

MGNREGA marks a paradigm shift from all earlier and existing wage employment programmes because it is an Act and not just a scheme. It provides a legal guarantee to work. The rural households in the notified districts will have the right to register themselves with the local gram panchayat as persons interested in getting employment under the Act. The gram panchayat upon verification will register the household and issue a job card which is a legal document entitling a person to ask for work under the Act. The Act is a very bold step of the Government to eradicate poverty from rural India in the era of liberalisation and globalisation.

Table 17.10

MGNREGA Household Status

Employment demanded	38.17 lakh	Total fund	₹ 2,109.32 crore
Employment provided	38.17 lakh	Expenditure	₹ 1,336.31 crore
Person days (in lakh)		Total works taken up	4,25,196
Total person days	1,265.8	Works completed	64,084
SCs	356.1 (28.13%)	Works in progress	3,61,112
STs	158.56 (12.53%)		
Women	715.98 (56.56%)		
Others	751.14 (59.34%)		

Source: Outcome Budget and website of MGNREGS of Rural Development, Govt. of Andhra Pradesh, 2012-13.

Performance of MGNREGS

MGNREGS is being implemented in 21,861 gram panchayats covering 69,010 rural habitations of the state in 1098 mandals. Since its inception, 91.3 lakh rural households have been provided employment; and a total of 1.8 crore rural labour have accessed the scheme. The total expenditure incurred under the scheme was ₹ 22,689 crore with wage expenditure of ₹ 16,785 crore and material expenditure of ₹ 4,332 crore. The average wage rate per day amounts to ₹ 93.3. The total person days generated is 180 crore. 48.6 lakh households were each provided 100 days of wage employment over the period of six years.

Table 17.11

Implementation Status of MGNREGA in Andhra Pradesh

Status	*Cumulative upto 2009-10*
Upto 2009-10	
No. of Job Cards Issued (in lakh)	120
HH Provided Employment (in lakh)	81.95
Individuals Provided Employment (in lakh)	153.7
Expenditure Wages (in crore)	
Total	6592.18
7827.5	
Person Days Generated (in lakh)	7827.5
Average No. of Days Employment Provided per HH	-
HH Completed 100 Days of Wage Employment (in lakh)	16.64

Source: Outcome Budget and website of MGNREGS of Rural Development, Govt. of Andhra Pradesh, 2012-13.

Total expenditure incurred under NREGA during 2012-13 was ₹ 3,535 crore out of which ₹ 2,830 crore is paid as wages to labourers and ₹ 431 crore was spent on material cost. 54.2 lakh households were provided wage employment with an average employment of 50.2 days per household. Number of wage seekers reporting to work was 98.2 lakh. Total man-days of employment generated during the year was 27.2 crore with an average wage rate of ₹ 105.8 per day per person. Total number of households which completed 100 days during the year were 6.28 lakhs.

Assets Created

Land development is taken up to develop fallow lands of SC/STs, to enhance and diversify livelihood options of the poor by bringing these lands under diversified farming systems. 34 lakh acres of fallow land and degraded cultivable land was taken up with an expenditure of ₹ 5,925 crore benefitting 26.5 lakh SC/ST/small and marginal farmers. 18131 minor irrigation (MI) tanks restoration works were taken up with an expenditure of ₹ 3,425 crore and 8.56 lakh acres of *ayacut* stabilised. To improve the connectivity to 17,388 rural unconnected habitations, 25,048 kms length of roads were taken up with an expenditure of ₹ 1,935.5 crore. To stabilise *ayacut* under field channels and feeder channels, ₹ 1,085 crore was spent.

An *ayacut* of 5.2 lakh acres was stabilised by desilting 1.5 lakh kms of canals, feeder channels etc. To improve the groundwater table thereby increasing the direct and indirect *ayacut*, 1.2 lakh percolation and mini percolation tanks were constructed with an expenditure of ₹ 793 crore, which resulted in storing 900 lakh cubic meters of water. Earthen bunding is taken up in 8.5 lakh acres for soil and water conservation and for improving the fertility of the soil with an expenditure of ₹ 760 crore.

For the purpose of water conservation, 1.2 lakh farm ponds were taken up with an expenditure of ₹ 280 crore, which resulted in 146 lakh cubic meters of rainwater storage. To create sustainable livelihood opportunities for SC/ST/small and marginal farmers, 6.1 lakh acres plantations were taken up with an expenditure of ₹ 721 benefitting 4.8 lakh SC/ST/small and marginal farmers. Bunds and boundaries taken up under MGNREGS for planting the long gestation timber species. In the year 2012, bund/boundary plantation was taken up in the lands of around 3 lakh farmers' lands. Beneficiaries were mainly SC/ST as well as small and marginal farmers. In total, around 5 crore of plants were planted. To support MGNREGS activities at the gram panchayat level and for record keeping, gram panchayat buildings were taken up. 218 gram panchayat building were completed and 4408 are in progress with an expenditure of ₹ 228 crore.

Social Audit: Social audits involve both the people as well as the administrative officers who come together to verify the processes under the scheme right from planning to implementation. Any programme under the scheme can be taken up for audit by the wage seekers and the related expenses and details can be examined. The performance of the village can be analysed and the concerned authorities and gram panchayats can be made accountable.

Jawaharlal Nehru National Urban Renewal Mission

The aim of the JNNURM is to encourage reforms and fast track planned development of identified cities. Focus is on efficiency in urban infrastructure and service delivery mechanisms, community participation, and accountability of urban local bodies (ULB)/parastatal agencies. The first sub-Mission is for urban infrastructure and governance namely

Urban Infrastructure Development Scheme for Small & Medium Towns (UIDSSMT) which focuses on infrastructure projects relating to water supply and sanitation, sewerage, solid waste management, road network, urban transport and redevelopment of old city areas with a view to upgrading infrastructure therein, shifting industrial and commercial establishments to conforming areas etc. The second sub-Mission is for Basic Services to the Urban Poor (BSUP) which mainly focuses on integrated development of slums through projects for providing shelter, basic services and other related civic amenities with a view to providing utilities to the urban poor.

During 2009-10, an expenditure of 287.15 crore was incurred under JNNURM against the available funds of 667.51 crore (includes unspent balance of ₹ 261.65 crore as on 01.04.2009 and release of ₹ 405.86 crore by Central and state governments) which was 43.02 per cent of the total available funds and 70.75 per cent of the released. A total provision of 615.92 crore was kept for the year 2010-11 under JNNURM. An expenditure of 140.45 crore was incurred up to November, 2010 which is 35.69 per cent of the total available funds and 1069.69 per cent of the released.

A comprehensive programme under JNNURM for affordable housing for the poor in cities and towns with special attention to the needs of slum dwellers is being undertaken. Total Hyderabad City Development Plan outlay is estimated at ₹ 20,017 crore for a period of 7 years under JNNURM. These funds shall be deployed for creation of urban infrastructure in and around Hyderabad city. The funding needs are projected to be met from Government of India to the extent of ₹ 7,692.08 crore, state government ₹ 2,533.76 crore and executing institutions ₹ 9,790.78 crore staggered over 7 years.

Allocations to the tune of ₹ 15,441.62 crore are made for urban infrastructure such as water supply, sewerage, storm water drains, traffic & transportation and urban renewal. To reap the benefit of expertise of ULBs and parastatals, various categories of project works are allotted for execution to Greater Hyderabad Municipal Corporation (GHMC), Hyderabad Metro Water Supply and Sewerage Board (HMWSSB), Hyderabad Metropolitan Development Authority (HMDA), AP State Housing Corporation and AP State Road Transport Corporation.

Table 17.12

Source of Funds for Execution of JNNURM Project Works

(₹ *in crore*)

Institutions	*2005-06*	*2006-07*	*2007-08*	*2008-09*	*2009-10*	*2010-11*	*2011-12*	*Total*
A. Sources of Funding								
Government of India	564.19	1,296.19	1,337.49	1,348.14	1,117.17	1,096.07	932.83	7,692.08
AP State Government	143.14	448.07	452.51	455.36	371.69	362.99	300.00	2,533.76
Total – A	707.33	1,744.26	1,790.00	1,803.50	1,488.86	1,459.06	1,232.83	10,225.84
B. Implementing Institutions Own Funds								
MCH & Surrounding Municipalities	231.75	680.60	754.45	689.90	397.80	383.10	378.23	3,515.80
HMWSB	252.68	588.60	517.80	601.30	605.55	591.05	380.80	3,537.78
HUDA	2.50	228.15	242.65	241.65	246.65	246.65	246.75	1,455.00
AP State Housing Corporation	191.00	167.50	167.50	167.50	167.50	167.50	171.50	1,200.00
APSRTC	-	17.00	22.00	14.55	9.55	9.55	9.55	82.20
Total – B	677.93	1,681.85	1,704.40	1,714.90	1,427.05	1,397.85	1,186.83	9,790.78
Grand Total (A+B)	1,385.26	3,426.11	3,494.40	3,518.40	2,915.91	2,856.91	2,419.66	20,016.62

Source: Andhra Pradesh Urban Finance and Infrastructure Development Corporation, Department of MA & UD, Govt. of A.P.

Table 17.13

Urban Basic Services for the Poor: JNNURM Sub-Mission

(₹ *in crore*)

Institutions	*2005-06*	*2006-07*	*2007-08*	*2008-09*	*2009-10*	*2010-11*	*2011-12*	*Total*
A. Urban Basic Services for the Poor								
Government of India (50%)	264.50	323.50	381.50	389.00	322.00	320.50	286.50	2,287.50
AP State Government (10%)	14.70	31.20	42.80	44.30	30.90	30.60	23.00	217.50
Total – A	279.20	354.70	424.30	433.30	352.90	351.10	309.50	2,505.00
B. Implementing Institutions Own Funds (40%)								
MCH & Surrounding Municipalities	58.80	108.80	112.40	116.40	60.80	57.60	51.20	566.00
HMWSB	-	16.00	58.80	60.80	62.80	64.80	40.80	304.00
AP State Housing Corporation*	191.00	167.50	167.50	167.50	167.50	167.50	171.50	1,200.00
Total – B	249.80	292.30	338.70	344.70	291.10	289.90	263.50	2,070.00
Grand Total (A+B)	529.00	647.00	763.00	778.00	644.00	641.00	573.00	4,575.00

Note: * For housing to the poor, 50 per cent component from GoI, 40 per cent borrowing by the APSHC and 10 per cent from the beneficiaries.

Source: Andhra Pradesh Urban Finance and Infrastructure Development Corporation, Department of MA & UD, Govt. of A.P.

Table 17.14

JNNURM Project Sanctions

(₹ in crore)

Programme	*No.*	*Value*	*Share of GoI*	*GoAP*	*ULB/Ben*
BSUP	36	3010.20	1497.50	602.22	910.47
IHSDP	77	1139.08	764.53	154.62	219.80
UI&G	54	5267.50	2235.64	820.50	2211.35
UIDSSMT	101	3111.43	2489.00	311.25	311.25
Total	268	12528.18	6986.67	1888.59	3652.87

Note: BUSP: Basic Service to Urban Poor; IHSDP: Integrated Housing and Slum Development programme; UI&G: Urban Infrastructure and Governance, UIDSSMT: Urban Infrastructure Development Scheme for Small & Medium Towns.

Source: Andhra Pradesh Urban Finance and Infrastructure Development Corporation, Department of MA & UD, Govt. of A.P.

Coverage of JNNURM

Out of 124 ULB (Urban Local Bodies) in the state, 95 ULBs are covered under various components of JNNURM including 4 Mission Cities. Of the remaining 11 Municipal Corporations, 10 are covered under National Urban Renewal Mission. Out of 109 small and medium towns, 81 towns are covered with UIDSSMT and IHSDP projects. Plantation programme is being taken up along important roads, EWS Housing colonies and in schools in 13 ULBs under Phase I. Under PPP Projects initiatives, a pilot project was taken up at Jagityal town providing drinking water

Table 17.15

Financial Utilisation by ULBs/Implementing Agencies

(₹ in crore)

S. No.	*Component*	*Project Cost*	*Releases made by GoI and GoAP*	*Funds adjusted to SLNA*	*Utilisation by ULBs/IAs*
1	UI&G	5344.81	2425.00	2275.99	3578.33
2	UIDSSMT	2459.96	2750.79	2514.15	2452.85
MoUD Total		7804.77	5175.79	4790.14	6031.18
3	BSUP	3732.12	1832.78	1816.41	2337.85
4	IHSDP	988.77	766.19	750.71	673.95
MoHUPA Total		4720.89	2598.97	2567.12	3011.80
Grand Total		12,525.66	7774.76	7357.26	9042.98

Source: Andhra Pradesh Urban Finance and Infrastructure Development Corporation, Department of MA & UD, Govt. of A.P.

connection for ₹ 2,000 per connection for urban poor. As a helping hand for BSUP beneficiaries, the APUFIDC tied-up with State Bank of Hyderabad to extend loan of ₹ 20,000 at 4 per cent interest to 90,622 BSUP beneficiaries and 8 per cent interest for loans above ₹ 20,000 for taking up some small business.

Table 17.16

Physical Progress: JNNURM

No.	*Component*	*Physical Progress*				
		Not Started	*< 50%*	*>50%*	*Completed*	*Total*
MoUD						
1	UI&G	2	9	22	23	56
2	UIDSSMT	0	5	24	55	84
MoUD Total		2	14	46	78	140
MoHUPA						
3	BSUP	1	10	17	11	39
4	IHSDP	1	12	51	10	74
MoHUPA Total		3	22	68	21	113
Grand Total		5	36	114	99	253

Source: Andhra Pradesh Urban Finance and Infrastructure Development Corporation, Department of MA & UD, Govt. of A.P.

Benefits Accrued from JNNURM Programme

Benefits of the programme are impressive across Andhra Pradesh. Under the Urban Infrastructure and Governance (UI&G) component, a population of 60 lakh in the Mission cities of Hyderabad, Visakhapatnam and Vijayawada have benefited with continuous water supply through the accrual of 685 MLD and 4.18 lakh water connections. While the completion of 193 kms of storm water drains has improved the living conditions of 70 lakh people, the addition of 85 MLD underground drainage in Visakhapatnam and Vijayawada has benefitted a population of 11 lakh through 85,000 connections issued. The last mile coverage through 100 per cent water supply to 47 towns has raised the bar to provide 3.5 lakh new water connections in 61 ULBs with the addition of 736 MLD to an existing capacity of 521 MLD in 61 towns. 292 kms have been covered through storm water drains in 9 ULBs covering 100 per cent of the area in towns.

Very few of the infrastructure projects planned have been fully delivered in the two years of the mission. Growing urban population and the consequent shortage of infrastructure and municipal services will tend to increase the number of urban poor. Majority of the slums are on private land (52 per cent). Other slums occupy land belonging to government, railways, defence, irrigation and other reserved land. A large number of people in slums live on riverbeds, hilltops and other environmentally dangerous areas. Major slum problems are related to security of tenure, good quality housing and access to social infrastructure. The GHMC has given top priority to slum rehabilitation under BSUP.

JNNURM addresses much of the infrastructure and service delivery needs. But monitoring mechanisms should be strengthened and decentralised to ensure that projects are taken up and executed responsibly. There is great scope for improvement and JNNURM is only a stepping stone towards attaining the vision envisaged.

Summary and Conclusion

Of the total allocation of ₹ 26,320.43 crore an amount of ₹ 9,782.89 crore (₹ 6,655.37 crore as Centre share and ₹ 3,127.52 crore as state share) was released. An amount of ₹ 8,143.14 crore has been spent.

The TSC programme basically follows a demand-driven approach. Transition from the principle of state-wise allocation to a demand-responsive rewards system creates incentives which encourage participation by the people. Community-driven and people-centred approach also makes the implementing agencies more accountable and transparent in their approach. PRIs (panchayati raj institutions), with the involvement of cooperatives, women's groups, youth clubs and NGOs, help mobilise cooperation and coordination among rural constituencies. The most effective methodology adopted in this programme is the campaign mode approach. The TSC's other project components include hygiene education in schools and awareness campaigns to sensitise the rural population about the importance of sanitation facilities for maintaining good health.

On the development of the IEC campaign, the interviews and focus groups discussions with stakeholders revealed that the importance of the information on health which focus on education and communication about the need for a strong and sustained commitment to improve the sanitation conditions.

School sanitation has been neglected badly in all Plans for which corrective action is urgently needed. The children of today are the citizens of tomorrow. The key person is the teacher. The primary and upper-primary school teachers should be trained and their capacity should be enhanced to enable them to transform their mind-set and attitude in such a way so that this message reaches the rural household. The teacher may also work as a motivator in his/her vicinity and be involved in the communication strategy for behaviour change. These findings suggest that social mobilisation is needed to improve overall sanitation.

The coverage of habitations with water supply and sanitation under NRDWP is dynamic and changes with time. In spite of sincere efforts by the Government, quality affected habitations and partially covered habitations are re-emerging due to human intervention and improper management. As a result, about 24,654 habitations slipped into either to PC or NSS or NC from FC category during the span of 10 years. The reasons for such slippage are: unsustainability of source, falling quality of groundwater, population increases and maintenance failures.

Rehabilitating the existing village tanks, creating detention basins by storing rain water in local depressions, abandoned mines/quarries etc., for water harvesting for the development of water resources needs to be encouraged. Small dams should be encouraged because the micro watershed area is more efficient for water conservation. Underground siphons which would conserve the water and recharge the aquifer should be used to avoid the evaporation losses from such small storages.

Despite good progress, improvement in rural water supply and increased outlay by the Government, particularly in the last decade, general satisfaction is quite low at the community level. Despite huge investments, the objective of providing access to water and sanitation to the entire population has remained distant. The water supply facilities installed often provide irregular and scanty supply of water. Besides, the appalling conditions of sanitation in most of the urban areas cause severe health hazards. Measures like prioritisation and adopting the norms of water-use efficiency should be taken up at the habitation level. Water rationing is also a useful instrument to control water use but this requires community participation.

An amount of ₹ 981.94 crore has been allocated, out of which 50 per cent was released so far in addition to the available opening balance of ₹ 301.30 crore. Out of the total amount available 37 per cent has been utilised so far by covering 628 habitations.

An amount of ₹ 524.66 crore of Central share has been allocated to NSAP, out of which 33 per cent was released so far and 126 per cent funds have been utilised. A substantial increase in the allocation for the social sector is only likely to happen when something changes in the budget-making process and in the effective implementation of checks and balances of public finance to fulfil the set targets of social development.

The progress under ARWSP and TSC is good but the amount of funds for the toilets i.e. ₹ 2500 seems to be inadequate.

Though the absolute position of Andhra Pradesh at the national level is average, the number of houses constructed per lakh population under IAY scheme in the state has always been higher than national average. The position of the state improved from 13 to 7 at the national level if we consider the number of houses constructed per lakh population as an indicator during the period 2003-04 to 2008-09. This is a positive indication that the programme is progressing well in the state. Within the state, the variations across districts are quite significant. The position of districts like Kadapa, Anantapur, Karimnagar and Vizianagaram, which are relatively less developed, is very low when we consider houses constructed per lakh population. On the other hand, West Godavari, East Godavari, Krishna and Guntur, which are all much more developed, are always among the top five districts in terms of number of houses constructed per lakh population during the study period. Clearly, the Government should place more emphasis on implementing the programme in less developed districts.

An amount of ₹ 1252.21 crore has been allocated, out of which nearly 50 per cent was released. Out of the total amount available of ₹ 724.24 crore, 89 per cent funds have been utilised. Construction of 0.65 lakh number of houses has been taken up against the target of 2.70 lakh.

Field observations show that major constraints for the IAY programme are lack of access to land i.e., ownership on the land; inadequate amount given by the Government for the construction of a house resulting in heavy borrowing from private money lenders at higher interest rates; and SC/ST beneficiaries are not able to complete the construction of houses compared to other category beneficiaries. However, beneficiaries expressed their full satisfaction about the programme since it is a good initiative that permits them to own a permanent house.

The matter of concern is that irrespective of the revenue account position, whether improving or, continuing the surplus situation, water supply and sanitation showed mixed trends (increase in one phase and decrease in another phase). Contrary to this, expenditure towards housing and urban development showed an increasing trend because of the increased expenditure towards these schemes. Housing expenditure showed a decline in terms of GSDP and total expenditure.

Though the PMGSY programme aimed at providing road connectivity to all unconnected habitations, a majority (79%) of unconnected habitations do not have road connectivity as yet. This number is high in Visakhapatnam district with 1,374 unconnected habitations and 3,726 habitations still to be connected by roads in the state. The percentage of habitations covered under PMGSY was the lowest in Visakhapatnam, Srikakulam, Adilabad and Vizianagaram. This may be because large tracts in Visakhapatnam, Srikakulam and Adilabad are hilly and a major part of these districts is under agency areas. The Government needs to focus on the agency districts like Visakhapatnam, Srikakulam, Vizianagaram, Khammam and Adilabad where the ST population is relatively high and which need better road connectivity. Out of the total amount available, ₹ 517.45 crore, 21 per cent has been utilised. Length of road covered is 231 kms against the target of 400 kms.

Under innovations in the implementation process of MGNREGS in payment of wages through banks, IT driven implementation and the social audit system for public vigilance in the implementation, the state is in the forefront at the national level. Continuing with the efforts to enhance efficiency and transparency in MGNREGS implementation, continuous innovations in both technology integration and processes streamlining have improved the Andhra Pradesh model of MGNREGS. The state has also taken up all the necessary steps to convey to the wage seekers that MGNREGS is a scheme not only aimed at providing wage employment to the unskilled labour but also intended at creating durable assets and thereby enhancing the livelihoods of the poorest of the poor in the rural areas. The durable assets created under the scheme include development of lands, water bodies, and also enhancing the productivity of their cultivable land. An amount of ₹ 7559 crore has been allocated, out of which 32 per cent funds have been released so far. Out of the total amount of ₹ 4013.40 crore available, 88 per cent of the funds have been utilised. 27.21 crore of person-days were generated, providing an average number of 50.12 days per household.

JNNURM has brought with itself immense responsibility on the ULBs, people and the city as a whole. Reforms need to be pursued vigorously for improved service delivery, to really exploit the massive inflow of funds coming into the city of Hyderabad. Very few of the infrastructure projects planned have been delivered fully in the first two years of the mission. Growing urban population and the consequent shortage of infrastructure and municipal services will tend to increase the number of urban poor. Majority of the slums are on private land (52 per cent). Other slums occupy land belonging to government, railways, defence, irrigation and other reserved land. A large number of slums are on riverbeds, hilltops and other environmentally dangerous areas.

An amount of ₹ 1855 crore has been allocated, out of which 28 per cent was released so far in addition to the available opening balance of ₹ 656.14 crore. Out of the total amount available 32 per cent funds have been utilised. Construction of 9,234 houses has been taken up against the target of 63,230.

The major slum dwellers are daily wage earners. Almost all slums have access to basic services. The major slum problems are related to security of tenure, good quality housing and access to social infrastructure. All these issues concerning JNNURM naturally leave doubts about the management and allocation of funds and resources. Progress should not

Table 17.17

Performance of Flagship Programmes 2012-13

No.	Scheme	Unit	Physical		Financial (₹ crore)		
			Target	Achievement	Available Funds	Exp.	%
1	Mahatma Gandhi National Rural Employment Guarantee Scheme (MGNREGS)	1) Works Completed (lakh)		3.14	4013.40	3535.52	88
		2) Employment provided to households (lakh)		54			
		3) Wage employment provided to persons (crore)		98.26			
		4) Person-days generated (crore)	33.00	27.21			
		5) Average no. of days provided per HH (Nos.)		50.12			
		6) Average wage rate per person per day (₹)		105.80			
2	Indira Awas Yojana (IAY)	Construction of houses (lakh)	2.70	0.65	599.95	302.86	50
3	Jawaharlal Nehru Urban Renewal Mission (JNNURM)	UI&G project works (Nos.)	29.00	1.00	1175.82	377.81	32
		BSUP houses (Nos.)	46909	8306			
		UIDSSMT project works (Nos.)	34	5			
		IHSDP houses (Nos.)	16321	928			
4	Pradhan Mantri Gram Sadak Yojana (PMGSY)	1) Road works (Nos.)		100	517.45	109.18	21
		2) Road length covered (kms.)	400	230.94			
5	National Rural Drinking Water Supply Programme (NRDWP)	Habitations covered (Nos.)	5266	628	797.80	298.89	37
6	Total Sanitation Campaign (TSC)	IHHLS and Toilets (lakh Nos.)	7.19	1.37	375.29	26.00	7
7	National Social Assistance Programme (NSAP)	IGNOAPS (Pensions)	1587813	1587813	171.93	216.29	126
		IGNWPS (Pensions)	303945	303945			
		IGNDPS (Pensions)	64595	64595			
		NFBS (Benfs.)	29000	17394			
		ANNAPURNA (Benfs.)	93200	93200			

go unnoticed and has to be appreciated. JNNURM addresses much of the infrastructure and service delivery needs, but monitoring mechanisms should be strengthened and decentralised to ensure that projects are taken up and executed responsibly. The JNNURM is only a stepping stone towards attaining the vision envisaged. However every good policy comes with its baggage of problems. With JNURM, the government of India answers the tricky question of the centre's involvement given that urban issues are a state subject, especially with limited resources and large rural demands, JNNURM is the best hope.

References

Government of Andhra Pradesh, *Outcome Budget*, 2008-09, 2009-10.

Government of Andhra Pradesh, *Budget Documents, 2012.*

Government of Andhra Pradesh, *Socio Economic Survey, 2012-13.*

Government of Andhra Pradesh (various years). *Annual Reports*, 2003-04 to 2008-09, 2011-12, 2012-13. Andhra Pradesh State Housing Corporation Ltd.

Government of Andhra Pradesh (various years). *Outcome Budgets*, 2008-09, 2009-10, 2011-12, 2012-13. Department of Housing.

Government of Andhra Pradesh (various years). *Outcome Budgets*, 2008-09, 2009-10, 2011-12, 2012-13. Department of Rural Development.

Government of Andhra Pradesh (various years). *Annual Plans*, 2008-09, 2009-10, 2010-11, 2011-12, 2012-13.

Website of the Department of Rural Water Supply and Sanitation, Government of Andhra Pradesh. *http://aprwssp.ap.nic.in/*

Website of Drinking Water Department, Government of India. *http://ddws.nic.in/mis_prog.htm*

Section V: Local Finances

18 Towards New Agenda for Fiscal Decentralisation

J.B. Rajan*

Decentralisation Continuum

Decentralisation plays an increasingly important role in assuring sound public service and democratic governance. Decentralisation reforms are being pursued in countries around the world in order to enhance the efficiency with which public services are provided to communities. Decentralisation can be in the form of de-concentration, delegation, and devolution; the continuum provides progressive degree of transfer of power in organising the public sector. De-concentration is the process of shifting decision-making power within the Central government structure from Central government officials in the capital to Central government officials that are located outside the capital, at the local (or regional) level (Anon, 2009). Although government services are produced by a (de-concentrated) local entity, all decision-making authority remains with the Central government. There is no need to have elected local government authorities in a de-concentrated system of governance as compared with delegation and devolution. Delegation is the process of shifting the responsibility of providing certain services from the Central government to local government that are not wholly controlled by the Central government, but that are ultimately fully accountable to it. Delegation requires local governments to be semi-autonomous (i.e. elected), but it does not give local governments substantive decision-making authority over how the services should be provided. Local governments are used as agents to produce the government service, but in the end the Central government is actually

* Special thanks are due to Dr Shaheena, Associate Professor, Kerala Agricultural University, Thrissur for sharing necessary data and information on this paper and also for providing technical advice. However, I shoulder the responsibility of any errors or mistakes that may have crept in the paper.

responsible for all facets of the provision of the service. Devolution, on the other hand, is the process of assigning substantive responsibility for the delivery of a public goods or services to a sub-national government level. Either the Central government could devolve the responsibility to provide a Central government service to the local government level, or the Central government could devolve responsibility over all aspects of a functional responsibility (Anon, 2009).

In a real decentralised system, there will be high degree of transfer of power—i.e. devolution. There will be clear role assignments, devolution of power to spend money, devolution of power to tax, discretion in spending money, power to fire and control staff, and direct accountability. If the degree of decentralisation is low, then there will be scheme bound expenditure, staff on deputation, limited power to collect resources, and no direct responsibility. One of the core components of decentralisation leading to real devolution of power is fiscal decentralisation; the others being political and administrative. According to Bahl (2008), fiscal decentralisation is the empowerment of people through fiscal empowerment of their local governments. By yielding greater fiscal responsibilities to local governments, the public sector can be more flexible in response to variations in local needs and demands for public services.

This paper discusses the concept of fiscal decentralisation and prevalent fiscal decentralisation in India. The paper explains how Kerala stood as the trendsetter and how it is the lost winner.

Pillars of Fiscal Decentralisation

There is a conventional wisdom on fiscal decentralisation—finance-follows-function. First should come the assignment of expenditure responsibility to sub-national governments, and then the assignment of revenue raising powers. There is a good logic to this finance-follows-function rule. Based on this rule, there are four pillars of fiscal decentralisation. They are assignment of expenditure responsibilities, assignment of revenue sources to sub-national governments, the allocation of inter-governmental fiscal transfers or grants, rules on sub-national budget deficits, and the incurrence of sub-national debt.

Expenditure Assignments

The starting point for fiscal decentralisation is expenditure assignments, which seeks to address the question what functions and expenditure responsibilities should be assigned to each level of government. Assigning expenditure responsibilities refers to the distribution of functions among the different government levels. It involves the delineation of roles and functional responsibility among levels of government for regulating, financing, administering, and producing public goods and services. It relates to the principle of subsidiarity, which deals with who should do what? What can be done best at a particular level and what should be done at that level, and assignment of expenditure responsibilities.

Revenue Assignments

Allocating revenue sources refers to the distribution of financial resources among the different levels of government. A comprehensive definition of a revenue assignment considers which government level (i) legislates each tax, (ii) defines the tax base and exemptions, (iii) determines the tax rate, (iv) collects/administers the tax, and (v) receives the revenues from the tax. The fundamental question is how the expenditure responsibilities are financed?

Inter-governmental Fiscal Transfers or Grants

The inter-governmental fiscal transfers refer to the transfer of finances from the Central government to lower government levels. Inter-governmental fiscal relations denote the extent of fiscal transfers between different tiers of governments; normally between higher-level to lower level government. Usually inter-governmental fiscal transfers are aimed at achieving vertical fiscal balance, horizontal equalisation, or other specific objectives of the payer. It is expected that the expenditure responsibilities of a government and its revenue capability should match. The mis-match if any has to be bridged through inter-governmental fiscal transfers or grants.

Rules on Sub-national Budget Deficits or Subnational Debts

Sub-national borrowing/debt refers to the capacity for sub-national governments to borrow money to cover their expenditure responsibilities. Borrowing allows a local entity to carry out a more ambitious capital programme than otherwise would be possible. It promotes inter-governmental equity by having the generation of citizens that benefits from a capital facility's services pay for its construction.

Fiscal Decentralisation in India

The 73rd and 74th Constitutional Amendment Act (CAA) of India has created a legal foundation for third tier of government in the federal structure of the country. With the CAA, the local governments in India (both rural and urban) have become constitutionalised since 1993. The Local Self Government Institutions (LSGIs) are enshrined in the Constitution like the two upper levels of government, *viz.*, Central and state governments and enable them to function as institutions of self-government. The state governments were made responsible for enacting conformity Acts to devolve functions listed in the XIth and XIIth Schedules[1] of the Constitution. The aforesaid CAA mandates to devolve power to LSGIs so as to render public services including drinking water, sanitation, street light, roads, etc. According to finance-follows-function rule, there should be adequate fiscal decentralisation to enable the LSGIs to provide the public services that are devolved to them. How far this has been attained? What is the extent of fiscal decentralisation after the 73rd and 74th CAA?. These are addressed hereunder based on indicators. The indicators used for assessing the extent of fiscal decentralisation are: (i) share of expenditure by different tiers of government, (ii) share of expenditure to GDP (gross domestic products), (iii) composition of revenue sources, and (iv) fiscal autonomy ratio.

Share of Expenditure

The expenditure assignment, the fundamental step in fiscal decentralisation, is characterised by the functions and relative expenditure shares of local governments. Of the total expenditure, the share of total expenditure of local governments in India is meager compared to the share of state and Central governments (Table 18.1). Not only that the local governments' share of expenditure declined from 8.6 per cent in 1976-77 to 2.5 per cent in 2007-08, but also the decline was substantial by one-third in three decades. Another striking point is that the substantial decline in

1. The schedules include 29 subjects to be devolved by the states to the LSGIs.

share of expenditure of local governments has taken place after the 73rd and 74th CAA! They were in the range of 6 to 9 per cent during 1976-77 to 1986-87 and 2 to 3 per cent during 1997-98 to 2007-08.

Table 18.1

Share of Expenditure by Tiers of Governments in India

(in %)

Tiers of Governments	*1976-77*	*1986-87*	*1997-98*	*2002-03*	*2007-08*
Local Governments	8.6	6.4	2.9	1.9	2.5
State Governments	59.1	44.4	48.2	59.9	59.9
Central Governments	32.3	49.2	48.9	38.2	37.6
Aggregate of All Tiers	100.0	100.0	100.0	100.0	100.0

Source: Shaheena and Isaac, 2007; 2013.

The local governments' share of expenditure in India is lowest compared to other countries too. In countries like Australia, Canada, Germany and Switzerland, the share of expenditure of local governments is two digit figures in the range of 14 to 21 per cent, while the share is hardly 2 per cent in India. (Table 18.2).

Table 18.2

Share of Expenditure of Local Governments: India versus Other Countries

(in %)

Countries	*1997*	*2002*	*2007*
Australia	16.40	14.00	13.85
Canada	18.35	18.09	19.19
Germany	15.26	14.77	15.93
Switzerland	21.36	19.54	20.02
India	*1997-98*	*2002-03*	*2007-08*
	2.9	1.9	2.5

Source: OECD, 2013.

Expenditure to GDP

Local governments' ratio of expenditure to GDP in India is meager compared to the share of state and Central governments. Both state and Central governments' share of expenditure to GDP shows two digit figures (with the exception of Central government in 1976-77), the same is hardly 2 per cent as far as local governments are concerned (Table 18.3).

Table 18.3

Ratio of Expenditure to GDP by Tiers of Governments in India

(in %)

Tiers of Governments	*1976-77*	*1986-87*	*1997-98*	*2002-03*	*2007-08*
Local Governments	1.60	2.10	1.01	1.71	2.30
State Governments	11.10	14.80	16.65	18.78	16.50
Central Governments	6.20	16.30	17.24	18.46	15.63.63

Source: Shaheena and Isaac, 2007; 2013.

Composition of Sources

Composition of the financial sources of panchayat raj institutions (PRIs) in India shows that they are heavily dependent on upper tiers of governments. The major chunk of revenue composition of PRIs in India is from grants and other revenues. This accounts for about 90 to 97 per cent in different years. (Table 18.4).

Table 18.4

Revenue Composition of PRIs in India

(in %)

Sources	*1976-77*	*1997-98*	*2002-03*	*2007-08*
Own Sources of Revenue	10.8	3.5	6.8	4.57
Grants and Other Revenues	89.2	96.5	93.2	95.43
Total	100.0	100.0	100.0	100.00

Source: Compiled from Shaheena and Issac, 2007; 2013.

Fiscal Autonomy Ratio

The level of fiscal autonomy of LSGIs can be assessed by computing fiscal autonomy ratio, the ratio of own revenue to total expenditure. As reflected by fiscal autonomy ratio, fiscal autonomy of local governments (rural) is not only very low but has also declined from 1998-99 onwards (Table 18.5).

From the four indicators analysed in this section, it is clear that the fiscal decentralisation to the lower tiers—local governments—is bleak. There is mismatch between fiscal requirements and availability, which puts more stress on local governments. It can be concluded from the analysis that the fiscal space of local governments in India is shrinking.

Table 18.5

Fiscal Autonomy Ratio

(in %)

Type of LSGIs	*1990-91*	*1995-96*	*1997-98*	*1998-99*	*1999-00*	*2000-01*	*2001-02*	*2002-03*
Rural	15.93	10.83	10.60	6.34	6.15	5.89	5.98	6.77
Urban	84.45	99.12	82.38	57.11	51.07	52.47	55.05	52.58

Source: Shaheena and Isaac, 2007.

Kerala the Trend Setter

The general trend of decentralisation in India is not satisfactory as revealed by the indicators discussed in the earlier section. However, Kerala has taken a lead role in decentralisation. Kerala is well known for decentralisation due to its distinctive features compared to other states. Decentralisation in Kerala is not deconcentration or delegation. The extent of decentralisation is assessed at national level based on 3 Fs (i.e., devolution of functions, functionaries, and finance). Kerala is not only the trend setter on these 3 Fs, but also other Fs—freedom (for LSGIs), fraternity (for decentralisation), flexibility (in procedures), future-oriented (effective local governance), and framework (for institutionalisation). Kerala has taken proactive steps for making local governments as institutions of self government, by conceiving the letter and spirit of 73rd and 74th CAA. The salient features of Kerala Model of Decentralisation are well narrated by Vijayanand (2009), the relevant portions are summarised below.

Big Bang Approach

Traditional wisdom calls for capacity building of local governments and then giving power to them in degrees to match the improvements in capacity. But real and effective decentralisation calls for a big bang approach—functions, powers and resources being transferred at one go in a political act of faith. To operationalise decentralisation, Kerala chose the path of participatory local level planning as the entry point. This succeeded to a considerable extent in harnessing public action in favour of decentralisation.

Principles of Devolution

The Committee on Decentralisation of Powers (popularly known as Sen Committee) laid down the key principles of devolution of functions which have been adhered to by government in practice (Government of Kerala, 1997). Accordingly, the local governance system in Kerala was reframed keeping the principles of autonomy, subsidiarity, role-clarity, complementarity, uniformity, people's participation, accountability, and transparency. These principles adopted by Kerala are of universal relevance. The LSGIs have been left to function freely with government supervision limited to the obligatory and regulatory functions.

Legislative Entitlements

The Kerala Panchayat Raj Act and Kerala Municipality Act, both of which were enacted in 1994, were thoroughly restructured in 1999 incorporating the lessons from experience of the initial years of 'big bang' decentralisation. Kerala is the only state which carved out the functional domain of different local governments with a great deal of precision. The functions have been divided into mandatory, general and sector-wise functions. Kerala pioneered activity-mapping by amending and of late has done a responsibility mapping that spells out an operational division of labour between Gram Panchayats, Block Panchayats, District Panchayats, Municipalities, and State. Grama Sabha have been given clear rights and responsibilities with absolute powers for identification of functionaries, wide powers for social audit and strong advisory powers for prioritising developmental needs. The elected heads of the local governments have been declared as the executive authority. The Acts provide for certain innovative features towards promoting good governance *viz.*, absolute right to information, mandatory publication of citizen charter, performance audit system, code of conduct for officials and elected functions, and powerful supportive institutions.

Amendment to Allied Acts

The state made a path-breaking amendment to 42 Acts dealing with subjects which are in the functional domain of local governments. This decision was taken to make it clear that local governments are not just the creatures of the panchayat raj and municipality acts; but they are entitled to legal space in all legislations having something to do with their functions, thus becoming the third tier of governments below the Central and state governments.

Transfer of Institutions

The hallmark of Kerala's administrative decentralisation is the transfer of public service delivery institutions to local governments. Important institutions of public services like Public Health Centres, Hospitals, Schools, Krishi Bhavans, Veterinary Institutions, Anganwadis, etc., have been transferred to LSGIs. No state in India, other than Kerala, has implemented institutional decentralisation.

Human Resource

When new functions were devolved the principle of work and worker going together was enunciated. This enabled the government to transfer institutions and offices along with staff to the local governments. The salaries of the staff transferred continue to be paid for by Government. The officials of 17 departments have either fully or partially deployed technical/administrative staff to LSGIs. The cadre of the staff transferred is not disturbed. Even the own staff of local governments i.e., village panchayats and municipal bodies who are paid for by the local governments themselves are recruited through the Public Service Commission (PSC).

Supplementary Systems

In order to eke out the human resource availability and supplement the skill sets available in local governments, a system of sourcing-in expertise from outside the governmental system has been put in place. For the preparation of projects for different local governments, working groups are set up for different sectors. The typical working group is headed by an elected member and has expert professionals, officials, practitioners, and other stakeholders. This facilitates a process of multiple points of view getting imbibed—political, professional, official, activist and primary stakeholder-based.

Responsibilities of Local Governments

The hallmark of decentralisation in Kerala is the transfer of well-defined developmental responsibilities to local governments. In the case of infrastructure, barring highways and major district roads connectivity has become an exclusive local government responsibility. In the case of power in addition to the traditional function of street light maintenance, extension of electricity lines to unserved areas is now by and large carried out by local governments. Sanitation including solid and liquid waste management is now totally under local governments. Almost all functions on agriculture & allied sectors, social welfare, education, health, poverty alleviation, etc. became local government responsibility.

Fiscal Decentralisation

As regards fiscal decentralisation, Kerala is the only state in India having separate budget window for LSGIs and devolving not less than 30 per cent of state plan funds to LSGIs. Fiscal transfers to local governments from government were done in systematic manner. Another feature of sub-state level devolution in Kerala is formula-based distribution of plan funds taking into account population and backwardness. Long before the term 'fiscal responsibility' came into vogue the state stipulated that local governments can pass budgets only if they showed a 5 per cent surplus. Kerala was the first state in the country to set up a statutory Rural Development Board to raise funds from the market through debentures and channel them to village panchayats for commercially viable projects.

Kerala, the Lost Winner

Kerala's initiatives for decentralisation in general and fiscal decentralisation in particular are a model for other states to emulate. The specific feature of decentralisation in Kerala has been a discourse at national and international level and renowned as Kerala Model of Decentralisation. Despite the fact that Kerala is far ahead in decentralisation when compared with other Indian states, it remains a loser as far as the grants of Union Finance Commission (UFC) are concerned. There is a paradox between the extent of devolution—represented by devolution index—by the states and the general basic grants provided to them by UFCs. The general basic grant by XIIIth UFC is a typical example. (See Table 18.6 for select states arranged in descending order of devolution index).

Kerala though it topped in devolution index (74) received only 3.1% of general basic grants by the XIIIth UFC, while Andhra Pradesh received

8.29% even though its devolution index was much lower than Kerala (lower by 24). This is due to the fact that the devolution index was not duly considered in the allocation formula.[2]

Table 18.6

Devolution Index versus General Basic Grant by XIIIth UFC

	State	*Devolution Index*[1]	*General Basic Grant by XIIIth UFC (%)*[2]
1	Kerala	74	3.11
2	Karnataka	69	7.54
3	Tamilnadu	67	6.33
4	West Bengal	66	6.68
5	Maharastra	61	10.07
6	Madhya Pradesh	59	6.51
7	Gujarat	53	4.22
8	Andhra Pradesh	50	8.29

Source: 1. Alok and Chaubey, 2010.
2. Government of India, 2009.

Need for Revamping

The federal fiscal system in India is designed for two tier system of governance that was in existence before the 73rd and 74th CAA. The Amendments to CAA by inserting Article 280 (3)(bb and c) is a firm affirmation of organic link between UFC, state, and sub-state. Considering the spirit of the 73rd and 74th CAA in general and Article 280 (3)(bb and c) in particular, the federal fiscal system needs to be revamped. The constitutionally created third tier of government—LSGIs—shall be given due place as they deserve. LSGIs are constitutionally eligible to get the financial support as that of states. In view of this:

i. The LSGIs shall also to be considered along with states in the central divisible pool.

ii. There shall be regular transfer arrangements to LSGIs instead of adhoc grants of UFC.

2. With the 73rd and 74th Amendments to Indian Constitution, third-tier of government, i.e. local governments come into existence. However devolution index does not takes into account, in fullest sense, the third-tier of governments and decentralisation process.

iii. The consolidated fund of a state enunciated in Article 280 shall be augmented to supplement the resources of the LSGIs.

iv. Hard budget constraints shall be insisted on, i.e. those LSGIs who are given autonomy will be asked to balance their budgets without recourse to any end-of-year assistance from the Central government.

v. Fiscal capacity equalisation shall be ensured so that the issues of shrinking fiscal space of LSGIs can be resolved. This will enable the LSGIs to discharge functions assigned to them.

vi. The uniformly designed Centrally Sponsored Schemes (CSSs) across the country creates burden for the LSGIs. The CSSs shall be reframed considering the state specific needs. Steps shall be taken to reduce burden of CSSs on LSGIs.

vii. Devolution index needs to be given at most importance by assigning appropriate weight to devolution index in the allocation formula.

References

Alok, V.N. and P.K. Chaubey (2010). *Panchayats in India: Measuring Devolution by States*. New Delhi: Macmillan.

Anon (2009). *Fiscal Decentralisation and Local Governance: Course Material*. Monograph. Atlanda: Andrew Young School of Policy Studies, Georgia State University.

Bahl, Roy (2008). *Fiscal Decentralisation and Local Governance: Course Material*. Monograph. Atlanda: Andrew Young School of Policy Studies, Georgia State University.

Government of India (2009). *Thirteenth Finance Commission 2010-2015*. Ministry of Finance, New Delhi: 13th Finance Commission.

Government of Kerala (1997). *Report of the Decentralisation of Powers: S.B. Sen Committee Report*. Volume 1.

Shaheena, P. and Isaac, Thomas T.M (2013). "Awards of Finance Commissions and Local Government Finances", *Economic and Political Weekly* (forthcoming).

———. (2007). "Fiscal Devolution to Local Self Governments and the Finance Commissions", National Seminar on *Democracy, Decentralisation, and Participatory Development in Kerala: A Decade Beyond*. April 24-25. Thiruvananthapuram.

OECD (2013). *Fiscal Decentralisation Database*. website.

Vijayanand, S.M. (2009). *Kerala: A Case Study of Classical Democratic Decentralisation*. Thrissur, Kerala: Kerala Institute of Local Administration (KILA).

19 Fiscal Transfers to Local Bodies

Andhra Pradesh Experience

M. Gopinath Reddy

Introduction

In recent times there is an increasing realisation that genuine decentralisation leads to development. It is also felt that decentralisation of power to the local units of government and management is one of the best ways of empowering people, promoting public participation and increasing efficiency. Decentralisation can help mobilise resources, introduce locally and regionally diverse solutions and promote equitable growth by bringing the poor into mainstream development.

It is also often argued that decentralisation is a more effective and efficient framework for delivering pro-poor programmes. The perceived benefits of decentralisation range from stimulation of economic growth and alleviation of rural poverty to strengthening civil society and reducing the responsibilities of the centre (Manor, 1999). It was observed that project costs are four times higher in centralised systems when compared to decentralised systems. Besides, asset maintenance is much better in the decentralised systems (Bardhan, 1996). Decentralisation with its potential benefits coupled with the declining legitimacy of centralised systems has attracted support from a diverse range of ideological schools. While decentralised systems are found to be superior in terms of intra-regional targeting efficiency, their delivery systems target better in low poverty regions and not as well in high poverty regions (Bardhan and Mookherjee, 2000).

In view of the importance of fiscal transfer to local bodies, the present paper briefs to understand the experience of Andhra Pradesh with regard to fiscal transfers to local bodies. The paper is organised in four sections besides the introduction and concluding sections. It discusses the status of devolution funds, functions and functionaries (3Fs) in major states of India *vis-á-vis* Andhra Pradesh and focuses on PRIs (panchayati raj Institutions) and their role in CSS (Centrally Sponsored Schemes) in several and key flagship programmes in particular. Further, it analyses the status of local finances in Andhra Pradesh, in particular the constitution of State Finance Commissions (SFCs) and their recommendations. The paper is primarily based on secondary information besides some primary data.

Status of Devolution of Funds, Functions and Functionaries: All India Scenario

It is realised that, decentralisation to rural local governments is meaningful only when the *panchayats* have adequate untied funds to provide the public services assigned to them. Assignment of adequate and appropriate revenue sources to rural local governments is extremely important in the Indian context. The inability to assign potent revenue sources has led to local governments carrying on unfunded mandates and this has resulted in poor service delivery. Inadequate assignments combined with low levels of effort by the rural local governments have led to high levels of transfer dependence and low fiscal autonomy (Rao and Rao, 2004).

Article 243G of the Constitution empowers *panchayats* to function as institutions of self-government for the purposes of preparing plans and implementing schemes for economic development and social justice in their respective areas for various matters, including those listed in the 11th Schedule which is merely illustrative and indicative.[1] Unlike the division of

1. 11th Schedule lists 29 Functions (Core functions: drinking water; roads, culverts, bridges, ferries, waterways, and other means of communication; rural electrification, including distribution of electricity; health and sanitation, including hospitals, primary health centres, and dispensaries; maintenance of community assets. Welfare functions: rural housing; non-conventional energy sources; poverty alleviation programmes; education, including primary and secondary schools; technical training and vocational education; adult and informal education; libraries; cultural activities; family welfare; woman and child development; social welfare, including welfare of the handicapped and mentally retarded; welfare of the weaker sections, and in particular, of the scheduled castes (SC) and scheduled tribes (ST); Public distribution system; agriculture and allied functions: agriculture, including agricultural extension; land improvement, implementation of land reforms, land consolidation, and soil conservation; minor irrigation, water management, and watershed development; animal husbandry, dairying, and poultry; fisheries; social forestry and farm forestry; minor forestry and farm forestry; minor forest produce; fuel and fodder; markets and

contd...

powers and functions enumerated in the Union List and State List, no clear demarcation exists between the state and *panchayats*. It is for the state legislature to make laws regarding the devolution of powers and functions to the *panchayats*. Almost all states and UTs (union territories) claim that they have transferred responsibilities in varying degrees to the *panchayats*, by enacting laws in conformity with the Constitutional Amendment Act (CAA). However, the functional domain of *panchayats* pertains only to traditional civic functions in several states.

Another challenge before the state government has been the allocation of activities to the appropriate tier of the *panchayat* system. Traditionally, the lowest-level *panchayat*—the village *panchayat*—has been the most active in almost all states. Generally, the village *panchayats* carry out major functions, including core functions, whereas intermediate and district *panchayats* in most states are allotted supervisory functions or act mainly as executing agents for the state government (Jha, 2004).

When the authority and power in respect of a certain activity is transferred from the state to the *panchayats*, the latter should have the prerogative of making 'decisions', in respect of planning and implementation of such activity. In the sphere of devolution of responsibilities to lower levels of governance, some important principles should be kept in view. In the first place, the principle of 'subsidiarity' needs to be given adequate attention. The principle of subsidiarity postulates that any function which can be performed by a lower tier, should be handled by that tier alone and not by any higher tier of PRI. Second, the state government should not unilaterally withdraw responsibilities and powers already granted to the *panchayats* without adequate justification and prior consultation with the latter. Third, responsibilities, authorities and powers granted to the *panchayats* should be extremely specific, clear and simple in order to be comprehended by the *panchayats*. Lastly, whenever, functions and responsibilities are transferred to the *panchayats*, it should be ensured that the necessary funds, functionaries and freedom in decision-making also accompany such transfer (Government of India, 2001).

...contd...

fairs; industries: small-scale industries, including food processing industries; *khadi*, village, cottage industries) that PRIs are mandated to have control and commensurate resources need to be allocated to discharge these functions.

Keeping the above framework in mind of the CAA, the status of devolution of functions, funds and functionaries has been analysed across major states of India (Table 19.1).

Table 19.1

Transfer of Subjects and its Coverage Under Activity Mapping: Few Indian Major States

State	*Transfer of Subjects through Legislation*	*Subjects Covered under Activity Mapping*
Andhra Pradesh[2]	17 Subjects	9 Subjects
Karnataka	29 Subjects	29 Subjects
Kerala	26 Subjects	26 Subjects
Bihar	25 Subjects	25 Subjects
Madhya Pradesh	23 Subjects	23 Subjects

Source: Ministry of Panchayat Raj (MoPR), Govt of India (2006).

Devolution Index for Major States

Further, a recent survey by the Indian Institute of Public Administration (IIPA, 2010) has updated the Devolution Index regularly done by National Council for Applied Economic Research (NCEAR) for the years 2006-07, 2007-08 and 2008-09. IIPA's survey constructs an index[3] for all the 23 states including Andhra Pradesh. The four dimensional sub-indices and the composite devolution index for important states is presented in Table 19.2 and Figure 19.1.

2. Latest Position: A Task Force constituted under the special Chief Secretary for Activity Mapping has prepared detailed formulations. Draft Government Orders incorporating activity mapping in accordance with the recommendations of the committee are under the consideration of a Group of Ministers for finalisation. After the completion of these discussions, departments have been directed to finalise the Government Orders for issue.
3. The index covered parameters such as: functions (D2), finances (D3) and functionaries (D4) besides using 'framework' (D1) as the fourth dimension to the existing 3F structure. The 'framework' dimension looked at four mandatory provisions, *viz.*, establishing the State Election Commission (SFCs), holding regular *panchayat* elections, establishing State Finance Commissions (SFCs) at regular intervals and getting up District Planning Committees (DPC) (Alok and Chaubey, 2010).

Table 19.2

Devolution Index (D) and Sub-indices

Rank	*States/UTs*	D_1	D_2	D_3	D_4	D
1	Kerala	92.59	80.76	69.62	61.25	74.73
2	Karnataka	90.74	77.95	56.11	64.08	69.45
3	Tamil Nadu	89.63	77.11	58.76	49.58	67.06
4	West Bengal	96.30	70.90	61.56	46.25	66.51
5	Maharashtra	73.52	65.52	62.78	44.17	61.49
6	Madhya Pradesh	74.44	63.52	53.50	54.17	59.78
7	Gujarat	54.44	59.78	51.56	44.58	53.07
8	Andhra Pradesh	70.74	45.01	53.77	35.83	50.10
National Average		69.37	47.76	36.65	37.40	45.04

Source: IIPA Survey; Alok and Chaubey, 2010.

Figure 19.1

Overall Devolution Index

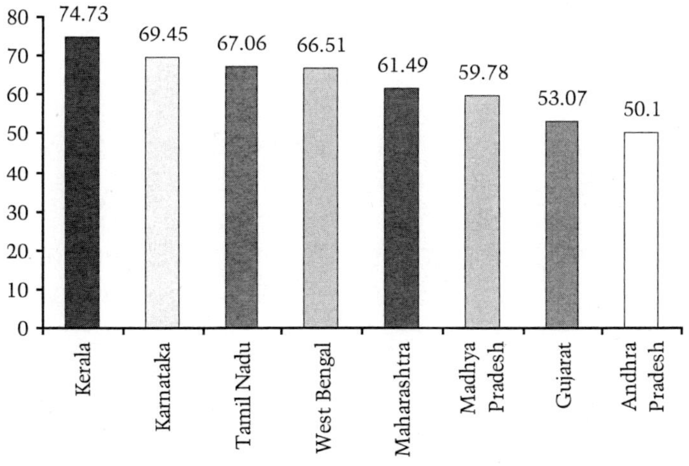

Source: IIPA Survey; Alok and Chaubey, 2010.

It is clear from the Table 19.2 and Figure 19.1 that Kerala is ranked first with value close to 75 per cent followed by Karnataka (69.5), Tamil Nadu (68.9), West Bengal (66.5). The scores of Maharastra and Madhya Pradesh are lower around 60 per cent whereas Gujarat and Andhra Pradesh scores are above 50 per cent.

Dependence on fiscal transfers could reduce fiscal autonomy and if the transfers are conditional and purpose specific, it could reduce the autonomy of local governments to allocate resources according to their own priorities.

It is a general perception that *panchayats* are financially and technically under equipped to perform even the core functions, much less the welfare functions and other economic functions related to agriculture and industries. Hence, many of the core functions that traditionally belonged to *panchayats*—drinking water, rural roads, street lighting, sanitation, primary health, and so forth—have not been transferred fully in some states and are being performed by the line departments of the state government or the parallel parastatals. As a result, the per capita total expenditure of *panchayats* remains abysmally low in all states except Andhra Pradesh, Chhattisgarh, Goa, Gujarat, Karnataka, Kerala, Maharashtra and Tamil Nadu.

The power of *panchayats* to impose taxes was considered imperative to be enshrined in the Constitution under Article 243H, to impart certainty, continuity, and strength to *panchayats*.

Devolution of taxes to *panchayats* can easily be linked with the activities assigned to them, which vary from state to state. From various lists including the list of the 11th Schedule, certain basic functions could be said to be in the exclusive domain of *panchayats*. Even these essential services require huge funds. To this end, the devolution of taxes to the three tiers of the *panchayats* needs to be linked to activity mapping for the devolution of functions and functionaries.

It is clear from the above data that proceeds from internal sources (own revenues) constitute a very insignificant share to the *panchayat* pool, when seen against the background of states own revenue sources during 2005-2008. Kerala stands first with 2.28 per cent followed by Andhra Pradesh (1.38%), Maharastra (1.15%), whereas *panchayats*' share for all states stands at 0.83 per cent. In other words, *panchayats* rely more on fiscal transfers from the state governments in the form of shared taxes and grants.

Table. 19.3

Own Revenue of Panchayats (All Tiers) as Percentage of Respective State Own Revenue of Selected States

(₹ crore)

No.	State	Sum of Own Revenues (2005-2008)	States Own Revenue (2005-2008)	Own Revenue of Panchayats as % of State Own Revenue
1.	Andhra Pradesh	415.4	30057.0	1.38
2.	Gujarat	111.5	22986.6	0.49
3.	Karnataka	198.0	26419.8	0.75
4.	Kerala	292.7	12824.4	2.28
5.	Madhya Pradesh	56.4	13070.3	0.43
6.	Maharashtra	582.3	50523.1	1.15
7.	Tamil Nadu	258.5	30014.6	0.86
	All States	2610.6	313749.3	0.83

Source: MoPR and IIPA, 2011-12.

PRIs and Centrally Sponsored Schemes

In the recent years, centrally sponsored programmes have come to dominate the *panchayat* resources in a majority of the states. Even though they add to the financial resources of the *panchayats*, these are mostly tied funds and PRIs do not have much discretion over its spending.

The Union Government, through the state governments, provides a majority of *panchayat* finances in most states. These grant-based transfers from the Planning Commission or Union Ministries are made in the form of CSSs. These schemes are quite large in number. Many pertain to the 29 subjects being implemented by different ministries and departments of the Union government. The viability of many schemes has been questioned time and again.

Substantial tied funds are being transferred to the *panchayats* through the CSSs and ACAs (additional central assistance). For long, the CSS transfers were administered and utilised mainly by the line departments. In recent years, the *panchayats* are being increasingly recognised as implementing institutions for the plan schemes of line ministries. The most important of these is the Mahatma Gandhi National Rural Employment Guarantee Act (MGNREGA), where the *panchayats* at the district, intermediate and village levels have been given specific responsibilities as principal authorities for planning and implementation.

Table 19.4

Allocation of Each Scheme that Entails a Role of the Panchayats

(₹ crore)

Scheme	*2004-05*	*2008-09*
National Rural Employment Guarantee Scheme/SGRY	10000	16000
National Rural Health Mission (NRHM)	-	11974
Mid Day Meal	1507	8000
Sarva Shiksha Abhiyan (SSA)	4754	13000
Pradhan Mantri Gram Sadak Yojana (PMGSY)	2468	7530
Accelerated Rural Drinking Water Supply Programme (ARDWSP)	2900	7300
Integrated Child Development Scheme (ICDS)	1934	5665
Indira Awas Yojana (IAY)	2500	5400
Swarnjayanti Gram Swarozgar Yojana (SGSY)	1000	2150
Rajiv Gandhi Grameen Vidyutikaran Yojana (RGGVY)	-	5055
Backward Region Grant Fund (BRGF)	-	4670

Source: IIPA (2009); Draft Joint Memorandum on behalf of *panchayats* to the 13th Finance Commission (ThFC) prepared by a Technical Committee of the Ministry of Panchayati Raj (Chairman: V. Ramachandran).

Since 2004, allocations to the programmes entailing the involvement of the *panchayats* have shown a substantial growth. It is a good augury that the institutional mechanisms tend to provide centrality to the *panchayats* in their planning and implementation.

The National Development Council's Empowered Committee on Panchayati Raj Issues, comprising several state Ministers of Panchayati Raj and chaired by Mr Mani Shanker Aiyar, the then Minister of Panchayati Raj, had in 2008 submitted their Report unanimously recommending a host of steps for promoting the centrality of PRIs, that is, inclusive governance for inclusive growth. Three years on, the Planning Commission is still to submit the Report for ratification to the National Development Council (Aiyar, n.d.). It is also mentioned by the Second Administrative Reforms Commission (ARC) that the schemes taken up under CSS programmes also need to find a place in the overall development plan of the *panchayat* body. While some of the schemes do give a crucial role to the PRIs in their implementation, some bypass them and create separate structures. Even the schemes which allow the participation of *panchayats*, often do not give them enough flexibility in decision-making. Such flexibility is essential to take care of the local specificities, which strait-jacketed schemes designed from above cannot accommodate. Further, a Second ARC mentions that parallel bodies created by conditions of CSSs should be wound up and merged with standing committees of the PRIs. Some of them may need to have organic linkage with the PRIs. (Second ARC Sixth Report, 2007).

Status of Local Finances: Andhra Pradesh Experience

The general fund budget or untied resources for the three tiers of local government derive from two sources: transfers from the state and local revenues. Transfers from the Centre have generally been low, sparking demands to the Finance Commission (FC) to revise these transfers, with little result (Reddy and Sreedevi, 2004). This reluctance to increase the level of transfers to local governments is partially attributed to the poor revenue-raising of local bodies in Andhra Pradesh, which in practice result in the bodies being under-funded. In recent years, partly because of fiscal constraints at the state level, CSSs have come to dominate planned expenditures even in what are traditionally state services such as education, health, and water and sanitation (in 2002-03, 58% of the planned spending on elementary education came from the Centre). CSSs are also an important source of funding for items that fall within the domain of PRIs (World Bank, 2006: 67).

In addition, analysis suggests that tax collection remains low because of both design and implementation issues. Although Gram Panchayats (GPs) have the power to levy taxes on some items, the lack of rules prescribing the maximum and minimum tax rates means there are no incentives for GPs to raise taxes and risk losing voters' support (Sarumathy, 1999), and they thus prefer to lobby for increased transfers. Additionally, low income levels in villages result in low tax revenue collection, so GPs income is meagre (Reddy and Sreedevi, 2004). This same situation is generated at the Mandal Parishad (MP) and Zilla Parishad (ZP) levels, with the additional constraint that the numbers of items for which the MPs and ZPs can levy taxes is limited.

In practice, therefore, internal revenue mobilisation at the *panchayat* level is weak, and *panchayats* are largely dependent on transfers from the state and Central government and have limited discretion regarding expenditure in Andhra Pradesh.

Establishment of SFCs and the Status of Its Reports

As mentioned above, *panchayats* rely more on fiscal transfers from the state governments in the form of shared taxes and grants. State taxes are shared according to the recommendations of the SFC. Constitution of the SFC at a regular interval of five years is a mandatory requirement for states. Besides tax sharing, the SFC is assigned the task of reviewing the financial position of *panchayats* and making recommendations on the assignment of various taxes, duties, tools, fees, and grants in-aid to be given to *panchayats* from the consolidated fund of the states (Alok, 2008).

The First SFC in Andhra Pradesh was constituted in 1995, which recommended that 39.24 per cent of the states revenue (both tax and non-tax) should be devolved to local bodies at the ratio of 70 per cent to PRIs and 30 per cent to ULBs (urban local bodies), respectively. The Report recommended that provisions related to percentage of devolution may be incorporated in the Andhra Pradesh Panchayati Raj Act. The SFC recommended categorisation of *panchayats* as advanced, ordinary, backward and tribal with weightage to be suggested by the Planning Department to measure the rate of development.

(i) A *panchayat* classified as backward gets 1.66 times the amount given to an 'ordinary' *panchayat*.

(ii) A tribal *Panchayat* gets 2.66 times the amount given to ordinary *panchayat*

(iii) An 'advanced *panchayat* gets 0.66 times state amount given to an ordinary *panchayat*

It is ascertained that the recommendations of the First SFC regarding sharing of taxes, duties, fees and grants to PRIs were not accepted. However, in compliance with the recommendations of the First SFC, the Second SFC was set up on 1998.

The Second SFC recommended a total additional devolution of ₹ 1793.94 crore, which amounted to 10.39 per cent of the total tax and non-tax revenues of the state, including the share of central taxes. Of this amount, 6.76 per cent was recommended to go to rural bodies and 3.63 per cent to urban bodies. Regarding the vertical sharing formula between the three levels of *panchayats*, the Second SFC recommended that GPs be given 50 per cent, MPs 30 per cent and ZPs 20 per cent.

Grants to *Panchayats*

The recommendations of Second SFC regarding grants to PRIs are as follows:

- The 11th Finance Commission (EFC) grant of ₹ 152.05 crore for providing civic amenities to GPs and municipal bodies, data bank, maintenance of accounts etc., might be distributed as per the formula of the SFC.
- Construction of office building for 177 *mandals* that did not have office buildings might be taken up and completed in a period of 3 years by allocating ₹ 12 crore per annum.
- Provision ought to be made of ₹ 2.41 and ₹ 2.07 crore respectively per annum as grants for providing toilet and drinking water facilities in schools.
- An amount of ₹ 6.50 crore ought to be provided per annum for special repairs to school buildings of PRIs.
- ₹ 4.88 crores ought to be provided per annum for maintenance of office buildings of MPs, ZPs and other buildings.
- A grant equivalent to 5 per cent of salary ought to be provided to meet the additional expenditure due to pay and DA (dearence allowance) revision.

The Second SFC recommended that the revenue foregone by the PRIs due to abolition of land cess should be given to them as compensation and distributed on population basis. It recommended the following distribution for transfer of ₹ 200 crore to PRIs on account of different state revenues.

No.	*Name of the Local Body*	*₹ in crore*
1	Zilla Parishad	40
2	Mandal Parishad	25
3	Zilla Parishad	135

There is no information as to whether these recommendations were accepted. According to the figures available on the transfer of funds to *panchayats*, it does not seem as if they have been accepted.

Constitution of Third SFC

As per the G.O. Ms.No. 13 (P.R & R.D Dept., dated: 16-1-2003) Government of Andhra Pradesh (GoAP) constituted the Third SFC under the Chairmanship of Prof D.L.Narayana with a condition that the Commission shall make its report available by 15-7-2004 covering a period of five years commencing from 1st April, 2005. The Commission could not submit their report for want of information from PRIs and municipal bodies and requested the Government for extension of one year period beyond 15-7-2004, but the Government rejected the request of the Commission. As per the G.O.Ms.No:322 (P.R & R.D Dept., dated: 8-10-2003), the Government re-constituted the Third SFC under the Chairmanship of Prof B. Satyanarayana with a period of 3 years from the date of commencement of the Commission i.e., up to 28-12-2007. The term of the re-constituted Commission was extended up to 31-01-2008 as per the G.O.Ms.No:390 (P.R & R.D Dept., dated: 23-12-2009).

The functions of the Commission, among other things, were to suggest the ways and means and the resources to augment the financial position of local bodies namely GPs, Mandal Praja Parishads, Zilla Praja Parishads, Municipal Councils, Notified Areas and Municipal Corporations in the state.

The report of the Third SFC covers RLBs (rural local bodies) coming under the Panchayati Raj Department and ULBs coming under the Municipal Administration Department. The recommendations of the Third SFC were examined by a Committee constituted as per the G.O.Rt. No:379 (P.R & R.D Dept., dated:10-3-2008). The Committee with the following Members examined the report of the Third SFC and suggested to the Government various steps to be taken on the recommendations of the Commission and various measures to improve the financial position of local bodies keeping in view the ways and means of the Government.

Minister (PR): Chairman; Minister (RD): Member; Minister (Home): Member; Minister (Revenue): Member; Minister (Law): Member; Prl. Secretary (RD): Member; Minister (MA & UD): Member; Minister (Finance): Member; Prl. Secretary (Finance): Member; Prl. Secretary (RD): Member; Prl. Secretary (MA & UD): Member; Spl. C.S. (PR): Member-Convener.

The Committee was requested to examine the report of the Third SFC in detail and suggest various steps to be taken by the Government on the recommendations of the Commission within 3 months. The Committee Report was not made public as the Committee constituted for the purpose was seized of the matter.

In Andhra Pradesh, as compared to other southern Indian states, the GPs income is very meager. District-wise classification of GPs as per income reveals this dismal picture more glaringly. Out of 21,809 GPs in Andhra Pradesh, a total of 13,455 (61.7%) GPs have an annual income of between ₹ 40,000 and 1,000,000; 13.7 per cent of GPs have income between ₹ 1,00,000 and ₹ 2,00,000; 6.2 per cent have between ₹ 2,00,000 and ₹ 3,00,000; 5.8 per cent between ₹ 3,00,000 and ₹ 4,00,000; 3.7 per cent between ₹ 4,00,000 and below ₹ 5,00,000; 4.3 per cent between ₹ 5,00,000 and below 10,00,000 and 1.3 per cent between ₹ 10,00,000 and below ₹ 15,00,000 and lastly 1.7 per cent of GPs have above ₹ 15,00,000. The income of the GPs mentioned in Table 19.5 includes income from all sources. One can imagine with such meager sources of income for a majority of the *panchayats*, what kind of developmental needs of the people can be meaningfully addressed. The income is not sufficient even to attend to core functions of the *panchayats* leave alone the large array of functions mentioned in the 11th Schedule of the CAA. In contrast to Andhra Pradesh village *panchayat* resources, in Tamil Nadu, the picture is better with as many as 7,400 GPs out of 12,618 *panchayats* having income between ₹ 1 lakh and 5 lakh and as many as 3,180 having income between ₹ 5,00,000 and ₹ 10,00,000. A substantial number (nearly 1,500) have income between

Table 19.5

District-wise Classification of Gram Panchayats as per Income in Andhra Pradesh

No.	Name of the District	Total Gram Panchayats	Upto 40,000	Above 40,000 below 1,00,000	Above 1,00,000 below 2,00,000	Above 2,00,000 below 3,00,000	Above 3,00,000 below 4,00,000	Above 4,00,000 below 5,00,000	Above 5,00,000 below 10,00,000	Above 10,00,000 below 15,00,000	Above 15,00,000
1	2	3	4	5	6	7	8	9	10	11	12
1	Srikakulam	1101	786	162	23	19	20	21	57	5	8
2	Vizianagaram	928	451	276	126	26	22	7	15	0	5
3	Visakhapatnam	944	215	88	126	220	170	71	14	22	18
4	East Godavari	1012	174	176	131	129	133	112	85	35	37
5	West Godavari	887	50	105	251	153	91	59	103	46	29
6	Krishna	972	38	165	239	114	97	74	179	25	41
7	Guntur	1022	71	129	260	203	173	94	68	11	13
8	Prakasam	1043	428	364	147	35	11	10	12	8	28
9	Nellore	961	383	371	133	24	11	10	16	7	6
10	Kadapa	808	345	79	208	76	56	15	11	11	7
11	Kurnool	898	379	306	77	42	32	13	20	11	18
12	Ananthapur	1001	717	195	18	20	10	8	24	4	5
13	Chittoor	1380	760	367	125	42	21	11	29	10	15
14	Karimnagar	1194	446	269	153	116	74	90	26	8	12
15	Adilabad	866	701	33	29	28	42	17	12	4	0
16	Khammam	770	172	157	184	108	59	40	36	5	9
17	Warangal	1014	88	255	249	120	100	52	96	18	36
18	Mahabubnagar	1348	1181	80	62	1	1	2	6	2	13
19	Medak	1059	631	284	73	17	11	5	10	6	22
20	Ranga Reddy	705	213	65	86	60	78	75	60	38	30
21	Nalgonda	1178	487	440	123	46	21	8	33	5	15
22	Nizamabad	718	124	249	168	71	51	15	28	8	4
	Total	21809	8840	4615	2991	1670	1284	809	940	289	371

Source: Commissioner of Panchayati Raj, Government of Andhra Pradesh.

₹ 10 lakh or 25 lakh. (Table 19.6). In Karnataka, the Government has developed a detailed range of activity mapping with the responsibility of implementing wide ranging development schemes. As a result, the average budget for a GP in Karnataka has increased to ₹ 35 lakh. The state government has transferred 435 plan and 230 non-plan items in about 26 development sectors to the *panchayats* (Babu and Sivanna, 2008).

Table 19.6

Income-wise Classification of Village Panchayats in Tamil Nadu (Average Income of 3 Years from 2003-04 to 2005-06)

No.	*Income Range (In Rupees)*	*No. of Village Panchayats*
1.	Up to 50,000	10
2.	50,000–1 lakh	178
3.	1–5 lakh	7,422
4.	5–10 lakh	3,181
5.	10–25 lakh	1,489
6.	25–50 lakh	252
7.	50 lakh–1 crore	60
8.	1–3 crore	24
9.	Above 3 crore	2
	Total	12,618

Source: Policy Note 2007-08, Government of Tamil Nadu, Rural Development and Panchayat Raj Department.

The case of Kerala, where PRI funds (GPs) are said to be robust and stable is presented for the year 2010-11 in Table 19.7.

In the state, the total available fund with the GPs in the year 2010-11 was calculated as ₹ 281784.40 lakh and out of which ₹ 179571.00 lakh (63.73%) was from 'Non-plan grant transferred by state to *panchayats* untied to any scheme', ₹ 49779.00 lakh (17.67%) was under the head of 'Non-plan grant transferred by state to *panchayats* tied to schemes', ₹ 46742.41 lakh (16.59%) was from '*panchayats* own revenue including collection from rental, lease etc.', ₹ 4694.00 lakh (1.67%) was under the head of 'Plan grant transferred by the state to the *panchayats* tied to schemes', ₹ 500.00 lakh (0.18%) was mentioned as 'fund from slaughter house' and ₹ 498.00 lakh (0.18%) was mentioned as 'fund from burning and burial ground'.

Table. 19.7

Fund Availability with the Gram Panchayats in Kerala, 2010-11

(₹ *in lakh)*

No	*Break Up of Revenue Financial Year 2010-11*	
	Revenue transferred to *panchayats* by state	
1	*Panchayats* own revenue including collection from rental, lease, etc.	46742.41
2	Plan grant transferred by the state to the *panchayats* untied to schemes	0
3	Plan grant transferred by state to *panchayats* tied to any scheme	4694
4	Non-plan grant transferred by state to *panchayats* untied to schemes	179571
5	Non-plan grant transferred by state to *panchayats* tied to any scheme	49799
6	Any others (Slaughter House for GP)	500
7	Any others (Burning and Burial Ground for GP)	498
	Total	281804.41

Source: Data Furnished by the Kerala State Local Self Govt. Department.

We now illustrate cases of a few *panchayats* in selected districts of Andhra Pradesh.

Table. 19.8

Income Details of Two Gram Panchayats in Nalgonda District:

A. Name of the Panchayat: Patelgudem

No	*Sources of Income*	*Details of the Income (in Rupees)*
1	Stamp duty	32,000.00
2	Population grant	4,200.00
3	President honorarium	1,200.00
4	Tax grant	15,000.00
5	Own source (House tax, tap tax, and land revenue)	56,000.00
6	ThFC grant	50,900.00
7	SFC grant	16,900.00
	Total	1,76,200.00

Source: Author's own field work.

B. Name of the Panchayat: Tangutoor

No	Sources of Income	Details of the Income (in Rupees)
1	Stamp duty	50,000.00
2	Population grant	7,500.00
3	President honorarium	1,200.00
4	Tax grant	12,000.00
5	Own source (House tax, tap tax, and land revenue)	39,000.00
6	ThFC grant	45,900.00
7	SFC grant	13,646.00
	Total:	1,68,346.00

Source: Author's own field work.

Table. 19.9

Income Details of Two Gram Panchayats in Ananthapur District

A. Name of the Panchayat: Boginapally

Sl. No	Sources of Income	Details of the Income (in Rupees)
1	Stamp duty	36,782.00
2	Population grant	2,120.00
3	President honorarium	900.00
4	Tax grant	8,632.00
5	Own source (House tax, tap tax, and land revenue)	10,521.00
6	ThFC grant	42,250.00
7	SFC grant	6,911.00
	Total:	1,08,116.00

Source: Author's own field work.

B. Name of the Panchayat: M.Cherlopally

Sl. No	Sources of Income	Details of the Income (in Rupees)
1	Stamp duty	23,400.00
2	Population grant	3,000.00
3	President honorarium	900.00
4	Tax grant	10,000.00
5	Own source (House tax, tap tax, and land revenue)	15,000.00
6	ThFC grant	35,600.00
	Total:	87,900.00

Source: Author's own field work.

It is evident from the above tables that village *panchayats'* income base is extremely meagre in Andhra Pradesh. In every *panchayat,* 30 to 40 per cent of the village *panchayat's* income is coming from ThFC and SFC grants. The resources of the village *panchayat* account for very little income. Unless the resource base is expanded, there is hardly any chance for the development public provisions.

Conclusion

Andhra Pradesh remains one of the 'decentralisation deficit' states in the country. Although on devolution index it scores 50 per cent, it is lagging behind all the southern states in India. Further, the picture is not encouraging when one observes the field level situation. Genuine devolution of 3Fs has still not taken place. Most of the recommendations of the First and Second SFC have not been accepted by the Government. Although DPC have been constituted, their functioning as agents for the preparation of comprehensive districts plans may be said to be poor and lacklustre. *Panchayats* are continued to be bypassed by Community Based Organisations (CBO) and line departments (Reddy, 2003). The functions enshrined in the 11th Schedule of the Constitution have not been fully entrusted to PRIs to plan and implement schemes at the grassroots level. As compared to the other southern states, the income base of village *panchayats* in Andhra Pradesh is very meager. Although centrality of PRIs institutions in the implementation of CSS is recognised in Andhra Pradesh, CSS are still mostly implemented by line departments. This goes against the spirit of CAA. Also, there should be provision for a separate *panchayat* line department in the state budget. Andhra Pradesh still has a long way to go in realising that PRIs need to be made genuine institutions of local self government for efficient service delivery.

References

Aiyar, Mani Shankar (n.d.). *Inclusive Governance for Inclusive Development: The History, Politics and Economics of Panchayat Raj.*

Alok, V.N. (2013). *Strengthening of Panchayats in India: Comparing Devolution across States—Empirical Assessment 2012-13.* Study sponsored by Ministry of Panchayati Raj (MoPR), Government of India. New Delhi- Indian Institute of Public Administration (IIPA). April.

————. (2012). *Devolution to Panchayats in India: Ranking Functional Environment at Sub-National Level—Empirical Assessment 2011-12.* Study sponsored by Ministry of Panchayati Raj (MoPR), Government of India. New Delhi- Indian Institute of Public Administration (IIPA). March.

————. (2008). "The Role of State Finance Commissions in Fiscal Decentralization in India", in M A Oommen (ed.), *Fiscal Decentralisation to Local Governments in India,* Newcastle: Cambridg Scholars Publishing.

Alok, V.N. and P.K. Chaubey (2010). *Panchayats in India: Measuring Devolution by States.* New Delhi: Macmillan.

Babu, Devendra M. and N. Sivanna (2008). "Finances of Rural Local Governments in Karnataka; Structure, Pattern and Policy Implications", Paper Presented at the conference on *Issues Before the Finance Commission: Empowering the Panchayati Raj Institutions.* December 22-23.

Bardhan, Pranab and Dilip Mookherjee (2000). "Capture and Governance at Local and National Levels., *American Economic Review* 90 (2): 135-39.

Bardhan, Pranab (1996). "Decentralized Development", *Indian Economic Review* XXXI(2): 139-56.

Government of India (2007). *Second Administrative Reforms Commission: Sixth Report—Local Governance.* October.

————. (2006). *Planning at the Grassroots Level: An Action Programme for the Eleventh Five Year Plan.* Report of the Expert Group. New Delhi: Ministry of Panchayati Raj.

————. (2001). *Report of the Working Group on 'Decentralised Planning and Panchayati Raj Institutions', for the Tenth Five-year Plan.* New Delhi: Ministry of Rural Development, Government of India.

IIPA (2009). Report of the Technical Committee of the Ministry of Panchayati Raj to prepare Draft Joint Memorandum on behalf of Panchayats to the 13th Finance Commission. New Delhi: Indian Institution of Public Administration (Chairman: V Ramachandran).

Jha, Shikha (2004). *Panchayats: Functions, Responsibilities, and Resources.* Paper commissioned by the National Institute of Rural Development (NIRD), Hyderabad on behalf of the 12th Finance Commission of India. January 23.

Manor, J. (1999). "The Political Economy of Democratic Decentralization", *Directions in Development Series.* Washington DC: World Bank.

Reddy, M. Gopinath (2003). "Status of Decentralised Local Bodies: Post-73rd Amendment Scenario", *Economic and Political Weekly* XXXVIII (12 and 13): 22-29, March.

Reddy, M. Gopinath and N. Sreedevi (2004). "Local Finances in Andhra Pradesh: A Situation Analysis", *Indian Journal of Public Administration* L(3): 829-39, July-September.

Rao, Govind and Vasanth Rao (2004). "Expanding the Resource Base of Panchayats: Augmenting Own Revenues", *Economic & Political Weekly*, January 26.

Sarumathy, M. (1999). "Andhra Pradesh", in R.C. Choudhury and S. P. Jain (eds.), *Patterns of Decentralised Governance in Rural India*. Vol. 1. Hyderabad: National Institute of Rural Development. pp.25-63.

Section VI: Panel Discussion

20 Issues Before Fourteenth Finance Commission

*A Panel Discussion**

A. Vaidyanathan

The Finance Commission's (FC) focus is on mitigating the differences between states in terms of administrative capacity and basic social amenities and services and the capacity to raise resources to address these deficiencies. Central plan assistance for states is for development programmes in their constitutional domain but within the framework of strategy and priorities of the national plan as approved by National Development Council (NDC). The distribution of total central assistance in each plan is determined on the basis of an agreed (modified Gadgil) formula which provides, to a limited extent, for a larger share of assistance to poorer states. A substantial and increasing part of central assistance is earmarked for several special programmes (such as basic literacy, health care, employment, rural and agricultural development, social protection) considered necessary to fulfil important national socio-economic objectives. The overall size of state plans and their sectoral and programme allocations are decided at the annual plan discussion between each state and the Planning Commission.

It is well-known that priorities of states are not in sync with those supposed to be the basis of the national plan. Therefore, the FC transfers and central plan assistance, being non-mandatory, are left to be decided by states. Political expediency makes the states reluctant to mobilise own resources for development activities that fall in their domain. Resources that they manage to mobilise are inadequate to maintain facilities already

* Chairman: Prof V. Vaidyanathan

Panellists: Sri V. Bhaskar, Prof M. Govinda Rao, Prof D.K. Srivastava, Prof Partha Mukhopadhyay and Dr Haseeb A. Drabu.

created and to manage them efficiently. At the same time, their propensity to expand the scope and scale of subsidies continues to grow. In many key areas new development programmes in sectors that are supposed to be their responsibility have come to depend on Centrally Sponsored Schemes (CSS).

States not only welcome the substantial volume of central funds available for their plans but also exert pressures to increase it. They have acquiesced in the expansion of CSS schemes despite reservations about their intrusion in the states' domain and for being too rigid to permit adaptation to local conditions. The size of state plans, their financing and the sectoral allocations, determined after discussions between their governments and the Planning Commission, are not mandatory. Actual allocations decided by the state governments according to their priorities invariably turn out to be different from approved plans. The Planning Commission has neither the authority nor the means to monitor the implementation of schemes. States are not only unwilling to provide information on physical progress of programmes/schemes, they also do not have an information system for collecting and verifying needed data (especially those which by their nature are small, localised and widely dispersed).

Because of these delays, inefficiencies and leakages in the state governments' use of resources, implementation of programmes have grown unchecked to their present alarming proportions. At present, it is impossible to even assess the magnitude and underlying reasons for all this, much less to enforce accountability or to plan corrective action. This is a systemic problem that covers both their own resources and those obtained from the Centre and therefore needs to be viewed in a wider perspective. For this purpose I would suggest that the discussion in this section be focussed on the following issues:

1. Lack of reliable and credible mechanism for objective monitoring of the level, content and quality of spending on different kinds of projects and achievement of physical targets. The scope and nature of such a system, the locus and modalities for implementing them. Whether to have administrative reporting or an empowered nodal monitoring agency in the government? Or the monitoring should be through an independent, continuing social audit?

2. Persuading/incentivising states to set up such systems and ensuring that the data are made available in the public domain.
3. Redesigning CSS for greater efficiency and accountability: rationalise schemes to avoid duplication, minimise soft elements (subsidies) and give states greater freedom and flexibility to adapt content and procedures to suit local conditions; ensure effective decentralisation of authority and resources for local development schemes, with mechanisms for maintenance and inspection of proper records, by elected *panchayats*.
4. More pro-active effort of the FC and Planning Commission to: (i) review whether and to what extent resources are used for objectives they are meant to achieve; (ii) consider renewal/ augmentation of transfers/assistance on the basis of actual achievements in these respects.
5. How to overcome the reluctance of states to provide the Centre reliable and validated data on the performance of their developmental programmes, especially those of high national priority and funded by the Centre. Should the Planning Commission be empowered to demand needed information/data from states and to verify the validity of information provided and/ or directly collect information?

These are some of the critical issues that need to be addressed to establish and nurture more transparent, healthier Centre-state financial relations and ensure effective management of public finances at all levels.

V. Bhaskar[1]

The terms of reference (ToR) of the Fourteenth Finance Commission (hereinafter FFC)[2] generally follow the pattern of the ToRs of the previous commissions. This paper examines four questions which will need to be considered by the FFC as it commences its work. The first question is, whether the FFC should confine itself to its constitutional mandate and not get distracted by other items in its ToR? Second, to provide a predictable incentive environment to states to improve their fiscal behaviour, should the Commission seek to develop incentive frameworks which will carry credibility with future commissions? Third, should the FFC encourage better fiscal performance in states more explicitly? Fourth, should the FFC provide fiscal headroom in its projections for accommodating unanticipated developments arising from uncertainty in the economic environment? These four questions may need to be examined by the FFC keeping in mind its diagnosis and prognosis of the present economic environment and the challenges being faced by the Centre and the states. These four questions may not be independent of each other, but adopting such an artifice enables laying out the ground for defining expectations from the FFC.

Only the Constitutional Mandate?

The FC is required to make recommendations consistent with sub-article 280(3) of the Constitution. This sub-article has five clauses. The first four of these clauses require that recommendations be made regarding (i) Extent and scope of vertical and horizontal devolution. (ii) Grants-in-aid of revenues to be provided to the states. (iii) Augmentation of the Consolidated Fund of the States to supplement the resources of the *panchayats* and the municipalities. (iv) These clauses, relating to intergovernmental finance, are the *raison d'être* of the Commission.

1. The author is grateful to V.L. Kelkar, Sumit Bose and an anonymous referee for insightful comments. The author thanks participants of the national seminar on "Centre-State Relations in Indian Fiscal Context" held at the Centre for Economic and Social Studies (CESS), Hyderabad on 5 November 2012 for their comments on a preliminary version of this article. The author also thanks P. Srinivasa Subrahmanyam (OSD), Finance Department, Government of Andhra Pradesh, for research assistance. The usual disclaimers apply. This paper is published in *Economic & Political Weekly* XLVIII(17), April 27, 2013.

2. Available at *http: //finmin.nic.in / press_ room / 2013 / Finance Commission Notification.pdf*

The fifth clause empowers the Commission to make additional recommendations on "any other matter referred to the Commission by the President in the interests of sound finance".

In Para 5 of its ToR, the FFC has been asked to review the state of finances, deficit and debt levels of the Union and the states, and suggest measures for maintaining a stable and sustainable fiscal environment including amending the Fiscal Responsibility and Budget Management (FRBM) Acts. The inclusion of this item in the ToR of the FFC is unassailable, being patently in the interests of sound finance.

However, this cannot be said of some other items which have crept into the ToR of the FFC. These inclusions seek justification by virtue of being part of the so-called "consideration items". Following precedent, Para 6 of the ToR of the FFC states, "In making these recommendations, the Commission shall have regard among other considerations to..." And a list of 11 items follows. These include issues like:

- The level of subsidies that are required with regard to the need for sustainable and inclusive growth, and equitable sharing of subsidies between the Central government and state governments.
- The need for insulating the pricing of public utility services like drinking water, irrigation, power and public transport from policy fluctuations through statutory provisions.
- The need to balance management of ecology, environment and climate change consistent with sustainable development.
- The need for making public sector enterprises competitive and market-oriented.
- Listing, disinvestment and relinquishing of non-priority enterprises.

Inclusion of these "consideration" items appear to be dictated more by an imperative to bring to closure on-going political debates on subsidies, cost recovery, environment protection and disinvestment rather than by the requirements of Article 280(3). There appears to be no constitutional authority for the inclusion of such "consideration" items in the ToR. Disregarding the extreme position that all such references can be tenuously linked to the interests of sound public finance, it can be argued that such mandates which have not been endorsed by the Constitution need not be taken into consideration at all by the FFC. However, it must be acknowledged that similar "consideration" items abound in the ToRs of earlier FCs.

Article 280(4) of the Constitution says, "The Commission shall determine their procedure and shall have such powers in the performance of their functions as Parliament may by law confer on them." This is further amplified by Section 8 of the Finance Commission (Miscellaneous Provisions) Act 1951, which provides that the Commissions shall determine their procedure and in the performance of their functions shall have all the powers of a civil court.

Thus, it is up to the Commission to set out the procedure by which it will fulfil its mandate outlined in Article 280(3). Undoubtedly, this procedure will and must include examination of many of the consideration items included in the FFC's ToR like the resources of the Centre and the states, their committed expenditure and the need for balancing the revenue account. It is however debatable whether the Commission need to be guided by all the consideration items, especially those items which do not have any explicit linkages with sound public finance

Historically, the ToR of the 1st Finance Commission did not include any consideration items. The ToRs of the 2nd to the 6th Finance Commissions confined the consideration items to the determination of the principles which should govern the grants-in-aid to states. From the 7th Finance Commission onwards, the consideration items started appearing in the ToRs as a broader swathe directed at influencing the commission's recommendations more expansively. This also led to successive Commissions recommending grants to address issues which were at best ancillary to their constitutional mandate. Some grants like the revenue deficit grant, the local bodies grant, the drought relief grant do fall within the core functions of the FC. However, other grants like the upgradation grant, the special problems grant, the health sector grants, the education sector grant may not fall under this core category. It may further be argued that award of these non-core grants can be considered redundant for two reasons. First, as revenue disparities and cost disabilities amongst states should already have been internalised by the Commission in its horizontal distribution formula, separate and distinct grants for upgradation and special problems may not be necessary. Second, costs like maintenance of roads and bridges should normally be subsumed in the overall non-plan revenue expenditure based on which the non-plan revenue deficit grant eligibility is worked out. A list of the non-core function grants awarded by various FCs in the past is listed in Table 20.1.

As can be seen in Table 20.1 the recommended outlay for grants to meet the "non-core" functions of the FC has been increasing linearly and steadily over the last six FCs. Disregarding this distraction to the commission's core mandate and resources, recommending such grants without any constitutional justification, merely because they find place in the ToR, also cuts into the fiscal space available for rule-based devolution to state governments.[3]

The consequential question which then arises is, should the FFC fulfil its constitutional duty as mandated under Article 280(3) with blinkers on, or devote equal attention to the "non-core" items, including those which have no explicit linkages with sound public finance? A commentator had urged the 13th Finance Commission (ThFC)[4] to treat such references in the ToR not mandated by the Constitution as a Protestant treats the biblical Apocrypha—consider it useful and good for reading but not necessarily to be followed.

On the other hand, there is an expectation from sitting governments that the FC champion systemic reform to provide additional lift to initiatives that have been unable to take off. Previous FCs have often fruitfully donned the mantle of a change agent. Through the adroit use of conditionality, the 12th Finance Commission (TwFC) successfully championed the cause of debt sustainability. The ThFC effectively championed reform in allocations to and utilisation of funds by local bodies. At present, there are a number of proposals relating to sound public finance which are hanging fire. These include the recommendations

3. The issue of the optimum mix of rule-based devolution and discretion-based grants to states as part of the FC's devolution process is not examined here.
4. B.P.R. Vithal's address to the Thirteenth Finance Commission, New Delhi, 3 May 2008.

Table 20.1

Allocation of Grants for Non-Core Functions by Different Finance Commissions

(₹ in crore)

No.	Finance Commission	Non-Core Function Grants		
		Item	Amount	Commission Total
1	7th	Upgradation	436.80	436.80
2	8th	Upgradation	967.33	
		Margin money grant	601.88	1,569.21
3	10th	Upgradation	1,362.50	
		Special problem	1,246.00	2,608.50
4	11th	Upgradation and special problems	4,972.63	4,972.63
5	12th	Health sector	5,887.08	
		Education	10,171.65	
		Roads and bridges	15,000.00	
		Buildings	5,000.00	
		Forests	1,000.00	
		Heritage conservation	625.00	
		State-specific grants	7,100.00	44,783.73
6	13th	Fiscal performance incentive	1,500.00	
		Elementary education	24,068.00	
		Improving outcomes	9,446.00	
		Environmental related	10,000.00	
		Roads and bridges maintenance	19,930.00	
		State-specific grants	27,945.00	
		GST compensation	50,000.00	
		For reduction of IMR	5,000.00	
		Renewable energy grant	5,000.00	1,52,889.00

Source: Reports of the various Finance Commissions.

of the Rangarajan Committee on improving management of public expenditure; the Chaturvedi Committee on the treatment of CSS and the Punchhi Commission on centre-state fiscal relations. Most states support their recommendations and look forward for their early implementation. No time line has been indicated by the GoI in this regard. The FFC could take a stand on endorsing these recommendations to accelerate their implementation. However, whether the FFC should give a finding on issues like the level of subsidies to be adopted and their sharing between the Union and the states—essentially a political issue—is open to debate.

Similarly, the pricing policy of public utilities can be seen to be within the ambit of the respective sector regulators.

Should the FFC Seek to Develop Incentive Frameworks to Improve States' Fiscal Behaviour?

The fact that traditionally all its recommendations[5] have been accepted by the Centre has been a powerful motivator for successive FCs to attempt to induce change in the fiscal behaviour of state governments through the use of incentives. Such incentives cannot be applied to the devolution component of the FC's award in view of the constitutional imperative of Article 280(3)(a). However, these incentives have been applied to determine eligibility for grants awarded by the Commission under Article 280(3)(b).

Such incentives can be put in place through two avenues:

(i) The use of conditionalities to determine eligibility of a state for a predetermined grant amount earmarked for it.

(ii) The use of forward-looking indicators (hereinafter FLI) to determine at a future date a particular state's share of a pre-determined lump sum provision.

The ThFC was the first to use FLI to determine at a future date a state's share of a lump sum provision made for a grant depending upon its performance up to that future date. These FLIs were to be used for determining the eligibility for three grants. These were:

(i) Grant for goods and services tax (GST) compensation: ₹ 50,000 crore.

(ii) Grant for reduction in Infant Mortality Rate (IMR): ₹ 5,000 crore.

(iii) Grant for renewable energy: ₹ 5,000 crore.

The total allocation for FLI grants was thus ₹ 60,000 crore of a total grant of ₹ 2,58,581 crore, i.e., 23 per cent. If the GST grant (which was abortive) were to be excluded, this figure reduces to only 4 per cent. This modest beginning in the use of FLIs has not yet generated adequate experience on its relevance and utility.

---

5. With limited exceptions proving the rule.

Criticism and Counter-Criticism

The use of conditionalities has often been criticised on the following grounds:

(i) They militate against the constitutional mandate in Article 275(1) that grants-in-aid be made to "such states as Parliament may determine, to be in need of assistance." This injunction requires that the award of grants should be solely focused on meeting the present needs of states and should not be shackled by the use of conditionalities.

(ii) They are used by FCs asymmetrically. Conditionalities have been imposed only on state governments. However, no conditionalities have been imposed nor can they be imposed by FCs on GoI to change its fiscal behaviour, as there is no enforcement mechanism available. In respect of the GoI, FCs merely substitute pious expressions of hope regarding what is expected of the Centre. In respect of the states, however, the GoI diligently monitors the compliance of states and punishes non-compliance of not only FC conditionalities but also FRBM commitments, by withholding the FC grants allocated to them.[6]

(iii) Expectations of the FC regarding performance of state governments are enshrined in a specific conditionality framework which often overshoots both the capacity and the willingness of the respective states to meet these expectations.

(iv) The amount of the grant is often not substantial enough to incentivise states to attempt the quantum leap into a reform orbit. For example, the water sector grant of the ThFC aggregates to only ₹ 5,000 crore across all states. Excluding Uttar Pradesh which was allocated ₹ 1,364 crore, this allocation does not exceed ₹ 368 crore (Maharashtra) for any state over a

---

6. Which is why the reference in the FFC's ToR requiring it to recommend "incentives and disincentives for States for observing the obligations laid down in the Fiscal Responsibility and Budget Management Acts" appears disjointed. This asymmetrical mandate ignores the fact that GoI is already monitoring the state's implementation of their respective FRBM Acts. In any case, it is not clear why incentives are needed for implementing a law duly passed by the State Legislature.

period of five years, i.e., an average of ₹ 74 crore per annum. For a state with an annual budget exceeding ₹ 1,00,000 crore, the fiscal cost of surrendering this grant evidently pales before the political cost of accessing it.

(v) Conditionalities are binary in nature. They do not allow for flexibility and gradualism in their compliance by states and they thus deter performance.

On the other hand, there are a number of arguments in favour of the application of conditionalities for disbursal of a grant. These include:

(i) Though Article 275(1) may not allow for the use of conditionalities, this does not preclude their application by FCs which can use the relatively greater flexibility afforded by Article 280(3)(b) which does not impose such limitations.

(ii) The fact that conditionalities cannot be imposed on the Centre and are therefore asymmetrical does not provide adequate justification for not applying them to states. Further, it can be argued that the ToR of the Commission itself is asymmetric dealing with only the sharing of the taxes levied, collected and appropriated by the Centre and not that of the states.

(iii) The use of conditionalities by FCs perhaps needs to be guided by the exhortation, "A man's reach should exceed his grasp; or what a Heaven is for?"[7] And a number of Heavens are often reachable. The seemingly stringent conditionalities put in place for drawing down the local bodies performance grant by the ThFC were criticised as over-ambitious and unattainable by critics. Nearly three years after submission of the ThFC report, a number of states have complied with these tough conditions and become eligible for the performance grant, concomitantly bringing in significant reform into the operating environment of local bodies.

(iv) The FC being a temporary body must ensure that verification of compliance with conditionalities can be undertaken in as objective a manner as possible especially as this will have

7. Robert Browning; Andrea del Sarto.

to be done by an interested party—the Union government. This is difficult to achieve using gradualistic conditionalities. Compliance with binary conditionalities are easier to assess and disbursal of such grants will consequently be more objective.

(v) Given the paradigm shift in the political environment across most states, coupled with a greater accent on pro-poor policies, it is difficult for states to undertake fiscal reform unless three conditions are satisfied, namely, (i) States are incentivised fiscally to accept politically difficult reform conditionalities, (ii) such reform conditionalities are applied uniformly across all states, (iii) such reform conditionalities can be attributed to an external agency by the state governments.[8] This may make these conditionalities politically acceptable.

The FC's conditional grants satisfy all these three conditions and are therefore ideally placed for incentivising reform. Different FCs adopting different incentive frameworks may not provide the states with a clear goal to aim for in the medium term. The second question should the Commission seek to develop incentive frameworks which will stand the test of time and carry credibility with future commissions?—therefore needs the answer "yes". The subsidiary questions—the extent to which these conditionalities should be applied and should FLI be deployed in this effort—however need careful consideration.

Should the Commission Encourage Better Fiscal Performance in States More Explicitly?

This is one of the oldest debates relating to the work of FCs. In the course of determining priorities for horizontal devolution, while accepting the need for incorporating both efficiency and equity into its analysis, what relative weights should it accord to these competing parameters?

The arguments for the use of equity and efficiency parameters are summarised below.

8. The ToR of the FFC seems to indicate that GoI itself endorses such an approach.

Arguments for Equity

(i) Equity considerations form the essence of inter-governmental transfer aimed at ensuring that each state provides comparable levels of public services at comparable tax rates. For this to be achieved, the gaps in the revenue-raising capacities across states and their cost disabilities have to be bridged. This is best done by allocating significant weights to equity-based parameters in the distribution formula.

(ii) Apart from income distance, population and area also significantly affect the levels of public service provided by a state and thus also need to be included in the computation.

(iii) The ToRs of the 7th Finance Commission and all subsequent commissions have carried the injunction that: "In making its recommendations on various matters, the Commission shall generally take the base of population figures as of 1971 in all cases where population is a factor for determination of devolution of taxes and duties, and grants in aid." This item also finds place as clause 7 of the ToR of the FFC. Freezing the

Table 20.2

Available Resources and Plan Performance Gap in Select States

(in ₹ crore)

No	State	Revenue Surplus(+)/ Deficit(-)		Available Debt while Maintaining 3% FD		Expenditure Shortfall (Annual Plan Outlay Minus Actual Expenditure)	
		2009-10	2010-11	2009-10	2010-11	2009-10	2010-11
1	Assam	1,348.00	-53.00	1,550.74	1,288.65	976.91	761.90
2	Bihar	2,943.00	6,316.00	0.00	1,415.00	1,816.49	1,282.42
3	Jharkhand	-10.00	836.00	414.00	2,107.00	1,671.12	972.41
4	Madhya Pradesh	5,498.00	6,843.00	466.00	691.00	1,564.16	1,156.84
5	Maharashtra	-8,006.00	-590.00	5,562.79	7,443.76	8,228.35	5,339.22
6	Meghalaya	302.00	248.00	77.36	57.39	682.13	120.80
7	Odisha	1,139.00	3,908.00	2,371.00	3,237.00	1,772.25	894.33
8	Punjab	-6,048.00	-5,289.00	570.71	NA	3,626.22	825.63
9	Rajasthan	-4,747.00	1,055.00	87.00	528.00	-700.68	2,459.72
10	Uttar Pradesh	7,047.00	3,508.00	0.00	0.00	1,788.48	699.30
11	Uttarakhand	-1,171.00	-13.00	0.00	0.00	2,286.72	2,324.90

Source: Finance Accounts of the respective States and RBI's *Study of State Finances* for Different Years.

population criterion to a level it was 40 years ago is seen as a significant dilution of the equity principle by the states with large populations. The smaller population states on the other hand see this as a necessary complement to their on-going reform efforts. The added mandate of the FFC that: "however, the Commission may also take into account the demographic changes that have taken place subsequent to 1971", appears to now muddy the waters, raising doubts on what exactly is expected from the FFC.

Arguments for Efficiency

(i) While equity is an important parameter for horizontal distribution, it leads to adoption of a gap-filling approach for determining eligibility for grants. Given that poor fiscal performance may lead to higher grant eligibility, states may then become susceptible to perverse incentives while managing their fisc. To resolve this, it is necessary to introduce efficiency parameters in the distribution formula.

(ii) In our resource-constrained economy, it is the duty of the FC to catalyse states to fully exploit and better utilise all available resources. This is best done by adopting the efficiency parameter in the horizontal distribution formula.

(iii) States which have received relatively higher devolution on equity considerations have often been unable to perform efficiently. This is demonstrated in Table 20.2, which details three parameters for 11 states. The revenue surplus is listed in column 3 for these states for the two years 2009-10 and 2010-11. In essence, this figure is the "free reserve" at the disposal of state government, which can be used to finance any expenditure without infringing on its FRBM commitments. The available debt in column 4 is the amount of further debt that can be drawn down by the state government without exceeding the 3 per cent GSDP (gross state domestic product) limit. Column 5 shows the shortfall in plan expenditure for the same two-year period. As can be seen, most of these states recorded significant shortfalls in Plan outlays despite having resources available either in the form of revenue surpluses or borrowing headroom. The analysis below shows that the problem may not be in the availability of resources but rather in their prompt and efficient utilisation. Also, it can be argued that the annual plans in these states are not optimistic enough, considering their available resources. Such issues can be best addressed through the use of an invariable efficiency parameter applied consistently across successive FCs.

(iv) A related issue is the problem of high general cash balances of all the states, which is presently estimated at about ₹ 1,00,000 crore. A recent paper[9] identifies 10 states which account for 80 per cent of total outstanding cash balances of all states between 2005-06 and 2007-08. The cash balances for these 10 states over the last five years have been placed in Table 20.3.

As can be seen, in some states the general cash balances are both substantial and continuing over the past five years. Holding these balances has a deleterious effect on the fiscal position of the states while affecting the market for the following reasons: (i) The negative carry between the cost of borrowing (now about 9%) and the interest earned on their short-term investments (now about 5%) is a significant drain on the resources of the state with no tangible benefit provided by these balances—which in a delicious irony[10] are invested in 14-day treasury bills. (ii) The high cash-balances are caused by excessive state borrowing which crowds out from the market more productive borrowing by the private sector.

States, however, are not adequately incentivised to dismount this fiscal tiger for the following reasons: (i) The proceeds of borrowing undertaken by a state are not included in the computation of the fiscal deficit until the money borrowed is actually spent. The definition presently adopted for the fiscal deficit is purely expenditure-driven (total expenditure minus the sum of total revenue and non-debt capital receipts). The actual borrowing undertaken by a state is not linked to this definition. If a state borrows money from the market and does not spend it, it will only result in its cash

9. *Determination of Surplus Cash Balances of States in India: A Panel Data Analysis*, RBI Staff Studies by Kumudini Hajra, Rajeev Jain and Dhirendra Gajbhiye.

10. The irony is delicious because 6 of these 10 states are ruled by political parties who are opposed to the ruling coalition at the Centre. Despite their political stance, they are effectively financing the Centre.

Table 20.3

State-wise General Cash Balances

(in ₹ crore) (As on 31 March)

No	State	2007	2008	2009	2010	2011
1	Maharashtra	4,651.10	7,501.62	16,479.53	19,082.56	22,757.71
2	Tamil Nadu	8,393.86	9,491.39	13,805.53	17,026.55	12,975.09
3	Uttar Pradesh	NA	15,183.78	9,056.15	3,392.82	10,292.43
4	Gujarat	5,907.49	9,185.03	8,564.67	6,471.53	9,372.84
5	Karnataka	5,755.65	3,570.39	7,160.86	8,782.31	6,214.38
6	Assam	2,697.00	3,955.67	8,030.71	6,773.48	5,774.58
7	Odisha	4,416.95	4,985.41	5,319.62	4,419.39	5,141.65
8	Andhra Pradesh	3,128.35	6,162.26	1,997.97	2,306.32	4,302.65
9	Bihar	1,197.94	2,070.85	3,238.84	1,810.59	1,868.42
10	Haryana	6,407.83	5,629.16	2,238.72	-1,028.32	-1,092.33

Source: Finance Accounts of the respective states for the respective years.

balance increasing. Its fiscal deficit will not increase till it actually spends this money. Thus, there is no deterrent in the present FRBM framework to prevent states from borrowing money from the market and parking it as cash balances. Further the "borrowing eligibility" of 3 per cent of GSDP permitted by the FRBM clothes this unutilised borrowing in unnecessary legality. (ii) If a state draws down its cash balance as an alternative to borrowing to meet its revenue expenditure, the downside is that this will adversely affect its revenue deficit.

Even though the cash balances "belong"[11] to the state government, spending them will increase the revenue deficit because the definition of revenue expenditure is also purely expenditure-driven (revenue expenditure minus revenue receipts). The definition does not allow for drawing down of a state's existing cash balances. (c) Some states have a strong need to protect themselves from the downside reputational risk of availing ways and means advances as well as going into an overdraft. This political risk of being accused of financial mismanagement by opposition parties is accentuated by the fact that the record of a state's borrowing from the Reserve Bank of India (RBI) is publicly available.[12] Therefore, these statcs

11. Public account balances which also form part of a state's cash balances do not "belong" to the state government, but they are utilised by it in a fiduciary capacity.
12. Statement 38 of the "State Finances: A Study of Budgets of 2011-12", Reserve Bank of India.

regard the maintenance of high cash balances as a lesser evil than going into an overdraft with the RBI.

It is clear that if the problem of high cash balances held by the states is to be addressed, the FFC may have to incentivise states to actively draw down their large cash balances. One of the options available is by reviewing the definitions of fiscal deficit and revenue deficit. Perhaps the mandate in item 5 of the FFC's ToR warranting it to recommend amendments to the FRBM Act may catalyse the FFC into doing so.

Another question relating to measuring efficiency relates to the indicators used to judge performance. Presently, performance is judged based upon historical data and a state is rewarded or penalised for its past actions—some or most of which could have been undertaken by a different government/political party in power. Ideally, states should be rewarded for future performance based upon well-set rules of the game announced in advance. Only this can influence future behaviour. This can best be done through the use of forward-looking indicators, but as noted earlier, not enough experience has been gained on the use of these two indicators to take a final view.

Based upon this discussion, it appears that the answer to the third question, "Should the FFC encourage better fiscal performance in states more explicitly?", requires the answer "Yes", as widely as possible not only to ensure better fiscal performance but also better financial management.

Should the FFC Provide Fiscal Headroom for Accommodating Unanticipated Developments?

Recent experience has shown that FC projections often go awry. These deviations are caused by unanticipated developments both in the international and the domestic spheres. The perturbations to the projections can arise through factors arising from either risk or uncertainty. Risk-based factors like an oil price increase, adverse seasonal conditions, political economy considerations can to some extent be anticipated by the FFC and built into its projections. However, the Commission may find it difficult to anticipate shocks arising from factors flowing from uncertainty including possible black swan events. The issue is whether the FC should provide in its projections a cushion for addressing the challenges arising from such uncertain events.

Internationally, while the impact of the 2008-09 crisis was factored in by the ThFC, the follow through Euro zone crisis and its impact on the Indian economy could not be anticipated. Further, the central government's domestic commitments additionally burdened the fisc. The current macroeconomic situation is thus not encouraging. Growth has moderated, inflation remains high, investment has decelerated and the twin deficits have yet to be effectively bridged. To address this situation, the government constituted the Kelkar Committee on a Road Map for Fiscal Consolidation which submitted its report in September 2012. This report identified fiscal consolidation as the key policy action required to avoid "the approaching fiscal precipice". The committee also outlined the key reform steps required to be taken while outlining a fiscal road map up to 2014-15 in a reform situation. Subsequently, the Union Finance Minister in a statement on 29 October 2012 outlined a fiscal consolidation plan that he proposed to adopt in terms of the fiscal deficit. As per this plan, the fiscal deficit would be gradually brought down to 3 per cent by 2016-17. All the three proposed fiscal consolidation paths are placed in Table 20.4.

Table 20.4

Fiscal Consolidation Road Map for Union Government
(Fiscal Deficit as % of GDP)

Financial Year	*Recommendations by*	*FD*
2012-13	ThFC Finance Commission	4.2
	Kelkar Committee	5.2
	Finance Minister's statement	5.3
2013-14	ThFC Finance Commission	3.0
	Kelkar Committee	4.6
	Finance Minister's Statement	4.8
2014-15	ThFC Finance commission	3.0
	Kelkar Committee	3.9
	Finance Minister's statement	4.2

Source: ThFC Report, Kelkar Committee Report, Statement of the Union Finance Minister on Fiscal Road Map and Consolidation on 29 October 2012.

As can be seen, since December 2009 when the ThFC report was submitted, there has been a successive decline in the expectations of fiscal performance during each successive assessment by the GoI itself. Predictably, the projections of union finances made by the ThFC for the period 2010-2015 are no longer relevant. However, such a situation can at least partly be attributed to the lack of policy reform by the GoI—for example in the matter of fertiliser subsidies. Keeping this in mind, should the FFC provide some fiscal headroom in its projections for accommodating uncertain economic developments? Should such accommodation be made in the FFC recommendations for both upside and downside deviations? Since the devolution to states will be affected by considering such a proposition, can this proposal be implemented objectively since the GoI is an interested party?

The fourth question needs to be answered more guardedly given the difficulty in anticipating such events as well as the impact such a provision may have on the devolution to the states.

Conclusions

Four questions relating to the functioning of the FFC have been posed in this paper. The answers suggested are summarised below.

The first question, "Should the FFC solely fulfil its Constitutional duty as mandated under Article 280(3)?", needs the answer, "The FFC need not necessarily be guided by all the consideration items, especially those items which do not have any explicit linkages with public finance."

The second question, "Should the Commission seek to develop incentive frameworks which will stand the test of time and carry credibility with future Commissions?" should be answered with a "Yes". The subsidiary questions, to what extent should these conditionalities be applied and should FLI be deployed in this effort however need careful consideration.

The third question, "Should the Commission encourage better fiscal performance in states more explicitly?" requires the answer, "Yes", as widely as possible to ensure not only better fiscal performance but also better financial management.

The fourth question, "Should the Finance Commission provide fiscal headroom in its recommendations for accommodating future uncertain economic developments?", cannot be answered unequivocally given the difficulty in anticipating such events as well as the impact this may have on the devolution to the states.

M. Govinda Rao

Introduction

The theme of this section is "Issues Before the 14th Finance Commission". As the Commission has not been constituted yet, one can make only some informed guess about the scope of work of the 14th Finance Commission (FFC) on the basis of the Constitutional provisions mandating the tasks under Article 280 and the pattern of the terms of reference (ToR) that have evolved over the years in keeping with economic and fiscal developments in the country. In particular, while the ToRs in Article 280(3)(a), and (b) dealing with tax devolution and grants-in-aid of revenues are clear and based on the past experience, it is possible to identify the important issues in respect of them. Similarly, the issues relating to augmenting the consolidated funds of the states to supplement the resources of rural and urban local bodies under Article 280(3)(bb) and (c) can also be guessed. It is the omnibus term under Article 280(3)(d), namely, "...any other matter referred to the Commission in the interests of sound finance", where a number of issues have been referred to the Commission to seek solutions to emerging inter-governmental fiscal problems in the country and to provide directives to the Commission in adopting the approach and methodology while dealing with its task.[13] The ThFC was asked to make recommendations on matters such as charting out a road map for fiscal consolidation for the Centre and states, assess the impact of the proposed GST and recommend issues relating to the management of ecology and environment, disaster relief, adequate provision for the maintenance of capital assets and issues relating to the transformation of expenditures into outputs and outcomes. Often, many fiscal issues which the central government cannot itself solve have been referred to the Commission and in the process there is a tendency to overload the Commission which it cannot deal with satisfactorily during its short tenure.

---

13. The Presidential ToR to the FCs have provided directives to the Commission for determining their scope as well as methodology. The directive to restrict the scope of the Commissions while assessing the states' requirements to non-plan sides from the 4th Finance Commission has been much debated. Similarly, the 9th Finance Commission was asked to adopt "normative approach" and this prescription of methodology to be adopted was a subject of considerable criticism. For details see, Rao and Singh (2005).

Fiscal Road Map

Irrespective of the ToRs that will be given, it is clear that the Commission will have an uphill task of recommending the transfer system and working out fiscal restructuring road map in the prevailing difficult fiscal environment. The situation continues to be precarious at the central level and slippage in the deficit targets is inevitable. In part, this was admitted when the Medium Term Fiscal Policy (MTFP) statement presented along with the 2012-13 Budget by the Finance Minister set the fiscal deficit target for 2014-15 at 3.9 per cent of GDP, a clear 0.9 percentage point higher than the FC's target. Subsequently, this has been endorsed in the revised target set by the Committee on Road Map for Fiscal Consolidation comprising essentially the ThFC team chaired by Dr Vijay Kelkar. Unfortunately, the Committee does not explain whether the earlier targets were inappropriate or there have been new developments warranting a revision after it submitted the report. In any case, the Finance Minister's restructuring plan closely follows the consolidation road map suggested by the Kelkar committee and according to this the fiscal deficit of the Union government will be compressed to 3 per cent of GDP by 2016-17, almost two years into the award of the FFC. If indeed, the FFC is asked to recommend fiscal consolidation strategy and road map, it will be constrained by the plan laid out by the Finance Minister.

At the state level, however, the fiscal situation is healthier. The aggregate fiscal deficit of the states in 2011-12 is estimated at 2.2 per cent of GDP and they do not have revenue deficits. The budgeted estimates for 2012-13 are broadly similar. Of course, this hides the fact that in some states such as Kerala, Punjab and West Bengal the situation is precarious and does not conform to the separate restructuring plans recommended by the ThFC. Even more important is the fact that while the states have contained their own deficits, the liabilities on account of losses of power utilities have continued to mount and these constitute at least one per cent of the GDP. In part, this is due to the fact that the incentive scheme of the FC requires compression of only the fiscal deficits of the states and not the liabilities from state utilities.

Substantive Terms of Reference

While the Constitution envisages the FC to be the agency for effecting Union transfers to states, the adoption of a planned development strategy and the introduction of specific purpose transfers for various schemes by various line ministries at the Union level have resulted in multiple agencies making the transfers with no proper coordination. The overlapping system of transfers given on multiple criteria results in blurring the objectives and the FC has no control over either the total volume of transfers or its distribution. The FCs in the past have expressed their concern on the issue and the TwFC prescribed the cap of total transfers from all agencies at 38 per cent of Union government revenues which was revised to 39.5 per cent by the ThFC. In the scheme of ThFC, its transfers would constitute about 32.2 per cent of Central revenues and the transfers by the Planning Commission and Central Ministries together should not exceed 7.3 per cent. However, this is only an indicative target and does not make much sense as the Commission cannot exercise any control over the Planning Commission or the Central Ministries in giving grants to states.

The ToR dealing with the augmentation of consolidated funds of the states to supplement the resources of *panchayats* and municipal bodies based on the recommendations of SFC has been a difficult area. The past commissions could not take account of the recommendations of the SFCs mainly because consistent and coordinated reports of SFCs are not available. There is no coordination whatsoever in the timing of the setting up of the SFCs and their submission of the reports, there are states that do not accept their recommendations even when submitted, and even when they are 'accepted in principle', they are not implemented. In fact, the quality of the reports varies widely across states. While it is impossible to consider the reports of SFCs to formulate the recommendations, independent assessment by the FC too is not possible because there is hardly any worthwhile information system on the finances of rural and urban local bodies (ULBs), the standards of local services provided in individual local bodies and their economic and demographic profiles even after 20 years of Constitutional amendment. The attempts by the past commissions to incentivise the states to build a proper information system has failed miserably and the states have preferred not to build the information system and utilise the grants meant for the purpose. The FCs have been simply making some ad hoc grants to the states for supplementing the resources of these local bodies and that has hardly served much purpose. Of course, the ThFC recommended that the states should be given half a percentage of the previous year's gross tax revenue of the Centre which is much higher than the past, but not founded in sound logic. There are questions on what are the requirements of the local bodies, how much of the requirements should be raised by the local bodies themselves, what should be the quantum of assistance by the states and how much should be supplemented by the Centre. The commissions have not considered any of these but simply have gone about giving ad hoc grants to the states.

Irrespective of the ToRs, the commission, to a considerable extent, was constrained by the past practices and conventions. Although there is no compulsion to follow the past, any significant deviation could destabilise the states' fiscal positions and therefore, any changes it will make can only be marginal, if the recommendations have to be accepted. Can it make a substantial departure from the previous commissions on the proportion of tax devolution and grants to be given? Can it substantially change the inter-state distribution of transfers, irrespective of the shortcomings of the past commissions? The theoretical arguments for inter-governmental transfers is that these should be given to offset vertical and horizontal fiscal imbalances and inter-state distribution is to enable comparable levels of public services at a comparable tax-price. At present, although the transfer system, particularly the transfers given by the FCs have been equalising, the fiscal disabilities of low income states are not completely offset and per capita expenditures on various services after the transfers are given varies widely across states, with the lowest per capita GSDP state having just about 45 per cent of the all-state average. Another important issue is what happens if the Government accepts the recommendation of the Committee on Expenditure Efficiency (Chaired by Dr Rangarajan) that the distinction between plan and non-plan expenditures in the budget should be done away with?

Other Terms of Reference

As mentioned earlier, the recent trend has been to assign the Commission with a number of tasks under "any other matter in the interest of sound finance". In fact, all politically difficult issues which the

Government is unable to deal with are assigned to the Commission. The most difficult issue to deal with perhaps will be to work out a revised road map for fiscal consolidation. The Kelkar Committee has recommended the fiscal deficit target for the Centre relative to GDP at 3.0 per cent in contrast to the ThFC's target of 3.0 per cent for 2014-15. The Finance Minister, in his road map has taken the deficit target of 3.9 per cent for 2014-15 and has extended his road map for a further period of two years to reach 3.0 per cent by 2016-17. If the fiscal consolidation issue is referred to the Commission, there are questions as to how the Commission should deal with the Finance Minister's target in working out its consolidation path.

It has become a practice to refer the task of ensuring efficiency in spending to the FCs and it is likely that the FFC will also be asked to make recommendations in this regard. Often commissions have been loaded with tasks which the governments themselves could not handle and this is one such area! The important issue is the time with the FC will be limited as it will have to submit the report latest by December 2014 because the 2015-16 budget will have to take these recommendations into account. Within the short time available, it is unwise to entrust the Commission with the task of tax reform commission, expenditure reform commission and of course, the basic work of the FC. Of course, the Rangarajan committee on expenditure efficiency has made extensive recommendations and it will be appropriate for the Union government to implement those recommendations rather than refer it to the next FC.

Another important issue in this regard is the treatment of revenue deficits. There have been arguments that the capital grants given by the Centre should not be considered as revenue expenditures and included in the revenue deficit. Based on this logic, the Union budgets have been showing "effective revenue deficits" separately from the revenue deficit numbers. The Rangarajan committee too has suggested that the capital grants should not be included in the revenue deficit targets. However, it is important to have a clear view on what constitutes capital grants. Surely, the grants given to employment guarantee cannot be considered capital grants!

Equally important is the introduction of the incentive scheme to ensure that fiscal consolidation is a commitment. The ThFC has stated that the MTFP which the Union and state governments present along with their annual budgets should be a commitment rather than a mere statement. The past experience has not been happy, and the MTFP targets have been violated with impunity by the Union government itself. While the Union government can monitor and punish the states for their violation, there is no monitoring of the targets of the Union government. Thus, while the FCs can only 'bark' at the Centre, they can 'bite' the states! Evolving an effective and workable incentive mechanism for prudent fiscal management and ensuring a uniformly effective treatment of Centre and States is a difficult challenge.

Another issue which the FC may be asked to address is the introduction of goods and services tax (GST). The Commission may be asked to devise a compensation mechanism when the reform is introduced. This, however, would require finalising the threshold, list of exemptions and the rate structure. It is not even clear that the Union and state governments will be able to conclude negotiations on these issues soon within two years when the Commission will be deliberating. Nevertheless, this will be one of the difficult areas the Commission may have to deal with.

The past practice has been to ask the commissions to take into account a variety of factors in finalising their recommendations on tax devolution and grants. One of the areas referred to the commission since the ThFC was the issue to compensate the states for protecting ecology and environment. Besides losing revenue on account of the forest cover, the states are required to spend on expanding the cover and face higher cost of providing services in areas where forest cover exists. Incentivising the states to maintain and expand forest cover therefore, requires additional incentives and the 13th Finance Commission provided some grants for the purpose which the states with large forest cover complain is too little. The issues of adequate compensation for loss of revenue and cost disabilities may have to be looked at afresh by the Commission.

Concluding Remarks

It is difficult to guess the scope of the FFC at this stage when the Commission has not been constituted and the ToR is not available. It is also not easy to hazard a guess about the methodology the Commission will adopt. What is however known is that the Commission will have to take into consideration the pattern of past distribution and cannot make significant deviations in terms of relative shares of the states in the interest of stability. Nevertheless, there is considerable uncertainty on the issues faced by the FFC.

Indeed, the appointment of the Commission comes at a time when the fiscal situation in the country is difficult. Besides dealing with large deficits and debt, the Union government may be faced with important unfunded liabilities in the medium term including large outlays on food security, universal health care and recapitalisation of nationalised banks. With many power generation projects facing fuel, land and environmental clearance uncertainly, discoms facing uncertain financial future despite the restructuring of short term loans and projects on slow progress in highways due to lock of various clearances, a considerable proportion of outstanding loans from the nationalised banks is likely to become non-performing assets (NPAs) and with stringent Basel 3 requirements, considerable amount of funds may have to be infused from the budget to these banks to meet the norms. The medium term fiscal situation does not look promising and it remains to be seen how the FFC will negotiate the difficult task of achieving fiscal consolidation while ensuring a fair share of resources between the Union and states, and among the states inter se.

D.K. Srivastava*

Introduction

In terms of the role that institutions have played in the smooth and efficient working of a federal economy like India, the FC has played a key role. The FC has a constitutional status; its members are generally professionals rather than politicians; and each commission has a finite life. The FCs in India have established a reputation for objectivity and transparency. Their reports are published and widely debated. In general, their recommendations have been accepted. The FFC will also no doubt maintain this rich tradition.

The tasks of a FC can be divided into two parts: core tasks and contextual tasks. The core tasks have been spelt out in the Constitution. These relate to the sharing of central taxes with the states and for determining grants-in-aid to the states and local bodies. Apart from these constitutionally mandated tasks, the Commission is also asked to address additional issues reflecting challenges emanating from the contemporary economic context. Such tasks emanate from issues that have a macroeconomic or inter-state context.

Macroeconomic Challenges

The ThFC was asked to suggest measures to maintain a stable and sustainable fiscal environment consistent with equitable growth. At that time the Indian economy was emerging out of the 2008-09 global crisis. From a high of more than 9 per cent growth, the growth had slipped to just about 6 per cent. Today the macroeconomic situation is much worse.

India is going through a phase of low growth and high inflation. Growth in 2012-13 was expected to be in the range of 5.5 to 6 per cent. However, the economy grew at a much slower pace (4.5%). In all likelihood the base year for the calculations leading to projections of revenues and expenditures undertaken by the FFC will be 2013-14. These projections will be used for the period 2015-16 to 2029-30. However, growth in 2013-14 is also likely to remain subdued around 6 per cent or so. Correspondingly, the

---

* The views expressed here are his personal views.

central tax revenues will also not show much surplus and the exercise for allocations of resources would be that much difficult.

The growth targets of the Twelfth Five year plan are also getting revised downwards from time to time. The revised target is being fixed at 8 per cent per annum for the Twelfth Plan period. Even this appears to be an overestimate. In fact, the potential growth rate appears to have fallen by about 2 percentage points from the 9 per cent achieved during 2005-2008. In such a context, conventional measures of monetary or fiscal stimulation would only exacerbate inflation. One has to go through the long haul of supply side measures of stimulating investment and improving productivity of resources. The supply side factors that need to be evaluated relate, among others, to saving and investment rates in the economy, the growing consumption of fixed capital stock, sectoral allocation of net fixed capital stock, and determinants of its productivity. From the year of previous peak growth in 2007-08, the savings rate has fallen by 5 percentage points of GDP at market prices. Two main contributors to this erosion of savings performance are government whose revenue deficit has increased by 4.5 percentage points and household sector whose savings, particularly that kept in the financial form, has fallen significantly. Investment has also fallen and, compared to 2007-08, its financing from the current account deficit has increased by about 4.5 percentage points. As the current account deficit is reduced, increase in investment will have to be financed by an adequate increase in domestic savings relative to GDP. These are long term factors and cannot be corrected quickly. Correspondingly, the FFC will have to make realistic assumptions about the growth rate that can be achieved, which has a bearing on the tax revenues that can be generated in their award period that is 2015-16 to 2019-20.

The FFC might also need to examine strategies to stimulate growth and make it more stable and equitable. The macroeconomic scenario has a direct bearing on central and state taxes since a high nominal growth of GDP translates into high tax revenues. Given the low growth and sluggish prospects of uplifting tax revenues relative to GDP, the Commission will find it quite a challenge to resolve the vertical imbalance between the Central and state governments, and the horizontal imbalance among the state governments. The Commission will need a robust exercise for projecting Central and state government revenues, and expenditures under alternative assumptions to formulate a realistic view on available resources and needs for all the three tiers of governments.

Fiscal Consolidation

Linked to macroeconomic stabilisation, there is the issue arising from the fiscal responsibility legislations. The Central and state governments have both committed to limiting fiscal deficit relative to GDP and GSDP respectively at 3 per cent, and achieving balance on the revenue account. While the state governments taken together appear to have achieved this, the Central government has slipped in achieving these targets in a significant way. Some of the state governments, considered individually, have slipped. The FFC will have to recast the fiscal consolidation path. A credible path would require hard fiscal discipline rules particularly for the Central government. Designing and implementing such rules will be a crucial challenge for the Commission. Further, rational ways of handling significant non-tax revenues arising from natural resources on the surface such as land and water, under-ground resources such as coal and other minerals, and in space such as the spectrum should also be reviewed by the FC. Non-tax revenues are likely to grow in importance.

Core Tasks and Dated Information Base

For the constitutionally mandated responsibility of dividing the shareable central tax revenues between the Centre and the states and determining grants to the states, revenue and expenditure assessment may yield a lower surplus with the Centre and higher deficit with the states. With a high subsidy bill and other committed expenditures, the Centre would have a dwindling surplus while the states need more resources for uplifting the deficient standards of services they are supposed to provide.

To resolve this imbalance, the Commission should take a comprehensive view of all transfers including those from the Planning Commission transfers and the central ministries that have progressively become larger and more ad hoc.

Using the 1971 population data for determining the share of states in the shareable tax revenues needs to be given up. This is hopelessly dated. It would be best to simply drop the clause mandating the Commission to use

1971 population data. The last year of the award of the FFC would be 2019-20. Using 1971 population data would be nearly 50 years out of date. The other main constituent of the information base, namely, the comparable gross state domestic product (GSDP) is also both dated and inadequate for the purpose at hand. GSDP is measured at factor cost and provides an indicator of production that takes place within the boundary of a state. It does not indicate either the income of its residents or their aggregate consumption. What we need is a macro indicator of fiscal capacity which can serve as a base for projecting expected revenues from a destination based tax system. Some of the previous commissions had recommended that the CSO may be asked to work on adjustments required on the GSDP data so that it can better serve as an indicator of fiscal capacity. However, no known work has been undertaken for this purpose. The GSDP data also happens to be dated. For 2019-20, the GSDP data likely to be used would possibly be for 2013-14. It can be shown that the combination of dated population data and dated GSDP data can result in large distortions.

In other major federations like Canada and Australia, not only is the equalisation principle used for determining unconditional transfers but also special care is taken that shares of states are determined using current information.

The use of a dated and distorted information base makes the task of achieving and assessing the extent of 'equalisation' achieved in any scheme of fiscal transfers extremely difficult. Equalisation has been accepted by most established federations as a guiding principle for determining unconditional transfers as it is consistent with both the equity and efficiency principles by ensuring that citizens in states are entitled to comparable standards of public services and merit services like education and health if they make comparable tax efforts.

Pursuing Tax Reforms

The ThFC was asked to examine the impact of the proposed implementation of GST with effect from 1st April, 2010. The GST has so far remained elusive. The proposed constitutional amendment and on-going discussions in the Empowered Committee of State Finance Ministers indicate a rate structure involving two rates for goods and a different one for services. The standard rate for goods is likely to be set high. These features are not desirable.

The FFC may be asked to examine the GST issue afresh and give an interim report for its implementation possibly within one year. New ways of setting at rest some of the concerns of the states should be explored. This can include a permanent mechanism for compensation for revenue losses of the net producing states on account of the abolition of the central sales tax, supplementary non-rebatable tax for demerit and polluting goods, bringing taxation of petroleum products within the GST ambit, and a low core GST rate for goods and services.

It is important to note that nearly 90 per cent of central excise revenues is derived from a list of 20 commodities that includes items like petroleum products, tobacco products, iron and steel, plastics and chemicals, which can all be included under the caption of 'demerit and polluting goods'. Once these goods are taken out for the calculation of revenue neutral rates and given a specific treatment such as the levy of a non-rebatable supplementary tax over and above the GST, almost every aspect of the design of GST falls in place. The RNR (renewable energy resources) for the vast majority of goods become low; both states and the Centre get an acceptable degree of autonomy since the goods under demerit and polluting goods are large revenue contributors with low price-elasticity of demand. The overall indirect system will also become more efficient from an optimal tax viewpoint since low demand elasticity goods will be taxed at higher rates. Thus, it would be possible to design a GST where the standard rate is low but revenue-risks are covered easily. In this kind of framework, the issue of compensation, arising mainly on account of withdrawal of the central sales tax and entry tax that mainly affects the so-called net producing states can be endogeneised since most of the mineral-producing states and industrial states that would lose revenue and suffer pollution will have a handle to recover revenue and discourage polluting activities. This would also avoid the difficult task of making calculations for compensation, which are bound to be based on a number of specific assumptions that are likely to be disputed. It would also be consistent with the objective of promoting environment and ecology, a task given to the ThFC. A similar task may be given to the FFC.

Partha Mukhopadhyay

Introduction

The importance of urban areas in economic activity has recently come into focus (HPEC 2011, Sankhe *et al.*, 2010; World Bank, 2013; Government of India, 2013). However, while there has been some progress in the autonomous functioning of village *panchayats*, subsequent to the 73rd amendment to the Constitution, progress in ULB has been much more limited. In most states, much of the 12th Schedule in the 74th Amendment has not devolved to the local government, with some exceptions to this trend, e.g., Gujarat and Maharashtra. The courts have also concurred with the position that such transfer is not mandated by the Constitution, but is at the option of state governments (Sivaramakrishnan, 2009).

In this context, the FFC will need to address the issue of financing of urban local government on a priority basis. Its predecessor created a new approach for sharing Union taxes with local governments in a buoyant manner (by indexing it to the previous year's collection) and thus some precedent for sharing of Union revenues with local governments has been established, though inter se allocations remain in the purview of state governments. SFCs too have begun to function in a more regular manner, thus putting the sharing of state taxes on a firmer footing. But, how feasible is such support?

The Thought Experiment

HPEC (2011) is the only recent document to attempt an estimate of the requirement of funds needed for urban infrastructure. For purposes of comparison and convenience, it seems to be as good a point of departure as any. One can start from the HPEC estimates and adopt a slightly different approach to the financing of urban services than that adopted in the Report, which relies on own revenue and revenue-shared taxes. Rather, one can ask what kind of tax-sharing is implied by such investment numbers.

The gross investment numbers in the HPEC report is ₹ 3,918,670 crore over the 20 year period, 2012-2031. The O&M requirement is another ₹ 1,993,902 crore. In this thought experiment, the focus is on capital expenditure. Table 20.5 provides the details by each sector. The next step is to simulate a time path for capital expenditure and implied tax requirements. The HPEC report itself has an assumed time path, but here a more direct assumption is used. This, and other assumptions used in the simulation are given below.

(i) Expenditure is assumed to be a constant proportion of urban GDP.

(ii) For this assumptions are needed about overall GDP growth, which is taken at 7 per cent per annum in real terms.

(iii) The share of GDP from urban areas is assumed at 60 per cent in 2012, increasing by 0.7 percentage points per year to reach 73.3 per cent by 2031.[14]

Based on a GDP (at current market prices) of ₹ 8,855,797 crore in 2011-12, these assumptions lead to a total urban GDP over 2012-2031 of ₹ 247,520,825 crore (at 2012 prices). This implies that HPEC estimated capital expenditure over this period generates a share of 1.58 per cent of urban GDP.

(iv) A part of this expenditure will be financed by user fees, which is assumed at 29 per cent of the total investment.

This estimate is based on the share of investment in water and sewerage, slum housing, solid waste management and half the investment in "others", in Table 20.5, i.e., on the supposition that these services can be provided on a cost-recovery basis, admittedly a strong assumption, but one which has a functional basis.

The remaining 71 per cent is to be financed through transfers from the Union and state government. In principle, this can also be done through providing urban local government an autonomous tax base, e.g., a share of the GST, but the focus here is on the amount of revenue that would be needed. The specific mechanisms are left for further discussion. The tax requirement

14. The HPEC assumes the following phasing of growth in real investment in urban infrastructure: 15 per cent p.a. during 2012-13 to 2016-17, 12 per cent p.a. during 2017-18 to 2021-22 and 8 per cent p.a. during 2022-23 to 2031-32. Throughout the period, annual real GDP growth is assumed at 8 per cent. There are no projections for urban GDP for the period.

is assumed as shared equally between the Union (net of tax transfers to the states) and the states (inclusive of tax transfers from the Union). The tax effort as a share of GDP is based on the shares in 2007-08, the peak of recent tax effort.

(e) Union taxes (net of transfers) is assumed at 8.9 per cent of GDP and state taxes (exclusive of share of Union taxes) at 5.8 per cent of GDP and 3.0 per cent of GDP (transfers to states), generating state tax revenue (inclusive of tax transfers from the Union) of 8.8 per cent of GDP. In addition, another 3.6 per cent of GDP is Union (2.1%) and state (1.5%) revenue from non-tax sources, which is not considered here.

(f) Finally, assuming that urban population grows at 2.5 per cent and total population by 1.1 per cent, implicit urbanisation in 2031 is 40.5 per cent. Concomitantly, the urban:rural per capita income ratio rises from 3.3 in 2012 to 4.0 in 2031 and urban per capita income rises to over USD 20,000 in PPP constant dollars in 2031.

Results

The results of the simulation based on these assumptions are provided in Table 20.6. The total investment in 2012 is ₹ 84,121 crore in 2012 rising to ₹ 371,664 crore in 2031. In 2012, this implies ₹ 29,863 crore each from Union and state, with the remaining ₹ 24,395 crore from user fees/ local taxes.

Now, as already noted, the constant investment profile equals 1.58 per cent of urban GDP or 0.95 per cent of current GDP in 2012. Once the revenue realisation from user fees, i.e., 29 per cent as noted above, is taken into account, the required revenue realisation from taxes is 0.67 per cent of GDP. Now, as already noted, the constant investment profile equals 1.58 per cent of urban GDP or 0.95 per cent of current GDP in 2012. Once the revenue realisation from user fees, i.e., 29 per cent as noted above, is taken into account, the required revenue realisation from taxes is 0.67 per cent of GDP, given the possible tax revenues (based on best-case tax effort) noted above, of 8.9 per cent and 8.8 per cent for Union and state taxes respectively.

This means that an equal allocation of the tax transfers from the Union and the states would imply about 3.8 per cent each of Union and state taxes would need to be transferred to local bodies to finance the HPEC investment profile in 2012. This rises to 4.6 per cent and 4.7 per cent (as the profile is an equal share of urban GDP, which is rising with respect to overall GDP over time, it is an increasing share of overall GDP) in the terminal year.

Feasibility

Are these implied shares of taxes to be transferred to the urban local governments feasible? In order to answer this question, two approaches are used. First, is the expenditure profile that is simulated capable of being absorbed by urban local government? This is tested by comparing the profile to the existing levels of expenditure by ULBs. This absorption capacity of urban local government is assessed based on current spending and the ability to spend under the projects of JNNURM. The second issue is if the state and Union governments would find the implied levels of transfers politically acceptable. This is inferred based on comparability with other expenditures and the contributions to state taxes from 'urban sources', such as revenue from stamp duties and registration fees.

As a comparison, the total expenditure by all ULBs was ₹ 47,026 crore in 2007-08 (1% of GDP) and of this, 40 per cent (₹ 18,594 crore) was capital expenditure.[15] So, at first sight, the HPEC profile implies a more than four-fold increase in capital expenditure in local bodies but this data does not include expenditure by development authorities or state agencies like water supply and sewerage boards and SPVs (special purpose vehicles) like metro rail companies and therefore the actual spending on urban infrastructure may be much higher. Indeed, the total expenditure on Delhi Metro is more than that on the Golden Quadrilateral.

In the states, the stamp duty and registration fees are assumed to be suitable for sharing with urban local governments, given that the revenues come significantly from the transfer of properties in urban areas. The state contribution of 3.8 per cent of total tax revenues (including transfers from the Union) is less than half of tax revenues from stamp duties and registration fees (8.5% in 2007-08, as a share of total tax revenues including transfers from the Union). In other words, the state contribution

15 Cumulative Union releases for JNNURM across all four schemes is ₹ 36,293 crore till FY 2012.

can be seen as transferring half the revenues from stamp duties and registration fees to urban local governments. As such, the extent of implied tax transfers from the states does not seem unreasonable. Similarly, the Union transfer of an equivalent amount is lesser in magnitude than a large CSS like the MGNREGS, on which ₹ 35,841 crore was spent in 2010-11. Thus, the broad numbers on the tax transfers implied by the time path of urban investment appear within the realm of feasibility. However, the level of transfers indicated in this approach far exceeds the level of transfers envisaged by the ThFC, which estimated transfers in 2011-12 at ₹ 12,724 crore for all local bodies including rural areas (Govt. of India 2009: 174).

Expenditure on Operations and Maintenance (O&M)

So far, the analysis has focused on capital expenditure. The O&M of these assets is equally important. As shown in Table 20.5, the HPEC estimated this over the same time period to be ₹ 1,993,902 crore, just over half of the capital expenditure requirement. Of this, 57.6 per cent is attributable to user-fee financed sectors, i.e., water and sewerage, solid waste management and half the investment in "others", as discussed above. The remaining will have to be financed from taxes. However, for O&M, prompt cash flow is important and it is here that an autonomous tax base for urban local governments would be most important. Using the same approach for capital expenditure, i.e., a constant share of urban GDP (admittedly a gross oversimplification, since O&M would be related to the capital stock), and excluding the user fee financed sectors, this indicates a tax requirement of 0.34 per cent of urban GDP. For this, new taxes in addition to property taxes, related more to economic activity can be considered, such as the local body tax in Maharashtra (replacing the octroi), which is a tax on transactions within the local body.

Land-based Finance

At this point, it is perhaps important to address the issue of land as a part of resource mobilisation. In the Indian experience, land is already a major source of revenue for development authorities or similar agencies. Often land is acquired from private landowners in the urban fringe by the development authority and sold by it after some infrastructure investments and a change in land use. Development authorities argue that their revenue model is based on value addition generated by their infrastructure investments, but in the hands of the private owner, the value of the land would be much less if it remained classified for agricultural use. If the land was not acquired but rezoned and infrastructure is provided, the increase in value accruing to the private landowner could have been alternatively captured by a tax increment financing type of instrument. This current kind of revenue raising from land development can thus be seen as a very extreme form of benefit financing where almost all the benefit is extracted from some landowners and none from others, e.g., those that are proximate to the land that has been acquired. Land based financing as currently practiced is therefore quite iniquitous.

Public private partnerships (PPP) are also often advocated as a solution. It is important to note that PPP does not generate new money, which comes from user fees and taxes and asset sales, like land auctions. It is merely a means of financing. However, if the private sector is more efficient at building assets and maintaining them and can operate facilities at a lower cost, this efficiency will reduce the fund requirement that needs to be a raised from user fees and taxes. This assumes that the higher financial costs[16] offset by the lower total cost of implementation.

Conclusion

To sum up, it is important to highlight the relative contributions of different sources that emerge out of this thought experiment or simulation exercise. To begin with, user fees finance 29 per cent of the capital expenditure and 57 per cent of the O&M expenditure. Local taxes, preferably autonomous tax sources, fund the remaining O&M expenditure. Union and state tax transfers fund 71 per cent of the capital expenditure in equal measure. Since capital expenditure is about twice that of O&M expenditure, this implies that Union and state transfers fund about 23.5 per cent each of the total capital and O&M expenditure, local taxes fund

16. While usually private sector raises financing at a higher cost than government, this may not be the case with respect to local government. Credible private sector firms may therefore be able to raise funds at comparable or lower rates than local government.

about 14.5 per cent and the remaining 38.5 per cent of the capital and O&M expenditure is financed through user fees. Thus, user fees play a key role, and with local taxes are more than half of financing. Disregarding the issue of scale, even compared to the current structure of revenue in Table 20.7, there are major differences. The existing sources of local revenue are biased more towards taxes and not towards user fees (non-tax revenues). The simulation indicates both a continuance and reversal of this pattern. With respect to support from Union and state transfers, the existing pattern is biased towards state transfers. To some extent, the ThFC has remedied this, but some further adjustment may need to take place. The simulation exercise therefore indicates a structural change in the way urban local government is financed.

It would however, appear from the above, admittedly simple and preliminary analysis, that revenue capacity does not appear to be the binding constraint in financing urban infrastructure. The implied share of state and Union taxes to be transferred to urban local governments too seems acceptable, given the revenue raised by states from city focused taxes, such as stamp duty and the size of Union CSS. While expenditure capability may currently be a hurdle since investment projections are a multiple of existing levels of activity, it may not necessarily be as high as may appear at first glance once expenditures of development authorities and state agencies are taken into account. The assurance of continued support can incentivise capacity building in this area much as the national highway spending created a whole new industry of road construction companies and eventually new infrastructure firms. Prima facie, this is feasible.

There are of course many ways in which this analysis can be further refined. For example, in addition to an autonomous tax base for local governments, the Union can transfer four per cent of its taxes to states, based on the population in their urban local bodies (as distinct from their urban population, to incentivise them to recognise urban population in Census towns). SFC can be provided guidelines to further transfer this amount onward to ULBs. The SFCs can additionally earmark portions of revenue from specified taxes, like half of stamp duties and registration fees for transfers to ULBs, in relation to their population. However, it is important to recognise such an approach would reinforce existing urbanisation patterns, since it directs resources to existing urban areas *vis-à-vis* emerging areas like the towns along the Delhi Mumbai Industrial Corridor (DMIC), which need support for infrastructure.

Further, such a basic structure can be modified to condition a part of the transfers on own revenue effort (both tax and user fees) by the urban local governments. Similarly, rather than city specific support for projects as in JNNURM, part of the Union support can be linked to regional projects and formation of effective regional governance entities, which would target support to large urban areas.

In conclusion, while there may be many ways to the same objective, it is likely that the broad magnitudes of fiscal transfers, in terms of share of taxes, would remain similar, to finance investments indicated in HPEC (2011). While these magnitudes are feasible, it is likely to need a fundamental restructuring of the way the FFC approaches local government finance.

References

Government of India (2009). *Thirteenth Finance Commission Vol. 1 Report.*

————. (2013). *Twelfth Five Year Plan Vol. 2.* New Delhi: Sage Publications.

High Powered Expert Committee (HPEC) for Estimating the Investment Requirements for Urban Infrastructure Services 2011: *Report on Indian Urban Infrastructure and Services*

Rao, M Govinda and Nirvikar Singh (2005). *Political Economy of Federalism in India*. New Delhi Oxford University Press.

Sankhe, Shirish, Ireena Vittal, Richard Dobbs, Ajit Mohan, Ankur Gulati, Jonathan Ablett, Shishir Gupta, Alex Kim, Sudipto Paul, Aditya Sanghvi, Gurpreet Sethy (2010). *India's Urban Awakening: Building Inclusive Cities, Sustaining Economic Growth* McKinsey. Global Institute.

Sivaramakrishnan, K.C. (2009). *Courts, Panchayats and Nagarpalikas: Background and Review of the Case Law*. New Delhi: Academic Foundation.

World Bank (2013). *Urbanization beyond Municipal Boundaries: Nurturing Metropolitan Economies and Connecting Peri-Urban Areas in India*. Directions in Development Washington, DC: World Bank.

Table 20.5

HPEC Estimates of Infrastructure Needs

(₹ crore)

Sector	*Capital Expenditure*	*O&M*
Urban Roads	1,728,941	375,267
Urban Transport	449,426	304,386
Renewal and Redevelopment	408,955	..
Water Supply	320,908	546,095
Sewerage	242,688	236,964
Storm Water and Drainage	191,031	34,612
Capacity Building	101,759	..
Traffic Support Infrastructure	97,985	36,690
Solid Waste Management	48,582	273,906
Street Lighting	18,580	4,717
Others	309,815	181,265
Total	3,918,670	1,993,902

Source: HPEC 2011: xv, 83.

Table 20.7

Structure of Revenue for Urban Local Government 2007-08

	₹ *crore*	*Relative Share (%)*	*% of GDP*	*Simulation (%)*
Own Revenue	23,522	53.0	0.50	53.0
'Exclusive Taxes'	15,278	34.4	0.32	14.5
Non-tax Revenue	8,244	18.6	0.18	38.5
Other Revenue	20,907	47.0	0.44	47.0
Transfers from SFC	9,171	20.6	0.19	23.5
Grants-in-aid from State Government	5,676	12.8	0.12	
Transfers from CFC	869	2.0	0.02	23.5
Grants-in-aid from Union Government	2,373	5.3	0.05	
Other	2,818	6.3	0.06	
Total	44,429	100.0	0.94	100.0

Source: HPEC 2011: 153.

Table 20.6

Simulation of Investment in Urban Infrastructure as a Share of Tax Revenues

				Investment in Urban infrastructure			As Share of Tax Revenue (%)				
	GDP Estimate	Urban Share of GDP (%)	Urban GDP	Profile of Investment	Share of GDP (%)	Net After User Fees (% of GDP) transfers)	Total Tax Revenues	Union Taxes	State Taxes (incl.	Urban Population (crore)	Implicit per capita Urban GDP (₹)
2012	8,855,797	60.0	5,313,478	84,121	0.9	0.67	3.81	3.79	3.83	37.71	140,904
2013	9,475,703	60.7	5,751,752	91,060	1.0	0.68	3.85	3.83	3.88	38.65	148,806
2014	10,139,002	61.4	6,225,347	98,558	1.0	0.69	3.90	3.88	3.92	39.62	157,130
2015	10,848,732	62.1	6,737,063	106,659	1.0	0.70	3.94	3.92	3.97	40.61	165,898
2016	11,608,143	62.8	7,289,914	115,412	1.0	0.71	3.99	3.97	4.01	41.62	175,134
2017	12,420,713	63.5	7,887,153	124,867	1.0	0.71	4.03	4.01	4.06	42.67	184,861
2018	13,290,163	64.2	8,532,285	135,080	1.0	0.72	4.08	4.05	4.10	43.73	195,104
2019	14,220,475	64.9	9,229,088	146,112	1.0	0.73	4.12	4.10	4.14	44.83	205,890
2020	15,215,908	65.6	9,981,636	158,026	1.0	0.74	4.17	4.14	4.19	45.95	217,247
2021	16,281,022	66.3	10,794,317	170,892	1.0	0.75	4.21	4.19	4.23	47.09	229,205
2022	17,420,693	67.0	11,671,864	184,785	1.1	0.75	4.25	4.23	4.28	48.27	241,794
2023	18,640,142	67.7	12,619,376	199,786	1.1	0.76	4.30	4.28	4.32	49.48	255,046
2024	19,944,952	68.4	13,642,347	215,981	1.1	0.77	4.34	4.32	4.37	50.72	268,996
2025	21,341,098	69.1	14,746,699	233,465	1.1	0.78	4.39	4.36	4.41	51.98	283,680
2026	22,834,975	69.8	15,938,813	252,338	1.1	0.78	4.43	4.41	4.46	53.28	299,134
2027	24,433,423	70.5	17,225,563	272,710	1.1	0.79	4.48	4.45	4.50	54.62	315,398
2028	26,143,763	71.2	18,614,359	294,697	1.1	0.80	4.52	4.50	4.55	55.98	332,514
2029	27,973,826	71.9	20,113,181	318,425	1.1	0.81	4.57	4.54	4.59	57.38	350,525
2030	29,931,994	72.6	21,730,628	344,032	1.1	0.82	4.61	4.58	4.64	58.81	369,476
2031	32,027,234	73.3	23,475,962	371,664	1.2	0.82	4.65	4.6	4.7	60.29	389,416

Note: The assumptions underlying the simulation are provided in the text.

Haseeb A. Drabu

Even as federalism has evolved in structure and form, fiscal federalism or federal policy making has stagnated. It has neither kept pace with changing politics nor with the economics of the system.

The framework of fiscal federalism has to change/adapt to the changed political economy of India. And that changed framework of fiscal federalism has to provide the overall context for the FFC in the form of the ToR.

First, it needs to be recognised that we now have a fiscal federal system in a market economy and not a controlled and regulated economy for which the present system of fiscal transfers was designed.

The FC as an institution was created in a situation where public finance was the key "development" driver. It was a state sponsored development strategy that was being pursued. Public investment was the major instrument and financing it was the major policy challenge. This is no longer the case. The state is no longer the largest investor in the economy.

This has many facets:

(i) First, of course, is the serious economic disempowerment of state governments under the new economic regime. The economic liberalisation in 1991 along with political decentralisation have put the state governments in a pincer: with Central government squeezing it from the top and the *panchayats* pushing it from below.

(ii) Major disconnect between politics and economics. In 1993, the political framework was decentralised but economic policy became more centralised.

(iii) Economic reforms and globalisation have resulted in a complete change in the nature of the tax and non-tax regime which has resulted in increased economic centralisation, at least on the revenue side.

(iv) In the market economy today, it is resources, regulations and Rupee/monetary policy that have become far more important.

(v) Resource federalism: Shares resources rather than revenues.

(vi) Rising protectionism at the state level

The big challenge for the FFC will be how to integrate fiscal federalism with resource federalism.

In the markets led growth paradigm, natural resources—minerals, oil, natural gas, and hydropower—are fast becoming the key revenue drivers for, and major constraints to macroeconomic growth and its spread across the sub-national economies. This change necessitates a change in the design of fiscal federalism.

As such, the fundamental change in the approach of the FC has to be spelt out in its ToR. The FFC must be asked to "design a framework for "resource revenue" sharing in addition to the "transactional revenue" sharing that it traditionally does. In other words, fiscal federalism must be now be linked to resource federalism in India.

This alternative framework can start with a fair scheme for distribution of resource rents, but it must eventually graduate towards a more robust and institutionalised system of resource federalism.

In doing so, the FC can also capture the changes needed for a fiscal federal set up to work in an open but regulated market economy as against a closed controlled one, the vestiges of which remain in this segment of the economy.

For instance, instead of restructuring the minerals sector along market lines, the amendments to the "Mines and Minerals (Development and Regulation) Act, 1957", has restricted states from exercising the powers of state governments even though they are the owners of minerals located within their respective boundaries.

Not only that, the Central government also extracts a substantial share of revenue directly and indirectly from these resources. At the pre-production stage, the Centre collects revenue as forest conservation charges and labour welfare cess, in the production stage in the form of custom duty, excise duty, income tax and corporate taxes, and in the post-production stage as central tax and export duty.

If this wasn't enough, the Central government undertakings being the biggest consumers of minerals are an additional source of revenue for the Centre! The Centre has been milking these minerals cows through dividend and can encash their embodied value by divesting its stake.

The net result is that the distribution of revenues emanating from natural resources is effectively 50:50. In other words, the Centre corners half of the revenues generated from natural resources. In some cases, like iron ore, it has been estimated that the share of state taxes (royalty and sales tax) in total revenues is in the range 20 per cent while the Centre's share (mainly income tax and dividend tax) is 80 per cent. This is because large profits are made by iron ore companies due to increased demand, high prices and the very low royalty payments that they make to states.

Ignoring this aspect is already having serious implications on the political economy of India.

There is a trend of rising "regional protectionism" within India which in the era of national liberalism is incongruous but not curious.

Even though India has been becoming an increasingly open country over the last 20 years, its constituent state economies are going in the opposite direction of increasing protectionism.

Consider the following: West Bengal imposes a 1 per cent entry tax on goods entering or passing through the state. Uttar Pradesh imposes a 5 per cent tax on crude oil being transported to IOC's Mathura refinery. Goa levies an "export" duty of 30 per cent on iron ore that leaves its shores. Assam is legislating levying a cess on the crude removed from its "domiciled" facilities. Orissa seeks an imposition of Mineral Resource Rent Tax (at the rate of 50% of the super normal profits being made by mines owners) which is earmarked for its tribal areas.

These restrictive fiscal measures apart, even physical controls are being enforced. Orissa has stipulated that 60 per cent of iron ore mined/ produced must be used within the state. Karnataka has taken it upon itself to decide on the actual quantity each iron ore mine can produce and supervises its utilisation.

All these new levies, be it in the form of entry tax, or extraction cess or export duty are in addition to existing taxes/duties by the state and not in line with the overall direction of tax regime that the country is moving towards. Little surprise then that consensus has eluded the imposition of a supra state tax like the GST.

Underlying the creation of these fiscal barriers is essentially a restrictive policy of economic protection. These state governments are imputing and adding an economic element to the administrative and political boundaries of a state. The administrative boundary of a state is being slowly but surely being converted into an economic border.

At the moment, it is being done by a few resource rich states to primarily prevent the outflow of scarce local raw material or the sale of non-locally produced goods within their areas. But there is nothing that prevents it from extending to other areas or states. There is now an unmistakable trend of rising "regional protectionism" within India.

No one seems to be thinking of the economic, legal and even constitutional implications of the state-level protectionist policies. They can affect macroeconomic liberalisation. A deeper internal economic integration of sub-national economies is a must for further globalisation. In fact, except in the financial sector, liberalisation is just a policy at the national level; its real operative arena is the markets in the states, be it the product market, land market or labour market.

A serious possibility is of some parts of the country becoming more closely integrated with the global economy than with their neighbouring states. This will be the beginning of the socio-political disarticulation of India which would in turn place an unbearable strain on the unity and integrity of India.

Section VII: Personal Tributes to B.P.R. Vithal

B.P.R. Vithal: Grip on State Finances and Founding of the CESS

C.H. Hanumatha Rao

Prof V.K.R.V. Rao once mentioned to me about Sri B.P.R. Vithal garu very warmly as one who chose to work for the state government with commitment disregarding enticements for working at the Centre. K. Rosaiah garu, the veteran Finance Minister in the state—now Governor of Tamil Nadu—told me that Vithal garu, because of his expertise in planning and finance, and the confidence he evoked, successive governments of diverse political persuasions found it comfortable to work with him. Apart from his grip on the subject, this speaks of his ability to convince the leaders on the merits of the issues at hand as well as accommodate the concerns of the elected representatives without compromising on the reasonableness of the proposals or the soundness of allocations.

The way he was trusted by the successive Chief Ministers and Finance Ministers enabled him to create an autonomous research institution like the Centre for Economic and Social Studies (CESS), initially with full financial support from the state government. The main objective of this Centre at that time was to do all the technical work needed for the Planning Department. Happily, a good deal of such work continues to be done at the Centre, to this day, thanks to the active interest shown by the secretaries of Planning as well as Finance who are also the members of the Board of Governors of the CESS.

Observations made at the National Seminar on Centre-State Relations in the Fiscal Context (In Honour of B.P.R. Vithal, Founder, CESS), Centre for Economic and Social Studies, Hyderabad, 5-6 November, 2012.

But Vithal garu's perspective was much wider. As he once explained, he was also inspired by the vision of Professors V.K.R.V. Rao, K.N. Raj and Malcolm Adiseshiah to decentralise research away from Delhi for focusing on the problems at the grassroots level. Our experience has been encouraging as the themes chosen for research at the CESS are relevant to the region, such as agriculture, poverty and environment, and there is a good interface with scholars working in other research centres and civil society organisations in the state.

Over the last two decades, including 12 years when I was the Chairman of the Board, I have had several occasions to closely interact and work with Vithal garu. I am struck by the active interest he has been taking, to this day, in the development of the Centre and, I must add, he has been doing this with a rare sense of detachment from its day-to-day functioning.

The sources of inspiration for his social commitments and widening of his horizons are deeper. Not many may be knowing that when he was barely 15, he chose Mahatma Gandhi's teachings as a way for his life style, corresponded with him, did spinning regularly, wore *khadi*, attended the Quit India Session of the Congress at Bombay in August, 1942, and was even witness to the number of votes cast for and against the Quit India resolution! His political digressions caused a three year break in his education, but, according to him, these have been both exhilarating and elevating!

Vithal Garu: A Scholar Administrator

R. Radhakrishna

I have had a very memorable and enriching association with Vithal garu since I joined the University of Hyderabad as Professor of Economics in 1980. He invited me to join the CESS Board and sought my help in initiating research activities at the Centre. On his suggestion, I joined the CESS as its Director in 1985 and continued in that position for over nine years. During this period, I got an opportunity to initiate a number of academic activities and build a committed research team at the Centre. This was possible only because I enjoyed his full confidence as well as freedom in managing the affairs of the institute. I also got the rare opportunity of interacting with eminent personalities associated with him. When I recollect back my association with him, I realise that it provided a turning point in my career.

Vithal garu is responsible for positioning CESS as an autonomous national institution providing a platform between academicians and policy makers. Even though governance of political parties changed in the state during the last three decades, CESS relationship with the government has remained mutually supportive. I admired the way he guided the proceedings of CESS Board Meetings in ensuring that collective wisdom prevailed in decision-making. It is admirable that he could persuade eminent scholars of national stature to serve CESS as Chairpersons. The Board has always acted as a catalyst for the growth of the Centre and created a conducive environment for academic pursuits of the faculty.

He has many admirers of his public speeches which are marked with wisdom, wit and anecdotes. I had many opportunities to listen to his speeches. He has the knack of making complex issues understandable to a lay man. In recent years, his public speeches have become rare, but compensated by his scholarly writings. This volume is a tribute to his contributions to public finance.

Sri Vithal: A Mentor

C.S. Rao

B.P.R. Vithal garu has been philosopher, mentor and guide to a large circle of people in various walks of life, especially the civil services. I was extremely fortunate to come into this circle early in my career as an Indian Administrative Service (IAS) officer, when I was posted as Deputy Secretary, Budget. Vithal garu was Finance Secretary, Government of Andhra Pradesh, at the time. It so happened that the late U.B. Ranghavendra Rao, my predecessor at the post, had suggested my name as successor. Vithal garu had asked Raghavendra Rao for a recommendation, and such was his faith in his judgement that he accepted it without even meeting me first! Two aspects of this opportunity gladdened me: the opportunity to fill the shoes of an outstanding officer like Raghavendra Rao; and the opportunity to work with an officer whom I'd admired since my stint as Assistant Collector in the Hyderabad district in the years 1968 and 1969.

As Assistant Collector, I first had occasion to listen to Vithal garu speak at the Collectors' Conference of 1968. He explained with lucidity a memorandum seeking assistance for drought relief and rehabilitation from the Central government. I was also amazed by the manner in which he handled the Ministers and Collectors present who wanted to secure as large an allocation as possible for their districts. His manner and tone were accommodative and he promised to address everyone's concerns to the extent possible, but he asserted that ultimately the memorandum had to be based on rational grounds supported by rainfall data and its periodicity. Vithal garu was able to persuade the Conference to approve the memorandum with the sole caveat that modifications, where considered necessary, may be made by the Chief Minister in the light of the discussions at the Conference. I am not sure what changes were incorporated into the memorandum finally submitted, but he had tactfully secured from the Conference an endorsement of the methodology and basic structure of the memorandum, and had also secured for the Government the final say on what could be included in it. Without a doubt, only those suggestions that did not affect the credibility of the state government, and did not alter the basic structure and integrity of the report would have been included in the submitted memorandum. He is an excellent consensus builder, and no doubt it is this trait, taken along with his unchallenged mastery over the field of public finance, that endeared him to successive Chief Ministers and Finance Ministers who ensured he remained, first, Planning Secretary and later Secretary of the integrated Department of Finance and Planning.

So, by the time I took charge as Deputy Secretary reporting directly to Vithal garu, I was already an admirer! As part of this assignment I was involved in areas concerning the budget, the financial position of the state, and issues relating to cash management. Reporting directly to him, I had the opportunity to observe closely the unfolding of a vision to place the state on a firm financial foundation and to usher in an era of rapid and sustainable economic growth.

Even back then, in a time of less volatile economic climates, he was grounded in the mantra of sustainability of economic growth. This objective of sustainability was key to his decision-making. It was common back then for Secretaries to seek large allocations for their departments on the ground that the state had generated surplus cash and if utilised fully the Center would grant additional funds. He was completely aware of the risks involved in sudden increases in outlays: they often resulted in wastages and created crises in the event of unforeseen stringencies. His decade as Secretary, Finance and Planning, witnessed a steady growth in our developmental outlays and gave us great credibility at the Center as a prudent but development-oriented state.

B.P.R. Vithal was—and is—a well-known figure in Delhi circles even though he did not choose to go to Delhi to work for the Government of India. In the meetings of the National Development Council (NDC) he played a crucial role, and the Finance Secretaries of various states sought his counsel on how to deal with the Planning Commission. The Planning Commission itself relied on his sound judgement while dealing with sensitive matters concerning states.

Working with him closely, especially in the formative years of my career, was not just an education in the complex field of public finance but also equal to a qualification in itself. The fact that I had worked with him was more than adequate for me to find a foothold in the Ministry of Finance at the Centre. It is no exaggeration to say that the fact that I was B.P.R. Vithal's *shishya* was a more eloquent testimonial than an outstanding remark in my confidential report. What I saw and learnt from Vithal garu, I tried to put in practice. And if I had any success in my career, it is entirely due to his training, wise counsel, and good wishes. I say 'good wishes' because 'blessings' is a word that he despises!

I greatly cherish Vithal garu's influence on me both as a civil servant and as an individual. I'm sure a very large number of other people feel the same way—that is the very nature of association with him! I learnt a great deal from Vithal garu and enjoyed an easy relationship with him from the very beginning. And my son, who is in his thirties and a writer, finds him very approachable, generous and feels greatly benefited by his insights. That is B.P.R. Vithal!

What I Learnt from Vithal Garu

Y.V. Reddy

I am fortunate to benefit from knowledge, wisdom, affection and love of Vithal garu. He enhanced my understanding of things, people, issues, institutions and ideas in a wholesome manner with a memorable built-in humour. The range of subjects that we discussed over five decades have indeed been wide and continues to encompass society, politics, religion, history, economics and of course public finance. Most of the learning happened in a chatty manner, through examples and anecdotes rather than pontification or enunciation.

I had the privilege of listening to Vithal garu in 1961 when he presented a paper in a Seminar on Applied Economics in Osmania University. At that time he was Registrar of Osmania University and I was a full time Research Fellow. His presentation combined a deep understanding of history, politics and economics, and I was very impressed with it because it went beyond the standard recourse to research methodologies or personal experiences. That approach had an influence on my subsequent presentations in various seminars.

I joined the IAS in 1964 and moved on to become Deputy Secretary, Planning in September 1969 which gave me a golden opportunity to work under Vithal garu. I came to know later that he brought me into his fold to spare the Chief Secretary from the predicament that he was facing due to my "difficult" way of functioning in Guntur district as Collector in charge at that time. In a sense, therefore, Vithal garu virtually took me under his protection and chose me to be one of his *shishyas*. I would like to recall a few memorable things that I learnt from Vithal garu during my days in Planning Department.

He never disagreed with his deputies on the file without discussing the matter. Early in my career, when he called me for discussion and expressed disagreement with what I proposed, I mentioned to him that he could overrule me on file and that I have no objection to his views at all. He clarified that in his view, all of us are endowed with similar intelligence and devotion to work. Therefore, he would like to discuss so that we appreciate each other's point of view. In his view, reasonable people should be able to come to an agreement once the facts and assumptions are clarified. He explained that the issue of overruling will arise only when differences cannot be resolved through discussions. He added that even when a subordinate is overruled, it does not mean that the superior in the office is more intelligent but that is the only convenient way in which organisations are run. Vithal garu always used to call for discussion whenever he disagreed. This has a lasting impact on me and I have internalised it, both in office and my home; even with my children and grandchildren. Whenever there are disagreements among my grandchildren they say "like tattaya, let us discuss and decide."

Vithal garu is politeness personified. He was equally pleasant, with the similar tone and tenor whether he was speaking to a Minister, a Secretary or his private secretary Bhavani Shankaram. He has, what I call and cherish, old world sentiments in his dealings in the workplace also. In administration, delays occur and often it provokes, in superiors, annoyance or even attribution of motives when delays occur. I found him never asking me or anybody as to why something was delayed. In a way, it increases the responsibility on the subordinates to ensure that there is no delay or to explain the delay even before being asked. I have religiously followed his example of not questioning the past but guiding the future.

Vithal garu also had a singular knack of distinguishing substance from sentiment or prejudices. Once a Minister asked him for a draft speech for an important occasion and the speech had some political implications. He called me and asked me to draft a speech for the Minister. I explained to him that I had already given the draft speech to the Minister. He asked me to show him a copy. He read it; called his PS and asked him to retype it with a different font and on a different size of paper. He made no corrections at all. He was simply giving a message to the Minister that he had full trust in my draft and it was inappropriate for the Minister to suspect my bonafides or capacities in regard to the draft. Being subtle but effective is an art that I tried to learn from Vithal garu.

Vithal garu is very soft spoken and pleasant, but he can be very assertive when warranted. There was an occasion when a political leader complained about delays at my level when I was Deputy Secretary, Planning. I was present and there was an accusation of some motives on my part for having delayed the papers. It is true that the papers were delayed and it was also true that it was deliberate. But it was done in what we considered to be public interest. The moment the political leader mentioned about a deliberate delay on my part, Vithal garu promptly asserted that he takes personal responsibility for any delay in his Department and that there should be no passing of responsibility on his deputies in such matters. Yet, I was annoyed and decided to resign from the service as a protest. Vithal garu appreciated that my feelings were hurt and persuaded the political leader to apologise to me so that I withdrew my intention to resign from service. This episode shows Vital garu's generosity as well as commitment to ensure that public interest is served, while respecting the professional roles and dignities of all people concerned. He could advise, assert and deliver, by virtue of the trust and confidence that he commanded from the political leadership and bureaucracy in equal measures. I tried to learn from him the art of expressing disagreement without being unpleasant.

When I started as Deputy Secretary Planning, I wanted to do significant analytical work on regional planning. At that time Vithal garu was not convinced that these were of any practical use. True to his nature, he did not keep his reservation a secret but at the same time he explained that I was at liberty to pursue what I thought was right course of action as long as there was no harm done to the system. I was granted freedom to pursue analytical and theoretical interests as long as they were of relevance to my job. He adopted a similar benign approach to my completing the thesis for PhD during my stint in Planning Department. Above all, he was very liberal in allowing me to participate in national or international seminars without demur, provided there was no financial burden on the State. He had trust and confidence in me that I would pursue academic interest in a way that does not adversely affect performance of official duties.

It should be clear from this that my career has been influenced by Vithal garu not only in terms of the way I conduct my official duties but also the manner in which I could equip myself intellectually over the entire career.

There has been one area in which, despite my best efforts, I could not reach the standards set by Vithal garu and that relates to the quality of drafting. From the time I started working with him in 1969, he was always urging me to improve my drafting, be it notes or papers. I think that I have been improving, but I am acutely aware that I am still short of the high standards that he sets. I have not given up the quest to improve my drafting and that is the assurance that I want to give to Vithal garu today.

I look up to him for guidance, wherever I happen to be—Government of India, Reserve Bank of India, World Bank, International Monetary Fund or Finance Commission. Vithal garu has bestowed on me the honour and privilege of being one of his *shishyas* (disciples).

Appendix

Bio-Sketch of B.P.R. Vithal

Date of Birth:

Born at Hyderabad on 30-11-1927

Education:

Studied at Madrasa-I-Aliya, Hyderabad and Madras Christian College, Madras.

Positions in Public Life:

Participated in the Freedom Movement. Attended the Quit India Session of the Indian National Congress at Bombay in August 1942. Elected as Chairman of the Madras Christian College Union in 1949 and Vice President of the Madras Students Congress in 1944.

Joined the Indian Administrative Service in 1950.

Registrar, Osmania University from 1961 to 1984.

In-charge of Planning and Development, Government of Andhra Pradesh from 1964 to 1982. In-charge of the Finance Department of Andhra Pradesh Government from 1974 to 1982, first as Secretary and then as Principal Secretary.

Deputy Chairman (Chief Secretary), State Planning Board, 1985.

From 1982 to 1984, worked for the International Monetary Fund (IMF) as a Fiscal Expert as IMF Budget Adviser to the Government of Sudan at Khartoum. From 1985 to 1986, worked in the same capacity to the Government of Malawi.

Member, Committee on Taxation of Agricultural Wealth and Income (K.N. Raj Committee), Ministry of Finance, Government of India February 24, 1972.

Member, High Power Pay Committee for Public Sector Undertakings, Ministry of Industry, Government of India, 1985-1988.

Chairman, Expenditure Commission, Government of Kerala, 1987-1989. (with the status of Cabinet Minister of the State).

Deputy Chairman, State Planning Board, Government of Andhra Pradesh, 1990-1993 (with the status of Cabinet Minister of the State).

Chairman, Expert Committee on Panchayati Raj Institutions, Government of Andhra Pradesh, 1991-92.

Chairman, Research Programmes Committee, Planning Department, Government of Andhra Pradesh, 1993-94, (with the status of Cabinet Minister of the State).

Member, Tenth Finance Commission, 1992-94, (with the status of Minister of State, Government of India).

Chairman, Reserve Bank of India, Informal Advisory Committee on Ways and Means Advances to State Governments, November 25, 1998.

Honorary Senior Fellow, Centre for Economic & Social Studies, Hyderabad.

Has written extensively on Public Finance, Federal Financial Relations and Planning.

Awarded honorary Doctorates by Osmania and Annamalai Universities.

Published Work:

1. "State Plan Outlays and Resource Mobilisation" in I.S. Gulati (ed.), *Centre-State Budgetary Transfers*. Oxford University Press. 1987.
2. "New Approaches to Planning", in Bidyut Sarkar (ed.), *P.N. Haksar: Our Times and the Man*. Allied Publishers 1989.
3. Re-considering Socialist Man. Vishalandhra Publishing House. 1990.
4. "Evolving Practices and Emerging Fissures", in R.V.R. Chandrasekhar Rao and V.S. Prasad (eds.), *Indian Constitution and Polity*. Sterling Publishers. 1991.
5. *Changing Role and Perceptions of the Bureaucracy*. U.B. Raghavender Rao Memorial Lecture, Waltair. 4 April 1991.
6. "Reducing Government Expenditure", Amaresh Bagchi, J.L. Bajaj and William A. Byrd (eds.), *State Finances in India*. Vikas Publishing House. 1992.
7. *Crises in Values*. DurgabaiDeshmukh 86th Birthday Memorial Lecture, Andhra Mahila Sabha, Hyderabad. 15 July 1994.
8. "Centre-State Financial Relations", in Ajit M. Bannerjee. and K.A. Chandrasekharan (eds.), *Renewing Governance: Issues and Options*. Tata-Megraw Hill. 1996.
9. "Evolving Trends in Bureaucracy", in Partha Chaterjee (ed.), *State and Politics in India*. Oxford. 1997.

10. *A Citizen of No Mean City*. First Foundation Lecture, Kuchibhotla Vasanthi Foundation, Kakinada. 20 March 1998.

11. "Andhra Pradesh: Two Contrasting Decades of Financial Management", *Man and Development* XX(1), March 1998.

12. "Sleep-walking into the Millennium", *Man and Development* XXII(3), September 2000.

13. *Fiscal Federalism in India* (co-author M.L. Sastry). Oxford University Press. 2001.

14. *The Telengana Surpluses: A Case Study*. Centre for Economic and Social Studies. June 2002.

15. *The Gadgil Formula* (co-Author, M.L. Sastry). Centre for Economic and Social Studies and Manohar Publishers. November 2002.

16. *A State in Periodic Crises: Andhra Pradesh*. New Delhi: Academic Foundation. 2012.

17. *In Retrospect: B.P.R. Vithal*. Centre for Economic and Social Studies. 2012.